GUIDE TO ATLASES:
World, Regional, National, Thematic

An International Listing of Atlases Published Since 1950

by

GERARD L. ALEXANDER

The Scarecrow Press, Inc.
Metuchen, N. J.   1971

Contents

NATIONAL ATLASES

iv

NORTH AMERICA

SOUTH AMERICA

THEMATIC ATLASES

Introduction

Though I trust it will have many other uses, this Guide to Atlases has been deliberately planned to fill a long felt need and to serve one specific purpose: namely, to list at a glance all atlases published since 1950, by whom and where, of what area, what type, in what language, and of what size and date.

In order to facilitate its use, perhaps a word is needed to explain the arrangement of the volume. For easy use as a reference tool, the atlas entries have been divided into four distinct groups: 1) World Atlases have been arranged chronologically by date and, within each year, alphabetically by publisher; 2) Regional Atlases, covering whole continents or major regions of same, are listed within each continent alphabetically by name of publisher; 3) National Atlases, those of individual countries as a whole, are located within each continent in alphabetic order by publishers; 4) Thematic Atlases are divided first alphabetically by subject, such as economy, geology, history, roads, and within each category alphabetically by publishers.

An atlas is listed more than once if it covers more than one area or subject. As an example, a Soil atlas of the Congo, Rwanda and Burundi will have the following four entries: under Soil (Thematic Atlases) and also within Africa (National Atlases) under the name of each individual country: Congo, Rwanda and Burundi. This facilitates the search for a certain type of atlas, as well as for the geographical area desired.

Each atlas entry lists the name of the publisher, title, edition, author, place of publication, date of publication, number of pages, colored maps and size of atlas.

In addition to a Publishers Index, arranged alphabetically and listing also the city and country of publication, there is a List of Publishers, divided first by continents, listing alphabetically by countries the various governmental agencies, as well as private enterprises. Also provided is

ix

an alphabetic Language Index, and an Authors, Cartographers, Editors Index.

The numbering of each atlas entry is consecutive throughout the entire volume. The numbers listed in the various indexes refer to the actual atlas entries, and not the page numbers.

No effort has been spared to date atlases accurately. Dates for undated atlases have been established from bibliographic sources, and when available, from internal evidence. Where a date is only deducted or conjectured it appears in square brackets. The earliest and latest dates have been supplied for composite atlases. In many instances the actual number of pages in an atlas was doubtful; these have therefore been listed as one volume. The dimensions of each atlas are given in centimeters, either height or width, whichever is greater.

Entries for oriental atlases in Chinese, Japanese, Korean, etc., have titles and names of publishers given in the romanization of the characters. Other non-roman languages (Albanian, Arabic, Greek, Hebrew, Russian, Serbo-Croatian, etc.), have likewise been transliterated. This was often problematic and made consistency difficult. The same applies to the use of accents and punctuations, some of which had to be omitted.

When I first undertook to compile this international survey of all atlases, irrespective of area and subject, published in every part of the world, in all languages, I knew only too well that I would be confronted with many problems. The vast number of atlases published over the years, and the unbelievable amount of research involved, made it imperative that I limit my work to the production of atlases since 1950. Another consideration was not to eliminate the possibility to purchase desired atlases. Many atlases published during the last twenty years may still be available, while others have long since gone out of print. Fortunately, however, the major library atlas collections throughout the world have preserved on their shelves a comprehensive selection for consultation.

As the work progressed, my task was made more difficult by the many conflicting data which were available to me. Invariably I found that different publishers in scattered corners of the world published the very same atlas with identical title, but with their own imprint and date.

Many atlases were translated from one language to another and reissued.

While I consulted literally thousands of possible sources, I was hard put to decide which seemed the most authoritative. Information varied frequently on titles, editions, names of publishers, number of pages, size of atlas, dates, and especially the inconsistency of spelling was most confusing. In many instances it was particularly difficult to find the actual number of pages and different sizes for the identical atlas. I tried to decide on the most authoritative source, but realize that occasional mistakes in judgment are unavoidable.

Additionally, a great handicap was the fact that I was unable personally to inspect physically each individual atlas listed.

The arduous nature of the task of bringing together titles of thousands of atlases, out of the enormous mass of literature from all over the world, in different languages, is sufficiently obvious. But the difficulties attending its performance by a single individual can only be estimated by those practically acquainted with the magnitude of this undertaking. Notwithstanding the time and care devoted, no one is more conscious than the compiler that the work cannot be free from errors and omissions. Suggestions for any factual corrections and additions, which may be appropriate for inclusion in a future edition, if and when one becomes a reality, would be much appreciated.

Gerard L. Alexander

Chief, Map Division
The Research Libraries
The New York Public Library

WORLD ATLASES

1950

1   Atlantik Verlag.
     Die Länder der Erde. Atlas für die deutsche Schule.
     By Willy Eggers. Hamburg, [1950].
     34 p. col. maps. 34 cm.

2   Atlantik Verlag.
     Kleiner Weltatlas. 2 ed. By Willy Eggers.
     Hamburg, [1950].
     36 p. col. maps. 28 cm.

3   Bartholomew, John & Son, Ltd.
     The world pocket atlas and gazetteer. Edinburgh,
     1950.
     160 p. col. maps. 15 cm.

4   Carlson, A. V.
     Atlas nr. 1 för allmänna läroverken. By Hans W.
     Ahlmann. Stockholm, [1950].
     64 p. col. maps. 32 cm.

5   Collins, William, Sons & Co., Ltd.
     Collins-Longmans clarion atlas. 3 ed. By K. H.
     Huggins. Glasgow, New York, [1950].
     64 p. col. maps. 23 cm.

6   Colorgravure.
     New Australian world atlas illustrated with political
     and resources-relief maps. By Horace Blanche.
     Melbourne, [1950].
     144 p. col. maps. 32 cm.

7   Columbus Verlag Oestergaard.
     Columbus Weltatlas. Berlin, [1950].
     209 p. col. maps. 43 cm.

8   Columbus Verlag Oestergaard.
     Columbus Weltatlas. E. Debes Handatlas.

Berlin, [1950].
211 p.   col. maps.   43 cm.

9   Cram, George F. Co.
     Quick reference atlas of the world.   Indianapolis,
     Ind., [1950].
     34 p.   col. maps.   31 cm

10   Cram, George F. Co.
     Student quick reference atlas of the world.
     Indianapolis, Ind., 1950.
     1 vol.   col. maps.   31 cm.

11   Crowell & Co.
     Atlas of world affairs.   By Clifford MacFadden.
     New York, 1950.
     1 vol.   28 cm.

12   Czechoslovakia. Komenium.
     Školní zeměpisný atlas.   1 ed.   By Bedřich Salamon
     and K. Kuchař.   Praha, 1950.
     38 p.   col. maps.   32 cm.

13   Droemer.
     Knaurs Welt Atlas.   By Günter Pahl.   München,
     [1950].
     463 p.   col. maps.   29 cm.

14   Edições Melhoramentos.
     Atlas geográfico Melhoramentos.   8 ed.   By
     Geraldo José Pauwels.   São Paulo, 1950.
     61 p.   col. maps.   36 cm.

15   Editorial Luis Vives, S. A.
     Atlas universal y de España.   Zaragoza, [1950].
     52 p.   col. maps.   32 cm.

16   Editorial Teide.
     Atlas de geografia general.   By J. Vicens Vives.
     Barcelona, [1950].
     32 p.   col. maps.   32 cm.

17   Editorial Teide.
     Atlas escolar, carpeta.   With Istituto Geografico
     De Agostini.   Barcelona, [195-].
     15 p.   col. maps.   38 cm.

18   Elsevier.
      Grote Elsevier atlas voor buitenlandse handel.
      Amsterdam, 1950-
      2 vol. col. maps. 36 cm.

19   Elsevier.
      Kleine wereld atlas met encyclopaedische informatie.
      Amsterdam, 1950.
      85 p. col. maps. 25 cm.

20   Elsevier.
      Winkler Prins atlas. Amsterdam, 1950-
      296 p. col. maps. 36 cm.

21   Freytag, Berndt & Artaria.
      Freytag-Berndt Taschen-Weltatlas. Wien, [1950].
      136 p. col. maps. 19 cm.

22   Geographia Map Co.
      The authentic atlas of the world. By Alexander
      Gross. New York, [1950].
      96 p. col. maps. 35 cm.

23   Geokarta.
      Shkolski atlas. Beograd, 1950.
      12 p. col. maps. 33 cm.

24   Gumperts Förlag.
      Fick atlas. With Philip. Göteborg, 1950.
      108 p. col. maps. 20 cm.

25   Gumperts Förlag.
      Record atlas. 14 ed. By George Godall. With
      Philip. Göteborg, 1950.
      342 p. col. maps. 29 cm.

26   Gyldendal.
      Atlas for folkeskolen. 22 ed. By C.C. Christen-
      sen. København, 1950.
      36 p. col. maps. 24 cm.

27   Gyldendal.
      Atlas uden navne. 13 ed. By C.C. Christensen.
      København, 1950-
      1 vol. col. maps. 23 cm.

28   Hachette.
        Atlas moderne. By Th. Waucomont. Paris, [1950].
        96 p. col. maps. 32 cm

29   Halcyon House.
        New standard world atlas.   With Geographia Map Co.
        Garden City, N.Y., [1950].
        96 p. col. maps. 35 cm.

30   Hammond, C. S. & Co., Inc.
        Advanced reference atlas, the modern, medieval and
        ancient world. New York, 1950.
        1 vol.   col. maps.   32 cm.

31   Hammond, C. S. & Co., Inc.
        Complete world atlas. New York, [1950].
        376 p.   col. maps.   25 cm.

32   Hammond, C. S. & Co., Inc.
        Library world atlas. New York, [1950].
        328 p.   col. maps.   32 cm.

33   Hammond, C. S. & Co., Inc.
        New era atlas of the world. New York, [1950].
        160 p.   col. maps.   32 cm.

34   Hammond, C. S. & Co., Inc.
        New international world atlas; the modern, medieval
        and ancient world. New York, [1950].
        124 p.   col. maps.   32 cm.

35   Hammond, C. S. & Co., Inc.
        Replogle world atlas. Chicago, [1950].
        200 p.   col. maps.   23 cm.

36   Hammond, C. S. & Co., Inc.
        Standard world atlas. New York, [1950].
        328 p.   col. maps.   32 cm.

37   Hammond, C. S. & Co., Inc.
        World wide atlas. New York, [1950].
        1 vol.   col. maps.   26 cm.

38   Hitt Label Co.
        Hitt's better maps of all danger zones.   Los
        Angeles, Calif., 1950.
        23 p.   24 cm.

39   Hölzel, Ed. Verlag.
      Österreichischer Mittelschulatlas.   74 ed.   By Hans
      Slanar.   Wien, 1950.
      146 p.   col. maps.   31 cm.

40   Istituto Geografico De Agostini.
      Atlante geografico muto fisico-politico a colori.
      Novara, 1950.
      1 vol.   col. maps.   27 cm.

41   JRO-Verlag.
      Grosser JRO Weltatlas, mit zahlreichen vielfarbingen
      Landkarten der ganzen Welt.   By Ernst Kremling.
      München, 1950.
      1 vol.   col. maps.   45 cm.

42   JRO-Verlag.
      JRO Weltatlas.   Handausgabe.   By Ernst Kremling.
      München, [1950].
      110 p.   col. maps.   31 cm.

43   Kanaat Kitabevi.
      Yeni orta atlas.   Yeni basi.   Istanbul, [1950].
      40 p.   col. maps.   30 cm.

44   Larousse.
      Atlas international Larousse; politique et économique.
      Paris, [1950].
      172 p.   col. maps.   50 cm.

45   Livraria popular de F. Franco.
      Atlas do mundo comercial e politico.   By J. R.
      Silva.   Lisboa, [1950].
      24 p.   col. maps.   27 cm.

46   Livraria Simões Lopes.
      Atlas geográfico para o estudo da geografia nos
      liceus, escolas comerciais, industriais e normais.
      Porto, [1950].
      30 p.   col. maps.   29 cm.

47   Longmans, Green.
      Clarion atlas.   By K. H. Huggins.   Toronto, New
      York, [1950].
      65 p.   col. maps.   22 cm.

48   Macmillan & Co. Ltd.
        A map book of world geography. By Alan Ferriday.
        London, 1950.
        70 p.   25 cm.

49   Mantnieks, P.
        Schoolatlas. Bruxelles, [1950].
        20 p. col. maps. 33 cm.

50   Mantnieks, P.
        World atlas. Bruxelles, [1950].
        32 p. col. maps. 17 cm.

51   McDougall's Educational Co. Ltd.
        School atlas. South African ed. Edinburgh, [1950].
        40 p. col. maps. 25 cm.

52   McGraw-Hill Book Co.
        The advanced atlas of modern geography. 1 ed.
        With Bartholomew. New York, 1950.
        155 p. col. maps. 39 cm.

53   McGraw-Hill Book Co.
        The advanced atlas of modern geography. 2 ed.
        With Bartholomew. New York, 1950.
        155 p. col. maps. 39 cm.

54   Meiklejohn.
        The advanced atlas of modern geography. 1 ed.
        With Bartholomew. London, 1950.
        155 p. col. maps. 39 cm.

55   Meiklejohn.
        The advanced atlas of modern geography. 2 ed.
        With Bartholomew, London, 1950.
        155 p. col. maps. 39 cm.

56   Merrill, C. E. Co.
        Current events [Atlas]. Maps and facts for world
        understanding. Columbus, Ohio, [1950].
        32 p. col. maps. 29 cm.

57   Milli Egitim Basimevi.
        Ilkokul cŏgrafya atlasi. Istanbul, [1950].
        1 vol. col. maps. 28 cm.

58   Nathan, Fernand.
      Atlas du Monde. In Encyclopédie Géographique du
      XX e. Siècle. Paris, [1950].
      71 p. col. maps. 34 cm.

59   Noordhoff, P.
      Atlas der gehele aarde. By P. R. Bos.
      Groningen, 1950.
      72 p. col. maps. 31 cm.

60   Odhams Press, Ltd.
      New atlas of the world. London, [1950].
      166 p. col. maps. 29 cm.

61   Permabooks.
      The Perma handy world atlas. By Alexander Gross.
      New York, [1950].
      190 p. col. maps. 17 cm.

62   Philip, George & Son, Ltd.
      Comparative commonwealth atlas for use in
      Australian schools. 10 ed. London, 1950.
      1 vol. col. maps. 23 cm.

63   Philip, George & Son, Ltd.
      Modern school atlas. 41 ed. By George Goodall.
      London, 1950.
      145 p. col. maps. 29 cm.

64   Philip, George & Son, Ltd.
      Record atlas. 14 ed. By George Goodall.
      London, 1950.
      342 p. col. maps. 29 cm.

65   Philip, George & Son, Ltd.
      The West African atlas. By George Goodall.
      London, 1950.
      31 p. col. maps. 24 cm.

66   Rand McNally & Co.
      Classroom atlas. Chicago, 1950.
      64 p. col. maps. 27 cm.

67   Rand McNally & Co.
      Goode school atlas, physical, political and economic.
      8 ed. By Edward B. Espenshade, Jr. Chicago, [1950].
      272 p. col. maps. 29 cm.

68   Rand McNally & Co.
      World atlas.   Chicago, 1950.
      30 p. col. maps. 36 cm.

69   Replogle Globes, Inc.
      Replogle world atlas.   Chicago, [1950].
      200 p. col. maps. 23 cm.

70   Robinson, H. E. C. pty, Ltd.
      Modern school atlas of the world.   17 ed.
      Sydney, [1950].
      57 p. col. maps. 23 cm.

71   Sadig Salih.
      [School atlas for elementary and middle schools].
      In Arabic.   Baghdad, [195-].
      36 p.   30 cm.

72   Schultz.
      Lille verdensatlas.   By Johannes Humlum.
      København, 1950.
      34 p. col. maps. 29 cm.

73   Učiḷa.
      Školski atlas.   By Josip C. Roglić.   Zagreb, 1950—
      1 vol. col. maps. 33 cm.

74   U.S.S.R. Glavnoe upravlenie geodezii i kartografii.
      Geograficheskii atlas zaribechnich stran dlya
      srednei shkoly. 1 ed.   Moskva, 1950.
      79 p. col. maps. 30 cm.

75   Ward, Lock.
      Ward Lock's handy world atlas and gazetteer.   With
      John Bartholomew.   London, [1950].
      160 p. col. maps. 15 cm.

76   Warne, F.
      Nuttall's simplified atlas of the world.   By Somers
      Gill.   London, [1950].
      32 p. col. maps. 28 cm.

77   Wenschow.
      Atlas für die höhere Lehranstalten.   München, [1950].
      73 p. col. maps. 36 cm.

78   Westermann, Georg.
      Atlas für Berliner Schulen.   Braunschweig, [1950].
      1 vol.   col.   maps.   32 cm.

79   Westermann, Georg.
      Atlas für die Schulen in Schleswig-Holstein.
      Braunschweig, [1950].
      2 parts.   col.   maps.   32 cm.

80   Westermann, Georg.
      Diercke Weltatlas.   83 ed.   Braunschweig, [1950].
      142 p.   col.   maps.   36 cm.

81   Westermann, Georg.
      Heimat und Welt [Atlas].   By Diercke.
      Braunschweig, 1950.
      42 p.   col.   maps.   32 cm.

82   Yavneh.
      Atlas amami.   By Moshe Brawer.   Tel Aviv,
      1950/51.
      49 p.   col.   maps.   31 cm.

83   Zanichelli, Nicola.
      Atlante geografico Zanichelli ad uso delle scuole.
      Bologna, 1950.
      183 p.   col.   maps.   35 cm.

                          1951

84   Atlantik Verlag.
      Kleiner Weltatlas.   3 ed.   By Willy Eggers.
      Frankfurt, 1951.
      36 p.   col.   maps.   28 cm.

85   Atlantik Verlag.
      Kleiner Weltatlas.   4 ed.   By Willy Eggers.
      Frankfurt, 1951.
      36 p.   col.   maps.   28 cm.

86   Atlantik Verlag.
      Schulatlas für den Regierungsbezirk Stade.
      Frankfurt, [1951].
      36 p.   col.   maps.   34 cm.

87   Bartholomew, John & Son, Ltd.
       The world pocket atlas and gazetteer.   Edinburgh,
       1951.
       128 p.   col. maps.   15 cm.

88   Bonnier.
       Bonniers stora världsatlas.   By Axel Elvin.   With
       Touring Club Italiano.   Stockholm, [1951].
       353 p.   col. maps.   50 cm.

89   Cappelens, J. W. Forlag, A. S.
       Cappelens atlas for folkeskolen.   By Knut Klokk.
       Oslo, 1951.
       40 p.   col. maps.   32 cm.

90   Colin.
       Atlas historique et géographique Vidal-Lablache.
       Paris, [1951].
       164 p.   col. maps.   40 cm.

91   Contact.
       Nieuwe geillustreerde wereldatlas.   By Jan Pieter
       Bakker.   Antwerpen, [1951].
       320 p.   col. maps.   36 cm.

92   Czechoslovakia.   Ústřední správa geodesie a kartografie.
       Politicko-hospodárský atlas sveta.   Praha, 1951-56.
       in parts.   col. maps.   37 cm.

93   Dent, J. M.
       World atlas; Everyman's encyclopaedia.   With
       Bartholomew.   London, [1951].
       415 p.   col. maps.   21 cm.

94   Djambatan.
       Tenah air dan dunja.   By Djamaludin Adinegoro.
       Djakarta, [1951].
       24 p.   col. maps.   23 cm.

95   Droemer.
       Knaurs Weltatlas.   By Günter Pahl.   München,
       1951/52.
       464 p.   col. maps.   20 cm.

96   Encyclopaedia Britannica.
       Encyclopaedia Britannica world atlas. Chicago, [1951].
       561 p.   col. maps.   38 cm.

97   Freytag, Berndt & Artaria.
       Atlas für Hauptschulen. Wien, [1951].
       68 p. col. maps. 31 cm.

98   Garden City Books.
       New comprehensive world atlas.   With Hammond.
       Garden City, N. Y., [1951].
       31 p. col. maps. 32 cm.

99   Geographia Map Co.
       Geographia atlas of the world.   By Alexander Gross.
       New York,]1951].
       40 p. col. maps. 34 cm.

100   Geokarta.
       Shkolni atlas.   By Dobrosav Ž. Šobić.   Beograd,
       1951.
       23 p. col. maps. 33 cm.

101   Gyldendal.
       Gyldendals verdensatlas.   By Aage Aagesen.   With
       Touring Club Italiano. København, 1951.
       2 vol. col. maps. 50 cm.

102   Hachette.
       Atlas rex; le tour du monde.   By Jean Martin.
       Paris, [1951].
       215 p. col. maps. 22 cm.

103   Haller Verlag.
       Weltforst Atlas.   Berlin, 1951.
       in parts. col. maps. 61 cm.

104   Hammond, C. S. & Co., Inc.
       Comparative world atlas.   Desk ed.   New York,
       [1951].
       48 p. col. maps. 32 cm.

105   Hammond, C. S. & Co., Inc.
       Complete world atlas.   New York, 1951.
       376 p. col. maps. 25 cm.

106   Hammond, C. S. & Co. Inc.
       Globemaster world atlas.   New York, [1951].
       48 p. col. maps. 32 cm.

107   Hammond, C.S. & Co., Inc.
       Hammond's library world atlas. New York, 1951.
       328 p. col. maps. 32 cm.

108   Hammond, C. S. & Co. Inc.
       Modern world atlas and gazetteer, with new census.
       New York, [1951].
       48 p. col. maps. 31 cm.

109   Hammond, C. S. & Co., Inc.
       New comprehensive world atlas. New York, 1951.
       31 p. col. maps. 32 cm.

110   Hammond, C. S. & Co. Inc.
       Reference atlas of the world. New York, [1951].
       128 p. col. maps. 32 cm.

111   Hammond, C. S. & Co., Inc.
       World atlas; an encyclopedic atlas of the world with
       latest and most authentic geographical and statistical
       information in map, word and picture. New York,
       1951.
       334 p. col. maps. 32 cm.

112   Hammond, C. S. & Co. Inc.
       World atlas and gazetteer. New York, [1951].
       48 p. col. maps. 31 cm.

113   Hammond, C. S. & Co., Inc.
       World atlas. Classics ed. New York, 1951.
       1 vol. col. maps. 32 cm.

114   Hernando.
       Atlas geográfico universal. 5 ed. By José Reinoso.
       Madrid, 1951.
       72 p. col. maps. 34 cm.

115   Hölzel, Ed. Verlag.
       Österreichischer Mittelschulatlas. 75 ed. By Hans
       Slanar. Wien, 1951.
       146 p. col. maps. 31 cm.

116   IAC.
       Le plus petit atlas du monde. By J. L. Sibert.
       Lyon, [1951].
       70 p. col. maps. 11 cm.

117   Indian Book Depot & Maps House.
       The new rashtriya atlas, geographical and historical.
       By Biba Singh Kaushal.   Delhi, [1951].
       120 p.   col. maps.   28 cm.

118   Istituto Geografico De Agostini.
       Nuovo atlante geografico metodico.   By Luigi
       Visintin.   Novara, [1951].
       113 p.   col. maps.   34 cm.

119   Johnston, W. & A. K., Ltd.
       Johnston's premier atlas of the world.   2 ed.
       Edinburgh, 1951.
       94 p.   col. maps.   28 cm.

120   JRO Verlag.
       Grosser JRO Weltatlas.   3 ed.   München, [1951].
       108 p.   col. maps.   44 cm.

121   Kümmerly & Frey.
       Wirtschaftsgeographischer Atlas der Welt.   By Hans
       Boesch.   Bern, 1951.
       87 p.   col. maps.   30 cm.

122   Larousse.
       Atlas international Larousse, politique et économique.
       Paris, [1951].
       170 p.   col. maps.   50 cm.

123   Litografía de Fernández.
       Atlas de geografia universal.   By Salvador Salinas
       Bellver.   Madrid, 1951.
       69 p.   col. maps.   35 cm.

124   Lloyd's Corp. of
       Lloyd's maritime atlas.   1 ed.   London, 1951.
       1 vol.   col. maps.   25 cm.

125   Mantnieks, P.
       Atlas classique.   2 ed.   Bruxelles, [1951].
       24 p.   col. maps.   33 cm.

126   McDougall's Educational Co., Ltd.
       Pictorial atlas.   Edinburgh, [1951].
       30 p.   col. maps.   26 cm.

127   Nijgh & van Ditmar.
      Onze wereld in kaart en beeld.   By K. Bosma.
      Rotterdam, [1951].
      39 p.   col. maps.   27 cm.

128   Oxford University Press.
      The American Oxford atlas.   New York, 1951.
      224 p.   col. maps.   40 cm.

129   Oxford University Press.
      The Canadian Oxford atlas.   Toronto, 1951.
      236 p.   col. maps.   40 cm.

130   Oxford University Press.
      The Oxford atlas.   London, 1951.
      210 p.   col. maps.   40 cm.

131   Peuser, Ediciones Geográficas.
      Nuevo atlas geográfico metódico universal.   10 ed.
      By José Anesi.   Buenos Aires, 1951.
      76 p.   col. maps.   37 cm.

132   Pfahl Verlag.
      Hansa Weltatlas.   6 ed.   Laupheim, 1951.
      293 p.   22 cm.

133   Philadelphia Inquirer.
      Atlas of the world today.   Philadelphia, [1951].
      20 p.   col. maps.   38 cm.

134   Philip, George & Son, Ltd.
      Junior school atlas for South Africa.   By George
      Goodall.   London, Cape Town, 1951.
      41 p.   col. maps.   24 cm.

135   Philip, George & Son, Ltd.
      Modern school atlas.   42 ed.   By George Goodall.
      London, 1951.
      157 p.   col. maps.   29 cm.

136   Philip, George & Son, Ltd.
      Record atlas.   15 ed.   By George Goodall.
      London, 1951.
      343 p.   col. maps.   29 cm.

137   Quillet, A.
      Atlas universal Quillet, physique, economique,
      politique. By Maurice Allain. Paris, 1951—
      in parts. col. maps. 46 cm.

138   Rand McNally & Co.
      Atlas and globe revision supplement. Chicago, 1951.
      16 p. col. maps. 36 cm.

139   Rand McNally & Co.
      Cosmopolitan world atlas. 2 ed. Chicago, [1951].
      376 p. col. maps. 37 cm.

140   Rand McNally & Co.
      Pocket world atlas. With Pocket Books. New York,
      [1951].
      232 p. col. maps. 17 cm.

141   Rand McNally & Co.
      Readers world atlas. Chicago, [1951].
      288 p. col. maps. 28 cm.

142   Rand McNally & Co.
      Standard world atlas. Chicago, [1951].
      384 p. col. maps. 28 cm.

143   Reed, A. W. & A. H.
      New world atlas. 5 ed. By Alfred Hamish Reed.
      Wellington, 1951.
      47 p. col. maps. 25 cm.

144   Romer, Eugeniusz.
      Maly atlas geograficzny. 15 ed. Wroclaw, 1951.
      12 p. col. maps. 30 cm.

145   Schweizer Volks-Buchgemeinde.
      Universal Weltatlas. Luzern, 1951.
      383 p. col. maps. 22 cm.

146   Seljačka Sloga.
      Geografski atlas i statističko geografski pregled
      svijeta. By Petar Mardešić. Zagreb, 1951.
      177 p. col. maps. 21 cm.

147   Seljačka Sloga.
      Geografski atlas i statističko geografski pregled
      svijeta. 2 ed. By Petar Mardešić. Zagreb, 1951.
      179 p. col. maps. 21 cm.

148   Svenska bokförlaget Norstedts.
       Nordisk skolatlas, folkskolupplagan.   By Hans Wil-
       helmsson Ahlmann.   Stockholm, [1951].
       36 p.   col.   maps.   34 cm.

149   Touring Club Italiano.
       Atlante internazionale del touring club Italiano.
       Milano, 1951.
       235 p.   col.   maps.   51 cm.

150   Trzaska, Evert, i Michalski, s. a.
       Atlas kieszonkowy.   2 ed.   By Karel Kuchař and
       Jerzy Kondracki.   Warszawa, 1951.
       64 p.   col.   maps.   20 cm.

151   Uitgeverij De Bezige Bij·
       De Bezige Bij wereldatlas.   By W. F. Heinemeyer.
       Amsterdam, [1951].
       329 p.   col.   maps.   36 cm.

152   U. S. S. R. Glavnoe upravlenie geodezii i kartografii.
       Geograficheski atlas chastei sveta i vazhneishikh
       gosudarstv. dla 6go - 7go klasov. Moskva, 1951.
       76 p.   col.   maps.   30 cm.

153   U. S. S. R. Glavnoe upravlenie geodezii i kartografii.
       Geograficheski atlas dla 5go i 6go klasov strednei
       shkoly.   Moskva, [1951].
       45 p.   col.   maps.   30 cm.

154   U. S. S. R. Glavnoe upravlenie geodezii i kartografii.
       Geograficheski atlas dla 7go i 8go klasov strednei
       shkoly.   Moskva, 1951.
       76 p.   col.   maps.   29 cm.

155   Velhagen & Klasing.
       Kleiner Schulatlas.   3 ed.   Bielefeld, [1951].
       42 p.   col.   maps.   33 cm.

156   Westermann, Georg.
       Atlas für die Schulen in Schleswig-Holstein.
       Braunschweig, [1950].
       2 vol.   col.   maps.   32 cm.

157   Westermann, Georg.
       Welt Atlas.   84 ed.   Braunschweig, [1951].
       146 p.   col.   maps.   36 cm.

158   Wolters, J. B.
      Schoolatlas der gehele aarde.   38 ed.   By Pieter
      Roelof Bos.   Groningen, 1951.
      44 p.   col. maps.   39 cm.

159   Zanichelli, Nicola.
      Atlante geografico sintefico Zanichelli.   Bologna, 1951.
      60 p.   col. maps.   34 cm.

                              1952

160   Atlantik Verlag.
      Die Länder der Erde.   Atlas für die deutsche
      Schule.   3 ed.   By Willy Eggers.   Frankfurt, 1952.
      49 p.   col. maps.   44 cm.

161   Bartholomew, John & Son, Ltd.
      The citizen's atlas of the world.   10 ed.   Edinburgh,
      1952.
      357 p.   col. maps.   37 cm.

162   Bergvalls Förlag.
      Bergvalls nya skolatlas.   By Magnus Lundquist.
      Stockholm, [1952].
      40 p.   col. maps.   26 cm.

163   Book Production Industries.
      The International standard world atlas.   By Franklin
      J. Meine.   Chicago, [1952].
      1 vol.   col. maps.   35 cm.

164   Colin.
      Atlas historique et géographique Vidal-La Blache.
      Paris, [1952].
      160 p.   col. maps.   40 cm.

165   Collins, William, Sons & Co., Ltd.
      Collins, Longmans study atlas.   9 ed.   By K. H.
      Huggins.   Glasgow, 1952.
      126 p.   col. maps.   30 cm.

166   Collins, William, Sons & Co., Ltd.
      Graphic atlas.   3 ed.   London, [1952].
      135 p.   col. maps.   28 cm.

167   Collins, William, Sons & Co., Ltd.
      The standardised South African atlas.   By B. A.
      Workman.   London, 1952.
      49 p.   col.   maps.   28 cm.

168   Columbus Verlag Oestergaard.
      Columbus Hausatlas in Wort und Bild.   Berlin,
      [1952].
      78 p.   col.   maps.   41 cm.

169   Cram, George F. Co.
      Unrivaled atlas, the world - indexed.   64 ed.
      Indianapolis, Ind., 1952.
      403 p.   col.   maps.   39 cm.

170   Czechoslovakia.   Státní nakl.   učebnic.
      Skolní zeměpisný atlas.   2 ed.   By Bedřich
      Šalamon and Karel Kuchař.   Praha, 1952.
      37 p.   col.   maps.   32 cm.

171   Dar al-ma' ārif.
      al Atlas al-Arabī.   By Muhammad 'Awad Ibrāhīm.
      Cairo, [1952].
      69 p.   col.   maps.   30 cm.

172   Denoyer-Geppert Co.
      Abridged elementary school atlas.   3 ed.   By
      Levinus Phillippus Denoyer.   Chicago, [1952].
      39 p.   col.   maps.   28 cm.

173   Djambatan.
      Atlas semesta dunia.   By Djamaludin Adinegorô.
      Djakarta, 1952.
      256 p.   col.   maps.   36 cm.

174   Dreyers forlag.
      Dreyers Verdensatlas.   1 ed.   By Kristian Gleditsch.
      Oslo, [1952].
      168 p.   col.   maps.   29 cm.

175   Državana založba slovenije.
      Gospodarski atlas sveta.   By Stane Zrimec.
      Ljubljana, 1952.
      120 p.   35 cm.

176   Editora Civilização Brasileira, S.A.
      Atlas de geografia moderna.   Rio de Janeiro, [1952].
      38 p.   col.   maps.   35 cm.

177 Empresa Editora Zig-Zag.
     Atlas universal. 2 ed. By Alejandro Rios Valdivia.
     Santiago de Chile, 1952.
     65 p. col. maps. 29 cm.

178 Encyclopaedia Britannica.
     Encyclopaedia Britannica world atlas. By G. Donald
     Hudson. Chicago, [1952].
     569 p. col. maps. 38 cm.

179 Fachbuchverlag, G. m. b. H.
     Weltspiegel. Taschenatlas. Leipzig, [1952].
     24 p. col. maps. 26 cm.

180 Falk Verlag.
     Welt-Seuchen-Atlas. [World atlas of epidemic
     diseases]. Hamburg, 1952-61.
     3 vol. col. maps. 48 cm.

181 Freytag, Berndt & Artaria.
     Atlas für Mittelschulen. Wien, [1952].
     89 p. col. maps. 32 cm.

182 Garden City Books.
     New supreme world atlas. With Hammond.
     Garden City, N. Y., [1952].
     176 p. col. maps. 32 cm.

183 Grolier Society.
     World atlas; an encyclopedic atlas of the world.
     With Hammond. Canadian classics ed. Toronto,
     1952.
     360 p. col. maps. 33 cm.

184 Gumperts Förlag.
     Skandinavisk världsatlas. By Karl Erik Bergsten.
     With Philip. Göteborg, [1952].
     168 p. col. maps. 29 cm.

185 Haack, Hermann.
     Weltatlas; die Staaten der Erde und ihre Wirtschaft.
     1 ed. Gotha, 1952 —
     in parts. col. maps. 35 cm.

186 Hammond, C. S. & Co., Inc.
     Comparative wall atlas. New York, [1952].
     16 p. col. maps. 73 cm.

187   Hammond, C. S. & Co., Inc.
       Complete world atlas. New York, [1952].
       376 p. col. maps. 25 cm.

188   Hammond, C. S. & Co., Inc.
       Hammond's world atlas. Classics ed. New York,
       1952.
       1 vol. col. maps. 32 cm.

189   Hammond, C. S. & Co., Inc.
       Library world atlas. New York, 1952.
       328 p. col. maps. 32 cm.

190   Hammond, C. S. & Co., Inc.
       New international world atlas; the modern medieval
       and ancient world. New York, [1952].
       120 p. col. maps. 32 cm.

191   Hammond, C. S. & Co., Inc.
       Reference atlas of the world. New York, [1952].
       128 p. col. maps. 32 cm.

192   Hammond, C. S. & Co., Inc.
       Standard world atlas; a geographic encyclopedia.
       New York, 1952.
       302 p. col. maps. 32 cm.

193   Hammond, C. S. & Co., Inc.
       Universal world atlas. New York, 1952.
       1 vol. col. maps. 32 cm.

194   Hammond, C. S. & Co., Inc.
       World atlas; an encyclopedic atlas of the world.
       New York, [1952].
       328 p. col. maps. 33 cm.

195   Hölzel, Ed. Verlag.
       Österreichischer Mittelschulatlas. 76 ed. By Hans
       Slanar. Wien, 1952.
       146 p. col. maps. 31 cm.

196   Jackson, W. M., Inc.
       Atlas manual del mundo Jackson. Mexico, D. F.,
       1952.
       80 p. col. maps. 25 cm.

197   JRO Verlag.
      JRO Weltatlas. Handausgabe. 3 ed. By Ernst
      Kremling. München, [1952].
      110 p. col. maps. 31 cm.

198   Ksiaznica-Atlas.
      Maly atlas geograficzny. 15 ed. By Engeniusz
      Romer. Wroclaw, 1952.
      12 p. col. maps. 30 cm.

199   Kümmerly & Fry.
      Pflanzengeographischer Welt Atlas. Bern, 1941-[52].
      1 vol. col. maps. 33 cm.

200   Orbis.
      Politicko-hospodářský atlas světa. 1 ed. Praha,
      [1952-54].
      in parts. col. maps. 33 cm.

201   Oxford University Press.
      Concise Oxford atlas. By D. P. Bickmore.
      London, 1952.
      97 p. col. maps. 26 cm.

202   Pan American Airways.
      Route maps, PAA. New York, [1952].
      12 p. col. maps. 23 cm.

203   Perthes, Justus.
      Taschenatlas der ganzen Welt. 80 ed. Gotha, 1952.
      148 p. col. maps. 18 cm.

204   Perthes, Justus.
      Taschenatlas der ganzen Welt. 81 ed. Gotha, 1952.
      148 p. col. maps. 18 cm.

205   Pfahl Verlag.
      Hansa Weltatlas. Laupheim, 1952.
      293 p. col. maps. 24 cm.

206   Philip, George & Son, Ltd.
      Comparative Commonwealth atlas for use in
      Australian schools. 11 ed. London, 1952.
      1 vol. col. maps. 23 cm.

207   Philip, George & Son, Ltd.
       Comparative Commonwealth atlas for use in
       Australian schools. 12 ed. London, 1952.
       1 vol. col. maps. 23 cm.

208   Philip, George & Son, Ltd.
       Philip's Australian Commonwealth atlas. By George
       Goodall. London, 1952.
       88 p. col. maps. 31 cm.

209   Philip, George & Son, Ltd.
       Philip's mercantile marine atlas. 14 ed. By
       Harold Fullard. London, 1952.
       96 p. col. maps. 53 cm.

210   Philip, George & Son, Ltd.
       Record atlas. 16 ed. By George Goodall.
       London, 1952.
       207 p. col. maps. 29 cm.

211   Politikens Forlag.
       Politikens' verdensatlas. By Axel Schou.
       København, 1952.
       168 p. col. maps. 29 cm.

212   Prentice-Hall.
       Atlas of the World's Resources Vol II. The
       Mineral Resources of the World. By William Van
       Royen, Oliver Bowles, Elmer W. Pehrson.
       New York, 1952.
       181 p.   40 cm.

213   Rand McNally & Co.
       Cosmopolitan world atlas. 2 ed. Chicago, [1952].
       375 p. col. maps. 37 cm.

214   Rand McNally & Co.
       Cosmo relief series maps. Chicago, 1952.
       1 vol. col. maps. 26 cm.

215   Rand McNally & Co.
       Current events world atlas. Chicago, 1952.
       36 p. col. maps. 27 cm.

216   Rand McNally & Co.
       Premier world atlas. Chicago, [1952].
       272 p. col. maps. 37 cm.

217   Söderström, Werner
      Kotien maailmankartasto.   Porvoossa, [1952].
      107 p.   col. maps.   35 cm.

218   Svenska bokförlaget Norstedts.
      Nordisk skolatlas; folkskolupplagen.   2 ed.   By Hans
      W. Ahlmann.   Stockholm, [1952].
      38 p.   col. maps.   34 cm.

219   Technical Press, Ltd.
      Oil-field atlas.   By Arthur Beeby-Thompson.
      London, 1952.
      15 p.   27 cm.

220   Tidens förlag.
      Tidens världsatlas.   With Generalstabens litografiska
      anstalt.   By M:son Mannerfelt.   Stockholm, [1952].
      160 p.   col. maps.   28 cm.

221   Učila.
      Školski atlas.   By Josip C. Roglić.   Zagreb, 1952.
      30 p.   col. maps.   33 cm.

222   Van Schaik's Bookstore.
      Van Schaik's large print atlas for South Africa.
      20 ed.   By George Goodall.   With Philip.   Pretoria,
      1952.
      71 p.   col. maps.   29 cm.

223   VEB Bibliographisches Institut.
      Weltatlas; die Staaten der Erde und ihre Wirtschaft.
      Leipzig, [1952].
      166 p.   col. maps.   33 cm.

224   Volk und Wissen Verlag.
      Atlas zur Erd-und Länderkunde.   By Fritz Haefke.
      Berlin, 1952.
      56 p.   col. maps.   31 cm.

225   Westermann, Georg.
      Atlas für Hamburger Schulen.   Braunschweig,
      1952-53.
      2 vol.   col. maps.   32 cm.

226   Westermann, Georg.
      Heimat und Welt [Atlas].   Braunschweig, 1952.
      42 p.   col. maps.   32 cm.

227   Westermann, Georg.
      Welt atlas.   86 ed.   Braunschweig,   [1952].
      146 p.   col. maps.   36 cm.

                              1953

228   Atlantik Verlag.
      Die Länder der Erde.   Atlas für die deutsche
      Schule.   4 ed.   By Willy Eggers.   Frankfurt, 1953.
      49 p.   col. maps.   44 cm.

229   Atlantik Verlag.
      Kleiner Weltatlas.   By Willy Eggers.   Frankfurt,
      [1953].
      41 p.   col. maps.   28 cm.

230   Atlantik Verlag.
      Kleiner Weltatlas für die bayerische Schule.
      München, [1953].
      41 p.   col. maps.   28 cm.

231   Atlantik Verlag.
      List's Taschenatlas der Welt.   München, [1953].
      68 p.   col. maps.   19 cm.

232   Bachtiar, A.
      Atlas Tanah Air Kita dan Dunia Luarnja Untuk
      Sekolah Rakjat.   Djakarta, 1953.
      43 p.   col. maps.

233   Bartholomew, John & Son, Ltd.
      The Columbus atlas; or, Regional atlas of the world.
      Edinburgh, 1953.
      297 p.   col. maps.   29 cm.

234   Bartholomew, John & Son, Ltd.
      The compact atlas of the world.   3 ed.
      Edinburgh, 1953.
      266 p.   col. maps.   17 cm.

235   Book Publishers Distributing Co.
      World atlas; an encyclopedic atlas of the world.
      With Hammond.   Cincinnati, Ohio, 1953.
      340 p.   col. maps.   32 cm.

236   Bordos, H.
       Nouvel atlas général. Wien, 1953.
       1 vol. col. maps. 31 cm.

237   Cappelens, J. W. Forlag, A.S.
       Cappelens atlas; større utgave for hjem og skole.
       By Ellef Ellefson and K. B. Sollesnes. Oslo, 1953.
       90 p. col. maps. 35 cm.

238   Collier, P. F. & Son, Corp.
       World atlas and gazetteer. New York, [1953].
       472 p. col. maps. 37 cm.

239   Collins, William, Sons & Co., Ltd.
       Collins-Longmans clarion atlas. 4 ed. By B. A.
       Workman. Glasgow, New York, [1953].
       64 p. col. maps. 23 cm.

240   Collins, William, Sons & Co., Ltd.
       Die gestandaardiseerde Suid-Afrikaanse atlas. By
       B. A. Workman and K. H. Huggins. Glasgow, [1953].
       49 p. col. maps. 28 cm.

241   Collins, William, Sons & Co., Ltd.
       The standardised South African atlas. By B. A.
       Workman and K. H. Huggins. Glasgow, [1953].
       49 p. col. maps. 28 cm.

242   Container Corporation of America.
       World geo-graphic atlas, a composite of man's en-
       vironment. By Herbert Bayer. Chicago, 1953.
       368 p. col. maps. 41 cm.

243   Czechoslovakia. Státní pedagogické nakl.
       Skolní zeměpisný atlas. 3 ed. By Bedřich
       Salamon and Karel Kuchař. Praha, 1953.
       37 p.   col. maps. 32 cm.

244   Czechoslovakia. Státní zeměměřicky a kartografický
       ústav.
       Maly politicky atlas světa. 2 ed. By Antonin
       Koláčný. Praha, 1953.
       316 p. col. maps. 32 cm.

245   Delagrave.
       Nouvel atlas classique. By M. Fallex and A.
       Gilbert. Paris, 1953.
       102 p. col. maps. 28 cm.

246   Djambatan.
      Atlas Indonesia dan dunia untuk sekolah rakjat.   By
      Djamaludin Adinegoro.   Djakarta, 1953.
      48 p.   col.   maps.   30 cm.

247   Djambatan.
      Atlas tanah air untuk sekolah rakjat.   4 ed.
      Djakarta, 1953
      24 p.   col.   maps.   29 cm.

248   Editions Bordas.
      Nouvel atlas général: la France, l'Union française,
      le monde.   By Pierre Serryn.   Paris, [1953].
      170 p.   col.   maps.   31 cm.

249   Editorial Seix Barral, S.A.
      Atlas universal y de Colombia.   Barcelona, 1953.
      20 p.   col.   maps.   29 cm.

250   Geographical Pub. Co.
      School and library atlas of the world.   By Fred W.
      Foster.   Chicago, [1953].
      324 p.   col.   maps.   56 cm.

251   Geokarta.
      Geografiski atlas.   By Dobrosav Ž. Šobić.
      Beograd, 1953.
      38 p.   col.   maps.   34 cm.

252   Grolier Society.
      World atlas; an encyclopedic atlas of the world.
      Canadian classics ed.   With Hammond.   Toronto,
      1953.
      340 p.   col.   maps.   32 cm.

253   Haack, Hermann.
      Atlas zur Erd- und Länderkunde.   Grosse Ausgabe.
      Gotha, 1953.
      1 vol.   col.   maps.   31 cm.

254   Haack, Hermann.
      Die Erde.   Taschenatlas.   Gotha, 1953 —
      1 vol.   col.   maps.   18 cm.

255   Hachette.
      Atlas classique de géographie ancienne et moderne.
      By F. Schrader and L. Gallouédec.   Paris, [1953].
      110 p.   col.   maps.   32 cm.

256   Hammond, C. S. & Co. , Inc.
       Comparative world atlas. New York, [1953].
       48 p. col. maps. 32 cm.

257   Hammond, C. S. & Co. , Inc.
       Global geography atlas. Maplewood, N. J., [1953].
       48 p. col. maps. 32 cm.

258   Hammond, C. S. & Co. , Inc.
       Hammond's Library world atlas. New York, 1953.
       328 p. col. maps. 32 cm.

259   Hammond, C. S. & Co. , Inc.
       Hammond's modern world atlas and gazetteer, with
       new census. New York, [1953].
       48 p. col. maps. 31 cm.

260   Hammond, C. S. & Co. , Inc.
       Hammond's universal world atlas. New York, 1953.
       176 p. col. maps. 32 cm.

261   Hammond, C. S. & Co. , Inc.
       Hammond's world history wall atlas. New York,
       1953.
       24 p. col. maps. 73 cm.

262   Hammond, C. S. & Co. , Inc.
       New home reference world atlas and gazetteer.
       New York, [1953].
       2 vol. col. maps. 25 cm.

263   Hammond, C. S. & Co. , Inc.
       New international world atlas; the modern medieval
       and ancient world. New York, [1953].
       120 p. col. maps. 32 cm.

264   Hammond, C. S. & Co. , Inc.
       Standard world atlas. New York, 1953.
       296 p. col. maps. 32 cm.

265   Hammond, C. S. & Co. , Inc.
       World atlas; an encyclopedic atlas of the world.
       New York, 1953.
       340 p. col. maps. 32 cm.

266   Hammond, C. S. & Co. , Inc.
       World atlas. Superior ed. Maplewood, N.J., 1953 —
       1 vol. col. maps. 32 cm.

267   Hölzel, Ed. Verlag.
       Österreichischer Mittelschulatlas.   77 ed. Wien, 1953.
       146 p. col. maps. 31 cm.

268   Hölzel, Ed. Verlag.
       Österreichischer Mittelschulatlas.   78 ed. Wien, 1953.
       146 p. col. maps. 31 cm.

269   Humboldt Verlag.
       Welt Atlas.   By Alfred Malaschofsky.   With
       Columbus Verlag Oestergaard.   Stuttgart, [1953].
       192 p. col. maps. 18 cm.

270   Importbøger.
       List's verdensatlas.   With Atlantik Verlag.
       København, [1953].
       74 p. col. maps. 19 cm.

271   Istituto Geografico De Agostini.
       Piccolo atlante della produzione e dei commerci.
       By L. Visintin.   Novara, [1953].
       86 p. col. maps. 26 cm.

272   Istituto geografico editoriale italiano.
       Atlantino I.G.E.I., con dizionario geografico.   By
       Riccardo Riccardi and Mario Riccardi.   Roma,
       [1953].
       228 p. col. maps. 16 cm.

273   Johnston, W. & A. K., Ltd.
       Pocket atlas of the world.   Edinburgh, 1953.
       158 p. col. maps. 18 cm.

274   JRO-Verlag.
       JRO Bildatlas der Welt.   1 ed.   By Ernst Kremling.
       München, [1953].
       219 p. col. maps. 31 cm.

275   Klett Verlag.
       Geographischer Weltatlas.   By W. Weber.
       Stuttgart, 1953.
       37 p. col. maps. 33 cm.

276   Kümmerly & Frey.
       Taschen Weltatlas.   Bern, [1953].
       40 p. col. maps. 18 cm.

277   Lloyd's Corp. of.
      Lloyd's maritime atlas. 2 ed. London, 1953.
      1 vol. col. maps. 25 cm.

278   McGraw Hill Book Co.
      The advanced atlas of modern geography. 3 ed.
      With Bartholomew. New York, 1953.
      159 p. col. maps. 38 cm.

279   Meiklejohn.
      The advanced atlas of modern geography. 3 ed.
      With Bartholomew. London, 1953.
      159 p. col. maps. 38 cm.

280   Meiklejohn.
      The comparative atlas of physical and political
      geography. 40 ed. With Bartholomew. London,
      1953.
      112 p. col. maps. 28 cm.

281   Noordhoff-Kolff, N.V.
      Atlas Indonesia dan Dunia Sekolah Rakjat. Djakarta,
      1953.
      1 vol. col. maps. 28 cm.

282. Orbis.
      Politicko-hospodarský atlas světa. 4 ed. Praha,
      1953 –
      in parts. col. maps. 33 cm.   ·

283   Philip, George & Son, Ltd.
      College atlas for South Africa. By George Goodall.
      London, 1953.
      127 p. col. maps. 29 cm.

284   Philip, George & Son, Ltd.
      Comparative Commonwealth atlas for use in
      Australian schools. 13 ed. London, 1953.
      1 vol. col. maps. 23 cm.

285   Philip, George & Son, Ltd.
      Modern world atlas. By George Goodall. London,
      1953.
      35 p. col. maps. 23 cm.

286   Philip, George & Son, Ltd.
      Philips' modern world atlas.   By George Goodall.
      London, 1953.
      24 p. col. maps. 23 cm.

287   Philip, George & Son, Ltd.
      The university atlas. 7 ed. London, 1953.
      148 p. col. maps. 38 cm.

288   Philip, George & Son, Ltd.
      Visual contour atlas. By George Goodall. London,
      1953.
      54 p. col. maps. 23 cm.

289   Poland. Państwowe przedsiębiorstwo wydawnictw
      kartograficznych.
      Maly atlas geograficzny. 15 ed. By E. Romer.
      Warszawa, 1953.
      12 p. col. maps. 30 cm.

290   Rand McNally & Co.
      Cosmopolitan world atlas. Chicago, [1953].
      375 p. col. maps. 37 cm.

291   Rand McNally & Co.
      Premier world atlas. Chicago, [1953].
      272 p. col. maps. 37 cm.

292   Rand McNally & Co.
      Rand McNally regional atlas. By Edward B.
      Espenshade, Jr. Chicago, [1953].
      60 p. col. maps. 29 cm.

293   Rand McNally & Co.
      World atlas; physical, political and economic. 9 ed.
      By Edward B. Espenshade, Jr. Chicago, [1953].
      272 p. col. maps. 29 cm.

294   Replogle Globes, Inc.
      Replogle comprehensive atlas of the world. With
      Hammond. Chicago, [1953].
      376 p. col. maps. 25 cm.

295   Romania. Editura de stat pentru literatură stiinţifică.
      Atlas geografic. Bucuresti, 1953.
      76 p. col. maps. 31 cm.

296 Svenska bokförlaget Norstedts.
Nordisk skolatlas, folkskolupplagan. 3 ed. By Hans
Wilhelmsson Ahlmann. Stockholm, [1953].
36 p. col. maps. 34 cm.

297 Svenska bokförlaget Norstedts.
Nordisk skolatlas; läroverksupplagan. By Hans
Wilhelmsson Ahlmann. Stockholm, [1953].
64 p. col. maps. 34 cm.

298 Teikoku-shoin Co., Ltd.
Shinsho koto chizu. [New atlas for colleges]. By
Kozo Iwata. Tokyo, 1953.
138 p. col. maps. 26 cm.

299 ten Brink, H.
Schoolatlas. By H. Boelmans. Meppel, 1953—
in parts. col. maps. 29 cm.

300 Tidens förlag.
Tidens världsatlas. With Generalstabens
litografiska anstalt. Stockholm, [1953].
100 p. col. maps. 28 cm.

301 Ti- t'u chu-pan she.
Shih- chieh yü ti - hsüeh she. Hsin shih - chieh ti-
t'u chi. [New atlas of the world]. Shanghai, 1953.
40 p. col. maps. 27 cm.

302 Universal Guild.
New home reference world atlas and gazetteer.
With Hammond. New York, [1953].
2 vol. col. maps. 25 cm.

303 U.S.S.R. Glavnoe upravlenie geodezii i kartografii.
Geograficheskii atlas dlya nachalnoi shkoly.
Moskva, 1953.
16 p. col. maps. 25 cm.

304 Verlag Lebendiges Wissen.
Weltatlas. By Alfred Malaschofsky. With Columbus
Verlag Oestergaard. München, [1953].
208 p. col. maps. 18 cm.

305 Volk und Wissen Verlag.
Atlas zur Erd-und Länderkunde. Grosse Ausgabe.
By Fritz Haefke. Berlin, 1953.
99 p. col. maps. 31 cm.

306   Wesmael-Charlier.
      Atlas classique. By Jean Tilmont. Namur, [1953].
      70 p. col. maps. 36 cm.

307   Westermann, Georg.
      Heimat und Welt. [Atlas]. Braunschweig, 1953.
      42 p. col. maps. 32 cm.

308   Wolters, J. B.
      Kleine schoolatlas der gehele aarde. 44 ed. By
      P. R. Bos. Groningen, 1953.
      64 p. col. maps. 31 cm.

                              1954

309   Aguilar, S.A. de Ediciones.
      Atlas universal Aguilar. By José Aguilar. Madrid,
      1954.
      386 p. col. maps. 42 cm.

310   Alves, Francisco.
      Novo atlas de geografia. By Julio Monteiro
      Aillaud. Rio de Janeiro, [1954].
      56 p. col. maps. 33 cm.

311   Atlantik Verlag.
      Deutschland und die Welt. By Willy Eggers.
      Frankfurt, [1954].
      75 p. col. maps. 34 cm.

312   Bartholomew, John & Son, Ltd.
      The Edinburgh world atlas or advanced atlas of
      modern geography. 1 ed. Edinburgh, 1954.
      159 p. col. maps. 39 cm.

313   Bertelsmann, C.
      Weltatlas. Gütersloh, [1954].
      498 p. col. maps. 20 cm.

314   Cram, George F. Co.
      Cram's student quick reference atlas of the world.
      Indianapolis, Ind., [1954].
      34 p. col. maps. 31 cm.

315 Doubleday.
     Hammond-Doubleday illustrated world atlas and
     gazetteer. Garden City, N.Y., 1954.
     128 p. col. maps. 32 cm.

316 Edições Melhoramentos.
     Atlas geográfico Melhoramentos. 12 ed. By José
     Geraldo Pauwels. São Paulo, 1954.
     95 p. col. maps. 35 cm.

317 Editions Bordas.
     Nouvel atlas général: la France, l'Union française,
     le monde. By Pierre Serryn. Paris, 1954.
     170 p. col. maps. 31 cm.

318 Editorial Luis Vives, S.A.
     Atlas universal. Zaragoza, [1954].
     36 p. col. maps. 32 cm.

319 Editorial Luis Vives, S. A.
     Atlas universal y de España. Zaragoza, [1954].
     52 p. col. maps. 31 cm.

320 Editorial Seix Barral, S.A.
     Atlas escolar universal y del Perú. Barcelona, 1954.
     20 p. col. maps. 29 cm.

321 Encyclopaedia Britannica.
     Encyclopaedia Britannica world atlas. Chicago,
     [1954].
     537 p. col. maps. 38 cm.

322 Evans Brothers.
     Visual geography atlas. London, [1954].
     36 p. 25 cm.

323 Falk Verlag.
     Weh-Bevölkerungs-Atlas. Hamburg, 1954-[1957].
     in parts. col. mpas. 47.5 cm.

324 Freytag, G.
     Beckmanns neues welt-lexikon. 4 ed. München,
     1954.
     2 vol. col. maps. 20 cm.

325 Geodéziai és kartográfiai intézet.
     GKI Zseb-atlasz. Budapest, [1954].
     32 p. col. maps. 17 cm.

326   Hachette.
       Atlas classique. By Pierre Gourou. Paris, [1954-
       56].
       2 vol. col. maps. 33 cm.

327   Hammond, C. S. & Co., Inc.
       Ambassador world atlas. Maplewood, N. J., 1954-
       1 vol. col. maps. 37 cm.

328   Hammond, C. S. & Co., Inc.
       Complete world atlas. New York, [1954].
       376 p. col. maps. 25 cm.

329   Hammond, C. S. & Co., Inc.
       Hammond-Doubleday illustrated world atlas and
       gazetteer. Garden City, N. Y., 1954.
       128 p. col. maps. 32 cm.

330   Hammond, C. S. & Co., Inc.
       New home reference world atlas and gazetteer.
       New York, [1954].
       2 vol. col. maps. 25 cm.

331   Hammond, C. S. & Co., Inc.
       New world atlas and gazetteer. New York, [1954].
       112 p. col. maps. 32 cm.

332   Hammond, C. S. & Co., Inc.
       Pictorial world atlas; an encyclopedic atlas of the
       world. New York, 1954.
       312 p. col. maps. 32 cm.

333   Hammond, C. S. & Co., Inc.
       Standard world atlas. New York, [1954].
       328 p. col. maps. 32 cm.

334   Hammond, C. S. & Co., Inc.
       Universal world atlas. New York, [1954].
       1 vol. col. maps. 32 cm.

335   Hammond, C. S. & Co., Inc.
       World atlas for students. New York, 1954.
       50 p. col. maps. 32 cm.

336   Hammond, C. S. & Co., Inc.
       World wide atlas. New York, [1954].
       31 p. col. maps. 27 cm.

337   Hölzel, Ed. Verlag.
      Österreichischer Mittelschulatlas. 79 ed.   By Hans
      Slanar. Wien, 1954.
      146 p. col. maps. 31 cm.

338   Istituto Geografico De Agostini.
      Atlante geografico commerciale.   By Luigi Visintin.
      Novara, [1954].
      64 p. col. maps. 33 cm.

339   Istituto Geografico De Agostini.
      Atlante storico. Novara, [1942-54].
      3 vol. col. maps. 33 cm.

340   Istituto Geografico De Agostini.
      Nouvo atlante geografico metodico.   By Luigi
      Visintin. Novara, [1954].
      110 p. col. maps. 34 cm.

341   Istituto geografico editoriale italiano.
      Atlante storico e geografico elementare.   By Riccardo
      Riccardi. Roma, [1954].
      16 p. col. maps. 26 cm.

342   JRO-Verlag.
      JRO Bildatlas der Welt.   2 ed.   By Ernst Kremling.
      München, [1954].
      219 p. col. maps. 31 cm.

343   Kantonaler Lehrmittel Verlag.
      Schweizerischer Sekundarschulatlas.   6 ed.   By Ed
      Imhof. Zürich, 1954.
      80 p. col. maps. 36 cm.

344   Keysersche Verlagsbuchhandlung, G. M. B. H.
      Atlas zur Erdkunde. 1 ed.   By Hermann
      Lautensach. Heidelberg, [1954].
      146 p. col. maps. 31 cm.

345   Kümmerly & Frey.
      Schweizerischer Schulatlas. 15 ed.   Bern, [1954].
      49 p. col. maps. 31 cm.

346   Kümmerly & Frey.
      Schweizerischer Volksschulatlas.   10 ed.   Bern,
      [1954].
      26 p. col. maps. 31 cm.

347   Livraria Sá da Costa.
      <u>Novo atlas escolar portugues.</u>   5 ed.   By João
      Soares.   Lisboa, [1954].
      80 p.   col. maps.   34 cm.

348   McGraw-Hill Book Co.
      <u>The Columbus atlas; or Regional atlas of the world.</u>
      With Bartholomew.   New York, [1954].
      297 p.   col. maps.   29 cm.

349   Noordhoff, P.
      <u>Atlas der gehele aarde.</u>   32 ed.   By P. R. Bos.
      Groningen, 1954.
      120 p.   col. maps.   31 cm.

350   Noordhoff, P.
      <u>Atlas seluruh dunia, untuk sekolah landjutan.</u>   By
      P. R. Bos.   Djakarta, 1954.
      42 p.   col. maps.   31 cm.

351   Oxford University Press.
      <u>Oxford economic atlas of the world.</u>   1 ed.
      London, 1954.
      279 p.   col. maps.   27 cm.

352   Pfahl Verlag.
      <u>Hansa   Weltatlas.</u>   8 ed.   By Oswald Muris and
      Hans Kleinert.   Laupheim, 1954.
      446 p.   col. maps.   24 cm.

353   Philip, George & Son, Ltd.
      <u>College atlas for South Africa.</u>   By George Goodall.
      London, [1954].
      127 p.   col. maps.   29 cm.

354   Philip, George & Son, Ltd.
      <u>Contemporary world atlas.</u>   By George Goodall.
      London, 1954.
      127 p.   col. maps.   29 cm.

355   Philip, George & Son, Ltd.
      <u>Modern school atlas.</u>   46 ed.   By George Goodall.
      London, 1954.
      127 p.   col. maps.   29 cm.

356 Philip, George & Son, Ltd.
New school atlas. 44 ed. By George Goodall.
London, 1954.
86 p. col. maps. 29 cm.

357 Poland. Wydawn. Ministerstwa Obrony Narodowej.
Podręczny atlas swiata. 1 ed. Warszawa, [1954-
61].
5 parts. col. maps. 25 cm.

358 Politikens forlag.
Politikens lommeatlas. By Axel Schou. København,
1954.
167 p. col. maps. 21 cm.

359 Prentice-Hall.
Atlas of the world's resources. Vol 1: The
agricultural resources of the world. By William
Van Royen. New York, 1954.
258 p. 40 cm.

360 Replogle Globes, Inc.
Replogle comprehensive atlas of the world. With
Hammond. Chicago, [1954].

361 Salinas Bellver, Salvador.
Atlas de geografía universal. 29 ed. Madrid, 1954.
70 p. col. maps. 35 cm.

362 Sears Roebuck.
New world atlas and gazetteer. With Hammond.
Chicago, [1954].
112 p. col. maps. 32 cm.

363 Sears Roebuck.
Sears family world atlas; an encyclopedic atlas of the
world. With Hammond. Chicago, [1954].
404 p. col. maps. 32 cm.

364 Svenska bokförlaget Norstedts.
Nordisk skolatlas, folkskolupplagen. 4 ed. By Hans
W:son Ahlmann. Stockholm, [1954].
38 p. col. maps. 34 cm.

365 Teikoku-shoin Co., Ltd.
Chûgakhô shakaika chizu. [Sociological atlas for
high schools]. Tokyo, 1954.
132 p. col. maps. 26 cm.

366   Universal Guild.
       New home reference world atlas and gazetteer.
       With Hammond.   New York, [1954].
       2 vol.   col.   maps.   25 cm.

367   U.S.S.R.   Glavnoe upravlenie geodezii i kartografii.
       Atlas mira.   Moskva, 1954.
       301 p.   col.   maps.   19 cm.

368   U.S.S.R.   Glavnoe upravlenie geodezii i kartografii.
       Atlas mira.   Moskva, 1954.
       373 p.   col.   maps.   51 cm.

369   U.S.S.R.   Glavnoe upravlenie geodezii i kartografii.
       Atlas mira.   By N. I. Svinarenko.   Moskva, 1954.
       152 p.   col.   maps.   26 cm.

370   U.S.S.R.   Glavnoe upravlenie geodezii i kartografii.
       Geograficheski atlas chastei sveta i vazhneishikh
       gosudarstv. dlya 6go 7go klasov.   Moskva, 1954.
       76 p.   col.   maps.   30 cm.

371   U.S.S.R.   Glavnoe upravlenie geodezii i kartografii.
       Geograficheski atlas dlya 5go i 6go klasov strednei
       shkoly.   Moskva, 1954.
       45 p.   col.   maps.   30 cm.

372   U.S.S.R.   Glavnoe upravlenie geodezii i kartografii.
       Geograficheski atlas dlya uchitelei srednei shkoly.
       Moskva, 1954.
       191 p.   col.   maps.   38 cm.

373   Volk und Wissen Verlag.
       Atlas zur Erd-und Länderkunde.   By Fritz Haefke.
       Berlin, 1954.
       98 p.   col.   maps.   31 cm.

374   Wenschow.
       Weltatlas.   München, [1954].
       48 p.   col.   maps.   34 cm.

375   Westermann, Georg.
       Der kleine Westermann atlas.   Braunschweig, [1954].
       32 p.   col.   maps.   29 cm.

376   Westermann, Georg.
      Der Lebensraum des Menschen; ein Westermann-
      Atlas für Schule und Haus. Braunschweig, 1954.
      70 p.   col. maps.   33 cm.

377   Westermann, Georg.
      Welt Atlas.   87 ed.   Braunschweig, [1954].
      142 p.   col. maps.   36 cm.

378   Wise, W. H.
      Pictorial world atlas; an encyclopedic atlas of the
      world.   With Hammond.   New York, 1954.
      312 p.   col. maps.   32 cm.

379   Yavneh.
      Atlas le-bate sefer amamiyim.   3 ed.   By Moshe
      Brawer.   Tel Aviv, [1954].
      48 p.   col. maps.   31 cm.

                              1955

380   Atlantik Verlag.
      Harms Schulatlas.   Frankfurt, [1955].
      41 p.   col. maps.   28 cm.

381   Bartholomew, John & Son, Ltd.
      The graphic atlas of the world.   10 ed.   Edinburgh,
      1955.
      180 p.   col. maps.   26 cm.

382   Cappelens, J. W.   Forlag, A. S.
      Hjemmenes verdensatlas med spesielle Norgeskart.
      Oslo, 1955.
      180 p.   col. maps.   28 cm.

383   Colin.
      Atlas historique et géographique Vidal-Lablache.
      Paris, 1955—
      1 vol.   col. maps.   40 cm.

384   Collier, P. F. & Son, Corp.
      World atlas and gazetteer, presenting the world in
      its geographical, physical, and commercial aspects.
      New York, [1955].
      480 p.   col. maps.   37 cm.

385   Collins, William, Sons & Co., Ltd.
      Collins-Longmans visible regions atlas.   10 ed.
      By K. H. Huggins.   London, New York, [1955].
      96 p.   col. maps.   30 cm.

386   Collins, William, Sons & Co., Ltd.
      Collins-Longmans world atlas for Malaya.   2 ed.
      By K. H. Huggins.   Glasgow, [1955].
      24 p.   col. maps.   29 cm.

387   Cram, George F. Co.
      Student quick reference atlas of the world.
      Indianapolis, Ind., [1954].
      34 p.   col. maps.   31 cm.

388   Djambatan.
      Atlas Indonesia dan dunia untuk sekolah rakjat.   By
      Djamaludin Adinegoro.   Djakarta, [1955].
      1 vol.   col. maps.   30 cm.

389   Encyclopaedia Britannica.
      Encyclopaedia Britannica world atlas.   Chicago,
      [1955].
      576 p.   col. maps.   38 cm.

390   Falk-Verlag.
      Falk Haus-Atlas.   Hamburg, [1955].
      142 p.   col. maps.   34 cm.

391   Freytag, Berndt & Artaria.
      Atlas für Lehrer-und Lehrerinnen Bildungsanstalten.
      Wien, [1955].
      89 p.   col. maps.   32 cm.

392   Freytag, G.
      Beckmanns neues Welt-Lexikon.   5 ed.
      München, [1955].
      2 vol.   col. maps.   20 cm.

393   Goldmann Verlag.
      Goldmanns Grosser Weltatlas.   By L. Visintin,
      Herbert Bayer and Wilhelm Goldmann.   München,
      [1955].
      323 p.   col. maps.   41 cm.

394   Haack, Hermann.
      Die Erde, Taschenatlas.   85 ed.   Gotha, 1955.
      214 p.   col. maps.   18 cm.

395   Haack, Hermann.
       Kleiner Weltatlas.   3 ed.   Gotha, [1955].
       124 p.   col. maps.   21 cm.

396   Hammond, C. S. & Co., Inc.
       Hammond's comparative world atlas.   Desk ed.
       New York, [1955].
       48 p.   col. maps.   31 cm.

397   Hammond, C. S. & Co., Inc.
       Hammond's modern world atlas and gazetteer.
       New York, [1955].
       48 p.   col. maps.   31 cm.

398   Hammond, C. S. & Co., Inc.
       Standard world atlas.   Canadian ed.   New York, 1955.
       328 p.   col. maps.   32 cm.

399   Hammond, C. S. & Co., Inc.
       World atlas, an encyclopedic atlas of the world,
       with latest and most authentic geographical and
       statistical information.   New York, 1955.
       388 p.   col. maps.   32 cm.

400   Hammond, C. S. & Co., Inc.
       World atlas for students.   New York, [1955].
       50 p.   col. maps.   32 cm.

401   Hammond, C. S. & Co., Inc.
       World wide atlas.   New York, [1955].
       31 p.   col. maps.   26 cm.

402   Hölzel, Ed. Verlag.
       Österreichischer Mittelschulatlas.   80 ed.   Wien,
       1955.
       146 p.   col. maps.   31 cm.

403   Houghton Mifflin Co.
       The Times atlas of the world.   With Bartholomew.
       Boston, 1955-59.
       5 vol.   col. maps.   50 cm.

404   Istituto Geografico De Agostini.
       Atlante universale.   By Luigi Visintin.   Novara,
       [1955].
       305 p.   col. maps.   28 cm.

405   Johnston, W. & A. K. and G. W. Bacon, Ltd.
      New world atlas. Edinburgh, [1955].
      143 p. col. maps. 29 cm.

406   JRO Verlag.
      Grosser JRO Weltatlas. 11 ed. München, 1955.
      137 p. col. maps. 43 cm.

407   Kartográfiai Vállalat.
      Földrajzi atlasz, a középiskolák számára.
      Budapest, 1955.
      48 p. col. maps. 28 cm.

408   Kartográfiai Vállalat.
      Földrajzi zsebatlasz. By Bognár Gábor.
      Budapest, 1955.
      48 p. col. maps. 17 cm.

409   Keysersche Verlagsbuchhandlung, G. M. B. H.
      Atlas zur Erdkunde. 2 ed. By Hermann
      Lautensach. Heidelberg, [1955].
      146 p. col. maps. 31 cm.

410   Knaur, Th. Nachf.
      Knaurs welt atlas. München, [1955].
      637 p. col. maps. 25 cm.

411   Librairie Payot.
      Atlas scolaire suisse pour l'enseignement secondaire.
      10 ed. By Ed. Imhof. Lausanne, 1955.
      144 p. col. maps. 36 cm.

412   Nathan, Fernand.
      Petit atlas universel Nathan. Paris, [1955].
      80 p. col. maps. 16 cm.

413   Noordhoff, P.
      Atlas selurah dunia untuk sekolah landjutan.
      Djakarta, 1955.
      49 p. col. maps. 31 cm.

414   Oxford University Press.
      Oxford economic atlas of the world. London, 1955.
      279 p. col. maps. 27 cm.

415   Oxford University Press.
      Oxford home atlas of the world. London, [1955].
      104 p. col. maps. 26 cm.

416 Oxford University Press.
Oxford school atlas. 1 ed. London, 1955.
104 p. col. maps. 26 cm.

417 Peuser, Ediciones Geográficas.
Nuevo atlas geográfico metódico universal. 13 ed.
By José Anesi. Buenos Aires, 1955.
76 p. col. maps. 37 cm.

418 Pfahl Verlag.
Hansa-Weltatlas. 9 ed. Laupheim, 1955.
446 p. col. maps. 24 cm.

419 Pfahl Verlag.
Welt Bildatlas, ein kartenwerk zum Verständnis des
zeitgeschehens. By Oswald Muris. Laupeim, 1955.
223 p. col. maps. 31 cm.

420 Philip, George & Son, Ltd.
Comparative Commonwealth atlas for use in
Australian schools. 14 ed. London, 1955.
1 vol. col. maps. 23 cm.

421 Philip, George & Son, Ltd.
Comparative Commonwealth atlas for use in
Australian schools. 15 ed. London, 1955.
1 vol. col. maps. 23 cm.

422 Philip, George & Son, Ltd.
Philips mercantile marine atlas. 15 ed. By
Harold Fullard. London, 1955.
96 p. col. maps. 53 cm.

423 Philip, George & Son, Ltd.
Record atlas. 17 ed. By George Goodall. London,
1955.
320 p. col. maps. 29 cm.

424 Poland. Centralny urząd geodezji i kartografii.
Atlas geograficzny. By Eugeniusz Romer.
Warszawa, 1955.
60 p. col. maps. 31 cm.

425 Poland. Centralny urząd geodezji i kartografii.
Maly atlas geograficzny. 16 ed. By Eugeniusz
Romer. Warszawa, 1955.
14 p. col. maps. 30 cm.

426   Rand McNally & Co.
      Cosmopolitan world atlas. Chicago, [1955].
      375 p. col. maps. 37 cm.

427   Rand McNally & Co.
      Premier world atlas. Chicago, [1955].
      303 p. col. maps. 37 cm.

428   Rand McNally & Co.
      Rand McNally encyclopedic world atlas.
      Chicago, [1955].
      246 p. col. maps. 22 cm.

429   Rand McNally & Co.
      Standard world atlas. Chicago, [1955].
      294p. col. maps. 28 cm.

430   Rand McNally & Co.
      World atlas, physical, political, and economic.
      9 ed. By Edward B. Espenshade, Jr. New York,
      [1955].
      272 p. col. maps. 29 cm.

431   Replogle Globes, Inc.
      Replogle world atlas. With Hammond. Chicago,
      [1955].
      200 p. col. maps. 23 cm.

432   Robinson, H. E. C. Pty, Ltd.
      Primary school world atlas, illus. in color.
      Sydney, [1955].
      62 p. col. maps. 23 cm.

433   Sadlier, W. H.
      Atlas of the world. With Hammond. New York, 1955.
      1 vol. col. maps. 26 cm.

434   Seljačka sloga.
      Geografski atlas i statističko-geografski pregled
      svijeta. 4 ed. By Petar Mardešić. Zagreb, 1955.
      308 p. col. maps. 22 cm.

435   Söderström, Werner.
      Jokamiehen maailmankartasto. Porvoossa, [1955].
      140 p. col. maps. 22 cm.

436 Switzerland. Konferenz der Kantonalen
Erziehungsdirektoren.
Schweizerischer Mittelschulatlas. 11 ed. Zürich,
1955.
144 p. col. maps. 36 cm.

437 The Times Publishing Co.
The Times atlas of the world. Mid-century ed.
With Bartholomew. London, 1955-59.
5 vol. col. maps. 50 cm.

438 Thieme, W. J.
Atlas van Europa en de werelddelen, voor de
lagere school. 45 ed. By G. Prop. Zutphen,
1955.
48 p. col. maps. 26 cm.

439 U. S. Weather Bureau.
U. S. Navy Marine climatic atlas of the world.
Washington, D. C., 1955-68.
8 vol. col. maps. 50 cm.

440 U.S.S.R. Glavnoe upravelenie geodezii i kartografii.
Atlas mira. Moskva, 1955.
230 p. col. maps. 20 cm.

441 U.S.S.R. Glavnoe upravelenie geodezii i kartografii.
Geograficheskii atlas dlya nachalnoi shkoly.
Moskva, [1955].
1 vol. col. maps. 25 cm.

442 U.S.S.R. Glavnoe upravelenie geodezii i kartografii.
Geograficheskii atlas dlya 5go i 6go klassov srednei
shkoly. Moskva, 1955.
43 p. col. maps. 30 cm.

443 U.S.S.R. Glavnoe upravelenie geodezii i kartografii.
Geograficheskii atlas dlya uchitelei srednei shkoly.
Moskva, 1955.
191 p. col. maps. 38 cm.

444 U.S.S.R. Glavnoe upravelenie geodezii i kartografii.
Geograficheskii atlas zaribechnich stran dlya srednei
shkoly. 2 ed. Moskva, 1955.
79 p. col. maps. 30 cm.

445   Volk und Wissen Verlag.
      Atlas zur Erd-und Länderkunde.   By Fritz Haefke.
      Berlin, 1955.
      56 p. col. maps. 31 cm.

446   Volk und Wissen Verlag.
      Atlas zur Erd-und Länderkunde.   Grosse Ausg.
      Berlin, 1955.
      99 p. col. maps. 31 cm.

447   Wenshow.
      Atlas for secondary schools in Afghanistan.
      München, [1955].
      33 p. col. maps. 34 cm.

448   Westermann, Georg.
      Atlas für Hamburger Schulen. Braunschweig, 1955.
      3 vol. in 2. col. maps. 32 cm.

449   Westermann, Georg.
      Der Lebensraum des Menschen; ein Westermann
      Atlas für Schule und Haus. Braunschweig, 1955.
      70 p. col. maps. 33 cm.

450   Wolters, I. B.
      Schoolatlas der gehele aarde. 39 ed. By P. R.
      Bos. Groningen, 1955.
      48 p. col. maps. 39 cm.

451   Yayneh.
      Atlas physi, medini ve-kalkali. 2 ed. By Moshe
      Brawer. Tel Aviv, [1955].
      83 p. col. maps. 31 cm.

                              1956

452   Aguilar, S. A. de Ediciones.
      Atlas medio universal y de España. Madrid, [1956].
      126 p. col. maps. 31 cm.

453   Atlantik Verlag.
      Deutschland und die Welt. By Willy Eggers.
      Frankfurt, [1956].
      75 p. col. maps. 34 cm.

454 Atlantik Verlag.
Die Länder der Erde. 7 ed. By Willy Eggers.
Frankfurt, [1956].
49 p. col. maps. 34 cm.

455 Atlantik Verlag.
Handelschulatlas. Atlas für Wirtschaftsschulen.
By Willy Eggers. Frankfurt, [1956].
61 p. col. maps. 34 cm.

456 Atlantik Verlag.
Kleiner Weltatlas. By Willy Eggers. Frankfurt,
[1956].
43 p. col. maps. 28 cm.

457 Bartholomew, John & Son, Ltd.
The graphic atlas of the world. 10 ed. Edinburgh,
1956.
180 p. col. maps. 27 cm.

458 Bergvalls Förlag.
Bergvalls nya skolatlas. By Magnus Lundquist.
Stockholm, [1956].
56 p. col. maps. 25 cm.

459 Brazil. Conselho Nacional de Geografia.
Atlas geográfico escolar. Rio de Janeiro, [1956].
60 p. col. maps. 32 cm.

460 Collins, William, Sons & Co., Ltd.
Collins-Longmans study atlas. Glasgow, New York,
[1956].
1 vol. col. maps. 30 cm.

461 Columbus Verlag Oestergaad.
Columbus Weltatlas. By Karlheinz Wagner.
Berlin, [1956].
217 p. col. maps. 32 cm.

462 Cram, George F. Co.
New modern world atlas. Indianapolis, Ind.,[1956].
336 p. col. maps. 32 cm.

463 Czechoslovakia. Ústřední správa geodesie a kartografie.
Malý atlas světa. 3 ed. By Antonín Koláčný.
Praha, 1956.
235 p. col. maps. 30 cm.

464   Czechoslovakia. Ústřední správa geodesie a kartografie.
      Skolní zeměpisný atlas. 5 ed. By Bedřich
      Šalamon and Karel Kuchař. Praha, 1956.
      1 vol. col. maps. 32 cm.

465   Dell Pub. Co.
      The new Hammond-Dell world atlas. With Hammond.
      New York, 1956.
      255 p. col. maps. 17 cm.

466   Doubleday.
      Hammond-Doubleday illustrated world atlas and
      gazetteer. With Hammond. Garden City, N. Y.,
      [1956].
      128 p. col. maps. 32 cm.

467   Doubleday.
      Hammond family reference world atlas. With
      Hammond. Garden City, N. Y., 1956—
      1 vol. col. maps. 32 cm.

468   Editions Rencontre.
      Nouvel atlas mondial géographique et économique de
      tous les pays. By Eugen Theodor Rimli. Lausanne,
      [1956-].
      1 vol. in parts. col. maps. 28 cm.

469   Editorial Seix Barral, S. A.
      Atlas escolar universal. Barcelona, 1956.
      24 p. col. maps. 29 cm.

470   Freytag, Berndt & Artaria.
      Welt atlas. Wien, [1956].
      181 p. col. maps. 19 cm.

471   Freytag, G.
      Beckmanns neues Welt-lexikon mit Welt atlas. 6 ed.
      München, 1956.
      85 p. col. maps. 20 cm.

472   Ganaco, N. V.
      Atlas teruna untuk sekolah rakjat. Bandung, 1956—
      1 vol. col. maps. 34 cm.

473   GEO Publishing Co.
      The Faber atlas. By Daniel James Sinclair.
      Oxford, [1956].
      198 p. col. maps. 31 cm.

474   Haack, Hermann.
        Kleiner Weltatlas. 4 ed.   Gotha, [1956].
        132 p.   col. maps.   21 cm.

475   Hachette.
        Atlas classique. By Pierre Gourou.   Paris, [1956].
        132 p.   col. maps.   33 cm.

476   Hachette.
        Atlas Hachette. By Jean Martin.   Paris, [1956].
        215 p.   col. maps.   22 cm.

477   Hammond, C. S. & Co. Inc.
        Advanced reference atlas.   Maplewood, N. J.,[1956].
        1 vol.   col. maps.   32 cm.

478   Hammond, C. S. & Co., Inc.
        Family reference world atlas.   Maplewood, N. J.,
        [1956].
        176 p.   col. maps.   32 cm.

479   Hammond, C. S. & Co., Inc.
        Hammond ambassador world atlas.   New York, 1956.
        416 p.   col. maps.   39 cm.

480   Hammond, C. S. & Co., Inc.
        Illustrated atlas for young America.   Maplewood,
        N. J., 1956−
        1 vol.   col. maps.   26 cm.

481   Hammond, C. S. & Co., Inc.
        New international world atlas; the modern medieval,
        and ancient world.   Maplewood, N. J., [1956].
        1 vol.   col. maps.   32 cm.

482   Hammond, C. S. & Co., Inc.
        Standard world atlas.   Maplewood, N. J., 1956.
        328 p.   col. maps.   32 cm.

483   Hammond, C. S. & Co., Inc.
        World atlas; and encyclopedic atlas of the world.
        Maplewood, N. J.,[1956].
        344 p.   col. maps.   32 cm.

484   Hammond, C. S. & Co., Inc.
        World atlas for students.   New York, [1956].
        50 p.   col. maps.   32 cm.

485   Hanover House.
       Family reference world atlas.   With Hammond.
       Garden City, N. Y., 1956–
       1 vol.   col.   maps.   32 cm.

486   Hanover House.
       New practical world atlas.   With Hammond.
       Garden City, N. Y., [1956].
       112 p.   col.   maps.   32 cm.

487   Hölzel, Ed. Verlag.
       Österreichischer Mittelschulatlas.   81 ed.   Wien,
       1956.
       146 p.   col.   maps.   31 cm.

488   Istituto Geografico De Agostini.
       Atlante mondiale.   By Luigi Visintin.   Novara,[1956].
       188 p.   col.   mpas.   34 cm.

489   Istituto Geografico De Agostini.
       Atlas mundial y de Venezuela.   By Marco Aurelio
       Vila.   Caracas, [1956].
       80 p.   col.   maps.   28 cm.

490   Johnston, W. & A. K. and G. W. Bacon, Ltd.
       The advanced modern school atlas.   Edinburgh, 1956.
       76 p.   col.   maps.   28 cm.

491   JRO Verlag.
       Grosse JRO Weltatlas.   Volksausgabe.   3 ed.
       München, 1956.
       1 vol.   col.   maps.   45 cm.

492   Klett Verlag.
       Geographischer Weltatlas.   2 ed.   Stuttgart, [1956].
       50 p.   col. maps.   33 cm.

493   McGraw Hill Book Co.
       The advanced atlas of modern geography.   3 ed.
       With Bartholomew.   New York, 1956.
       169 p.   col.   maps.   38 cm.

494   Meiklejohn.
       The advanced atlas of modern geography.   3 ed.
       With Bartholomew.   London, 1956.
       169 p.   col.   maps.   38 cm.

495 Natur och kultur bokförlaget.
Världsatlas by Filip Hultblad. Stockholm, [1956].
39 p. col. maps. 35 cm.

496 Oxford University Press.
Oxford economic atlas of the world. London, 1956.
279 p. col. maps. 27 cm.

497 Oxford University Press.
The Little Oxford atlas. London, [1956].
69 p. col. maps. 26 cm.

498 Oxford University Press.
The Oxford Atlas. By Clinton Lewis and J. D.
Campbell. London, [1956].
214 p. col. maps. 39 cm.

499 Penguin Books.
The Penguin atlas of the world. By J. S. Keates.
Harmondsworth, [1956].
156 p. col. maps. 21 cm.

500 Philip, George & Son, Ltd.
Comparative Commonwealth atlas for use in
Australian schools. 16 ed. By George Goodall and
Harold Fullard. London, 1956.
1 vol. col. maps. 23 cm.

501 Philip, George & Son, Ltd.
Record atlas. 17 ed. By George Goodall. London,
1956.
320 p. col. maps. 29 cm.

502 Philip, George & Son, Ltd.
The Standard reference atlas. By George Goodall,
with Harold Fullard. London, 1956.
222 p. col. maps. 41 cm.

503 Poland. Centralny urzad geodezji i kartografii.
Maly atlas geograficzny. By Eugeniusz Romer.
Warszawa, 1956.
14 p. col. maps. 30 cm.

504 Poland. Państwowe przedsiębiorstwo wydawn
kartograficznych.
Atlas geograficzny. By Eugeniusz Romer.
Warszawa, 1956.
91 p. col. maps. 31 cm.

505 Replogle Globes, Inc.
Replogle world atlas. With Hammond. Chicago,
[1956].
200 p. col. maps. 23 cm.

506 Sadlier, W. H.
World atlas. With Hammond. New York, [1956].
1 vol. col. maps. 26 cm.

507 Sears, Roebuck.
Sears family world atlas; an encyclopedic atlas of
the world. With Hammond. Chicago, [1956].
393 p. col. maps. 38 cm.

508 Smulders' Drukkerijen, N.V.
Zakatlas. De werelddeln, de landen van Europa.
's Gravenhage, [1956].
28 p. col. maps. 16 cm.

509 Standard International Library.
New home reference world atlas and gazetteer.
With Hammond. New York, [1956].
2 vol. col. maps. 25 cm.

510 Thieme, W. J.
Atlas van Europa en de werelddelen. 46 ed. By
G. Prop. Zutphen, 1956.
48 p. col. maps. 26 cm.

511 Touring Club Italiano.
Atlante internazionale. Milano, 1956.
2 vol. col. maps. 51 cm.

512 U.S.S.R. Glavnoe upravlenie geodezii i kartografii.
Atlas mira. 2 ed. Moskva, 1956.
301 p. col. maps. 19 cm.

513 U.S.S.R. Glavnoe upravlenie geodezii i kartografii.
Geograficheskii atlas dlya srednei shkoly.
Moskva, 1956.
191 p. col. maps. 38 cm.

514 Wheaton & Co., Ltd.
Wide world atlas. Exeter, [1956].
32 p. col. maps. 28 cm.

515   Wolters, J. B.
      Atlas de Nederlandse Antilen, Suriname, Nederland,
      en de wereld.   Groningen, 1956.
      40 p. col. maps. 31 cm.

                        1957

516   Anokh, Hanokh.
      Atlas le-talmidim be-Yisrael.   Tel Aviv, [1957].
      36 p. col. maps. 30 cm.

517   Bartholomew, John & Son, Ltd.
      The compact atlas of the world.   4 ed.
      Edinburgh, 1957.
      160 p. col. maps. 17 cm.

518   Bartholomew, John & Son, Ltd.
      The Edinburgh world atlas or Advanced atlas of
      modern geography.   2 ed.   Edinburgh, 1957.
      159 p. col. maps. 39 cm.

519   Bosch.
      Atlas geográfico mundial y especial de España.
      Barcelona, [1957].
      74 p. col. maps. 38 cm.

520   Buchgemeinschaft Donauland.
      Donauland Weltatlas.   By Ernst Kremling.
      Wien, [1957].
      92 p. col. maps. 31 cm.

521   Collier, P. F. & Son, Corp.
      World atlas and gazetteer, presenting the world in
      its geographical, physical and commercial aspects.
      New York, [1957].
      472 p. col. maps. 37 cm.

522   Collins, William, Sons & Co., Ltd.
      Westminster atlas & gazetteer of the world.
      London, 1957.
      63 p. col. maps. 28 cm.

523   Czechoslovakia.   Ústřední správa geodesie a kartografie.
      Malý atlas sveta.   1 ed.   Praha, [1957].
      185 p. col. maps. 22 cm.

524   Czechoslovakia. Ústřední správa geodesie a kartografie.
      <u>Maly atlas sveta.</u> 1 ed.   By Antonín Koláčný.
      Bratislava, 1957.
      2 vol.   col.   maps.   30 cm.

525   Czechoslovakia. Ústřední správa geodesie a kartografie.
      <u>Školský zeměpisný atlas.</u> 6 ed.   By Bedrich
      Šalamon and Karel Kuchar.   Praha, 1957.
      41 p.   col.   maps.   32 cm.

526   Czechoslovakia. Ústřední správa geodesie a kartografie.
      <u>Zeměpisný cvicentí pro 7. postupný ročník.</u> 1 ed.
      Praha, [1957].
      24 p.   col.   maps.   30 cm.

527   Djambatan.
      <u>Atlas untuk sekolah landjutan.</u>   By Adam Bachtiar.
      Djakarta, 1957.
      56 p.   col.   maps.   35 cm.

528   Doubleday.
      <u>Hammond-Doubleday new illustrated world atlas and
      gazetteer.</u>   With Hammond.   Garden City, N. Y.,
      1957.
      128 p.   col.   maps.   32 cm.

529   Droemer.
      <u>Knaurs Welt Atlas.</u>   Ausführlicher geographischer,
      bevölkerungs-und wirtschaftlicher text.   München,
      [1957].
      537 p.   col.   maps.   25 cm.

530   Ediciones Libreria del Colegio.
      <u>Atlas Ibero-Americano de geografia mundial.</u>   By
      Jaime Vincens Vives.   Buenos Aires, [1957].
      121 p.   col.   maps.   34 cm.

531   Edições Melhoramentos.
      <u>Atlas geográfico Melhoramentos.</u> 15 ed.   By
      Geraldo José Pauwels.   São Paulo, 1957.
      67 p.   col.   maps.   36 cm.

532   Editions Bordas.
      <u>Nouvel atlas général, la France, l'Union française,
      le monde.</u>   By Pierre Serryn.   Paris, [1957].
      150 p.   col.   maps.   31 cm.

533   Editorial Francisco Seix, S.A.
        Geografía y atlas universal.   Barcelona, 1957.
        271 p.   col. maps.   28 cm.

534   Elsevier.
        Winkler Prins Atlas.   3 ed.   By M. E. Dumont and
        G. G. M. Miermans.   Amsterdam, 1957.
        336 p.   col. maps.   32 cm.

535   Empresa Editora Zig Zag.
        Atlas universal, edición escolar.   4 ed.   (con
        nuevos mapas de Chile).   By Alejandro Ríos Valdavia.
        Santiago de Chile, 1957.
        43 p.   col. maps.   29 cm.

536   Europäischer Buchklub.
        Klub Weltatlas; E. Debes Handatlas.   By Karlheinz
        Wagner.   Stuttgart, [1957].
        231 p.   col. maps.   42 cm.

537   Falk-Verlag.
        Falk Haus-Atlas.   3 ed.   Hamburg, [1957].
        152 p.   col. maps.   34 cm.

538   Goldmann Verlag.
        Handatlas.   By L. Visintin and Wilhelm Goldmann.
        München, [1957].
        158 p.   col. maps.   41 cm.

539   Haack, Hermann.
        Die Erde, Taschenatlas.   87 ed.   Gotha, 1957.
        205 p.   col. maps.   18 cm.

540   Hachette.
        Atlas classique de géographie ancienne et moderne.
        By F. Schrader and L. Gallouédec.   Paris, [1957].
        126 p.   col. maps.   32 cm.

541   Hachette.
        Atlas Hachette.   Paris, [1957].
        195 p.   col. maps.   22 cm.

542   Hammond, C. S. & Co., Inc.
        Atlas moderno universal Hammond.   Maplewood,
        N. J., [1957].
        47 p.   col. maps.   31 cm.

543   Hammond, C. S. & Co., Inc.
       Complete world atlas. New York, [1957].
       400 p. col. maps. 25 cm.

544   Hammond, C. S. & Co., Inc.
       Globemaster world atlas. New York, [1957].
       48 p. col. maps. 32 cm.

545   Hammond, C. S. & Co., Inc.
       Hammond ambassador world atlas. Maplewood,
       N. J., [1957].
       1 vol. col. maps. 39 cm.

546   Hammond, C. S. & Co., Inc.
       Hammond's library world atlas. Maplewood,
       N. J., [1957].
       312 p. col. maps. 33 cm.

547   Hammond, C. S. & Co., Inc.
       New era atlas of the world. New York, [1957].
       160 p. col. maps. 32 cm.

548   Hammond, C. S. & Co., Inc.
       Standard world atlas. Maplewood, N. J., 1957.
       328 p. col. maps. 32 cm.

549   Hanover House.
       Family reference world atlas. With Hammond.
       Garden City, N. Y., [1957].
       176 p. col. maps. 32 cm.

550   Hanover House.
       Hammond's new practical world atlas. With
       Hammond. Garden City, N. Y., [1957].
       112 p. col. maps. 32 cm.

551   Hölzel, Ed. Verlag.
       Österreichischer Mittelschulatlas. 82 ed. Wien,
       1957.
       146 p. col. maps. 31 cm.

552   JRO Verlag.
       Weltwirtschafts Atlas: Atlas für Politik und
       Zeitgeschichte. By Ernst Kremling. München, 1957-
       in parts. col. maps. 30 cm.

553   Kantonaler Lehrmittelverlag.
      Schweizerischer Sekundarschulatlas.   7 ed.   By Ed.
      Imhof.   Zürich, 1957.
      80 p.   col. maps.   36 cm.

554   Kartográfiai Vállalat.
      Földrajzi atlasz as általános iskolák számára.
      Budapest, 1957.
      32 p.   col. maps.   29 cm.

555   Keysersche Verlagsbuchhandlung, G. M. B. H.
      Atlas zur Erdkunde.   Grosse Ausgabe.   3 ed.   By
      Hermann Lautensach.   Heidelberg, [1957].
      207 p.   col. maps.   31 cm.

556   Keysersche Verlagsbuchhandlung, G. M. B. H.
      Atlas zur Erdkunde, Kurzausgabe.   1 ed.   By
      Hermann Lautensach.   Heidelberg, [1957].
      100 p.   col. maps.   32 cm.

557   Larousse.
      Atlas international Larousse, politique et économique.
      By Jean Chardonnet and Ivan Du Jonchay.   Paris,
      [1957].
      239 p.   col. maps.   50 cm.

558   Meiklejohn.
      The advanced atlas of modern geography.   4 ed.
      With Bartholomew.   London, 1957.
      159 p.   col. maps.   38 cm.

559   Nathan, Fernand.
      Petit atlas universel Nathan.   Paris, [1957].
      80 p.   col. maps.   16 cm.

560   Newnes, George, Ltd.
      Newnes pictorial knowledge atlas.   By Peter Finch
      and H. Fullard.   London, [1957].
      1 vol.   col. maps.   26 cm.

561   Noordhoff-Kolff, N. V.
      Atlas seluruh dunia.   By R. Bos and K. Zeeman.
      Djakarta, 1957.
      42 p.   col. maps.   31 cm.

562   Odhams Press, Ltd.
      New illustrated atlas of the world.   London, [1957].
      1 vol.   col. maps.   29 cm.

563   Oxford University Press.
      The Canadian Oxford desk atlas of the world.
      Toronto, 1957.
      137 p. col. maps. 26 cm.

564   Oxford University Press.
      The Canadian Oxford atlas of the world.   2 ed.
      Toronto, 1957.
      1 vol. col. maps. 39 cm.

565   Oxford University Press.
      The Oxford atlas. London, 1957.
      210 p. col. maps. 40 cm.

566   Pfahl Verlag.
      Hansa Universal Atlas. 1 ed.   By Oswald Muris.
      Baden-Baden, 1957.
      480 p. col. maps. 24 cm.

567   Pfahl Verlag.
      Hansa Weltatlas. By Oswald Muris.   Baden-Baden,
      1957.
      390 p. col. maps. 24 cm.

568   Philip, George & Son, Ltd.
      Comparative Commonwealth atlas for use in
      Australian schools.   17 ed.   By George Goodall
      and Harold Fullard.   London, 1957.
      1 vol. col. maps. 23 cm.

569   Philip, George & Son, Ltd.
      Contemporary world atlas.   By Harold Fullard.
      London, 1957.
      143 p. col. maps. 29 cm.

570   Philip, George & Son, Ltd.
      Record atlas.   19 ed.   By Harold Fullard.
      London, 1957.
      320 p. col. maps. 29 cm.

571   Philip, George & Son, Ltd.
      Secondary school atlas.   96 ed.   By Harold Fullard.
      London, [1957].
      64 p. col. maps. 28 cm.

572   Poland. Państwowe przedsiębiorstwo wydawn.
       kartograficznych.
       Atlas geograficzny.   By E. Romer.   Warszawa,
       1957.
       108 p.   col. maps.   31 cm.

573   Poland. Państwowe przedsiębiorstwo wydawn.
       kartograficznych.
       Maly atlas geograficzny.   16 ed.   By E. Romer.
       Warszawa, 1957.
       14 p.   col. maps.   31 cm.

574   Praeger, Frederick A.
       An atlas of world affairs.   1 ed.   By Andrew Boyd.
       New York, [1957].
       160 p.   21 cm.

575   Rand McNally & Co.
       Classroom atlas.   Chicago, 1957.
       64 p.   col. maps.   26 cm.

576   Rand McNally & Co.
       Contemporary world atlas.   Chicago, 1957.
       96 p.   col. maps.   35 cm.

577   Rand McNally & Co.
       Cosmopolitan world atlas.   New York, 1957.
       375 p.   col. maps.   37 cm.

578   Rand McNally & Co.
       Rand McNally regional atlas.   Chicago, 1957.
       60 p.   col. maps.   29 cm.

579   Rand McNally & Co.
       Readers world atlas.   Chicago, [1957].
       288 p.   col. maps.   28 cm.

580   Rand McNally & Co.
       Standard world atlas.   Chicago, [1957].
       400 p.   col. maps.   28 cm.

581   Rand McNally & Co.
       World atlas; physical, political and economic.
       10 ed.   By Edward B. Espenshade, Jr.   Chicago,
       [1957].
       272 p.   col. maps.   29 cm.

582 Replogle Globes, Inc.
Replogle comprehensive atlas of the world. With
Hammond. Chicago, [1957].
400 p. col. maps. 25 cm.

583 Replogle Globes, Inc.
Replogle world atlas. With Hammond. Chicago,
[1957].
200 p. col. maps. 23 cm.

584 Romania. Editura di Stat Didactică și Pedagogică.
Atlas geografic școlar. By N. Gheorghiu.
Bucuresti, 1957.
34 p. col. maps. 33 cm.

585 Savremena shkola.
Zemijopisni atlas. By Slobadan Mitić. Beograd,
1957.
16 p. col. maps. 34 cm.

586 Società editrice internazionale.
Nuova atlante geografico SEI. By Dino Gribaudi.
Torino, [1957].
259 p. col. maps. 24 cm.

587 Sohlmans förlag, a.b.
Sohlmans världsatlas. By Karl Erik Bergsten.
With Philip. Stockholm, 1957.
163 p. col. maps. 29 cm.

588 Thieme, W. J.
Atlas van Europa en de werelddelen. 47 ed. By
G. Prop. Zutphen, 1957.
48 p. col. maps. 26 cm.

589 Tidens förlag.
Tidens världsatlas. 2 ed. With Generalstabens
litografiska anstalt. Stockholm, [1957].
169 p. col. maps. 28 cm.

590 U.S.S.R. Glavnoe upravlenie geodezii i kartografii.
Geograficheskii atlas dlya 4 go klassa. Moskva, 1957.
16 p. col. maps. 25 cm.

591 U.S.S.R. Glavnoe upravlenie geodezii i kartografii.
Geograficheskii atlas dlya 5 go klassa. Moskva, [1957].
16 p. col. maps. 28 cm.

592 Vallardi, A.
Atlante scolastico di geografia moderna. By Olinto
Marinelli. Milano, [1957].
132 p. col. maps. 32 cm.

593 Verlag Enzyklopädie.
Weltatlas; die staaten der erde und ihre wirtschaft.
2 ed. By Edgar Lehmann. Leipzig, 1957.
170 p. col. maps. 35 cm.

594 Volk und Wissen Verlag.
Atlas zur Erd-und Länderkunde. By Fritz Haefke.
Berlin, 1957.
56 p. col. maps. 31 cm.

595 Volk und Wissen Verlag.
Atlas zur Erd-und Länderkunde. Grosse Ausgabe.
13 ed. By Fritz Haefke. Berlin, 1957.
99 p. col. maps. 31 cm.

596 Westermann, Georg.
Der Lebensraum des Menschen; ein Westermann
Atlas für Schule und Haus. Braunschweig, 1957.
70 p. col. maps. 33 cm.

597 Westermann, Georg.
Weltatlas. 91 ed. Braunschweig, 1957.
222 p. col. maps. 34 cm.

1958

598 Aguilar, S. A. de Ediciones.
Atlas universal Aguilar. By José Aguilar.
Madrid, 1958.
514 p. col. maps. 42 cm.

599 Aguilar S. A. de Ediciones.
Nuevo atlas mundial. 1 ed. Madrid, 1958.
392 p. col. maps. 32 cm.

600 Aguilar S. A. de Ediciones.
Nuevo atlas mundial. 2 ed. Madrid, 1958.
392 p. col. maps. 32 cm.

601 Bartholomew, John & Son, Ltd.
The world pocket atlas and gazetteer. Edinburgh, 1958.
160 p. col. maps. 15 cm.

602   Bertelsmann, C.
        Weltatlas. Gütersloh, 1958.
        498 p. col. maps. 20 cm.

603   Book Production Industries.
        International standard atlas of the world. With
        Rand McNally. Chicago, [1958].
        448 p. col. maps. 35 cm.

604   Cartographia.
        Pocket atlas. International ed. Budapest, [1958].
        40 p. col. maps. 17 cm.

605   Collier, P. F. & Son, Corp.
        Collier's world atlas and gazetteer. New York, 1958.
        130 p. col. maps. 37 cm.

606   Columbus Verlag Oestergaard.
        Columbus Hausatlas in Wort and Bild. By Karlheinz
        Wagner. Berlin, [1958].
        1 vol. col. maps. 41 cm.

607   Czechoslovakia. Ústřední správa geodesie a kartografie.
        Malý atlas světa. 2 ed. Praha, 1958.
        188 p. col. maps. 21.5 cm.

608   Czechoslovakia. Ústřední správa geodesie a kartografie.
        Školní zeměpisný atlas. 7 ed. By Bedřich Šalamon
        and Karel Kuchař. Praha, 1958.
        1 vol. col. maps. 32 cm.

609   Czechoslovakia. Ústřední správa geodesie a kartografie.
        Školní zeměpisný atlas pro 4 a 5. ročník všeobecné
        vzdělavacích škol. 3 ed. Praha, [1958].
        18 p. col. maps. 30 cm.

610   Czechoslovakia. Ústřední správa geodesie a kartografie.
        Školní zeměpisný atlas pro 6. a 7. postupný ročník
        všeobecné vzdělávacích škol. 1 ed. Praha, 1958.
        81 p. col. maps. 31 cm.

611   Delagrave.
        Nouvel atlas classique. By Maurice Fallex and A.
        Gilbert. Paris, 1958.
        102 p. col. maps. 28 cm.

612 Dent, J. M.
    Dent's Canadian school atlas.   Toronto, 1958.
    115 p.   col. maps.   29 cm.

613 Dent, J. M.
    Everyman's encyclopaedia, Edinburgh world atlas.
    With Bartholomew.   London, [1958].
    163 p.   col. maps.   38 cm.

614 Dent, J. M.
    Historical and geographical atlas.   Toronto, [1958].
    148 p.   col. maps.   29 cm.

615 Doubleday.
    Hammond-Doubleday new illustrated world atlas and
    gazetteer.   With Hammond.   Garden City, N. Y.,
    [1958].
    128 p.   col. maps.   32 cm.

616 Editions Bordas.
    Nouvel atlas général, la France, l'Union française,
    le monde.   By Pierre Serryn.   Paris, 1958.
    168 p.   col. maps.   31 cm.

617 Editions Bordas.
    Petit atlas général.   By Pierre Serryn.   Paris, [1958].
    48 p.   col. maps.   31 cm.

618 Éditions Stauffacher.
    Nouvel atlas mondial.   2 ed.   By Eugene Th. Rimli
    and Louis Visintin.   Zürich, [1958-].
    1 vol.   col. maps.   28 cm.

619 Editorial Grijalbo.
    Pocket atlas.   With Kartográfiai Vállalat.
    Mexico, 1958.
    40 p.   col. maps.   17 cm.

620 Editorial Teide.
    Atlas de geografía general.   3 ed.   By J. Vincens
    and S. Sobrequés.   Barcelona, [1958].
    60 p.   col. maps.   32 cm.

621 Freytag, Berndt & Artaria.
    Atlas für Mittelschulen.   Wien, [1958].
    97 p.   col. maps.   32 cm.

622   Ganaco, N. V.
      Atlas teruna untuk sekolah rakjat. Bandung, 1958—
      in parts. col. maps. 34 cm.

623   Generalstabens litografiska anstalt.
      Kartboken; världsatlas för den 9 årige skolan. By
      Gösta Lundqvist. Stockholm, [1958].
      70 p. col. maps. 28 cm.

624   Geokarta.
      Geografisk atlas. By Dobrosav Ž. Šobić.
      Beograd, 1958.
      36 p. col. maps. 34 cm.

625   Germany. Deutscher Wetterdienst.
      World weather maps. Hamburg, 1958—
      in parts. col. maps. 58 cm.

626   Haack, Hermann.
      Agrarwirtschaftsatlas der Erde. Gotha, 1958.
      248 p. col. maps. 41 cm.

627   Haack, Hermann.
      Die Erde. Taschenatlas. 88 ed. Gotha, 1958.
      206 p. col. maps. 17 cm.

628   Hammond, C. S. & Co., Inc.
      Atlas moderno universal Hammond. Maplewood, N. J.,
      [1958].
      47 p. col. maps. 31 cm.

629   Hammond, C. S. & Co., Inc.
      Hammond ambassador world atlas. Maplewood,
      N. J., [1958].
      1 vol. col. maps. 39 cm.

630   Hammond, C. S. & Co., Inc.
      Illustrated atlas for young America. Maplewood,
      N. J., [1958].
      96 p. col. maps. 26 cm.

631   Hammond, C. S. & Co., Inc.
      Library world atlas. Maplewood, N. J., [1958].
      1 vol. col. maps. 32 cm.

632 Hammond, C. S. & Co., Inc.
World atlas, an encyclopedic atlas of the world.
Maplewood, N. J., 1958
394 p. col. maps. 33 cm.

633 Hanover House.
Family reference world atlas. With Hammond.
Garden City, N. Y., [1958].
258 p. col. maps. 27 cm

634 Herder Verlag.
Grosser Herder Atlas. By Carl Troll. Freiburg,
1958.
792 p. col. maps. 27 cm.

635 Hölzel, Ed. Verlag.
Österreichischer Hauptschulatlas. 3 ed. Wien, 1958.
76 p. col. maps. 31 cm.

636 Hölzel, Ed. Verlag.
Österreichischer Mittelschulatlas. 83 ed. Wien, 1958.
146 p. col. maps. 31 cm.

637 Johnston, W. & A. K. and G. W. Bacon, Ltd.
Johnston's premier atlas of the world. 3 ed.
Edinburgh, [1958].
94 p. col. maps. 28 cm.

638 Kanaat Yayinlari.
Büyük atlas. With Hölzel. Istanbul, [1958].
96 p. col. maps. 30 cm.

639 Kantonaler Lehrmittel Verlag.
Atlante svizzero per le scuole medie. 7 ed. By
Ed. Imhof. Zürich, 1958.
144 p. col. maps. 36 cm.

640 Kantonaler Lehrmittel Verlag.
Schweizerischer Mittelschulatlas. 12 ed. By
Ed. Imhof. Zürich, 1958.
144 p. col. maps. 36 cm.

641 Kartográfiai Vállalat.
Földrajzi atlasz az általános iskolák számára. 2 ed.
Budapest, 1958.
32 p. col. maps. 29 cm.

642   Kartográfiai Vállalat.
      Pocket atlas. International ed. Budapest, 1958.
      40 p. col. maps. 17 cm.

643   Kartográfiai Vállalat.
      Zsebatlasz. Budapest, 1958.
      72 p. col. maps. 17 cm.

644   Keysersche Verlagsbuchhandlung, G. M. B. H.
      Unsere Erde; eine Darstellung in Wort, Bild und
      Karte. By H. R. Fischer. Heidelberg, [1958].
      419 p. col. maps. 31 cm.

645   Kümmerly & Frey.
      Schweizerischer Volksschulatlas. 11 ed.
      Bern, [1958].
      34 p. col. maps. 33 cm.

646   Kümmerly & Frey.
      Taschen Weltatlas. Bern, [1958].
      48 p. col. maps. 18 cm.

647   Librairie Payot.
      Atlas scolaire suisse pour l'enseignement
      secondaire. 11 ed. By Ed. Imhof. Lausanne,
      [1958].
      144 p. col. maps. 36 cm.

648   Livraria Simões Lopes.
      Novo atlas geográfico para o estudo da geografia
      nos liceus, escolas comerciais, industriais e
      normais. 3 ed. By Augusto C. G. Soeiro and
      Carlos C. A. Vilamariz. Porto, [1958].
      32 p. col. maps. 33 cm.

649   Lloyd's Corp. of.
      Lloyd's maritime atlas. 3 ed. London, 1958.
      1 vol. col. maps. 25 cm.

650   Macdonald & Co., Ltd.
      The world is round. By Frank Debenham.
      London, 1958.
      97 p. col. maps. 41 cm.

651   National Geographic Society.
      National Geographic Society atlas folio. By James M.
      Darley. Washington, 1958—
      in parts. col. maps. 50 cm.

652 Nelson, Thomas & Sons, Ltd.
     Nelson's Canadian school atlas. By J. Wreford
     Watson. Toronto, [1958].
     92 p. col. maps. 29 cm.

653 Noordhoff-Kolff, N. V.
     Atlas sekolah rakjat. Djakarta, 1958.
     24 p. col. maps. 28 cm.

654 Oxford University Press.
     Concise Oxford atlas. 2 ed. By D. P. Bickmore.
     London, 1958.
     248 p. col. maps. 27 cm.

655 Oxford University Press.
     Oxford home atlas of the world. 2 ed. London,
     1958.
     138 p. col. maps. 26 cm.

656 Oxford University Press.
     The Oxford atlas. By Clinton Lewis and J. D.
     Campbell. London, [1958].
     188 p. col. maps. 39 cm.

657 Paravia, G. B.
     Atlante geografico, fisico, politico. By Giuseppe
     Pennesi. Torino, [1958].
     55 p. col. maps. 32 cm.

658 Pfahl Verlag.
     Hansa Handatlas. By Oswald Muris. Baden-Baden,
     1958.
     332 p. col. maps. 24 cm.

659 Pfahl Verlag.
     Hansa universal atlas. 2 ed. By Oswald Muris.
     Baden-Baden, 1958.
     380 p. col. maps. 24 cm.

660 Pfahl Verlag.
     Hansa Weltatlas. 10 ed. By Oswald Muris.
     Baden-Baden, 1958.
     380 p. col. maps. 24 cm.

661 Philip, George & Son, Ltd.
     Comparative Commonwealth atlas for use in
     Australian schools. 18 ed. By Harold Fullard. London, 1958.
     1 vol. col. maps. 23 cm.

662   Philip, George & Son, Ltd.
      Record atlas.   20 ed.   By Harold Fullard,
      London, 1958.
      184 p.   col. maps.   29 cm.

663   Philip, George & Son, Ltd.
      The university atlas.   8 ed.   London, 1958.
      200 p.   col. maps.   29 cm.

664   Poland.   Państwowe przedsiębiorstwo wydawnictw
      kartograficznych.
      Atlas geograficzny.   Warszawa, 1958.
      92 p.   col. maps.   31 cm.

665   Poland.   Państwowe przedsiębiorstwo wydawnictw
      kartograficznych.
      Atlas swiata.   Warszawa, 1958.
      293 p.   col. maps.   18 cm.

666   Poland.   Państwowe przedsiębiorstwo wydawnictw
      kartograficznych.
      Maly atlas geograficzny.   16 ed.   By Eugeniusz
      Romer.   Warszawa, 1958.
      14 p.   col. maps.   31 cm.

667   Prentice-Hall.
      Prentice-Hall world atlas.   By Joseph E. Williams.
      New York, 1958.
      100 p.   col. maps.   32 cm.

668   Rand McNally & Co.
      Classroom atlas.   Chicago, [1958].
      1 vol.   col. maps.   27 cm.

669   Rand McNally & Co.
      Cosmopolitan world atlas.   New York, [1958].
      376 p.   col. maps.   37 cm.

670   Rand McNally & Co.
      Popular world atlas.   Chicago, 1958.
      180 p.   col. maps.   27 cm.

671   Rand McNally & Co.
      Rand McNally world atlas, premier ed.   Chicago,
      1958.
      120 p.   col. maps.   41 cm.

672   Salinas Bellver, Salvador.
      Atlas de geografía universal.   32 ed.
      Madrid, 1958.
      70 p.   col. maps.   35 cm.

673   Silva, T. R.
      Atlas do mundo comercial e politico.   3 ed.
      Lisboa, 1958.
      24 p.   col. maps.   27 cm.

674   Simon & Schuster.
      The Global Atlas: A New View of the World from
      Space.   By Frank Debenham.   New York, 1958.
      97 p.   col. maps.   34 cm.

675   Stanford, Edward.
      The Whitehall atlas.   By Harold Fullard.   With
      Philip.   London, 1958.
      382 p.   col. maps.   285 cm.

676   Studio F. M. B.
      Nuovo atlante geografico.   Bologna, [1958].
      16 p.   col. maps.   22 cm.

677   Svenska bokförlaget.
      Kartboken; världsatlas för den 9 årige skolan.
      By Gösta Lundquist.   With Generalstabens
      litografiska anstalt.   Stockholm, [1958].
      70 p.   col. maps.   28 cm.

678   Thieme, W. J.
      Atlas van Europa en de werelddelen.   48 ed.
      By G. Prop.   Zutphen, 1958.
      48 p.   col. maps.   26 cm.

679   Tjempaka, P. T.
      Atlas ringkas untuk sekolah rakjat.   Djakarta,[1958].
      24 p.   col. maps.   32 cm.

680   Učila.
      Školski atlas za više razrede osmogodišnijh škola
      i za niže razrede gimnazija.   6 ed.   By
      Zvonimir Dugački.   Zagreb, 1958.
      48 p.   col. maps.   34 cm.

681   U.S.S.R. Glavnoe upravlenie geodezii i kartografii.
      Atlas mira.   3 ed.   Moskva, 1958.
      165 p.   col. maps.   20 cm.

682   U.S.S.R. Glavnoe upravlenie geodezii i kartografii.
      Geograficheskii atlas dlya 5 go i 6 go klassov
      srednei shkoly.   Moskva, [1958].
      1 vol.   col.   maps.   30 cm.

683   U.S.S.R. Glavnoe upravlenie geodezii i kartografii.
      Geograficheskii atlas dlya 6 go klassa.
      Moskva, 1958.
      32 p.   col.   maps.   29 cm.

684   U.S.S.R. Glavnoe upravlenie geodezii i kartografii.
      Geograficheskii atlas zaribechnich stran dlya
      strednei shkoly.   3 ed.   Moskva, 1958.
      79 p.   col.   maps.   30 cm.

685   U.S.S.R. Voyenno-topograficheskoe upravlenie.
      Atlas mira.   Moskva, 1958.
      459 p.   col.   maps.   23 cm.

686   Verlag Enzyklopädie·
      Pocket atlas.   International ed.   With Cartographia.
      Leipzig, [1958].
      40 p.   col.   maps.   17 cm.

687   Verlag Enzyklopädie.
      Pocket atlas.   International ed.   With Kartográfiai
      Vállalat.   Leipzig, 1958.
      40 p.   col.   maps.   17 cm.

688   Verlag Enzyklopädie.
      Weltatlas; die Staaten der Erde und ihre Wirtschaft.
      3 ed.   By Edgar Lehmann.   Leipzig, 1958.
      170 p.   col.   maps.   35 cm.

689   Verlag Lebendiges Wissen.
      Weltatlas.   5 ed.   By Alfred Malaschofsky.   With
      Columbus Verlag Oestergaard.   München, [1958].
      208 p.   col.   maps.   18 cm.

690   Volk und Wissen Verlag·
      Atlas zur Erd und Länderkunde.   14 ed.   By Fritz
      Haefke.   Berlin, 1958.
      99 p.   col.   maps.   31 cm.

691   Wenschow.
      Weltatlas.   München, [1958].
      43 p.   col.   maps.   34 cm.

692 Westermann, Georg.
Atlas für Hamburger Schulen. Braunschweig, 1958—
1 vol. col. maps. 32 cm.

693 Westermann, Georg.
Der Lebensraum des Menschen; ein Westermann
Atlas für Schule und Haus. Braunschweig, 1958.
90 p. col. maps. 33 cm.

694 Westermann, Georg.
Weltatlas. 93 ed. Braunschweig, 1958.
222 p. col. maps. 34 cm.

695 Westermann, Georg.
Westermanns Hausatlas. By Carl Diercke and
R. Dehmel. Braunschweig, [1958].
238 p. col. maps. 34 cm.

696 Westermann, Georg.
Westermanns Hausatlas. 3 ed. Braunschweig,
[1958].
259 p. col. maps. 35 cm.

697 Yavneh.
Atlas fisi, medini ve-kalkali. (In Hebrew). By
Moshe Brawer. Tel Aviv, 1958.
80 p. col. maps. 31 cm.

698 Zanichelli, Nicola.
Atlante geografico Zanichelli, ad uso delle scuole.
6 ed. By Giuseppe Nangeroni and Leonardo Ricci.
Bologna, 1958.
256 p. col. maps. 35 cm.

1959

699 Aguilar, S. A. de Ediciones.
Atlas medio universal y de Colombia. Madrid, 1959.
140 p. col. maps. 31 cm.

700 Aguilar, S. A. de Ediciones.
Atlas medio universal y de la República Argentina.
Madrid, [1959].
140 p. col. maps. 31 cm.

701 Aguilar, S. A. de Ediciones.
Nuevo atlas muudial. 3 ed. Madrid, 1959.
392 p. col. maps. 32 cm.

702 Albania. Ministria e aresimit dhe kultures.
Atlas për shkollat fillore. Tiranë, 1959.
15 p. col. maps. 25 cm.

703 Allhem.
Allhems värdsatlas. By S. S. Paterson.
Malmö, [1959].
205 p. col. maps. 32 cm.

704 American Map Co., Inc.
Colorprint general atlas of the world. New York,
[1959].
16 p. col. maps. 32 cm.

705 Atlantik Verlag.
Deutschland und die Welt. By Willy Eggers.
Frankfurt, [1959].
97 p. col. maps. 34 cm.

706 Bartholomew, John & Son, Ltd.
The Edinburgh world atlas or advanced atlas of
modern geography. 3 ed. Edinburgh, 1959.
159 p. col. maps. 39 cm.

707 Brug Uitgeversbedrijf, N. V.
Atlas van Nederland en de wereld voor het
voortgezet onderwijs. Amsterdam, 1959.
162 p. col. maps. 32 cm.

708 Brug Uitgeversbedrijf, N. V.
Nederlandse wereldatlas; de wereld in kaart,
woord en beeld. Amsterdam, [1959].
292 p. col. maps. 32 cm.

709 Bulgaria. Glavno upravlenie po geodeziā i kartografiā
Ucheben geografsky atlas. Sofia, [1959].
114 p. col. maps. 35 cm.

710 Czechoslovakia. Ústřední správa geodesie a kartografie
Malý atlas světa. 2 ed. By Antonîn Koláčný.
Bratislava, 1959.
2 vol. col. maps. 30 cm.

711   Czechoslovakia. Ústřední správa geodesie a kartografie
      Malý atlas světa. 3 ed.   Praha, 1959.
      189 p.   col.   maps.   22 cm.

712   Czechoslovakia. Ústřední správa geodesie a kartografie
      Školní zeměpisný atlas pro 4 a 5 ročník všeobecné
      vzdělavacích škol.   4 ed.   Praha, [1959].
      18 p.   col.   maps.   30 cm.

713   Denoyer-Geppert Co.
      Denoyer's student atlas.   By Philip Denoyer.
      Chicago, 1959.
      41 maps.   col.   maps.   28 cm.

714   Denoyer-Geppert Co.
      Library atlas.   With Philip.   Chicago, Ill., 1959.
      208 p.   col.   maps.   29 cm.

715   Editorial Luis Vives, S. A.
      Atlas universal y de España.   Zaragoza, [1959].
      1 vol.   col.   maps.   32 cm.

716   Editors Press Service.
      Atlas mundial Gea.   By Eduardo Cardenas.
      New York, 1959.
      192 p.   col.   maps.   20 cm.

717   Edizioni Cremonese.
      Atlante geografico; per le scuole medie.   2 ed.
      By Riccardo Riccardi.   Roma, [1959].
      1 vol.   col.   maps.   34 cm.

718   Encyclopedia Britannica.
      Encyclopedia Britannica world atlas.   Chicago, 1959.
      180 p.   col.   maps.   38 cm.

719   GEO Publishing Co.
      The Faber atlas.   2 ed.   By Daniel James Sinclair.
      Oxford, [1959].
      210 p.   col.   maps.   31 cm.

720   Gyldendal.
      Gyldendal verdensatlas.   By Hallstein Myklebost.
      Oslo, [1959].
      319 p.   col.   maps.   32 cm.

721   Hammond, C. S. & Co., Inc.
      Clear-relief wall atlas. Maplewood, N. J., 1959.
      22 p. col. maps. 73 cm.

722   Hammond, C. S. & Co., Inc.
      Hammond's ambassador world atlas. Maplewood,
      N. J., 1959.
      150 p. col. maps. 37 cm.

723   Hammond, C. S. & Co., Inc.
      Hammond's family reference world atlas.
      Maplewood, N. J., 1959.
      112 p. col. maps. 27 cm.

724   Hammond, C. S. & Co., Inc.
      Hammond's library world atlas. Maplewood, N. J.,
      1959.
      100 p. col. maps. 32 cm.

725   Hammond, C. S. & Co., Inc.
      My first world atlas. Maplewood, N. J., [1959].
      48 p. col. maps. 26 cm.

726   Hammond, C. S. & Co., Inc.
      New era atlas of the world. New York, [1959].
      160 p. col. maps. 32 cm.

727   Hanover House.
      Family reference world atlas. With Hammond.
      Garden City, N. Y., 1959.
      112 p. col. maps. 27 cm.

728   Hanover House.
      Family reference world atlas. New ed. With
      Hammond. Garden City, N. Y., [1959].
      256 p. col. maps. 27 cm.

729   Hirschsprungs forlag.
      Verdensatlas. København, 1959.
      305 p. col. maps. 32 cm.

730   Hölzel, Ed. Verlag.
      Österreichischer Mittelschulatlas. 84 ed. Wien,
      1959.
      146 p. col. maps. 31 cm.

731 Istituto Geografico De Agostini.
Grande atlante geografico. 5 ed. By Luigi
Visintin. Novara, [1959].
323 p. col. maps. 42 cm.

732 JRO Verlag.
JRO universal Weltatlas. By Ernst Kremling.
München, [1959].
1 vol. col. maps. 31 cm.

733 Kartográfiai Vállalat·
Világatlasz. By Radó Sándor. Budapest, [1959].
192 p. col. maps. 34 cm.

734 Kümmerly & Frey·
Schweizerischer Schulatlas. 16 ed. Bern, [1959].
51 p. col. maps. 33 cm.

735 Larousse·
Atlas general Larousse. Paris, [1959].
456 p. col. maps. 30 cm.

736 Librairie Payot·
Atlas scolaire suisse pour l'enseignement secondaire.
Lausanne, [1959].
1 vol. col. maps. 36 cm.

737 List, P.
List Taschenatlas München, [1959].
150 p. col. maps. 18 cm.

738 Livraria Popular de F. Franco·
Atlas de geografia para uso dos alunos dos liceus
e dos escolas industriais e comerciais. By
Augusto de Nascimento. Lisboa, [1959].
1 vol. col. maps. 30 cm.

739 Livraria Sá da Costa·
Novo atlas escolar português; histórico-geográfico.
7 ed. By João Soares. Lisboa, [1959].
83 p. col. maps. 34 cm.

740 Mairs Geographischer Verlag.
Mair Weltatlas Europa und Welt. Stuttgart, [1959].
160 p. col. maps. 24 cm.

741   Meulenhoff, I. M.
      Atlas van Nederland en de wereld. 1 ed. With
      Hölzel. Amsterdam, 1959.
      162 p. col. maps. 32 cm.

742   Nathan, Fernand.
      Atlas du XXe siècle. By René Ozouf. Paris,[1959].
      77 p. col. maps. 34 cm.

743   Nathan, Fernand.
      Petit atlas universal Nathan. Paris, [1959].
      80 p. col. maps. 16 cm.

744   Oliver & Boyd.
      Oliver and Boyd general atlas; physical and
      political geography. 1 ed. With Bartholomew.
      Edinburgh, [1959].
      112 p. col. maps. 29 cm.

745   Oxford University Press.
      Oxford Economic atlas of the world. 2 ed.
      London, 1959.
      279 p. col. maps. 27 cm.

746   Paravia, G. B.
      Atlante geografico, fisico, politico. By Giuseppe
      Pennesi. Torino, [1959].
      55 p. col. maps. 32 cm.

747   Philip, George & Son, Ltd.
      Comparative commonwealth atlas for use in
      Australian schools. 19 ed. By Harold Fullard.
      London, 1959.
      109 p. col. maps. 23 cm.

748   Philip, George & Son, Ltd.
      Philip's library atlas. 6 ed. By Harold Fullard
      and H. C. Darby. London, [1959].
      295 p. col. maps. 29 cm.

749   Philip, George & Son, Ltd.
      Philips mercantile marine atlas. 16 ed. By
      Harold Fullard. London, 1959.
      96 p. col. maps. 53 cm.

750   Philip, George & Son, Ltd.
      The new comprehensive world atlas.   By Harold
      Fullard.   London, [1959].
      312 p.   col. maps.   29 cm.

751   Philip, George & Son, Ltd.
      World-wide atlas.   99 ed.   By Harold Fullard.
      London, 1959.
      51 p.   col. maps.   29 cm.

752   Poland.   Państwowe przedsiębiorstwo wydawnictw
      kartograficznych.
      Atlas świata.   2 ed.   Warszawa, 1959.
      314 p.   col. maps.   18 cm.

753   Politikens Forlag.
      Politikens verdensatlas.   8 ed.   By Axel Schou.
      København, 1959.
      151 p.   col. maps.   29 cm.

754   Praeger, Frederick A.
      An atlas of world affairs.   2 ed.   By Andrew Boyd.
      New York, 1959.
      160 p.   21 cm.

755   Rand McNally & Co.
      CM political and terrain series maps.   Chicago,
      1959.
      1 vol.   col. maps.   26 cm.

756   Rand McNally & Co.
      Cosmopolitan world atlas.   Chicago, [1959].
      376 p.   col. maps.   37 cm.

757   Rand McNally & Co.
      International world atlas.   Chicago, 1959.
      24 p.   col. maps.   26 cm.

758   Rand McNally & Co.
      Premier world atlas.   Chicago [1959].
      304 p.   col. maps.   37 cm.

759   Rand McNally & Co.
      Space age atlas.   Chicago, 1959.
      48 p.   col. maps.   37 cm.

760 Replogle Globes, Inc.
     Replogle comprehensive atlas of the world. With
     Hammond. Chicago, [1959].
     400 p. col. maps. 25 cm.

761 Sallinas Bellver, Salvador.
     Atlas de geografía universal. Madrid, [1959].
     1 vol. col. maps. 36 cm.

762 Scholastic Book Service.
     Scholastic/Hammond world atlas. With Hammond.
     New York, 1959.
     1 vol. col. maps. 26 cm.

763 Società editrice internazionale.
     Nuovo atlante geografico SEI. 2 ed. By Dino
     Gribaudi. Torino, [1959].
     245 p. col. maps. 24 cm.

764 Thieme, W. J.
     Atlas van Europa en de werelddelen. 49 ed. By
     G. Prop. Zutphen, 1959.
     48 p. col. maps. 26 cm.

765 Thomas, A.
     The new comprehensive world atlas. By Harold
     Fullard. With Philip. Preston, [1959].
     312 p. col. maps. 29 cm.

766 U.S.S.R. Glavnoe upravlenie geodezii i kartografii.
     Atlas mira. Moskva, 1959.
     325 p. col. maps. 35 cm.

767 U.S.S.R. Glavnoe upravlenie geodezii i kartografii.
     Geograficheskii atlas dlya 4go klassa.
     Moskva, [1959].
     1 vol. col. maps. 25 cm.

768 U.S.S.R. Glavnoe upravlenie geodezii i kartografii.
     Geograficheskii atlas dlya 5go klassa. Moskva,
     [1959].
     1 vol. col. maps. 28 cm.

769 U.S.S.R. Glavnoe upravlenie geodezii i kartografii.
     Geograficheskii atlas dlya uchitelei srednei shkoly.
     2 ed. Moskva, 1959.
     191 p. col. maps. 38 cm.

770   Verlag Sport & Technik.
      Funkatlas. Radiotlas. By Ernst Georg Berends.
      Berlin, 1959.
      198 p. col. maps. 31 cm.

771   Wolters, J. B.
      De grote bosatlas. 40 ed. By F. J. Ormeling.
      Groningen, 1959.
      1 vol. col. maps. 37 cm.

                              1960

772   Barnes & Noble, Inc.
      The Barnes and Noble world atlas. By Harold
      Fullard. With Philip. New York, [1960].
      123 p. col. maps. 20 cm.

773   Bartholomew, John & Son, Ltd.
      The Graphic atlas of the world. 11 ed. Edin-
      burgh, 1960.
      180 p. col. maps. 26 cm.

774   Bartholomew, John & Son, Ltd.
      The world pocket atlas and gazetteer. Edinburgh,
      1960.
      210 p. col. maps. 15 cm.

775   Bergvalls Förlag.
      Bergvalls atlas. By Magnus Lundqvist and Olof
      Hedbom. Stockholm, [1960].
      72 p. col. maps. 25 cm.

776   Bertelsmann, C.
      Hausatlas. 1 ed. Gütersloh, [1960].
      318 p. col. maps. 33 cm.

777   Brazil. Instituto Brasileiro de Geografia e
      Estatistica.
      Atlas de relaçoes internacionais. Rio de Janeiro,
      1960.
      160 p. col. maps. 32 cm.

778   Brockhaus, F. A.
      Der grosse Brockhaus Atlas. Wiesbaden, 1960.
      664 p. col. maps. 25 cm.

779 Brown, W. C. Co.
Atlas for anthropology. By Robert F. Spencer and
Elden Johnson. Dubuque, Iowa, [1960].
1 vol. 28 cm.

780 Caxton Pub. Co.
The Caxton world atlas. By William Gordon East.
London, New York, [1960].
532 p. col. maps. 41 cm.

781 Colin.
Atlas historique et géographique Vidal-Lablache.
Paris, [1960].
187 p. col. maps. 40 cm.

782 Czechoslovakia. Ústřední správa geodésie a kartografie.
Kapesní atlas světa. 1 ed. Praha, 1960.
116 p. col. maps. 17 cm.

783 Czechoslovakia. Ústřední správa geodésie a kartografie.
Malý školní atlas. 5 ed. By Jan Musílek.
Praha, 1960.
20 p. col. maps. 30 cm.

784 Czechoslovakia. Ústřední správa geodésie a kartografie.
Malý školský atlas. 5 ed. By Jan Musílek.
Slovak ed. Praha, 1960.
20 p. col. maps. 30 cm.

785 Discolar.
Atlas de Venezuela y del mundo. With American
Map Co. Caracas, [196-].
23 p. col. maps. 31 cm.

786 Éditions Sequoia.
Petite encyclopédie géographique. Paris, [1960].
239 p. col. maps. 19 cm.

787 Editora Minerva.
Atlas geográfico escolar. By Juan E. Schaeffer.
Rio de Janeiro, [1960].
1 vol. col. maps. 28 cm.

788 Editorial Bello.
Atlas universal. 1 ed. Valencia, [1960].
85 p. col. maps. 24 cm.

789   Editors Press Service.
      Nuevo atlas mundial.   With Hammond.   New York,
      1960.
      32 p.   col. maps.   26 cm.

790   Fischer, G.
      Klimadiagramm-Weltatlas.   By Heinrich Walter and
      Helmut Lieth.   Jena, 1960-
      in 3 pts.   col. maps.   62 cm.

791   Ganaco, N. V.
      Atlas nasional seluruh dunia untuk sekolah landjutan.
      By J. E. Romein.   Djakarta, 1960.
      72 p.   col. maps.   39 cm.

792   Geographia Map Co.
      Geographia atlas of the world.   By Alexander Gross.
      New York, 1960.
      40 p.   col. maps.   34 cm.

793   Geokarta.
      Geografski atlas.   By Ratimir Kalmeta.   Beograd,
      1960.
      27 p.   col. maps.   34 cm.

794   Hammond, C. S. & Co., Inc.
      Clear-relief wall atlas.   Maplewood, N. J., 1960.
      20 p.   col. maps.   73 cm.

795   Hammond, C. S. & Co., Inc.
      Hammond ambassador world atlas.   Maplewood,
      N. J., [1960].
      1 vol.   col. maps.   39 cm.

796   Hammond, C. S. & Co., Inc.
      New home reference world atlas and gazetteer.
      New York, [1960].
      2 vol.   col. maps.   24 cm.

797   Hammond, C. S. & Co., Inc.
      Nuevo atlas mundial.   New York, 1960.
      32 p.   col. maps.   26 cm.

798   Hammond, C. S. & Co., Inc.
      The first book atlas.   New York, 1960.
      96 p.   col. maps.   23 cm.

799 Hölzel, Ed. Verlag.
     Österreichischer Mittelschulatlas.   85 ed.   Wien,
     1960.
     146 p.   col. maps.   31 cm.

800 IAC.
     Le plus petit atlas du monde.   By J. L. Sibert.
     Lyon, [1960].
     127 p.   col. maps.   13 cm.

801 JRO Verlag.
     Der Grosse JRO Weltatlas.   2 ed.   By Ernst
     Kremling.   München, [1960].
     1 vol.   col. maps.   45 cm.

802 Kaplán Cojano, Oscar.
     Geografía atlas universal.   Santiago de Chile, 1960.
     249 p.   col. maps.   26 cm.

803 Kümmerly & Frey.
     Schweizerischer Volksschulatlas.   12 ed.   Bern,
     [1960].
     34 p.   col. maps.   33 cm.

804 Kümmerly & Frey.
     Taschen-Weltatlas.   Zürich.   [1960].
     40 p.   col. maps.   18 cm.

805 Livros Cadernos.
     Atlas didático.   By Juan E. Schaeffer.   Rio de
     Janeiro, [1960].
     16 p.   col. maps.   32 cm.

806 Macmillan & Co., Ltd.
     World atlas for Uganda schools.   By J. T. Gleave.
     London, 1960.
     32 p.   col. maps.   28 cm.

807 Nelson, Thomas & Sons, Ltd.
     Nelson's Canadian school atlas.   2 ed.   By J.
     Wreford Watson.   Toronto, [1960].
     92 p.   col. maps.   29 cm.

808 Oliver & Boyd.
     The advanced atlas of modern geography.   5 ed.
     With Bartholomew.   Edinburgh, 1960.
     108 p.   col. maps.   38 cm.

809   Oliver & Boyd.
      The comparative atlas of physical and political
      geography. 45 ed. With Bartholomew. Edinburgh,
      1960.
      112 p. col. maps. 29 cm.

810   Oxford University Press.
      Oxford Economic atlas of the world. London, 1960.
      279 p. col. maps. 27 cm.

811   Oxford University Press.
      Oxford school atlas. 3 ed. By D. P. Bickmore
      and F. C. Couzens. London, 1960.
      130 p. col. maps. 26 cm.

812   Paravia, G. B.
      Atlante geografico, fisico, politico. By G. Pennesi
      and R. Almagià. Torino, [1960].
      55 p. col. maps. 32 cm.

813   Pfahl Verlag.
      Hansa Weltatlas. 11 ed. By Oswald Muris.
      Baden-Baden, 1960.
      390 p. col. maps. 24 cm.

814   Philip, George & Son, Ltd.
      Modern world atlas. By Harold Fullard. London,
      1960.
      24 p. col. maps. 24 cm.

815   Philip, George & Son, Ltd.
      Record atlas. 21 ed. By Harold Fullard.
      London, 1960.
      311 p. col. maps. 29 cm.

816   Philip, George & Son, Ltd.
      The library atlas. 7 ed. London, [1960].
      319 p. col. maps. 29 cm.

817   Philip, George & Son, Ltd.
      The university atlas. 9 ed. London, [1960].
      200 p. col. maps. 29 cm.

818   Poland. Państwowe przedsiębiorstwo wydawnictw
      kartograficznych.
      Atlas geograficzny dla klasy IV. Warszawa, 1960.
      38 p. col. maps. 26 cm.

819 Praeger, Frederick A.
     An atlas of world affairs. 3 ed. By Andrew Boyd.
     New York, 1960.
     160 p. 21 cm.

820 Rand McNally & Co.
     Rand McNally book of nations. Chicago, 1960.
     93 p. col. maps. 35 cm.

821 Rand McNally & Co.
     World atlas. 11 ed. By Edward B. Espenshade,
     Jr. Chicago, [1960].
     288 p. col. maps. 29 cm.

822 Simmons-Boardman Books.
     Simmons-Boardman world atlas. 1 ed. With
     Bartholomew. New York, [1960].
     112 p. col. maps. 29 cm.

823 Stanford, Edward.
     The Whitehall atlas. By Harold Fullard. With
     Philip. London, 1960.
     381 p. col. maps. 28 cm.

824 Südwest Verlag.
     Neuer grosser Weltatlas für Heim, Unterricht und
     Reise. By H. R. Fischer. München, [1960].
     160 p. col. maps. 32 cm.

825 Thieme, W. J.
     Atlas van Europa en de werelddelen. 50 ed. By
     G. Prop. Zutphen, 1960.
     48 p. col. maps. 26 cm.

826 Učila.
     Novi atlas za osnovno šolo. By Zvonimir Dugački.
     Zagreb, 1960.
     36 p. col. maps. 28 cm.

827 Učila.
     Sholski atlas. 3 ed. By Zvonimir Dugački.
     Zagreb, 1960.
     51 p. col. maps. 33 cm.

828 Vallardi, A.
     Atlante scolastico di geografia moderna. By Olinto
     Marinelli. Milano, [1960].
     1 vol. col. maps. 32 cm.

829 Volk und Wissen Verlag.
   Atlas der Erdkunde. 3 ed. By Walter
   Heidenreuter. With Haack. Berlin, 1960.
   135 p. col. maps. 31 cm.

830 Watts.
   The first book atlas. With Hammond. New York,
   1960.
   96 p. col. maps. 23 cm.

831 Westermann, Georg.
   Der Lebensraum des Menschen. Braunschweig, 1960.
   88 p. col. maps. 32 cm.

832 Westermann, Georg.
   Weltatlas. 98 ed. Braunschweig, [1960].
   222 p. col. maps. 34 cm.

833 Yavneh.
   Atlas fisi, medini ve-kalkali. (In Hebrew). By
   Moshe Brawer. Tel Aviv, 1960.
   80 p. col. maps. 31 cm.

834 Yavneh.
   Atlas kis, entsiklopedia geo-grafit, kalkalit,
   u-medinit. By Moshe Brawer. Tel Aviv, [1960].
   630 p. col. maps. 17 cm.

835 Yavneh.
   Atlas kis, entsiklopedia geo-grafit, kalkalit,
   u-medinit. 2 ed. By Moshe Brawer. Tel Aviv,
   [1960].
   633 p. col. maps. 17 cm.

                          1961

836 Aguilar, S. A. de Ediciones.
   Nuevo atlas mundial. 4 ed.
   Madrid, 1961.
   392 p. col. maps. 32 cm.

837 Akademiförlaget.
   Atlas of the world commodities; production, trade
   and consumption. By Olof Jonasson. Göteborg,
   [1961].
   81 p. col. maps. 22 cm.

838   Albania.   Ministria e aresimit dhe kultures.
      <u>Atlas për shkollat fillore.</u>   2 ed.   Tiranë, 1961.
      16 p.   col.   maps.   25 cm.

839   Bertelsmann, C.
      <u>Bertelsmann Atlas International.</u>   By Werner
      Bormann.   Gütersloh, 1961.
      171 p.   col.   maps.   41 cm.

840   Bertelsmann, C.
      <u>Der Grosse Bertelsmann Weltatlas.</u>   By W.
      Bormann.   Gütersloh, [1961].
      357 p.   col.   maps.   33 cm.

841   Bir Yayinevi.
      <u>Renkli, resimli ortaokul atlasi.</u>   By U. Bonapace.
      Istanbul, [1961].
      43 p.   col.   maps.   33 cm.

842   Bir Yayinevi.
      <u>Resimli ilk atlas.</u>   By Luigi Visintin.   Istanbul,
      [1961].
      28 p.   col.   maps.   27 cm.

843   Cassell.
      <u>Cassell's new atlas of the world; the world in</u>
      <u>physical, political, and economic maps.</u>   By
      Harold Fullard.   London, [1961].
      233 p.   col.   maps.   35 cm.

844   Collins Clear-Type Press.
      <u>Collins graphic atlas.</u>   By G. B. Young.   Glasgow,
      [1961].
      136 p.   col.   maps.   28 cm.

845   Collins Clear-Type Press.
      <u>Essential world atlas.</u>   London, New York, [1961].
      24 p.   col.   maps.   28 cm.

846   Collins, William, Sons & Co., Ltd.
      <u>Collins graphic atlas.</u>   By G. B. Young.   Glasgow,
      [1961].
      136 p.   col.   maps.   28 cm.

847   Collins, William, Sons & Co., Ltd.
      <u>Collins-Longmans clarion atlas.</u>   7 ed.   By B. A.
      Workman.   Glasgow, New York, [1961].
      64 p.   col.   maps.   22 cm.

848 Collins, William, Sons & Co., Ltd.
Essential world atlas. London, New York, [1961].
24 p. col. maps. 28 cm.

849 Collins, William, Sons & Co., Ltd.
Pocket atlas of the world. Glasgow, New York,
[1961].
160 p. col. maps. 18 cm.

850 Collins, William, Sons & Co., Ltd.
The standardised South African atlas. By K. H.
Huggins and B. A. Workman. Glasgow, [1961].
49 p. col. maps. 28 cm.

851 Columbus Verlag Oestergaard.
Grosser Columbus Weltatlas. By Karlheinz Wagner.
Berlin, [1961].
259 p. col. maps. 42 cm.

852 Cram, George F. Co.
Cram student atlas: earth science and outer space.
Indianapolis, Ind., [1961].
34 p. col. maps. 31 cm.

853 Cram, George F. Co.
Modern world atlas. Indianapolis, Ind., 1961.
368 p. col. maps. 31 cm.

854 Czechoslovakia. Ústřední správa geodesie a kartografie.
Malý školni atlas. 6 ed. By Jan Musílek.
Praha, 1961.
20 p. col. maps. 30 cm.

855 Czechoslovakia. Ústřední správa geodesie a kartografie.
Školní zeměpisný atlas světa. 3 ed. By Vladimír
Vokálek. Praha, 1961.
81 p. col. maps. 31 cm.

856 Dell Pub. Co.
The New Hammond-Dell world atlas. With Hammond. New York, [1961].
255 p. col. maps. 17 cm.

857 Denoyer-Geppert Co.
Student atlas, with map reading suggestions. By
L. P. Denoyer. Chicago, 1961.
1 vol. col. maps. 28 cm.

858   Dent, J. M.
      Canadian school atlas.   By H. E. Mindak.
      Toronto, [1961].
      115 p.   col. maps.   29 cm.

859   Dent, J. M.
      The Aldine world atlas; geography and history.
      1 ed.   By J. W. Hamilton and G. E. Tait.   With
      Bartholomew.   Toronto, 1961.
      166 p.   col. maps.   29 cm.

860   Editions Bordas.
      Atlas de poche, établi d'après le Nouvel atlas
      général.   By G. Tocqueville.   Paris, [1961].
      62 p.   col. maps.   14 cm.

861   Editorial Miguel A. Salvatella.
      Atlas escolares Salvatella.   Barcelona, [1961].
      1 vol.   col. maps.   33 cm.

862   Educational Book Club.
      World and space age atlas.   With Rand McNally.
      Des Moines, [1961].
      1 vol.   col. maps.   37 cm.

863   Encyclopaedia Britannica.
      Encyclopaedia Britannica world atlas.   By G.
      Donald Hudson.   Chicago, London, 1961.
      388 p.   col. maps.   37.5 cm.

864   Faber & Faber.
      The Faber Atlas.   3 ed.   By D. J. Sinclair.
      London, [1961].
      198 p.   col. maps.   31 cm.

865   Geographical Pub. Co.
      School and library atlas of the world.   By Fred
      William Foster.   Cleveland, [1961].
      324 p.   col. maps.   57 cm.

866   GEO Publishing Co.
      The Faber atlas.   3 ed.   By Daniel James Sinclair.
      Oxford, [1961].
      198 p.   col. maps.   31 cm.

867   Goldmann Verlag.
      Goldmanns Handatlas.   5 ed.   München, 1961.
      160 p.   col. maps.   41 cm.

868   Grafisk Forlag.
      Mentor verdensatlas.   With Bertelsmann.
      København, [1961].
      285 p.   col. maps.   33 cm.

869   Grosset & Dunlap.
      The International standard atlas of the world.   By
      Anthony M. Kronbauer.   With Rand McNally.   New
      York, [1961].
      448 p.   col. maps.   36 cm.

870   Gumperts Förlag.
      Atlas of the world commodities: production, trade
      and consumption.   By Olof Jonasson.   Göteborg,
      1961.
      82 p.   col. maps.   21 cm.

871   Gyldendal.
      Gyldendals Reliefatlas.   By Ib Rønne Kejlbo and
      Poul Holmelund.   København, 1961.
      1 vol.   col. maps.   27 cm.

872   Haack, Hermann.
      Weltatlas die Staaten der Erde und ihre Wirtschaft.
      Leipzig, 1961.
      105 p.   col. maps.   34 cm.

873   Hammond, C. S. & Co., Inc.
      Ambassador world atlas.   2 ed.   Maplewood, N. J.,
      [1961].
      500 p.   col. maps.   37 cm.

874   Hammond, C. S. & Co., Inc.
      Diplomat world atlas.   Maplewood, N. J., [1961].
      320 p.   col. maps.   37 cm.

875   Hammond, C. S. & Co., Inc.
      Hammond's complete world atlas. New York, 1961.
      400 p.   col. maps.   24 cm.

876   Hammond, C. S. & Co., Inc.
      Library world atlas.   60 anniversary ed.   Maple-
      wood, N. J., [1961].
      336 p.   col. maps.   32 cm.

877   Hammond, C. S. & Co., Inc.
      New era atlas of the world.   Maplewood, N.J.,[1961].
      176 p.   col. maps.   32 cm.

878   Hammond, C. S. & Co., Inc.
      Our world in space atlas. Maplewood, N.J.,1961.
      1 vol. col. maps. 32 cm.

879   Hammond, C. S. & Co., Inc.
      Universal world atlas. Maplewood, N.J.,[1961].
      232 p. col. maps. 32 cm.

880   Hölzel, Ed. Verlag.
      Österreichischer Hauptschulatlas.   4 ed.   Wien,
      [1961].
      76 p. col. maps. 31 cm.

881   Hölzel, Ed. Verlag.
      Österreichischer Mittelschulatlas.   86 ed.   Wien,
      1961.
      146 p. col. maps. 31 cm.

882   India. Survey of India.
      School atlas. Dehra Dūn, 1961.
      62 p. col. maps. 31 cm.

883   Johnston, W. & A. K. and G. W. Bacon, Ltd.
      New world atlas. 3 ed. Edinburgh, [1961].
      146 p. col. maps. 29 cm.

884   JRO Verlag.
      Der Kleine JRO Weltatlas.   By Ernst Kremling.
      München, [1961].
      451 p. col. maps. 22 cm.

885   JRO Verlag.
      Weltwirtschafts-Atlas.   Atlas für Politik und
      Zeitgeschichte. Permanente Ausgabe. München,
      1961.
      2 vol. col. maps. 30 cm.

886   Kanaat Yayinlari·
      Büyük atlas. Düzeltilmis yeni basi.   By Faik Sabri
      Duran. Istanbul, [1961].
      96 p. col. maps. 32 cm.

887   Kartográfiai Vállalat·
      Politikai és gazdasági világatlasz.   By Radó Sándor·
      Budapest, 1961.
      353 p. col. maps. 35 cm.

888   Leksikografski zavod FNRJ.
      Atlas svijeta. Zagreb, 1961.
      282 p. col. maps. 30 cm.

889   Lloyd's Corp. of.
      Lloyd's maritime atlas. 4 ed. London, 1961.
      1 vol. col. maps. 25 cm.

890   Martins forlag.
      Verdensatlas. By Henry Bjørn and Jack Petersen.
      København, [1961].
      1 vol. col. maps. 31 cm.

891   Monteverde, A.
      Atlas esquemático de ciencias geográficas. By
      Cayetano di Leoni and Omar I. Genovese.
      Montevideo, 1961.
      1 vol. 33 cm.

892   Nelson, Thomas & Sons, Ltd.
      Nelson's concise world atlas. By James Wreford
      Watson. London, New York, [1961].
      60 p. col. maps. 29 cm.

893   Oxford University Press.
      Concise Oxford atlas. London, 1961.
      288 p. col. maps. 26 cm.

894   Oxford University Press.
      The Oxford atlas. By Clinton Lewis and J. D.
      Campbell. London, [1961].
      192 p. col. maps. 39 cm.

895   Philip, George & Son, Ltd.
      Commercial course atlas. By Harold Fullard.
      London, [1961].
      120 p. col. maps. 29 cm.

896   Philip, George & Son, Ltd.
      Falcon atlas of the world. By Harold Fullard.
      London, [1961].
      119 p. col. maps. 20 cm.

897   Philip, George & Son, Ltd.
      Practical atlas. By Harold Fullard. London, 1961.
      176 p. col. maps. 29 cm.

898   Philip, George & Son, Ltd.
      Record atlas. 22 ed. By Harold Fullard. London,
      1961.
      301 p. col. maps. 29 cm.

899   Philip, George & Son, Ltd.
      World wide atlas. 99 ed. By Harold Fullard.
      London, [1961].
      51 p. col. maps. 29 cm.

900   Pocket Books.
      The new Rand McNally pocket world atlas. With
      Rand McNally. New York, [1961].
      295 p. col. maps. 18 cm.

901   Poland. Państwowe przedsiębiorstwo wydawnictw
      kartograficznych.
      Atlas geograficzny dla klasy IV. By Jan Slowik and
      Halina Tyc. Warszawa, 1961.
      35 p. col. maps. 26 cm.

902   Rand McNally & Co.
      Atlas of the world. Chicago, [1961].
      50 p. col. maps. 32 cm.

903   Rand McNally & Co.
      Collegiate world atlas. Chicago, [1961].
      404 p. col. maps. 28 cm.

904   Rand McNally & Co.
      Goode's world atlas. By Edward B. Espenshade,
      Jr. Chicago, 1961.
      207 p. col. maps. 29 cm.

905   Rand McNally & Co.
      International world atlas. Chicago, [1961].
      296 p. col. maps. 37 cm.

906   Rand McNally & Co.
      Readers world atlas. Chicago, [1961].
      284 p. col. maps. 28 cm.

907   Rand McNally & Co.
      The new Rand McNally pocket world atlas. New
      York, [1961].
      295 p. col. maps. 18 cm.

908   Rand McNally & Co.
      World and space age atlas.   Chicago, 1961.
      1 vol. col. maps. 37 cm.

909   Rand McNally & Co.
      World atlas.   Chicago, [1961].
      15 p. col. maps. 32 cm.

910   Rand McNally & Co.
      Worldmaster atlas.   Chicago, [1961].
      180 p. col. maps. 28 cm.

911   Reader's Digest Association, Ltd.
      The Reader's Digest great world atlas.   1 ed.   By
      Frank Debenham.   London, [1961].
      179 p. col. maps. 41 cm.

912   Sears, Roebuck.
      Sears family world atlas.   With Hammond.
      Chicago, 1961.
      368 p. col. maps. 32 cm.

913   Siemens & Halske, A. G.
      Welt-Telex-Atlas.   München, 1961.
      119 p. col. maps. 30 cm.

914   Simmons-Boardman Books.
      Simmons-Boardman world atlas.   2 ed.   With
      Bartholomew.   New York, 1961.
      112 p. col. maps. 29 cm.

915   Söderström, Werner.
      Suuri maailman kartasto.   With Bertelsmann.
      Porvoo, [1961].
      285 p. col. maps. 33 cm.

916   Thieme, W. J.
      Atlas van Europa en de werelddelen.   51 ed.   By
      G. Prop.   Zutphen, 1961.
      48 p. col. maps. 26 cm.

917   Time, Inc.
      Life pictorial atlas of the world.   With Rand
      McNally.   New York, 1961.
      600 p. col. maps. 36 cm.

918   University of Chicago Press.
      Atlas of economic development.   By Norton S.
      Ginsburg.   Chicago,   [1961].
      119 p.   col.   maps.   36 cm.

919   U.S.S.R.   Glavnoe upravlenie geodezii i kartografii.
      Atlas mira.   Moskva, 1961.
      301 p.   col.   maps.   19 cm.

920   U.S.S.R.   Glavnoe upravlenie geodezii i kartografii.
      Geograficheskii atlas chastei sveta i vazhneishikh
      gosudarstv dlya 6go-7go klasov.   Moskva, [1961].
      1 vol.   col.   maps.   29 cm.

921   Vallardi, A.
      Atlante geografico illustrato.   By C. Sulzer.
      Milano, [1961].
      29 p.   col.   maps.   37 cm.

922   Van Nostrand Co.
      Atlas of the world.   With Elsevier.   Princeton,
      N. J., [1961].
      240 p.   col.   maps.   19 cm.

923   Volk und Wissen Verlag.
      Atlas der Erdkunde.   4 ed.   With Haack.   By
      Walter Heidenreuter and Walter Krämer.   Berlin,
      1961.
      135 p.   col.   maps.   31 cm.

924   Westermann, Georg.
      Westermanns Hausatlas.   3 ed.   By C. Diercke
      and R. Dehmel.   Braunschweig, [1961].
      259 p.   col.   maps.   35 cm.

925   Wolters, J. B.
      De grote wereldatlas.   41 ed.   By F. J. Ormeling.
      Groningen, 1961.
      302 p.   col.   maps.   37 cm.

926   Wolters, J. B.
      Schoolatlas der gehele aarde.   41 ed.   By F. J.
      Ormeling.   Groningen, 1961.
      203 p.   col.   maps.   32 cm.

927 World Pub. Co.
The Meridian compact atlas of the world. With
Bartholomew. Cleveland, [1961].
158 p. col. maps. 18 cm.

1962

928 Aguilar, S. A. de Ediciones.
Atlas bachillerato universal y de España. 1 ed.
By A. L. Gómez. Madrid, 1962.
132 p. col. maps. 35 cm.

929 Aguilar, S. A. de Ediciones.
Nuevo atlas mundial. 5 ed. Madrid, 1962.
393 p. col. maps. 32 cm.

930 Aldus.
Aldus världsatlas. By Karin Öhman. Stockholm,
[1962].
240 p. col. maps. 19 cm.

931 Australian Educational Foundation, Pty. Ltd.
The Visual world atlas. Sydney, 1962.
272 p. col. maps. 26 cm.

932 Bartholomew, John & Son, Ltd.
The Edinburgh world atlas, or, Advanced atlas of
modern geography. 4 ed. Edinburgh, 1962.
161 p. col. maps. 28 cm.

933 Bergvalls Förlag.
Bergvalls atlas för den 9 -ärige skolan. By Magnus
Lundqvist and Olof Hedbom. Stockholm, [1962].
74 p. col. maps. 25 cm.

934 Bernces Förlag.
Bernces atlas, hela världen i er hand. Malmö,
[1962].
240 p. col. maps. 19 cm.

935 Brazil. Conselho Nacional de Geografia.
Atlas geográfico escolar. 2 ed. Rio de Janeiro,
[1962].
60 p. col. maps. 32 cm.

936 Brug Uitgeversbedrijf, N.V.
Atlas van Nederland en de wereld voor het voortgezet onderwijs. 2 ed. Amsterdam, 1962.
162 p. col. maps. 32 cm.

937   Caxton Pub. Co.
      The Caxton world atlas.   By W. Gordon East.
      London, New York, [1962].

938   Cram, George F. Co.
      Modern world atlas.   Indianapolis, Ind., 1962.
      368 p. col. maps. 32 cm.

939   Curcio, A.
      Atlante universale Curcio.   By Riccardo Riccardi.
      Roma, [1962].
      248 p. col. maps. 25 cm.

940   Czechoslovakia. Ústřední správa geodésie a kartografie.
      Školní zeměpisný atlas světa.   4 ed.   By Vladimír
      Vokálek. Praha, 1962.
      78 p. col. maps. 31 cm.

941   Doubleday.
      New supreme world atlas.   With Hammond.
      Garden City, N. Y., [1962].
      176 p. col. maps. 32 cm.

942   Doubleday.
      The Curtis-Doubleday world atlas.   With Hammond.
      Garden City, N. Y., 1962.
      1 vol. col. maps. 31 cm.

943   Edições Melhoramentos.
      Atlas geográfico Melhoramentos.   20 ed.   By José
      Geraldo Pauwels. São Paulo, 1962.
      95 p. col. maps. 35 cm.

944   Éditions Sequoia.
      Grand atlas international Sequoia.
      Paris, [1962].
      346 p. col. maps. 33 cm.

945   Éditions Stauffacher.
      Nouvel atlas mondial.   3 ed.   By E. T. Rimli and
      Louis Visintin. Zürich, [1962].
      1 vol. col. maps. 28 cm.

946   Editorial Vergara.
      Gran atlas Vergara.   With Bertelsmann.   Barcelona,
      [1962].
      287 p. col. maps. 33 cm.

947 Educational Book Club.
     The new world atlas. With Hammond. Des
     Moines, [1962].
     312 p. col. maps. 32 cm.

948 Educational Book Club.
     World and space age atlas. With Rand McNally.
     Des Moines, [1962].
     1 vol. col. maps. 37 cm.

949 Esselte Map Service.
     Scandinavian Airline system route atlas. Stock-
     holm, [1962].
     34 p. col. maps. 34 cm.

950 Ezy Index.
     Ezy reference world atlas for looseleaf notebooks.
     With Hammond. New York, [1962].
     31 p. col. maps. 28 cm.

951 Field Enterprises Educational Corp.
     The world book atlas. With Rand McNally.
     Chicago, [1962].
     1 vol. col. maps. 37 cm.

952 Fonna.
     Norsk allkunnebok atlas. By Kristian Gleditisch.
     Oslo, [1962].
     184 p. col. maps. 29 cm.

953 Generalstabens litografiska anstalt.
     Världsatlas. Stockholm, 1962.
     40 p. col. maps. 11 cm.

954 Geographia Map Co.
     Geographia world atlas. New York, 1962.
     40 p. col. maps. 33 cm.

955 Geokarta.
     Geografski atlas. 4 ed. By Mihailo Radovanocić.
     Beograd, 1962.
     91 p. col. maps. 34 cm.

956 Gyldendal.
     Gyldendal lommeatlas. With Djambatan. By Bjørn
     Søvik Berg and Arnulf Ursin-Holm. Oslo, [1962].
     240 p. col. maps. 19 cm.

957   Gyldendal.
      Verdens atlas.   With Djambatan N.V.   By Ib
      Kejlbo.   Kóbenhavn, 1962.
      240 p.   col.   maps.   18.5 cm.

958   Haack, Hermann.
      Kleiner Weltatlas.   Gotha, [1962].
      1 vol.   col.   maps.   21 cm.

959   Hammond, C. S. & Co., Inc.
      Ezy reference world atlas for looseleaf notebooks.
      New York, [1962].
      31 p.   col.   maps.   28 cm.

960   Hammond, C. S. & Co., Inc.
      Hammond's Globemaster world atlas.   Maplewood,
      N. J., 1962.
      48 p.   col.   maps.   32 cm.

961   Hammond, C. S. & Co., Inc.
      Library world atlas.   Maplewood, N. J., [1962].
      312 p.   col.   maps.   32 cm.

962   Hammond, C. S. & Co.
      Our world in space atlas.   Maplewood, N.J., [1962].
      50 p.   col.   maps.   32 cm.

963   Hilâl.
      [Atlas of climates, politics, and economics of the
      earth].   In Arabic.   By Ahmad Hafiz.   Cairo, [1962].
      84 p.   col.   maps.   29 cm.

964   Hölzel, Ed. Verlag.
      Österreichischer Mittelschulatlas.   87 ed.   Wien,
      1962.
      146 p.   col.   maps.   31 cm.

965   India.   Survey of India.
      School atlas.   Dehra Dūn, 1962.
      62 p.   col.   maps.   31 cm.

966   Informations et Coujoncture.
      Atlas mondial du pétrole et du gaz naturel.   By
      Jacques Bloch-Morhange.   Paris, 1962.
      1 vol.   col.   maps.   45 cm.

967 Istituto Geografico De Agostini.
Atlante geopolitico. By Luigi Visintin. Novara,
[1962].
500 p. col. maps. 34 cm.

968 Istituto Geografico De Agostini.
Atlante mondiale. By Luigi Visintin. Novara, [1962].
106 p. col. maps. 34 cm.

969 Istituto Geografico De Agostini.
Piccolo atlante geografico metodico. By U.
Bonapace and L. Visintin. Novara, [1962].
71 p. col. maps. 33 cm.

970 Kantonaler Lehrmittel Verlag.
Schweizerischer Mittelschulatlas. 13 ed. By Ed.
Imhof. Zürich, 1962.
144 p. col. maps. 34 cm.

971 Kartográfiai Vállalat.
Földrajzi atlasz a középiskolák számára. Budapest,
1962.
60 p. col. maps. 28 cm.

972 Kartográfiai Vállalat.
Földrajzi atlasz as áltatános iskolák számára. 6 ed.
By Radó Sándor. Budapest, 1962.
32 p. col. maps. 29 cm.

973 Kartográfiai Vállalat.
Gazdasagi es polilitikai vilagatlasz. Budapest, 1962.
353 p. col. maps. 35 cm.

974 Keysersche Verlagsbuchhandlung, G. M. B. H.
Keysers Grosser Weltatlas. By H. J. Neumann.
With Hölzel. Heidelberg, [1962].
352 p. col. maps. 35 cm.

975 Kümmerly & Frey.
Schweizerischer Schulatlas. 17 ed. Bern, [1962].
51 p. col. maps. 31 cm.

976 Kümmerly & Frey.
Taschen Weltatlas. Bern, [1962].
40 p. col. maps. 18 cm.

977   List, P.
      Harms Atlas, Deutschland und die Welt.   By W.
      Eggers.   München, [1962].
      97 p.   col. maps.   34 cm.

978   McGraw Hill Book Co.
      The advanced atlas of modern geography.   6 ed.
      With Bartholomew.   New York, 1962.
      163 p.   col. maps.   39 cm.

979   Meyer, Kartographisches Institut.
      Meyers Duden-Weltatlas.   Mannheim, [1962].
      636 p.   col. maps.   29 cm.

980   Nelson, Thomas & Son, Ltd.
      Junior atlas.   By J. W. Watson.   London, New
      York, [1962].
      51 p.   col. maps.   29 cm.

981   Ottenheimer Publishers, Inc.
      Ottenheimer world atlas.   By Chung-jun Kao.
      Baltimore, Md., [1962].
      16 p.   col. maps.   28 cm.

982   Oxford University Press.
      The little Oxford atlas.   2 ed.   London, 1962.
      67 p.   col. maps.   26 cm.

983   Philip, George & Son, Ltd.
      Philip's record atlas.   23 ed.   By Harold Fullard.
      London, 1962.
      341 p.   col. maps.   29 cm.

984   Philip, George & Son, Ltd.
      The university atlas.   10 ed.   London, [1962].
      200 p.   col. maps.   29 cm.

985   Poland.   Państwowe przedsiębiorstwo wydawnictw
      kartograficznych.
      Atlas geograficzny.   By Henryk Górski.
      Warszawa, [1962].
      149 p.   col. maps.   32 cm.

986   Poland.   Państwowe wydawnictwo naukowe.
      Atlas świata.   Warszawa, 1962—
      in parts.   col. maps.   42 cm.

987   Politikens forlag.
      Lommeatlas i farver.   By Axel Schou and Merete
      Rentsch. København, 1962.
      160 p. col. maps. 19 cm.

988   Praeger, Frederick A.
      An atlas of world affairs.   By Andrew Boyd. New
      York, [1962].
      160 p.   21 cm.

989   Rand McNally & Co.
      Atlas du monde. Chicago, [1962].
      15 p. col. maps. 31 cm.

990   Rand McNally & Co.
      Cosmopolitan world atlas. Chicago, [1962].
      360 p. col. maps. 37 cm.

991   Rand McNally & Co.
      Rand McNally collegiate atlas.   Chicago, 1962.
      1 vol. col. maps. 28 cm.

992   Rand McNally & Co.
      Rand McNally illustrated atlas of today's world.
      Encyclopedic ed. Chicago, [1962].
      1152 p. col. maps. 30 cm.

993   Rand McNally & Co.
      Rand McNally regional atlas. By Edward B.
      Espenshade, Jr. Chicago, 1962.
      64 p. col. maps. 29 cm.

994   Rand McNally & Co.
      Space age atlas. Chicago, [1962].
      40 p. col. maps. 36 cm.

995   Rand McNally & Co.
      World and space age atlas. Chicago, [1962].
      1 vol. col. maps. 37 cm.

996   Rand McNally & Co.
      World atlas. Chicago, [1962].
      15 p. col. maps. 31 cm.

997   Reader's Digest Association, Ltd.
      The Reader's Digest great world atlas. 1 ed.
      7 rev. London, 1962.
      179 p. col. maps. 41 cm.

998 Rikisútgáfa námsbóka.
Landabréfabók. Reykjavîk, 1962.
52 p. col. maps. 25 cm.

999 Romania. Editura di Stat Didacticā şi Pedagogicā.
Atlas geografic şcolar. By N. Gheorghiu.
Bucuresti, 1962.
34 p. col. maps. 33 cm.

1000 Romania. Editura Stiintificā.
Mic atlas geografic. By A. Barsan. Bucuresti,
1962.
301 p. col. maps. 17 cm.

1001 Skandinavisk Bogforlag.
Munksgaards Verdens atlas. With Elsevier.
Kǿbenhavn, 1962.
236 p. col. maps. 18.5 cm.

1002 Skrifola.
Sesam verdensatlas. With Generalstabens
litografiska anstalt. Kǿbenhavn, [1962].
160 p. col. maps. 28 cm.

1003 Söderström, Werner.
Suuri maailmankartasto. Helsinki, 1962.
187 p. col. maps. 33 cm.

1004 Ta chung shu chu.
Piao-chun shih-chieh k'o kuo ti-t'u. [Standard
maps of the countries of the world]. Hong Kong,
[1962].
31 p. col. maps. 27 cm.

1005 Thieme, W. J.
Atlas van Europa en de werelddelen. 52 ed. By
G. Prop. Zutphen, 1962.
48 p. col. maps. 26 cm.

1006 U.S.S.R. Glavnoe upravlenie geodezii i kartografii.
Atlas mira. Moskva, 1962.
64 p. col. maps. 19 cm.

1007 U.S.S.R. Glavnoe upravlenie geodezii i kartografii.
Atlas mira. Moskva, 1962.
293 p. col. maps. 20 cm.

1008 U.S.S.R. Glavnoe upravlenie geodezii i kartografii.
Atlas narodov mira. Moskva, 1962.
112 p. col. maps. 34 cm.

1009 Verlag Die Gabe.
Weltatlas. By W. Bormann. Gütersloh, [1962].
318 p. col. maps. 33 cm.

1010 Volk und Wissen Verlag.
Atlas der Erdkunde für die allgemein bildenden
polytechnischen Oberschulen. Berlin, [1962].
129 p. col. maps. 31 cm.

1011 Westermann, Georg.
Weltatlas. 110 ed. Braunschweig, [1962].
222 p. col. maps. 34 cm.

1012 Yavneh.
Atlas fisi, medini ve-kalkali. (In Hebrew). By
Moshe Brawer. Tel Aviv, 1962.
128 p. col. maps. 31 cm.

1013 Znanje.
Geografski atlas i statističkogeografski pregled
svijeta. 7 ed. By Petar Mardešić, Zvonimir
Dugački and Josip Zoričić. Zagreb, 1962.
533 p. col. maps. 22 cm.

1963

1014 Aguilar, S. A. de Ediciones.
Atlas bachillerato, universal y de España. 2 ed.
By A. L. Gómez. Madrid, 1963.
132 p. col. maps. 35 cm.

1015 Aguilar, S. A. de Ediciones.
Atlas bachillerato universal y de España. 3 ed.
By A. L. Gómez. Madrid, 1963.
132 p. col. maps. 35 cm.

1016 American Map Co., Inc.
Colorprint student's atlas of the world. New York,
[1963].
23 p. col. maps. 32 cm.

1017 Bartholomew, John & Son, Ltd.
The advanced atlas of modern geography. 7 ed.
Edinburgh, 1963.
159 p. col. maps. 38 cm.

1018 Bartholomew, John & Son, Ltd.
 The Edinburgh world atlas of modern geography.
 5 ed. Edinburgh, 1963.
 168 p. col. maps. 38 cm.

1019 Bartholomew, John & Son, Ltd.
 The pocket world atlas. Edinburgh, 1963.
 160 p. col. maps. 15 cm.

1020 Bertelsmann, C.
 Atlas der Oberflachenformen. Gütersloh, 1963.
 64 p. col. maps. 40 cm.

1021 Bertelsmann, C.
 Atlas international. By W. Bormann. Gütersloh,
 1963.
 426 p. col. maps. 41 cm.

1022 Bertelsmann, C.
 Kleiner Bertelsmann Weltatlas. By W. Bormann
 and W. Lenz. Gütersloh, 1963.
 435 p. col. maps. 19 cm.

1023 Beste, A. S.
 Der Grosse Reader's Digest Weltatlas. Adapted
 from English ed. Stuttgart, 1963.
 216 p. col. maps. 21.5 cm.

1024 Bulgaria. Glavno upravlenie po geodeziā i kartografiā.
 Atlas na sveta. Sofia, 1963.
 1 vol. col. maps. 31 cm.

1025 Collins, William, Sons & Co., Ltd.
 Collins-Longmans world atlas for Malaya. 8 ed.
 By K. H. Huggins. Glasgow, [1963].
 24 p. col. maps. 29 cm.

1026 Columbus Verlag Oestergaard.
 Columbus Hausatlas in Wort und Bild. Stuttgart,
 1963.
 189 p. col. maps. 41 cm.

1027 Czechoslovakia. Ústřední správa geodézie a kartografie.
 Kapesní atlas svĕta. 2 ed. Praha, 1963.
 120 p. col. maps. 17 cm.

1028 Czechoslovakia. Ústřední správa geodézie a kartografie.
Školský zemepianý atlas sveta. 5 Slovak ed. By
Kanštantín Zelenský. Praha, 1963.
79 p. col. maps. 31 cm.

1029 Delagrave.
Nouvel atlas classique. By M. Fallex and A.
Gilbert. Paris, 1963.
102 p. col. maps. 28 cm.

1030 Dent, J. M.
The Aldine world atlas; geography and history.
2 ed. By J. W. Hamilton and G. E. Tait. With
Bartholomew. Toronto, [1963].
166 p. col. maps. 29 cm.

1031 Educational Book Club.
The new world atlas. With Hammond. Des
Moines, [1963].
312 p. col. maps. 32 cm.

1032 Elsevier.
Elsevier Wereldatlas. 4 ed. By A. H. Symons.
Amsterdam, 1963.
179 p. col. maps. 26 cm.

1033 Elsevier.
Landen en volken; handboek over alle landen der
wereld. Samengesteld door de redactie van de
Nieuwe Winkler Prins atlas. Amsterdam, 1963.
156 p. col. maps. 33 cm.

1034 Elsevier.
Nieuwe Winkler Prins atlas. 6 ed. By A. H.
Symons. Amsterdam, 1963.
404 p. col. maps. 33 cm.

1035 Encyclopaedia Britannica.
Encyclopaedia Britannica world atlas. Chicago, 1963.
518 p. col. maps. 38 cm.

1036 Generalstabens litografiska anstalt.
En delad värld världspolitisk atlas. By Tor S.
Ahman and Gunnar Schalin. Stockholm, [1963].
64 p. col. maps. 22 cm.

1037 Generalstabens litografiska anstalt.
Sesam verdensatlas. Danish ed. Stockholm, 1963.
88 p. col. maps. 27.5 cm.

1038 Ginn & Co.
The Ginn world atlas. By Richard Edes Harrison
and staff. Boston, [1963].
62 p. col. maps. 26 cm.

1039 Ginn & Co.
The Ginn world atlas workbook. By Richard Edes
Harrison. Boston, [1963].
48 p. col. maps. 26 cm.

1040 Gjellerups Forlag.
Atlas for hoveskolen. 2 ed. København, 1963.
23 p. col. maps. 24 cm.

1041 Gjellerups Forlag.
Gjellerups skoleatlas II. With Generalstabens
litografiska anstalt. København, 1963.
73 p. col. maps. 33 cm.

1042 Goldmann Verlag.
Goldmann's Grosser Weltatlas. München, 1963.
332 p. col. maps. 41 cm.

1043 Gyldendal.
Atlas for folkeskolen. 28 ed. København, 1963.
34 p. col. maps. 24 cm.

1044 Gyldendal.
Gyldendals lommeatlas. Oslo, 1963.
240 p. col. maps. 19 cm.

1045 Gyldendal.
Kulturgeografisk atlas. 3 ed. By Johannes
Humlum. København, 1963.
2 vol. col. maps. 27 cm.

1046 Haack, Hermann.
Die Erde. Taschenatlas. 92 ed. Gotha, 1963.
295 p. col. maps. 16.5 cm.

1047 Haack, Hermann.
Taschenatlas Staaten und Wirtschaft. 1 ed.
Gotha, 1963.
400 p. col. maps. 16.5 cm.

1048 Haack, Hermann.
       Weltatlas. Die Staaten der Erde und ihre Wirtschaft.
       7 ed. By E. Lehmann. Gotha, 1963.
       181 p. col. maps. 34 cm.

1049 Hammond, C. S. & Co., Inc.
       Atlas internacional. (Atlas mundial). Mexico, [1963].
       224 p. col. maps. 37 cm.

1050 Hammond, C. S. & Co., Inc.
       Atlas moderno universal Hammond. Maplewood,
       N. J., 1963.
       45 p. col. maps. 31 cm.

1051 Hammond, C. S. & Co., Inc.
       Diplomat world atlas. Maplewood, N. J., [1963].
       276 p. col. maps. 37 cm.

1052 Hammond, C. S. & Co., Inc.
       Ezy-reference world atlas for looseleaf notebooks.
       New York, [1963].
       31 p. col. maps. 27 cm.

1053 Hammond, C. S. & Co., Inc.
       Family reference world atlas. Maplewood, N. J.,
       1963.
       256 p. col. maps. 26.5 cm.

1054 Hammond, C. S. & Co., Inc.
       Family world atlas. N. Y., [1963].
       2 vol. col. maps. 32 cm.

1055 Hammond, C. S. & Co., Inc.
       Hammond's comparative world atlas. Maplewood,
       N. J., 1963.
       48 p. col. maps. 31 cm.

1056 Hammond, C. S. & Co., Inc.
       Hammond's library world atlas. Maplewood, N. J.,
       1963.
       324 p. col. maps. 31 cm.

1057 Hammond, C. S. & Co., Inc.
       Hammond's new era atlas of the world. Maple-
       wood, N. J., 1963.
       176 p. col. maps. 31 cm.

1058 Hammond, C. S. & Co., Inc.
    Hammond's new home reference world atlas and
    gazetteer. Maplewood, N. J., 1963.
    2 vol. col. maps. 24 cm.

1059 Hammond, C. S. & Co., Inc.
    Hammond's new international world atlas. Maple-
    wood, N. J., 1963.
    96 p. col. maps. 31 cm.

1060 Hammond, C. S. & Co., Inc.
    Hammond's our world in space atlas. Maplewood,
    N. J., 1963.
    50 p. col. maps. 31 cm.

1061 Hammond, C. S. & Co., Inc.
    Hammond's standard world atlas. Maplewood,
    N. J., 1963.
    304 p. col. maps. 31 cm.

1062 Hammond, C. S. & Co., Inc.
    Hammond's world atlas. Maplewood, N. J., 1963.
    384 p. col. maps. 31 cm.

1063 Hammond, C. S. & Co., Inc.
    Hammond's world atlas. Superior ed. Maplewood,
    N. J., 1963.
    312 p. col. maps. 31 cm.

1064 Hammond, C. S. & Co., Inc.
    My first world atlas. Maplewood, N. J., 1963.
    49 p. col. maps. 25 cm.

1065 Herder - Verlag.
    Herders illustrierter Weltatlas. Freiburg, 1963.
    256 p. col. maps. 35 cm.

1066 Hölzel, Ed. Verlag.
    Österreichischer Mittelschulatlas. 88 ed. Wien,
    1963.
    146 p. col. maps. 31 cm.

1067 India. Survey of India.
    School atlas. Dehra Dŭn, 1963.
    62 p. col. maps. 31 cm.

1068 Istituto Geografico De Agostini.
Atlante geografico metodico. Novara, 1963.
109 p. col. maps. 33 cm.

1069 Istituto Geografico De Agostini.
Atlante geografico moderno. Novara, 1963.
76 p. col. maps. 33 cm.

1070 Istituto Geografico De Agostini.
Calendario atlante de Agostini. Novara, 1963.
544 p. col. maps. 16 cm.

1071 Istituto Geografico De Agostini.
Modern büyük atlas. Novara, 1963.
108 p. col. maps. 33 cm.

1072 Istituto Geografico De Agostini.
Modern Ilk atlas. Novara, 1963.
11 p. col. maps. 27 cm.

1073 Istituto Geografico De Agostini.
Novo atlas escolar Português. Novara, 1963.
125 p. col. maps. 34 cm.

1074 Istituto Geografico De Agostini.
Piccolo atlante della produzione e dei commerci.
By L. Visintin. Novara, [1963].
90 p. col. maps. 26 cm.

1075 Istituto Geografico De Agostini.
Resimli Ilk atlas. Novara, 1963.
28 p. col. maps. 27 cm.

1076 Jugoslavenski leksikografski zavod.
Atlas svijeta. 2 ed. By Petar Mardešić and Oto
Oppitz. Zagreb, 1963.
441 p. col. maps. 30 cm.

1077 Kartográfiai Vállalat.
Földrajzi atlasz as általános iskolák számará. By
Radó Sándor. Budapest, 1963.
32 p. col. maps. 29 cm.

1078 Kartográfiai Vállalat.
Földrajzi atlasz középiskolak számará. Budapest,
1963.
60 p. col. maps. 28 cm.

1079 Keysersche Verlagsbuchhandlung, GMBH.
     Grosser Weltatlas. By H. R. Fischer. Berlin,
     [1963].
     352 p. col. maps. 35 cm.

1080 Kiplinger-Washington Editors, Inc.
     The Kiplinger-Hammond forecast atlas of the world.
     With Hammond. Washington, D. C., 1963.
     1 vol. col. maps. 32 cm.

1081 List, P.
     Harms Atlas, die Länder der Erde. By W. Eggers
     and F. Pfrommer. München, [1963].
     65 p. col. maps. 33 cm.

1082 List, P.
     Harms Wirtschaftsatlas. By W. Eggers. München,
     [1963].
     73 p. col. maps. 33 cm.

1083 Martins Forlag.
     Martin Verdensatlas. 2 ed. Kφbenhavn, 1963.
     342 p. col. maps. 30.5 cm.

1084 McGraw Hill Book Co.
     McGraw-Hill international atlas. By W. Bormann.
     With Bertelsmann. New York, [1963].
     1 vol. col. maps. 41 cm.

1085 McGraw Hill Book Co.
     The advanced atlas of modern geography. 7 ed.
     With Bartholomew. New York, 1963.
     159 p. col. maps. 38 cm.

1086 Meulenhoff, J. M.
     Atlas van Nederland en de wereld. 2 ed. With
     Hölzel. Amsterdam, 1963.
     162 p. col. maps. 32 cm.

1087 Meyer, Kartographisches Institut.
     Meyers neuer Handatlas für Zeitungsleser,
     Rundfunkhörer und Fernsehteilnehmer. Mannheim,
     [1963].
     76 p. col. maps. 31 cm.

1088 Murray, John.
Murray's classical atlas for schools. By G. B.
Grundy. London, 1963.
37 p. col. maps. 32 cm.

1089 Nathan, Fernand.
Petit atlas universel. With Istituto Geografico De
Agostini. Paris, 1963.
71 p. col. maps. 15.5 cm.

1090 National Geographic Society.
National Geographic atlas of the world. Washington,
D. C., 1963.
300 p. col. maps. 50 cm.

1091 Nelson, Thomas & Sons, Ltd.
Nelson's Canadian school atlas. 3 ed. By J.
Wreford Watson. Toronto, 1963.
92 p. col. maps. 29 cm.

1092 New York Herald Tribune.
World wide atlas; complete with new nations. With
Hammond. New York, [1963].
31 p. col. maps. 26 cm.

1093 Oceana Publications.
Focus on maps of world crisis. By Jack Bloomfield. Dobbs Ferry, N. Y., 1963.
90 p. 28.5 cm.

1094 Otava.
Kolumbus maailamkartasto. 2 ed. Helsinki, 1963.
281 p. col. maps. 29 cm.

1095 Otava.
Otavan koulukartasto. 14 ed. Helsinki, 1963.
44 p. col. maps. 28 cm.

1096 Otava.
Otavan maailmankartasto. 4 ed. Helsinki, 1963.
168 p. col. maps. 28.5 cm.

1097 Otava.
Otavan taskukartasto. Helsinki, 1963.
240 p. col. maps. 29 cm.

1098 Oxford University Press.
     Shorter Oxford school atlas.   3 ed.   London, [1963].
     67 p.   col.   maps.   26 cm.

1099 Oxford University Press.
     The Canadian Oxford desk atlas of the world.   2 ed.
     Toronto, 1963.
     155 p.   col.   maps.   26 cm.

1100 Philip, George & Son, Ltd.
     Philips' new school atlas.   5 ed.   By Harold Fullard.
     London, 1963.
     94 p.   col.   maps.   29 cm.

1101 Philip, George & Son, Ltd.
     Philips' record atlas.   24 ed.   By Harold Fullard.
     London, 1963.
     257 p.   col.   maps.   29 cm.

1102 Poland.   Państwowe przedsiębiorstwo wydawnictw
     kartograficznych.
     Atlas geograficzny.   Warszawa, 1963.
     120 p.   col.   maps.   31 cm.

1103 Poland.   Państwowe przedsiębiorstwo wydawinctw
     kartograficznych.
     Atlas geograficzny dla klasy IV szkol podstawowych.
     Warszawa, 1963.
     1 vol.   col.   maps.   26 cm.

1104 Poland.   Państwowe przedsiębiorstwo wydawnictw
     kartograficznych.
     Atlas świata.   Warszawa, 1963.
     in parts.   col.   maps.   42 cm.

1105 Poland.   Państwowe przedsiębiorstwo wydawnictw
     kartograficznych.
     Maly atlas geograficzny.   Warszawa, 1963.
     1 vol.   col.   maps.   30 cm.

1106 Poland.   Państwowe przedsiębiorstivo wydawnictw
     kartograficznych.
     Maly atlas swiata.   Warszawa, [1963].
     1 vol.   col.   maps.   23 cm.

1107 Politikens Forlag.
     Politikens Verdensatlas.   With Philip.   København, 1963.
     15 p.   col.   maps.   28 cm.

1108 Praeger, Frederick A.
An atlas of world affairs. 4 ed. By Andrew Boyd.
New York, 1963.
160 p. 21 cm.

1109 Prentice-Hall.
Prentice-Hall world atlas. 2 ed. By Joseph E.
Williams. Englewood Cliffs, N. J., 1963.
137 p. col. maps. 32 cm.

1110 Rand McNally & Co.
Rand McNally book of nations. Chicago, 1963.
95 p. col. maps. 35 cm.

1111 Rand McNally & Co.
Rand McNally classroom atlas. 4 ed. Chicago,
1963.
84 p. col. maps. 25.5 cm.

1112 Rand McNally & Co.
Rand McNally cosmopolitan world atlas. Chicago,
1963.
370 p. col. maps. 36 cm.

1113 Rand McNally & Co.
Rand McNally world atlas. Chicago, 1963.
30 p. col. maps. 32 cm.

1114 Rand McNally & Co.
World portrait atlas. Chicago, 1963.
93 p. col. maps. 38 cm.

1115 Reader's Digest Association, Ltd.
Det Bedste store verdensatlas. Adapted from
English ed. København, [1963].
216 p. col. maps. 40 cm.

1116 Reader's Digest Association, Ltd.
Det bästas stora världatlas. By Hans W. Ahlmann.
Adapted from English ed. Stockholm, [1963].
216 p. col. maps. 40 cm.

1117 Reader's Digest Association, Ltd.
Reader's Digest great world atlas. 2 ed.
Pleasantville, N. Y., [1963].
232 p. col. maps. 41 cm.

1118 Siemens & Halske, A. G.
Welt-Texlex-Atlas. München, 1963.
205 p. col. maps. 30 cm.

1119 Söderström, Werner.
Kansakoulun kartasto. 4 ed. Helsinki, 1963.
36 p. col. maps. 27 cm.

1120 Söderström, Werner.
Oppikoulun kartasto. 5 ed. Helsinki, 1963.
67 p. col. maps. 27 cm.

1121 Sohlmans förlag, a. b.
Sohlmans världsatlas. By Karl Erik Bergsten.
With Philip. Stockholm, 1963.
163 p. col. maps. 29 cm.

1122 Springer Verlag.
Weltkarte zur klimakunde. By H. E. Landsberg.
Berlin, 1963.
28 p. col. maps. 30 cm.

1123 Südwest Verlag.
Neuer Taschenatlas. Die Erde und ihre Länder in
polit. und wirtschaftl. Darstellung. By Hans R.
Fischer. München, [1963].
156 p. col. maps. 32 cm.

1124 Svenska bokförlaget.
Ekonomisk geografi. Statistik atlas för den
ekonomiska geografin. 4 ed. By Sven Olof
Garland. Stockholm, [1963].
32 p. col. maps. 27 cm.

1125 Texana.
This wonderful world. Maps by areas. Los
Angeles, 1963.
32 p. col. maps. 15 cm.

1126 Thieme, W. J.
Atlas van Europa en de werelddelen. 53 ed. By
G. Prop. Zutphen, 1963.
48 p. col. maps. 26 cm.

1127 Učila.
Veliki školski atlas. 12 ed. By Zvonimir
Dugački. Zagreb, 1963.
58 p. col. maps. 35 cm.

1128 Volk und Wissen Verlag.
      Atlas für die 5. und 6. Klasse.   By W. Krämer.
      With Haack.   Berlin, 1963.
      26 p.   col. maps.   31 cm.

1129 Wenschow.
      Wenschow Weltatlas.   München, 1963.
      43 p.   col. maps.   34 cm.

1130 Westermann, Georg.
      Atlas für die Berliner Schulen.   8 ed.
      Braunschweig, 1963.
      36 p.   col. maps.   32 cm.

1131 Westermann, Georg.
      Atlas für die Hamburger Schulen.   Braunschweig,
      1963.
      56 p.   col. maps.   32 cm.

1132 Westermann, Georg.
      Der Lebensraum des Menschen.   Braunschweig, 1963.
      93 p.   col. maps.   33 cm.

1133 Westermann, Georg.
      Weltatlas.   113 ed.   By C. Diercke and R. Dehmel.
      Braunschweig, 1963.
      243 p.   col. maps.   34 cm.

1134 Westermann, Georg.
      Westermann Atlas.   Heimat und Welt.
      Braunschweig, 1963.
      45 p.   col. maps.   32 cm.

1135 Weststadt Verlag.
      The world shipping scene; atlas of shipping, ship-
      building, seaports and sea-borne trade.   By G.A.
      Theel.   München, 1963.
      1 vol.   col. maps.   31 cm.

1136 Wjedza Powszechna.
      Swiat w mapach i wykresach—Europa.   Krakow, 1963.
      341 p.   24 cm.

1137 Wolters, J. B.
      School atlas der gehele aarde.   42 ed.   By F. J.
      Ormeling.   Groningen, 1963.
      205 p.   col. maps.   38 cm.

1964

1138 Aguilar, S. A. de Ediciones.
Atlas bachillerato universal y de España.   4 ed.
By A. L. Gómez.   Madrid, 1964.
132 p. col. maps. 35 cm.

1139 Aguilar, S. A. de Ediciones.
Atlas bachillerato universal y de España.   5 ed.
By A. L. Gómez.   Madrid, 1964.
132 p. col. maps. 35 cm.

1140 Aguilar, S. A. de Ediciones.
Atlas bachillerato universal y de España.   6 ed.
By A. L. Gómez.   Madrid, 1964.
132 p. col. maps. 35 cm.

1141 American Map Co. , Inc.
Atlas de Venezuela y del mundo.   New York, [1964].
23 p. col. maps. 31 cm.

1142 American Map Co. , Inc.
Colorprint student's atlas of the world.   New York,
1964.
23 p. col. maps. 31 cm.

1143 American Map Co. , Inc.
Physical world atlas.   With Bartholomew.   Tarry-
town, N. Y. , 1964.
231 p. col. maps. 37.5 cm.

1144 Aschchoug & Co.
Skole-atlas.   20 ed.   Oslo, 1964.
86 p. col. maps. 29 cm.

1145 Bantam Books.
New Hammond world atlas.   With Hammond.   New
York, [1964].
272 p. col. maps. 18 cm.

1146 Bartholomew, John & Son. , Ltd.
The Edinburgh world atlas.   Edinburgh, 1964.
208 p. col. maps. 37.5 cm.

1147 Bergvalls Förlag.
Bergvalls atlas för den 9-årige skolan.   By
Magnus Lundqvist and Olof Hedbom.   Stockholm,
[1964].
85 p. col. maps. 25 cm.

1148 Bertelsmann, C.
    Kleiner Bertelsmann Weltatlas. 50 ed. Gütersloh,
    1964.
    435 p. col. maps. 19 cm.

1149 Beste, A. S.
    Det Bestes store verdensatlas. With Reader's
    Digest Association, Ltd. Oslo, 1964.
    216 p. col. maps. 40 cm.

1150 Brockhaus, F. A.
    Der Grosse Brockhaus Atlas. Wiesbaden, 1964.
    664 p. col. maps. 25 cm.

1151 Buchgemeindschaft Donauland.
    Weltatlas von heute. With Westermann. Wien, 1964.
    121 p. col. maps. 31 cm.

1152 Cappelens, J. W. Forlag, A. S.
    Cappelens atlas for folkeskolen. Oslo, 1964.
    90 p. col. maps. 32 cm.

1153 Cappelens, J. W. Forlag, A. S.
    Hjemmenes nye verdensatlas. Oslo, 1964.
    184 p. col. maps. 28 cm.

1154 Collins Clear-Type Press.
    The world-where, how, and why. 1 ed. By Allan
    Murray. London, [1964].
    64 p. col. maps. 26 cm.

1155 Consolidated Book Publishers.
    The Universal standard atlas of the world. With
    Rand McNally. Chicago, [1964].
    400 p. col. maps. 35 cm.

1156 Cram, George F. Co.
    Student-quick reference atlas of the world.
    Indianapolis, Ind., 1964.
    34 p. col. maps. 30.5 cm.

1157 Droemer.
    Knaurs Weltatlas. München, 1964.
    226 p. col. maps. 29 cm.

1158 Edições Melhoramentos.
    Atlas Geográfico Melhoramentos. São Paulo, 1964.
    89 p. col. maps. 36 cm.

1159 Editions Bordas.
    Atlas général Bordas, historique et géographique.
    Paris, 1964.
    164 p. col. maps. 30.5 cm.

1160 Editions Bordas.
    Atlas général Bordas: La France, le monde.   By
    Pierre Serryn. Paris, [1964].
    140 p. col. maps. 31 cm.

1161 Editorial Teide.
    Atlas universal Teide: geográfico, estadístico,
    ilustrado. By Luigi Visintin. With Istituto
    Geografico De Agostini. Barcelona, [1964].
    120 p. col. maps. 34 cm.

1162 Educational Book Club.
    World and space age atlas.   With Rand McNally.
    Des Moines, [1964].
    323 p. col. maps. 32 cm.

1163 Elsevier.
    Elseviers moderne atlas. Amsterdam, 1964.
    240 p. col. maps. 26 cm.

1164 Elsevier.
    Winkler Prins Wereldatlas. Amsterdam, 1964.
    241 p. col. maps. 33 cm.

1165 Encyclopaedia Britannica.
    Encyclopaedia Britannica International atlas. With
    Istituto Geografico De Agostini. Novara, 1964.
    256 p. col. maps. 42 cm.

1166 Encyclopaedia Britannica.
    Encyclopaedia Britannica world atlas.   Chicago, 1964.
    428 p. col. maps. 38 cm.

1167 English University Press, Ltd.
    The Teach Yourself Atlas of the World.   By Harold
    Fullard. With Philip. London, 1964.
    192 p. col. maps. 20 cm.

1168 Field Enterprises Educational Corp.
    The World book atlas. With Rand McNally.
    Chicago, [1964].
    412 p. col. maps. 37 cm.

1169 Generalstabens litografiska anstalt.
Svensk världs atlas. Stockholm, 1964.
158 p. col. maps. 27 cm.

1170 GEO Publishing Co.
The Faber atlas. 4 ed. By D. J. Sinclair. With
Hölzel. Oxford, [1964].
201 p. col. maps. 31 cm.

1171 Gjellerups Forlag.
Hovedskolens atlas. Med geografisk handbogsafsnit.
København, 1964.
72 p. col. maps. 30 cm.

1172 Gyldendal.
Atlas 3 for gymmasiet og seminariet samt anden
hojere undervisning. By Willy Frits Hellner.
København, 1964.
83 p. col. maps. 31.5 cm.

1173 Gyldendal.
Kulturgeografisk atlas. 4 ed. By Johannes Humlum.
København, 1964.
2 vol. col. maps. 27 cm.

1174 Haack, Hermann.
Die Erde. Taschenatlas. 93 ed. Gotha, 1964.
271 p. col. maps. 18 cm.

1175 Haack, Hermann.
Geographie für Jedermann. Gotha, 1964.
285 p. col. maps. 22.5 cm.

1176 Haack, Hermann.
Weltatlas. Die staaten der Erde und ihre
Wirtschaft. 8 ed. Gotha, [1964].
172 p. col. maps. 35 cm.

1177 Hammond, C. S. & Co., Inc.
Advanced reference atlas. Maplewood, N. J., 1964.
189 p. col. maps. 31 cm.

1178 Hammond, C. S. & Co., Inc.
Comparative world atlas. New desk ed. Maplewood, N. J., 1964.
48 p. col. maps. 31 cm.

1179 Hammond, C. S. & Co., Inc.
Ezy-reference atlas for looseleaf notebooks. New

York, 1964.
31 p. col. maps. 28 cm.

1180 Hammond, C. S. & Co. , Inc.
Family reference world atlas. Space age ed.
With Doubleday. Maplewood, N. J. , 1964.
256 p. col. maps. 27 cm.

1181 Hammond, C. S. & Co. , Inc.
Hammond's library world atlas. Maplewood, N. J. ,
1964.
336 p. col. maps. 31 cm.

1182 Hammond, C. S. & Co. , Inc.
Hammond universal world atlas. Canadian ed.
Maplewood, N. J. , [1964].
160 p. col. maps. 32 cm.

1183 Hammond, C. S. & Co. , Inc.
Illustrated atlas for young America. Maplewood,
N. J. , 1964.
96 p. col. maps. 27 cm.

1184 Hammond, C. S. & Co. , Inc.
New era atlas of the world. Maplewood, N. J. ,
1964.
152 p. col. maps. 31 cm.

1185 Hammond, C. S. & Co. , Inc.
Standard world atlas. Maplewood, N. J. , 1964.
312 p. col. maps. 31 cm.

1186 Hammond, C. S. & Co. , Inc.
Universal world atlas. Maplewood, N. J. , 1964.
192 p. col. maps. 31 cm.

1187 Hammond, C. S. & Co. , Inc.
World atlas. Classics ed. Maplewood, N. J. , 1964.
384 p. col. maps. 31 cm.

1188 Hammond, C. S. & Co. , Inc.
World atlas. Superior ed. Maplewood, N. J. , 1964.
286 p. col. maps. 31 cm.

1189 Hammond, C. S. & Co. , Inc.
World atlas, an encyclopedic atlas of the world.
With Nelson-Doubleday. Maplewood, N. J. , [1964].
264 p. col. maps. 32 cm.

1190 Hammond, C. S. & Co., Inc.
World atlas, an encyclopedic atlas of the world.
Grolier International ed. Maplewood, N. J., [1964].
232 p. col. maps. 32 cm.

1191 Hammond, C. S. & Co., Inc.
World atlas for students. Maplewood, N. J., 1964.
51 p. col. maps. 31 cm.

1192 Herder Verlag.
Herders illustrierter Weltatlas. 2 ed. Freiburg,
1964.
256 p. col. maps. 35 cm.

1193 Hölzel, Ed. Verlag.
Büyük atlas. By Faik Sabri Duran. (in Turkish).
Wien, 1964.
96 p. col. maps. 31 cm.

1194 Hölzel, Ed. Verlag.
Ilk atlas. (in Turkish). Wien, 1964.
16 p. col. maps. 27 cm.

1195 Hölzel, Ed. Verlag.
Österreichischer Hauptschulatlas. 5 ed. Wien,
1964.
76 p. col. maps. 31 cm.

1196 Hölzel, Ed. Verlag.
Österreichischer Mittelschulatlas. 89 ed. Wien,
1964.
146 p. col. maps. 31 cm.

1197 Hölzel, Ed. Verlag.
Österreichischer Mittelschulatlas. 90 ed. Wien,
1964.
226 p. col. maps. 31 cm.

1198 Hölzel, Ed. Verlag.
Yeni orta atlas. (in Turkish). Wien, 1964.
40 p. col. maps. 31 cm.

1199 India. Survey of India.
School atlas. Dehra Dūn, 1964.
62 p. col. maps. 31 cm.

1200 Istituto Geografico De Agostini.
Atlante geografico metodico. Novara, 1964.

190 p.   col. maps.   34 cm.

1201 Istituto Geografico De Agostini.
     Atlante geografico moderno.   Novara, 1964.
     150 p.   col. maps.   34 cm.

1202 Istituto Geografico De Agostini.
     Ilkokul atlasi.   (in Turkish). Novara, 1964.
     18 p.   col. maps.   26 cm.

1203 Istituto Geografico De Agostini.
     Modern ilkokul atlasi.   (in Turkish). Novara, 1964.
     64 p.   col. maps.   25.5 cm.

1204 Istituto Geografico De Agostini.
     Piccolo atlante della produzione e dei commerci.
     Novara, 1964.
     86 p.   col. maps.   26 cm.

1205 Istituto Geografico De Agostini.
     Renkli Resimli ortaokul atlasi.   (in Turkish).
     Novara, 1964.
     28 p.   col. maps.   27 cm.

1206 Johnston, W. & A. K. and G. W. Bacon, Ltd.
     Johnston's new premier atlas of the world.   3 ed.
     Edinburgh, 1964.
     94 p.   col. maps.   29 cm.

1207 Journaux, André.
     Atlas mondial.   Caen, 1964.
     15 p.   col. maps.   31 cm.

1208 Kapelusz y Cía.
     Atlas mundi, astronómico-general: Asia, Africa,
     Europa, Oceanía, América; físico, político,
     económico.   Buenos Aires, [1964].
     40 p.   col. maps.   27 cm.

1209 Keysersche Verlagsbuchhandlung, GMBH.
     Atlas zur Erdkunde.   4 ed.   By H. Lautensach.
     München, 1964.
     129 p.   col. maps.   31 cm.

1210 Keysersche Verlagsbuchhandlung, GMBH.
     Atlas zur Erdkunde.   6 ed.   By H. Lautensach.
     München, [1964].
     174 p.   col. maps.   31 cm.

1211 Kiplinger Washington Editors, Inc.
   The Kiplinger. Hammond forecast atlas of the
   world. With Hammond. Maplewood, N. J., [1964].
   386 p. col. maps. 31.5 cm.

1212 Kümmerly & Frey.
   Geteilte Welt. Weltpolitischer Atlas. By Tor S.
   Ahman and Gunnar Schalin. Transl. from Swedish.
   Bern, [1964].
   96 p. col. maps. 21 cm.

1213 Larousse.
   Atlas Larousse classique. By Donald Curran and
   Michel Coquery. Paris, [1964].
   158 p. col. maps. 31 cm.

1214 List, P.
   Harms' Atlas. Die Länder der Erde. München,
   1964.
   65 p. col. maps. 33 cm.

1215 Lloyd's, Corp. of.
   Lloyd's maritime atlas. 5 ed. London, 1964.
   1 vol. col. maps. 25 cm.

1216 Merrill, C. E. Co.
   Merrill school atlas. By P. F. Griffin. Columbus,
   Ohio, [1964].
   96 p. col. maps. 29 cm.

1217 Minerva Books.
   Atlas de Venezuela y del mundo. With American
   Map Co. Caracas, [1964].
   23 p. col. maps. 31 cm.

1218 Nathan, Fernand.
   Atlas du xxe siècle. By Rand M. Ozouf. With
   Istituto Geografico De Agostini. Paris, [1964].
   140 p. col. maps. 35 cm.

1219 Nelson Doubleday.
   World atlas; an encyclopedic atlas of the world.
   Australian ed. With Hammond. St. Leonards,
   N. S. W., [1964].
   264 p. col. maps. 32 cm.

1220 Newnes, George, Ltd.
   Newnes world atlas. With Hammond. London,

[1964].
210 p. col. maps. 31.5 cm.

1221 Oliver & Boyd.
The new comparative atlas. 47 ed. With
Bartholomew. Edinburgh, [1964].
120 p. col. maps. 29 cm.

1222 Otava.
Otavan koulukartasto. Helsinki, 1964.
44 p. col. maps. 28 cm.

1223 Oxford University Press.
Oxford junior atlas. London, 1964.
55 p. col. maps. 26 cm.

1224 Paravia, G. B.
Atlante geografico Paravia.   Torino, 1964.
96 p. col. maps. 33 cm.

1225 Pfahl Verlag.
Minerva-Weltatlas.   By A. Zimmermann.   Baden-
Baden, 1964.
218 p. col. maps. 24 cm.

1226 Philip, George & Son, Ltd.
Philips' First venture atlas; how and where people
live. By Harold Fullard. London, [1964].
24 p. col. maps. 23 cm.

1227 Philip, George & Son, Ltd.
Philips' Record atlas. 25 ed. By Harold Fullard.
London, 1964.
267 p. col. maps. 29 cm.

1228 Philip, George & Son, Ltd.
The University atlas. 11 ed. London, 1964.
187 p. col. maps. 29 cm.

1229 Poland. Państwowe przedsiębiorstwo wydawnictw
kartograficznych.
Atlas geograficzny. Warszawa, 1964.
158 p. col. maps. 33 cm.

1230 Poland. Państwowe przedsiębiorstwo wydawnictw
kartograficznych.
Atlas geograficzny dla klasy IV. Warszawa, 1964.
1 vol. col. maps. 26 cm.

1231 Poland. Państwowe p|rzedsiębiorstwo |wydawnictw kartograficznych.
Atlas geograficzny. V-VIII Klasy. Warszawa, 1964.
60 p. col. maps. 30.5 cm.

1232 Poland. Sluzba topograficzna wojska polskiego.
Atlas swiata. Warszawa, [1964].
1 vol. col. maps. 31 cm.

1233 Praeger, Frederick A.
An atlas of world affairs. 5 ed. By Andrew Boyd.
New York, 1964.
160 p. 21 cm.

1234 Principato, Giuseppe.
Atlante geografico Principato. Milano, 1964.
142 p. col. maps. 33.5 cm.

1235 Rand McNally & Co.
Atlas of nations. Chicago, 1964.
32 p. col. maps. 35 cm.

1236 Rand McNally & Co.
Cosmopolitan world atlas. Chicago, [1964].
360 p. col. maps. 37 cm.

1237 Rand McNally & Co.
Goode's world atlas. 12 ed. By Edward B.
Espenshade, Jr. Chicago, 1964.
288 p. col. maps. 29 cm.

1238 Rand McNally & Co.
Rand McNally book of nations. Chicago, 1964.
93 p. col. maps. 35 cm.

1239 Rand McNally & Co.
Rand McNally collegiate world atlas. Chicago, 1964.
416 p. col. maps. 27 cm.

1240 Rand McNally & Co.
Rand McNally geographical world atlas. Chicago,
1964.
96 p. col. maps. 29 cm.

1241 Rand McNally & Co.
Rand McNally regional atlas. 3 ed. By Edward
B. Espenshade, Jr. Chicago, 1964.
64 p. col. maps. 29 cm.

1242 Rand McNally & Co.
     Rand McNally space age atlas. Chicago, [1964].
     40 p. col. maps. 36 cm.

1243 Rand McNally & Co.
     Rand McNally world atlas. Chicago, 1964.
     29 p. col. maps. 33 cm.

1244 Rand McNally & Co.
     Student's political atlas of the world. Chicago, 1964.
     48 p. col. maps. 28 cm.

1245 Reader's Digest Association, Ltd.
     The Reader's Digest Association great world atlas.
     1 ed. London, 1964.
     183 p. col. maps. 40 cm.

1246 Reader's Digest Association, Ltd.
     The Reader's Digest great world atlas. 1 ed.
     3 rev. London, 1964.
     183 p. col. maps. 40 cm.

1247 Reader's Digest Mexico, S. A.
     El atlas de nuestro tiempo de selecciones del
     Reader's Digest. Mexico, [1964].
     207 p. col. maps. 40 cm.

1248 Romania. Editura di Stat Didactică si Pedagogică.
     Atlas geografic pentru clasele III-IV ale scolii
     generale de 8 ani. By Elena Papatănese and
     Florica Vornicescu. Bucuresti, 1964.
     51 p. col. maps. 34 cm.

1249 Scholastic Book Services.
     Scholastic Hammond world atlas. With Hammond.
     New York, 1964.
     62 p. col. maps. 25 cm.

1250 Südwest Verlag.
     Der Neue Hausatlas. München, [1964].
     192 p. col. maps. 32 cm.

1251 Südwest Verlag.
     Neuer Grosser Weltatlas. Für Heim, Unterricht
     und Reise. München, 1964.
     161 p. col. maps. 32 cm.

1252 Südwest Verlag.
Neuer Taschenatlas. Die Erde und ihre Länder
in politischer und wirtschaftlicher Darstellung.
By H. R. Fischer. München, 1964.
156 p. col. maps. 32 cm.

1253 Thieme, W. J.
Atlas van Europa en de werelddelen. 54 ed. By
G. Prop. Zutphen, 1964.
48 p. col. maps. 26 cm.

1254 U.S.S.R. Glavnoe upravlenie geodezii i kartografii.
Atlas mira. Moskva, 1964.
64 p. col. maps. 18 cm.

1255 U.S.S.R. Glavnoe upravlenie geodezii i kartografii.
Atlas narodov mira. Moskva, 1964.
184 p. col. maps. 34.5 cm.

1256 U.S.S.R. Glavnoe upravlenie geodezii i kartografii.
Atlas zaribechnich stran. Moskva, 1964.
40 p. col. maps. 28 cm.

1257 U.S.S.R. Glavnoe upravlenie geodezii i kartografii.
Fiziko-geograficheskii atlas mira. Moskva, 1964.
298 p. col. maps. 51 cm.

1258 U.S.S.R. Glavnoe upravlenie geodezii i kartografii.
Geograficheski atlas chastei sveta i vazhneishich
gosudarstv dla 6go-7go klasov. Moskva, [1964].
48 p. col. maps. 29 cm.

1259 U.S.S.R. Glavnoe upravlenie geodezii i kartografii.
Geograficheskii atlas dla 5go klassa. Moskva, 1964.
16 p. col. maps. 28 cm.

1260 Volk und Wissen Verlag.
Atlas für die 5. und 6. klasse. By W. Krämer.
With Haack. Berlin, 1964.
26 p. col. maps. 31 cm.

1261 Westermann, Georg.
Atlas für Berliner Schulen. 9 ed. Braunschweig,
1964.
36 p. col. maps. 32 cm.

1262 Westermann, Georg.
Atlas für Hamburger Schulen. Braunschweig, 1964.

121 p. col. maps. 32 cm.

1263 Westermann, Georg.
Der Lebensraum des Menschen. Ein Westermann
Atlas für Schule und Haus. Braunschweig, 1964.
93 p. col. maps. 33 cm.

1264 Westermann, Georg.
Hausatlas. 4 ed. Braunschweig, 1964.
240 p. col. maps. 34 cm.

1265 Westermann, Georg.
Heimat und Welt. Braunschweig, 1964.
45 p. col. maps. 33 cm.

1266 Westermann, Georg.
Weltatlas. Braunschweig, 1964.
224 p. col. maps. 36 cm.

1267 Wolters, J. B.
De grote Bosatlas. 43 ed. By F. J. Ormeling.
Groningen, 1964.
202 p. col. maps. 37 cm.

1268 Wolters, J. B.
Bos-Niermeyer schoolatlas der gehele aarde. 43 ed.
By F. J. Ormeling. Groningen, 1964.
172 p. col. maps. 38 cm.

1269 Zanichelli, Nicola.
Piccolo atlante geografico Zanichelli. Bologna, 1964.
70 p. col. maps. 31 cm.

1965

1270 Aguilar, S. A. de Ediciones.
Atlas bachillerato universal y de España. 7 ed.
By A.L. Gómez. Madrid, 1965.
132 p. col. maps. 35 cm.

1271 Aguilar, S. A. de Ediciones.
Atlas bachillerato universal y de España. 8 ed.
By A. L. Gómez. Madrid, 1965.
132 p. col. maps. 35 cm.

1272 American Map Co., Inc.
Colorprint world atlas. New York, [1965].
16 p. col. maps. 31 cm.

1273 Aschehoug & Co.
Aschehougs verdens atlas. 2 ed. Oslo, 1965.
214 p. col. maps. 33 cm.

1274 Bancroft & Co.
The New Bancroft world atlas. London, 1965.
126 p. col. maps. 17 cm.

1275 Bertelsmann, C.
Bertelsmann atlas international. Gütersloh, 1965.
564 p. col. maps. 40 cm.

1276 Bertelsmann, C.
Bertelsmann Hausatlas. Gütersloh, 1965.
320 p. col. maps. 32 cm.

1277 Bertelsmann, C.
Der Grosse Bertelsmann Weltatlas. Gütersloh, 1965.
392 p. col. maps. 32 cm.

1278 Bertelsmann, C.
Kleiner Bertelsmann Weltatlas. Gütersloh, 1965.
440 p. col. maps. 19 cm.

1279 Bir Yayinevi.
Büyük atlas. With Istituto Geografico De Agostini.
Istanbul, 1965.
88 p. col. maps. 33 cm.

1280 Bir Yayinevi.
Ilkokul atlas. With Istituto Geografico De Agostini.
Istanbul, 1965.
20 p. col. maps. 26 cm.

1281 Bir Yayinevi.
Resimli Ilk atlas. With Istituto Geografico De
Agostini. Istanbul, 1965.
56 p. col. maps. 26 cm.

1282 Brazil. Campanha Nacional de Material de Ensino.
Atlas geográfico escolar. 3 ed. Rio de Janeiro,
1965.
61 p. col. maps. 31 cm.

1283 British Sulphur Corp. Ltd.
World fertilizer atlas, 1964. London, [1965].
82 p. 28 cm.

1284 Buchgemeinschaft Donauland.
     Grosser Hausatlas der Buchgemeinschaft Donauland.
     With Hölzel.   Wien, [1965].
     294 p. col. maps. 33 cm.

1285 China. National war college.
     The grand atlas of the world. With the Chinese
     geographical institute. Taipei, Taiwan, 1965—
     in parts. col. maps. 39 cm.

1286 Collins, William, Sons, & Co., Ltd.
     Collins-Longmans Study atlas. 15 ed. London, 1965.
     126 p. col. maps. 30 cm.

1287 Collins, William, Sons & Co., Ltd.
     Collins Westminster atlas. Glasgow, [1965].
     176 p. col. maps. 28 cm.

1288 Columbus Verlag Oestergaard.
     Grosser Columbus-Weltatlas.   8 ed.   Berlin,
     Stuttgart, [1965].
     182 p. col. maps. 41 cm.

1289 Czechoslovakia. Ústřední správa geodesie a kartografie.
     Československý vojenský atlas. Praha, 1965.
     386 p. col. maps. 40 cm.

1290 Czechoslovakia. Ústřední správa geodesie a kartografie.
     Školný zeměpisný atlas světa. Praha, 1965.
     67 p. col. maps. 31 cm.

1291 Damm, N. W. & Søn.
     Kartboka for den ni-årige skolen. Oslo, [1965].
     32 p. col. maps. 26 cm.

1292 Denoyer-Geppert Co.
     Our world, its geography in maps. Chicago, [1965].
     96 p. col. maps. 28 cm.

1293 Dent, J. M.
     Dent's Canadian school atlas. Toronto, 1965.
     115 p. col. maps. 29 cm.

1294 Dreyers forlag.
     Dreyers verdensatlas med Norges atlas. 4 ed. By
     Kr. Gleditsch. With Philip. Oslo, London, 1965.
     197 p. col. maps. 28 cm.

1295 Dutton, E. P. & Co.
    Classical atlas. By J. O. Thomson. New York,
    [1965].
    61 p. col. maps. 20 cm.

1296 Editions Bordas.
    Atlas général Bordas: la France, le monde. By
    Pierre Serryn. Paris, [1965].
    140 p. col. maps. 31 cm.

1297 Editions Stauffacher.
    Nouvel atlas mondial. 4 ed. By E. T. Rimli.
    Zürich, [1965].
    1 vol. col. maps. 28 cm.

1298 Elsevier.
    De wereld in kaarten en cifers. Amsterdam,
    Brussels, 1965.
    1 vol. col. maps. 31 cm.

1299 Encyclopaedia Britannica.
    Encyclopaedia Britannica International atlas.
    Chicago, London, 1965.
    380 p. col. maps. 29 cm.

1300 Fabritius.
    Fabritius atlas. Oslo, [1965].
    44 p. col. maps. 30 cm.

1301 Field Enterprises Educational Corp.
    The world book atlas. With Rand McNally.
    Chicago, 1965.
    392 p. col. maps. 37 cm.

1302 Generalstabens litografiska anstalt.
    En delad värld; världspolitisk atlas. By Tor S.
    Ahman. Stockholm, [1965].
    80 p. col. maps. 22 cm.

1303 Geokarta.
    Geografski atlas. By Ratimir Kalmeta. Beograd,
    1965.
    35 p. col. maps. 34 cm.

1304 Goldmann Verlag.
    Goldmanns Handatlas. 6 ed. München, 1965.
    160 p. col. maps. 41 cm.

1305 Gyldendal.
Atlas 2 for realafdelingen og tilsvarende
undervisningstrin. 2 ed. København, [1965].
61 p. col. maps. 29.5 cm.

1306 Gyldendal.
Kulturgeografisk atlas. 5 ed. By Johannes Humlum.
[Atlas of economic geography.] København, [1965-67].
2 vol. col. maps. 27 cm.

1307 Haack, Hermann.
Atlas der Erdkunde für die allegemeinbildenden
polytechnischen Oberschulen. 7 ed. By Walter
Krämer and Wilfried Görtler. Gotha, 1965.
128 p. col. maps. 30 cm.

1308 Haack, Hermann.
Grosser Weltatlas. By Rudolf Habel. Gotha,
[1965-].
in parts. col. maps. 34 cm.

1309 Haack, Hermann.
Haack Hausatlas. 1 ed. Gotha, Leipzig, 1965.
298 p. col. maps. 35 cm.

1310 Hachette.
Nouvel atlas du monde. By Pierre Gourou. Paris,
[1965].
142 p. col. maps. 33 cm.

1311 Hammond, C. S. & Co., Inc.
Advanced reference atlas. Maplewood, N.J., 1965.
47 p. col. maps. 31 cm.

1312 Hammond, C. S. & Co., Inc.
Atlas internacional. Atlas mundial. Mexico,
D. F., [1965].
224 p. col. maps. 37 cm.

1313 Hammond, C. S. & Co., Inc.
Atlas moderno universal Hammond. Maplewood,
N. J., [1965].
47 p. col. maps. 31 cm.

1314 Hammond, C. S. & Co., Inc.
Comparative world atlas. New desk ed.
Maplewood, N. J., 1965.
48 p. col. maps. 31 cm.

1315 Hammond, C. S. & Co., Inc.
Hammond modern world atlas and gazetteer.
Canadian ed. Maplewood, N. J., 1965.
40 p. col. maps. 31 cm.

1316 Hammond, C. S. & Co., Inc.
Hammond new supreme world atlas. Maplewood,
N. J., 1965.
192 p. col. maps. 32 cm.

1317 Hammond, C. S. & Co., Inc.
Hammond world atlas; an encyclopedic atlas of the
world. Australian and New Zealand reference ed.
Maplewood, N. J., [1965].
1 vol. col. maps. 32 cm.

1318 Hammond, C. S. & Co., Inc.
Hammond's family reference world atlas. Space
age ed. Maplewood, N. J., 1965.
256 p. col. maps. 27 cm.

1319 Hammond, C. S. & Co., Inc.
Modern world atlas. Maplewood, N. J., 1965.
40 p. col. maps. 31 cm.

1320 Hammond, C. S. & Co., Inc.
New international world atlas. Maplewood, N. J.,
1965.
1 vol. col. maps. 32 cm.

1321 Hammond, C. S. & Co., Inc.
Standard world atlas. Maplewood, N. J., 1965.
1 vol. col. maps. 32 cm.

1322 Hammond, C. S. & Co., Inc.
The new Hammond world atlas. New York, 1965.
272 p. col. maps. 18 cm.

1323 Hammond, C. S. & Co., Inc.
World atlas, and encyclopedic atlas of the world.
Grolier International ed. Maplewood, N. J., [1965].
236 p. col. maps. 32 cm.

1324 Hammond, C. S. & Co., Inc.
World atlas, an encyclopedic atlas of the world with
latest and most authentic geographical and statistical
information. Maplewood, N. J., 1965.
1 vol. col. maps. 32 cm.

1325 Hammond, C. S. & Co., Inc.
World atlas. Classical ed. Maplewood, N. J.,
1965.
1 vol. col. maps. 32 cm.

1326 Hölzel, Ed. Verlag.
Österreichischer Mittelschulatlas. 91 ed. Wien,
1965.
165 p. col. maps. 31 cm.

1327 Istituto Geografico De Agostini.
Atlante geografico metodico. Novara, 1965/66.
232 p. col. maps. 33 cm.

1328 Istituto Geografico De Agostini.
Atlante geografico moderno. Novara, 1965/66.
178 p. col. maps. 33 cm.

1329 Istituto Geografico De Agostini.
Büyük atlas. Novara, 1965.
88 p. col. maps. 33 cm.

1330 Istituto Geografico De Agostini.
Calendario atlante de Agostini 1965. Novara, 1965.
784 p. col. maps. 16 cm.

1331 Istituto Geografico De Agostini.
Grande atlante geografico, economico, storico.
Novara, 1965.
1 vol. col. maps. 42 cm.

1332 Istituto Geografico De Agostini.
Novo atlas escolar portuguese. Novara, 1965.
101 p. col. maps. 33 cm.

1333 JRO Verlag.
Der Grosse JRO Weltatlas, Luxusausgabe.
München, [1965].
128 p. col. maps. 44 cm.

1334 JRO Verlag.
Der Kleine JRO Weltatlas. München, [1965].
592 p. col. maps. 21.5 cm.

1335 JRO Verlag.
Grosser JRO Weltatlas, Permanentausgabe.
München, [1965].
301 p. col. maps. 45 cm.

1336 JRO Verlag.
JRO Hausatlas. München, [1965].
366 p. col. maps. 31 cm.

1337 JRO Vcrlag.
JRO Taschen Weltatlas. München, [1965].
150 p. col. maps. 17.5 cm.

1338 JRO Verlag.
JRO Universal Weltatlas. München, [1965].
128 p. col. maps. 30.5 cm.

1339 JRO Verlag.
JRO Weltatlas Handausgabe. München, [1965].
366 p. col. maps. 31 cm.

1340 JRO Verlag.
Volksausgabe des Grossen JRO Weltatlas.
München, [1965].
1 vol. col. maps. 44 cm.

1341 Kaiser.
Weltatlas von heute. Klagenfurt [1965].
109 p. col. maps. 30 cm.

1342 Kanaat Yayinlari.
Büyük atlas. With Hölzel. Istanbul, 1965.
103 p. col. maps. 31 cm.

1343 Kanaat Yayinlari.
Ilk atlas. With Geographisches Institut, Wien.
Istanbul, 1965.
16 p. col. maps. 27 cm.

1344 Kanaat Yayinlari.
Yeni arta atlas. With Geographisches Institut, Wien.
Istanbul, 1965.
40 p. col. maps. 30.5 cm.

1345 Kartográfiai Vállalat.
Földrajzi atlasz as altanos iskolak számará. By
Radó Sándor. Budapest, 1965.
32 p. col. maps. 29 cm.

1346 Kartográfiai Vállalat.
Földrajzi atlasz középiskolak számará. Budapest,
1965.
60 p. col. maps. 28 cm.

1347 Kartográfiai Vállalat.
      Kis Világatlasz.   Budapest, 1965.
      291 p. col. maps. 19 cm.

1348 Larousse.
      Atlas international Larousse politique et économique.
      2 ed. Paris, 1965.
      272 p. col. maps. 49 cm.

1349 List, P.
      Harms Atlas Deutschland und die Welt.   By Willy
      Eggers. München, [1965].
      118 p. col. maps. 33 cm.

1350 Mantnieks, P.
      Fabritius atlas. Bruxelles, Oslo, 1965.
      44 p. col. maps. 30 cm.

1351 Meyer, Kartographisches Institut.
      Meyers grosser physischer Weltatlas. Mannheim,
      1965 –
      in 8 vol. col. maps. 30 cm.

1352 Monteverde, A.
      Atlas esquemático de ciencias geográficas.   7 ed.
      By Cayetano di Leoni and Omar I. Genovese.
      Montevideo, 1965.
      24 p. 33 cm.

1353 Moore, William L.
      Outline maps of the world.   Mt. Vernon, Ill., 1965.
      41 p. 28 cm.

1354 Nelson, Thomas & Sons, Ltd.
      Ghana Junior atlas. By E. A. Boateng.   London,
      Edinburgh, New York, 1965.
      33 p. col. maps. 29 cm.

1355 Nelson, Thomas & Sons, Ltd.
      Nelson's Canadian school atlas.   4 ed.   By J.
      Wreford Watson. Don Mills, Ont., 1965.
      92 p. col. maps. 29 cm.

1356 Oliver & Boyd.
      Oliver and Boyd general atlas; physical and political
      geography.   3 ed.   With John Bartholomew & Son,
      Ltd. Edinburgh, 1965.
      112 p. col. maps. 29 cm.

1357 Oliver & Boyd.
    The new comparative atlas. 48 ed. With John
    Bartholomew & Son, Ltd. Edinburgh, [1965].
    112 p. col. maps. 29 cm.

1358 Otava.
    Otavan koulukartasto. Helsinki, 1965.
    44 p. col. maps. 28 cm.

1359 Oxford University Press.
    Oxford economic atlas of the world. 3 ed. London,
    New York, 1965.
    286 p. col. maps. 27 cm.

1360 Oxford University Press.
    The shorter Oxford economic atlas of the world.
    3 ed. London, New York, 1965.
    128 p. col. maps. 26 cm.

1361 Philip, George & Son, Ltd.
    Philip's commercial course atlas. By Harold
    Fullard. London, [1965].
    117 p. col. maps. 29 cm.

1362 Philip, George & Son, Ltd.
    Philip's modern school atlas. By Harold Fullard.
    Liverpool, 1965.
    1 vol. col. maps. 29 cm.

1363 Philip, George & Son, Ltd.
    Philip's record atlas. 26 ed. By Harold Fullard.
    London, [1965].
    257 p. col. maps. 29 cm.

1364 Philip, George & Son, Ltd.
    Venture atlas. By Harold Fullard. London, [1965].
    49 p. col. maps. 28 cm.

1365 Poland. Państwowe przedsiębiorstwo wydawnictw
    kartograficznych.
    Atlas geograficzny. Warszawa, 1965.
    120 p. col. maps. 31 cm.

1366 Poland. Państwowe przedsiębiorstwo wydawnictw
    kartograficznych.
    Atlas geograficzny dla klasy IV. Warszawa, 1965.
    1 vol. col. maps. 26 cm.

1367 Poland. Państwowe przedsiębiorstwo wydawnictw
     kartograficznych.
     Atlas geograficzny. V-VIII kl. Warszawa,1965.
     1 vol. col. maps. 30.5 cm.

1368 Politikens Forlag.
     Politikens verdensatlas. With George Philip & Son,
     Ltd. Kφbenhavn, 1965.
     148 p. col. maps. 28 cm.

1369 Porto Editora.
     Atlas editora. With Aguilar. Porto, 1965.
     129 p. col. maps. 32 cm.

1370 Rand McNally & Co.
     Classroom atlas. 5 ed. Chicago, 1965.
     84 p. col. maps. 25.5 cm.

1371 Rand McNally & Co.
     Collegiate world atlas. Chicago, 1965.
     1 vol. col. maps. 28 cm.

1372 Rand McNally & Co.
     Rand McNally new cosmopolitan world atlas.
     Chicago, 1965.
     1 vol. col. maps. 35 cm.

1373 Rand McNally & Co.
     Rand McNally readers world atlas. Chicago, [1965].
     300 p. col. maps. 28 cm.

1374 Rand McNally & Co.
     Rand McNally regional atlas. By Edward B.
     Espenshade, Jr. Chicago, 1965.
     64 p. col. maps. 29 cm.

1375 Rand McNally & Co.
     Rand McNally world atlas. Chicago, 1965.
     32 p. col. maps. 33 cm.

1376 Rand McNally & Co.
     Rand McNally world atlas. Family ed. Chicago,
     [1965].
     325 p. col. maps. 32 cm.

1377 Rand McNally & Co.
     Rand McNally world atlas. Imperial ed. Chicago,
     [1965].

325 p.   col.   maps.   32 cm.

1378 Reader's Digest Association, Ltd.
Det Bestes store verdensatlas.   With Beste.   Oslo,
[1965].
216 p.   col.   maps.   40 cm.

1379 Reader's Digest Association, Ltd.
[Great world atlas].   in Japanese.   Tokyo, 1965.
With Reader's Digest of Japan, Ltd.
216 p.   col.   maps.   40 cm.

1380 Robinson, H. E. C. Pty., Ltd.
Robinson's primary world atlas.   14 ed.   Sydney,
[1965].
93 p.   col.   maps.   23 cm.

1381 Söderström, Werner.
Oppikoulun kartasto.   6 ed.   Helsinki, 1965.
67 p.   col.   maps.   27 cm.

1382 Standard Reference Works Pub. Co.
Hammond family world atlas.   With Hammond.
Brooklyn, [1965].
2 vol.   col.   maps.   32 cm.

1383 Thieme, W. J.
Atlas van Europa en de werelddelen.   55 ed.   By
G. Prop. Zutphen, 1965.
48 p.   col.   maps.   26 cm.

1384 U.S.S.R. Glavnoe upravlenie geodezii i kartografii.
Atlas zarubezhnykh stran dlya srednei shkoly.
Kurs ekonomicheskoi geografii.   Moskva, [1965].
40 p.   col.   maps.   28 cm.

1385 U.S.S.R. Galvnoe upravlenie geodezii i kartografii.
Geograficheskii atlas dlya 6go- 7go klassov.
Moskva, 1965.
48 p.   col.   maps.   28.5 cm.

1386 U.S.S.R. Glavnoe upravlenie geodezii i kartografii.
Malyi atlas mira.   Moskva, 1965.
1 vol.   col.   maps.   20 cm.

1387 Velhagen & Klasing.
Unsere Welt.   Atlas für die Schule.   Berlin, [1965].
104 p.   col.   maps.   28 cm.

1388 Volk und Wissen Verlag.
     Atlas der Erdkunde für die allgemeinbildenden
     polytechnischen Oberschulen. Berlin, [1965].
     129 p. col. maps. 31 cm.

1389 Volk und Wissen Verlag.
     Atlas für die 5. und 6. Klasse.   With Haack.
     Berlin, 1965.
     26 p. col. maps. 31 cm.

1390 Vuk Karadžić.
     Svet u džepu; geografski atlas sveta.   Beograd,
     [1965].
     70 p. col. maps. 17 cm.

1391 Weilin & Co.
     Maailmanpolitikan kartasto.   Världspolitisk atlas.
     Helsinki, 1965.
     77 p. 28 cm.

1392 Westermann, Georg.
     Diercke Weltatlas.   Braunschweig, 1965.
     168 p. col. maps. 36 cm.

1393 Wolters, J. B.
     De Grote Wereldatlas.   Groningen, [1965].
     104 p. col. maps. 32 cm.

1394 Wolters, J. B.
     De landen der wereld.   By J. A. J. Nonnekens and
     C. Hoogvorst.   Groningen, 1965.
     48 p. col. maps. 31 cm.

1395 Wolters, J. B.
     Kleine schoolatlas der gehele aarde.   By P. R.
     Bos and C. L. van Balen.   Groningen, 1965.
     64 p. col. maps. 31 cm.

                              1966

1396 Aguilar, S. A. de Ediciones.
     Atlas bachillerato universal y de España.   9 ed.
     By A. L. Gómez.   Madrid, 1966.
     132 p. col. maps. 35 cm.

1397 Aguilar, S. A. de Ediciones.
     Atlas bachillerato universal y de España.   10 ed.
     By A. L. Gómez.   Madrid, 1966.
     132 p. col. maps. 35 cm.

1398 Aguilar, S. A. de Ediciones.
    Atlas bachillerato, universal y de España.   11 ed.
    By A. L. Gómez.   Madrid, 1966.
    132 p.   col. maps.   35 cm.

1399 Aguilar, S. A. de Ediciones.
    Atlas Universal Aguilar.   4 ed.   Madrid, 1966.
    1 vol.   col. maps.   42 cm.

1400 American Map Co.
    Physical world atlas.   With Bartholomew.   Edin-
    burgh, New York, 1966.
    168 p.   col. maps.   37.5 cm.

1401 Bartholomew, John & Son, Ltd.
    The Pocket world atlas.   Edinburgh, 1966.
    164 p.   col. maps.   15 cm.

1402 Bertelsmann, C.
    Der Grosse Bertelsmann Weltatlas.   Gütersloh,
    [1966].
    400 p.   col. maps.   33 cm.

1403 Bertelsmann, C.
    Der Grosse Universal Atlas.   Die Welt in Karten.
    Gütersloh, 1966.
    480 p.   col. maps.   32 cm.

1404 Bertelsmann, C.
    Neuer Atlas der Welt.   By W. Bormann.
    Gütersloh, 1966.
    224 p.   col. maps.   33 cm.

1405 Cappelens, J. W., Forlag, A. S.
    Cappelens atlas større utg. for hjem og skole.
    4 ed.   By Ellef Ellefsen and K. B. Sollesnes.
    Oslo, 1966.
    64 p.   col. maps.   34 cm.

1406 Cappelens, J. W., Forlag, A. S.
    Cappelens verdensatlas for skolen.   Oslo, [1966].
    79 p.   col. maps.   31 cm.

1407 Collins, William, Sons & Co., Ltd.
    Collins-Longmans atlas two.   Glasgow, [1966].
    64 p.   col. maps.   26 cm.

1408 Columbus Verlag Oestergaard.
     Columbus Hausatlas in Wort und Bild.   8 ed.
     Berlin, Stuttgart, [1966].
     160 p.   col.   maps.   41 cm.

1409 Czechoslovakia.   Ústřední správa geodezie a kartografie.
     Československý vojenský atlas.   Seznam názvů.
     (Index)   Praha, 1966.
     256 p.   col.   maps.   40 cm.

1410 Czechoslovakia.   Ústřední správa geodezie a kartografie.
     Kapesní atlas světa.   5 ed.   Praha, 1966.
     120 p.   col.   maps.   17 cm.

1411 Denoyer-Geppert Co.
     Visual relief atlas of world continents.   By
     Clarence B. Odell.   Chicago, 1966.
     32 p.   col.   maps.   28 cm.

1412 De Sikkel.
     Schoolatlas.   De Wereld.   2 ed.   By F. Lauwers.
     Antwerpen, 1966.
     32 p.   col.   maps.   31 cm.

1413 Edições Melhoramentos.
     Atlas geográfico Melhoramentos.   24 ed.   São
     Paulo, 1966.
     89 p.   col.   maps.   35 cm.

1414 Editions Bordas.
     Atlas général Bordas, historique et géographique.
     Paris, [1966].
     208 p.   col.   maps.   33 cm.

1415 Editions Bordas.
     Petit atlas politique et économique de la France et
     du monde.   Paris, [1966].
     32 p.   col.   maps.   27 cm.

1416 Editions Sequoia.
     Grand atlas international Sequoia.   Paris, [1966].
     354 p.   col.   maps.   32 cm.

1417 Elsevier.
     Elsevier atlas van de gehele wereld.   16 ed.
     Amsterdam, Bruxelles, 1966.
     240 p.   col.   maps.   18 cm.

1418 Encyclopaedia Britannica.
Encyclopaedia Britannica world atlas. Chicago,
[1966].
418 p. col. maps. 38 cm.

1419 Fawcett Publications.
Crest colorprint world atlas. With American Map
Co. By Gwen M. Schultz. Greenwich, Conn.,
[1966].
255 p. col. maps. 38 cm.

1420 Field Enterprises Educational Corp.
The world book atlas. With Rand McNally & Co.
Chicago, [1966].
392 p. col. maps. 37 cm.

1421 Generalstabens litografiska anstalt.
En delad värld. Världspolitisk atlas. 3 ed. By
Tor S. Ahman. Stockholm, [1966].
96 p. col. maps. 22 cm.

1422 Geographical Projects, Ltd.
Hamlyn's new relief world atlas. London, 1966.
205 p. col. maps. 30 cm.

1423 Ginn & Co.
The Ginn world atlas. By Richard Edes Harrison.
Boston, [1966].
62 p. col. maps. 26 cm.

1424 Greystone Press.
The world and its people: illustrated world atlas.
With Hammond, Inc. New York, [1966].
310 p. col. maps. 32 cm.

1425 Haack, Hermann.
Haack Grosser Weltatlas. Gotha, 1966—
in parts. col. maps. 34 cm.

1426 Haack, Hermann.
Hausatlas. 1 ed. Gotha, 1965.
298 p. col. maps. 35 cm.

1427 Hachette.
Nouvel atlas du monde. By Pierre Gourou.
Paris, 1966.
114 p. col. maps. 33 cm.

1428 Hammond, Inc.
    Ambassador world atlas. New perspective ed.
    Maplewood, N. J., [1966].
    364 p. col. maps. 39 cm.

1429 Hammond, Inc.
    Atlas internacional. (Atlas mundial). México, [1966].
    224 p. col. maps. 37 cm.

1430 Hammond, Inc.
    Atlas mundial. Maplewood, N. J., [1966].
    16 p. col. maps. 32 cm.

1431 Hammond, Inc.
    Hammond citation world atlas. New perspective ed.
    Maplewood, N. J., [1966].
    364 p. col. maps. 32 cm.

1432 Hammond, Inc.
    Hammond international world atlas. New perspective
    ed. Maplewood, N. J., [1966].
    204 p. col. maps. 32 cm.

1433 Hammond, Inc.
    Hammond medallion world atlas. New perspective
    ed. Maplewood, N. J., [1966].
    464 p. col. maps. 39 cm.

1434 Hammond, Inc.
    Hammond's clear-relief world atlas. Maplewood,
    N. J., 1966.
    26 p. col. maps. 73 cm.

1435 Hammond, Inc.
    My first world atlas. Maplewood, N. J., 1966.
    48 p. col. maps. 31 cm.

1436 Hammond, Inc.
    Panoramic world atlas. With Geographical Projects,
    Ltd. Maplewood, N. J., 1966.
    208 p. col. maps. 32 cm.

1437 Hammond, Inc.
    World atlas and gazetteer. Maplewood, N. J., 1966.
    48 p. col. maps. 31 cm.

1438 Herder Verlag.
    Der Neue Herder-Handatlas. By C. Troll.

Freiburg, Basel, Wien, 1966.
200 p. col. maps. 59 cm.

1439 Hölzel, Ed. Verlag.
Österreichischer Mittelschulatlas. 92 ed. Wien,
1966.
165 p. col. maps. 31 cm.

1440 International Bank for Reconstruction and Development.
World Bank atlas of per capita product and population. Washington, D. C., 1966.
14 p. col. maps. 28 cm.

1441 Istituto Geografico De Agostini.
Grande atlante geografico economico. Novara, 1966.
351 p. col. maps. 25 cm.

1442 Istituto Geografico De Agostini.
Modern Orta atlas. Istanbul, [1966].
43 p. col. maps. 34 cm.

1443 JRO Verlag.
Der Grosse JRO Weltatlas. 25 ed. München, 1966.
128 p. col. maps. 31 cm.

1444 JRO Verlag.
Grosser JRO Weltatlas. 8 ed. München, 1966.
146 p. col. maps. 45 cm.

1445 Jugoslavenski leksikografski zavod.
Atlas svijeta. Zagreb, 1966.
274 p. col. maps. 30 cm.

1446 Jugoslavenski leksikografski zavod.
Atlas svijeta. 3 ed. Zagreb, 1966.
548 p. col. maps. 30 cm.

1447 Kartográfiai Vállalat.
Földrajzi atlasz a középiskolák számára.
Budapest, [1966].
62 p. col. maps. 28 cm.

1448 Kartográfiai Vállalat.
Földrajzi atlasz as általános iskolák számára.
Budapest, 1966.
32 p. col. maps. 28 cm.

1449 Kartográfiai Vállalat.

Képes politikai és gazdasági, világatlasz.   By
Radó Sándor.   Budapest, 1966.
1 vol.   col. maps.   34 cm.

1450 Kümmerly & Frey.
Geteilte Welt; weltpolitischer atlas.   2 ed.   By Tor
S. Ahman.   Transl. from Swedish.   Bern, 1966.
112 p.   col. maps.   21 cm.

1451 Larousse.
Atlas classique Larousse.   Paris, [1966].
168 p.   col. maps.   30.5 cm.

1452 Larousse.
Atlas international Larousse.   Paris, 1966.
272 p.   col. maps.   50 cm.

1453 Larousse.
Atlas international Larousse, politico y economico.
Paris, 1966.
272 p.   col. maps.   50 cm.

1454 List, P.
Harms Weltatlas für die bayerische Schule.
München, [1966].
55 p.   col. maps.   31 cm.

1455 Lloyd's Corp. of.
Lloyd's maritime atlas.   6 ed.   London, 1966.
1 vol.   col. maps.   25 cm.

1456 Meyer, Kartographisches Institut.
Meyers Neuer Geographischer Handatlas.   Mannheim, 1966.
450 p.   col. maps.   37 cm.

1457 National Geographic Society.
National Geographic atlas of the world.   2 ed.
Washington, D. C., 1966.
343 p.   col. maps.   49 cm.

1458 Nelson, Thomas & Sons, Ltd.
Atlas universal y de Mexico.   London, 1966.
33 p.   col. maps.   28 cm.

1459 Nelson, Thomas & Sons, Ltd.
Ghana junior atlas.   By E. A. Boateng.   London,
1966.

33 p. col. maps. 29 cm.

1460 News Map of the Week, Inc.
Pivot-page atlas of the world. Skokie, Ill., 1966.
52 p. col. maps. 32 cm.

1461 Noordhoff, P.
Atlas der gehele aarde. 38 ed. By P. R. Bos and
K. Zeeman. Groningen, 1966.
64 p. col. maps. 31 cm.

1462 Odyssey Books.
Odyssey world atlas. With General Drafting Co.,
Inc. New York, 1966.
317 p. col. maps. 42 cm.

1463 Oxford University Press.
Concise Oxford atlas. London, 1966.
288 p. col. maps. 26 cm.

1464 Oxford University Press.
The Oxford atlas. London, 1966.
93 p. col. maps. 40 cm.

1465 Oxford University Press.
The Oxford atlas. London, 1966.
202 p. col. maps. 40 cm.

1466 Pergamon Press, Ltd.
Pergamon General world atlas. Oxford, New York,
1966.
132 p. col. maps. 27 cm.

1467 Philip, George & Son, Ltd.
Philip's modern school atlas. 64 ed. By Harold
Fullard. London, 1966.
132 p. col. maps. 29 cm.

1468 Philip, George & Son, Ltd.
Philip's new school atlas. 54 ed. London, 1966.
72 p. col. maps. 29 cm.

1469 Philip, George & Son, Ltd.
Philip's senior atlas for Canada. London, [1966].
80 p. col. maps. 29 cm.

1470 Poland. Państwowe przedsiębiorstwo wydawnictw
kartograficznych.
Atlas geograficzny. Warszawa, 1966.

60 p.   col.   maps.   31 cm.

1471 Poland.   Państwowe wydawnictwo naukowe.
Atlas swiata.   Warszawa, 1966.
364 p.   col.   maps.   42 cm.

1472 Rand McNally & Co.
Goode's world atlas.   12 ed.   By Edward B.
Espenshade, Jr.   Chicago, 1966.
310 p.   col.   maps.   29 cm.

1473 Rand McNally & Co.
Rand McNally atlas of nations.   Chicago, 1966.
32 p.   col.   maps.   35 cm.

1474 Rand McNally & Co.
Rand McNally collegiate world atlas.   Chicago,
[1966].
386 p.   col.   maps.   21 cm.

1475 Rand McNally & Co.
Rand McNally continental world atlas.   Chicago,
[1966].
314 p.   col.   maps.   28 cm.

1476 Rand McNally & Co.
Rand McNally new cosmopolitan world atlas.
Chicago, 1966.
386 p.   col.   maps.   37 cm.

1477 Reader's Digest Association, Ltd.
Det Bästas stora världsatlas.   Stockholm, [1966].
216 p.   col.   maps.   40 cm.

1478 Sadlier, W. H.
Atlas of the world.   With Hammond.   New York,
1966.
29 p.   col.   maps. 32 cm.

1479 Sélection du Reader's Digest, S.A.R.L.
Grand atlas mondial.   Paris, [1966].
1 vol.   col.   maps.   41 cm.

1480 Teikoku-Shoin Co., Ltd.
[World].   New detailed atlas for high school
students.   In Japanese.   Tokyo, 1966.
150 p.   col.   maps.   31 cm.

1481 Thieme, W. J.
      Atlas van Europa en de werelddelen. 56 ed. By
      G. Prop. Zutphen, 1966.
      48 p. col. maps. 26 cm.

1482 Time, Inc.
      Atlas of the world. By Life and Rand McNally &
      Co. New York, [1966].
      160 p. col. maps. 28 cm.

1483 Učila.
      Veliki školski atlas. 15 ed. Zagreb, 1966.
      59 p. col. maps. 34 cm.

1484 U.S.S.R. Glavnoe upravlenie geodezii i kartografii.
      Atlas mira. Moskva, 1966.
      64 p. col. maps. 18 cm.

1485 U.S.S.R. Glavnoe upravlenie geodezii i kartografii.
      Atlas mira. Moskva, 1966.
      250 p. col. maps. 50 cm.

1486 U.S.S.R. Glavnoe upravlenie geodezii i kartografii.
      Atlas zarubezhnykh stran dlya srednei shkoly.
      Kurs ekonomicheskoi geografii. Moskva, [1966].
      40 p. col. maps. 28 cm.

1487 U.S.S.R. Glavnoe upravlenie geodezii i kartografii.
      Maly atlas mira. Moskva, 1966.
      302 p. col. maps. 20 cm.

1488 Velhagen & Klasing.
      Unsere Welt. Atlas für die Schule. 4 ed.
      Berlin, 1966.
      109 p. col. maps. 28 cm.

1489 Volk und Wissen Verlag.
      Unser atlas. Atlas für die achtstufige allgemein-
      bildende polytechnische Hilfschule. Berlin, [1966].
      38 p. col. maps. 31 cm.

1490 Welch Scientific Co.
      Pivot-page atlas of the world. Chicago, 1966.
      52 p. col. maps. 32 cm.

1491 Wesmael-Charlier.
      Atlas classique. By J. Tilmont and M. DeRoeck.

Namur, 1966.
54 p. col. maps. 36 cm.

1492 Wesmael-Charlier.
Atlas elementaire. By J. Tilmont and M. DeRoeck.
Namur, 1966.
34 p. col. maps. 32 cm.

1493 Wesmael-Charlier.
Vereenvoudigde atlas. By M. DeRoeck and J.
Tilmont. Namur, 1966.
34 p. col. maps. 32 cm.

1494 Westermann, Georg.
Erdöl Weltatlas. By F. Mayer. Braunschweig,
1966.
152 p. col. maps. 31 cm.

1495 Westermann, Georg.
Westermann-Atlas. Heimat und Welt. Braunschweig, Berlin, Hamburg, 1966.
1 vol. col. maps. 33 cm.

1496 Wolters, J. B.
Atlas der gehele aarde. 44 ed. By F. J.
Ormeling. Groningen, 1967.
202 p. col. maps. 37 cm.

1497 Wolters, J. B.
Kleine schoolatlas der gehele aarde. Groningen,
1966.
112 p. col. maps. 31 cm.

1967

1498 Aguilar, S. A. de Ediciones.
Atlas bachillerato universal y de España. 12 ed.
By A. L. Gómez. Madrid, 1967.
117 p. col. maps. 35 cm.

1499 Aguilar, S. A. de Ediciones.
Atlas bachillerato universal y de España. 13 ed.
By A. L. Gómez. Madrid, 1967.
117 p. col. maps. 35 cm.

1500 Aguilar, S. A. de Ediciones.
Atlas bachillerato universal y de España. 14 ed.
By A. L. Gómez. Madrid, 1967.
117 p. col. maps. 35 cm.

1501 American Map Co. , Inc.
    Colorprint scholastic world atlas.   New York, [1967].
    47 p.   col. maps.   31 cm.

1502 Atheneum.
    Atlas geografico mundial Atheneum.   Barcelona,
    [1967].
    1 vol.   col. maps.   32 cm.

1503 Bartholomew, John & Son, Ltd.
    The Edinburgh world atlas.   6 ed.   Edinburgh, 1967.
    159 p.   col. maps.   38 cm.

1504 Bertelsmann, C.
    Atlas der Oberflächeformen.   Gütersloh, [1967].
    120 p.   col. maps.   60 cm.

1505 Bertelsmann, C.
    Bertelsmann atlas international.   Gütersloh, 1967.
    560 p.   col. maps.   41 cm.

1506 Bertelsmann, C.
    Das Antlitz unserer Erde; der neuartige Universal-
    Atlas.   Gütersloh, 1967.
    640 p.   col. maps.   33 cm.

1507 Bertelsmann, C.
    Der Grosse Universatlas.   Die Welt in Karte, Wort
    und Bild.   Gütersloh, 1967.
    480 p.   col. maps.   32 cm.

1508 Brug Uitgeversbedrijf, N.V.
    Atlas van Nederland en de wereld voor het
    voortgezet onderwijs.   Amsterdam, 1967.
    162 p.   col. maps.   32 cm.

1509 Buchclub Ex Libris.
    Ex Libris Weltatlas.   Das grosse Kartenwerk
    unserer Zeit.   Zürich, [1967].
    250 p.   col. maps.   40 cm.

1510 Collet.
    Collet's world atlas.   London, 1967.
    250 p.   col. maps.   32 cm.

1511 Collins, William, Sons & Co. , Ltd.
    A new secondary school atlas for Hong Kong.   2 ed.
    Glasgow, 1967.

87 p.   col. maps.   29 cm.

1512 Collins, William, Sons & Co., Ltd.
     Collins-Longmans visible regions atlas.   16 ed.
     By K. H. Huggins.   London, [1967].
     80 p.   col. maps.   29 cm.

1513 Deutscher Bücherbund.
     Der neue Weltatlas.   Das grosse Kartenwerk
     unseres Zeit.   Stuttgart, Hamburg, [1967].
     250 p.   col. maps.   32 cm.

1514 Edições Melhoramentos.
     Pequeño atlas escolar.   13 ed.   São Paulo, 1967.
     32 p.   col. maps.   23 cm.

1515 Éditions du renouveau pédagogique.
     Atlas du monde contemporain.   By Pierre Gourou.
     Montréal, [1967].
     88 p.   col. maps.   36 cm.

1516 Editôra Ypiranga.
     Grande atlas mundial.   With Reader's Digest
     Association.   Rio de Janeiro, [1967].
     195 p.   col. maps.   40 cm.

1517 Editorial F. T. D.
     Atlas universal y del Perú.   Lima, [1967].
     88 p.   col. maps.   32 cm.

1518 Encyclopaedia Britannica.
     Britannica world atlas international.   Chicago, [1967].
     367 p.   col. maps.   41 cm.

1519 Field Enterprises Educational Corp.
     The world book atlas.   Chicago, 1967.
     412 p.   col. maps.   37 cm.

1520 Freytag-Berndt & Artaria.
     Neuer Schulatlas für Hauptschulen und Unterstufen
     der Höheren Schulen.   Wien, 1967.
     126 p.   col. maps.   32 cm.

1521 Generalstabens litografiska anstalt.
     En delt verden, utenrikspolitisk atlas.   By Tor S.
     Ahman.   Oslo, 1967.
     96 p.   col. maps.   22 cm.

1522 Generalstabens litografiska anstalt.
Skolans Världsatlas. Stockholm, 1967.
95 p. col. maps. 31 cm.

1523 Geographical Projects, Ltd.
Hamlyn's new relief world atlas. London, 1967.
295 p. col. maps. 30 cm.

1524 Golden Press.
The Odyssey world atlas. With General Drafting
Co., Inc. New York, [1967].
317 p. col. maps. 35 cm.

1525 Grosset & Dunlop.
The new Grosset world atlas and gazetteer. New
York, [1967].
105 p. col. maps. 17 cm.

1526 Gyldendal.
Kulturgeografisk atlas. 6 ed. By Johannes Humlum.
København, 1967.
2 vol. col. maps. 27 cm.

1527 Haack, Hermann.
Kleiner Weltatlas. Gotha, Leipzig, 1967.
204 p. col. maps. 17 cm.

1528 Haack, Hermann.
Taschenatlas. Die Erde. Gotha, Leipzig, 1967.
380 p. col. maps. 17 cm.

1529 Hallwag, A. G.
Weltatlas. Bern, Stuttgart, 1967.
49 p. col. maps. 32 cm.

1530 Hammond, Inc.
Atlas moderno universal Hammond. Maplewood,
N. J., [1967].
1 vol. col. maps. 31 cm.

1531 Hammond, Inc.
Hammond Academic world atlas. Maplewood,
N. J., [1967].
351 p. col. maps. 27.5 cm.

1532 Hammond, Inc.
Hammond Comparative world atlas. Maplewood,

N. J., 1967.
48 p. col. maps. 31 cm.

1533 Hammond, Inc.
Hammond Headline world atlas. Maplewood, N. J.,
1967.
36 p. col. maps. 31 cm.

1534 Hammond, Inc.
Hammond illustrated atlas for young America.
Maplewood, N. J., 1967.
1 vol. col. maps. 26 cm.

1535 Hammond, Inc.
Hammond space age world atlas. Maplewood, N. J.,
[1967].
32 p. col. maps. 31 cm.

1536 Hammond, Inc.
Hammond world atlas for students. Maplewood,
N. J., [1967].
52 p. col. maps. 31 cm.

1537 Hammond, Inc.
Pacesetter world atlas. Maplewood, N. J., 1967.
38 p. col. maps. 31 cm.

1538 Hammond, Inc.
Profile of the nations. Atlas. Maplewood, N. J.,
[1967].
64 p. col. maps. 32 cm.

1539 Hammond, Inc.
Standard world atlas. Maplewood, N. J., 1967.
332 p. col. maps. 31 cm.

1540 Hammond, Inc.
World atlas, classic ed. Maplewood, N. J., 1967.
400 p. col. maps. 31 cm.

1541 Hölzel, Ed. Verlag.
Österreichischer Hauptschulatlas. Wien, 1967.
76 p. col. maps. 32 cm.

1542 Hölzel, Ed. Verlag.
Österreichischer Mittelschulatlas. 93 ed. Wien,
1967.
167 p. col. maps. 31 cm.

1543 Houghton, Mifflin Co.
     The Times atlas of the world. Comprehensive ed.
     With Bartholomew and Times of London. Boston,
     1967.
     558 p. col. maps. 46 cm.

1544 International Bank for Reconstruction and Development.
     World bank atlas; per capita product; population;
     main urban centers. Washington, D. C., 1967.
     7 p. col. maps. 28 cm.

1545 Istituto Geografico De Agostini.
     Geoatlante. By Umberto Bonapace. Novara, 1967.
     134 p. col. maps. 30 cm.

1546 Johnston, W. & A. K. and G. W. Bacon, Ltd.
     World study atlas. Edinburgh, 1967.
     64 p. col. maps. 27.5 cm.

1547 JRO Verlag.
     JRO Hausatlas. 2 ed. München, 1967.
     365 p. col. maps. 31 cm.

1548 JRO Verlag.
     JRO Weltatlas. 17 ed. München, 1967.
     349 p. col. maps. 31 cm.

1549 JRO Verlag.
     Neuer JRO Weltatlas. München, 1967.
     215 p. col. maps. 31 cm.

1550 Kartográfiai Vállalat.
     Kis világatlasz. Budapest, [1967].
     48 p. col. maps. 18.5 cm.

1551 Keysersche Verlagsbuchhandlung, G. M. B. H.
     Keysers Handatlas für Geographie und Geschichte.
     With Hölzel. München, [1967].
     96 p. col. maps. 31 cm.

1552 List, P.
     Harms Weltatlas. München, [1967].
     55 p. col. maps. 33 cm.

1553 Literarisches Institut.
     Herders Grosser Weltatlas. Basel, 1967.
     250 p. col. maps. 40 cm.

1554 Livraria Sá da Costa.
      Novo atlas escolar português.   Lisboa, 1967/68.
      1 vol. col. maps. 34 cm.

1555 Meulenhoff, J. M.
      Atlas van Nederland en de wereld.   3 ed.   With
      Hölzel. Amsterdam, 1967.
      162 p. col. maps. 32 cm.

1556 Meyer, Kartographisches Institut.
      Rororo Weltatlas.   Hamburg, 1967.
      152 p. col. maps. 32 cm.

1557 Nelson, Thomas & Sons, Ltd.
      Ghana junior atlas.   By E. A. Boateng.   London,
      1967.
      33 p. col. maps. 29 cm.

1558 Newnes, George, Ltd.
      Newnes international world atlas.   New perspective
      ed. With Hammond. London, [1967].
      197 p. col. maps. 31.5 cm.

1559 Oxford University Press.
      Oxford school atlas.   London, 1967.
      142 p. col. maps. 26 cm.

1560 Oxford University Press.
      The Oxford atlas.   London, 1967.
      215 p. col. maps. 40 cm.

1561 Peuser, Ediciones Geográficas.
      Nuevo atlas geográfico metódico universal.   3 ed.
      By José Anesi. Buenos Aires, 1967.
      96 p. col. maps. 38 cm.

1562 Philip, George & Son, Ltd.
      Contemporary world atlas.   By Harold Fullard.
      London, [1967].
      48 p. col. maps. 28.5 cm.

1563 Philip, George & Son, Ltd.
      Philip's library atlas.   London, 1967.
      319 p. col. maps. 29 cm.

1564 Philip, George & Son, Ltd.
      Philip's new school atlas.   55 ed.   By Harold

Fullard.   London,   [1967].
64 p.   col.   maps.   28 cm.

1565 Philip, George & Son, Ltd.
Philip's practical atlas.   London, 1967.
1 vol.   col.   maps.   29 cm.

1566 Philip, George & Son, Ltd.
Philip's record atlas.   27 ed.   By Harold Fullard.
London, [1967].
129 p.   col.   maps.   29 cm.

1567 Philip, George & Son, Ltd.
Secondary school atlas.   London, [1967].
1 vol.   col.   maps.   28 cm.

1568 Philip, George & Son, Ltd.
University atlas.   12 ed.   London, 1967.
288 p.   col.   maps.   29 cm.

1569 Poland. Państwowe przedsiębiorstwo wydawnictw
kartograficznych.
Atlas geograficzny.   3 ed.   By Henryk Górski.
Warszawa, [1967].
149 p.   col.   maps.   33 cm.

1570 Poland. Państwowe przedsiębiorstwo wydawnictw
kartograficznych.
Atlas geograficzny.   By Jan Rzedowski.   Warszawa,
1967.
38 p.   col.   maps.   31 cm.

1571 Porto Editora.
Atlas editora.   With Aguilar.   Porto, [1967].
135 p.   col.   maps.   32 cm.

1572 Rand McNally & Co.
Atlas mundial.   Chicago, [1967].
239 p.   col.   maps.   37 cm.

1573 Rand McNally & Co.
Rand McNally current events world atlas.   Chicago,
1967.
332 p.   col.   maps.   32 cm.

1574 Rand McNally & Co.
Rand McNally new cosmopolitan world atlas.

Chicago, [1967].
367 p. col. maps. 37 cm.

1575 Rand McNally & Co.
Rand McNally pictorial world atlas.   Chicago, 1967.
160 p. col. maps. 31 cm.

1576 Rand McNally & Co.
Rand McNally premier world atlas.   Chicago, 1967.
280 p. col. maps. 31 cm.

1577 Rand McNally & Co.
Rand McNally world atlas.   Chicago, 1967.
32 p. col. maps. 33 cm.

1578 Reader's Digest Association, Ltd.
Il grande atlante di selezione.   2 ed.   Milano, [1967].
211 p. col. maps. 40 cm.

1579 Reader's Digest Association, Ltd.
Reader's atlas de nuestro tiempo.   Madrid, 1967/68.
211 p. col. maps. 40 cm.

1580 Romania.   Editura di Stat Didactică si Pedagogică.
Atlas geografic scolar.   Bucuresti, 1967.
34 p. col. maps. 33 cm.

1581 Romania.   Editura Stiintifica.
Mic atlas geografic.   By A. Barsan.   Bucuresti,
1967.
301 p. col. maps. 17 cm.

1582 Schaeffer, Juan E.
Atlas geográfico mundial.   Rio de Janeiro, 1967.
60 p. col. maps. 28 cm.

1583 Thieme, W. J.
Atlas van Europa en de werelddelen.   57 ed.   By
G. Prop.   Zutphen, 1967.
1 vol. col. maps. 26 cm.

1584 Times of London.
The Times atlas of the world.   With Bartholomew.
London, 1967.
558 p. col. maps. 46 cm.

1585 U.S.S.R. Glavnoe upravlenie geodezii i kartografii.
Atlas dlya uchitelei strednei shkoly.   3 ed.

Moskva, 1967.
164 p.   col. maps.   38 cm.

1586 U.S.S.R. Glavnoe upravlenie geodezii i kartografii.
Atlas mira. Moskva, 1967.
64 p.   col. maps.   24 cm.

1587 U.S.S.R. Glavnoe upravlenie geodezii i kartografii.
Atlas mira. 2 ed.   Moskva, 1967.
250 p.   col. maps.   50 cm.

1588 U.S.S.R. Glavnoe upravlenie geodezii i kartografii.
Atlas naselenia mira. Moskva, 1967.
1 vol.   col. maps.   37 cm.

1589 U.S.S.R. Glavnoe upravlenie geodezii i kartografii.
Geograficheskii atlas dlya uchitelei strednei shkoly.
3 ed.   Moskva, 1967.
198 p.   col. maps.   38 cm.

1590 U.S.S.R. Glavnoe upravlenie geodezii i kartografii.
Malyi atlas mira. Moskva, 1967.
159 p.   col. maps.   19 cm.

1591 U.S.S.R. Glavnoe upravlenie geodezii i kartografii.
The world atlas. 2 ed.   (in English). Moskva, 1967.
250 p.   col. maps.   50 cm.

1592 U.S.S.R. Glavnoe upravlenie geodezii i kartografii.
Uchebnyi atlas mira. Moskva, 1967.
147 p.   col. maps.   32 cm.

1593 Velhagen & Klasing.
Unsere Welt. Atlas für die Schule. Berlin, [1967].
122 p.   col. maps.   28 cm.

1594 Volk und Wissen Verlag.
Atlas der Erdkunde für die allgemeinbildenden polytechnischen Oberschulen. 8 ed.   With Haack.
Berlin, 1967.
104 p.   col. maps.   31 cm.

1595 Westermann, Georg.
Der Lebensraum des Menschen. Mit Heimatatlas.
Braunschweig, 1967.
1 vol.   col. maps.   33 cm.

1596 Westermann, Georg.
Weltatlas. Braunschweig, [1967].
225 p. col. maps. 36 cm.

1597 Westermann, Georg.
Westermanns Hausatlas. 5 ed. Braunschweig,
[1967].
267 p. col. maps. 35 cm.

1598 Wolters, J. B.
Atlas der gehele aarde. 45 ed. By F. J.
Ormeling. Groningen, 1967.
172 p. col. maps. 37 cm.

1599 Wolters, J. B.
De Kleine wereldatlas. By M. Goossens. Leuven,
1967.
56 p. col. maps. 31 cm.

1600 Wolters, J. B.
Kleine schoolatlas der gehele aarde. 52 ed. By
P. R. Bos. Groningen, 1967.
112 p. col. maps. 31 cm.

1968

1601 Aguilar, S. A. de Ediciones.
Atlas bachillerato universal y de España. 15 ed.
By A. L. Gómez. Madrid, 1968.
117 p. col. maps. 35 cm.

1602 Aguilar, S. A. de Ediciones.
Atlas bachillerato universal y de España. 16 ed.
By A. L. Gómez. Madrid, 1968.
117 p. col. maps. 35 cm.

1603 Aguilar, S. A. de Ediciones.
Atlas bachillerato universal y de España. 17 ed.
By A. L. Gómez. Madrid, 1968.
117 p. col. maps. 35 cm.

1604 Aguilar, S. A. de Ediciones.
Atlas bachillerato universal y de España. 18 ed.
By A. L. Gómez. Madrid, 1968.
117 p. col. maps. 35 cm.

1605 Aguilar, S. A. de Ediciones.
Atlas universal Aguilar. Madrid, 1968.
390 p. col. maps. 42 cm.

1606 Alves, Francisco.
Nóvo atlas de geografia.   Rio de Janeiro, 1968.
56 p.   col.   maps.   31 cm.

1607 American Map Co., Inc.
Colorprint student's atlas of the world.   New York,
[1968].
24 p.   col.   maps.   31 cm.

1608 Asedi.
Atlas de géographie.   La Belgique, le monde.   By
José A. Sporck and Luc Piérard.   With Hölzel.
Bruxelles, [1968].
144 p.   col.   maps.   33 cm.

1609 Bartholomew, John & Son, Ltd.
The Aldine world atlas; geography and history.   3 ed.
Toronto, Vancouver, [1968].
166 p.   col.   maps.   29 cm.

1610 Beste, G. M. B. H.
Der Grosse Reader's Digest Welt Atlas.   6 ed.
With Reader's Digest Association, Ltd.   Stuttgart,
1968.
217 p.   col.   maps.   40 cm.

1611 Brown, W. C., Co.
Atlas for anthropology.   By Robert F. Spencer and
Elden Johnson.   Dubuque, Iowa, 1968.
61 p.   28 cm.

1612 Bulgaria.   Glavno upravlenie po geodeziā i kartografiā.
Geografski atlas za osmi klas.   Sofia, [1968].
65 p.   col.   maps.   31 cm.

1613 Cappelens, J. W., Forlag, A. S.
Cappelens handatlas.   Oslo, 1968.
134 p.   col.   maps.   21 cm.

1614 Collins, William, Sons & Co., Ltd.
Collins-Longmans advanced atlas.   Glasgow, 1968.
160 p.   col.   maps.   28 cm.

1615 Collins, William, Sons & Co., Ltd.
Collins-Longmans atlas one.   Glasgow, [1968].
32 p.   col.   maps.   26 cm.

1616 Collins, William, Sons & Co., Ltd.

The Daily Telegraph world atlas. London, 1968.
121 p. col. maps. 27 cm.

1617 Delagrave.
Atlas classique. By R. Kienast and A. J. C.
Bertrand. Paris, [1968].
120 p. col. maps. 31.5 cm.

1618 Deutsche Lufthansa.
Lufthansa streckenatlas. With Mairs. Köln,[1968].
19 p. col. maps. 24 cm.

1619 Deutscher Bücherbund.
Handatlas für Geographie und Geschichte. By Hans
Prechtl. With Hölzel. Stuttgart, Hamburg, [1968].
96 p. col. maps. 32 cm.

1620 E.D.A.F.
El Universo en color: gran atlas geografia EDAF;
fisico-politico-económico. Madrid, [1968].
395 p. col. maps. 40 cm.

1621 Edições Melhoramentos.
Atlas geográfico Melhoramentos. 28 ed. By
Geraldo José Pauwels. São Paulo, 1968.
95 p. col. maps. 35 cm.

1622 Editions Bordas.
Atlas illustré Bordas. By Pierre Serryn. Paris,
1968.
208 p. col. maps. 33 cm.

1623 Editora Liceu.
Atlas contemporâneo. By Nilo Bernardes and
Pierre Gourou. Rio de Janeiro, 1968.
67 p. col. maps. 34 cm.

1624 Elsevier.
Elsevier atlas van de gehele wereld. Amsterdam,
1968.
237 p. col. maps. 18 cm.

1625 Elsevier.
Niewe Winkler Prins. Atlas. 6 ed. Amsterdam,
1968.
408 p. col. maps. 32 cm.

1626 Encyclopaedia Britannica.

Britannica world atlas international.   Chicago, [1968].
367 p.   col. maps.   41 cm.

1627 Fabbri.
Grande atlante geografico.   By Piero Dagradi.
Milano, [1968].
190 p.   col. maps.   32.5 cm.

1628 Field Enterprises Educational Corp.
The world book atlas.   Chicago, 1968.
392 p.   col. maps.   37 cm.

1629 Freytag, Berndt & Artaria.
Neuer Schulatlas für Hauptschulen und Unterstufen
der Höheren Schulen.   Wien, 1968.
110 p.   col. maps.   32 cm.

1630 Generalstabens litografiska anstalt.
En delad värld; världspolitisk atlas.   By Tor S.
Ahman.   Stockholm, 1968.
96 p.   col. maps.   22 cm.

1631 Generalstabens litografiska anstalt.
Världen i ett nötskal.   Stockholm, 1968.
1 vol.   col. maps.   17 cm.

1632 Generalstabens litografiska anstalt.
Vär värld atlas.   Stockholm, 1968.
183 p.   col. maps.   31 cm.

1633 Generalstabens litografiska anstalt.
Vär värld.   Politisk-ekonomisk atlas.   Stockholm,
1968 -
in 6 vol.   col. maps.   31 cm.

1634 Geographical Pub. Co.
School and library atlas of the world.   By Fred W.
Foster.   Cleveland, [1968].
324 p.   col. maps.   57 cm.

1635 Goldmann Verlag.
Handatlas.   8 ed.   München, [1968].
161 p.   col. maps.   41 cm.

1636 Granda, J. C.
Atlas universal ilustrado.   By Ernesto Reguera
Sierra.   Buenos Aires, 1968.
300 p.   col. maps.   35 cm.

1637 Gyldendal.
  Atlas for folkeskolen. 30 ed. By C. C.
  Christensen and A. M. R. Krogsgaard. København,
  1968.
  34 p. col. maps. 23 cm.

1638 Gyldendal.
  Gyldendals relief atlas. 2 ed. By Paul Holmelund
  and Ib Kejlbo. København, 1968.
  125 p. col maps. 35 cm.

1639 Haack, Hermann.
  Haack Grosser Weltatlas. Gotha, Leipzig, 1968.
  718 p. col. maps. 34 cm.

1640 Haack, Hermann.
  Haack Hausatlas. 2 ed. Gotha, Leipzig, 1968.
  296 p. col. maps. 35 cm.

1641 Hammond, Inc.
  Advanced reference atlas. Maplewood, N. J., 1968.
  196 p. col. maps. 31 cm.

1642 Hammond, Inc.
  Atlas moderno universal Hammond. Maplewood,
  N. J., 1968.
  47 p. col. maps. 31 cm.

1643 Hammond, Inc.
  Hammond illustrated family world atlas. With
  Bobley Pub. Corp. Glen Cove, N. Y., [1968].
  2 vol. col. maps. 32 cm.

1644 Hammond, Inc.
  Intermediate world atlas. Maplewood, N. J., 1968.
  63 p. col. maps. 28 cm.

1645 Hammond, Inc.
  My first world atlas. Maplewood, N. J., 1968.
  48 p. col. maps. 31 cm.

1646 Hammond, Inc.
  The first book atlas. New York, 1968.
  96 p. col. maps. 23 cm.

1647 Hammond, Inc.
  World atlas. Classics ed. Maplewood, N. J., 1968.
  352 p. col. maps. 31 cm.

1648 Hatier.
Atlas mondial. By André Journaux. Paris, 1968.
188 p. col. maps. 34 cm.

1649 Herder Verlag.
Herders grosser Weltatlas. Freiburg, [1968].
266 p. col. maps. 40 cm.

1650 Hölzel, Ed. Verlag.
Atlas de Géographie, La Belgique et le Monde.
Wien, 1968.
112 p. col. maps. 33 cm.

1651 Hölzel, Ed. Verlag.
Österreichischer Mittelschulatlas. 94 ed. Wien,
1968.
167 p. col. maps. 31 cm.

1652 International Bank for Reconstruction and Development.
World bank atlas; population and per capita product.
3 ed. Washington, D. C., 1968.
16 p. col. maps. 28 cm.

1653 Kartográfiai Vállalat.
Képes politikai és gazdasági. Világatlasz. Budapest, 1968.
1 vol. col. maps. 34 cm.

1654 Kartográfiai Vállalat.
Kis világatlasz. By Radó Sándor. Budapest, 1968.
350 p. col. maps. 19 cm.

1655 Kartográfiai Vállalat.
Világatlasz. Budapest [1968].
192 p. col. maps. 35 cm.

1656 Keysersche Verlagsbuchhandlung, G. M. B. H.
Atlas zur Erdkunde. By H. Lautensach. München,
1968.
168 p. col. maps. 31 cm.

1657 Kümmerly & Fry.
Wirtschaftsgeographischer Weltatlas. By Hans
Boesch. Zürich, 1968.
90 p. col. maps. 34 cm.

1658 Lingen.
Grosser Weltatlas für Schule und Heim. Köln, 1968.

100 p.   col. maps.   31 cm.

1659 List, P.
     Harms Weltatlas.   München, 1968.
     55 p.   col. maps.   33 cm.

1660 List, P.
     Wirtschaftsgeographischer Weltatlas.   By Hans
     Boesch.   With Kümmerly & Frey.   München, 1968.
     89 p.   col. maps.   34 cm.

1661 Livre de poche.
     Atlas de poche.   Paris, 1968.
     238 p.   col. maps.   17 cm.

1662 McGraw-Hill Book Co.
     Man's domain.   A thematical atlas of the world.
     With General Drafting Co.   New York, 1968.
     76 p.   col. maps.   33 cm.

1663 Meulenhoff, J. M.
     Beknopte atlas voor het voortgezet onderwijs.   1 ed.
     With Svenska Bokförlaget.   Amsterdam, 1968.
     78 p.   col. maps.   32 cm.

1664 Meulenhoff, J. M.
     Meulenhoff atlas voor de mammoet.   With Hölzel.
     Amsterdam, 1968.
     128 p.   col. maps.   32 cm.

1665 Meyer, Kartographisches Institut.
     Rororo Weltatlas.   Hamburg, 1968.
     224 p.   col. maps.   32 cm.

1666 Munksgaard.
     Atlas til orienteringsfagene.   By Keld Irgens.
     København, [1968].
     32 p.   col. maps.   30 cm.

1667 Nagel Publishers.
     New Horizons: Maps of the world.   With Pan
     American Airways.   Geneva, [1968].
     336 p.   col. maps.   16 cm.

1668 Nathan, Fernand.
     Atlas du XXe siècle.   By R. and M. Ozouf.
     Paris, 1968.
     140 p.   col. maps.   35 cm.

1669 Nelson, Thomas & Sons, Ltd.
Atlas Universal y de México.   London, [1968].
30 p. col. maps. 28 cm.

1670 Nelson, Thomas & Sons, Ltd.
Atlas universal y del Peru.   London, 1968.
25 p. col. maps. 28 cm.

1671 Ottenheimer Publishers, Inc.
Atlas and gazetteer of the world.   Baltimore, Md.,
189 p. col. maps. 28 cm.

1672 Oxford University Press.
Concise Oxford atlas.   London, 1968.
288 p. col. maps. 26 cm.

1673 Oxford University Press.
Concise Oxford atlas.   2 ed.   London, 1968.
249 p. col. maps. 26 cm.

1674 Oxford University Press.
Shorter Oxford school atlas.   London, 1968.
1 vol. col. maps. 26 cm.

1675 Pergamon Press, Ltd.
Pergamon world atlas.   With Sluzba topograficzna
wojska Polskego.   Oxford, New York, 1968.
525 p. col. maps. 42 cm.

1676 Philip, George & Son, Ltd.
Philip's modern home atlas.   By Harold Fullard.
London, 1968.
48 p. col. maps. 29 cm.

1677 Philip, George & Son, Ltd.
Philip's pocket atlas of the world.   By Harold
Fullard.   London, 1968.
120 p. col. maps. 20 cm.

1678 Poland.   Państwowe przedsiębiorstwo wydawnictw
kartograficznych.
Atlas geograficzny.   4 ed.   Warszawa, [1968].
159 p. col. maps. 37 cm.

1679 PUMA.
Atlas mundial.   By Murillo Alves da Cunba.   Rio
de Janeiro, [1968].
95 p. col. maps. 18 cm.

1680 Radio Amateur Callbook, Inc.
    Radio amateurs' world atlas.   Chicago, 1968.
    16 p. col. maps. 31 cm.

1681 Rand McNally & Co.
    Rand McNally answer atlas.   Chicago, [1968].
    71 p. col. maps. 29 cm.

1682 Rand McNally & Co.
    Rand McNally currents events world atlas.
    Chicago, 1968.
    32 p. col. maps. 32 cm.

1683 Rand McNally & Co.
    Rand McNally new cosmopolitan world atlas.
    Chicago, 1968.
    376 p. col. maps. 37 cm.

1684 Rand McNally & Co.
    Rand McNally premier world atlas.   Chicago, Ill.,
    [1968].
    350 p. col. maps. 31 cm.

1685 Rand McNally & Co.
    Rand McNally standard world atlas.   Chicago, Ill.,
    [1968].
    264 p. col. maps. 28 cm.

1686 Rand McNally & Co.
    Rand McNally world atlas.   Family Edition.
    Chicago, Ill., [1968].
    324 p. col. maps. 32 cm.

1687 Rand McNally & Co.
    The World book atlas.   With Field Enterprises
    Educational Corp.   Chicago, [1968].
    392 p. col. maps. 37 cm.

1688 Reader's Digest Association, Ltd.
    Reader's Digest great world atlas.   London, [1968].
    232 p. col. maps. 40 cm.

1689 Reader's Digest Association, Ltd.
    Reader's Digest great world atlas.   3 ed.
    Pleasantville, N. Y., [1968].
    232 p. col. maps. 40 cm.

1690 Tallandier.
Atlas Tallandier en relief. With Geographical
Projects. Paris, 1968.
205 p. col. maps. 30 cm.

1691 Time-Life Books.
Atlas of the world. With Rand McNally. New
York, [1968].
160 p. col. maps. 28 cm.

1692 Times of London.
The Time atlas of the world. 2 ed. With
Bartholomew. London, 1968.
558 p. col. maps. 46 cm.

1693 Touring Club Italiano.
Atlante Internazionale del Touring Club Italiano.
8 ed. Milano, 1968.
2 vol. col. maps. 50 cm.

1694 Touring Club Italiano.
Planisfero politico. Con notizie sugli stati e sulle
organizzazioni internazionali. Milano, [1968].
24 p. col. maps. 22 cm.

1695 U.S.S.R. Glavnoe upravlenie geodezii i kartografii.
Atlas mira. Moskva, 1968.
64 p. col. maps. 24 cm.

1696 U.S.S.R. Glavnoe upravlenie geodezii i kartografii.
Atlas mira. With index vol. Moskva, 1968.
2 vol. col. maps. 50 cm. & 30 cm.

1697 U.S.S.R. Glavnoe upravlenie geodezii i kartografii.
Atlas zarubezhnykh stran dlya strednei shkoly.
Moskva, 1968.
48 p. col. maps. 29 cm.

1698 U.S.S.R. Glavnoe upravlenie geodezii i kartografii.
Malyi atlas mira. Moskva, 1968.
159 p. col. maps. 29 cm.

1699 U.S.S.R. Glavnoe upravlenie geodezii i kartografii.
The world atlas. English ed. With vol 2: Index.
Moskva, 1968.
250 p. col. maps. 50 cm.

1700 U.S.S.R. Glavnoe upravlenie geodezii i kartografii.

Uchebnii atlas mira.   By F. M. Kozlov.   Moskva,
1968.
179 p.   col. maps.   34 cm.

1701 Vallardi, A.
     Atlante geografico illustrato fisico politico economico.
     By Cesare Saibene.   Milano, 1968.
     282 p.   col. maps.   32 cm.

1702 Volk und Wissen Verlag.
     Atlas der Erdkunde für die allgemeinbildenden poly-
     technischen Oberschulen.   9 ed.   With Haack.
     Berlin, 1968.
     104 p.   col. maps.   31 cm.

1703 Westermann, Georg.
     Der Lebensraum des Menschen.   Ein Westermann
     Atlas.   Braunschweig, 1968.
     154 p.   col. maps.   33 cm.

1704 Westermann, Georg.
     Weltatlas.   Braunschweig, [1968].
     244 p.   col. maps.   36 cm.

1705 Wolters, J. B.
     De grote bosatlas.   46 ed.   By F. T. Ormeling.
     Groningen, 1968.
     202 p.   col. maps.   37 cm.

1706 Zenkoku Kyoiku Tosho.
     New world atlas.   By Keiji Tanaka.   Tokyo, [1968].
     182 p.   col. maps.   42 cm.

1969

1707 Aguilar, S. A. de Ediciones.
     Atlas bachillerato universal y de España.   19 ed.
     By A. L. Gómez.   Madrid, 1969.
     117 p.   col. maps.   35 cm.

1708 Aguilar, S. A. de Ediciones.
     Atlas bachillerato universal y de España.   20 ed.
     By A. L. Gómez.   Madrid, 1969.
     117 p.   col. maps.   35 cm.

1709 Aguilar, S. A. de Ediciones.
     Atlas bachillerato, universal y de España.   21 ed.
     By A. L. Gómez.   Madrid, 1969.
     117 p.   col. maps.   35 cm.

1710 Aguilar, S. A. de Ediciones.
       Atlas bachillerato universal y de España.   22 ed.
       By A. L. Gómez.   Madrid, 1969.
       117 p.   col. maps.   35 cm.

1711 Aguilar, S. A. de Ediciones.
       Gran atlas Aguilar.   Madrid, 1969.
       3 vol.   col. maps.   49.5 cm.

1712 Aldine Pub. Co.
       Aldine university atlas.   1 ed.   By Norton Ginsburg.
       With George Philip & Son Ltd.   Chicago, [1969].
       309 p.   col. maps.   29 cm.

1713 American Map Co., Inc.
       Colorprint scholastic world atlas.   New York, [1969].
       48 p.   col. maps.   31 cm.

1714 Bobley Pub. Corp.
       Hammond illustrated family world atlas.   With
       Hammond, Inc.   Glen Cove, N. Y., [1969].
       2 vol.   col. maps.   32 cm.

1715 British Sulphur Corporation, Ltd.
       World fertilizer atlas.   3 ed.   London, 1969.
       82 p.   28 cm.

1716 Collins, William, Sons & Co., Ltd.
       Collins-Longmans Atlas Four.   Glasgow, [1969].
       110 p.   col. maps.   26 cm.

1717 Collins, William, Sons & Co., Ltd.
       Fontana pocket atlas of the world.   London, 1969.
       192 p.   col. maps.   18 cm.

1718 Collins, William, Sons & Co., Ltd.
       Pathfinder atlas.   London, 1969.
       1 vol.   col. maps.   23 cm.

1719 Doubleday.
       Hammond contemporary world atlas.   New perspec-
       tive ed.   Garden City, N. Y., [1969].
       256 p.   col. maps.   29 cm.

1720 E.D.A.F.
       Gran atlas y geografia EDAF.   Madrid, [1969].
       400 p.   col. maps.   39 cm.

1721 Editions Bordas.
     Petit atlas Bordas: la France, le monde. By René
     Canët, Pierre Serryn and Marc Vincent.   Paris,
     1969.
     78 p. col. maps. 33 cm.

1722 Encyclopaedia Britannica.
     Britannica atlas. London, Chicago, 1969.
     542 p. col. maps. 37 cm.

1723 Encyclopaedia Britannica.
     The international atlas. With Rand McNally.
     Chicago, 1969.
     556 p. col. maps. 37.5 cm.

1724 Field Enterprises Educational Corp.
     The world book atlas. Chicago, [1969].
     392 p. col. maps. 37 cm.

1725 Follett Educational Corp.
     Follett classroom atlas. By Herbert H. Gross.
     Chicago, [1969].
     64 p. col. maps. 26 cm.

1726 Freytag, Berndt & Artaria.
     Neuer Schulatlas für Hauptschulen und Unterstufen
     der Höheren Schulen. Wien, 1969-70.
     110 p. col. maps. 31 cm.

1727 Geographical Pub. Co.
     School and library atlas of the world.   By Fred
     W. Foster. Cleveland, 1969.
     366 p. col. maps. 57 cm.

1728 Gyldendal.
     Kulturgeografisk atlas. 6 ed. By Johannes Humlum.
     København, 1969.
     2 vol. col. maps. 27 cm.

1729 Hammond, Inc.
     Ambassador world atlas. New perspective ed.
     Maplewood, N. J., 1969.
     352 p. col. maps. 39 cm.

1730 Hammond, Inc.
     Atlas moderno universal. Maplewood, N. J., 1969.
     47 p. col. maps. 31 cm.

1731 Hammond, Inc.
    Hammond citation world atlas. New perspective ed.
    Maplewood, N. J., [1969].
    352 p. col. maps. 32 cm.

1732 Hammond, Inc.
    Hammond contemporary world atlas. New perspec-
    tive ed. Maplewood, N. J., [1969].
    256 p. col. maps. 29 cm.

1733 Hammond, Inc.
    Hammond Medallion world atlas. New perspective
    edition. Maplewood, N. J., 1969.
    415 p. col. maps. 39 cm.

1734 Hammond, Inc.
    Hammond standard world atlas. Maplewood, N. J.,
    [1969].
    192 p. col. maps. 32 cm.

1735 Hammond, Inc.
    Hammond world atlas. Collector's ed. Maplewood,
    N. J., [1969].
    352 p. col. maps. 32 cm.

1736 Hammond, Inc.
    Hammond world atlas. Prestige ed. Maplewood,
    N. J., [1969].
    192 p. col. maps. 32 cm.

1737 Hammond, Inc.
    Headline world atlas. Maplewood, N. J., [1969].
    68 p. col. maps. 27.5 cm.

1738 Hammond, Inc.
    Large-type Hammond-Jennison world atlas. Maple-
    wood, N. J., 1969.
    144 p. col. maps. 32 cm.

1739 Hammond, Inc.
    My first world atlas. Maplewood, N. J., 1969.
    48 p. col. maps. 31 cm.

1740 Hammond, Inc.
    New world atlas: Hammond/Scholastic. Maplewood,
    N. J., [1969].
    64 p. col. maps. 28 cm.

1741 Hammond, Inc.
     Standard world atlas.   Collector's ed.   Maplewood,
     N. J., 1969.
     352 p. col. maps. 32 cm.

1742 Herder Verlag.
     Der Neue Herder Handatlas.   2 ed.   By Carl Troll.
     Freiburg, [1969].
     200 p. col. maps. 59 cm.

1743 Hölzel, Ed. Verlag.
     Österreichischer Mittelschulatlas.   95 ed.   Wien,
     1969.
     167 p. col. maps. 31 cm.

1744 International Bank for Reconstruction and Development.
     World bank atlas; population, per capita product and
     growth rate.   4 ed.   Washington, D. C., 1969.
     16 p. col. maps. 28 cm.

1745 Istituto Geografico De Agostini.
     Atlante geografici moderno.   By Umberto Bonapace.
     Novara, [1969].
     133 p. col. maps. 36 cm.

1746 Istituto Geografico De Agostini.
     Atlante geografico metodico.   By Umberto Bonapace
     and Giuseppe Motta.   Novara, [1969].
     194 p. col. maps. 36 cm.

1747 Istituto Geografico De Agostini.
     Nuovo atlante mondiale.   By Umberto Bonapace.
     Novara, 1969.
     530 p. col. maps. 35.5 cm.

1748 Istituto Geografico De Agostini.
     World atlas of agriculture.   Novara, 1969—
     in parts. col. maps. 69 cm.

1749 Larousse
     Atlas moderne Larousse.   By Donald Curran and
     Michael Coquery.   Paris, [1969].
     175 p. col. maps. 31 cm.

1750 Meyer, Kartographisches Institut.
     Grosses Duden-Lexikon Weltatlas.   Mannheim, [1969].
     485 p. col. maps. 32 cm.

1751 Meyer, Kartographisches Institut.
     Rororo Weltatlas. Hamburg, [1969].
     224 p. col. maps. 32 cm.

1752 Oxford University Press.
     Oxford home atlas of the world. London, 1969.
     138 p. col. maps. 26 cm.

1753 Oxford University Press.
     The little Oxford atlas. London, 1969.
     67 p. col. maps. 26 cm.

1754 Peuser, Ediciones Geográficas.
     Nuevo atlas geográfico metódico universal. 32 ed.
     By José Anesi. Buenos Aires, 1969.
     96 p. col. maps. 38 cm.

1755 Philip, George & Son, Ltd.
     Philips' new school atlas. 56 ed. London, 1969.
     64 p. col. maps. 28 cm.

1756 Philip, George & Son, Ltd.
     Philips' practical atlas. 4 ed. London, 1969.
     97 p. col. maps. 29 cm.

1757 Philip, George & Son, Ltd.
     The international atlas. London, [1969].
     558 p. col. maps. 37.5 cm.

1758 Philip, George & Son, Ltd.
     The university atlas. 13 ed. By H. Fullard and
     H. C. Darby. London, 1969.
     288 p. col. maps. 28 cm.

1759 Poland. Państwowe przedsiębiorstwo wydawnictw
     kartograficznych.
     Maly atlas swiata. Warszawa, 1969.
     1 vol. col. maps. 23 cm.

1760 Rand McNally & Co.
     Goode's world atlas. 13 ed. By Edward B.
     Espenshade, Jr. Chicago, [1969].
     315 p. col. maps. 29 cm.

1761 Rand McNally & Co.
     Rand McNally new cosmopolitan world atlas.
     Chicago, Ill., 1969.
     420 p. col. maps. 37 cm.

1762 Rand McNally & Co.
  The International atlas. Chicago, 1969.
  556 p. col. maps. 37.5 cm.

1763 Reader's Digest Association, Ltd.
  Reader's Digest Taschen Weltatlas. Stuttgart,
  Zurich, Wien, 1969.
  48 p. col. maps. 19 cm.

1764 Robinson, H.E.C., Pty. Ltd.
  Robinson's world atlas. By Harry Tierney.
  Sydney, 1969.
  130 p. col. maps. 28 cm.

1765 Scott, Foresman & Co.
  Aldine university atlas. By Harold Fullard and
  H. C. Darby. Glenview, Ill., 1969.
  318 p. col. maps. 29 cm.

1766 Sélection du Reader's Digest, S.A.R.L.
  Atlas du monde. 1 ed. With Kümmerly & Frey.
  Paris, [1969].
  55 p. col. maps. 29 cm.

1767 U.S.S.R. Glavnoe upravlenie geodezii i kartografii.
  Atlas naselenia mira. Moskva, 1969-70.
  160 p. col. maps. 37 cm.

1768 Velhagen & Klasing.
  Unsere Welt. Atlas für die Schule. Berlin, [1969].
  112 p. col. maps. 28 cm.

1769 Westermann, Georg.
  Atlas für Hamburger Schulen. Braunschweig, 1969.
  1 vol. col. maps. 32 cm.

1770 Westermann, Georg.
  Der Lebensraum des Menschen. Atlas für Schule
  und Haus. Braunschweig, [1969].
  99 p. col. maps. 33 cm.

1771 Westermann, Georg.
  Diercke Weltatlas. Braunschweig, [1969].
  224 p. col. maps. 36 cm.

1772 Westermann, Georg.
  Westermann Schulatlas. Braunschweig, [1969].
  124 p. col. maps. 32 cm.

1970

1773 Aguilar, S. A. de Ediciones.
     Atlas bachillerato, universal y de España.   23 ed.
     By A. L. Gómez.   Madrid, 1970.
     117 p.   col. maps.   35 cm.

1774 Aschehoug & Co.
     Aschehougs verdens atlas.   3 ed.   With Bertelsmann.
     Oslo, [1970].
     288 p.   col. maps.   33 cm.

1775 Cappelens, J. W. Forlag, A. S.
     Cappelens internasionale atlas.   Oslo, 1970.
     1 vol.   col. maps.   32 cm.

1776 Collins, William, Sons & Co., Ltd.
     Collins-Longmans atlas three.   Glasgow, [1970].
     1 vol.   col. maps.   26 cm.

1777 Encyclopaedia Britannica.
     Britannica atlas.   Chicago, [1970].
     543 p.   col. maps.   39 cm.

1778 Field Enterprises Educational Corp.
     The world book atlas.   Chicago, [1970].
     392 p.   col. maps.   37 cm.

1779 Hölzel, Ed. Verlag.
     Österreichischer Mittelschulatlas.   96 ed.   Wien,
     1970.
     167 p.   col. maps.   31 cm.

1780 Istituto Geografico De Agostini.
     Calendario atlante de Agostini.   Novara, 1970.
     785 p.   col. maps.   16 cm.

1781 Meyer, Kartographisches Institut.
     Meyers universalatlas.   By Adolf Hanle.   Mannheim,
     [1970].
     227 p.   col. maps.   32 cm.

1782 Rand McNally & Co.
     Rand McNally regional atlas.   4 ed.   By Edward
     B. Espenshade, Jr.   Chicago, [1970].
     64 p.   col. maps.   29 cm.

1783 Rand McNally & Co.
     World atlas.   13 ed.   By Edward B. Espenshade,

Jr.   Chicago, 1970.
315 p.   col. maps.   29 cm.

1784 U.S.S.R.   Gidronet.
Agroklimatocheski atlas mira.   Leningrad, 1970.
512 p.   col. maps.   32 cm.

1785 U.S.S.R.   Glavnoe upravlenie geodezii i kartografii.
Ekonomicheskii atlas mira.   Moskva, 1970-71.
1 vol.   col. maps.   50 cm.

1786 Westermann, Georg.
Diercke Weltatlas.   64 ed.   Braunschweig, 1970.
226 p.   col. maps.   36 cm.

AFRICA

1787 Afrika Instituut.
Africa; maps and statistics.   Pretoria, 1962-65.
10 vol. col. maps. 35 cm.

1788 Arnold, E.
An atlas of African history. By J. D. Fage.
London, [1958].
64 p. 29 cm.

1789 Automobile Association of South Africa.
Road atlas and touring guide of southern Africa.
2 ed. Johannesburg, [1963].
200 p. col. maps. 25 cm.

1790 Automobile Association of South Africa.
Trans-African highways; a route book of the
main trunk roads in Africa. 5 ed. Johannesburg, 1963.
352 p. col. maps. 28 cm.

1791 B. P. Southern Africa Pty., Ltd.
Padkaarte. Road maps. Union of South Africa,
South West Africa. Capetown, [196-].
10 p. col. maps. 29 cm.

1792 Brown, W. C. Co.
Africa in maps. By Geoffrey J. Martin.
Dubuque, Iowa, [1962].
124 p. 28 cm.

1793 Collins, William, Sons & Co., Ltd.
Collins-Longmans atlas for Central Africa. 1 ed.
By K. H. Huggins. Glasgow, [1950].
46 p. col. maps. 23 cm.

1794 Collins, William, Sons & Co., Ltd.
     Die gestandaardiseerde Suid-Afrikaanse atlas.   By
     B. A. Workman and K. H. Huggins.   Glasgow,
     [1953].
     49 p.   col. maps.   28 cm.

1795 Collins, William, Sons & Co., Ltd.
     Pathfinder atlas for West Africa.   2 ed.   Glasgow,
     1950.
     48 p.   col. maps.   23 cm.

1796 Collins, William, Sons & Co., Ltd.
     Pathfinder atlas for West Africa.   3 ed.   Glasgow,
     [1952].
     48 p.   col. maps.   23 cm.

1797 Collins, William, Sons & Co., Ltd.
     Pathfinder atlas for West Africa.   4 ed.   Glasgow,
     1954.
     48 p.   col. maps.   23 cm.

1798 Collins, William, Sons & Co., Ltd.
     Pathfinder atlas for West Africa.   5 ed.   Glasgow,
     1955.
     48 p.   col. maps.   23 cm.

1799 Collins, William, Sons & Co., Ltd.
     Pathfinder atlas for West Africa.   6 ed.   Glasgow,
     1956.
     56 p.   col. maps.   23 cm.

1800 Collins, William, Sons & Co., Ltd.
     Pathfinder atlas for West Africa.   7 ed.   Glasgow,
     [1957].
     56 p.   col. maps.   23 cm.

1801 Collins, William, Sons & Co., Ltd.
     Pathfinder atlas for West Africa.   8 ed.   Glasgow, [1959]
     56 p.   col. maps.   23 cm.

1802 Collins, William, Sons & Co., Ltd.
     Pathfinder atlas for West Africa.   9 ed.   Glasgow,
     1960.
     56 p.   col. maps.   23 cm.

1803 Collins, William, Sons & Co., Ltd.
Pathfinder atlas for West Africa. 10 ed. Glasgow,
[1962].
56 p. col. maps. 23 cm.

1804 Collins, William, Sons & Co., Ltd.
Pathfinder atlas for West Africa. 11 ed. Glasgow,
1964.
56 p. col. maps. 23 cm.

1805 Collins, William, Sons & Co., Ltd.
The standardised South African atlas. By B. A.
Workman. London, 1952.
49 p. col. maps. 28 cm.

1806 Collins, William, Sons & Co., Ltd.
The standardised South African atlas. By B. A.
Workman and K. H. Huggins. Glasgow,
[1953].
49 p. col. maps. 28 cm.

1807 Collins, William, Sons & Co., Ltd.
The standardised South African atlas. By K. H.
Huggins and B. A. Workman. Glasgow,
[1961].
49 p. col. maps. 28 cm.

1808 Commission for Technical Cooperation in Africa South
of the Sahara.
Climatological atlas of Africa. Lagos, 1961.
55 p. col. maps. 60 cm.

1809 Czechoslovakia. Ústřední správa geodesie a kartografie.
Kapesní atlas "Afrika". Praha, 1967.
53 p. col. maps. 17 cm.

1810 Denoyer-Geppert Co.
Philip's modern college atlas for Africa. 6 ed.
By Harold Fullard. Chicago, 1965.
168 p. col. maps. 29 cm.

1811 Denoyer-Geppert Co.
The history of Africa in maps. By Harry A.
Gailey, Jr. Chicago, [1967].
96 p. 28 cm.

1812 Djambatan.
     Atlas of the Arab world and the Middle East.
     Amsterdam, [1960].
     55 p.   col. maps. 35 cm.

1813 Djambatan.
     Atlas of the Arab world and the Middle East.
     Amsterdam, [1966].
     55 p.   col. maps. 35 cm.

1814 East African institute of social research.
     Tribal maps of East Africa and Zanzibar.   By
     E. J. Goldthrope and F. B. Wilson.   Kampala,
     Uganda, 1960.
     14 p.   col. maps. 25 cm.

1815 Elsevier.
     Atlas van Afrika.   By L. Dudley Stamp and Gouv.
     H. Deschamps.   Amsterdam, [1956].
     200 p.   col. maps. 36 cm.

1816 Falk Verlag.
     Niederschlag, Temperatur und Schwule in Afrika
     [Atlas].   Hamburg, 1955.
     15 p.   col. maps. 47.5 cm.

1817 Gollancz, Victor.
     An atlas of Africa.   By J. F. Horrabin.   London,
     1960.
     126 p.   18 cm.

1818 Hulton Educational Publications, Ltd.
     A sketch-map history of West Africa.   By Norah
     Latham.   London, [1959].
     80 p.   25 cm.

1819 Hulton Educational Publications, Ltd.
     Outlines of Africa.   By M. R. Morgan.   London,
     1964.
     64 p.   23 cm.

1820 Institut fondamental d'Afrique noire.
     West African international atlas.   Atlas international
     de l'ouest africain.   Dakar, 1968—
     in parts.   col. maps. 53 cm.

1821 Institut Français d'Afrique Noire.
     Cartes ethno-demographique de l'Afrique Occidentale.

Dakar, 1952.
12 p.   col. maps.   28 cm.

1822 International Publications Service.
 Climatological atlas of Africa.   New York, 1963.
 55 p.   col. maps.   60 cm.

1823 Istituto Italiano per l'Africa.
 L'Africa nei suoi aspetti geografici, storici ed
 umani.   By Luchino Franciosa.   Roma,   [1953].
 149 p.   col. maps.   30 cm.

1824 Longmans, Green.
 The standardised South African atlas.   By B. A.
 Workman, K. H. Huggins and J. C. B. Redfearn.
 London, 1952.
 49 p.   col. maps.   28 cm.

1825 Macmillan & Co., Ltd.
 A map book of Africa.   By Alan Ferriday.   London,
 1966.
 80 p.   col. maps.   25 cm.

1826 Macmillan & Co., Ltd.
 A map book of Africa and South America.   1 ed.
 By A. Ferriday.   London, [1951].
 64 p.   col. maps.   25 cm.

1827 Macmillan & Co., Ltd.
 A map book of Africa and South America.   2 ed.
 By A. Ferriday.   London, 1954.
 64 p.   col. maps.   25 cm.

1828 Macmillan & Co., Ltd.
 A map book of Africa and South America.   2 ed.
 By A. Ferriday.   London, [1955].
 64 p.   col. maps.   25 cm.

1829 Macmillan & Co., Ltd.
 A map book of Africa and South America.   3 ed.
 By A. Ferriday.   London, 1958.
 64 p.   col. maps.   25 cm.

1830 Macmillan & Co., Ltd.
 A map book of Africa and South America.   4 ed.
 By A. Ferriday.   London, 1960.
 64 p.   col. maps.   25 cm.

1831 Macmillan & Co., Ltd.
       A map book of Africa and South America.   5 ed.
       By A. Ferriday.   London, 1962.
       64 p.   col. maps.   25 cm.

1832 Macmillan & Co., Ltd.
       A map book of Africa and South America.   6 ed.
       By A. Ferriday.   London, [1964].
       64 p.   col. maps.   25 cm.

1833 Macmillan & Co., Ltd.
       A map book of Africa and South America.   7 ed.
       By A. Ferriday.   London, 1965.
       64 p.   col. maps.   25 cm.

1834 Macmillan & Co., Ltd.
       A map book of Africa and South America.   8 ed.
       By Alan Ferriday.   London, 1967.
       65 p.   col. maps.   25 cm.

1835 Macmillan & Co., Ltd.
       My East African atlas.   London, 1960.
       48 p.   col. maps.   28 cm.

1836 Map Studio Productions, pty., Ltd.
       BP Padkaarte.   Road maps.   Cape Town, [1963].
       22 p.   col. maps.   28 cm.

1837 Marco Surveys, Ltd.
       Marketing maps: East Africa; cash crops and
       harvest times.   Nairobi, 1962.
       1 vol.   37 cm.

1838 Methuen.
       An atlas of African affairs.   By Andrew Boyd and
       Patrick van Rensburg.   London, [1962].
       133 p.   21 cm.

1839 Munger Oil Information Service.
       Munger map book: petroleum developments and
       generalized geology of Africa and Middle East.
       Los Angeles, 1960.
       115 p.   45 cm.

1840 Nelson, Thomas & Sons, Ltd.
       West African secondary school atlas.   By J.
       Wreford Watson and A. K. Wareham.   London,
       New York, 1963.

76 p.   col.   maps.   29 cm.

1841 Nelson, Thomas & Sons, Ltd.
West African secondary school atlas.   2 ed.   By J.
Wreford Watson and A. K. Wareham.   London,
New York, 1966.
80 p.   col.   maps.   29 cm.

1842 Oxford University Press.
Oxford atlas for East Africa.   Oxford, London,
Nairobi, 1966.
65 p.   col.   maps.   26 cm.

1843 Oxford University Press.
Oxford atlas for East Africa.   London, 1967.
64 p.   col.   maps.   26 cm.

1844 Oxford University Press.
The climate of Africa. [Atlas].   By B. W.
Thompson.   Nairobi, New York, 1965.
132 p.   col.   maps.   52 cm.

1845 Oxford University Press.
The Middle East and North Africa.   London, [1960].
135 p.   col.   maps.   27 cm.

1846 Oxford University Press.
The Middle East and North Africa.   London, [1964].
135 p.   col.   maps.   27 cm.

1847 Oxford University Press.
The Oxford regional economic atlas of Africa.   By
P. H. Andy and A. H. Hazlewood.   London, 1965.
244 p.   col.   maps.   26 cm.

1848 Oxford University Press.
Twenty West African maps for certificate geography.
London, 1967.
52 p.   col.   maps.   24.5 cm.

1849 Philip, George & Son, Ltd.
Juta se kollege atlas vir suidelike Afrika.   By
Harold Fullard and C. Potgieter.   Kaapstad, 1959.
167 p.   col.   maps.   29 cm.

1850 Philip, George & Son, Ltd.
Juta se springbok groot-druk atlas vir suidelike
Afrika.   3 ed.   By Harold Fullard and C. Potgieter.

Kaapstad, [1960].
79 p.   col. maps.   29 cm.

1851 Philip, George & Son, Ltd.
Juta's springbok large print atlas for Southern Africa.
2 ed.   By Harold Fullard.   Cape Town, [1957].
79 p.   col. maps.   29 cm.

1852 Philip, George & Son, Ltd.
Large print atlas for southern Africa.   22 ed.   By
George Goodall.   London, 1955.
79 p.   col. maps.   29 cm.

1853 Philip, George & Son, Ltd.
Large print atlas for southern Africa.   24 ed.
London, 1957.
79 p.   col. maps.   29 cm.

1854 Philip, George & Son, Ltd.
Large print atlas for southern Africa.   34 ed.   By
Harold Fullard.   London, 1969.
65 p.   col. maps.   28 cm.

1855 Philip, George & Son, Ltd.
New age atlas for West Africa.   4 ed.   By Harold
Fullard.   London, 1960.
40 p.   col. maps.   23 cm.

1856 Philip, George & Son, Ltd.
Philip se kollege atlas vir suidelike Afrika.   2 ed.
By Harold Fullard and C. Potgieter.   London, 1961.
167 p.   col. maps.   29 cm.

1857 Philip, George & Son, Ltd.
Philip's college atlas for southern Africa.   By
Harold Fullard.   London, 1962.
1 vol.   col. maps.   29 cm.

1858 Philip, George & Son, Ltd.
Philip's college atlas for southern Africa.   By
Harold Fullard.   London, [1963].
1 vol.   col. maps.   29 cm.

1859 Philip, George & Son, Ltd.
Philip's college atlas for southern Africa.   By
Harold Fullard.   London, 1967.
1 vol.   col. maps.   29 cm.

1860 Philip, George & Son, Ltd.
     Philip's junior school atlas for southern Africa. By
     Harold Fullard. London, 1968.
     30 p. col. maps. 23 cm.

1861 Philip, George & Son, Ltd.
     Philip's modern college atlas for Africa.   London,
     1959.
     168 p. col. maps. 29 cm.

1862 Philip, George & Son, Ltd.
     Philip's modern college atlas for Africa.   6 ed. By
     Harold Fullard. London, 1965.
     168 p. col. maps. 29 cm.

1863 Philip, George & Son, Ltd.
     Philip's modern college atlas for Africa.   7 ed. By
     Harold Fullard. London, 1966.
     197 p. col. maps. 29 cm.

1864 Philip, George & Son, Ltd.
     Philip's modern college atlas for Africa.   8 ed. By
     Harold Fullard. London, 1967.
     168 p. col. maps. 29 cm.

1865 Philip, George & Son, Ltd.
     Philip's school atlas for East Africa.   By Harold
     Fullard. London, 1956.
     32 p. col. maps. 28 cm.

1866 Philip, George & Son, Ltd.
     Philip's school atlas for East Africa.   By Harold
     Fullard. London, [1967].
     32 p. col. maps. 28 cm.

1867 Philip, George & Son, Ltd.
     Philip's venture atlas for southern Africa.   London,
     [1966].
     1 vol. col. maps. 28.5 cm.

1868 Philip, George & Son, Ltd.
     The pictorial atlas for West Africa.   By George
     Goodall. London, 1951.
     1 vol. col. maps. 23 cm.

1869 Philip, George & Son, Ltd.
     The West African atlas.   By George Goodall.
     London, 1950.

31 p. col. maps.   24 cm.

1870 Praeger, Frederick A.
     An atlas of Africa. By J. F. Horrabin. New York,
     [1960].
     126 p. 21 cm.

1871 Praeger, Frederick A.
     An atlas of Africa. 2 ed. By J. F. Horrabin.
     New York, 1961.
     126 p. 21 cm.

1872 Praeger, Frederick A.
     An atlas of African affairs. By Andrew Boyd and
     Patrick van Rensburg. New York, 1962.
     133 p. 21 cm.

1873 Praeger, Frederick A.
     An atlas of African affairs. By Andrew Boyd and
     Patrick van Rensburg. New York, [1965].
     133 p. 21 cm.

1874 Royal East African Automobile Assoc.
     Road book of East Africa. Nairobi, 1952.
     227 p. col. maps.   24 cm.

1875 Shell Company of South Africa, Ltd.
     Shell road map of southern Africa. Cape Town, 1953.
     48 p. col. maps.   28 cm.

1876 South Africa. Government Printer Office.
     Climatological atlas of Africa. By Stanley P.
     Jackson. Pretoria, 1962.
     56 p. col. maps.   60 cm.

1877 South Africa. Government Printer Office.
     Climatological atlas of Africa. By Stanley P.
     Jackson. Pretoria, 1964.
     56 p. col. maps.   60 cm.

1878 Spain. Dirreción general de Marrnecos y Colonias e
     instituto de estudios Africanos.
     Atlas histórico y geográfico de Africa Española.
     Madrid, 1955.
     197 p. col. maps.   42 cm.

1879 St. Martin's Press.
     A map book of Africa. By Alan Ferriday. New

York, 1966.
80 p. col. maps. 25 cm.

1880 St. Martin's Press.
A map book of Africa and South America.   6 ed.
By A. Ferriday. New York, [1964].
64 p. col. maps. 25 cm.

1881 St. Martin's Press.
A map book of Africa and South America.   7 ed.
By A. Ferriday. New York, 1965.
64 p. col. maps. 25 cm.

1882 St. Martin's Press.
A map book of Africa and South America.   8 ed.
By Alan Ferriday. New York, 1967.
65 p. col. maps. 25 cm.

1883 United Nations. Food and Agricultural Organization.
Crop ecological survey in West Africa. By J.
Papadakis. Roma, 1965.
1 vol. col. maps. 58 cm.

1884 United Nations. Food and Agricultural Organization.
East African livestock survey. Regional-Kenya,
Tanzania, Uganda. Firenze, 1967.
1 vol. col. maps. 58 cm.

1885 University of Chicago Press.
Atlas of African prehistory. By J. Desmond Clark.
Chicago, 1967.
112 p. col. overlays. 61 cm.

1886 University Tutorial Press.
The map approach to African history. By A. M.
Healy and E. R. Vere-Hodge. London, [1959].
64 p. 21 cm.

1887 U.S.S.R. Glavnoe upravlenie geodezii i kartografii.
Atlas Afriki. Moskva, 1967.
64 p. col. maps. 32 cm.

1888 U.S.S.R. Glavnoe upravlenie geodezii i kartografii.
Atlas Afriki. By S. I. Shurov. Moskva, 1968.
118 p. col. maps. 32 cm.

1889 Warszawa Uniwersytet.
Atlas podziałów administracyjnych krajów Afryki.

Warszawa, 1964.
63 p.   43 cm.

1890 Wheaton, A. & Co., Ltd.
New West African atlas.   Exeter, England, 1962.
48 p.   col. maps.   28 cm.

1891 Wheaton, A. & Co., Ltd.
New West African atlas.   Exeter, England, 1963.
48 p.   col. maps.   28 cm.

1892 Wheaton, A. & Co., Ltd.
New West African atlas.   Exeter, England, 1967.
48 p.   col. maps.   28 cm.

ANTARCTICA

1893 American Geographical Society.
Anarctic map folio series.   New York, 1964—
in parts.   col. maps.   44 cm.

1894 Poligrafiche Bolis.
Atlante polare.   Bergamo, 1958.
28 p.   col. maps.   34 cm.

1895 U. S. Navy Hydrographic Office.
Oceanographic atlas of the polar seas.   Antarctic,
Arctic. Washington, D.C., 1957-58.
2 vol.   col. maps.   40 cm.

1896 U.S.S.R. Glavnoe upravlenie geodezii i kartografii.
Atlas antarktiki.   Moskva, 1966—
2 vol.   col. maps.   60 cm.

ASIA

1897 Arnold, E.
An outline atlas of eastern history.   By R. R.
Sellman.   London, [1954].
63 p.   28 cm.

1898 Codex Verlag.
Kulturatlas von Palästina.   Gundholzen, [1970].
in 4 parts.   col. maps.   43 cm.

1899 Denoyer-Geppert Co.
Historical atlas of the Far East in modern times.
By Michael P. Ohorato.   Chicago, [1967].
32 p.   28 cm.

1900 Denoyer-Geppert Co.
     Southeast Asia in Maps.   By Thomas F. Barton.
     Chicago, [1970].
     96 p.   28 cm.

1901 Djambatan.
     Atlas of South-east Asia.   By D.G.E. Hall.
     Amsterdam, [1964].
     84 p.   col. maps.   35 cm.

1902 Djambatan.
     Atlas of the Arab World and the Middle East.
     Amsterdam, [1960].
     55 p.   col. maps.   35 cm.

1903 Djambatan.
     Atlas of the Arab World and the Middle East.
     Amsterdam, [1966].
     55 p.   col. maps.   35 cm.

1904 Hai kuang ch'u pan shê.
     Tung-nan Ya ti t'u chi. 2 ed. [Southeast-Asia in
     maps]. By Min-Fei Li. Hong Kong, 1958.
     80 p.   col. maps.   27 cm.

1905 Hai kuang ch'u pan shê.
     Tung-nan Ya tsui hsin ta ti t'u chi. [Southeast Asia
     in maps]. By Min-Fei Li. Hong Kong, [1955].
     30 p.   39 cm.

1906 Macmillan & Co. Ltd.
     A map book of Asia.   5 ed.   By Alan Ferriday.
     London, [1961].
     68 p.   25 cm.

1907 Macmillan & Co., Ltd.
     A map book of Asia.   5 ed.   By A. Ferriday.
     London, [1964].
     68 p.   25 cm.

1908 Macmillan & Co., Ltd.
     A map book of Australasia.   2 ed.   By Alan
     Ferriday.   London, 1959.
     48 p.   25 cm.

1909 Macmillan & Co., Ltd.
     A map book of Australasia.   3 ed.   By Alan
     Ferriday.   London, Melbourne, 1966.

52 p.   25 cm.

1910 Macmillan & Co. , Ltd.
A map book of Australasia.   4 ed.   By Alan
Ferriday.   London, Melbourne, 1969.
52 p.   25 cm.

1911 Macmillan & Co. , Ltd.
Atlas of South-East Asia.   London, 1964.
102 p.   col. maps.   35 cm.

1912 Macmillan & Co. , Ltd.
Atlas of the Arab World and Middle East.   With
Djambatan.   London, 1960.
68 p.   col. maps.   35 cm.

1913 Macmillan & Co. , Ltd.
Macmillan's atlas for South-East Asia.   1 ed.   By
Roy Edgardo Parry.   London, 1953.
32 p.   col. maps.   28 cm.

1914 Macmillan & Co. , Ltd.
Macmillan's atlas for South-East Asia.   By Roy
Edgardo Parry.   London, 1961.
32 p.   col. maps.   28 cm.

1915 Munger Oil Information Service.
Munger map book: Petroleum developments and
generalized geology of Africa and Middle East.
Los Angeles, 1960.
115 p.   45 cm.

1916 Nelson, Thomas & Sons, Ltd.
Atlas of Mesopotamia.   By D. R. Welsh and H. H.
Rowley.   London, 1962.
164 p.   col. maps.   36 cm.

1917 Oxford University Press.
Oxford regional economic atlas of the Middle East.
Oxford, 1956.
1 vol.   col. maps.   26 cm.

1918 Oxford University Press.
The Australasian school atlas, physical, political,
economic and historical.   4 ed.   With Bartholomew.
Melbourne, [1954].
84 p.   col. maps.   28 cm.

1919 Oxford University Press.
The Australasian school atlas, physical, political,
economic, and historical. 4 ed. With Bartholomew.
Melbourne, [1959].
68 p. col. maps. 28 cm.

1920 Oxford University Press.
The Middle East and North Africa. London, [1960].
135 p. col. maps. 27 cm.

1921 Oxford University Press.
The Middle East and North Africa. London, [1964].
135 p. col. maps. 27 cm.

1922 Praeger, Frederick A.
An atlas of Middle Eastern affairs. By Norman
J.G. Pounds and Robert C. Kingsbury. New York,
London, 1963.
117 p. 21 cm.

1923 Praeger, Frederick A.
An atlas of Middle Eastern affairs. By Norman
J.G. Pounds and Robert C. Kingsbury. New York,
London, 1966.
117 p. 21 cm.

1924 St. Martin's Press.
A map book of Asia. By A. Ferriday. New York,
[1961].
68 p. 25 cm.

1925 St. Martin's Press.
A map book of Asia. 5 ed. By A. Ferriday.
New York, [1964].
68 p. 25 cm.

1926 St. Martin's Press.
A map book of Australasia. 3 ed. By A. Ferriday.
New York, 1966.
52 p. 25 cm.

1927 St. Martin's Press.
A map book of Australasia. 4 ed. By Alan
Ferriday. New York, 1969.
52 p. 25 cm.

1928 St. Martin's Press.
Atlas of South-East Asia. By D. G. E. Hall. With

Djambatan. New York, 1964.
84 p. col. maps. 35 cm.

1929 St. Martin's Press.
     Atlas of South-East Asia. By D. G. E. Hall.
     With Djambatan. New York, 1965.
     84 p. col. maps. 35 cm.

1930 St. Martin's Press.
     Atlas of the Arab World and the Middle East. New
     York, 1960.
     68 p. col. maps. 35 cm.

1931 U. S. Army Natick Laboratories.
     Climatic atlas of Southeast Asia. Natick, Mass.,
     1967.
     1 vol. col. maps. 46 cm.

1932 U.S.S.R. Glavnoe upravlenie geodezii i kartografii.
     Atlas blizhnego i srednego vostoka. Moskva, 1970.
     1 vol. col. maps. 32 cm.

1933 U. S. S. R. Glavnoe upravlenie geodezii i kartografii.
     Atlas yuzhnoi Azii. Moskva, 1970.
     1 vol. col. maps. 32 cm.

1934 Yavneh.
     Atlas ha-mizrah ha-tikhon. By Moshe Brawer.
     Tel Aviv, [1964].
     80 p. col. maps. 35 cm.

1935 Yavneh.
     Atlas ha-mizrah ha-tikhon. 2 ed. By Yehuda
     Karmon and Moshe Brawer. Tel Aviv, [1967].
     80 p. col. maps. 35 cm.

AUSTRALIA

1936 Australia. Bureau of Mineral Resources. Geology
     and Geophysics.
     South Australia geological atlas series. Adelaide,
     1962 –
     in parts. col. maps. 31 cm.

1937 Jacaranda.
     Atlas of the southwest Pacific. 1 ed. By Ian
     Geoffrey Ord. Brisbane, 1967.
     59 p. col. maps. 26 cm.

1938 Jacaranda.
    Atlas of the southwest Pacific. 2 ed. By Ian
    Geoffrey Ord. Brisbane, [1968].
    59 p. col. maps. 26 cm.

1939 Macmillan & Co., Ltd.
    A map book of Australasia. 2 ed. By Alan
    Ferriday. London, 1959.
    48 p. 25 cm.

1940 Macmillan & Co., Ltd.
    A map book of Australasia. 3 ed. By Alan
    Ferriday. London, Melbourne, 1966.
    52 p. 25 cm.

1941 Macmillan & Co., Ltd.
    A map book of Australasia. 4 ed. By Alan
    Ferriday. London, Melbourne, 1969.
    52 p. 25 cm.

1942 Oxford University Press.
    The Australasian school atlas, physical, political,
    economic and historical. 4 ed. With Bartholomew.
    Melbourne, [1954].
    84 p. col. maps. 28 cm.

1943 Oxford University Press.
    The Australasian school atlas, physical, political,
    economic and historical. 4 ed. With Bartholomew.
    Melbourne, [1959].
    68 p. col. maps. 28 cm.

1944 Praeger, Frederick A.
    A descriptive atlas of the Pacific Islands. New
    Zealand, Australia, Polynesia, Melanesia, Micro-
    nesia, Philippines. By T. F. Kennedy. New York,
    [1968].
    64 p. 24 cm.

1945 Reed, A. H. & A. W.
    A descriptive atlas of the Pacific Islands. New
    Zealand, Australia, Polynesia, Melanesia, Micro-
    nesia, Philippines. By T. F. Kennedy. Wellington,
    1966.
    64 p. 24 cm.

1946 St. Martin's Press.
    A map book of Australasia. 3 ed. By A. Ferriday.

New York, 1966.
52 p.   25 cm.

1947 St. Martin's Press.
     A map book of Australasia.   4 ed.   By Alan
     Ferriday.   New York, 1969.
     52 p.   25 cm.

EUROPE

1948 American Map Co., Inc.
     Itinerary and diary atlas of Western Europe.   New
     York, 1955.
     7 p.   29 cm.

1949 Angus & Robertson.
     The German speaking countries of central Europe.
     By Richard H. Samuel and J. G. Hajdu.   Sydney,
     [1969].
     31 p.   col. maps.   25 cm.

1950 Automobile Club d'Italia.
     Atlante automobilistico d'Europa.   Roma, [1958].
     90 p.   col. maps.   27 cm.

1951 Automobile Club d'Italia.
     Atlante automobilistico d'Europa.   Roma, [1965].
     51 p.   col. maps.   26 cm.

1952 Auto-Motor-und Radfahrerbund Österreichs.
     Auto-Atlas Europa.   With Ravenstein.   Wien, 1966.
     80 p.   col. maps.   38 cm.

1953 Auto-Motor-und Radfahrerbund Österreichs.
     Auto-Atlas Europa.   With Ravenstein.   Wien, 1967.
     80 p.   col. maps.   38 cm.

1954 Bartholomew, John & Son, Ltd.
     Bartholomew road atlas Europe.   Edinburgh, [1969].
     40 p.   col. maps.   25 cm.

1955 Bartholomew, John & Son, Ltd.
     Bartholomew road atlas Europe.   Edinburgh, 1970.
     40 p.   col. maps.   25 cm.

1956 Bertelsmann, C.
     Atlas of Central Europe.   By W. Bormann.
     Gütersloh, [1963].
     172 p.   col. maps.   33 cm.

1957 Bertelsmann, C.
Autoatlas Bertelsmann. Deutschland-Europe.
Gütersloh, [1964].
388 p. col. maps. 27 cm.

1958 Bertelsmann, C.
Autoatlas Bertelsmann. Deutschland-Europe.
Gütersloh, 1965.
388 p. col. maps. 27 cm.

1959 Bertelsmann, C.
Autoatlas Bertelsmann. Deutschland-Europe.
Gütersloh, 1966.
388 p. col. maps. 27 cm.

1960 Blackie & Son, Ltd.
A paleogeographical atlas of the British Isles and
adjacent parts of Europe. By Leonard J. Wills.
London, 1951.
64 p. col. maps. 22 cm.

1961 Blackie & Son, Ltd.
A paleogeographical atlas of the British Isles and
adjacent parts of Europe. 4 ed. By Leonard J.
Wills. London, 1962.
64 p. col. maps. 22 cm.

1962 Blondel La Rougery.
Europe, routes, highways. Paris, [1952].
215 p. col. maps. 15 cm.

1963 BLV Verlagsgesellschaft.
Bildatlas der Kultur und Geschichte der slawischen
Welt. By P. Kovalewsky. München, [1964].
215 p. col. maps. 35 cm.

1964 Buchgemeinschaft Donauland.
Donauland Autoatlas. Wien, [1965].
1 vol. col. maps. 27 cm.

1965 Collins, William, Sons & Co., Ltd.
Collins road atlas, Europe. London, [1965].
232 p. col. maps. 25 cm.

1966 Continental Gummiwerke Kartographischer Verlag.
Continental atlas. 32 ed. Hannover, 1963.
757 p. col. maps. 26 cm.

1967 Continental Gummiwerke Kartographischer Verlag.
     <u>Continental atlas.</u> 35 ed. Hannover, 1964.
     644 p. col. maps. 26 cm.

1968 Continental Gummiwerke Kartographischer Verlag.
     <u>Continental atlas.</u> Hannover, 1966/67.
     531 p. col. maps. 26 cm.

1969 Continental Gummiwerke Kartographischer Verlag.
     <u>Continental atlas.</u> Hannover, 1968-69.
     531 p. col. maps. 26 cm.

1970 Continental Gummiwerke Kartographischer Verlag.
     <u>Continental atlas.</u> Deutschland, Europa. 34 ed.
     Hannover, [1966].
     531 p. col. maps. 26 cm.

1971 Continental Gummiwerke Kartographischer Verlag.
     <u>Continental atlas.</u> Deutschland, Europa. 35 ed.
     Hannover, 1968-69.
     531 p. col. maps. 26 cm.

1972 Denoyer-Geppert Co.
     <u>European history atlas; ancient, medieval, and</u>
     <u>modern European and world history.</u> 9 ed. By
     J. H. Breasted. Chicago, 1951.
     62 p. col. maps. 28 cm.

1973 Denoyer-Geppert Co.
     <u>European history atlas; ancient, medieval and</u>
     <u>modern European and world history.</u> 10 ed. By
     J. H. Breasted. Chicago, 1954.
     1 vol. col. maps. 28 cm.

1974 Denoyer-Geppert Co.
     <u>European history atlas; ancient, medieval and</u>
     <u>modern European and world history.</u> 11 ed. By
     J. H. Breasted. Chicago, 1964.
     1 vol. col. maps. 28 cm.

1975 Denoyer-Geppert Co.
     <u>European history atlas.</u> Student edition. Ancient,
     medieval and modern European and world history.
     1 ed. By J. H. Breasted. Chicago, [1951].
     62 p. col. maps. 28 cm.

1976 Dijkstra.
     <u>Ons werelddeel; atlas van Europa.</u> 37 ed. Zeist,

[1964].
20 p. col. maps. 31 cm.

1977 Dijkstra.
Ons werelddeel. Atlas van Europa. 38 ed. By
Wijbren Bakker and H. Rusch. Zeist, [1969].
23 p. col. maps. 31 cm.

1978 Éditions de l'École.
L'Europe et l'Asie Russe. [Atlas]. By François
Pinardel. Paris, [1957].
40 p. col. maps. 27 cm.

1979 Editions de Lyon.
Atlas de l'Europe occidentale. By Jean Chardonnet.
Lyon, [1963].
50 p. col. maps. 31 cm.

1980 Editions Meddens.
Atlas historique et culturel de l'Europe. By
Fernand Vercauteren. Bruxelles, [1962].
245 p. col. maps. 35 cm.

1981 Editions Sequoia.
Atlas de la grande armée. By J. C. Quennevat.
Paris, [1969].
304 p. col. maps. 27.5 cm.

1982 Elsevier.
Agro-Climatic atlas of Europe. By P. Thran and
S. Broekhuizen. Amsterdam, 1965.
in parts. col. maps. 44 cm.

1983 Elsevier.
Agro-ecological atlas of cereal growing in Europe.
New York, 1965—
1 vol. col. maps. 46 cm.

1984 Elsevier.
Atlas de la civilisation occidentale. By Frederik
van der Meer. Paris, 1952.
227 p. col. maps. 36 cm.

1985 Elsevier.
Atlas historique et culturel de l'Europe. By
Fernand Vercauteren. Paris, [1962].
245 p. col. maps. 35 cm.

1986 Elsevier.
      Atlas of the cereal growing areas in Europe.
      Amsterdam, London, New York, 1969.
      1 vol. col. maps. 46 cm.

1987 Elsevier.
      Atlas van de westerse beschaving. By Frederik van
      der Meer. Amsterdam, 1951.
      228 p. col. maps. 36 cm.

1988 Esso, A. G.
      Esso Europa atlas. Hamburg, 1965.
      204 p. col. maps. 27 cm.

1989 Esso, A. G.
      Europa atlas. Hamburg, 1967.
      96 p. col. maps. 30 cm.

1990 Europa im Automobile A. G.
      Reiseführer und atlas. Zürich, 1966.
      584 p. col. maps. 27 cm.

1991 European Communities. Press and Information Service.
      Die Europäische Gemeinschaft in Karten. Bruxelles,
      [1962].
      12 p. col. maps. 28 cm.

1992 European Communities. Press and Information Service.
      The European community in maps. Bruxelles,
      [1962].
      16 p. col. maps. 28 cm.

1993 European Communities. Press and Information Service.
      The European community in maps. Bruxelles,
      [1967].
      12 p. col. maps. 28 cm.

1994 European Road Guide, Inc.
      European motoring atlas, 1967-68. Larchmont,
      N. Y., 1967.
      23 p. col. maps. 28 cm.

1995 European Road Guide, Inc.
      Motoring atlas: Europe and Israel 1968/1969.
      Larchmont, N. Y., 1968.
      48 p. col. maps. 28 cm.

1996 European Road Guide, Inc.
     Motoring atlas of Europe and Israel.   1969-70 ed.
     Larchmont, N. Y., 1969.
     68 p. col. maps. 28 cm.

1997 Falk Verlag.
     Falk autoatlas Nr. 355. Von Kopenhagen bis
     Mailand. 19 ed. Hamburg, 1963.
     70 p. col. maps. 27 cm.

1998 Falk Verlag.
     Niederschlag und Temperatur in Europe. [Atlas].
     Hamburg, [1956].
     1 vol. col. maps. 48 cm.

1999 Fédération internationale de l'automobile.
     Atlas camping and caravaning. Roma, 1966.
     66 p. col. maps. 30 cm.

2000 Flemmings Verlag.
     2000 Jahre Europäische Geshichte.   Geschichtsatlas.
     By A. Koselleck. Hamburg, 1957.
     35 p. col. maps. 31 cm.

2001 Frankfurt. Institut für Angewandte Geodäsie.
     Atlas of European triangulation networks. By Max
     Kneisel. Frankfurt, 1965.
     28 p. col. maps. 69 cm.

2002 Generalstabens litografiska anstalt.
     Ekonomisk karta över Europa. Stockholm, 1953.
     33 p. col. maps. 35 cm.

2003 Generalstabens litografiska anstalt.
     Euroatlas fysisk. Stockholm, [1969].
     96 p. col. maps. 22 cm.

2004 Generalstabens litografiska anstalt.
     Vär värld Europa. Politisk-ekonomisk atlas.   By
     Leif Söderström and Gunnar Schalin. Stockholm,
     1968.
     72 p. col. maps. 22 cm.

2005 Geographia, Ltd.
     Geographia European motoring atlas and guide.
     London, [1969].
     1 vol. col. maps. 26 cm.

2006 Hallwag, A. G.
        Europa auto atlas.   Bern, [1967].
        124 p.   col.   maps.   26 cm.

2007 Hallwag, A. G.
        Europa touring; motoring guide of Europe.   Bern,
        1962.
        740 p.   col.   maps.   26 cm.

2008 Hallwag, A. G.
        Europa touring; motoring guide to Europe.   Bern,
        1966.
        788 p.   col.   maps.   26 cm.

2009 Hallwag, A. G.
        Europa touring; motoring guide to Europe.   Bern,
        1967.
        788 p.   col.   maps.   26 cm.

2010 Hallwag, A. G.
        Europa touring; motoring guide to Europe.   Bern,
        1968.
        788 p.   col.   maps.   26 cm.

2011 Hallwag, A. G.
        Europa touring; motoring guide to Europe.   Bern,
        1969.
        788 p.   col.   maps.   26 cm.

2012 Heinemann.
        An atlas of Russian and East European history.   By
        Arthur E. Adams and William O. McCagg.   London,
        1966.
        204 p.   21 cm.

2013 Heinemann.
        An atlas of Russian and East European history.   By
        Arthur E. Adams.   London, 1967.
        204 p.   21 cm.

2014 Indiana University.   Department of Geography.
        An atlas of the European Economic Council.
        Bloomington, Ind., 1964.
        45 p.   28 cm.

2015 International Telecommunication Union.
        Atlas des circuits internationaux d'Europe sous
        câble.   Geneva, 1953.

1 portf. col. maps. 31 cm.

2016 Istituto Geografico De Agostini.
      Atlante delle regioni d'Europa. Novara, 1962.
      80 p. col. maps. 29 cm.

2017 Istituto Geografico De Agostini.
      Atlante delle regioni d'Europa. Novara, 1965.
      80 p. col. maps. 29 cm.

2018 JRO Verlag.
      Der Grosse JRO Europa autoatlas. München, [1965].
      630 p. col. maps. 24.5 cm.

2019 JRO Verlag.
      JRO atlas für Kraftfahrer und alle Reisenden.
      München, [1950].
      344 p. col. maps. 25 cm.

2020 JRO Verlag.
      JRO autoatlas. Deutschland, Europäische Reise-
      länder. München, [1954].
      514 p. col. maps. 25 cm.

2021 JRO Verlag.
      JRO autoatlas. Deutschland, Europäische Reise-
      länder. München, [1955].
      515 p. col. maps. 25 cm.

2022 JRO Verlag.
      JRO autoatlas Österreich, Südost-deutschland,
      Oberitalien, Nordwest Jugoslawien, Ostschweiz.
      München, [1956].
      239 p. col. maps. 25 cm.

2023 JRO Verlag.
      JRO Strassen atlas. Deutschland. Europa.
      München, [1968].
      78 p. col. maps. 29.5 cm.

2024 Kanaat Yayinlari.
      Tarih atlasi. By Faik Reşit Unat. Istanbul, [1958].
      56 p. col. maps. 25 cm.

2025 Kanaat Yayinlari.
      Tarih atlasi. Genişletilmis basim. By Faik Reşit
      Unat. Istanbul, [1967].
      56 p. col. maps. 25 cm.

2026 Kartográfiai Vállalat.
     Európa autóatlasza.   Budapest, [1968].
     192 p.   col. maps.   26 cm.

2027 Katholiek Sociaal-Kerkelijk Instituut.
     Étude cartographique de la structure économique et
     démographique de l'Europe occidentale. 's-Graven-
     hage, [1959].
     10 p.   col. maps.   29 cm.

2028 König,   Hans, Verlag.
     Fina Europa atlas.   1 ed.   Frankfurt am Main,
     [1963].
     114 p.   col. maps.   25 cm.

2029 König,   Hans, Verlag.
     Reiseatlas Deutschland, Europa.   Enkheim, 1965.
     61 p.   col. maps.   29 cm.

2030 König,   Hans, Verlag.
     Reiseatlas.   Deutschland-Europa.   Frankfurt am
     Main, [1966].
     64 p.   col. maps.   29 cm.

2031 Kümmerly & Frey.
     Auto-Europa.   Bern, 1965.
     216 p.   col. maps.   26 cm.

2032 Kümmerly & Frey.
     Auto-Europa.   Bern, 1966.
     216 p.   col. maps.   26 cm.

2033 Kümmerly & Frey.
     Euroatlas; Strassen-und Reise atlas.   Bern, 1961.
     152 p.   col. maps.   30 cm.

2034 Kümmerly & Frey.
     Euroatlas; Strassen-und Reise atlas.   Bern, [1963].
     150 p.   col. maps.   30 cm.

2035 Kümmerly & Frey.
     Euroatlas; Strassen-und Reise atlas.   Bern, 1966.
     150 p.   col. maps.   30 cm.

2036 Kümmerly & Frey.
     Europa, Europe.   Strassenatlas.   Bern, 1962.
     218 p.   col. maps.   26 cm.

2037 Kümmerly & Frey.
       Europa, Europe. Strassenatlas. Bern, [1965].
       140 p. col. maps. 26 cm.

2038 Kümmerly & Frey.
       Europa, Europe. Strassenatlas. 4 ed. Bern, 1967.
       218 p. col. maps. 26 cm.

2039 Kümmerly & Frey.
       Europa. Strassenatlas. 19 ed. Bern, [1965].
       43 p. col. maps. 26 cm.

2040 Kümmerly & Frey.
       Europe, atlas routier. Bern, [1955].
       140 p. col. maps. 23 cm.

2041 Kümmerly & Frey.
       Europe, atlas routier. Bern, [1957].
       140 p. col. maps. 23 cm.

2042 Les Éditions de Lyon.
       Atlas de l'Europe occidentale. By Jean Chardonnet.
       Lyon, [1953].
       50 p. col. maps. 31 cm.

2043 Macmillan & Co., Ltd.
       A map book of Europe. 2 ed. By A. Ferriday.
       London, 1950.
       65 p. 25 cm.

2044 Macmillan & Co., Ltd.
       A map book of Europe. 3 ed. By A. Ferriday.
       London, 1959.
       65 p. 25 cm.

2045 Macmillan & Co., Ltd.
       A map book of Europe. 4 ed. By A. Ferriday.
       65 p. 25 cm.

2046 Macmillan & Co., Ltd.
       A map book of Europe. 5 ed. By A. Ferriday.
       London, 1963.
       65 p. 25 cm.

2047 Macmillan & Co., Ltd.
       A map book of Europe. By A. Ferriday. London,
       1966.
       65 p. 25 cm.

2048 Macmillan & Co., Ltd.
     A map book of Europe. 6 ed. By A. Ferriday.
     London, 1968.
     64 p. col. maps. 25 cm.

2049 Mairs Geographischer Verlag.
     Continental atlas. Deutschland, Europa. 36 ed.
     Stuttgart, 1969.
     555 p. col. maps. 27 cm.

2050 Mairs Geographischer Verlag.
     Der Grosse Shell Atlas. 1 ed. Stuttgart, [1960].
     419 p. col. maps. 27 cm.

2051 Mairs Geographischer Verlag.
     Der Grosse Shell Atlas. 8 ed. Stuttgart, 1963.
     335 p. col. maps. 26.5 cm.

2052 Mairs Geographischer Verlag.
     Der Grosse Shell Atlas. 9 ed. Stuttgart, 1964.
     335 p. col. maps. 26.5 cm.

2053 Mairs Geographischer Verlag.
     Der Grosse Shell Atlas. 11 ed. Stuttgart, 1965.
     460 p. col. maps. 26.5 cm.

2054 Mairs Geographischer Verlag.
     Der Grosse Shell Atlas. 12 ed. Stuttgart, 1966.
     460 p. col. maps. 26.5 cm.

2055 Mairs Geographischer Verlag.
     Der Grosse Shell Atlas. Stuttgart, 1969/70.
     460 p. col. maps. 26.5 cm.

2056 Mairs Geographischer Verlag.
     Der Grosse Shell Atlas. Deutschland und Europa.
     10 ed. Stuttgart, [1965].
     259 p. col. maps. 27 cm.

2057 Mairs Geographischer Verlag.
     Der Grosse Shell Atlas. Deutschland und Europa.
     11 ed. Stuttgart, [1966].
     283 p. col. maps. 27 cm.

2058 Mairs Geographischer Verlag.
     Der Grosse Shell Atlas. Deutschland und Europa.
     12 ed. Stuttgart, [1967].
     283 p. col. maps. 27 cm.

2059 Mairs Geographischer Verlag.
    Der Grosse Shell Atlas. Deutschland und Europa.
    13 ed. Stuttgart, [1968].
    283 p. col. maps. 27 cm.

2060 Mairs Geographischer Verlag.
    Der Grosse Shell Atlas. Deutschland und Europa.
    14 ed. Stuttgart, 1969.
    283 p. col. maps. 27 cm.

2061 Mairs Geographischer Verlag.
    Europa Shell Atlas. Stuttgart, 1964.
    178 p. col. maps. 27 cm.

2062 Mairs Geographischer Verlag.
    Mair Weltatlas. Europa und Welt. Stuttgart, [1959].
    160 p. col. maps. 24 cm.

2063 Mairs Geographischer Verlag.
    Shell Atlas. 20 ed. Stuttgart, [1957].
    272 p. col. maps. 27 cm.

2064 Mairs Geographischer Verlag.
    Shell Atlas. Stuttgart, [1961].
    1 vol. col. maps. 27 cm.

2065 Mairs Geographischer Verlag.
    Shell Autoatlas. 10 ed. Stuttgart, [1952].
    206 p. col. maps. 27 cm.

2066 Mairs Geographischer Verlag.
    Shell Autoatlas. 11 ed. Stuttgart, [1952].
    206 p. col. maps. 27 cm.

2067 Mairs Geographischer Verlag.
    Shell Autoatlas. 12 ed. Stuttgart, [1954].
    266 p. col. maps. 27 cm.

2068 Mairs Geographischer Verlag.
    Shell Autoatlas. 14 ed. Stuttgart, [1954].
    266 p. col. maps. 27 cm.

2069 Mairs Geographischer Verlag.
    Shell Autoatlas. 15 ed. Stuttgart, [1955].
    268 p. col. maps. 27 cm.

2070 Mairs Geographischer Verlag.
    Shell Autoatlas. Maps of Germany, maps of

European countries. Stuttgart, [1954].
266 p. col. maps. 27 cm.

2071 Mairs Geographischer Verlag.
Shell Autoatlas. Maps of Germany, maps of
European countries. Stuttgart, [1956].
268 p. col. maps. 27 cm.

2072 Murray, John.
Atlas of Central Europe. With C. Bertelsmann.
London, [1963].
65 p. col. maps. 33 cm.

2073 Newnes, George, Ltd.
Newnes' motorist's touring maps and gazetteer of
Western Europe. London, [1963].
51 p. col. maps. 29 cm.

2074 Nomos Verlagsgesellschaft.
Atlas sozialökonomischer Regionen Europas. With
Soziographisches Institut der Universität Frankfurt.
By L. Neundörfer. Baden-Baden, 1964 –
in parts. col. maps. 60 cm.

2075 Nuffield Organization.
Motoring atlas and touring guide to the Continent.
2 ed. By K. G. Cleveley. Oxford, [1964].
88 p. col. maps. 28 cm.

2076 Odhams Press, Ltd.
Odhams new road atlas of Great Britain, Ireland
and Western Europe. London, [1963].
239 p. col. maps. 24 cm.

2077 Oxford University Press.
Atlas of European history. By Edward Whiting Fox.
London, 1957.
64 p. col. maps. 26 cm.

2078 Oxford University Press.
Atlas of European history. By Edward Whiting Fox.
London, [1964].
64 p. col. maps. 26 cm.

2079 Oxford University Press.
Atlas of European History. By Edward Whiting Fox.
New York, 1968.
76 p. col. maps. 26 cm.

2080 Oxford University Press.
     Atlas of European History.   By E. W. Fox and H.
     S. Deighton. London, 1969.
     96 p. col. maps. 26 cm.

2081 Oxford University Press.
     Oxford regional economic atlas of the U.S.S.R. and
     Eastern Europe. Oxford, 1956.
     140 p. col. maps. 26 cm.

2082 Oxford University Press.
     Oxford regional economic atlas of the U.S.S.R. and
     Eastern Europe. Oxford, [1963].
     1 vol. col. maps. 26 cm.

2083 Plantyn.
     Atlas. Europa, staten van Europa, de wereld buiten
     Europa. 6 ed. By D. Praet. Antwerpen, [1966].
     36 p. 25.5 cm.

2084 Praeger, Frederick A.
     An atlas of European affairs.   By Norman J. G.
     Pounds. New York, 1964.
     142 p. 22 cm.

2085 Praeger, Frederick A.
     An atlas of Russian and East European history. By
     Arthur E. Adams, Ian M. Matley, William O.
     McCagg. New York, 1966.
     204 p. 21 cm.

2086 Rabén & Sjögren.
     Europa guide. With Royal Automobile Club, Sweden.
     Stockholm, [1964].
     448 p. col. maps. 25 cm.

2087 Rand McNally & Co.
     Europe Rand McNally & Co.   Chicago, 1963.
     31 p. col. maps. 35 cm.

2088 Ravenstein Geographische Verlagsanstalt.
     Autoatlas Benelux und Europa.   Frankfurt am Main,
     1964.
     36 p. col. maps. 29 cm.

2089 Ravenstein Geographische Verlagsanstalt.
     Autoatlas Benelux und Europa.   Frankfurt am Main,

[1965].
56 p.   col.   maps.   29 cm.

2090 Ravenstein Geographische Verlagsanstalt.
     Autoatlas Europa.   Frankfurt am Main, [1966].
     80 p.   col.   maps.   38 cm.

2091 Ravenstein Geographische Verlagsanstalt.
     Frisia Reise atlas.   Deutschland und Europa.
     Frankfurt, 1967.
     66 p.   col.   maps.   29 cm.

2092 Ravenstein Geographische Verlagsanstalt.
     Strassen; der aktuelle Auto-Atlas Deutschland und
     Europa.   Frankfurt am Main, [1966].
     1 vol.   col.   maps.   29 cm.

2093 Ravenstein Geographische Verlagsanstalt.
     Strassen, der aktuelle Auto-Atlas Deutschland   und
     Europa.   Frankfurt am Main, [1969].
     66 p.   col.   maps.   29 cm.

2094 Ravenstein Geographische Verlagsanstalt.
     Strassen Deutschland und Europa.   2 ed.   Frank-
     furt am Main, [1962].
     51 p.   col.   maps.   29 cm.

2095 Ravenstein Geographische Verlagsanstalt.
     Strassen Deutschland und Europa.   3 ed.   Frankfurt
     am Main, 1963.
     55 p.   col.   maps.   29 cm.

2096 Ravenstein Geographische Verlagsanstalt.
     Strassen Deutschland und Europa.   5 ed.   Frank-
     furt am Main, 1964.
     57 p.   col.   maps.   29 cm.

2097 Ravenstein Geographische Verlagsanstalt.
     Strassen Deutschland und Europa.   Frankfurt am
     Main, [1966].
     1 vol.   col.   maps.   29 cm.

2098 Royal Automobile Club.
     Camping and caravaning guide and atlas of Europe.
     3 ed.   London, 1966.
     66 p.   col.   maps.   30 cm.

2099 Royal Automobile Club.
      Camping and caravaning guide and atlas of Europe.
      4 ed. London, 1967.
      66 p. col. maps. 30 cm.

2100 Royal Automobile Club.
      Camping and caravaning guide and atlas of Europe.
      5 ed. London, 1968.
      66 p. col. maps. 30 cm.

2101 Royal Automobile Club.
      Camping and caravaning guide and atlas of Europe.
      6 ed. London, 1969.
      66 p. col. maps. 30 cm.

2102 Schweizer Reisekasse.
      Reiseatlas Schweiz und Ausland.   Bern, [1957].
      72 p. col. maps. 21 cm.

2103 Skrifola.
      Sesam bilatlas europa.   With Kümmerly & Frey.
      København, 1963.
      96 p. col. maps. 30 cm.

2104 Smulders' Doukkerijen, N.V.
      Zakatlas.   De werelddeln, de landen van Europa.
      's-Gravenhage, [1956].
      28 p. col. maps. 16 cm.

2105 Société européenne d'études et d'informations.
      Atlante dell'Europa occidentale.   By Jean Dollfus.
      Paris, [1961].
      46 p. col. maps. 34 cm.

2106 Société européenne d'études et d'informations.
      Atlas de l'Europe de l'Ouest.   By Jean Dollfus.
      Paris, 1961.
      46 p. col. maps. 34 cm.

2107 Société européenne d'études et d'informations.
      Atlas of Western Europe.   By Jean Dollfus.   Paris,
      46 p. col. maps. 34 cm.

2108 St. Martin's Press.
      A map book of Europe.   6 ed.   By A. Ferriday.
      New York, 1968.
      64 p. col. maps. 25 cm.

2109 Südwest-Verlag.
    Neuer Europa Auto Atlas.   München, [1964].
    246 p. col. maps. 24 cm.

2110 Tammi.
    Europaan autoilukartasto.   With Kümmerly & Frey.
    Helsinki, 1963.
    156 p. col. maps. 31 cm.

2111 Tammi.
    Euroopan matkaopas.   Helsinki, 1964.
    368 p. col. maps. 31 cm.

2112 Thieme, W. J.
    Atlas van Europa en de werelddelen, voor de lagere
    school. 45 ed. By G. Prop. Zutphen, 1955.
    48 p. col. maps. 26 cm.

2113 Thieme, W. J.
    Atlas van Europa en de werelddelen.   46 ed. By
    G. Prop. Zutphen, 1956.
    48 p. col. maps. 26 cm.

2114 Thieme, W. J.
    Atlas van Europa en de werelddelen.   47 ed. By
    G. Prop. Zutphen, 1957.
    48 p. col. maps. 26 cm.

2115 Thieme, W. J.
    Atlas van Europa en de werelddelen.   48 ed. By
    G. Prop. Zutphen, 1958.
    48 p. col. maps. 26 cm.

2116 Thieme, W. J.
    Atlas van Europa en de werelddelen.   49 ed. By
    G. Prop. Zutphen, 1959.
    48 p. col. maps. 26 cm.

2117 Thieme, W. J.
    Atlas van Europa en de werelddelen. 50 ed. By
    G. Prop. Zutphen, 1960.
    48 p. col. maps. 26 cm.

2118 Thieme, W. J.
    Atlas van Europa en de werelddelen. 51 ed. By
    G. Prop. Zutphen, 1961.
    48 p. col. maps. 26 cm.

2119 Thieme, W. J.
       Atlas van Europa en de werelddelen. 52 ed. By
       G. Prop. Zutphen, 1962.
       48 p. col. maps. 26 cm.

2120 Thieme, W. J.
       Atlas van Europa en de werelddelen. 53 ed. By
       G. Prop. Zutphen, 1963.
       48 p. col. maps. 26 cm.

2121 Thieme, W. J.
       Atlas van Europa en de werelddelen. 54 ed. By
       G. Prop. Zutphen, 1964.
       48 p. col. maps. 26 cm.

2122 Thieme, W. J.
       Atlas van Europa en de werelddelen. 55 ed. By
       G. Prop. Zutphen, 1965.
       48 p. col. maps. 26 cm.

2123 Thieme, W. J.
       Atlas van Europa en de werelddelen. 56 ed. By
       G. Prop. Zutphen, 1966.
       48 p. col. maps. 26 cm.

2124 Thieme, W. J.
       Atlas van Europa en de werelddelen. 57 ed. By
       G. Prop. Zutphen, 1967.
       1 vol. col. maps. 26 cm.

2125 Ullstein.
       Europa atlas. Berlin, [1955].
       78 p. col. maps. 30 cm.

2126 Ullstein.
       Unser Europa. Der Sammelatlas der Berliner
       Morgenspost. Berlin, [1954].
       48 p. col. maps. 30 cm.

2127 U. S. Army Map Service.
       Atlas of magnetic declination of Europe for 1944-5.
       Washington, D.C., [1951].
       86 p. col. maps. 82 cm.

2128 Velhagen & Klasing.
       Atlas östliches Mitteleuropa. Bielefeld, Berlin,
       Hannover, 1959.
       68 p. col. maps. 55 cm.

2129 Verlag Enzyklopädie.
Historisch-geographisches Kartenwerk. Wirtschafs-
historische Entwicklung. By Edgar Lehmann.
Leipzig, 1960.
81 p.   col. maps.   41 cm.

2130 Walker, Gerald E.
A short atlas of European economic history.
Berkeley, Calif., [1963].
1 vol.   28 cm.

2131 Walker, Gerald E.
A short atlas of European economic history.
Berkeley, Calif., 1964.
41 p.   28 cm.

2132 Wesmael-Charlier.
Cartographie de l'Europe.   By Jean Tilmont.
Namur, 1967.
32 p.   36 cm.

2133 Wjedza Powszechna.
Swiat w mapach i wykresach-Europa.   Krakow, 1963.
341 p.   24 cm.

NORTH AMERICA

2134 Abercrombie & Fitch.
The complete Abercrombie & Fitch vacation atlas
for all North America. New York, 1965.
142 p.   col. maps.   34 cm.

2135 Barnes & Noble, Inc.
An atlas of North American affairs. By D. K.
Adams and H. B. Rodgers. New York, 1969.
135 p.   22 cm.

2136 Diversified Map Corporation.
The complete Abercrombie & Fitch vacation atlas
for all North America. New York, 1965.
142 p.   col. maps.   34 cm.

2137 Diversified Map Corporation.
This week magazine's vacation planner and speedy
flipout road atlas ... to all North America. New
York, [1965].
142 p.   col. maps.   34 cm.

2138 Fondo de cultura económica.

Atlas del Nuevo Mundo. 1 ed.   By Jorge Millares
Hernández.   México, [1962].
96 p.   col. maps.   18 cm.

2139 Goushá, H. M. Co.
American highway atlas.   Chicago, 1962.
112 p.   col. maps.   43 cm.

2140 Goushá, H. M. Co.
North American vacation guide and road atlas.   San
Jose, Calif., 1967.
64 p.   col. maps.   28 cm.

2141 Goushá, H. M. Co.
Trip plan (atlas), Allstate Motor Club travel service.
Skokie, Ill., 1965.
1 vol.   col. maps.   29 cm.

2142 Hammond, Inc.
North American Bicycle Atlas.   Maplewood, N. J.,
1969.
128 p.   24 cm.

2143 Harper & Row.
Historical atlas of religion in America.   1 ed.   By
Edwin Scott Gaustad.   New York, [1962].
179 p.   col. maps.   31 cm.

2144 Macmillan & Co., Ltd.
A map book of North America.   4 ed.   By A.
Ferriday.   London, [1963].
69 p.   25 cm.

2145 Macmillan & Co., Ltd.
A map book of North America.   4 ed.   By A.
Ferriday. London, [1965].
69 p.   25 cm.

2146 Macmillan & Co., Ltd.
Carribbean atlas.   London, [1953].
16 p.   col. maps.   25 cm.

2147 Methuen.
An atlas of North American affairs.   By David Keith
Adams and H. B. Rodgers.   London, 1969.
135 p.   22 cm.

2148 Novoe Vremya.

Atlas novogo vremeni.   Moskva, 1965.
48 p.   27 cm.

2149 St. Martin's Press.
A map book of North America.   4 ed.   By A.
Ferriday.   New York, [1963].
69 p.   25 cm.

2150 St. Martin's Press.
A map book of North America.   4 ed.   By A.
Ferriday.   New York, [1965].
69 p.   25 cm.

2151 St. Martin's Press.
Caribbean atlas.   New York, [1953].
16 p.   col. maps.   25 cm.

2152 World Pub. Co.
World's road atlas and vacation guide of North
America for 1966-67.   Cleveland, 1966.
64 p.   col. maps.   28 cm.

2153 World Pub. Co.
World's road atlas and vacation guide of North
America for 1967-68.   Cleveland, 1967.
64 p.   col. maps.   28 cm.

2154 World Pub. Co.
World's road atlas and vacation guide of North
America for 1968-69.   Cleveland, 1968.
64 p.   col. maps.   28 cm.

SOUTH AMERICA

2155 Argentina.   Instituto Geográfico Militar.
Atlas Argentina y Americano.   By Roberto Manuel
Cayo.   Buenos Aires, [1966].
78 p.   col. maps.   32 cm.

2156 Cooper Square Publishers.
Historical atlas of Latin America.   Political,
geographic, economic, cultural.   By A. Curtis
Wilgus.   New York, 1967.
365 p.   24 cm.

2157 Ediciones Condarco.
Atlas histórico de America.   La Paz, 1968.
186 p.   col. maps.   26 cm.

2158 Editorial Campano.
  Campano atlas de América.   Buenos Aires, [1965].
  88 p.   col. maps.   31 cm.

2159 Elsevier.
  Atlas van Zuid-Amerika.   By W. J. van Balen.
  Amsterdam, 1957.
  230 p.   col. maps.   35 cm.

2160 Fondo de cultura económica.
  Atlas del Nuevo Mundo.   1 ed.   By Jorge Millares
  Hernández.   Mexico, [1962].
  96 p.   col. maps.   18 cm.

2161 Macmillan & Co., Ltd.
  A map book of Africa and South America.   1 ed.
  By A. Ferriday.   London, [1951].
  64 p.   col. maps.   25 cm.

2162 Macmillan & Co., Ltd.
  A map book of Africa and South America.   2 ed.
  By A. Ferriday.   London, 1954.
  64 p.   col. maps.   25 cm.

2163 Macmillan & Co., Ltd.
  A map book of Africa and South America.   2 ed.
  By A. Ferriday.   London, [1955].
  64 p.   col. maps.   25 cm.

2164 Macmillan & Co., Ltd.
  A map book of Africa and South America.   3 ed.
  By A. Ferriday.   London, 1958.
  64 p.   col. maps.   25 cm.

2165 Macmillan & Co., Ltd.
  A map book of Africa and South America.   4 ed.
  By A. Ferriday.   London, 1960.
  64 p.   col. maps.   25 cm.

2166 Macmillan & Co., Ltd.
  A map book of Africa and South America.   5 ed.
  By A. Ferriday.   London, 1962.
  64 p.   col. maps.   25 cm.

2167 Macmillan & Co., Ltd.
  A map book of Africa and South America.   6 ed.
  By A. Ferriday.   London, [1964].
  64 p.   col. maps.   25 cm.

2168 Macmillan & Co., Ltd.
     A map book of Africa and South America.   7 ed.
     By A. Ferriday.   London, 1965.
     64 p.   col. maps.   25 cm.

2169 Macmillan & Co., Ltd.
     A map book of Africa and South America.   8 ed.
     By Alan Ferriday.   London, 1967.
     65 p.   col. maps.   25 cm.

2170 Macmillan & Co., Ltd.
     A map book of South America.   1 ed.   By A.
     Ferriday.   London, 1966.
     56 p.   col. maps.   25 cm.

2171 Macmillan & Co., Ltd.
     A map book of South America.   By A. Ferriday.
     New York, 1967.
     56 p.   col. maps.   25 cm.

2172 Methuen.
     An atlas of Latin American affairs.   By Ronald M.
     Schneider.   London, 1966.
     136 p.   20.5 cm.

2173 Novoe Vremya.
     Atlas novogo vremeni.   Moskva, 1965.
     48 p.   27 cm.

2174 Praeger, Frederick A.
     An atlas of Latin American affairs.   By Ronald M.
     Schneider.   New York, 1965.
     136 p.   22 cm.

2175 St. Martin's Press.
     A map book of Africa and South America.   6 ed.
     By A. Ferriday.   New York, [1964].
     64 p.   col. maps.   25 cm.

2176 St. Martin's Press.
     A map book of Africa and South America.   7 ed.
     By A. Ferriday.   New York, 1965.
     64 p.   col. maps.   25 cm.

2177 St. Martin's Press.
     A map book of Africa and South America.   8 ed.
     By Alan Ferriday.   New York, 1967.
     65 p.   col. maps.   25 cm.

2178 U.S.S.R. Glavnoe upravlenie geodezii i kartografii.
Atlas Latinskoi Ameriki. Moskva, 1967.
54 p. col. maps. 32 cm.

2179 U.S.S.R. Glavnoe upravlenie geodezii i kartografii.
Atlas Latinskoi Ameriki. Moskva, 1968.
54 p. col. maps. 32 cm.

AFRICA

Angola

2180 Edições Spal.
Angola; e os seus 15 distritos (Atlas). Luanda,
[1966].
15 p. 27 cm.

Burundi

2181 Belgium. Académie royale des sciences d'Outre-Mer.
Atlas général du Congo et du Rwanda-Burundi.
Bruxelles, 1964.
16 p. col. maps. 37 cm.

2182 Belgium. Centre d'Information et de Documentation du
Congo Belge et du Ruanda-Urundi.
Cartes géographiques du Congo belge et du Ruanda-
Urundi. 2 ed. Bruxelles, 1953.
5 p. col. maps. 24 cm.

2183 Belgium. Centre d'Information et de Documentation du
Congo Belge et du Ruanda-Urundi.
Cartes géographiques du Congo belge et du Ruanda-
Urundi. 3 ed. Bruxelles, 1954.
6 p. col. maps. 24 cm.

2184 Editions R-de Rouck.
Atlas géographique et historique du Congo Belge et
des territoires sous mandat du Ruanda-Urundi.
4 ed. Bruxelles, [1951].
11 p. col. maps. 36 cm.

2185 Elsevier.
Atlas du Congo belge et du Ruanda-Urundi. By
Gaston Derkinderen. Bruxelles, 1955.
204 p. col. maps. 36 cm.

2186 Elsevier.
   Atlas van Belgisch Congo en Ruanda-Urundi.   By
   G. Derkinderen.   Amsterdam, [1955].
   196 p.   col. maps.   36 cm.

2187 L'Institut National Pour L'Étude Agronomique du Congo.
   Atlas des sols et de la vegetation du Congo, du
   Rwanda et du Burundi.   Bruxelles, 1966 —
   in parts.   col. maps.   46 cm.

2188 Visscher.
   Atlas du Ruanda-Urundi.   Bruxelles, [1951].
   21 p.   col. maps.   30 cm.

Cameroon

2189 Institut de recherches scientifiques du Cameroun.
   Atlas du Cameroun.   Paris, Yaoundé, [1956-59].
   7 p.   col. maps.   47 cm.

2190 Institut de recherches scientifiques du Cameroun.
   Atlas du Cameroun.   Yaoundé, 1960 —
   in parts.   col. maps.   46 cm.

2191 Nathan, Fernand.
   République fédérale du Cameroun.   Paris, 1967.
   16 p.   23 cm.

Congo

2192 Belgium.   Académie royale des sciences d'Outre-Mer.
   Atlas géneral du Congo.   Bruxelles, 1963 —
   in parts.   col. maps.   37 cm.

2193 Belgium.   Académie royale des sciences d'Outre-Mer.
   Atlas général du Congo et du Rwanda-Burundi.
   Bruxelles, 1964.
   16 p.   col. maps.   37 cm.

2194 Belgium.   Centre d'Information et de Documentation du
   Congo Belge et du Ruanda-Urundi.
   Cartes géographiques du Congo belge et du Ruanda-
   Urundi.   2 ed.   Bruxelles, 1953.
   5 p.   col. maps.   24 cm.

2195 Belgium.   Centre d'Information et de Documentation du
   Congo Belge et du Ruanda-Urundi.

Cartes géographiques du Congo belge et du Ruanda-
Urundi. 3 ed. Bruxelles, 1954.
6 p. col. maps. 24 cm.

2196 Editions R. de Rouck.
Atlas géographique et historique du Congo Belge et
des territoires sous mandat du Ruanda-Urundi.
4 ed. Bruxelles, [1951].
11 p. col. maps. 36 cm.

2197 Elsevier.
Atlas du Congo belge et du Ruanda-Urundi. By
Gaston Derkinderen. Bruxelles, 1955.
204 p. col. maps. 36 cm.

2198 Elsevier.
Atlas van Belgisch Congo en Ruanda-Urundi. By
G. Derkinderen. Amsterdam, [1955].
196 p. col. maps. 36 cm.

2199 L'Institut National Pour L'Étude Agronomique du Congo.
Atlas des sols et de la végétation du Congo, du
Rwanda et du Burundi. Bruxelles, 1954.
in parts. col. maps. 46 cm.

2200 Wesmael-Charlier.
Cartographie de la Belgique et du Congo. By Jean
Tilmont. Namur, 1967.
32 p. 36 cm.

Dahomey

2201 Nathan, Fernand.
Le Dahomey. By T. A. Djivo. Paris, 1967.
16 p. 23 cm.

Ethiopia

2202 Mariam, Mesfin Wolde.
A preliminary atlas of Ethiopia. Addis Ababa,
[1962].
34 p. col. maps. 28 cm.

Gabon

2203 Editions Alain.
Petit atlas du Gabon. By Francis Lafont. Paris,

[1958].
45 p. col. maps. 28 cm.

Ghana

2204 Gatrell, A. W. & Co., Ltd.
     Ghana junior atlas. By E. A. Boateng. London,
     New York, 1967.
     33 p. col. maps. 29 cm.

2205 Ghana. Census Office.
     1960 population census of Ghana; atlas of population
     characteristics. Accra, 1964.
     29 p. col. maps. 43 cm.

2206 Ghana. Survey Dept.
     Portfolio of Ghana maps. Accra, 1961.
     13 p. col. maps. 44 cm.

2207 Nelson, Thomas & Sons, Ltd.
     Ghana junior atlas. By E. A. Boateng. London,
     Edinburgh, New York, 1965.
     33 p. col. maps. 29 cm.

2208 Nelson, Thomas & Sons, Ltd.
     Ghana junior atlas. By E. A. Boateng. London,
     1966.
     33 p. col. maps. 29 cm.

2209 Nelson, Thomas & Sons, Ltd.
     Ghana junior atlas. By E. A. Boateng. London,
     1967.
     33 p. col. maps. 29 cm.

2210 Nelson, Thomas & Sons, Ltd.
     Ghana population atlas. By T. E. Hilton. Edin-
     burgh, 1960.
     40 p. col. maps. 40 cm.

Ivory Coast

2211 Société pour le développement de la Côte d'Ivoire.
     Atlas de la Côte d'Ivoire. Abidjan, 1965.
     11 p. 30 cm.

Kenya

2212 Collins, William, Sons & Co., Ltd.

The new Kenya primary atlas. Nairobi, [1968].
48 p. col. maps. 27 cm.

2213 Nelson, Thomas & Sons, Ltd.
     Nelson's school atlas for Kenya, Malawi, Tanzania,
     Uganda, Zambia. London, 1968.
     76 p. col. maps. 29 cm.

2214 Survey of Kenya.
     Atlas of Kenya; a comprehensive series of new and
     authentic maps. By R. J. Butler. Nairobi, 1959.
     44 p. col. maps. 46 cm.

2215 Survey of Kenya.
     Atlas of Kenya: a comprehensive series of new and
     authentic maps. Nairobi, 1962.
     55 p. col. maps. 46 cm.

2216 United Nations. Food and Agricultural Organization.
     East African livestock survey. Regional-Kenya,
     Tanzania, Uganda. Firenze, 1967.
     1 vol. col. maps. 58 cm.

Lesotho

2217 Macmillan & Co., Ltd.
     Basutoland atlas. London, [1960].
     16 p. col. maps. 28 cm.

Lybia

2218 Codex Verlag.
     Kulturatlas von Lybien. Gundholzen, [1970-].
     in 3 parts. col. maps. 43 cm.

Malagasy Republic

2219 Malagasy. Bureau pour le développement de la produc-
     tion agricole.
     Atlas de Madagascar. Tananarive, 1969.
     1 vol. 40 cm.

Malawi

2220 Collins, William, Sons & Co., Ltd.
     Atlas for Malawi. Limbe, [1968].
     36 p. col. maps. 27 cm.

2221 Map Studio Productions, pty., Ltd.
     BP Padkaarte. Road maps. Cape Town, [1963].
     22 p. col. maps. 28 cm.

2222 Nelson, Thomas & Sons, Ltd.
     Nelson's school atlas for Kenya, Malawi, Tanzania,
     Uganda, Zambia. London, 1968.
     76 p. col. maps. 29 cm.

2223 Rhodesia. Department of Trigonometrical and Topo-
     graphical Surveys.
     Federal atlas Rhodesia & Nyasaland. Salisbury,
     1960-
     in parts. col. maps. 76 cm.

Morocco

2224 Morocco. Comité national de Géographie.
     Atlas du Maroc. Rabat 1954-
     in parts. col. maps. 51 cm.

Mozambique

2225 Empresa Moderna.
     Atlas de Moçambique. Lourenço Marques, 1962.
     43 p. col. maps. 39 cm.

2226 Map Studio Productions, pty., Ltd.
     BP Padkaarte. Road maps. Cape Town, [1963].
     22 p. col. maps. 28 cm.

2227 Shell Moçambique, Ltd.
     Estradas de Moçambique. Laurenço Marques, [1968].
     12 p. col. maps. 23 cm.

Nigeria

2228 Collins, William, Sons & Co., Ltd.
     Pathfinder atlas for Nigeria. By A. L. Mabogunje.
     London, 1965.
     57 p. col. maps. 22.5 cm.

2229 Collins, William, Sons & Co., Ltd.
     Pathfinder atlas for Nigeria. By A. L. Mabogunje.
     London, 1967.
     57 p. col. maps. 22.5 cm.

2230 Nelson, Thomas & Sons, Ltd.
     Nigeria junior atlas. By E. E. Soladoye. London,
     Edinburgh, New York, 1965.
     33 p. col. maps. 28 cm.

2231 Nigeria. Federal Surveys.
     Atlas Nigeria. Lagos, [1964-].
     in parts. col. maps. 54 cm.

2232 Nigeria. Federal Surveys.
     Nigeria. Lagos, [1962].
     16 p. col. maps. 55 cm.

2233 Nigeria. Survey Dept.
     Nigeria. Lagos, [1959].
     22 p. col. maps. 54 cm.

Rhodesia

2234 Atlantik Refining Company of Africa.
     Union of South Africa, South-West Africa and
     Rhodesia road maps. Cape Town, [195-].
     24 p. col. maps. 29 cm.

2235 Collins, M. O. (pvt), Ltd.
     Rhodesia. [Atlas]. Its natural resources and
     economic development. Salisbury, 1965.
     52 p. col. maps. 33 cm.

2236 Collins, William Sons & Co., Ltd.
     New junior atlas for Rhodesia. Salisbury, 1967.
     48 p. col. maps. 27 cm.

2237 Map Studio Productions, pty., Ltd.
     BP Padkaarte. Road maps. Cape Town, [1963].
     22 p. col. maps. 28 cm.

2238 Rhodesia. Department of Trigonometrical and Topo-
     graphical Surveys.
     Federal atlas Rhodesia & Nyasaland. Salisbury,
     1960—
     in parts. col. maps. 76 cm.

Rwanda

2239 Belgium. Académie royale des sciences d'Outre-Mer.
     Atlas général du Congo et du Rwanda-Burundi.

Bruxelles, 1964.
16 p. col. maps. 37 cm.

2240 Belgium. Centre d'Information et de Documentation du
Congo Belge et du Ruanda-Urundi.
Cartes géographiques du Congo belge et du Ruanda-
Urundi. 2 ed. Bruxelles, 1953.
5 p. col. maps. 24 cm.

2241 Belgium. Centre d'Information et de Documentation du
Congo Belge et du Ruanda-Urundi.
Cartes géographiques du Congo belge et du Ruanda-
Urundi. 3 ed. Bruxelles, 1954.
6 p. col. maps. 24 cm.

2242 Editions R. de Rouck.
Atlas géographique et historique du Congo Belge et
des territoires sous mandat du Ruanda-Urundi.
4 ed. Bruxelles, [1951].
11 p. col. maps. 36 cm.

2243 Elsevier.
Atlas du Congo belge et du Ruanda-Urundi. By
Gaston Derkinderen. Bruxelles, 1955.
204 p. col. maps. 36 cm.

2244 Elsevier.
Atlas van Belgisch Congo en Ruanda-Urundi. By
G. Derkinderen. Amsterdam, [1955].
196 p. col. maps. 36 cm.

2245 L'Institut National Pour L'Étude Agronomique du Congo.
Atlas des sols et de la végétation du Congo, du
Rwanda et du Burundi. Bruxelles, 1966—
in parts. col. maps. 46 cm.

2246 Visscher.
Atlas du Ruanda-Urundi. Bruxelles, [1951].
21 p. col. maps. 30 cm.

Senegal

2247 Senegal. Ministère du plan et du développement.
[Atlas du Senegal]. Cartes pour servir à
l'aménagement du territoire. Dakar, 1965.
40 p. 38.5 cm.

Sierra Leone

2248 Collins, William, Sons & Co., Ltd.
      School atlas for Sierra Leone. By Milton Harvey.
      London, [1967].
      27 p. col. maps. 26.5 cm.

2249 Collins, William, Sons & Co., Ltd.
      School atlas for Sierra Leone. Glasgow, [1968].
      26 p. col. maps. 26.5 cm.

2250 Nelson, Thomas & Sons, Ltd.
      Sierra Leone atlas. By M. I. Cran. London,
      [1965].
      26 p. col. maps. 28 cm.

2251 Nelson, Thomas & Sons, Ltd.
      Sierra Leone atlas. By M. I. Cran. London,
      New York, [1966].
      26 p. col. maps. 28 cm.

2252 Sierra Leone. Survey and Lands Dept.
      Atlas of Sierra Leone. 1 ed. Freetown, 1953.
      16 p. col. maps. 39 cm.

2253 Sierra Leone. Surveys and Lands Division.
      Atlas of Sierra Leone. 2 ed. Freetown, 1966.
      16 p. col. maps. 39 cm.

2254 Stanford, Edward.
      Atlas of Sierra Leone. By Surveys and Lands
      Department Sierra Leone. London, 1953.
      16 p. col. maps. 39 cm.

2255 University of London Press.
      Sierra Leone in maps. By John I. Clarke.
      London, [1966].
      119 p. 29 cm.

2256 University of London Press.
      Sierra Leone in maps. 2 ed. By John I. Clarke.
      London, 1969.
      111 p. 29 cm.

South Africa

2257 Atlantik Refining Company of Africa.

Union of South Africa, South-West Africa and
Rhodesia road maps. Cape Town, [195-].
24 p. col. maps. 29 cm.

2258 Automobile Association of South Africa.
Road atlas and touring guide of Southern Africa.
2 ed. Johannesburg, [1963].
200 p. col. maps. 25 cm.

2259 B. P. Southern Africa Pty., Ltd.
Padkaarte. Road Maps. Union of South Africa,
South West Africa. Cape Town, [196-].
10 p. col. maps. 29 cm.

2260 Collins, William, Sons & Co., Ltd.
Die gestandaardiseerde Suid-Afrikaanse atlas. By
B. A. Workman and K. H. Huggins. Glasgow,
[1953].
49 p. col. maps. 28 cm.

2261 Collins, William, Sons & Co., Ltd.
The standardised South African atlas. By B. A.
Workman. London, 1952.
49 p. col. maps. 28 cm.

2262 Collins, William, Sons & Co., Ltd.
The standardised South African atlas. By B. A.
Workman and K. H. Huggins. Glasgow, [1953].
49 p. col. maps. 28 cm.

2263 Collins, William, Sons & Co., Ltd.
The standardised South African atlas. By K. H.
Huggins and B. A. Workman. Glasgow, [1961].
49 p. col. maps. 28 cm.

2264 Juta & Co., Ltd.
An historical atlas for South African schools. By
W. Dale and T. A. Rennard. Cape Town, Johannesburg, [195-].
47 p. col. maps. 18 cm.

2265 Longmans, Green.
The standardised South African atlas. By B. A.
Workman, K. H. Huggins and J. C. B. Redfearn.
London, 1952.
49 p. col. maps. 28 cm.

2266 Map Studio Productions, pty. , Ltd.
      BP Padkaarte. Road maps. Cape Town, [1963].
      22 p. col. maps. 28 cm.

2267 McDougall's Educational Co. , Ltd.
      School atlas. South African ed. Edinburgh, [1950].
      40 p. col. maps. 25 cm.

2268 Nationale boekhandel.
      Geskiedenis-atlas vir Suid-Afrika. 2 ed. By A. J.
      Böeseken. Kaapstad, [1953].
      92 p. 31 cm.

2269 Philip, George & Son, Ltd.
      College atlas for South Africa. By George Goodall.
      London, 1953.
      127 p. col. maps. 29 cm.

2270 Philip, George & Son, Ltd.
      College atlas for South Africa. By George Goodall.
      London, [1954].
      127 p. col. maps. 29 cm.

2271 Philip, George & Son, Ltd.
      Junior school atlas for South Africa. By George
      Goodall. London, Cape Town, 1951.
      41 p. col. maps. 24 cm.

2272 Philip, George & Son, Ltd.
      Juta se kollege atlas vir Suidelike Africa. By
      Harold Fullard and C. Potgieter. Kaapstad, 1959.
      167 p. col. maps. 29 cm.

2273 Philip, George & Son, Ltd.
      Juta se springbok groot-druk atlas vir Suidelike
      Afrika. 3 ed. By Harold Fullard and C. Potgieter.
      Kaapstad, [1960].
      79 p. col. maps. 29 cm.

2274 Philip, George & Son, Ltd.
      Juta's springbok large print atlas for Southern
      Africa. 2 ed. By Harold Fullard. Cape Town,
      [1957].
      79 p. col. maps. 29 cm.

2275 Philip, George & Son, Ltd.
      Large print atlas for southern Africa. 22 ed. By

George Goodall. London, 1955.
79 p. col. maps. 29 cm.

2276 Philip, George & Son, Ltd.
Large print atlas for southern Africa. 24 ed.
London, 1957.
79 p. col. maps. 29 cm.

2277 Philip, George & Son, Ltd.
Large print atlas for southern Africa. 34 ed. By
Harold Fullard. London, 1969.
65 p. col. maps. 28 cm.

2278 Philip, George & Son, Ltd.
Philip se kollege atlas vir Suidelike Africa. 2 ed.
By Harold Fullard and C. Potgieter. London, 1961.
167 p. col. maps. 29 cm.

2279 Philip, George & Son, Ltd.
Philip's College atlas for southern Africa. By
Harold Fullard. London, 1962.
1 vol. col. maps. 29 cm.

2280 Philip, George & Son, Ltd.
Philip's college atlas for southern Africa. By
Harold Fullard. London, [1963].
1 vol. col. maps. 29 cm.

2281 Philip, George & Son, Ltd.
Philip's college atlas for southern Africa. By
Harold Fullard. London, 1967.
1 vol. col. maps. 29 cm.

2282 Philip, George & Son, Ltd.
Philip's junior school atlas for southern Africa. By
Harold Fullard. London, 1968.
30 p. col. maps. 23 cm.

2283 Philip, George & Son, Ltd.
Philip's Venture atlas for southern Africa. London,
[1966].
1 vol. col. maps. 28.5 cm.

2284 Philip, George & Son, Ltd.
Student's atlas for South Africa. By George
Goodall. London, [1953].
94 p. col. maps. 29 cm.

2285 Philip, George & Son, Ltd.
      Van Schaik's large print atlas for South Africa.
      20 ed. By George Goodall. Pretoria, 1952.
      71 p. col. maps. 29 cm.

2286 Shell Company of South Africa, Ltd.
      Shell road map of southern Africa. Cape Town, 1953.
      48 p. col. maps. 28 cm.

2287 South Africa. Department of Planning.
      Ontwikkelingsatlas. Pretoria, 1966 —
      1 vol. col. maps. 57 cm.

2288 South Africa. National Council for Social Research.
      Atlas of the Union of South Africa. By A. M.
      Talbot and W. J. Talbot. Pretoria, 1960.
      177 p. col. maps. 55 cm.

2289 Timmins, H. B.
      Large print atlas for South Africa. 18 ed. By
      George Goodall. With Philip. Cape Town, 1950.
      71 p. col. maps. 29 cm.

2290 Tourist Publications.
      South Africa in maps and a guide to the caravan
      parks. By Denis Conolly. Cape Town, 1966.
      51 p. 25 cm.

2291 Van Schaik's Bookstore.
      Van Schaik's large print atlas for South Africa.
      20 ed. By George Goodall. With Philip. Pretoria,
      1952.
      71 p. col. maps. 29 cm.

Tanzania

2292 East African institute of social research.
      Tribal maps of East Africa and Zanzibar. By
      E. J. Goldthorpe and F. B. Wilson. Kampala,
      Uganda, 1960.
      14 p. col. maps. 25 cm.

2293 Nelson, Thomas & Sons, Ltd.
      Nelson's school atlas for Kenya, Malawi, Tanzania,
      Uganda, Zambia. London, 1968.
      76 p. col. maps. 29 cm.

2294 Tanganyika. Department of Lands and Surveys.
     Atlas of Tanganyika. 3 ed. Dar Es Salaam, 1956.
     29 p. col. maps. 60 cm.

2295 Tanzania. Ministry of Lands, Housing & Urban De-
     velopment. Survey and Mapping Division.
     Atlas of Tanzania. 4 ed. Dar Es Salaam, 1969.
     1 vol. col. maps. 60 cm.

2296 Tanzania. Ministry of Lands, Settlement and Water
     Development.
     Atlas of Tanzania. Dar Es Salaam, 1967.
     58 p. col. maps. 52 cm.

2297 United Nations. Food and Agricultural Organization.
     East African Livestock Survey. Regional-Kenya,
     Tanzania, Uganda. Firenze, 1967.
     1 vol. col. maps. 58 cm.

Togo

2298 Nathan, Fernand.
     Le Togo. Paris, [1968].
     16 p. 23 cm.

Uganda

2299 Macmillan & Co. , Ltd.
     World atlas for Uganda schools. By J. T. Gleave.
     London, 1960.
     32 p. col. maps. 28 cm.

2300 Nelson, Thomas & Sons, Ltd.
     Nelson's school atlas for Kenya, Malawi, Tanzania,
     Uganda, Zambia. London, 1968.
     76 p. col. maps. 29 cm.

2301 Nelson, Thomas & Sons, Ltd.
     Uganda junior atlas. By Yunia Mugahya. London,
     New York, [1966].
     47 p. col. maps. 28 cm.

2302 Oxford University Press.
     Land Systems of Uganda. [Atlas]. Oxford, 1969.
     129 p. col. maps. 50 cm.

2303 Uganda. Department of Lands and Surveys.
     Atlas of Uganda. Kampala, 1962.

        83 p.   col. maps.   49 cm.

2304 Uganda.   Department of Lands and Surveys.
     Atlas of Uganda.   2 ed.   Entebbe, 1967.
     81 p.   col. maps.   49 cm.

2305 United Nations.   Food and Agricultural Organization.
     East African Livestock Survey.   Regional-Kenya,
     Tanzania, Uganda.   Firenze, 1967.
     1 vol.   col. maps.   58 cm.

U. A. R. -Egypt

2306 Codex Verlag.
     Kulturatlas von Ägypten.   Gundholzen, [1970].
     in 10 parts.   col. maps.   43 cm.

2307 Codex Verlag.
     Kulturatlas von Syrien.   Gundholzen, [1970].
     in 4 parts.   col. maps.   43 cm.

2308 Elsevier.
     Atlas van Egypte.   By A. Klasens.   Amsterdam, [1956].
     220 p.   col. maps.   36 cm.

2309 Institut français d'archéologie orientale.
     Atlas of Christian sites in Egypt.   By Otto
     Meinardus.   Cairo, 1962.
     13 p.   28 cm.

Zambia

2310 Map Studio Productions, pty., Ltd.
     BP Padkaarte.   Road maps.   Cape Town, [1963].
     22 p.   col. maps.   28 cm.

2311 Nelson, Thomas & Sons, Ltd.
     Nelson's school atlas for Kenya, Malawi, Tanzania,
     Uganda, Zambia.   London, 1968.
     76 p.   col. maps.   29 cm.

2312 Northern Rhodesia Survey Dept.
     Northern Rhodesia.   Lusaka, 1962.
     17 p.   col. maps.   72 cm.

2313 Zambia.   Ministry of Lands and Mines.
     Atlas of Zambia.   Lusaka, 1966—
     in parts.   col. maps.   90 cm.

ASIA

Afghanistan

2314 Wenschow.
Atlas for secondary schools in Afghanistan.
München, [1955].
33 p. col. maps. 34 cm.

Burma

2315 Oxford University Press.
The Oxford school atlas for India, Pakistan, Burma,
and Ceylon. 20 ed. Bombay, [1958].
63 p. col. maps. 28 cm.

Cambodia

2316 Vietnam. Nha g'ám dôc khí-tu'o'ng
Gian-dồ khi-hâu; cao dồ mu'a trung-bính tai
Vietnam, Ailao và Cambodge. Saigon, 1958.
13 p. col. maps. 33 cm.

Ceylon

2317 Oxford University Press.
Oxford economic atlas of India and Ceylon.
London, 1953.
97 p. col. maps. 25.5 cm.

2318 Oxford University Press.
The Oxford school atlas for India, Pakistan, Burma,
and Ceylon. 20 ed. Bombay, [1958].
63 p. col. maps. 28 cm.

China

2319 Aldine Pub. Co.
An historical atlas of China. By Albert Herrmann
and Norton Ginsburg. With Djambatan. Chicago,
[1966].
88 p. col. maps. 30 cm.

2320 China. Academy of Sciences.
        [Paleogeographic maps of China]. In Chinese.
        Peking, 1955.
        21 p. col. maps. 37 cm.

2321 China. Geographical Institute.
        Chung-Hua Jen-Min Kung-Ho-Kou Fen-Sheng Ti-T'u.
        By Ching-Yu Chin. Shanghai, 1950.
        103 p. col. maps. 35 cm.

2322 China. National War College.
        Atlas of the Republic of China. By Chang Chi-Yun.
        Taipei, 1960-63.
        in 5 vol. col. maps. 43 cm.

2323 Chinese Map Publ.
        [Atlas of the People's Republic of China]. In
        Chinese. Peking, 1957.
        152 p. col. maps. 30 cm.

2324 Denoyer-Geppert Co.
        China in maps. By Harold Fullard. Chicago, 1968.
        25 p. col. maps. 28 cm.

2325 Djambatan.
        An historical atlas of China. By Albert Herrmann.
        Amsterdam, 1966.
        88 p. col. maps. 30 cm.

2326 Edinburgh University Press.
        An historical atlas of China. By Albert Herrmann.
        Edinburgh, [1966].
        88 p. col. maps. 30 cm.

2327 Hsin kuang yü ti hsüeh she.
        Chung-kuo ti li chiao k'o t'u. 2 ed. [Textbook
        atlas of China]. Hong Kong, 1955.
        134 p. col. maps. 27 cm.

2328 Hsin kuang yü ti hsüeh she.
        Tsui hsin Chung-kuo fên shêng t'u. [New Pro-
        vincial atlas of China]. Topographic ed. Hong
        Kong, 1956.
        31 p. col. maps. 19 cm.

2329 Hsin ya shu tien.
        Chung-kuo li shih ti t'u. [Historical atlas of China].

By Shu-shih Wang. Shanghai, 1953.
6 p. col. maps. 40 cm.

2330 Kuang hua yü ti hsüeh shê.
Chung-hua jên min kung ho kuo hsin ti t'u. [New
atlas of the People's Republic of China]. Peking,
1950.
58 p. col. maps. 27 cm.

2331 Kuang hua yü ti hsüeh shê.
Chung-hua jên min kung ho kuo hsin ti t'u. [New
atlas of the People's Republic of China]. Shanghai,
1951.
58 p. col. maps. 27 cm.

2332 Kuang hua yü ti hsüeh shê.
Hsin Chung-kuo fên shêng ti t'u; hsiao hsüeh chi
ch'u chung shih yung. [New Provincial atlas of
China]. Peking, 1950.
36 p. col. maps. 21 cm.

2333 Liang, Ch'i-Shan.
Chung-kuo ti li hsin t'u chi; tzu jan jên wên fen lei
t'u chieh. [New geographical atlas of China].
Hong Kong, 1956.
36 p. col. maps. 27 cm.

2334 Philip, George & Son, Ltd.
China in maps. By Harold Fullard. London, 1968.
25 p. col. maps. 28 cm.

2335 Sha, Hsüeh-chün.
Chung-kuo ti li t'u chi. Chung têng hsüeh hsiao
shih yung. [Geographical atlas of China]. Taipei,
[1953].
64 p. col. maps. 39 cm.

2336 Shih chieh ch'u pan shê.
Chung-kuo fên shêng t'u; chung hsiao hsüeh shih
yung. [New Provincial atlas of China]. Hong Kong,
1957.
32 p. col. maps. 19 cm.

2337 Shih chieh yü ti hsüeh shê.
Hsin Chung-kuo fên shêng t'u. [New pocket provincial atlas of China]. 1 ed. Shanghai, 1953.
30 p. col. maps. 15 cm.

2338 Shih chieh yü ti hsüeh shê.
     Hsin Chung-kuo fên shêng t'u. [New pocket pro-
     vincial atlas of China]. 7 ed. Shanghai, 1953.
     30 p. col. maps. 15 cm.

2339 Shih chieh yü ti hsüeh shê.
     Hsin Chung-kuo fên shêng t'u. [New pocket pro-
     vincial atlas of China]. 21 ed. Shanghai, 1953.
     30 p. col. maps. 15 cm.

2340 Ta chung shu chü.
     Tsui hsin Chung-kuo fên shêng ti t'u. [New pro-
     vincial atlas of China]. Hong Kong, 1955.
     67 p. col. maps. 27 cm.

2341 Ta chung shu chü.
     Tsui hsin Chung-kuo fên shêng ti t'u. [New pro-
     vincial atlas of China]. Hong Kong, 1958.
     66 p. col. maps. 27 cm.

2342 Ta chung shu chü.
     Tsui hsiu Chung-kuo fên shêng ti t'u. [New pro-
     vincial atlas of China]. Topographic ed. Hong
     Kong, 1958.
     66 p. col. maps. 20 cm.

2343 Ta chung shu chü.
     Tsui hsiu Chung-kuo fên shêng ti t'u. [New pro-
     vincial atlas of China]. Hong Kong, [1959].
     129 p. col. maps. 27 cm.

2344 Ta chung shu chü.
     Tsui hsin Chung-kuo ti li chiao hsüeh t'u ts'ê.
     Ch'u chung shih yung. [New atlas of China. For
     Junior High School]. Hong Kong, 1957.
     40 p. col. maps. 21 cm.

2345 Ta chung shu chü.
     Tsui hsin Chung-kuo ti t'u ts'ê. Hsiao hsüeh shih
     yung. [New atlas of China. For Elementary School
     use]. Hong Kong, 1957.
     18 p. col. maps. 21 cm.

2346 Ta chung ti hsüeh shê.
     Hsin Chung-kuo fên shêng t'u; hsiang chu wu ch'an
     fên pu. Ch'u chung shih yung. [New provincial
     atlas of China]. 1 ed. Shanghai, 1953.
     70 p. 20 cm.

2347 Ta chung ti hsüeh shê.
Hsin Chung-kuo fên shêng t'u; hsiang chu wu ch'an
fen pu. Ch'u chung shih yung. [New provincial
atlas of China]. 3 ed. Shanghai, 1953.
70 p. 20 cm.

2348 T'ai-wan ta hsüeh.
Chien ming Chung-kuo yen ko ti t'u. [Simplified
historical atlas of China]. Taipei, [1952].
27 p. 26 cm.

2349 Ta lu yü ti shê.
Hsin Chung-kuo ti t'u; kao hsiao ch'u chung shih
yung. [New atlas of China]. By Yung-ju Chang.
Shanghai, 1950.
32 p. col. maps. 17 cm.

2350 Ti t'u ch'u pan shê.
Chung-hua jên min kung ho kuo fên shêng ching t'u.
[Detailed provincial atlas of the People's Republic
of China]. Popular ed. Shanghai, 1955.
67 p. col. maps. 37 cm.

2351 Ti t'u ch'u pan shê.
Chung-hua jên min kung ho kuo ti t'u chi. [Atlas
of the People's Republic of China]. Shanghai, 1957.
152 p. col. maps. 27 cm.

2352 Ti t'u ch'u pan shê.
Chung-kuo fên shêng ti t'u. [Provincial atlas of
China]. Shanghai, [195-].
33 p. col. maps. 18 cm.

2353 Ti t'u ch'u pan shê.
Chung-kuo fên shêng ti t'u. [Provincial atlas of
China]. De luxe ed. Shanghai, [195-].
33 p. col. maps. 18 cm.

2354 Ti t'u ch'u pan shê.
Chung-kuo fên shêng ti t'u. [Provincial atlas of
China]. Pocket ed. Shanghai, [1953].
33 p. col. maps. 15 cm.

2355 Ti t'u ch'u pan shê.
Chung-kuo fên shêng ti t'u. [Provincial atlas of
China]. Deluxe ed. Shanghai, [1957].
33 p. col. maps. 18 cm.

2356 Ti t'u ch'u pan shê.
     Chung-kuo ti li chiao hsüeh t'u; ch'u chung shih
     yung. [Textbook atlas of China]. Shanghai, 1953.
     48 p. col. maps. 31 cm.

2357 U.S. Central Intelligence Agency.
     China; provisional atlas of Communist administrative
     units. Washington, D.C., 1959.
     29 p. col. maps. 60 cm.

2358 U.S. Central Intelligence Agency.
     Communist China administrative atlas. Washington,
     D.C., 1969.
     27 p. col. maps. 60 cm.

2359 U.S. Central Intelligence Agency.
     Communist China map folio [Atlas]. Washington,
     D.C., 1967.
     20 p. col. maps. 54 cm.

2360 Ya kuang yü ti hsüeh shê.
     Chung-hua jên min kung ho kuo fên shêng ching t'u.
     [Detailed provincial atlas of the People's Republic of
     China]. Popular ed. By Ch'ing-Yü Chin.
     Shanghai, 1951.
     126 p. col. maps. 18 cm.

2361 Ya kuang yü ti hsüeh shê.
     Chung-hua jên min kung ho kuo fên shêng ching t'u.
     [Detailed provincial atlas of the People's Republic
     of China]. 2 ed. Shanghai, 1952.
     1 vol. col. maps. 18 cm.

2362 Ya kuang yü ti hsüeh shê.
     Chung-hua jên min kung ho kuo fên shêng ching t'u.
     [Detailed provincial atlas of the People's Republic
     of China]. Popular pocket ed. Shanghai, 1952.
     33 p. col. maps. 15 cm.

2363 Ya kuang yü ti hsüeh shê.
     Chung-hua jên min kung ho kuo fên shêng ching t'u.
     [Detailed provincial atlas of the People's Republic
     of China]. Deluxe ed. Shanghai, 1953.
     134 p. col. maps. 18 cm.

2364 Ya kuang yü ti hsüeh shê.
     Chung-hua jên min kung ho kuo fên shêng ching t'u.

[Detailed provincial atlas of the People's Republic of China]. Popular ed. Shanghai, 1953.
132 p. col. maps. 18 cm.

2365 Ya kuang yü ti hsüeh shê.
Chung-hua jên min kung ho kuo fên shêng ti t'u.
[Provincial atlas of the People's Republic of China].
Rev. popular ed. Shanghai, 1953.
175 p. col. maps. 27 cm.

2366 Ya kuang yü ti hsüeh shê.
Chung-hua jên min kung ho kuo fên shêng ti t'u.
4 ed. [Provincial atlas of the People's Republic of China]. By Ch-ing'yü Chin. Shanghai, 1951.
162 p. col. maps. 26 cm.

2367 Ya kuang yü ti hsüeh shê.
Chung-hua jên min kung ho kuo fên shêng ti t'u.
[Provincial atlas of the People's Republic of China].
6 ed. Shanghai, 1952.
1 vol. col. maps. 27 cm.

2368 Ya kuang yü ti hsüeh shê.
Hsiu chên Chung-hua jên min kung ho kuo fên shêng ching t'u. [Detailed pocket atlas of the People's Republic of China]. By Ch'ing Yü Chin. Shanghai, 1950.
31 p. col. maps. 15 cm.

2369 Ya kuang yü ti hsüeh shê.
Hsiu chên Chung-hua jên min kung ho kuo fên shêng ching t'u. [Detailed pocket atlas of the People's Republic of China]. Popular ed. By Ch'ing-yü Chin. Shanghai, 1951.
31 p. col. maps. 15 cm.

Hong Kong

2370 Collins, William, Sons & Co., Ltd.
A new secondary school atlas for Hong Kong. 2 ed.
Glasgow, 1967.
87 p. col. maps. 29 cm.

2371 Hong Kong. Govt. Printer.
Road maps of Hong Kong. Hong Kong, 1953.
1 vol. 29 cm.

2372 Hong Kong University Press.
     The development of Hong Kong and Kowloon as told
     in maps. 1 ed. By T. R. Tregear and L. Berry.
     Hong Kong, 1959.
     31 p. col. maps. 28 cm.

India

2373 India. Directorate General of Health Services.
     Health atlas of India. Delhi, [1953].
     54 p. 36 cm.

2374 India. Directorate of Economics and Statistics.
     Indian agricultural atlas. [Delhi], 1952.
     55 p. col. maps. 30 cm.

2375 India. Directorate of Economics and Statistics.
     Indian agricultural atlas. 2 ed. [New Delhi], 1958.
     59 p. col. maps. 31 cm.

2376 India. Information and broadcasting ministry.
     India in maps. Calcutta, [1950].
     81 p. 32 cm.

2377 India. Ministry of Education and Scientific Research.
     National atlas of India. By S. P. Chatterjee.
     Calcutta, 1957—
     in parts. col. maps. 78 cm.

2378 India. National Atlas Organization.
     National atlas of India. [Selected Maps]. By S. P.
     Chatterjee. Calcutta, 1968.
     16 p. col. maps. 55 cm.

2379 India. Survey of India.
     School atlas. Dehra Dūn, 1961.
     62 p. col. maps. 31 cm.

2380 India. Survey of India.
     School atlas. Dehra Dūn, 1962.
     62 p. col. maps. 31 cm.

2381 India. Survey of India.
     School atlas. Dehra Dūn, 1963.
     62 p. col. maps. 31 cm.

2382 India. Survey of India.

School atlas. Dehra Dūn, 1964.
62 p. col. maps. 31 cm.

2383 Indian Book Depot & Map House.
Coloured states atlas of India. With useful notes.
By Biba Singh Kaushal. Delhi, 1958.
34 p. col. maps. 25 cm.

2384 Indian Book Depot & Map House.
The new rashtriya atlas, geographical and historical.
By Biba Singh Kaushal. Delhi, [1951].
120 p. col. maps. 28 cm.

2385 Indian Central Cotton Committee.
Cotton atlas of India. Bombay, 1957.
100 p. 34 cm.

2386 Indian Central Oilseeds Committee.
The Indian oilseed atlas. Hyderabad, 1958.
118 p. 31 cm.

2387 Oxford University Press.
An historical atlas of the Indian peninsula. Madras,
New York, [1953].
141 p. col. maps. 25 cm.

2388 Oxford University Press.
An historical atlas of the Indian peninsula. 2 ed.
Madras, New York, 1959.
141 p. col. maps. 25 cm.

2389 Oxford University Press.
Oxford economic atlas of India and Ceylon. London,
1953.
97 p. col. maps. 25.5 cm.

2390 Oxford University Press.
The Oxford school atlas for India, Pakistan, Burma,
& Ceylon. 20 ed. Bombay, [1958].
63 p. col. maps. 28 cm.

2391 Verlag Enzyklopädie.
Indien. Entwicklung seiner Wirtschaft und Kultur.
Historisch-geographisches Kartenwerk. Leipzig,
1958.
1 vol. col. maps. 42.5 cm.

Indonesia

2392 Bachtiar, A.
Atlas Tanah air kita dan dunia lurnja untuk sekolah
rakjat. Djakarta, 1953.
43 p.   col.   maps.   29 cm.

2393 Djambatan.
Atlas Indonesia dan dunia untuk sekolah rakjat.   By
Djamaludin Adinegoro.   Djakarta, 1953.
48 p.   col.   maps.   30 cm.

2394 Djambatan.
Atlas Indonesia dan dunia untuk sekolah rakjat.   By
Djamaludin Adinegoro.   Djakarta, [1955].
1 vol.   col.   maps.   30 cm.

2395 Djambatan.
Atlas sedjarah.   By Muhammad Yamin.   Amsterdam, 1956.
88 p.   col.   maps.   29 cm.

2396 Djambatan.
Atlas tanah air untuk sekolah rakjat.   4 ed.
Djakarta, 1953.
24 p.   col.   maps.   29 cm.

2397 Djambatan.
Atlas untuk sekolah landjutan.   By Adam Bachtiar.
Djakarta, 1957.
56 p.   col.   maps.   35 cm.

2398 Ganaco, N. V.
Atlas nasional seluruh dunia untuk sekolah landjutan.
By J. E. Romein.   Djakarta, 1960.
72 p.   col.   maps.   39 cm.

2399 Ganaco, N. V.
Atlas teruna untuk sekolah rakjat.   Bandung, 1956–
1 vol.   col.   maps.   34 cm.

2400 Ganaco, N. V.
Atlas teruna untuk sekolah rakjat.   Bandung, 1958–
in parts.   col.   maps.   34 cm.

2401 Ichtiar.
Atlas Indonesia untuk sekolah rakjat kelas IV-V-VI.

By C. S. Soekarno. Djakarta, 1958.
1 vol. col. maps. 30 cm.

2402 Indonesia. Army Topographical Directorate.
Atlas of Indonesian Resources. Djakarta, 1963.
1 vol. col. maps. 112 cm.

2403 Indonesia. Badan Atlas Nacional.
Atlas sumber2 kemakmuran Indonesia. [Atlas of
Indonesian resources]. Djakarta, 1965 –
in parts. col. maps. 112 cm.

2404 Noordhoff-Kolff, N. V.
Atlas Indonesia dan dunia sekolah rakjat. Djakarta,
1953.
1 vol. col. maps. 28 cm.

2405 Noordhoff-Kolff, N. V.
Atlas sekolah rakjat. Djakarta, 1958.
24 p. col. maps. 28 cm.

2406 Noordhoff-Kolff, N. V.
Atlas seluruh dunia. By R. Bos and K. Zeeman.
Djakarta, 1957.
42 p. col. maps. 31 cm.

2407 Noordhoff, P.
Atlas seluruh dunia untuk sekolah landjutan. By
R. Bos. Djakarta, 1954.
42 p. col. maps. 31 cm.

2408 Noordhoff, P.
Atlas selurah dunia untuk sekolah landjutan.
Djakarta, 1955.
49 p. col. maps. 31 cm.

2409 Pemusatan.
Kepulauan di seluruh Indonesia. Bandung, [1952].
32 p. col. maps. 19 cm.

2410 Pemusatan.
Kepulauan di seluruh Indonesia. Bandung, 1955.
18 p. col. maps. 19 cm.

2411 Pradnja-Paramita.
Atlas Indonesia untuk sekolah rakjat. Djakarta, 1961.
16 p. col. maps. 29 cm.

2412 Thieme, W. J.
Atlas van Nederland, de West en Indonesië, voor de
lagere school. 53 ed. By G. Prop. Zutphen, 1951.
42 p. col. maps. 26 cm.

2413 Thieme, W. J.
Atlas van Nederland, de West en Indonesië. By G.
Prop. Zutphen, 1953.
42 p. col. maps. 26 cm.

2414 Thieme, W. J.
Atlas van Nederland, de West en Indonesië, voor de
lagere school. 58 ed. By G. Prop. Zutphen, 1955.
42 p. col. maps. 26 cm.

2415 Tjempaka, P. T.
Atlas ringkas untuk sekolah rakjat. Djakarta, [1958].
24 p. col. maps. 32 cm.

2416 Wolters, J. B.
Atlas Indonesia. By C. Lekkerkerker. Djakarta,
Groningen, [1957].
16 p. col. maps. 29 cm.

2417 Wolters, J. B.
Atlas Indonesia untuk sekolah rendah. 2 ed. By
C. Lekkerkerker. Groningen, Djakarta, [195-].
16 p. col. maps. 29 cm.

2418 Wolters, J. B.
Atlas van Indonesië voor de lagere school. By C.
Lekkerkerker. Groningen, [195-].
16 p. col. maps. 29 cm.

Iran

2419 Guruhi Jughrafiya.
Atlas-i Iglimi-yi Iran. By Ahmad Mustaufi.
Teheran, [1969].
1 vol. col. maps. 30 cm.

Iraq

2420 Surveys Press.
Atlas of Iraq, showing administrative boundaries,
areas & population. 1 ed. By Ahmed Sousa.
Baghdad, 1953.
40 p. col. maps. 35 cm.

Israel

2421 Ahiever.
The Hebrew maps of the Holy Land. 2 ed. By
Zev Vilnay. Jerusalem, 1968.
30 p. col. maps. 40 cm.

2422 Ben-Eliyahu, Ephraim.
Atlas li-yedi'at Erets-Yisrael veha-TaNakH. Jerusalem, [1957/58].
136 p. 34 cm.

2423 Carta.
Cartás. Atlas of the Bible. By Yohanan Aharoni.
Jerusalem, 1964.
1 vol. col. maps. 30 cm.

2424 Carta.
Carta's Israel road guide. Jerusalem, 1963.
68 p. co. maps. 24 cm.

2425 Carta.
Carta's Israel road guide. Jerusalem, 1969.
68 p. col. maps. 24 cm.

2426 Codex Verlag.
Kulturatlas von Palästina. Gundholzen, [1970-].
in 4 parts. col. maps. 43 cm.

2427 Elsevier.
Atlas of Israel. [English ed.]. With Israel. Department of Surveys. Amsterdam, 1970.
290 p. col. maps. 47.5 cm.

2428 European Road Guide, Inc.
Motoring atlas: Europe and Israel 1968/69. Larchmont, N. Y., 1968.
48 p. col. maps. 28 cm.

2429 European Road Guide, Inc.
Motoring atlas of Europe and Israel. 1969-70 ed.
Larchmont, N. Y., 1969.
68 p. col. maps. 28 cm.

2430 Humphrey, H. A. Ltd.
The new Israel atlas. By Zev Vilnay. London,
1968.
114 p. col. maps. 30 cm.

2431 Israel. Department of Surveys.
     Atlas of Israel. (in Hebrew). Jerusalem, 1956-
     1964.
     1 vol. col. maps. 47.5 cm.

2432 Israel. Department of Surveys.
     Israel in pictorial maps. By Friedel Stern. Tel
     Aviv, [1957].
     35 p. col. maps. 35 cm.

2433 Israel. Mahleket ha-medidot.
     Atlas Yisrael. Jerusalem, [1956].
     1 vol. col. maps. 50 cm.

2434 Israel. Ministry of Labour.
     Atlas of Israel; cartography, physical, geography,
     human and economic geography, history. 2 ed.
     Jerusalem, 1970.
     296 p. col. maps. 49 cm.

2435 Israel. Ministry of Survey.
     Official National atlas of Israel. Tel Aviv, 1970.
     71 p. col. maps. 47.5 cm.

2436 Israel. Tseva haganah le-Yisrael.
     Atlas geografi-histori shel Erets-Yisrael. By
     Michael Avi-Yonah. Jerusalem, [195-].
     60 p. col. maps. 36 cm.

2437 Israel University Press.
     The new Israel atlas; Bible to present. By Zev
     Vilnay. Jerusalem, 1968.
     112 p. col. maps. 30 cm.

2438 Macmillan & Co.
     Jewish history atlas. By Martin Gilbert. New
     York, [1969].
     126 p. 24 cm.

2439 McGraw-Hill Book Co.
     The new Israel atlas. Bible to present. By Zev
     Vilnay. New York, 1969.
     112 p. col. maps. 30 cm.

2440 Szapiro, J.
     Atlas histori shel 'am Yisrael. Tel Aviv, 1960.
     71 p. col. maps. 28 cm.

2441 Universitas.
Israel pocket atlas and handbook. Jerusalem, [1961].
79 p. col. maps. 25 cm.

2442 Universitas.
Israel Taschenatlas und Handbuch. 2 ed. By
Michael Avi-Yonah. Jerusalem, 1965.
1 vol. col. maps. 24 cm.

2443 Weidenfeld & Nicolson.
Jewish history atlas. By Martin Gilbert. London,
1969.
112 p. 25.5 cm.

2444 Yavneh.
Atlas ha-mizrah ha-tikhon. By Moshe Brawer.
Tel Aviv, [1964].
80 p. col. maps. 35 cm.

2445 Yavneh.
Atlas ha-mizrah ha tikhon. 2 ed. By Yehuda
Karmon and Moshe Brawer. Tel Aviv, [1967].
80 p. col. maps. 35 cm.

Japan

2446 Japan. Un'yushŏ Kankŏkyoku.
Nihon kankŏ chizu. Kaiteiban. [Tourist atlas of
Japan]. Tokyo, [1950].
33 p. col. maps. 38 cm.

2447 Jimbunsha.
Nihon bunken chizu chimei sōran harabini kōkyō
shisetsun benran. [Prefectural atlas of Japan with
gazetteer]. Tokyo, [1958].
1 vol. col. maps. 38 cm.

2448 Jimbunsha.
Nihon bunken chizu chimei sōran narabini kŏkyō
shisetsun benran. [Prefectural atlas of Japan with
gazetteer]. Tokyo, [1959].
1 vol. col. maps. 38 cm.

2449 Jimbunsha.
Saikin chōsa zenkoku kembetsu jitsuyŏ hakuchizu;
dōro tetsudō shi-chō-sommei meisai. [Perfectural
atlas . . . showing roads, railroads, cities, towns,

and villages]. Tokyo, [1954].
47 p. 61 cm.

2450 Jimbunsha.
Saishin nihon bunken chizu. [New perfectural atlas
of Japan]. Tokyo, [195-].
23 p. col. maps. 21 cm.

2451 Kishō Kyōkai.
Nihon no kikōzu; me de miru Nihon no shiki.
[Meteorological atlas of Japan]. Tokyo, [1957].
75 p. col. maps. 27 cm.

2452 Kokusai Chicaku Kyōkai.
Atlas and gazetteer of the perfectures of Japan.
Tokyo, 1952.
1 vol. col. maps. 38 cm.

2453 Nihon Kyōzu Kabushiki Kaisha.
Nihon bunken seizu. [Detailed prefectural atlas of
Japan]. Tokyo, [1958].
273 p. col. maps. 45 cm.

2454 Nitchi Shuppan Kabushiki Kaisha.
Handĭ Nihon bunken chizuchō. Tsuketari, ryokō
annaiki. Kaiteiban. [Handy prefectural atlas of
Japan]. Tokyo, [1953].
73 p. col. maps. 18 cm.

2455 Nitchi Shuppan Kabushiki Kaisha.
Handĭ Nihon bunken chizuchō. Tsuketari, ryokō
annaiki. Kaiteiban. [Handy prefectural atlas of
Japan]. Tokyo, [1954].
66 p. col. maps. 18 cm.

2456 Nitchi Shuppan Kabushiki Kaisha.
Saishin Nihon bunken chizu. [New prefectural atlas
of Japan]. Tokyo, 1951.
47 p. col. maps. 37 cm.

2457 Nitchi Shuppan Kabushiki Kaisha.
Saishin Nihon bunken chizu. [New prefectural atlas
of Japan]. Tokyo, 1952.
47 p. col. maps. 37 cm.

2458 Nitchi Shuppan Kabushiki Kaisha.
Saishin Nihon bunken chizu. [New prefectural atlas

of Japan]. Tokyo, 1953.
48 p. col. maps. 37 cm.

2459 Nitchi Shuppan Kabushiki Kaisha.
Saishin Nihon bunken chizu. [New prefectural atlas
of Japan]. Tokyo, 1954.
50 p. col. maps. 37 cm.

2460 Nitchi Shuppan Kabushiki Kaisha.
Saishin Nihon bunken chizu. [New prefectural atlas
of Japan]. Tokyo, 1955.
52 p. col. maps. 37 cm.

2461 Nitchi Shuppan Kabushiki Kaisha.
Saishin Nihou bunken chizu. [New prefectural atlas
of Japan]. Tokyo, 1957.
78 p. col. maps. 37 cm.

2462 Nitchi Shuppan Kabushiki Kaisha.
Saishin Nihon bunken chizu. [New prefectural atlas
of Japan]. Tokyo, 1959.
105 p. col. maps. 37 cm.

2463 Nitchi Shuppan Kabushiki Kaisha.
Saishin shōmitsn Nihon chizu. [A new detailed atlas
of Japan]. Tokyo, [1955].
1 vol. col. maps. 38 cm.

2464 Teikoku-Shoin Co., Ltd.
Complete atlas of Japan. (in English) Tokyo, 1964.
55 p. col. maps. 31 cm.

2465 Teikoku-Shoin Co., Ltd.
Kihan Nihon dai chizu [Standard atlas of Japan].
Tokyo, 1957.
103 p. col. maps. 38 cm.

2466 Teikoku-Shoin Co., Ltd.
Kihan Nihon dai chizu. [Standard atlas of Japan].
Tokyo, 1958.
64 p. col. maps. 38 cm.

2467 Teikoku-Shoin Co., Ltd.
Saishin Nihon shi seizu. Kaiteiban. [New detailed
historical atlas of Japan]. Tokyo, [1954].
51 p. col. maps. 26 cm.

2468 Teikoku-Shoin Co. , Ltd.
      Teikoku's complete atlas of Japan. By Yoshio
      Moriya. Tokyo, 1968.
      55 p. col. maps. 31 cm.

2469 Tōbunsha.
      Poketto bunken chizuchō. [Pocket prefectural atlas].
      Tokyo, [1957].
      105 p. col. maps. 21 cm.

2470 Tōbunsha.
      Poketto bunken chizuchō. [Pocket prefectural atlas].
      Tokyo, [1959].
      105 p. col. maps. 21 cm.

2471 Tokyo Chizu K. K.
      Zen Nihon Doro Chiaucho. Tokyo, 1967.
      1 vol. col. maps. 31 cm.

2472 Tōsei Shuppan Kabushiki Kaisha.
      Dai Nihon bunken chizu narabini chimei sōran.
      [Prefectural atlas of Japan with gazetteer]. Tokyo,
      [1953].
      1 vol. col. maps. 38 cm.

2473 Tōsei Shuppan Kabushiki Kaisha.
      Dai Nihon bunken chizu narabini chimel sōran.
      [Prefectural atlas of Japan with gazetteer]. Tokyo,
      [1955].
      1 vol. col. maps. 38 cm.

2474 Tōsei Shuppan Kabushiki Kaisha.
      Dai Nihon bunken chizu narabini chimei sōran.
      [Prefectural atlas of Japan with gazetteer]. Tokyo,
      [1956].
      1 vol. col. maps. 38 cm.

2475 Tōsei Shappan Kabushiki Kaisha.
      Dai Nihon bunken chizu narabini chimei sōran.
      [Prefectural atlas of Japan with gazetteer]. Tokyo,
      [1957].
      1 vol. col. maps. 38 cm.

2476 Tōsei Shappan Kabushiki Kaisha.
      Dai Nihon bunken chizu narabini chimei sōran.
      [Prefectural atlas of Japan with gazetteer]. Tokyo,
      [1959].
      1 vol. col. maps. 38 cm.

2477 U.S.S.R. Glavnoe upravlenie geodezii i kartografii.
Atlas yaponii. Moskva, 1970-71.
1 vol. col. maps. 32 cm.

2478 Zenkoku Jichitai Kenkyūkai.
Shinsei bunken chizu zuki zenkoku shi-chō-son sōran
narabini gakkō meikan. [New prefectural atlas with
gazetteer]. Tokyo, [1957].
679 p. col. maps. 27 cm.

2479 Zenkoku kyóiku tosho.
Nippon keizai chizu. [The economic atlas of Japan].
By Kôichi Aki. Tokyo, 1954.
186 p. col. maps. 37 cm.

2480 Zenkoku ryokaku jidōsha yōran henshūshitsu.
Zenkoku basu rosenzu sōran. Un'yushō jidōshakyoku
kanshū. [Atlas of national motor bus routes].
Tokyo, [1957].
48 p. col. maps. 37 cm.

Korea

2481 Kim, Sang-jin.
Taehan Minguk tobyol haengjoug yo. [Administrative
atlas of Korean provinces]. Seoul, [1958].
15 p. col. maps. 31 cm.

2482 Sosŏ Publishing Co.
Standard atlas of Korea. (in Korean). By Pong Su Yi.
Seoul, 1960.
47 p. col. maps. 38 cm.

2483 Taehan Sŏrim.
Hoejung Hanguk chŏngmilto. Pu haengjŏng kuyo
p'yŏllam. [Detailed pocket atlas of Korean pro-
vinces]. Seoul, [1953].
10 p. col. maps. 15 cm.

Laos

2484 U.S. Aid Mission to Laos.
Laos. [Washington, D.C., 1965].
11 p. 97 cm.

2485 Vietnam. Nha g'ám-dôc Khí-tu'o'ng.
Gian-dô khi-hâu; cao dô mu'a trung-bính tai Vietnam,

Ailao và Cambodge.   Saigon, 1958.
13 p.   col. maps.   33 cm.

Lebanon

2486 Lebanon.   Direction des affaires géographiques.
     Liban: carte routière.   Beyrouth, [1967].
     21 p.   col. maps.   30 cm.

2487 Lebanon.   Ministère du Plan.
     Atlas du Liban.   Beyrouth, 1964.
     24 p.   col. maps.   42 cm.

2488 Lebanon.   Service météorologique.
     Atlas climatique du Liban.   Beyrouth, 1966–
     in parts.   col. maps.   33 cm.

Malaysia

2489 Automobile Association of Malaya.
     Malaysia road atlas.   Penang, [1967].
     16 p.   col. maps.   25 cm.

2490 Borneo Literature Bureau.
     Map book of Malaysia.   By Peter Collenette.
     Kuching, Sarawak, [1963].
     17 p.   30 cm.

2491 Borneo Literature Bureau.
     Map book of Malaysia.   By P. Collenette.   Kuching,
     Sarawak, 1966.
     26 p.   30 cm.

2492 Borneo Literature Bureau.
     Map book of Malaysia.   By P. Collenette.   Kuching,
     Sarawak, 1968.
     26 p.   30 cm.

2493 Collins, William, Sons & Co., Ltd.
     Atlas rendah baharu Malaysia.   Glasgow, 1969.
     32 p.   col. maps.   26 cm.

2494 Collins, William, Sons & Co., Ltd.
     Collins-Longmans new secondary atlas for Malaya.
     3 ed.   By K. H. Huggins.   Glasgow, [1961].
     96 p.   col. maps.   29 cm.

2495 Collins, William, Sons & Co., Ltd.
Collins-Longmans new secondary atlas for Malaysia
and Singapore. 2 ed. By R. B. Bunnett. Glasgow,
1967.
88 p. col. maps. 29 cm.

2496 Collins, William, Sons & Co., Ltd.
Collins-Longmans world atlas for Malaya. 2 ed.
By. K. H. Huggins. Glasgow, [1955].
24 p. col. maps. 29 cm.

2497 Collins, William, Sons & Co., Ltd.
Collins-Longmans world atlas for Malaya. 8 ed.
By K. H. Huggins. Glasgow, [1963].
24 p. col. maps. 29 cm.

2498 Collins, William, Sons & Co., Ltd.
Junior atlas for Malaysia and Singapore. Glasgow,
1967.
1 vol. col. maps. 29 cm.

2499 Hai kuang ch'u pan shê.
Ma-lai-ya lien ho pang fên chou t'u. [Maps of the
States of the Federation of Malay]. By Min-fei Li.
Hong Kong, 1958.
44 p. col. maps. 27 cm.

2500 Malaysia. Directorate of National Mapping.
Caltex motorist's guide & map book. Singapore,
[1969].
24 p. col. maps. 23 cm.

2501 Tien Wah Press, Ltd.
Primary school atlas for Malaya and Singapore.
Singapore, 1965.
28 p. col. maps. 28 cm.

Nepal

2502 Nepal. Ministry of Information and Broadcasting.
Nepal in maps. Kathmandu, 1966.
41 p. 28 cm.

Pakistan

2503 Oxford University Press.
Oxford economic atlas for Pakistan. By C. F. W. R.

Gullick.   Oxford, 1955.
131 p.   col. maps.   26 cm.

2504 Oxford University Press.
Oxford economic atlas for Pakistan.   By C. F.W. R.
Gullick.   New York, 1958.
131 p.   col. maps.   26 cm.

2505 Oxford University Press.
Oxford school atlas for Pakistan.   By Kazi S.
Ahmad and Nafis Ahmad.   Karachi, 1959.
57 p.   col. maps.   26 cm.

2506 Oxford University Press.
The Oxford school atlas for India, Pakistan, Burma
& Ceylon.   20 ed.   Bombay, [1958].
63 p.   col. maps.   28 cm.

2507 Pakistan.   Dept. of Advertising, Films and Publications.
Atlas of Pakistan; information in maps.   Karachi,
[195-].
20 p.   44 cm.

Philippines

2508 Caltex (Philippines).
Road map of the Philippines.   Manila, 1957.
60 p.   col. maps.   25 cm.

2509 Phil-Asian Publishers, Inc.
Atlas of the Philippines.   By Robert S. Hendry.
Manila, 1959.
228 p.   col. maps.   48 cm.

2510 Philippines.   Agriculture and natural resources dept.
Philippine agricultural atlas, 1957.   Quezon City,
[1960].
108 p.   38 cm.

2511 Philippines.   Bureau of Public Works.
Official road map of the Philippines.   Manila, [1952].
15 p.   52 cm.

2512 Philippines.   Office of the President.
The Philippine economic atlas.   Manila, [1965].
163 p.   col. maps.   37 cm.

2513 Praeger, Frederick A.
A descriptive atlas of the Pacific Islands. New
Zealand, Australia, Polynesia, Melanesia,
Micronesia, Philippines. By T. F. Kennedy. New
York, [1968].
64 p. 24 cm.

2514 Reed, A. H. and A. W.
A descriptive atlas of the Pacific Islands. New
Zealand, Australia, Polynesia, Melanesia,
Micronesia, Philippines. By T. F. Kennedy.
Wellington, 1966.
64 p. 24 cm.

Singapore

2515 Collins, William, Sons & Co., Ltd.
Collins-Longmans new secondary atlas for Malaysia
and Singapore. 2 ed. By R. B. Bunnett. Glasgow,
1967.
88 p. col. maps. 29 cm.

2516 Collins, William, Sons & Co., Ltd.
Junior atlas for Malaysia and Singapore. Glasgow,
1967.
1 vol. col. maps. 29 cm.

2517 Tien Wah Press, Ltd.
Primary school atlas for Malaya and Singapore.
Singapore, 1965.
28 p. col. maps. 28 cm.

Taiwan

2518 China. National War College.
Atlas of the Republic of China. By Chang Chi-Yun.
Taipei, 1960-63.
in 5 vol. col. maps. 43 cm.

2519 Fu-Min Geographical Institute of Economic Development.
Geographical atlas of Taiwan. By Cheng-Siang Cheng.
Taipei, 1959.
164 p. col. maps. 26 cm.

2520 Taiwan. National University.
Atlas of land utilization in Taiwan. By Chêng-hsiang
Ch'en. Taipei, 1950.
121 p. col. maps. 38 cm.

Thailand

2521 Collins, William, Sons & Co., Ltd.
     A school atlas for Thailand. Glasgow, 1969.
     41 p. col. maps. 26 cm.

2522 Thailand. Department of Commercial Intelligence.
     An atlas of Thailand's agricultural resources.
     Bangkok, [1959].
     73 p. 25 cm.

2523 Thailand. Royal Thai Survey Department.
     Natural resources atlas. Bangkok, 1966.
     in parts. 34 cm.

2524 Thailand. Royal Thai Survey Department.
     Natural resources atlas. Bangkok, 1970.
     1 vol. 34 cm.

Vietnam

2525 Vietnam. Dept. of Survey and Mapping.
     Atlas Vietnam. Hanoi, 1964.
     19 p. col. maps. 26 cm.

2526 Vietnam. Nha g'ám-dôc khí-tu'o'ng.
     Gian-dô khi-hâu; cao dô mu'a trung-bính tai Vietnam,
     Ailao và Cambodge. Saigon, 1958.
     13 p. col. maps. 33 cm.

AUSTRALIA

Australia

2527 Ampol Petroleum, Ltd.
The Ampol touring atlas of Australia.　Sydney,
[1969].
93 p.　col. maps.　32 cm.

2528 Angus & Robertson.
Australia, a map geography.　By Barry Cohen.
Sydney, [1968].
90 p.　25 cm.

2529 Australia.　Department of National Development.
Atlas of Australian resources.　First Series.
Canberra, 1952-60.
in parts.　col. maps.　71 cm.

2530 Australia.　Department of National Development.
Atlas of Australian resources.　Second series.
Canberra, 1962 —
in parts.　col. maps.　71 cm.

2531 Australia.　Division of Soils, Commonwealth Scientific
and Industrial Research Organization.
Atlas of Australian soils.　Canberra, 1960-68.
in parts.　col. maps.　77 cm.

2532 Australian Educational Foundation, Pty., Ltd.
The visual world atlas.　Sydney, 1962.
272 p.　col. maps.　26 cm.

2533 B. P. Australia, Ltd.
Roads of Australia with insets of main towns.　Melbourne, 1966.
76 p.　col. maps.　22 cm.

2534 Clapsy, E. M.
An atlas of political parties in Australia published
in 1944, 1958 supplement.　Dowagiac, Mich., [1958].
28 p.　28 cm.

2535 Collins, William Sons & Co., Ltd.
     Australia, New Zealand and the Pacific.   By Allan
     Murray.   London, [1956].
     96 p.   26 cm.

2536 Collins, William Sons & Co., Ltd.
     Australian junior atlas.   Sydney, [1967].
     67 p.   col. maps.   27 cm.

2537 Colorgravure.
     New Australian world atlas illustrated with political
     and resources-relief maps.   By Horace Blanche.
     Melbourne, [1950].
     144 p.   col. maps.   32 cm.

2538 Colorgravure
     The new Elizabethan world atlas illustrated.   By
     Horace Blanche.   Melbourne, [1955].
     152 p.   col. maps.   32 cm.

2539 Hammond, C. S. & Co., Inc.
     Hammond world atlas; an encyclopedic atlas of the
     world.   Australian and New Zealand reference ed.
     Maplewood, N. J., [1965].
     1 vol.   col. maps.   32 cm.

2540 Hammond, C. S. & Co., Inc.
     Illustrated atlas of Australia.   Maplewood, N. J.,
     [196-].
     16 p.   col. maps.   31 cm.

2541 Hammond, C. S. & Co., Inc.
     World atlas, an encyclopedic atlas of the world.
     Australian ed.   With Nelson-Doubleday.   Maple-
     wood, N. J., [1964].
     264 p.   col. maps.   32 cm.

2542 Macmillan & Co., Ltd.
     Atlas for Australian secondary schools.   1 ed.
     London, 1960.
     68 p.   col. maps.   28 cm.

2543 Macmillan & Co., Ltd.
     Atlas for Australian secondary schools.   2 ed.
     London, [1961].
     68 p.   col. maps.   28 cm.

2544 Motor Manual.
      Highways of Australia.   Melbourne, [1949-50].
      208 p.   25 cm.

2545 Motor Manual.
      Highways of Australia.   4 ed.   By Keith Winser.
      Melbourne, 1954.
      240 p.   25 cm.

2546 Motor Manual.
      Highways of Australia.   5 ed.   By Keith Winser.
      Melbourne, [1956].
      248 p.   25 cm.

2547 Motor Manual.
      Highways of Australia, road atlas.   6 ed.   By Keith
      Winser.   Melbourne, [1958].
      250 p.   25 cm.

2548 Motor Manual.
      Highways of Australia, road atlas.   6 ed.   By Keith
      Winser.   Melbourne, [1959].
      248 p.   25 cm.

2549 Motor Manual.
      Highways of Australia, road atlas.   7 ed.   By
      Keith Winser.   Melbourne, 1960/61.
      205 p.   25 cm.

2550 Motor Manual.
      Highways of Australia, road atlas.   8 ed.   By
      Keith Winser.   Melbourne, 1966.
      248 p.   25 cm.

2551 Nelson Doubleday.
      World atlas; an encyclopedic atlas of the world.
      Australian ed.   With Hammond.   St. Leonards,
      N.S.W., [1964].
      264 p.   col. maps.   32 cm.

2552 Nelson, Thomas & Sons, Ltd.
      Nelson's atlas for Australia.   London, 1968.
      40 p.   col. maps.   32 cm.

2553 Oxford University Press.
      A map history of Australia.   By Ian Wynd and Joyce
      Wood.   Melbourne, [1963].
      60 p.   col. maps.   25 cm.

2554 Oxford University Press.
     The Oxford Australian atlas.   Melbourne, New York,
     1957.
     71 p.   col. maps.   26 cm.

2555 Oxford University Press.
     The Oxford Australian atlas.   2 ed.   Melbourne,
     New York, 1966.
     75 p.   col. maps.   26 cm.

2556 Oxford University Press.
     The shorter Oxford Australian atlas.   London, 1962.
     32 p.   col. maps.   26 cm.

2557 Philip, George & Son, Ltd.
     Australian Commonwealth atlas.   By George Goodall
     and George M. Philip.   London, 1952.
     107 p.   col. maps.   23 cm.

2558 Philip, George & Son, Ltd.
     Comparative Commonwealth atlas for use in
     Australian schools.   10 ed.   London, 1950.
     1 vol.   col. maps.   23 cm.

2559 Philip, George & Son, Ltd.
     Comparative Commonwealth atlas for use in
     Australian schools.   11 ed.   London, 1952.
     1 vol.   col. maps.   23 cm.

2560 Philip, George & Son, Ltd.
     Comparative Commonwealth atlas for use in
     Australian schools.   12 ed.   London, 1952.
     1 vol.   col. maps.   23 cm.

2561 Philip, George & Son, Ltd.
     Comparative Commonwealth atlas for use in
     Australian schools.   13 ed.   London, 1953.
     1 vol.   col. maps.   23 cm.

2562 Philip, George & Son, Ltd.
     Comparative Commonwealth atlas for use in
     Australian schools.   14 ed.   London, 1955.
     1 vol.   col. maps.   23 cm.

2563 Philip, George & Son, Ltd.
     Comparative Commonwealth atlas for use in
     Australian schools.   15 ed.   London, 1955.
     1 vol.   col. maps.   23 cm.

2564 Philip, George & Son, Ltd.
     Comparative Commonwealth atlas for use in
     Australian schools. 16 ed. By George Goodall and
     Harold Fullard. London, 1956.
     1 vol. col. maps. 23 cm.

2565 Philip, George & Son, Ltd.
     Comparative Commonwealth atlas for use in
     Australian schools. 17 ed. By George Goodall and
     Harold Fullard. London, 1957.
     1 vol. col. maps. 23 cm.

2566 Philip, George & Son, Ltd.
     Comparative Commonwealth atlas for use in
     Australian schools. 18 ed. By Harold Fullard.
     London, 1958.
     1 vol. col. maps. 23 cm.

2567 Philip, George & Son, Ltd.
     Comparative Commonwealth atlas for use in
     Australian schools. 19 ed. By Harold Fullard.
     London, 1959.
     109 p. col. maps. 23 cm.

2568 Philip, George & Son, Ltd.
     Philip's Australian Commonwealth atlas. By George
     Goodall. London, 1952.
     88 p. col. maps. 31 cm.

2569 Praeger, Frederick A.
     A descriptive atlas of the Pacific Islands. New
     Zealand, Australia, Polynesia, Melanesia,
     Micronesia, Philippines. By T. F. Kennedy.
     New York, [1968].
     64 p. 24 cm.

2570 Reader's Digest Association Pty, Ltd.
     The Reader's Digest complete atlas of Australia.
     Sydney, [1968].
     183 p. col. maps. 40 cm.

2571 Reed, A. H. and A. W.
     A descriptive atlas of the Pacific Islands. New
     Zealand, Australia, Polynesia, Melanesia,
     Micronesia, Philippines. By T. F. Kennedy.
     Wellington, 1966.
     64 p. 24 cm.

2572 The Age.
      Highways of Australia road atlas to every town in
      Australia. 9 ed. By Keith Winser. Melbourne,
      1968.
      190 p. 25 cm.

New Zealand

2573 Collins, William Sons & Co., Ltd.
      Australia, New Zealand and the Pacific. By Allan
      Murray. London, [1956].
      96 p. 26 cm.

2574 Hammond, C. S. & Co., Inc.
      Hammond world atlas; an encyclopedic atlas of the
      world. Australian and New Zealand reference ed.
      Maplewood, N. J., [1965].
      1 vol. col. maps. 32 cm.

2575 Macmillan & Co., Ltd.
      A map book of Australasia. 2 ed. By Alan Ferri-
      day. London, 1959.
      48 p. 25 cm.

2576 Macmillan & Co., Ltd.
      A map book of Australasia. 3 ed. By Alan
      Ferriday. London, Melbourne, 1966.
      52 p. 25 cm.

2577 Macmillan & Co., Ltd.
      A map book of Australasia. 4 ed. By Alan
      Ferriday. London, Melbourne, 1969.
      52 p. 25 cm.

2578 New Zealand. Atlas committee.
      A descriptive atlas of New Zealand. By A. H.
      McLintock. Wellington, 1959.
      130 p. col. maps. 32 cm.

2579 New Zealand. Atlas committee.
      A descriptive atlas of New Zealand. By A. H.
      McLintock. Wellington, 1960.
      130 p. col. maps. 32 cm.

2580 New Zealand. National Airways Corporation.
      NAC air atlas. Wellington, [1965].
      15 p. col. maps. 25.5 cm.

2581 New Zealand. National Airways Corporation.
      NAC air atlas of New Zealand. Wellington, [1968].
      18 p. col. maps. 25.5 cm.

2582 New Zealand. Town and Country Planning Branch.
      Atlas of New Zealand regional statistics. Wellington,
      [1968].
      62 p. 37 cm.

2583 Oxford University Press.
      Oxford social studies atlas for New Zealand. By
      R. G. Lister. London, 1963.
      32 p. col. maps. 26 cm.

2584 Oxford University Press.
      The Oxford atlas for New Zealand. By R. G.
      Lister. London, 1959.
      71 p. col. maps. 26 cm.

2585 Oxford University Press.
      The Oxford atlas for New Zealand. 2 ed. London,
      Wellington, 1966.
      75 p. col. maps. 26 cm.

2586 Praeger, Frederick A.
      A descriptive atlas of the Pacific Islands. New
      Zealand, Australia, Polynesia, Melanesia,
      Micronesia, Philippines. By T. F. Kennedy.
      New York, [1968].
      64 p. 24 cm.

2587 Reed, A. H. & A. W.
      A descriptive atlas of the Pacific Islands. New
      Zealand, Australia, Polynesia, Melanesia,
      Micronesia, Philippines. By T. F. Kennedy.
      Wellington, 1966.
      64 p. 24 cm.

2588 Reed, A. H. & A. W.
      Atlas of New Zealand geography. By G. J. R.
      Linge and R. M. Frazer. Wellington, 1965.
      64 p. 25 cm.

2589 Reed, A. H. & A. W.
      Atlas of New Zealand geography. By G. J. R.
      Linge and R. M. Frazer. Wellington, 1966.
      64 p. 25 cm.

2590 Reed, A. H. & A. W.
      Atlas of New Zealand geography. By G. J. R.
      Linge and R. M. Frazer. 2 ed. Wellington, 1968.
      64 p. 25 cm.

2591 Reed, A. H. & A. W.
      Reed's atlas of New Zealand. Wellington, [1952].
      71 p. col. maps. 26 cm.

2592 Shell Oil New Zealand, Ltd.
      New Zealand road maps. Wellington, 1953.
      22 p. col. maps. 24 cm.

2593 Shell Oil New Zealand, Ltd.
      Shell road maps of New Zealand. Wellington,
      [1950-].
      1 vol. col. maps. 27 cm.

2594 Shell Oil New Zealand, Ltd.
      Shell road maps, New Zealand. Wellington, [1956].
      32 p. col. maps. 25 cm.

2595 St. Martin's Press.
      A map book of Australasia. 3 ed. By A. Ferri-
      day. New York, 1966.
      52 p. 25 cm.

2596 St. Martin's Press.
      A map book of Australasia. 4 ed. By Alan Ferri-
      day. New York, 1969.
      52 p. 25 cm.

Papua and New Guinea

2597 Jacaranda.
      Atlas of the southwest Pacific. 1 ed. By Ian
      Geoffrey Ord. Brisbane, 1967.
      59 p. col. maps. 26 cm.

2598 Jacaranda.
      Atlas of the southwest Pacific. 2 ed. By Ian
      Geoffrey Ord. Brisbane, [1968].
      59 p. col. maps. 26 cm.

2599 Netherlands. Ministerie van Marine.
      Meteorolgie Nederlands Nieuw Guinea: Voorlopige
      atlas. 's Gravenhage, 1959.
      1 vol. 34 cm.

2600 Reader's Digest Association Pty., Ltd.
The Reader's Digest complete atlas of Australia.
Sydney, [1968].
183 p. col. maps. 40 cm.

2601 Stenvert.
Stenverts atlas Nederland, de West en Nederland's
Nieuw-Guinea. 4 ed. By Wijbren Bakker and
J. M. Bosch. Apeldoorn, [1962].
94 p. 22 cm.

2602 Versluys, W.
Schoolatlas van Nederlands Nieuw-Guinea. By
H. Eggink. Amsterdam, [1956].
28 p. col. maps. 31 cm.

EUROPE

Albania

2603 N. I. Sh. Mjete Mesimore e Sportive "Hamid Shijaku".
Atlas i luftes nacional çlirimatare. Tiranë, 1969.
38 p. col. maps. 32 cm.

Austria

2604 Austria. Akademie der Wissenschaften.
Atlas der Republik Osterreich. By Hans Bobek.
Wien, 1961-.
in parts. col. maps. 73 cm.

2605 Austria. Akademie der Wissenschaften.
Osterreichischer Volkskundeatlas. Wien, 1959-
in parts. col. maps. 60 cm.

2606 Buchgemeinschaft Donauland.
Donauland autoatlas. Wien, [1965].
1 vol. col. maps. 27 cm.

2607 Buchgemeinschaft Donauland.
Grosser Hausatlas der Buchgemeinschaft Donauland.
With Hölzel. Wien, [1965].
294 p. col. maps. 33 cm.

2608 Continental Gummiwerke Kartographischer Verlag.
Continental atlas. Deutschland, Benelux, Schweiz,
Österreich, Norditalian. 33 ed. Hannover, 1964.
635 p. col. maps. 26 cm.

2609 Dom Verlag.
Kirchenhistorischer atlas von Österreich. By E.
Bernleithner. Wien, 1966-
in parts. col. maps. 63 cm.

2610 Falk-Verlag.
Falk auto-atlas Österreich. Hamburg, [1959].
32 p. col. maps. 25 cm.

2611 Falk Verlag.
Falk Plan Österreich; auto-atlas Österreich. 4 ed.

Hamburg, [1964].
32 p. col. maps. 25 cm.

2612 Freytag-Berndt & Artaria.
Autoatlas von Österreich. Wien, [1950].
85 p. col. maps. 26 cm.

2613 Freytag-Berndt & Artaria.
Autoatlas von Österreich. Wien, [1954].
87 p. col. maps. 26 cm.

2614 Freytag-Berndt & Artaria.
Autoatlas von Österreich. Wien, [1956].
87 p. col. maps. 26 cm.

2615 Freytag-Berndt & Artaria.
Autoatlas von Österreich. Wien, [1958].
67 p. col. maps. 26 cm.

2616 Freytag-Berndt & Artaria.
Autoatlas von Österreich. Wien, [1962].
67 p. col. maps. 26 cm.

2617 Freytag-Berndt & Artaria.
Autoatlas von Österreich. Wien, 1964.
105 p. col. maps. 26 cm.

2618 Freytag-Berndt & Artaria.
Autoatlas von Österreich. Wien, [1966].
67 p. col. maps. 26 cm.

2619 Freytag-Berndt & Artaria.
Autoatlas von Österreich. Wien, 1968.
105 p. col. maps. 26 cm.

2620 Freytag-Berndt & Artaria.
Luftbildatlas Österreich. By Leopold Scheidl.
Wien, 1969.
1 vol. 26 cm.

2621 Freytag-Berndt & Artaria.
Neuer Schulatlas für Hauptschulen und Unterstufen
der Höheren Schulen. Wien, 1969-70.
110 p. col. maps. 31 cm.

2622 Hölder, Pichler, Tempsky.
Atlas zur allgemeinen und Österreichischen

Geschichte. By Wilhelm Franz Schier. Wien, 1951.
63 p. col. maps. 28 cm.

2623 Hölder, Pichler, Tempsky.
Atlas zur allgemeinen und Österreichischen
Geschichte. By Wilhelm Franz Schier. Wien,
[1958].
63 p. col. maps. 28 cm.

2624 Hölder, Pichler, Tempsky.
Atlas zur allgemeinen und Österreichischen
Geschichte. 7 ed. By Wilhelm Franz Schier.
Wien, 1964.
63 p. col. maps. 28 cm.

2625 Hölder, Pichler, Tempsky.
Atlas zur allgemeinen und Österreichischen
Geschichte. 8 ed. By Wilhelm Franz Schier.
Wien, [1966].
68 p. col. maps. 28 cm.

2626 Hölder, Pichler, Tempsky.
Historischer Schul-atlas zur allgemeinen und
Österreichischen Geschichte. By F. W. Putzger.
Wien, [1961].
146 p. col. maps. 27 cm.

2627 Hölder, Pichler, Tempsky.
Historischer Schul-atlas zur allgemeinen und
Österreichischen Geschichte. 43 ed. By F. W.
Putzger. Wien, 1963.
146 p. col. maps. 27 cm.

2628 Hölzel, Ed. Verlag.
Österreichischer Hauptschulatlas. 3 ed. Wien, 1958.
76 p. col. maps. 31 cm.

2629 Hölzel, Ed. Verlag.
Österreichischer Hauptschulatlas. 4 ed. Wien,
[1961].
76 p. col. maps. 31 cm.

2630 Hölzel, Ed. Verlag.
Österreichischer Hauptschulatlas. 5 ed. Wien, 1964.
76 p. col. maps. 32 cm.

2631 Hölzel, Ed. Verlag.
Österreichischer Hauptschulatlas. Wien, 1967.

76 p. col. maps. 32 cm.

2632 Hölzel, Ed. Verlag.
Österreichischer Mittelschulatlas. 74 ed. By Hans
Slanar. Wien, 1950.
146 p. col. maps. 31 cm.

2633 Hölzel, Ed. Verlag.
Österreichischer Mittelschulatlas. 75 ed. By Hans
Slanar. Wien, 1951.
146 p. col. maps. 31 cm.

2634 Hölzel, Ed. Verlag.
Österreichischer Mittelschulatlas. 76 ed. By Hans
Slanar. Wien, 1952.
146 p. col. maps. 31 cm.

2635 Hölzel, Ed. Verlag.
Österreichischer Mittelschulatlas. 77 ed. Wien,
1953.
146 p. col. maps. 31 cm.

2636 Hölzel, Ed. Verlag.
Österreichischer Mittelschulatlas. 78 ed. Wien,
1953.
146 p. col. maps. 31 cm.

2637 Hölzel, Ed. Verlag.
Österreichischer Mittelschulatlas. 79 ed. By Hans
Slanar. Wien, 1954.
146 p. col. maps. 31 cm.

2638 Hölzel, Ed. Verlag.
Österreichischer Mittelschulatlas. 80 ed. Wien,
1955.
146 p. col. maps. 31 cm.

2639 Hölzel, Ed. Verlag.
Österreichischer Mittelschulatlas. 81 ed. Wien,
1956.
146 p. col. maps. 31 cm.

2640 Hölzel, Ed. Verlag.
Österreichischer Mittelschulatlas. 82 ed. Wien,
1957.
146 p. col. maps. 31 cm.

2641 Hölzel, Ed. Verlag.
  Österreichischer Mittelschulatlas. 83 ed. Wien,
  1958.
  146 p. col. maps. 31 cm.

2642 Hölzel, Ed. Verlag.
  Österreichischer Mittelschulatlas. 84 ed. Wien,
  1959.
  146 p. col. maps. 31 cm.

2643 Hölzel, Ed. Verlag.
  Österreichischer Mittelschulatlas. 85 ed. Wien,
  1960.
  146 p. col. maps. 31 cm.

2644 Hölzel, Ed. Verlag.
  Österreichischer Mittelschulatlas. 86 ed. Wien,
  1961.
  146 p. col. maps. 31 cm.

2645 Hölzel, Ed. Verlag.
  Österreichischer Mittelschulatlas. 87 ed. Wien,
  1962.
  146 p. col. maps. 31 cm.

2646 Hölzel, Ed. Verlag.
  Österreichischer Mittelschulatlas. 88 ed. Wien,
  1963.
  146 p. col. maps. 31 cm.

2647 Hölzel, Ed. Verlag.
  Österreichischer Mittelschulatlas. 89 ed. Wien,
  1964.
  146 p. col. maps. 31 cm.

2648 Hölzel, Ed. Verlag.
  Österreichischer Mittelschulatlas. 90 ed. Wien,
  1964.
  226 p. col. maps. 31 cm.

2649 Hölzel, Ed. Verlag.
  Österreichischer Mittelschulatlas. 91 ed. Wien,
  1965.
  165 p. col. maps. 31 cm.

2650 Hölzel, Ed. Verlag.
  Österreichischer Mittelschulatlas. 92 ed. Wien,

1966.
165 p. col. maps. 31 cm.

2651 Hölzel, Ed. Verlag.
Österreichischer Mittelschulatlas.   93 ed.   Wien,
1967.
167 p. col. maps. 31 cm.

2652 Hölzel, Ed. Verlag.
Österreichischer Mittelschulatlas.   94 ed.   Wien,
1968.
167 p. col. maps. 31 cm.

2653 Hölzel, Ed. Verlag.
Österreichischer Mittelschulatlas.   95 ed.   Wien,
1969.
167 p. col. maps. 31 cm.

2654 Hölzel, Ed. Verlag.
Österreichischer Mittelschulatlas.   96 ed.   Wien,
1970.
167 p. col. maps. 31 cm.

2655 Internationaler Holzmarkt.
Österreichischer Sägewerksatlas.   1 ed.   Wien,
[1951].
1 vol. col. maps. 26 cm.

2656 Internationaler Holzmarkt.
Österreichischer Sägewerksatlas.   2 ed.   Wien,
[1960].
1 vol. col. maps. 26 cm.

2657 JRO Verlag.
JRO Autoatlas Österreich, Südostdeutschland,
Oberitalien, Nordwest-Jugoslawien, Ostschweiz.
München, [1956].
239 p. col. maps. 25 cm.

2658 Velhagen & Klasing.
Putzger Historischer Schul-atlas zur allgemeinen und
Österreichischen Geschichte.   43 ed.   Berlin,
Bielefeld, 1964.
190 p. col. maps. 26.5 cm.

Belgium

2659 Asedi.
    Atlas de géographie. La Belgique, le monde. By
    José A. Sprock and Luc Piérard. With Hölzel.
    Bruxelles, [1968].
    144 p. col. maps. 33 cm.

2660 Belgium. Centre national de recherches scientifiques
    souterraines.
    Atlas des grottes de Belgique. Liège, [1961-].
    1 vol. 30 cm.

2661 Belgium. Comité National de Géographie.
    Atlas de Belgique. Bruxelles, 1951—
    1 vol. col. maps. 62 cm.

2662 Belgium. Ministère des travaux publics et de la
    reconstruction.
    Atlas du survey national. Bruxelles, 1954—
    in parts. col. maps. 38 cm.

2663 Continental Gummiwerke Kartographischer Verlag.
    Continental atlas. Deutschland, Benelux, Alpen-
    länder. 26 ed. Hannover, [1956].
    453 p. col. maps. 26 cm.

2664 Continental Gummiwerke Kartographischer Verlag.
    Continental atlas. Deutschland, Benelux, Schweiz,
    Österreich, Norditalian. 33 ed. Hannover, 1964.
    635 p. col. maps. 26 cm.

2665 Elsevier.
    Atlas culturel et historique de Belgique. By Theo
    Luykx. New York, 1954.
    192 p. col. maps. 35 cm.

2666 Elsevier.
    Culturhistorische atlas van Belgie. By Theo Luykx.
    Amsterdam, [1954].
    226 p. col. maps. 36 cm.

2667 Elsevier.
    Elsevier atlas van Nederland, Belgie en Luxemburg.
    By M. E. Dumont, G. Peeters and A. H. Sijmonds.
    Amsterdam, 1960.
    195 p. col. maps. 19 cm.

2668 Hölzel, Ed. Verlag.
    Atlas de Géographie. La Belgique et le monde.
    Wien, 1968.
    112 p. col. maps. 33 cm.

2669 Netherlands. Staatsdrukkerij-en Uitgeverijbedrijf.
    Gemeentenatlas Benelux. 's Gravenhage, [1952].
    58 p. 35 cm.

2670 Ravenstein Geographische Verlagsanstalt.
    Autoatlas Benelux und Europa. Frankfurt am Main,
    1964.
    36 p. col. maps. 29 cm.

2671 Ravenstein Geographische Verlagsanstalt.
    Autoatlas Benelux und Europa. Frankfurt am Main,
    [1965].
    56 p. col. maps. 29 cm.

2672 Transportikroniek.
    Nijverheids-en handels-atlas der Belgische water-
    wegen. Antwerpen, 1951.
    257 p. 23 cm.

2673 Wesmael-Charlier.
    Atlas der algemene geschiedenis. By F. Hayt.
    Namur, 1968.
    144 p. col. maps. 26 cm.

2674 Wesmael-Charlier.
    Atlas d'histoire universelle. By Paul Schmets.
    Namur, [1962].
    126 p. col. maps. 26 cm.

2675 Wesmael-Charlier.
    Atlas d'histoire universelle. By Paul Schmets and
    Franz Hayt. Namur, [1965].
    126 p. col. maps. 26 cm.

2676 Wesmael-Charlier.
    Atlas d'histoire universelle (et d'histoire de Belgi-
    que). By Franz Hayt. Namur, 1967.
    144 p. col. maps. 26 cm.

2677 Wesmael-Charlier.
    Atlas d'histoire universelle. By F. Hayt. Namur,
    1968.
    132 p. col. maps. 26 cm.

2678 Wesmael-Charlier.
Cartographie de la Belgique et du Congo. By Jean
Tilmont. Namur, 1967.
32 p. 36 cm.

Bulgaria

2679 Bulgaria. Akademiya na naukite.
Atlas po bŭlgarska istoriya. Sofia, 1963.
87 p. col. maps. 32 cm.

2680 Bulgaria. Glavno upravlenie po geodezià i kartografià.
Avtumobilei atlas Bulgaria. Sofia, 1967.
56 p. col. maps. 20.5 cm.

2681 Bulgaria. Glavno upravlenie po geodezià i kartografià.
Geografski atlas na Bulgarija. Sofia, 1965.
40 p. col. maps. 30.5 cm.

2682 Bulgaria. Glavno upravlenie po geodezià i kartografià.
Geografski atlas za osmi klas i purvi kurs na
tekhnikumite. Sofia, [1968].
65 p. col. maps. 31 cm.

2683 Bulgaria. Muzei na revoliutsionnoto dvizhenie v
Bŭlgariiá.
Atlas na partizanskoto dvizhenie v Bŭlgariiá. Sofia,
[1968].
96 p. col. maps. 34 cm.

Czechoslovakia

2684 Czechoslovakia. Kartografické nakladatelství.
Autoatlas ČSSR. Praha, 1963.
163 p. col. maps. 31 cm.

2685 Czechoslovakia. Kartografické nakladatelství.
Autoatlas ČSSR. Praha, 1966.
163 p. col. maps. 31 cm.

2686 Czechoslovakia. Kartografické nakladatelství.
Autoatlas ČSSR. Praha, [1967].
163 p. col. maps. 31 cm.

2687 Czechoslovakia. Kartografické nakladatelství.
Mapový lexikon obcí ČSSR. Praha, 1968.
1 vol. col. maps. 30 cm.

2688 Czechoslovakia. Kartografické nakladatelství.
Školni atlas Československých dějin. Praha, 1967.
1 vol. col. maps. 30 cm.

2689 Czechoslovakia. Ministerstro národní obrany.
ČSSR; soubor map z čs. vojenského atlasu. 1 ed.
Praha, [1966].
16 p. col. maps. 42 cm.

2690 Czechoslovakia. Ústřední správa geodézie a kartografie.
Atlas Československé Socialistické Republiky. By
Antonin Götz. Praha, 1966.
83 p. col. maps. 50 cm.

2691 Czechoslovakia. Ústřední správa geodézie a kartografie.
Atlas Československých dějin. 1 ed. Praha, [1965].
58 p. col. maps. 52 cm.

2692 Czechoslovakia. Ústřední správa geodésie a kartografie.
Atlas obyvatelstva ČSSR. 1 ed. By Jindrich
Svoboda. Praha, [1962].
91 p. col. maps. 22 cm.

2693 Czechoslovakia. Ústřední správa geodézie a kartografie.
Atlas podnebí Československé republiky. Praha, 1958.
1 vol. col. maps. 45 cm.

2694 Czechoslovakia. Ústřední správa geodésie a kartografie.
Autoatlas ČSSR. Praha, 1963.
165 p. col. maps. 25 cm.

2695 Czechoslovakia. Ústřední správa geodésie a kartografie.
Autoatlas ČSSR. Praha, 1965.
163 p. col. maps. 25 cm.

2696 Czechoslovakia. Ústřední správa geodésie a kartografie.
Automapa ČSR. 1 ed. Praha, 1957.
98 p. col. maps. 22 cm.

2697 Czechoslovakia. Ústřední správa geodésie a kartografie.
Automapa ČSR. 2 ed. Praha, 1958.
98 p. col. maps. 22 cm.

2698 Czechoslovakia. Ústřední správa geodésie a kartografie.
Automapa ČSR. 3 ed. Praha, 1959.
98 p. col. maps. 22 cm.

2699 Czechoslovakia. Ústřední správa geodesie a kartografie. Československý vojenský atlas. Praha, 1965. 386 p. col. maps. 40 cm.

2700 Czechoslovakia. Ústřední správa geodézie a kartografie. Geological atlas. Regional Geology of Czechoslovakia. Praha, 1967. 15 p. col. maps. 24 cm.

2701 Czechoslovakia. Ústřední správa geodésie a kartografie. Historický atlas revolučního hnutí. Praha, 1956. 180 p. col. maps. 33 cm.

2702 Czechoslovakia. Ústřední správa geodésie a kartografie. Lesnický a myslivecký atlas. 1 ed. Praha, 1955. 120 p. col. maps. 33 cm.

2703 Czechoslovakia. Ústřední správa geodézie a kartografie. Malý školní zeměpisný atlas. 3 ed. By Konštantín Zelenský. Bratislava, 1966. 16 p. col. maps. 30 cm.

2704 Czechoslovakia. Ústřední správa geodézie a kartografie. Školní atlas Československých dějin. 2 ed. By Ivan Beneš. Praha, 1964. 63 p. col. maps. 31 cm.

2705 Czechoslovakia. Ústřední správa geodézie a kartografie. Školní atlas Československých dějin. Praha, 1965. 45 p. col. maps. 42.5 cm.

2706 Czechoslovakia. Ústřední správa geodézie a kartografie. Školní zeměpisný atlas Československé Socialistické Republiky. 1 ed. By Jindřich Svoboda. Praha, 1960. 35 p. col. maps. 31 cm.

2707 Czechoslovakia. Ústřední správa geodézie a kartografie. Školní zeměpisný atlas Československé Socialistické Republiky. By Jindřich Svoboda. Praha, 1962. 51 p. col. maps. 31 cm.

2708 Czechoslovakia. Ústřední správa geodézie a kartografie. Školský zeměpisný atlas Československé Socialistické Republiky. Praha, 1967. 40 p. col. maps. 31 cm.

2709 Czechoslovakia. Ústřední správa geodézie a kartografie.
Školský zeměpisný atlas Československé Socialistické Republiky. 2 ed. By Jindřich Svoboda.
Praha, 1962.
51 p. col. maps. 31 cm.

2710 Czechoslovakia. Ústřední správa geodézie a kartografie.
Školský zeměpisný atlas Československé Socialistické Republiky. Praha, 1965.
51 p. col. maps. 31 cm.

2711 Czechoslovakia. Ústřední ústav geologický.
Geologický atlas ČSSR. 1 ed. Praha, 1966.
1 vol. col. maps. 51 cm.

2712 Orbis.
Československo v mapách. Praha, 1953.
60 p. col. maps. 32 cm.

2713 Orbis.
Československo v mapách. Praha, [1954].
60 p. col. maps. 32 cm.

Denmark

2714 Denmark. Geodaetisk Institut.
Atlas kort over Denmark. København, 1969.
1 vol. col. maps. 27.5 cm.

2715 Denmark. Geodaetisk Institut.
Denmark. [Atlas]. København, 1963.
1 vol. col. maps. 27.5 cm.

2716 Denmark. Geodaetisk Institut.
FDM Kortbog. Denmark. 25 ed. København, 1964.
208 p. col. maps. 24 cm.

2717 Denmark. Geodaetisk Institut.
Generalstabskort Denmark. København, 1963.
1 vol. col. maps. 23.5 cm.

2718 Denmark. Geodaetisk Institut.
Generalstabskort Denmark. København, 1965.
1 vol. col. maps. 23.5 cm.

2719 Denmark. Geodaetisk Institut.
Geodaetisk Instituts Kort, Denmark. København,

1955.
53 p.   col. maps.   22 cm.

2720 Denmark.   Geodaetisk Institut.
Geodaetisk Instituts Kort, Denmark.   København,
1956.
53 p.   col. maps.   22 cm.

2721 Denmark.   Geodaetisk Institut.
Geodaetisk Instituts Kort.   København, 1965.
32 p.   col. maps.   27.5 cm.

2722 Gyldendal.
Denmark-atlas med Faerøerne og Grønland.   By
Johannes Humlum and Knud Nygard.   København,
1961.
1 vol.   col. maps.   30 cm.

2723 Imperial Press.
Atlas guide Denmark.   København, [1963].
40 p.   col. maps.   24 cm.

2724 Imperial Press.
Atlas guide Denmark.   København, 1964.
1 vol.   col. maps.   24 cm.

2725 Reitzels, C. A. Forlag.
Atlas over Denmark.   København, 1950—
in 5 vols.   col. maps.   55 cm.

Finland

2726 Generalstabens litografiska anstalt.
Joka Kodin Kartasto.   Helsinki, [1966].
145 p.   col. maps.   28 cm.

2727 Maanmittanshallitus.
Suomi.   Finland.   Yleiskartta 1:400,000 general
karta.   Helsinki, 1950.
166 p.   col. maps.   25 cm.

2728 Suomen Maantieteellinen Seura.
Suomen Kartasto, 1960.   Atlas of Finland.   4 ed.
Helsinki, [1960-62].
2 vol.   col. maps.   25 cm and 46 cm.

2729 Yhtyneet Kuvalehdet.
Suomen Kuvalehden Kartlakiya.   Helsinki, 1965.

72 p. col. maps. 25 cm.

France

2730 Blondel La Rougery.
Atlas des routes de France. Paris, 1967.
31 p. col. maps. 24 cm.

2731 Blondel La Rougery.
Atlas Simca des routes de France. Paris, [1950].
32 p. col. maps. 23 cm.

2732 Blondel La Rougery.
Atlas Simca des routes de France. Paris, [1952].
32 p. col. maps. 23 cm.

2733 Colin.
Atlas de la France rurale. By Jean Duplex.
Paris, 1968.
176 p. 34 cm.

2734 Colin.
Atlas historique. Paris, 1969.
258 p. col. maps. 32 cm.

2735 Colin.
Atlas historique de la France contemporaine, 1800-
1965. Paris, 1966.
235 p. col. maps. 23 cm.

2736 Didot-Bottin.
Atlas Bottin. Tome 1. 3 ed. Paris, 1951.
704 p. col. maps. 27 cm.

2737 Didot-Bottin.
Atlas du Bottin. Paris, 1950.
644 p. col. maps. 27 cm.

2738 Editions Bordas.
Atlas général Bordas: la France, le monde. By
Pierre Serryn. Paris, [1964].
140 p. col. maps. 31 cm.

2739 Editions Bordas.
Atlas général Bordas: la France, le monde. By
Pierre Serryn. Paris, [1965].
140 p. col. maps. 31 cm.

2740 Editions Bordas.
     Atlas schématique Bordas; France.   By M. Rouable
     and P. Gillardot.   Paris, [1968].
     47 p.   col. maps.   24 cm.

2741 Editions Bordas.
     Nouvel atlas général: La France, L'Union française,
     le monde.   By Pierre Serryn.   Paris, 1954.
     170 p.   col. maps.   31 cm.

2742 Editions Bordas.
     Nouvel atlas général, La France, L'Union française,
     le monde.   By Pierre Serryn.   Paris, [1957].
     150 p.   col. maps.   31 cm.

2743 Editions Bordas.
     Nouvel atlas général, la France, l'Union française,
     le monde.   By Pierre Serryn.   Paris, 1958.
     168 p.   col. maps.   31 cm.

2744 Editions Bordas.
     Petit atlas Bordas: la France, le monde.   By René
     Canët, Pierre Serryn and Marc Vincent.   Paris,
     1969.
     78 p.   col. maps.   33 cm.

2745 Editions Bordas.
     Petit atlas politique et économique de la France et
     du monde.   Paris, [1966].
     32 p.   col. maps.   27 cm.

2746 Elsevier.
     Atlas historique et culturel de la France.   By
     Jacques Boussard.   Paris, [1957].
     214 p.   col. maps.   35 cm.

2747 Foldex (France), Ltd.
     France: atlas des grandes routes.   Paris, [1966].
     32 p.   col. maps.   19 cm.

2748 France.   Comité National de Géographie.
     Atlas de France.   Paris, [1951-58].
     80 p.   col. maps.   50 cm.

2749 France.   Commissariat général à la productivité.
     Atlas de la productivité.   Paris, [1958].
     1 vol.   col. maps.   43 cm.

2750 France.   Conseil national du patronat français.
      Atlas de l'industrie française.   Paris, 1959.
      354 p.   col.   maps.   38 cm.

2751 France.   La Documentation Française.
      Atlas de la polution des eaux en France métropoli-
      taine.   By Louis Coin.   Paris, 1963.
      126 p.   col.   maps.   27 cm.

2752 France.   La Documentation Française.
      Atlas des eaux souterraines de la France.   Paris,
      [1970].
      360 p.   col.   maps.   28 cm.

2753 France.   La Documentation Française.
      Atlas économique et social pour l'aménagement du
      territoire.   By T. Hautreux.   Paris, 1966 –
      in parts.   col.   maps.   56 cm.

2754 France.   La Documentation Française.
      Atlas industriel de la France.   By Robert Giry.
      Paris, 1959.
      201 p.   col.   maps.   39 cm.

2755 France.   Ministère de L'Équipment.
      Cartes annuelle et mensuelles de la Hauteur
      Moyenne Des Précipitations.   Extraites de l'Atlas
      Climatique de la France.   Paris, 1966.
      1 vol.   col.   maps.   52 cm.

2756 France.   Ministère des postes et télécommunications.
      Mémento de nomenclature géographique.   Paris,
      1964.
      81 p.   31 cm.

2757 France.   Service de l'économie forestière.
      Atlas forestièr, année 1963.   Paris, [1964].
      65 p.   col.   maps.   32 cm.

2758 France.   Société nationale des chemins de fer français.
      Atlas des lignes ouvertes au trafic marchandises.
      Paris, 1964.
      14 p.   col.   maps.   31 cm.

2759 Gallimard.
      Atlas aérien: France.   By Pierre Defontaines.
      Paris, [1955-62].
      4 vol.   28 cm.

2760 Hachette.
    Atlas classique. By Pierre Gourou. Paris,
    [1954-56].
    2 vol. col. maps. 33 cm.

2761 Imprimeries Oberthur.
    Atlas des départements français. Rennes, [1961].
    1 vol. col. maps. 27 cm.

2762 Imprimeries Oberthur.
    Atlas des départements français. Rennes, 1966.
    1 vol. col. maps. 27 cm.

2763 Imprimeries Oberthur.
    Atlas des départements français. Rennes, 1967.
    1 vol. col. maps. 27 cm.

2764 Imprimeries Oberthur.
    Atlas des départements français et de l'union
    française. Rennes, 1958.
    114 p. col. maps. 27 cm.

2765 Imprimeries Oberthur.
    Atlas des départements français et territoires
    d'outre-mer. Rennes, [1954].
    101 p. col. maps. 31 cm.

2766 Imprimeries Oberthur.
    Index-atlas des départements français. Rennes,
    1968.
    210 p. col. maps. 27 cm.

2767 Le Carrousel Publicité.
    Gastronomical roads (Atlas) of the French provinces.
    Tours, 1967.
    36 p. col. maps. 27 cm.

2768 Librairie Mellottée.
    Atlas de route Mellottée. Paris, [1950].
    157 p. col. maps. 19 cm.

2769 Michelin et Cie.
    Atlas des routes de France. Paris, 1951-52.
    40 p. col. maps. 26 cm.

2770 Michelin et Cie.
    Atlas des routes de France. Paris, 1953-54.
    40 p. col. maps. 26 cm.

2771 Michelin et Cie.
Atlas des routes de France. Paris, [1955]. ·
40 p. col. maps. 26 cm.

2772 Michelin et Cie.
Atlas des routes de France. Paris, [1956].
40 p. col. maps. 26 cm.

2773 Michelin et Cie.
Atlas des routes de France. Paris, [1958].
40 p. col. maps. 26 cm.

2774 Michelin et Cie.
Camping en France. [Atlas]. Paris, 1957.
85 p. 25 cm.

2775 Nouvelles de l'Enseignement.
Synthèse de la vie économique en France. Petit
atlas de la France et de l'Union Française. By
Robert Poirier. Paris, [1956].
92 p. 27 cm.

2776 Peugeot.
Atlas routier Peugeot. Paris, [1954].
19 p. col. maps. 29 cm.

2777 Sélection du Reader's Digest, S.A.R.L.
Grand atlas de la France. 1 ed. Paris, 1969.
244 p. col. maps. 41 cm.

2778 Société des pétroles Shell Berre.
Cartoguide Shell Berre: France. Paris, 1962-64.
14 p. col. maps. 24 cm.

2779 Société française des pétroles BP.
France B. P. Courbevoie, Seine, [1964].
20 p. col. maps. 28 cm.

2780 U.S.S.R. Glavnoe upravlenie geodezii i kartografii.
Atlas Frantsii. Moskva, 1970-71.
1 vol. col. maps. 32 cm.

Germany

2781 Accumulatoren-Fabrik A. G.
Varta Auto-atlas. Hannover, [1950].
174 p. col. maps. 30 cm.

2782 Accumulatoren-Fabrik, A. G.
     <u>Varta Auto-atlas.</u> 3 ed. Frankfurt, 1952.
     164 p. col. maps. 30 cm.

2783 Akademie Verlag.
     <u>Klima Atlas für das Gebiet der Deutschen Demo-
     kratischen Republik.</u> Berlin, 1953—
     in parts. col. maps. 67 cm.

2784 Allgemeiner Deutscher Automobil-Club.
     <u>ADAC Auto-atlas.</u> Kiel, [1950-51].
     2 vol. col. maps. 28 cm.

2785 Atlantik Verlag.
     <u>Deutschland und die Welt.</u> By Willy Eggers.
     Frankfurt, [1954].
     75 p. col. maps. 34 cm.

2786 Atlantik Verlag.
     <u>Deutschland und die Welt.</u> By Willy Eggers.
     Frankfurt, [1956].
     75 p. col. maps. 34 cm.

2787 Atlantik Verlag.
     <u>Deutschland und die Welt.</u> By Willy Eggers.
     Frankfurt, [1959].
     97 p. col. maps. 34 cm.

2788 Atlantik Verlag.
     <u>Harms Heimatatlas.</u> Frankfurt, [1955].
     41 p. col. maps. 28 cm.

2789 Atlantik Verlag.
     <u>Harms Heimatatlas.</u> By C. H. Lübbert. Frank-
     furt, [1958].
     65 p. col. maps. 28 cm.

2790 Autokarten und Reiseführer Verlag.
     <u>Der neue Auto-Strassen Atlas.</u> Kiel, [1952].
     3 vol. inl. col. maps. 28 cm.

2791 Bertelsmann, C.
     <u>Autoatlas Bertelsmann.</u> Deutschland-Europe.
     Gütersloh, [1964].
     388 p. col. maps. 27 cm.

2792 Bertelsmann, C.
     <u>Autoatlas Bertelsmann.</u> Deutschland-Europe.

Gütersloh, 1965.
388 p. col. maps. 27 cm.

2793 Bertelsmann, C.
Autoatlas Bertelsmann. Deutschland-Europa.
Gütersloh, 1966.
388 p. col. maps. 27 cm.

2794 BLV Verlagsgesellschaft.
BLV-Atlas. Die Landwirtschaft der Bundesrepublik
Deutschland. By Inge Kloppenburg. München,
Basel, Wien, [1968-].
1 vol. col. maps. 44 cm.

2795 BP Benzin & Petroleum Gesellschaft.
BP Dieselatlas Deutschland. Hamburg, [195-].
39 p. col. maps. 21 cm.

2796 Columbus Verlag Oestergaard.
Columbus Auto-atlas für Reise, Verkehr und Handel.
Berlin, [1950].
40 p. col. maps. 28 cm.

2797 Continental Gummiwerke Kartographischer Verlag.
Continental Atlas. 27 ed. Hannover, [1957].
485 p. col. maps. 26 cm.

2798 Continental Gummiwerke Kartographischer Verlag.
Continental Atlas. 28 ed. Hannover, [1958].
489 p. col. maps. 26 cm.

2799 Continental Gummiwerke Kartographischer Verlag.
Continental Atlas. Deutschland, Benelux, Alpen-
länder. 26 ed. Hannover, [1956].
453 p. col. maps. 26 cm.

2800 Continental Gummiwerke Kartographischer Verlag.
Continental Atlas. Deutschland, Benelux, Schweiz,
Österreich, Norditalian. 33 ed. Hannover, 1964.
635 p. col. maps. 26 cm.

2801 Continental Gummiwerke Kartographischer Verlag.
Continental Atlas. Deutschland, Europa. 34 ed.
Hannover, [1966].
531 p. col. maps. 26 cm.

2802 Continental Gummiwerke Kartographischer Verlag.
Continental Atlas. Deutschland, Europa. 35 ed.

Hannover, 1968-69.
551 p. col. maps. 26 cm.

2803 Continental Gummiwerke Kartographischer Verlag.
Der grosse Continental Atlas. 21 ed. Hannover,
[1951].
212 p. col. maps. 26 cm.

2804 Continental Gummiwerke Kartographischer Verlag.
Der grosse Continental Atlas. 22 ed. Hannover,
[1951].
212 p. col. maps. 26 cm.

2805 Continental Gummiwerke Kartographischer Verlag.
Der grosse Continental Atlas. 23 ed. Hannover,
[1952].
212 p. col. maps. 26 cm.

2806 Continental Gummiwerke Kartographischer Verlag.
Der grosse Continental Atlas. 24 ed. Hannover,
[1953].
269 p. col. maps. 26 cm.

2807 Continental Gummiwerke Kartographischer Verlag.
Der grosse Continental Atlas. 25 ed. Hannover,
[1955].
318 p. col. maps. 26 cm.

2808 Continental Gummiwerke Kartographischer Verlag.
Der grosse Continental Atlas für Kraftfahrer. 20
ed. Hannover, [1950].
61 p. col. maps. 26 cm.

2809 Deutsche Viscobil Öl Gesellschaft.
Viscobil Auto Tourenkarte. Hamburg, 1953.
49 p. col. maps. 22 cm.

2810 Deutscher Zentralverlag VEB.
Strassen Atlas von Deutschland. 3 ed. Berlin,
[1952].
26 p. col. maps. 22 cm.

2811 Elwert Verlag.
Atlas der Deutschen Volkskunde. Neue Folge. By
Matthias Zender. Marburg, 1958—
in parts. col. maps. 72 cm.

2812 Elwert Verlag.
Deutscher Sprachatlas. Marburg, -1967.
in parts. col. maps. 69 cm.

2813 ESSO, A. G.
Esso Reise-Atlas für Kraftfahrer. München, [1956].
164 p. col. maps. 24 cm.

2814 ESSO, A. G.
Esso Reise-Atlas von Deutschland. München, [1955].
156 p. col. maps. 24 cm.

2815 Falk Verlag.
Autoatlas der Bundesrepublik Deutschland. 15 ed.
Hamburg, [1952].
57 p. col. maps. 25 cm.

2816 Falk Verlag.
Autoatlas der Bundesrepublik Deutschland. 51 and
53 ed. Hamburg, 1963.
68 p. col. maps. 24.5 cm.

2817 Falk Verlag.
Autoatlas der Bundesrepublik Deutschland. 54 and
55 ed. Hamburg, 1964.
68 p. col. maps. 24.5 cm.

2818 Falk Verlag.
Autoatlas der Bundesrepublik Deutschland. Hamburg, 1968.
68 p. col. maps. 24.5 cm.

2819 Falk Verlag.
Autostrassen Atlas der Bundesrepublik Deutschland.
Hamburg, [1955].
51 p. col. maps. 25 cm.

2820 Falk Verlag.
Falk Autoatlas Nr. 355. Von Kopenhagen bis
Mailand. 19 ed. Hamburg, 1963.
70 p. col. maps. 27 cm.

2821 Falk Verlag.
Falk Auto-Atlas, Bundesrepublik Deutschland. 2 ed.
Köln, 1953.
52 p. col. maps. 25 cm.

2822 Falk Verlag.
 Ford Auto-Atlas. Bundesrepublik Deutschland. 2 ed.
 Köln, [1953].
 52 p. col. maps. 25 cm.

2823 Akademie für Raumforschung und Landesplannung.
 Deutscher Plannungsatlas. Hannover, 1956-
 10 vol. col. maps. 60 cm.

2824 Germany. Statistisches Bundesamt, Institut für
 Landeskunde und Institut für Raumforschung.
 Atlas. Die Bundesrepublik Deutschland in Karten.
 Mainz, 1961-
 in parts. col. maps. 87 cm.

2825 Haack, Hermann.
 Agraratlas über das Gebiet der Deutschen Demokratischen Republik. By R. Matz. Gotha, 1956.
 1 vol. col. maps. 63 cm.

2826 Haack, Hermann.
 Atlas der Deutschen Demokratischen Republik.
 Gotha, Leipzig, 1966.
 17 p. col. maps. 27 cm.

2827 Haack, Hermann.
 Atlas der Deutschen Demokratischen Republik.
 2 ed. Leipzig, 1968.
 17 p. col. maps. 27 cm.

2828 Haack, Hermann.
 Autoatlas der Deutschen Demokratischen Republik.
 1 ed. Gotha, 1962.
 80 p. col. maps. 27 cm.

2829 Haack, Hermann.
 Autoatlas der Deutschen Demokratischen Republik.
 2 ed. Gotha, 1963.
 97 p. col. maps. 27 cm.

2830 Haack, Hermann.
 Deutschland. Taschenatlas. 14 ed. Gotha, 1950.
 142 p. col. maps. 18 cm.

2831 Haack, Hermann.
 Deutschland. Taschenatlas. 15 ed. Gotha, 1951.
 142 p. col. maps. 18 cm.

2832 Haack, Hermann.
      Deutschland.   Taschenatlas. 16 ed. Gotha, 1952.
      142 p. col. maps. 18 cm.

2833 Haack, Hermann.
      Deutschland.   Taschenatlas. 17 ed. Gotha, 1952.
      143 p. col. maps. 18 cm.

2834 Haack, Hermann.
      Deutschland.   Taschenatlas. 18 ed. Gotha, 1953.
      160 p. col. maps. 18 cm.

2835 Haack, Hermann.
      Deutschland.   Taschenatlas. 19 ed. Gotha, 1954.
      159 p. col. maps. 18 cm.

2836 Haack, Hermann.
      Deutschland.   Taschenatlas. 20 ed. Gotha, 1955.
      159 p. col. maps. 18 cm.

2837 Haack, Hermann.
      Deutschland.   Taschenatlas. 21 ed. Gotha, 1956.
      159 p. col. maps. 18 cm.

2838 Haack, Hermann.
      Deutschland.   Taschenatlas. 21 ed. Gotha, 1957.
      159 p. col. maps. 18 cm.

2839 Haack, Hermann.
      Deutschland.   Taschenatlas. 22 ed. Gotha, 1958.
      159 p. col. maps. 18 cm.

2840 Haack, Hermann.
      Deutschland.   Taschenatlas. 23 ed. Gotha, 1959.
      159 p. col. maps. 18 cm.

2841 Haack, Hermann.
      Deutschland.   Taschenatlas. Gotha, 1966.
      182 p. col. maps. 18 cm.

2842 Haack, Hermann.
      Die beiden Deutschen Staaten. Taschenatlas. 24 ed.
      Gotha, 1961.
      127 p. col. maps. 18 cm.

2843 Haack, Hermann.
      Die beiden Deutschen Staaten. Taschenatlas. 27 ed.

Gotha, 1965.
314 p. col. maps. 18 cm.

2844 Haack, Hermann.
Die beiden Deutschen Staaten. Taschenatlas.
Gotha, 1966.
314 p. col. maps. 18 cm.

2845 Haack, Hermann.
Verkehrsatlas. Deutsche Demokratische Republik.
1 ed. Gotha, 1959.
115 p. col. maps. 18 cm.

2846 Haack, Hermann.
Verkehrsatlas. Deutsche Demokratische Republik.
2 ed. Gotha, 1960.
115 p. col. maps. 18 cm.

2847 Haack, Hermann.
Verkehrsatlas. Deutsche Demokratische Republik.
3 ed. Gotha, 1961.
83 p. col. maps. 18 cm.

2848 Haack, Hermann.
Verkehrsatlas. Deutsche Demokratische Republik.
4 ed. Gotha, 1962.
87 p. col. maps. 18 cm.

2849 Haack, Hermann.
Verkehrsatlas. Deutsche Demokratische Republik.
5 ed. Gotha, 1963.
111 p. col. maps. 18 cm.

2850 Haack, Hermann.
Verkehrsatlas. Deutsche Demokratische Republik.
6 ed. Gotha, 1966.
220 p. col. maps. 18 cm.

2851 JRO Verlag.
JRO Atlas für Kraftfahrer und alle Reisenden.
München. [1950].
344 p. col. maps. 25 cm.

2852 JRO Verlag.
JRO Autoatlas. Deutschland, Europäische Reise-
länder. München, [1954].
514 p. col. maps. 25 cm.

2853 JRO Verlag.
JRO Autoatlas. Deutschland, Europäische Reise-
länder. München, [1955].
515 p. col. maps. 25 cm.

2854 JRO Verlag.
JRO Autoatlas. Deutschland, Schweiz, Westöster-
reich. München, [1953].
468 p. col. maps. 25 cm.

2855 JRO Verlag.
JRO Deutschland Spezialatlas für Organisation,
Handel und Verkehr. München, [1950].
38 p. col. maps. 45 cm.

2856 JRO Verlag.
JRO Strassen Atlas. Deutschland, Europa. München,
[1968].
78 p. col. maps. 29.5 cm.

2857 JRO Verlag.
JRO Strassen Taschenatlas. München, [1951].
160 p. col. maps. 21 cm.

2858 JRO Verlag.
JRO Strassen Taschenatlas. 2 ed. München, [1954].
162 p. col. maps. 21 cm.

2859 JRO Verlag.
JRO Verkehrsatlas für Strasse, Eisenbahn und Büro;
Deutschland. München, [1953].
271 p. col. maps. 25 cm.

2860 Kohlhammer Verlag.
Die Bundesrepublik Deutschland in Karten. Mainz,
1965—
in parts. col. maps. 29 cm.

2861 König, Hans, Verlag.
Caltex Städte und Reiseatlas der Bundesrepublik
Deutschland. 4 ed. Bergen-Enkheim, 1964.
273 p. col. maps. 29 cm.

2862 König, Hans, Verlag.
Deutscher Ferien Atlas. Frankfurt am Main, [1960].
84 p. col. maps. 24 cm.

2863 König, Hans, Verlag.
      Reiseatlas Deutschland, Europa.   Enkheim, 1965.
      61 p. col. maps. 29 cm.

2864 König, Hans, Verlag.
      Reiseatlas. Deutschland, Europa.   Frankfurt am
      Main, [1966].
      64 p. col. maps. 29 cm.

2865 Kümmerly & Frey.
      Kleinatlas Deutschland.   Bern, 1964.
      32 p. col. maps. 15 cm.

2866 Landkartenverlag VEB.
      Atlas für Motortouristik der Deutschen Demo-
      kratischen Republik.   1 ed. Berlin, 1963.
      228 p. col. maps. 23 cm.

2867 Landkartenverlag VEB.
      Atlas für Motortouristik der Deutschen Demo-
      kratischen Republik.   2 ed. Berlin, 1964.
      228 p. col. maps. 23 cm.

2868 Landkartenverlag VEB.
      Autoatlas der Deutschen Demokratischen Republik.
      4 ed. Berlin, [1966].
      133 p. col. maps. 25.5 cm.

2869 Landkartenverlag, VEB.
      Reiseatlas der Deutschen Demokratischen Republik.
      Berlin, 1967.
      100 p. col. maps. 26 cm.

2870 Landkartenverlag, VEB.
      Reiseatlas der Deutschen Demokratischen Republik.
      Berlin, [1969].
      100 p. col. maps. 26 cm.

2871 List, P.
      Harms Atlas, Deutschland und die Welt.   By W.
      Eggers. München, [1962].
      97 p. col. maps. 34 cm.

2872 List, P.
      Harms Atlas, Deutschland und die Welt.   By Willy
      Eggers. München, [1965].
      118 p. col. maps. 33 cm.

2873 List, P.
Harms Heimatatlas Köln. München, [1967].
49 p. col. maps. 30 cm.

2874 List, P.
Harms Ostdeutsche Heimat in Karte, Bild und Wort.
8-10 ed. By F. Dörr. München, [1961].
53 p. col. maps. 30 cm.

2875 List, P.
Harms Ostdeutsche Heimat in Karte, Bild und Wort.
By F. Dörr. Frankfurt, 1964.
51 p. col. maps. 30 cm.

2876 List, P.
Harms Ostdeutsche Heimat in Karte, Bild und Wort.
By F. Dörr. München, 1965.
49 p. col. maps. 30 cm.

2877 List, P.
Harms Ostdeutsche Heimat in Karte, Bild und Wort.
By F. Dörr. München, 1967.
49 p. col. maps. 30 cm.

2878 Mairs Geographischer Verlag.
Continental Atlas. Deutschland, Europa. 36 ed.
Stuttgart, 1969.
555 p. col. maps. 27 cm.

2879 Mairs Geographischer Verlag.
Der Grosse Shell Atlas. 1 ed. Stuttgart, [1960].
419 p. col. maps. 27 cm.

2880 Mairs Geographischer Verlag.
Der Grosse Shell Atlas. 8 ed. Stuttgart, 1963.
335 p. col. maps. 26.5 cm.

2881 Mairs Geographischer Verlag.
Der Grosse Shell Atlas. 9 ed. Stuttgart, 1964.
335 p. col. maps. 26.5 cm.

2882 Mairs Geographischer Verlag.
Der Grosse Shell Atlas. 11 ed. Stuttgart, 1965.
460 p. col. maps. 26.5 cm.

2883 Mairs Geographischer Verlag.
Der Grosse Shell Atlas. 12 ed. Stuttgart, 1966.
460 p. col. maps. 26.5 cm.

2884 Mairs Geographischer Verlag.
        Der Grosse Shell Atlas. Stuttgart, 1969/70.
        460 p. col. maps. 26.5 cm.

2885 Mairs Geographischer Verlag.
        Der Grosse Shell Atlas. Deutschland und Europa.
        10 ed. Stuttgart, [1965].
        259 p. col. maps. 27 cm.

2886 Mairs Geographischer Verlag.
        Der Grosse Shell Atlas. Deutschland und Europa.
        11 ed. Stuttgart, [1966].
        283 p. col. maps. 27 cm.

2887 Mairs Geographischer Verlag.
        Der Grosse Shell Atlas. Deutschland und Europa.
        12 ed. Stuttgart, [1967].
        283 p. col. maps. 27 cm.

2888 Mairs Geographischer Verlag.
        Der Grosse Shell Atlas. Deutschland und Europa.
        13 ed. Stuttgart, [1968].
        283 p. col. maps. 27 cm.

2889 Mairs Geographischer Verlag.
        Der Grosse Shell Atlas. Deutschland und Europa.
        14 ed. Stuttgart, 1969.
        283 p. col. maps. 27 cm.

2890 Mairs Geographischer Verlag.
        Deutscher Generalatlas. Stuttgart, 1967/8.
        450 p. col. maps. 37.5 cm.

2891 Mairs Geographischer Verlag.
        Shell atlas. 20 ed. Stuttgart, [1957].
        272 p. col. maps. 27 cm.

2892 Mairs Geographischer Verlag.
        Shell atlas. Stuttgart, [1961].
        1 vol. col. maps. 27 cm.

2893 Mairs Geographischer Verlag.
        Shell Autoatlas. 10 ed. Stuttgart, [1952].
        206 p. col. maps. 27 cm.

2894 Mairs Geographischer Verlag.
        Shell Autoatlas. 11 ed. Stuttgart, [1952].
        206 p. col. maps. 27 cm.

2895 Mairs Geographischer Verlag.
Shell Autoatlas. 12 ed. Stuttgart, [1954].
266 p. col. maps. 27 cm.

2896 Mairs Geographischer Verlag.
Shell Autoatlas. 14 ed. Stuttgart, [1954].
266 p. col. maps. 27 cm.

2897 Mairs Geographischer Verlag.
Shell Autoatlas. 15 ed. Stuttgart, [1955].
268 p. col. maps. 27 cm.

2898 Mairs Geographischer Verlag.
Shell Autoatlas. A new atlas of Germany. Stuttgart, [1951].
109 p. col. maps. 27 cm.

2899 Mairs Geographischer Verlag.
Shell Autoatlas, ein neues Kartenwerk von Deutschland. Stuttgart, [1950].
109 p. col. maps. 27 cm.

2900 Mairs Geographischer Verlag.
Shell Autoatlas; ein neues Kartenwerk von Deutschland. 5 ed. Stuttgart, [1951].
129 p. col. maps. 27 cm.

2901 Mairs Geographischer Verlag.
Shell Autoatlas; ein neues Kartenwerk von Deutschland. Stuttgart, [1952].
129 p. col. maps. 27 cm.

2902 Mairs Geographischer Verlag.
Shell Autoatlas. Maps of Germany, maps of European countries. Stuttgart, [1954].
266 p. col. maps. 27 cm.

2903 Mairs Geographischer Verlag.
Shell Autoatlas. Maps of Germany, maps of European countries. Stuttgart, [1956].
268 p. col. maps. 27 cm.

2904 Mairs Geographischer Verlag.
Varta Autoatlas. Deutschland. Stuttgart, 1963.
166 p. col. maps. 29 cm.

2905 Ravenstein Geographische Verlagsanstalt.
Frisia Reise Atlas. Deutschland und Europa.

Frankfurt, 1967.
66 p. col. maps. 29 cm.

2906 Ravenstein Geographische Verlagsanstalt.
Jugendherbergs. Taschenatlas der Bundesrepublik.
Frankfurt, [1953].
10 p. col. maps. 15 cm.

2907 Ravenstein Geographische Verlagsanstalt.
Strassen Atlas Bundesrepublik Deutschland. Frankfurt, [1955].
128 p. col. maps. 25 cm.

2908 Ravenstein Geographische Verlagsanstalt.
Strassen Atlas Bundersrepublik Deutschland. Frankfurt, [1957].
128 p. col. maps. 25 cm.

2909 Ravenstein Geographische Verlagsanstalt.
Strassen; der aktuelle Auto-Atlas Deutschland und
Europa. Frankfurt am Main, [1966].
1 vol. col. maps. 29 cm.

2910 Ravenstein Geographische Verlagsanstalt.
Strassen; der aktuelle Auto-Atlas Deutschland und
Europa. Frankfurt, [1969].
66 p. col. maps. 29 cm.

2911 Ravenstein Geographische Verlagsanstalt.
Strassen Deutschland und Europa. 2 ed.   Frankfurt am Main, [1962].
51 p. col. maps. 29 cm.

2912 Ravenstein Geographische Verlagsanstalt.
Strassen Deutschland und Europa. 3 ed.   Frankfurt am Main, 1963.
55 p. col. maps. 29 cm.

2913 Ravenstein Geographische Verlagsanstalt.
Strassen Deutschland und Europa. 5 ed.   Frankfurt am Main, 1964.
57 p. col. maps. 29 cm.

2914 Ravenstein Geographische Verlagsanstalt.
Strassen Deutschland und Europa. Frankfurt am
Main, [1966].
1 vol. col. maps. 29 cm.

2915 Ruhr-Stickstoff, A. G.
Landwirtschaftsatlas. Bochum, [1955].
62 p. col. maps. 43 cm.

2916 Steiner Verlag.
Atlas der Deutschen Agrarlandschaft. By Erich
Otremba. Wiesbaden, 1962—
in parts. col. maps. 57 cm.

2917 Steiner Verlag.
Die Bundesrepublik Deutschland in Karten.
Wiesbaden, 1966.
1 vol. col. maps. 29 cm.

2918 VEB Bibliographisches Institut.
Auto-Atlas "Neues Deutschland." Leipzig, 1951.
55 p. col. maps. 27 cm.

2919 VEB Bibliographisches Institut.
Auto-Atlas "Neues Deutschland." Leipzig, 1953.
55 p. col. maps. 27 cm.

2920 VEB Bibliographisches Institut.
Auto-Atlas "Neues Deutschland." Leipzig, 1954.
56 p. col. maps. 27 cm.

2921 VEB Bibliographisches Institut.
Auto-Atlas "Neues Deutschland." Leipzig, 1955.
59 p. col. maps. 27 cm.

2922 VEB Bibliographisches Institut.
Auto-Atlas "Neues Deutschland." Leipzig, 1956.
59 p. col. maps. 27 cm.

2923 VEB Bibliographisches Institut.
Auto-Atlas "Neues Deutschland." Leipzig, 1957.
59 p. col. maps. 27 cm.

2924 VEB Bibliographisches Institut.
Auto-Atlas "Neues Deutschland." Leipzig, 1958.
59 p. col. maps. 27 cm.

2925 Velhagen & Klasing.
Atlas zur Geschichte der deutschen Ostsiedlung.
2 ed. By Wilfried Krallert. Bielefeld, [1958].
56 p. col. maps. 27 cm.

2926 Westermann, Georg.
     Atlas für Berliner Schulen. Braunschweig, [1950].
     1 vol. col. maps. 32 cm.

2927 Westermann, Georg.
     Atlas für die Schulen in Schleswig-Holstein.
     Braunschweig, [1950].
     2 parts. col. maps. 32 cm.

2928 Westermann, Georg.
     Der Lebensraum des Menschen. Mit Heimatatlas.
     Braunschweig, 1967.
     1 vol. col. maps. 33 cm.

2929 Westermann, Georg.
     Heimat und Welt [Atlas]. By Diercke. Braun-
     schweig, 1950.
     42 p. col. maps. 32 cm.

2930 Westermann, Georg.
     Heimat und Welt. [Atlas]. Braunschweig, 1952.
     42 p. col. maps. 32 cm.

2931 Westermann, Georg.
     Heimat und Welt. [Atlas]. Braunschweig, 1953.
     42 p. col. maps. 32 cm.

2932 Westermann, Georg.
     Heimat und Welt. Braunschweig, 1964.
     45 p. col. maps. 33 cm.

2933 Westermann, Georg.
     Westermann Atlas. Heimat und Welt. Braun-
     schweig, 1963.
     45 p. col. maps. 32 cm.

2934 Westermann, Georg.
     Westermann-Atlas. Heimat und Welt. Braun-
     schweig. Berlin, Hamburg, 1966.
     1 vol. col. maps. 33 cm.

Greece

2935 Codex Verlag.
     Kulturatlas von Griechenland. Gundholzen, [1970].
     in 6 parts. col. maps. 43 cm.

2936 Greece. Ministry of National Economy.
Atlas holon ton Epiarchon tis Hellados. Athens,
1950-1952.
2 vol. col. maps. 42 cm.

2937 Greece. National Statistical Service.
Atlas of Greece. (in Greek). Athens, 1965.
50 p. col. maps. 50 cm.

2938 Greece. National Statistical Service.
Industrial atlas of Greece. (in Greek). Athens, 1966.
46 p. col. maps. 58 cm.

2939 Greece. Statistikon graphelon.
Economic and social atlas of Greece. (in Greek).
Athens, 1964.
508 p. col. maps. 48 cm.

2940 Hellēnikē Leschē Autokinētou Kai Periēgēsēon.
Road maps and tourist guide of Greece. (in Greek).
Athens, 1959.
42 p. col. maps. 22 cm.

2941 Hellēnikē Leschē Autokinētou Kai Periēgēsēon.
Road maps and tourist guide of Greece. (in Greek).
7 ed. Athens [1965].
44 p. col. maps. 22 cm.

2942 Hellenikē Leschē Autokinētou Kai Periēgēsēon.
Road maps and tourist guide of Greece. (in Greek).
Athens, [1967].
44 p. col. maps. 22 cm.

Great Britain

2943 Allan.
British rail atlas. London, 1967.
45 p. col. maps. 24 cm.

2944 Austin Motor Co., Ltd.
Austin road atlas of Great Britain. Birmingham,
[1955].
72 p. col. maps. 27.5 cm.

2945 Austin Motor Co., Ltd.
Austin road atlas of Great Britain. 3 ed. Birmingham, [1956].
75 p. col. maps. 27.5 cm.

2946 Austin Motor Co., Ltd.
 　　　Austin road atlas of Great Britain.   4 ed.   Bir-
 　　　mingham, [1957].
 　　　75 p. col. maps. 27.5 cm.

2947 Austin Motor Co., Ltd.
 　　　Austin road atlas of Great Britain.   6 ed.   Bir-
 　　　mingham, 1963.
 　　　31 p. col. maps. 27.5 cm.

2948 Austin Motor Co., Ltd.
 　　　Great Britain road atlas and touring guide.   With
 　　　Geographia, Ltd. Birmingham, [1967].
 　　　1 vol. col. maps. 27.5 cm.

2949 Austin Motor Co., Ltd.
 　　　Motoring through Britain.   2 ed.   With Geographia,
 　　　Ltd. London, 1964.
 　　　93 p. col. maps. 27.5 cm.

2950 Austin Motor Co., Ltd.
 　　　Road atlas of Great Britain.   With Geographia, Ltd.
 　　　London, 1964.
 　　　93 p. col. maps. 27.5 cm.

2951 Bartholomew, John & Son, Ltd.
 　　　Bartholomew's road atlas of England and Wales.
 　　　London, 1963.
 　　　59 p. col. maps. 25 cm.

2952 Bartholomew, John & Son, Ltd.
 　　　Road atlas of Great Britain.   9 ed.   Edinburgh,
 　　　1952.
 　　　112 p. col. maps. 25 cm.

2953 Bartholomew, John & Son, Ltd.
 　　　Road atlas of Great Britain.   16 ed.   Edinburgh,
 　　　1963.
 　　　95 p. col. maps. 25 cm.

2954 Bartholomew, John & Son, Ltd.
 　　　Road atlas of Great Britain.   17 ed.   Edinburgh,
 　　　1964.
 　　　95 p. col. maps. 25 cm.

2955 Bartholomew, John & Son, Ltd.
 　　　Road atlas of Great Britain.   18 ed.   Edinburgh,

1965.
112 p. col. maps. 25 cm.

2956 Bartholomew, John & Son, Ltd.
     Road atlas of Great Britain. 19 ed. Edinburgh,
     1966.
     112 p. col. maps. 25 cm.

2957 Bartholomew, John & Son, Ltd.
     Road atlas of Great Britain. 20 ed. Edinburgh,
     1967.
     112 p. col. maps. 25.5 cm.

2958 Bartholomew, John & Son, Ltd.
     Road atlas of Great Britain. 21 ed. Edinburgh,
     1968.
     112 p. col. maps. 25.5 cm.

2959 Bartholomew, John & Son, Ltd.
     Road atlas of Great Britain. Edinburgh, 1970.
     112 p. col. maps. 25 cm.

2960 Bartholomew, John & Son, Ltd.
     Roadmaster atlas of Great Britain. 3 ed. Edin-
     burgh, 1964.
     72 p. col. maps. 25 cm.

2961 Bartholomew, John & Son, Ltd.
     Roadmaster motoring atlas of Great Britain. Edin-
     burgh, 1958.
     38 p. col. maps. 25 cm.

2962 Bartholomew, John & Son, Ltd.
     Roadmaster travel maps of Britain. Edinburgh,
     1970.
     1 vol. col. maps. 25 cm.

2963 Bartholomew, John & Son, Ltd.
     The British Isles pocket atlas for touring. 14 ed.
     Edinburgh, 1952.
     120 p. col. maps. 16 cm.

2964 Blackie & Son, Ltd.
     A paleogeographical atlas of the British Isles and
     adjacent parts of Europe. By Leonard J. Wills.
     London, 1951.
     64 p. col. maps. 22 cm.

2965 Blackie & Son, Ltd.
        A paleogeographical atlas of the British Isles and
        adjacent parts of Europe. By Leonard J. Wills.
        London, 1952.
        64 p. col. maps. 22 cm.

2966 Blackie & Son, Ltd.
        A paleogeographical atlas of the British Isles and
        adjacent parts of Europe. 4 ed. By Leonard J.
        Wills. London, 1962.
        64 p. col. maps. 22 cm.

2967 British Motor Corp., Ltd.
        B.M.C. route planner, including motorways.
        London, [1968].
        50 p. col. maps. 28 cm.

2968 Cranfield & Bonfiel Books.
        Waterways atlas of the British Isles.   London, 1966.
        54 p. col. maps. 24 cm.

2969 Daily Express.
        Daily Express road book and gazetteer of Great
        Britain. London, [1950].
        128 p. col. maps. 25 cm.

2970 Deseret Book Co.
        A genealogical atlas of England and Wales. By
        David E. Gardner, Derek Harland and Frank Smith.
        Salt Lake City, Utah, [1960].
        88 p. 27 cm.

2971 Faber & Faber.
        An agricultural atlas of England and Wales. By
        J. T. Coppock. London, 1964.
        255 p. 25 cm.

2972 Geographers' Map Co.
        Geographers' road atlas: Great Britain and Northern
        Ireland. By Phyllis Pearsall. Sevenoaks, Kent,
        [1964].
        158 p. col. maps. 28 cm.

2973 Geographia, Ltd.
        Austin Great Britain road atlas and touring guide.
        7 ed. London, [1970].
        1 vol. col. maps. 28 cm.

2974 Geographia, Ltd.
      Commercial gazetteer & atlas of Great Britain.
      London, 1969.
      2 vol. col. maps. 25 cm.

2975 Geographia, Ltd.
      Geographia road atlas of Great Britain. London,
      [1969].
      1 vol. col. maps. 26 cm.

2976 Geographia, Ltd.
      Great Britain road atlas; showing new and projected
      pass roads and motorways. London, [1960].
      30 p. col. maps. 26 cm.

2977 Geographia, Ltd.
      Pocket road map of the British Isles. London,
      [1966].
      64 p. col. maps. 14 cm.

2978 Geographia, Ltd.
      Road atlas and route guide. London, [195-].
      6 vol. 16 cm.

2979 Geographia, Ltd.
      Road atlas and route guide. London, [1951].
      6 vol. 16 cm.

2980 Gt. Britain. Meteorological Office.
      Climatological atlas of the British Isles. London,
      1952.
      139 p. col. maps. 31 cm.

2981 Gt. Britain. Ministry of Agriculture, Fisheries & Food.
      Atlas of Long-Term Irrigation needs for England
      and Wales. London, 1967.
      1 vol. 32 cm.

2982 Gt. Britain. Ministry of Housing and Local Govern-
      ment.
      Desk atlas of planning maps of England and Wales.
      London, 1953 —
      in parts. col. maps. 43.5 cm.

2983 Johnston, W. & A. K. & G.W. Bacon, Ltd.
      Autoway atlas. Great Britain and Ireland. London,
      1967.
      1 vol. col. maps. 26 cm.

2984 Johnston, W. & A. K. & G. W. Bacon, Ltd.
     Johnston's A and B roads motoring atlas of Great
     Britain. Edinburgh, [1958].
     48 p. col. maps. 34 cm.

2985 Johnston, W. & A. K. & G. W. Bacon, Ltd.
     Johnston's A and B roads motoring atlas of Great
     Britain. Edinburgh, 1968.
     1 vol. col. maps. 34 cm.

2986 Johnston, W. & A. K. & G. W. Bacon, Ltd.
     Johnston's county motoring atlas of Great Britain
     and Ireland. Edinburgh, [1965].
     64 p. col. maps. 28 cm.

2987 Johnston, W. & A. K. & G. W. Bacon, Ltd.
     Johnston's handy road atlas of Great Britain and
     Ireland. Edinburgh, [1953].
     72 p. col. maps. 19 cm.

2988 Johnston, W. & A. K. & G. W. Bacon, Ltd.
     Johnston's Pocket road atlas of Great Britain and
     Ireland. London, [1969].
     64 p. col. maps. 13.5 cm.

2989 Johnston, W. & A. K. & G. W. Bacon, Ltd.
     Johnston's Road atlas of Great Britain. Edinburgh,
     [1964].
     16 p. col. maps. 25 cm.

2990 Johnston, W. & A. K. & G. W. Bacon, Ltd.
     Road atlas of Great Britain. 3 miles to 1 inch.
     Edinburgh, [1954].
     370 p. col. maps. 22 cm.

2991 Johnston, W. & A. K. & G. W. Bacon, Ltd.
     Road atlas of Great Britain. 4 ed. Edinburgh,
     [1957].
     370 p. col. maps. 22 cm.

2992 Johnston, W. & A. K. & G. W. Bacon, Ltd.
     3 miles to 1 inch road atlas of Great Britain. 5 ed.
     Edinburgh, London, 1965.
     1 vol. col. maps. 28 cm.

2993 Macmillan & Co., Ltd.
     A map book of the British Isles. 6 ed. By A.
     Ferriday. London, 1967.

69 p.   25 cm.

2994 Macmillan & Co., Ltd.
British weather in maps. By James A. Taylor and
R. A. Yates. London, 1958.
256 p.   col. maps.   23 cm.

2995 Macmillan Co.
British history atlas. By Martin Gilbert.   New
York, [1969].
118 p.   24 cm.

2996 Map Productions, Ltd.
Motorways: a new atlas to illustrate the motorway
system of Great Britain.   London, [1969].
1 vol.   col. maps.   27 cm.

2997 Michelin Tyre Co.
Michelin motoring atlas [of Great Britain].   Stoke-
on-Trent, [1954].
37 p.   col. maps.   25 cm.

2998 National Trust.
The National Trust Atlas showing places of historic
architectual & scenic interest in England, Wales
and Northern Ireland.   With Bartholomew. London,
1964.
80 p.   col. maps.   25 cm.

2999 National Trust.
The National Trust maps.   London, 1957.
48 p.   22 cm.

3000 Nelson, Thomas & Sons, Ltd.
Atlas of the British flora. By F. H. Perring and
S. M. Walters.   London, 1962.
432 p.   34 cm.

3001 Nelson, Thomas & Sons, Ltd.
National atlas of disease mortality in the United
Kingdom. By G. M. Howe.   London, Edinburgh,
1963.
111 p.   col. maps.   29 cm.

3002 Nelson, Thomas & Sons, Ltd.
National atlas of disease mortality in the United
Kingdom.   2 ed.   By G. M. Howe.   London,

Edinburgh, 1968.
120 p. col. maps. 29 cm.

3003 Nelson, Thomas & Sons, Ltd.
National atlas of disease mortality in the United
Kingdom. 2 ed. By G. M. Howe. London, 1970.
197 p. col. maps. 29 cm.

3004 Nelson, Thomas & Sons, Ltd.
The British Isles in map and diagram. By D. G.
Luxon and J. A. Morris. London, [1966].
67 p. col. maps. 29 cm.

3005 Nelson, Thomas & Sons, Ltd.
The Sunday Times road atlas. London, 1968.
188 p. col. maps. 29 cm.

3006 Newnes, George, Ltd.
Newnes Motorists touring maps and gazetteer. With
Bartholomew. London, [1950].
160 p. col. maps. 29 cm.

3007 Newnes, George, Ltd.
Newnes motorists' touring maps and gazetteer.
London, [1965].
48 p. col. maps. 29 cm.

3008 Nuffield Organization.
Great Britain road atlas and touring guide. 7 ed.
Oxford, [196-].
1 vol. col. maps. 29 cm.

3009 Nuffield Organization.
Nuffield road atlas of Great Britain. 4 ed. Oxford,
[1957].
75 p. col. maps. 28 cm.

3010 Odhams Press, Ltd.
Odhams new road atlas of Great Britain, Ireland
and Western Europe. London, [1963].
239 p. col. maps. 24 cm.

3011 Oxford University Press.
Oxford travel atlas of Britain. London, New York,
1953.
33 p. col. maps. 20 cm.

3012 Oxford University Press.
     The atlas of Britain and Northern Ireland.   By
     D. P. Bickmore and M. A. Shaw.   Oxford, 1963.
     222 p.   col. maps.   53 cm.

3013 Oxford University Press.
     The atlas of Britain and Northern Ireland.   By D.
     P. Bickmore and M. A. Shaw.   Oxford, 1964.
     236 p.   col. maps.   53 cm.

3014 Philip, George & Son, Ltd.
     National road atlas of Great Britain.   London, [1963].
     103 p.   col. maps.   28 cm.

3015 Philip, George & Son, Ltd.
     National road atlas of Great Britain.   London, 1967.
     103 p.   col. maps.   28 cm.

3016 Philip, George & Son, Ltd.
     Philip's road atlas of Great Britain.   London, 1963.
     47 p.   col. maps.   28 cm.

3017 Philip, George & Son, Ltd.
     Road atlas of Great Britain.   With Shell-Mex and
     BP Ltd.   London, 1964.
     143 p.   col. maps.   28 cm.

3018 Philip, George & Son, Ltd.
     Road atlas of Great Britain.   With Shell-Mex and
     BP Ltd.   London, 1965.
     143 p.   col. maps.   28 cm.

3019 Philip, George & Son, Ltd.
     Road atlas of Great Britain.   With Shell-Mex and
     BP Ltd.   London, 1966.
     144 p.   col. maps.   28.5 cm.

3020 Philip, George & Son, Ltd.
     Road atlas of Great Britain.   With Shell-Mex and
     BP Ltd.   London, [1968].
     144 p.   col. maps.   28 cm.

3021 Philip, George & Son, Ltd.
     Road atlas of Great Britain, with special London
     section & town plans.   London, [1968].
     176 p.   col. maps.   29 cm.

3022 Railway Publications, Ltd.
       British Rail atlas and gazetteer.   London, 1965.
       83 p.   col.   maps.   25 cm.

3023 Railway Publications, Ltd.
       British Rail atlas and gazetteer.   London, 1967.
       1 vol.   col.   maps.   25 cm.

3024 Railway Publications, Ltd.
       British railways pre-grouping atlas and gazetteer.
       3 ed.   London, 1963.
       45 p.   col.   maps.   25 cm.

3025 Railway Publications, Ltd.
       British railways pre-grouping atlas and gazetteer.
       4 ed.   London, [1965].
       84 p.   col.   maps.   25 cm.

3026 Reader's Digest Association, Ltd.
       The Reader's Digest A. A. book of the road.
       London, 1966.
       1 vol.   col.   maps.   28 cm.

3027 Reader's Digest Association, Ltd.
       The Reader's Digest A. A. book of the road.   2 ed.
       London, 1968.
       1 vol.   col.   maps.   28 cm.

3028 Reader's Digest Association, Ltd.
       The Reader's Digest complete atlas of the British
       Isles.   1 ed.   London, 1965.
       230 p.   col.   maps.   40 cm.

3029 Shell-Mex & BP Ltd.
       Shell nature lovers' atlas of England, Scotland and
       Wales.   By James Fisher.   London, 1966.
       1 vol.   col.   maps.   28 cm.

3030 Stanford, Edward.
       Esso road atlas of Great Britain and Ireland.
       London, 1970.
       1 vol.   col.   maps.   25 cm.

3031 Stanford, Edward.
       Standford's geological atlas of Great Britain.   By
       T. Eastwood.   London, 1964.
       288 p.   25 cm.

3032 St. Martin's Press.
A map book of the British Isles. 6 ed. By A.
Ferriday. New York, 1967.
69 p. 25 cm.

3033 Thomas, A.
National road atlas of Great Britain. Preston,
[1954].
370 p. col. maps. 22 cm.

3034 Weidenfeld & Nicolson.
British history atlas. London, 1968.
118 p. 26 cm.

3035 Wheaton & Co., Ltd.
History teaching atlas and note book of British and
world history from the earliest times to 1960.
Exeter, 1968.
88 p. col. maps. 28 cm.

Hungary

3036 Cartographia.
National atlas of Hungary. [In English]. By Sándor
Radó. Budapest, 1967.
112 p. col. maps. 41 cm.

3037 Kartográfiai Vállalat.
A dél-alföld atlasza. By Sándor Radó. Budapest,
1968.
in parts. col. maps. 49 cm.

3038 Kartográfiai Vállalat.
Magyarország autóatlasza. Budapest, 1966.
135 p. col. maps. 28 cm.

3039 Kartográfiai Vállalat.
Magyarország autóatlasza. Budapest, 1968.
135 p. col. maps. 28 cm.

3040 Kartográfiai Vállalat.
Magyarország autóatlasza. Budapest, 1960.
39 p. col. maps. 20.5 cm.

3041 Kartográfiai Vállalat.
Magyarország autóatlasza. Budapest, 1962.
39 p. col. maps. 20.5 cm.

3042 Kartográfiai Vállalat.
      Magyarország autóatlasza. By Sándor Radó.
      Budapest, 1963.
      39 p. col. maps. 20.5 cm.

3043 Kartográfiai Vállalat.
      Magyarország autóatlasza. By Sándor Radó.
      Budapest, 1968.
      40 p. col. maps. 20.5 cm.

3044 Kartográfiai Vállalat.
      Magyarország nemzeti atlasza. By Sándor Radó.
      Budapest, 1967.
      112 p. col. maps. 41 cm.

3045 Kartográfiai Vállalat.
      Magyarországi autóutak térképe. Budapest, 1955.
      75 p. col. maps. 22 cm.

3046 Kartográfiai Vállalat.
      Magyarországi autóutak térképe. 2 ed. Budapest,
      1956.
      75 p. col. maps. 22 cm.

3047 Országos Meteorológiai Intézet.
      Magyarország éghajlati atlasza. Klima-atlas von
      Ungarn. By J. Kakas. Budapest 1960-67.
      2 vol. col. maps. 50 cm.

3048 Ronai, Andras.
      As alföld talajvizterkepe. Magyarazö a talajviztükör
      felszinalatti mélységének 1:200,000- es méretü
      térképéhez. Budapest, 1961.
      102 p. col. maps. 25 cm.

3049 Tervgazdasági Könyvkiadó.
      Magyarország mezögazdasági földrajaza. By László
      Görög. Budapest, 1954.
      179 p. col. maps. 30 cm.

Iceland

3050 Rikisútgáfa námsbóka.
      Landabréfabók. Reykjavík, 1962.
      52 p. col. maps. 25 cm.

Ireland

3051 Automobile Association.
       The Automobile Association atlas of Ireland.
       London, 1963.
       31 p.   col. maps.   26 cm.

3052 Deseret Book Co.
       A genealogical atlas of Ireland.   By David E.
       Gardner, Derek Harland and Frank Smith.   Salt
       Lake City, Utah, 1964.
       41 p.   26 cm.

3053 Dublin Institute for Advanced Studies
       Linguistic atlas and survey of Irish dialects.   By
       Heinrich Wagner.   Dublin, 1958.
       300 p.   col. maps.   43 cm.

3054 Educational Company of Ireland, Ltd.
       Irish student's atlas.   By Elenor Butler, Dublin, [1960].
       66 p.   col. maps.   28 cm.

3055 Johnston, W. & A. K. & G. W. Bacon, Ltd.
       Autoway atlas.   Great Britain and Ireland.   London,
       1967.
       1 vol.   col. maps.   26 cm.

3056 Johnston, W. & A. K. & G. W. Bacon, Ltd.
       Johnston's county motoring atlas of Great Britain
       and Ireland.   Edinburgh, [1965].
       64 p.   col. maps.   28 cm.

3057 Johnston, W. & A. K. & G. W. Bacon, Ltd.
       Johnston's handy road atlas of Great Britain and
       Ireland.   Edinburgh, [1953].
       72 p.   col. maps.   19 cm.

3058 Johnston, W. & A. K. & G. W. Bacon, Ltd.
       Johnston's pocket road atlas of Great Britain and
       Ireland.   London, [1969].
       64 p.   col. maps.   13. 5 cm.

3059 Johnston W. & A. K. & G. W. Bacon, Ltd.
       Pocket road atlas of Ireland.   London, 1966.
       1 vol.   col. maps.   18 cm.

3060 Odhams Press, Ltd.
       Odhams new road atlas of Great Britain, Ireland

and Western Europe. London, [1963].
239 p. col. maps. 24 cm.

3061 Stanford, Edward.
      Esso road atlas of Great Britain and Ireland.
      London, 1970.
      1 vol. col. maps. 25 cm.

Italy

3062 AGIP.
      Carta automobilistica d'Italia. By Giuseppe Vallardi.
      Milano, [1963].
      32 p. col. maps. 24 cm.

3063 Automobile Club d'Italia.
      Autostrade d'Italia. Roma, 1965.
      12 p. col. maps. 27 cm.

3064 Automobile Club d'Italia.
      Italia; atlante automobilistico. Roma, [1957].
      72 p. col. maps. 27 cm.

3065 Consociazione Turistica Italiana.
      Atlante fisico economico d'Italia. Milano, 1950.
      1 vol. col. maps. 40 cm.

3066 Continental Gummiwerke Kartographischer Verlag.
      Continental atlas. Deutschland, Benelux, Schweiz,
      Österreich, Norditalian. 33 ed. Hannover, 1964.
      635 p. col. maps. 26 cm.

3067 Istituto Geografico De Agostini.
      Atlante delle regioni d'Italia. Novara, 1963.
      44 p. col. maps. 29 cm.

3068 Istituto Geografico De Agostini.
      Atlante stradale d'Italia. Novara, 1964.
      1 vol. col. maps. 24 cm.

3069 Istituto Geografico De Agostini.
      Atlantino delle regioni d'Italia. Novara, 1965.
      64 p. col. maps. 21 cm.

3070 Istituto Geografico De Agostini.
      Italia: atlante delle regioni. Novara, [1962].
      63 p. col. maps. 29 cm.

3071 Italatlas.
    Atlas. Guida atlante delle strade d'Italia. Roma,
    [1956].
    84 p. col. maps. 25 cm.

3072 Italgeo.
    Italy is waiting for you; artistic atlas with com-
    mentary. Milano, [1950].
    25 p. col. maps. 22 cm.

3073 Italy. Direzione generale della statistica.
    Atlante dei comuni d'Italia. Roma, 1951.
    1 vol. 35 cm.

3074 Italy. Istituto Geografico Militare.
    Atlante aerofotografico delle sedi umane in Italia.
    Firenze, 1964.
    1 vol. 52.5 cm.

3075 JRO Verlag.
    JRO Autoatlas Italien, Französische Riviera, West-
    österreich. München, [1955].
    260 p. col. maps. 25 cm.

3076 Poligratiche Bolis.
    Atlante delle regioni d'Italia. Beganmo, [1950].
    1 vol. col. maps. 27 cm.

3077 Reise und Verkehrsverlag.
    Atlas + Führer Italien. Stuttgart, [1957].
    216 p. col. maps. 26 cm.

3078 Società cartografica G. De Agostini.
    Atlante turistico d'Italia. Milano, [1960].
    114 p. col. maps. 15 cm.

3079 Società cartografica G. De Agostini.
    Italia, carta stradale 1: 650, 000. Milano, [1957].
    13 p. col. maps. 28 cm.

3080 Studi geo-cartografici.
    Atlante econometrico delle regioni d'Italia. By
    Frederico de Agostini. Milano, [196-].
    1 vol. col. maps. 41 cm.

3081 Touring Club Italiano.
    Atlante automobilistico. Milano, 1969—
    in parts. col. maps. 32 cm.

Luxembourg

3082 Continental Gummiwerke Kartographischer Verlag.
     Continental atlas. Deutschland, Benelux,
     Alpenländer. 26 ed. Hannover, [1956].
     453 p. col. maps. 26 cm.

3083 Continental Gummiwerke Kartographischer Verlag.
     Continental atlas. Deutschland, Benelux, Schweiz,
     Österreich, Norditalian. 33 ed. Hannover, 1964.
     635 p. col. maps. 26 cm.

3084 Elsevier.
     Elsevier atlas van Nederland, Belgie en Luxemburg.
     By M. E. Dumont, G. Peeters and A. H. Sijmonds.
     Amsterdam, 1960.
     195 p. col. maps. 19 cm.

3085 Elwert Verlag.
     Luxemburgischer Sprachatlas. By R. Bruch.
     Marburg, 1963.
     174 p. col. maps. 50 cm.

3086 France. Institut géographique national.
     Grande-Duché de Luxembourg. Atlas. Paris, 1965.
     30 p. col. maps. 71 cm.

3087 Netherlands. Staatsdrukkerij-en Uitgeverij bedrijf.
     Gemeentenatlas Benelux. 's Gravenhage, [1952].
     58 p. 35 cm.

3088 Ravenstein Geographische Verlagsanstalt.
     Autoatlas Benelux und Europa. Frankfurt am Main,
     1964.
     36 p. col. maps. 29 cm.

3089 Ravenstein Geographische Verlagsanstalt.
     Autoatlas Benelux und Europa. Frankfurt am Main,
     [1965].
     56 p. col. maps. 29 cm.

Netherlands

3090 Bootsma.
     Autokaart Nederland. 1 ed. 's Gravenhage, [1952].
     48 p. col. maps. 29 cm.

3091 Brug Uitgeversbedrijf, N. V.
Atlas van Nederland en de wereld voor het voortgezet onderwijs. Amsterdam, 1959.
162 p. col. maps. 32 cm.

3092 Brug Uitgeversbedrijf, N. V.
Atlas van Nederland en de wereld voor het voortgezet onderwijs. 2 ed. Amsterdam, 1962.
162 p. col. maps. 32 cm.

3093 Brug Uitgeversbedrijf, N. V.
Atlas van Nederland en de wereld voor het voortgezet onderwijs. Amsterdam, 1967.
162 p. col. maps. 32 cm.

3094 Dijkstra.
Ons eigen land. Eenvoudige atlas van Nederland.
By W. Bakker and H. Rusch. Zeist, [1966].
1 vol. col. maps. 26 cm.

3095 Duwaer, J. F. & Zonen.
Platen-atlas Nederland. Amsterdam, [1967].
40 p. col. maps. 27.5 cm.

3096 Elsevier.
Atlas van de Nederlandse beschaving. By J. J. M.
Timmers. Amsterdam, 1957.
246 p. col. maps. 35 cm.

3097 Elsevier.
Elsevier atlas van Nederland, Belgie en Luxemburg.
By M. E. Dumont, G. Peeters and A. H. Sijmonds.
Amsterdam, 1960.
195 p. col. maps. 19 cm.

3098 Meulenhoff, J. M.
Atlas van Nederland en de wereld. 1 ed. With
Hölzel. Amsterdam, 1959.
162 p. col. maps. 32 cm.

3099 Meulenhoff, J. M.
Atlas von Nederland en de wereld. 2 ed. With
Hölzel. Amsterdam, 1963.
162 p. col. maps. 32 cm.

3100 Meulenhoff, J. M.
Atlas von Nederland en de wereld. 3 ed. With

Hölzel.   Amsterdam, 1967.
162 p.   col. maps.   32 cm.

3101 Meulenhoff, J. M.
Beknopte atlas voor het voortgezet underwijs.   1 ed.
With Svenska Bokförlaget.   Amsterdam, 1968.
78 p.   col. maps.   32 cm.

3102 Meulenhoff, J. M.
Meulenhoff atlas voor de mammoet.   With Hölzel.
Amsterdam, 1968.
128 p.   col. maps.   32 cm.

3103 Netherlands.   Bureau voor Wegenen Verkeersstatistiek.
Atlas van de rijkswegen, 1949.   's Gravenhage,
[1950].
39 p.   col. maps.   30 cm.

3104 Netherlands.   Department van landbouwen visscherij.
Landbouwatlas van Nederland.   Zwolle, [1959].
79 p.   col. maps.   36 cm.

3105 Netherlands.   Dienst Verkeersonderzoek.
Atlas van de rijkswegen, 1954.   3 ed.   's Gravenhage, [1954].
14 p.   col. maps.   30 cm.

3106 Netherlands.   Staatsdrukkerij-en Uitgeverijbedrijf.
Atlas rijkswegen, 1960.   's Gravenhage, 1962.
15 p.   col. maps.   29 cm.

3107 Netherlands.   Staatsdrukkerij-en Uitgeverijbedrijf.
Atlas van de rijkswegen.   's Gravenhage, 1955.
56 p.   col. maps.   29 cm.

3108 Netherlands.   Staatsdrukkerij-en Uitgeverijbedrijf.
Atlas van Nederland.   's Gravenhage, 1963—
in parts.   col. maps.   57.5 cm.

3109 Netherlands.   Staatsdrukkerij-en Uitgeverijbedrijf.
Gemeentenatlas.   Benelux.   's Gravenhage, [1952].
58 p.   35 cm.

3110 Netherlands.   Staatsdrukkerij-en Uitgeverijbedrijf.
Stroomatlas Nederland.   2 ed.   's Gravenhage, 1963—
1 vol.   col. maps.   37 cm.

3111 Netherlands. Volkskundecommissie der Koninklijke
     Nederlandse Akademie van Wetenschappen.
     Volkskunde-atlas. By Pieter Jacobus Meertens.
     's Gravenhage, 1959—
     in parts. col. maps. 50 cm.

3112 Noordhoff, P.
     Atlas algemene en vaderlandse geschiedenis. 17 ed.
     Groningen, 1963.
     96 p. col. maps. 29.5 cm.

3113 Ravenstein Geographische Verlagsanstalt.
     Autoatlas Benelux und Europa. Frankfurt am Main,
     1964.
     36 p. col. maps. 29 cm.

3114 Ravenstein Geographische Verlagsanstalt.
     Autoatlas Benelux und Europa. Frankfurt am Main,
     [1965].
     56 p. col. maps. 29 cm.

3115 Stenvert.
     Stenverts atlas, Nederland, de West en Nederlands
     Nieuw-Guinea. 4 ed. By Wijbren Bakker and
     J. M. Bosch. Apeldoorn, [1962].
     94 p. 22 cm.

3116 Ten Brink, H.
     Ten Brink's Nieuwe zakatlasje van Nederland.
     Meppel, [1954].
     12 p. col. maps. 14 cm.

3117 Ten Brink, H.
     Ten Brink's Reiseatlas van Nederland. Meppel,
     [1954].
     23 p. col. maps. 25 cm.

3118 Thieme, W. J.
     Atlas van Nederland, de West en Indonesië. By
     G. Prop. Zutphen, 1953.
     42 p. col. maps. 26 cm.

3119 Thieme, W. J.
     Atlas van Nederland, de West en Indonesië, voor de
     lagere school. 53 ed. By G. Prop. Zutphen, 1951.
     42 p. col. maps. 26 cm.

3120 Thieme, W. J.
Atlas van Nederland, de West en Indonesië, voor de
lagere school. 58 ed. By G. Prop. Zutphen,
1955.
42 p. col. maps. 26 cm.

3121 Thieme, W. J.
Atlas van Nederland en de West voor het voortgezet
onderwijs. By G. Prop and B. J. ter Beek.
Zutphen, 1967.
1 vol. col. maps. 26 cm.

3122 Thieme, W. J.
Beginatlas van Nederland. 23 ed. By G. Prop.
Zutphen, 1953.
27 p. col. maps. 22 cm.

3123 Thieme, W. J.
Beginatlas van Nederland. By G. Prop. Zutphen,
1966.
32 p. col. maps. 22 cm.

3124 Wolters, J. B.
Atlas algemene en vaderlandse geschiedenis. By
B. A. Vermaseren. Groningen, 1966.
96 p. col. maps. 31 cm.

3125 Wolters, J. B.
Atlas de Nederlandse Antilen, Suriname, Nederland,
en de wereld. Groningen, 1956.
40 p. col. maps. 31 cm.

3126 Wolters, J. B.
Nederland. By J. A. J. Nonnekeus and C. Hoog-
vorst. Groningen, 1965.
32 p. col. maps. 31 cm.

3127 Wolters, J. B.
Thematische atlas Nederland. 1 ed. Groningen,
1967.
17 p. col. maps. 31 cm.

Norway

3128 Cappelens, J. W. Forlag, A. S.
Cappelen Bilkartbok. Oslo, 1967.
56 p. col. maps. 27.5 cm.

3129 Cappelens, J. W.   Forlag, A. S.
     Cappelens Norges atlas.   Oslo, 1965.
     185 p. col. maps. 31 cm.

3130 Cappelens, J. W.   Forlag, A. S.
     Cappelens Norges atlas for skolen.   Oslo, 1966.
     24 p. col. maps. 30 cm.

3131 Cappelens, J. W.   Forlag, A. S.
     Hjemmenes verdensatlas med spesielle Norgeskart.
     Oslo, 1955.
     180 p. col. maps. 28 cm.

3132 Cappelens, J. W.   Forlag, A. S.
     Kartbok over Norge.   By Ellef Ellefsen.   Oslo, 1954.
     31 p. col. maps. 28 cm.

3133 Cappelens, J. W.   Forlag, A. S.
     Kartbok over Norge.   By Ellef Ellefsen.   Oslo, 1955.
     32 p. col. maps. 28 cm.

3134 Cappelens, J. W.   Forlag, A. S.
     Kartbok over Norge.   By Ellef Ellefsen.   Oslo, 1963.
     31 p. col. maps. 28 cm.

3135 Dreyers forlag.
     Dreyers verdensatlas med Norges atlas.   4 ed.   By
     Kr. Gleditsch.   With Philip.   Oslo, London, 1965.
     197 p. col. maps. 28 cm.

3136 Fonna.
     Norsk allkunnebok atlas.   By Kristian Gleditisch.
     Oslo, [1962].
     184 p. col. maps. 29 cm.

3137 Kongelik Norsk automobilklub.
     Kartbok for Norge.   2 ed.   Oslo, 1954.
     103 p. col. maps. 26 cm.

3138 Kongelig Norsk automobilklub.
     KNA Kart-og reisehåndbok.   Oslo, [1967].
     1 vol. col. maps. 26 cm.

3139 Norway.   Post styret.
     Postkart over Norge, 1:400, 000.   Oslo, [1952].
     10 p. col. maps. 49 cm.

3140 Norway. Statistik Sentralbyrå.
Bosettingskart over Norge, 1:400,000. Oslo, [1955].
15 p. col. maps. 25 cm.

3141 Norway. Vegdirektoratet.
Trafikkart over Norge. Oslo, [1962].
19 p. col. maps. 49 cm.

3142 Poståpnernes Landsforbund.
Post-, vej- og fylkeskarte. Oslo, [1950].
43 p. col. maps. 23 cm.

Poland

3143 Ksiąznica- Atlas.
Atlas Polski wspólczesnej. 4 ed. By E. Romer
and J. Wąsowicz. Wrocľaw, 1950.
16 p. col. maps. 23 cm.

3144 Ksiąznica-Atlas.
Atlas Polski wspólczesnej. By E. Romer and J.
Wąsowicz. Wrocľaw, 1951.
16 p. col. maps. 23 cm.

3145 Ksiąznica-Atlas.
Atlas Polski wspólszesnej. 5 ed. By E. Romer
and J. Wąsowicz. Wrocľaw, 1952.
16 p. col. maps. 23 cm.

3146 Poland. Akademia nauk.
Atlas flory polskiej i ziem osciennych. Warszawa,
1965.
in parts. col. maps. 34 cm.

3147 Poland. Akademia nauk.
Atlas historyczny Polski. Warszawa, [1958].
2 vol. col. maps. 31 cm.

3148 Poland. Akademia nauk.
Atlas rozmieszczenia drzew i krzewów v Polsce.
Poznań, 1963—
in parts. col. maps. 33 cm.

3149 Poland. Akademia nauk.
Historia Polski. 1 ed. Warszawa, [1955]-63.
3 vol. col. maps. 25 cm.

3150 Poland. Akademia nauk.
Maly atlas gwar polskich. 1 ed. Wrocław, 1957-
in parts. col. maps. 50 cm.

3151 Poland. Akademia nauk.
Polski atlas etnograficzny. Warszawa, 1964-
in parts. col. maps. 49 cm.

3152 Poland. Centralny urzad geodezii i kartografii.
Atlas Polski. Warszawa, 1953-
in parts. col. maps. 34 cm.

3153 Poland. Instytut geologiczny.
Atlas geologiczny Polski. Warszawa, 1957-
in parts. col. maps. 43 cm.

3154 Poland. Instytut geologiczny.
Atlas geologiczny Polski. Warszawa, 1968.
11 p. col. maps. 59 cm.

3155 Poland. Instytut geologiczny.
Atlas géologique de Pologne (1:2,000,000). Text in
French. Prepared for the Geological Congress in
Mexico City. Warszawa, 1956.
1 portfolio. col. maps. 37 cm.

3156 Poland. Instytut geologiczny.
Geological atlas of Poland. By Jerzy Znosko.
Warszawa, 1968.
7 p. col. maps. 31 cm.

3157 Poland. Instytut geologiczny.
Mineralogenic atlas of Poland. [In English].
Warszawa, 1970.
1 vol. col. maps. 30 cm.

3158 Poland. Państwowe przedsiębiorstwo wydawnictw
kartograficznych.
Atlas historyczny Polski. Warszawa, 1967.
105 p. col. maps. 31 cm.

3159 Poland. Państwowe przedsiębiorstwo wydawnictw
kartograficznych.
Atlas samochodowy Polski. 1 ed. Warszawa, 1958.
155 p. col. maps. 23 cm.

3160 Poland. Państwowe przedsiębiorstwo wydawnictw
kartograficznych.

Atlas samochodowy Polski. 3 ed. Warszawa, 1964.
155 p. col. maps. 23 cm.

3161 Poland. Państwowe przedsiębiorstwo wydawnictw
kartograficznych.
Atlas samochodowy Polski. 4 ed. Warszawa, 1965.
155 p. col. maps. 23 cm.

3162 Poland. Państwowe przedsiębiorstwo wydawnictw
kartograficznych.
Atlas samochodowy Polski. 5 ed. Warszawa, 1967.
155 p. col. maps. 23 cm.

3163 Poland. Państwowe przedsiębiorstwo wydawnictw
kartograficznych.
Atlas samochodowy Polski. 6 ed. Warszawa, 1968.
155 p. col. maps. 23 cm.

3164 Poland. Państwowe przedsiębiorstwo wydawnictw
kartograficznych.
Atlas samochodowy Polski. Warszawa, 1969.
155 p. col. maps. 23 cm.

3165 Poland. Państwowe przedsiębiorstwo wydawnictw
kartograficznych.
Geograficzny atlas Polski. 1 ed. By Michael
Janiszewki. Warszawa, 1952.
28 p. col. maps. 34 cm.

3166 Poland. Państwowe przedsiębiorstwo wydawnictw
kartograficznych.
Geograficzny atlas Polski. 2 ed. Warszawa, 1953.
28 p. col. maps. 34 cm.

3167 Poland. Państwowe przedsiębiorstwo wydawnictw
kartograficznych.
Geograficzny atlas Polski. 3 ed. Warszawa, 1954.
28 p. col. maps. 34 cm.

3168 Poland. Państwowe przedsiębiorstwo wydawnictw
kartograficznych.
Geograficzny atlas Polski. 4 ed. Warszawa, 1955.
28 p. col. maps. 34 cm.

3169 Poland. Państwowe przedsiębiorstwo wydawnictw
kartograficznych.
Geograficzny atlas Polski. 5 ed. Warszawa, 1956.
28 p. col. maps. 34 cm.

3170 Poland. Państwowe przedsiębiorstwo wydawnictw kartograficznych.
<u>Geograficzny atlas Polski.</u> 6 ed. Warszawa, 1957.
28 p. col. maps. 34 cm.

3171 Poland. Państwowe przedsiębiorstwo wydawnictw kartograficznych.
<u>Geograficzny atlas Polski.</u> 7 ed. Warzawa, 1958.
28 p. col. maps. 34 cm.

3172 Poland. Państwowe przedsiębiorstwo wydawnictw kartograficznych.
<u>Geograficzny atlas Polski.</u> 8 ed. Warszawa, 1959.
28 p. col. maps. 34 cm.

3173 Poland. Państwowe przedsiębiorstwo wydawnictw kartograficznych.
<u>Geograficzny atlas Polski.</u> Warszawa, 1961.
28 p. col. maps. 34 cm.

3174 Poland. Państwowe przedsiębiorstwo wydawnictw kartograficznych.
<u>Geograficzny atlas Polski.</u> Warszawa, 1963.
28 p. col. maps. 34 cm.

3175 Poland. Państwowe przedsiębiorstwo wydawnictw kartograficznych.
<u>Geograficzny atlas Polski.</u> Warszawa, 1964.
28 p. col. maps. 34 cm.

3176 Poland. Państwowe przedsiębiorstwo wydawnictw kartograficznych.
<u>Geograficzny atlas Polski.</u> Warszawa, 1966.
37 p. col. maps. 34 cm.

3177 Poland. Państwowe przedsiębiorstwo wydawnictw kartograficznych.
<u>Geograficzny atlas Polski.</u> Warszawa, 1967.
37 p. col. maps. 34 cm.

3178 Poland. Państwowe przedsiębiorstwo wydawnictw kartograficznych.
<u>Geograficzny atlas Polski.</u> Warszawa, 1968.
37 p. col. maps. 34 cm.

3179 Poland. Państwowe przedsiębiorstwo wydawnictw kartograficznych.

Geograficzny atlas Polski. Warszawa, 1969.
37 p. col. maps. 34 cm.

3180 Poland. Państwowe przedsiębiorstwo wydawnictw
kartograficznych.
Geograficzny atlas Polski. Warszawa, 1970.
37 p. col. maps. 34 cm.

3181 Poland. Państwowe wydawnictw naukowe.
Atlas rozmieszcenia roslin zarodnikowych w Polsce.
Poznan, 1964.
23 p. 34 cm.

Portugal

3182 Firestone-Hispania, S. A.
Atlas de España y Portugal. 3 ed. Bilbao, [1964].
79 p. col. maps. 28 cm.

3183 Firestone-Hispania, S. A.
Atlas de España y Portugal. Bilbao, 1969.
1 vol. col. maps. 28 cm.

3184 Firestone-Hispania, S. A.
Firestone-Hispania nuevo atlas de España y Portugal.
Bilbao, [1961].
79 p. col. maps. 28 cm.

3185 Instituto de Estudos Geograficos.
Atlas de Portugal. 2 ed. By Aristides de Amorim
Girão. Coimbra, 1958.
40 p. col. maps. 42.5 cm.

3186 Instituto de Estudos Geograficos.
Atlas de Portugal. 2 ed. By Aristides de Amorim
Girão. Coimbra, [1960].
1 vol. col. maps. 42.5 cm.

3187 Instituto de Estudos Geograficos.
Mapa-oro-hidrográfico de Portugal. Lisbon, 1965.
37 p. 46 cm.

3188 Instituto Geografico De Agostini.
Novo atlas escolar portugués. Novara, 1963.
125 p. col. maps. 34 cm.

3189 Livraria Sá da Costa.
Novo atlas escolar portugués. 5 ed. By João

Soares. Lisboa, [1954].
80 p. col. maps. 34 cm.

3190 Livraria Sá da Costa.
Novo atlas escolar portugués. Lisboa, 1967/68.
1 vol. col. maps. 34 cm.

3191 Livraria Sá da Costa.
Novo atlas escolar portugués, histórico-geográfico.
7 ed. By João Soares. Lisboa, [1959].
83 p. col. maps. 34 cm.

3192 Spain. Consejo Superior de Investigaciones Científicas.
Atlas lingüístico de la Península Ibérica. Madrid,
1962 —
1 vol. col. maps. 62 cm.

3193 Spain. Ministerio de Obras Públicas.
Mapa oficial de carreteras. 4 ed. Madrid, 1961.
104 p. col. maps. 32 cm.

3194 Spain. Ministerio de Obras Públicas.
Mapa oficial de carreteras. 6 ed. Madrid, 1964.
118 p. col. maps. 32 cm.

Romania

3195 Romania. Academia Republicii Socialiste.
Noul atlas lingvistic român pe regiuni. By Boris
Cazacu. Bucuresti, 1967—
in parts. col. maps. 53 cm.

3196 Romania. Asociatia Automobiliştilor din R.P.R.
Republica populară Romînă. Hartă automobilistica.
Bucuresti, 1965.
32 p. col. maps. 19 cm.

3197 Romania. Editura Academiei Republicii Populare
Romîne.
Micul atlas lingvistic romîn. By Ioan Patrut.
Bucuresti, 1956—
in parts. col. maps. 25 cm.

3198 Romania. Editura di stat Didactică şi Pedagogică.
Atlas geografic: Republica Socialistă România. By
Victor Tufescu. Bucuresti, 1965.
144 p. col. maps. 34 cm.

3199 Romania. Editura di stat Didacticā şi Pedagogicā.
     Atlas geografic şcolar. By N. Gheorghiu.
     Bucuresti, 1957.
     34 p. col. maps. 33 cm.

3200 Romania. Editura di stat Didacticā si Pedagogicā.
     Atlas geografic şcolar. By N. Gheorghiu.
     Bucuresti, 1962.
     34 p. col. maps. 33 cm.

3201 Romania. Institutul Meteorologie.
     Atlasul climatologic al Republicii Socialiste
     Romānia. Bucuresti, 1966.
     180 p. col. maps. 58 cm.

Scotland

3202 Bookcraft.
     A genealogical atlas of Scotland. By David E.
     Gardner, Derek Harland, and Frank Smith. Salt
     Lake City, Utah, [1962].
     32 p. 27 cm.

3203 Ebury Press.
     The Shell guide to Scotland. By Moray McLaren.
     London, 1967.
     496 p. col. maps. 26 cm.

3204 Newnes, George, Ltd.
     Newnes motorists touring maps and gazetteer. With
     Bartholomew. London, [1950].
     160 p. col. maps. 29 cm.

3205 Newnes, George, Ltd.
     Newnes' motorists' touring maps and gazetteer.
     London, [1965].
     48 p. col. maps. 29 cm.

3206 Newnes, George, Ltd.
     Newnes' motorists' touring maps and gazetteer of
     Scotland. 1 ed. With Bartholomew. London,
     [1965].
     74 p. col. maps. 29 cm.

3207 Shell-Mex & BP Ltd.
     Shell Nature Lovers' Atlas of England Scotland
     and Wales. By James Fisher. London, 1966.
     1 vol. col. maps. 28 cm.

3208 University of London Press.
  An atlas notebook of Scotland. By Gordon Rae.
  London, [1960].
  48 p. 28 cm.

Spain

3209 Aguilar, S. A. de Ediciones.
  Atlas bachillerato universal y de España. 1 ed.
  By A. L. Gómez. Madrid, 1962.
  132 p. col. maps. 35 cm.

3210 Aguilar, S. A. de Ediciones.
  Atlas bachillerato universal y de España. 2 ed.
  By A. L. Gómez. Madrid, 1963.
  132 p. col. maps. 35 cm.

3211 Aguilar, S. A. de Ediciones.
  Atlas bachillerato universal y de España. 3 ed.
  By A. L. Gómez. Madrid, 1963.
  132 p. col. maps. 35 cm.

3212 Aguilar, S. A. de Ediciones.
  Atlas bachillerato universal y de España. 4 ed.
  By A. L. Gómez. Madrid, 1964.
  132 p. col. maps. 35 cm.

3213 Aguilar, S. A. de Ediciones.
  Atlas bachillerato universal y de España. 5 ed.
  By A. L. Gómez. Madrid, 1964.
  132 p. col. maps. 35 cm.

3214 Aguilar, S. A. de Ediciones.
  Atlas bachillerato universal y de España. 6 ed.
  By A. L. Gómez. Madrid, 1964.
  132 p. col. maps. 35 cm.

3215 Aguilar, S. A. de Ediciones.
  Atlas bachillerato universal y de España. 7 ed.
  By A. L. Gómez. Madrid, 1965.
  132 p. col. maps. 35 cm.

3216 Aguilar, S. A. de Ediciones.
  Atlas bachillerato universal y de España. 8 ed.
  By A. L. Gómez. Madrid, 1965.
  132 p. col. maps. 35 cm.

3217 Aguilar, S. A. de Ediciones.
      Atlas bachillerato universal y de España.   9 ed.
      By A. L. Gómez. Madrid, 1966.
      132 p. col. maps. 35 cm.

3218 Aguilar, S. A. de Ediciones.
      Atlas bachillerato universal y de España.   10 ed.
      By A. L. Gómez. Madrid, 1966.
      132 p. col. maps. 35 cm.

3219 Aguilar, S. A. de Ediciones.
      Atlas bachillerato universal y de España.   11 ed.
      By A. L. Gómez. Madrid, 1966.
      132 p. col. maps. 35 cm.

3220 Aguilar, S. A. de Ediciones
      Atlas bachillerato universal y de España.   12 ed.
      By A. L. Gómez. Madrid, 1967.
      117 p. col. maps. 35 cm.

3221 Aguilar, S. A. de Ediciones.
      Atlas bachillerato universal y de España.   13 ed.
      By A. L. Gómez. Madrid, 1967.
      117 p. col. maps. 35 cm.

3222 Aguilar, S. A. de Ediciones.
      Atlas bachillerato universal y de España.   14 ed.
      By A. L. Gómez. Madrid, 1967.
      117 p. col. maps. 35 cm.

3223 Aguilar, S. A. de Ediciones.
      Atlas bachillerato universal y de España.   15 ed.
      By A. L. Gómez. Madrid, 1968.
      117 p. col. maps. 35 cm.

3224 Aguilar, S. A. de Ediciones.
      Atlas bachillerato universal y de España.   16 ed.
      By A. L. Gómez. Madrid, 1968.
      117 p. col. maps. 35 cm.

3225 Aguilar, S. A. de Ediciones.
      Atlas bachillerato universal y de España.   17 ed.
      By A. L. Gómez. Madrid, 1968.
      117 p. col. maps. 35 cm.

3226 Aguilar, S. A. de Ediciones.
      Atlas bachillerato universal y de España.   18 ed.

By A. L. Gómez. Madrid, 1968.
117 p. col. maps. 35 cm.

3227 Aguilar, S. A. de Ediciones.
Atlas bachillerato universal y de España. 19 ed.
By A. L. Gómez. Madrid, 1969.
117 p. col. maps. 35 cm.

3228 Aguilar, S. A. de Ediciones.
Atlas bachillerato universal y de España. 20 ed.
By A. L. Gómez. Madrid, 1969.
117 p. col. maps. 35 cm.

3229 Aguilar, S. A. de Ediciones.
Atlas bachillerato universal y de España. 21 ed.
By A. L. Gómez. Madrid, 1969.
117 p. col. maps. 35 cm.

3230 Aguilar, S. A. de Ediciones.
Atlas bachillerato universal y de España. 22 ed.
By A. L. Gómez. Madrid, 1969.
117 p. col. maps. 35 cm.

3231 Aguilar, S. A. de Ediciones.
Atlas bachillerato universal y de España. 23 ed.
By A. L. Gómez. Madrid, 1970.
117 p. col. maps. 35 cm.

3232 Aguilar, S. A. de Ediciones.
Atlas medio de España. Madrid, 1957.
38 p. col. maps. 31 cm.

3233 Aguilar, S. A. de Ediciones.
Atlas medio universal y de España. Madrid, [1956].
126 p. col. maps. 31 cm.

3234 Aguilar, S. A. de Ediciones.
Nuevo atlas de España. Madrid, 1961.
455 p. col. maps. 32 cm.

3235 Bosch.
Atlas elemental de España, geográfico y estadístico.
Barcelona, [1950].
13 p. col. maps. 22 cm.

3236 Bosch.
Atlas geográfico mundial y especial de España.

Barcelona, [1957].
74 p.   col. maps.   38 cm.

3237 Compañia Mercantil Anónima Líneas Aéreas Españolas.
Rutas de España.   Madrid, 1960.
16 p.   col. maps.   36 cm.

3238 Editorial Luis Vives, S. A.
Atlas historico Edelvives.   Zaragoza, [1962].
68 p.   col. maps.   21 cm.

3239 Editorial Luis Vives, S. A.
Atlas universal y de España.   Zaragoza, [1950].
52 p.   col. maps.   32 cm.

3240 Editorial Luis Vives, S. A.
Atlas universal y de España.   Zaragoza, [1954].
52 p.   col. maps.   31 cm.

3241 Editorial Seix Barral, S. A.
Atlas geográfico de España, físico, político y
estadistíco.   Barcelona, 1950.
64 p.   col. maps.   34 cm.

3242 Editorial Seix Barral, S. A.
Atlas geográfico de España, físico, político y
estadístico.   Barcelona, 1953.
64 p.   col. maps.   34 cm.

3243 Editorial Seix Barral, S. A.
Atlas geográfico de España, físico, político y
estadístico.   Barcelona, 1957.
64 p.   col. maps.   34 cm.

3244 Editorial Teide.
Atlas de historia de España.   3 ed.   By Jaime
Vicens Vives.   Barcelona, [1963].
74 p.   col. maps.   26 cm.

3245 Firestone-Hispania, S. A.
Atlas de España y Portugal.   3 ed.   Bilbao, [1964].
79 p.   col. maps.   28 cm.

3246 Firestone-Hispania, S. A.
Atlas de España y Portugal.   Bilbao, 1969.
1 vol.   col. maps.   28 cm.

3247 Firestone-Hispania, S. A.
Firestone-Hispania nuevo atlas de España y Portugal.
Bilbao, [1961].
79 p. col. maps. 28 cm.

3248 Hernando.
Atlas de España con nociones de geografía. Madrid,
1965.
32 p. col. maps. 32 cm.

3249 Martín, A.
Atlas geográfico de España. 6 ed. Barcelona, 1953.
78 p. col. maps. 38 cm.

3250 Nathan, Fernand.
España, bella desconocide, descubierta en 46 mapas.
By Rooul J. Michel. Paris, 1968.
46 p. col. maps. 21 cm.

3251 Spain. Cámeras Oficiales de Comercio, Industria y
Navegación.
Atlas comercial de España. Madrid, 1963.
182 p. col. maps. 49 cm.

3252 Spain. Cámeras Oficiales de Comercio, Industria y
Navegación.
Atlas industrial de España. Madrid, 1964-66.
2 vol. col. maps. 44, 32 cm.

3253 Spain. Comité Español de Riegos y Drenajes.
Los riegos en España; datos para su estudio.
Madrid, 1956.
1 vol. col. maps. 31 cm.

3254 Spain. Dirección General de Montes, Caza y Pesca
Fluvial.
Mapa forestal de España. Madrid, 1966.
50 p. col. maps. 54 cm.

3255 Spain. Ejercito. Servicio Geografico.
Agenda. Madrid, 1964.
122 p. col. maps. 11 cm.

3256 Spain. Instituto Geográfico y Catastral.
Atlas nacional de España. Madrid, 1965—
in 3 parts. col. maps. 56 cm.

3257 Spain.   Ministerio de Obras Públicas.
     <u>Mapa oficial de carreteras.</u>   4 ed.   Madrid, 1961.
     104 p.   col. maps.   32 cm.

3258 Spain.   Ministerio de Obras Públicas.
     <u>Mapa oficial de carreteras.</u>   6 ed.   Madrid, 1964.
     118 p.   col. maps.   32 cm.

3259 Villarroya San Mateo, Antonio.
     <u>Atlas de geografía postal de España.</u>   Madrid, [1961].
     57 p.   28 cm.

3260 Villarroya San Mateo, Antonio.
     <u>Atlas de geografía postal de España.</u>   [Madrid], 1962.
     55 p.   35 cm.

<u>Sweden</u>

3261 Carlson, A. V.
     <u>Sverige nu; AVC:s atlas över Sveriges folk, land och</u>
     <u>näringar.</u>   2 ed.   By H. W. Ahlmann.   Stockholm,
     [1950].
     63 p.   col. maps.   28 cm.

3262 Carlson, A. V.
     <u>Sverige nu; AVC:s atlas över Sveriges folk, land</u>
     <u>och näringar.</u>   By H. W. Ahlmann.   Stockholm,
     [1961].
     43 p.   col. maps.   28 cm.

3263 Carlson, A. V.
     <u>Sverige nu; AVC:s atlas över Sveriges folk, land</u>
     <u>och näringar.</u>   2 ed.   By H. W. Ahlmann.
     Stockholm, 1967.
     47 p.   col. maps.   28 cm.

3264 Generalstabens litografiska anstalt.
     <u>Atlas över Sverige.</u>   Utgiven av Svenska Sällskapet
     för Antropologi och Geografi.   Stockholm, 1953-64.
     300 p.   col. maps.   43 cm.

3265 Generalstabens litografiska anstalt.
     <u>KAKs Bilatlas över Sverige.</u>   Stockholm, 1955.
     297 p.   col. maps.   26 cm.

3266 Generalstabens litografiska anstalt.
     <u>KAK Bilatlas.</u>   Stockholm, 1966.
     202 p.   col. maps.   31 cm.

3267 Generalstabens litografiska anstalt.
KAK Bilatlas. Stockholm, [1967].
202 p. col. maps. 31 cm.

3268 Generalstabens litografiska anstalt.
KAK bilkartor. Stockholm, 1968.
92 p. col. maps. 31 cm.

3269 Generalstabens litografiska anstalt.
Post-och järnvägs karta över Sverige. Stockholm,
[1957].
21 p. col. maps. 22.5 cm.

3270 Generalstabens litografiska anstalt.
Post-och järnvägs karta över Sverige. Stockholm,
1966.
15 p. col. maps. 22.5 cm.

3271 Generalstabens litografiska anstalt.
S-N bilkarta över Sverige. Stockholm, 1957.
104 p. col. maps. 24 cm.

3272 Generalstabens litografiska anstalt.
S-N bilatlas över Sverige. Stockholm, 1964.
123 p. col. maps. 24 cm.

3273 Kungliga Automobil Klubben.
Kungl. Automobilklubbens karta över Sverige.
Stockholm, 1954.
15 p. col. maps. 26 cm.

3274 Kungliga Automobil Klubben.
Road atlas, Sweden. With Generalstabens litografiska
anstalt. Stockholm, 1961.
128 p. col. maps. 26 cm.

3275 Lantbruksförbundets Tidskriftsaktiebolag.
Jordbruksatlas över Sverige. Stockholm, 1952.
183 p. 26 cm.

3276 Motormännens riksförbund.
M:s vägvisare: Sverige. Stockholm, 1957.
352 p. col. maps. 25 cm.

3277 Motormännens riksförbund.
M:s vägvisare: Sverige. Stockholm, [1961].
1 vol. col. maps. 25 cm.

3278 Motormännens riksförbund.
     M:s vägvisare: Sverige. Stockholm, [1963].
     1 vol. col. maps. 25 cm.

3279 Motormännens riksförbund.
     M:s vägvisare: Sverige. 7 ed. Stockholm, [1965].
     1 vol. col. maps. 25 cm.

3280 Motormännens riksförbund.
     M:s vägvisare: Sverige. 8 ed. Stockholm, 1968.
     1 vol. col. maps. 25 cm.

3281 Sveriges Köpmannaförbund.
     Handelsmoraden i Sverige. Ekonomisk-geografisk
     atlas. By Sven Dahl and Hans Jalinder. Stockholm,
     1966.
     43 p. col. maps. 40 cm.

Switzerland

3282 Buchverlag Verlandsdruckerei.
     Atlas der schweizerischen Landwirtschaft. By W.
     Bäggli. Bern, 1954.
     92 p. col. maps. 24 cm.

3283 Continental Gummiwerke Kartographischer Verlag.
     Continental Atlas. Deutschland, Benelux, Schweiz,
     Österreich, Norditalian. 33 ed. Hannover, 1964.
     635 p. col. maps. 26 cm.

3284 JRO Verlag.
     JRO Autoatlas. Deutschland, Schweiz, Westöster-
     reich. München, [1953].
     468 p. col. maps. 25 cm.

3285 Kantonaler Lehrmittel Verlag.
     Atlante svizzero per le scuole medie. 7 ed. By
     Ed. Imhof. Zürich, 1958.
     144 p. col. maps. 36 cm.

3286 Kantonaler Lehrmittel Verlag.
     Schweizerischer Mittelschulatlas. 12 ed. By Ed.
     Imhof. Zürich, 1958.
     144 p. col. maps. 36 cm.

3287 Kantonaler Lehrmittel Verlag.
     Schweizerischer Mittelschulatlas. 13 ed. By Ed.

Imhof. Zürich, 1962.
144 p. col. maps. 34 cm.

3288 Kantonaler Lehrmittel Verlag.
Schweizerischer Sekuudarschulatlas. 6 ed. By Ed.
Imhof. Zürich, 1954.
80 p. col. maps. 36 cm.

3289 Kantonaler Lehrmittel Verlag.
Schweizerischer Sekundarschulatlas. 7 ed. By Ed.
Imhof. Zürich, 1957.
80 p. col. maps. 36 cm.

3290 Kümmerly & Frey.
All about Switzerland. [Atlas]. Bern, [1957].
24 p. col. maps. 13 cm.

3291 Kümmerly & Frey.
Autoatlas Schweiz. Bern, [1952].
48 p. col. maps. 23 cm.

3292 Kümmerly & Frey.
Autoatlas Schweiz. Bern, [1954].
48 p. col. maps. 23 cm.

3293 Kümmerly & Frey.
Autoatlas Schweiz, Mitteleuropa. Bern, [1955].
48 p. col. maps. 24 cm.

3294 Kümmerly & Frey.
Autoatlas Schweiz, Mitteleuropa. Bern, [1956].
48 p. col. maps. 24 cm.

3295 Kümmerly & Frey.
Autokarte Schweiz und angrenzende Gebiete.
Zürich, [1955].
48 p. col. maps. 22 cm.

3296 Kümmerly & Frey.
Geologischer atlas der Schweiz. Bern, 1962 —
in parts. col. maps. 70 cm.

3297 Kümmerly & Frey.
Schweiz. [Atlas]. Bern, [1956].
28 p. col. maps. 15 cm.

3298 Kümmerly & Frey.
Schweiz und angrenzende Länder; Strassenatlas.

Bern, [1961].
60 p. col. maps. 23 cm.

3299 Kümmerly & Frey.
Schweiz, angrenzende Länder und Stadtpläne. Bern,
[1962].
60 p. col. maps. 23 cm.

3300 Kümmerly & Frey.
Schweiz, angrenzende Länder und Stadtpläne. Bern,
[1965].
60 p. col. maps. 23 cm.

3301 Kümmerly & Frey.
Schweiz, angrenzende Länder und Stadtpläne. Bern,
[1966].
60 p. col. maps. 23 cm.

3302 Kümmerly & Frey.
Schweizerischer Schulatlas. 15 ed. Bern, [1954].
49 p. col. maps. 31 cm.

3303 Kümmerly & Frey.
Schweizerischer Schulatlas. 16 ed. Bern, [1959].
51 p. col. maps. 33 cm.

3304 Kümmerly & Frey.
Schweizerischer Schulatlas. 17 ed. Bern, [1962].
51 p. col. maps. 31 cm.

3305 Kümmerly & Frey.
Schweizerischer Volksschulatlas. 10 ed. Bern,
[1954].
26 p. col. maps. 31 cm.

3306 Kümmerly & Frey.
Schweizerischer Volksschulatlas. 11 ed. Bern,
[1958].
34 p. col. maps. 33 cm.

3307 Kümmerly & Frey.
Schweizerischer Volksschulatlas. 12 ed. Bern,
[1960].
34 p. col. maps. 33 cm.

3308 Librairie Payot.
Atlas scolaire suisse pour l'enseignement secondaire.

10 ed. By Ed. Imhof. Lausanne, 1955.
144 p. col. maps. 36 cm.

3309 Librairie Payot.
Atlas scolaire suisse pour l'enseignement secondaire.
11 ed. By Ed. Imhof. Lausanne, [1958].
144 p. col. maps. 36 cm.

3310 Librairie Payot.
Atlas scolaire suisse pour l'enseignement secondaire.
Lausanne, [1959].
1 vol. col. maps. 36 cm.

3311 Orell Füssli, A. G.
Atlante svizzero por le suole medie. By Edward
Imhof. Zürich, 1965.
152 p. col. maps. 33.5 cm.

3312 Orell Füssli, A. G.
Schweizerischer Mittelschulatlas. By Edward Imhof.
Zürich, 1962.
152 p. col. maps. 33.5 cm.

3313 Orell Füssli, A. G.
Schweizerischer Mittelschulatlas. By Edward Imhof.
Zürich, 1965.
152 p. col. maps. 33.5 cm.

3314 Sauerländer, H. R.
Historischer atlas der Schweiz. By Hektor Ammann
and Karl Schib. Aarau, 1951.
95 p. col. maps. 35 cm.

3315 Sauerländer, H. R.
Historischer atlas der Schweiz. 2 ed. By Hektor
Ammann and Karl Schib. Aarau, 1958.
103 p. col. maps. 35 cm.

3316 Sauerländer, H. R.
Historischer atlas zur Welt- und Schweizer
Geschichte. 6 ed. By F. W. Putzger. Aarau,
[1965].
158 p. col. maps. 27 cm.

3317 Schweizer Reisekasse.
Reiseatlas Schweiz und Ausland. Bern, [1957].
72 p. col. maps. 21 cm.

3318 Schweizerische Gesellschaft für Volkskunde.
     Atlas der Schweizerischen Volkskunde.   Basle,
     [1950-].
     in parts.   col.   maps.   40 cm.

3319 Switzerland.   Konferenz der Kantonalen Erziehungs-
     direktoren.
     Schweizerischer Mittelschulatlas.   11 ed.   Zürich,
     1955.
     144 p.   col.   maps.   36 cm.

3320 Switzerland.   Landestopographie.
     Atlas der Schweiz.   Hersg. im Auftrag des
     Schweizerischen Bundestages.   Wabern-Bern, 1965-
     in parts.   col.   maps.   54 cm.

Turkey

3321 Codex Verlag.
     Kulturatlas der Türkei.   Gundholzen, [1967].
     in 12 parts.   col.   maps.   43 cm.

3322 Milli Egitim Basimevi.
     Türkiye Atlasi.   With Faculty of Letters, Univ. of
     Istanbul.   Istanbul, [1961].
     87 p.   47 cm.

U.S.S.R.

3323 Czechoslovakia.   Ústrední správa geodézie a kartografie.
     Prírucní atlas SSSR.   1 ed.   Praha, 1951.
     88 p.   col.   maps.   26 cm.

3324 Czechoslovakia.   Ústrední správa geodézie a kartografie.
     Prírucní atlas SSSR.   Praha, 1952.
     1 vol.   col.   maps.   26 cm.

3325 Denoyer-Geppert Co.
     Soviet Union in maps, its origin and development.
     By George Goodall.   Chicago, 1954.
     32 p.   col.   maps.   26 cm.

3326 Denoyer-Geppert Co.
     Soviet Union in maps; its origin and development.
     By Harold Fullard.   Chicago, 1965.
     32 p.   col.   maps.   26 cm.

3327 Denoyer-Geppert Co.

Soviet Union in maps; its origin and development.
By Harold Fullard.   Chicago, 1968.
32 p.   col. maps.   26 cm.

3328 Elsevier.
Atlas historique et culturel de la Russie et du monde
slave.   By Pierre Kovalewsky.   Paris, [1961].
216 p.   col. maps.   35 cm.

3329 Heinemann.
An atlas of Russian and East-European history.   By
Arthur E. Adams and William O. McCagg.   London,
1966.
204 p.   21 cm.

3330 Heinemann.
An atlas of Russian and East European history.   By
Arthur E. Adams.   London, 1967.
204 p.   21 cm.

3331 Melantrich.
Atlas SSSR.   Praha, 1951.
62 p.   col. maps.   31 cm.

3332 Methuen.
An atlas of Soviet affairs.   By Robert N. Taaffe.
London, [1965].
143 p.   21 cm.

3333 Orbis Terrarum.
Atlas skhem zheleznykh dorog SSSR.   New York,
1964.
143 p.   16 cm.

3334 Oxford University Press.
Oxford regional economic atlas of the U. S. S. R. and
Eastern Europe.   Oxford, 1956.
140 p.   col. maps.   26 cm.

3335 Oxford University Press.
Oxford regional economic atlas of the U.S.S.R. and
Eastern Europe.   Oxford, [1963].
1 vol.   col. maps.   26 cm.

3336 Philip, George & Son, Ltd.
Soviet Union in maps; its origin and development.
By George Goodall.   London, 1954.
32 p.   col. maps.   26 cm.

3337 Philip, George & Son, Ltd.
     Soviet Union in maps; its origin and development.
     By Harold Fullard. London, 1965.
     32 p. col. maps. 26 cm.

3338 Praeger, Frederick A.
     An atlas of Russian and East European history. By
     Arthur E. Adams, Ian M. Matley, William O.
     McCagg. New York, 1966.
     204 p. 21 cm.

3339 Praeger, Frederick A.
     An atlas of Soviet affairs.   By Robert N. Taaffee.
     New York, [1965].
     143 p. 21 cm.

3340 University of Michigan Press.
     Economic atlas of the Soviet Union.   By George
     Kish. Ann Arbor, Michigan [1960].
     96 p. col. maps. 27 cm.

3341 U.S.S.R. Akademiia nauk.
     Atlas paleogeograficheskikh kart SSSR.   Kiev, 1965-
     in parts. col. maps. 66 cm.

3342 U.S.S.R. Glavnoe upravlenie geodezii i kartografii.
     Atlas avtomobilnykh dorog SSSR.   Moskva, 1961.
     130 p. col. maps. 27 cm.

3343 U.S.S.R. Glavnoe upravlenie geodezii i kartografii.
     Atlas avtomobilnykh dorog SSSR.   Moskva, 1963.
     130 p. col. maps. 27 cm.

3344 U.S.S.R. Glavnoe upravlenie geodezii i kartografii.
     Atlas avtomobilnykh dorog SSSR.   Moskva, 1966.
     166 p. col. maps. 27 cm.

3345 U.S.S.R. Glavnoe upravlenie geodezii i kartografii.
     Atlas avtomobilnykh dorog SSSR.   Moskva, 1967.
     166 p. col. maps. 27 cm.

3346 U.S.S.R. Glavnoe upravlenie geodezii i kartografii.
     Atlas avtomobilnykh dorog SSSR.   Moskva, 1968.
     168 p. col. maps. 27 cm.

3347 U.S.S.R. Glavnoe upravlenie geodezii i kartografii.
     Atlas istorii SSSR.   Moskva, 1968.
     38 p. col. maps. 26 cm.

3348 U.S.S.R. Glavnoe upravlenie geodezii i kartografii.
Atlas istorii SSSR dlya IV klassa. Moskva, 1967.
12 p. col. maps. 26 cm.

3349 U.S.S.R. Glavnoe upravlenie geodezii i kartografii.
Atlas istorii SSSR dlya IV klassa. Moskva, 1968.
12 p. col. maps. 26 cm.

3350 U.S.S.R. Glavnoe upravlenie geodezii i kartografii.
Atlas istorii SSSR dlya VII klassa. Moskva, 1967.
18 p. col. maps. 26 cm.

3351 U.S.S.R. Glavnoe upravlenie geodezii i kartografii.
Atlas istorii SSSR dlya VII klassa. Moskva, 1968.
16 p. col. maps. 26 cm.

3352 U.S.S.R. Glavnoe upravlenie geodezii i kartografii.
Atlas istorii SSSR dlya VIII klassa. Moskva, 1967.
12 p. col. maps. 26 cm.

3353 U.S.S.R. Glavnoe upravlenie geodezii i kartografii.
Atlas istorii SSSR dlya VIII klassa. Moskva, 1968.
11 p. col. maps. 26 cm.

3354 U.S.S.R. Glavnoe upravlenie geodezii i kartografii.
Atlas istorii SSSR dlya IX klassa. Moskva, 1967.
20 p. col. maps. 26 cm.

3355 U.S.S.R. Glavnoe upravlenie geodezii i kartografii.
Atlas istorii SSSR dlya IX klassa. Moskva, 1968.
20 p. col. maps. 26 cm.

3356 U.S.S.R. Glavnoe upravlenie geodezii i kartografii.
Atlas istorii SSSR dlya 7go i 8go klassov. Moskva,
1964.
40 p. col. maps. 26 cm.

3357 U.S.S.R. Glavnoe upravlenie geodezii i kartografii.
Atlas istorii SSSR dlya 7go i 8go klassov. Moskva,
1967.
40 p. col. maps. 26 cm.

3358 U.S.S.R. Glavnoe upravlenie geodezii i kartografii.
Atlas istorii SSSR dlya V klassa srednei shkoly.
Moskva, 1968.
12 p. col. maps. 26 cm.

3359 U.S.S.R. Glavnoe upravlenie geodezii i kartografii.
Atlas istorii SSSR dlya srednei shkoly. Moskva,
1950.
1 vol.   col. maps.   30 cm.

3360 U.S.S.R. Glavnoe upravlenie geodezii i kartografii.
Atlas istorii SSSR dlya srednei shkoly. Moskva,
1951.
1 vol.   col. maps.   30 cm.

3361 U.S.S.R. Glavnoe upravlenie geodezii i kartografii.
Atlas istorii SSSR dlya srednei shkoly. Moskva,
1953.
2 vol.   col. maps.   30 cm.

3362 U.S.S.R. Glavnoe upravlenie geodezii i kartografii.
Atlas istorii SSSR dlya srednei shkoly. Moskva,
1954.
3 vol.   col. maps.   30 cm.

3363 U.S.S.R. Glavnoe upravlenie geodezii i kartografii.
Atlas istorii SSSR dlya srednei shkoly. Moskva,
1955.
2 vol.   col. maps.   30 cm.

3364 U.S.S.R. Glavnoe upravlenie geodezii i kartografii.
Atlas istorii SSSR dlya srednei shkoly. Moskva,
1964.
20 p.   col. maps.   27 cm.

3365 U.S.S.R. Glavnoe upravlenie geodezii i kartografii.
Atlas istorii SSSR dlya srednei shkoly. Part I.
Moskva, 1964.
16 p.   col. maps.   27 cm.

3366 U.S.S.R. Glavnoe upravlenie geodezii i kartografii
Atlas istorii SSSR dlya srednei shkoly. Part II.
Moskva, 1964.
12 p.   col. maps.   27 cm.

3367 U.S.S.R. Glavnoe upravlenie geodezii i kartografii.
Atlas lesov SSSR. Moskva, 1970-71.
1 vol.   col. maps.   34 cm.

3368 U.S.S.R. Glavnoe upravlenie geodezii i kartografii.
Atlas narodov SSSR. Moskva, 1969-70.
1 vol.   col. maps.   37 cm.

3369 U.S.S.R. Glavnoe upravlenie geodezii i kartografii.
Atlas razvita khoziaistva i kultury SSSR. Moskva,
1967.
172 p. col. maps. 34 cm.

3370 U.S.S.R. Glavnoe upravlenie geodezii i kartografii.
Atlas sel'skovo khozyaystva SSSR. Moskva, 1960.
308 p. col. maps. 35 cm.

3371 U.S.S.R. Glavnoe upravlenie geodezii i kartografii.
Atlas skhem zheleznykh dorog SSSR. Moskva, 1963.
143 p. col. maps. 16 cm.

3372 U.S.S.R. Glavnoe upravlenie geodezii i kartografii.
Atlas SSSR. Moskva, 1950.
147 p. col. maps. 26 cm.

3373 U.S.S.R. Glavnoe upravlenie geodezii i kartografii.
Atlas SSSR. Moskva, 1954.
147 p. col. maps. 26 cm.

3374 U.S.S.R. Glavnoe upravlenie geodezii i kartografii.
Atlas SSSR. Moskva, 1955.
147 p. col. maps. 26 cm.

3375 U.S.S.R. Glavnoe upravlenie geodezii i kartografii.
Atlas SSSR. Moskva, 1956.
194 p. col. maps. 16 cm.

3376 U.S.S.R. Glavnoe upravlenie geodezii i kartografii.
Atlas SSSR. Moskva, 1962.
147 p. col. maps. 26 cm.

3377 U.S.S.R. Glavnoe upravlenie geodezii i kartografii.
Atlas SSSR. Moskva, 1962.
185 p. col. maps. 39 cm.

3378 U.S.S.R. Glavnoe upravlenie geodezii i kartografii.
Atlas SSSR. 2 ed. Moskva, 1969.
199 p. col. maps. 38 cm.

3379 U.S.S.R. Glavnoe upravlenie geodezii i kartografii.
Atlas SSSR dlya srednei shkoly. Moskva, 1960.
50 p. col. maps. 28 cm.

3380 U.S.S.R. Glavnoe upravlenie geodezii i kartografii.
Atlas SSSR dlya srednei shkoly. Moskva, [1961].
50 p. col. maps. 28 cm.

3381 U.S.S.R. Glavnoe upravlenie geodezii i kartografii.
Atlas SSSR dlya srednei shkoly. 3 ed. Moskva,
[1967].
50 p. col. maps. 28 cm.

3382 U.S.S.R. Glavnoe upravlenie geodezii i kartografii.
Atlas SSSR dlya srednei shkoly. Moskva, 1968.
48 p. col. maps. 28 cm.

3383 U.S.S.R. Glavnoe upravlenie geodezii i kartografii.
Atlas uglenakoplenia na territorii SSSR. Moskva,
1962.
528 p. col. maps. 60 cm.

3384 U.S.S.R. Glavnoe upravlenie geodezii i kartografii.
Atlas vulkanov SSSR. Moskva, 1959.
174 p. col. maps. 28 cm.

3385 U.S.S.R. Glavnoe upravlenie geodezii i kartografii.
Atlas zdravookhranenia SSSR. Moskva, 1970-71.
1 vol. col. maps. 34 cm.

3386 U.S.S.R. Glavnoe upravlenie geodezii i kartografii.
Atlas zemletriasenii SSSR. Moskva, 1962.
337 p. col. maps. 34 cm.

3387 U.S.S.R. Glavnoe upravlenie geodezii i kartografii.
Geograficheskii atlas dlya 4go klassa srednei shkoly.
Moskva, 1964.
1 vol. col. maps. 28 cm.

3388 U.S.S.R. Glavnoe upravlenie geodezii i kartografii.
Geograficheskii atlas dlya 4go klassa. Moskva,
1967.
16 p. col. maps. 28 cm.

3389 U.S.S.R. Glavnoe upravlenie geodezii i kartografii.
Geograficheskii atlas dlya 4go klassa. Moskva,
[1968].
16 p. col. maps. 28 cm.

3390 U.S.S.R. Glavnoe upravlenie geodezii i kartografii.
Geograficheskii atlas dlya 5go klassa. Moskva,
1967.
16 p. col. maps. 28 cm.

3391 U.S.S.R. Glavnoe upravlenie geodezii i kartografii.
Geograficheskii atlas dlya 5go klassa. Moskva,

[1968].
16 p. col. maps. 28 cm.

3392 U.S.S.R. Glavnoe upravlenie geodezii i kartografii.
Geograficheskii atlas dlya 6go - 7go klassov.
Moskva, 1967.
48 p. col. maps. 28 cm.

3393 U.S.S.R. Glavnoe upravlenie geodezii i kartografii.
Geograficheskii atlas dlya 6go - 7go klassov.
Moskva, 1968.
48 p. col. maps. 28 cm.

3394 U.S.S.R. Glavnoe upravlenie geodezii i kartografii.
Geograficheskii atlas dlya 7go - 8go klassov.
Moskva, 1951.
76 p. col. maps. 30 cm.

3395 U.S.S.R. Glavnoe upravlenie geodezii i kartografii.
Geograficheskii atlas dlya 7go - 8go klassov.
Moskva, 1953.
76 p. col. maps. 30 cm.

3396 U.S.S.R. Glavnoe upravlenie geodezii i kartografii.
Geograficheskii atlas dlya 7go - 8go klassov.
Moskva, 1954.
76 p. col. maps. 30 cm.

3397 U.S.S.R. Glavnoe upravlenie geodezii i kartografii.
Geograficheski atlas dlya srednei shkoly. Moskva,
1950.
42 p. col. maps. 30 cm.

3398 U.S.S.R. Glavnoe upravlenie geodezii i kartografii.
Geograficheskii atlas dlya uchitelei srednei shkoly.
Moskva, 1967.
164 p. col. maps. 37 cm.

3399 U.S.S.R. Glavnoe upravlenie geodezii i kartografii.
Geograficheskii atlas dlya uchilelei srednei shkoly.
Moskva, 1968.
164 p. col. maps. 37 cm.

3400 U.S.S.R. Glavnoe upravlenie geodezii i kartografii.
Geograficheskii atlas malerikov dlya 6go kl. Moskva,
1969.
37 p. col. maps. 28 cm.

3401 U.S.S.R. Glavnoe upravlenie geodezii i kartografii.
Geograficheskii atlas SSSR dlya 7 - 8 klassov.
Moskva, 1962.
36 p. col. maps. 28 cm.

3402 U.S.S.R. Glavnoe upravlenie geodezii i kartografii.
Geograficheskii atlas SSSR dlya 7 - 8 klassov.
Moskva, 1964.
36 p. col. maps. 28 cm.

3403 U.S.S.R. Glavnoe upravlenie geodezii i kartografii.
Geograficheskii atlas SSSR dlya 7 - 8 klassov.
Moskva, 1966.
36 p. col. maps. 28 cm.

3404 U.S.S.R. Glavnoe upravlenie geodezii i kartografii.
Geograficheskii atlas SSSR dlya 7 - 8 klassov.
Moskva, 1967.
36 p. col. maps. 28 cm.

3405 U.S.S.R. Glavnoe upravlenie geodezii i kartografii.
Geograficheskii atlas SSSR dlya 7 - 8 klassov.
Moskva, 1968.
36 p. col. maps. 28 cm.

3406 U.S.S.R. Glavnoe upravlenie geodezii i kartografii.
Litologo-paleogeograficheskii atlas SSSR. Moskva,
1967-68.
2 vol. col. maps. 66 cm.

3407 U.S.S.R. Glavnoe upravlenie geodezii i kartografii.
Zheleznye dorogi SSSR. Moskva, 1965.
150 p. col. maps. 16 cm.

3408 U.S.S.R. Glavnoe upravlenie geodezii i kartografii.
Zheleznye dorogi SSSR. Moskva, 1966.
150 p. col. maps. 16 cm.

3409 U.S.S.R. Glavnoe upravlenie geodezii i kartografii.
Zheleznye dorogi SSSR. Moskva, 1967.
148 p. col. maps. 16 cm.

3410 U.S.S.R. Glavnoe upravlenie geodezii i kartografii.
Zheleznye dorogi SSSR. Moskva, 1968.
148 p. col. maps. 16 cm.

3411 Yale University Press.
An atlas of Russian history. By Allen F. Chew.

New Haven, Conn., 1967.
111 p.   27.5 cm.

3412 Yale University Press.
An atlas of Russian history.   2 ed.   By Allen F.
Chew.   New Haven, Conn., 1970.
111 p.   27.5 cm.

Wales

3413 Bartholomew, John & Son, Ltd.
Bartholomew's road atlas of England and Wales.
London, 1963.
59 p.   col. maps.   25 cm.

3414 Deseret Book Co.
A genealogical atlas of England and Wales.   By
David E. Gardner, Derek Harland and Frank Smith.
Salt Lake City, Utah, [1960].
88 p.   27 cm.

3415 Faber & Faber.
An agricultural atlas of England and Wales.   By
J. T. Coppock.   London, 1964.
255 p.   25 cm.

3416 Faber & Faber.
An historical atlas of Wales.   2 ed.   By William
Rees.   Cardiff, 1951.
70 p.   26 cm.

3417 Faber & Faber.
An historical atlas of Wales.   By William Rees.
London, [1959].
71 p.   26 cm.

3418 Faber & Faber.
An historical atlas of Wales from early to modern
times.   London, 1966.
73 p.   26 cm.

3419 Faber & Faber.
An historical atlas of Wales from early to modern
times.   3 ed.   London, 1967.
73 p.   26 cm.

3420 Gt. Britain.   Ministry of Agriculture, Fisheries & Food.
Atlas of long-term irrigation needs for England and

Wales.   London, 1967.
1 vol.   32 cm.

3421 Gt. Britain.   Ministry of Housing and Local Government.
Desk atlas of planning maps of England and Wales.
London, 1953—
in parts.   col. maps.   43.5 cm.

3422 Gwasg Prifysgol Cymru.
Atlas hanesyddol o gymru.   By James Idwal Jones.
Caerdydd, 1952.
99 p.   25 cm.

3423 Hughes & Son.
An atlas of Wales.   By J. Idwal Jones.   Wrexham,
[1957].
2 vol.   29 cm.

3424 National Trust.
The National Trust atlas showing places of historic,
architectual & scenic interest in England, Wales
and Northern Ireland.   With Bartholomew.   London,
1964.
80 p.   col. maps.   25 cm.

3425 Shell-Mex & BP Ltd.
Shell nature lover's atlas of England, Scotland and
Wales.   By James Fisher.   London, 1966.
1 vol.   col. maps.   28 cm.

3426 University of Wales Press.
Wales in maps.   By Margaret Davies.   Cardiff,
1951.
111 p.   25 cm.

3427 University of Wales Press.
Wales in maps.   2 ed.   By Margaret Davies.
Cardiff, 1958.
111 p.   25 cm.

Yugoslavia

3428 Geokarta.
Atlas Federativne Narodne Republike Jugoslavije.
By Jossip J. Uhlik.   Beograd, 1952.
63 p.   col. maps.   18 cm.

3429 Jugoslavenski leksikografski zavod.
Jugoslavija; auto atlas. Zagreb, [1967].
1 vol. col. maps. 28 cm.

3430 Jugoslavenski leksikografski zavod.
Jugoslavija; auto atlas. Zagreb, [1968].
1 vol. col. maps. 28 cm.

3431 Turistička Štampa.
Autokarta Jugoslavije. 2 ed. Beograd, 1956.
102 p. col. maps. 29 cm.

3432 Turistička Štampa
Road map, Yugoslavia. Beograd, 1955.
132 p. col. maps. 29 cm.

3433 Turistička Štampa.
Yougoslavie, carte routière. Beograd, 1954.
122 p. col. maps. 29 cm.

3434 Učila.
Autoatlas Jugoslavije. Zagreb, 1962.
29 p. col. maps. 23 cm.

3435 Učila.
Autoatlas Jugoslavije. Zagreb, 1966.
30 p. col. maps. 23 cm.

3436 Učila.
Autoatlas Jugoslavije. 4 ed. Zagreb, 1967.
29 p. col. maps. 23 cm.

3437 Učila
Autoatlas Jugoslavije. Zagreb, 1968.
29 p. col. maps. 23 cm.

3438 Učila
Istorijski atlas za niže razrede srednijih škol.
Zagreb, 1954.
36 p. col. maps. 22 cm.

3439 Yugoslavia. Vojno-istoriski institut.
Historical atlas of the liberation war of the peoples
of Yugoslavia, 1941-1945. Beograd, 1957.
41 p. col. maps. 41 cm.

3440 Yugoslavia. Vojno-istoriski institut.
Istoriski atlas oslobodilačkog rata naroda Jugoslavije, 1941-1945. Beograd, 1952.
41 p. col. maps. 41 cm.

3441 Znanje.
Geografski atlas Jugoslavije. By Petar Mardešić
and Zvonimir Dugački. Zagreb, 1961.
256 p. col. maps. 22 cm.

3442 Znanje.
Istoricki atlas nacionalni istorii. Beograd, 1953.
18 p. col. maps. 34 cm.

3443 Znanje.
Istoricki atlas nacionalni istorii. Beograd, 1956.
18 p. col. maps. 34 cm.

3444 Znanje.
Istoricki atlas za III i IV razred osnovne shkole.
By Slobodan Dukič. Beograd, 1953.
1 vol. col. maps. 31 cm.

Canada

3445 Abercrombie & Fitch.
The complete Abercrombie & Fitch vacation atlas
for all of North America. New York, 1965.
142 p. col. maps. 34 cm.

3446 Alpine Geographical Press.
Campground atlas of the United States and Canada.
Champaign, Ill., [1960].
176 p. col. maps. 28 cm.

3447 Alpine Geographical Press.
Campground atlas of the United States and Canada.
Champaign, Ill., [1962].
182 p. col. maps. 28 cm.

3448 Alpine Geographical Press.
Campground atlas of the United States and Canada.
Champaign, Ill., [1964].
186 p. col. maps. 28 cm.

3449 Alpine Geographical Press.
Campground atlas of the United States and Canada.
Champaign, Ill., 1966.
204 p. col. maps. 28 cm.

3450 Alpine Geographical Press.
Campground atlas of the United States and Canada.
Champaign, Ill., 1966-67.
157 p. col. maps. 28 cm.

3451 Alpine Geographical Press.
Campground atlas of the United States and Canada.
Champaign, Ill., 1967-68.
260 p. col. maps. 28 cm.

3452 Alpine Geographical Press.
Campground atlas of the United States and Canada.
Champaign, Ill., 1968-69.
260 p. col. maps. 28 cm.

3453 Alpine Geographical Press.
        Campground atlas of the United States and Canada.
        Champaign, Ill., 1969-70
        260 p. col. maps. 28 cm.

3454 American Hotel Register Co.
        Leahy's hotel-motel guide and travel atlas of the
        United States, Canada and Mexico. 75 ed. Chicago,
        1950.
        256 p. col. maps. 38 cm.

3455 American Hotel Register Co.
        Leahy's hotel-motel guide and travel atlas of the
        United States, Canada and Mexico. 76 ed.
        Chicago, 1951.
        256 p. col. maps. 38 cm.

3456 American Hotel Register Co.
        Leahy's hotel-motel guide and travel atlas of the
        United States, Canada and Mexico. 77 ed.
        Chicago, 1952.
        256 p. col. maps. 38 cm.

3457 American Hotel Register Co.
        Leahy's hotel-motel guide and travel atlas of the
        United States, Canada and Mexico. 78 ed.
        Chicago, 1953.
        256 p. col. maps. 38 cm.

3458 American Hotel Register Co.
        Leahy's hotel-motel guide and travel atlas of the
        United States, Canada and Mexico. 79 ed.
        Chicago, 1954.
        256 p. col. maps. 38 cm.

3459 American Hotel Register Co.
        Leahy's hotel-motel guide and travel atlas of the
        United States, Canada and Mexico. 80 ed.
        Chicago, 1955.
        256 p. col. maps. 38 cm.

3460 American Hotel Register Co.
        Leahy's hotel-motel guide and travel atlas of the
        United States, Canada and Mexico. 81 ed.
        Chicago, 1956.
        256 p. col. maps. 38 cm.

3461 American Hotel Register Co.
　　　Leahy's hotel-motel guide and travel atlas of the
　　　United States, Canada and Mexico.　82 ed.
　　　Chicago, 1957.
　　　256 p.　col. maps.　38 cm.

3462 American Hotel Register Co.
　　　Leahy's hotel-motel guide and travel atlas of the
　　　United States, Canada and Mexico.　83 ed.
　　　Chicago, 1958.
　　　256 p.　col. maps.　38 cm.

3463 American Hotel Register Co.
　　　Leahy's hotel-motel guide and travel atlas of the
　　　United States, Canada and Mexico.　84 ed.
　　　Chicago, 1959.
　　　256 p.　col. maps.　38 cm.

3464 American Hotel Register Co.
　　　Leahy's hotel-motel guide and travel atlas of the
　　　United States, Canada and Mexico.　85 ed.
　　　Chicago, 1960.
　　　256 p.　col. maps.　38 cm.

3465 American Hotel Register Co.
　　　Leahy's hotel-motel guide and travel atlas of the
　　　United States, Canada and Mexico.　86 ed.
　　　Chicago, 1961.
　　　256 p.　col. maps.　38 cm.

3466 American Hotel Register Co.
　　　Leahy's Hotel-motel guide and travel atlas of the
　　　United States, Canada and Mexico.　87 ed.
　　　Chicago, 1962.
　　　256 p.　col. maps.　38 cm.

3467 American Hotel Register Co.
　　　Leahy's hotel-motel guide and travel atlas of the
　　　United States, Canada and Mexico.　88 ed.
　　　Chicago, 1963.
　　　256 p.　col. maps.　38 cm.

3468 American Hotel Register Co.
　　　Leahy's hotel-motel guide and travel atlas of the
　　　United States, Canada and Mexico.　89 ed.
　　　Chicago, 1964.
　　　257 p.　col. maps.　38 cm.

3469 American Hotel Register Co.
     Leahy's hotel-motel guide and travel atlas of the
     United States, Canada and Mexico.   90 ed.
     Chicago, 1965.
     257 p.   col.   maps.   38 cm.

3470 American Hotel Register Co.
     Leahy's hotel-motel guide and travel atlas of the
     United States, Canada and Mexico.   91 ed.
     Chicago, 1966.
     258 p.   col.   maps.   38 cm.

3471 American Hotel Register Co.
     Leahy's hotel-motel guide and travel atlas of the
     United States, Canada and Mexico.   92 ed.
     Chicago, 1967.
     258 p.   col.   maps.   38 cm.

3472 American Hotel Register Co.
     Leahy's hotel-motel guide and travel atlas of the
     United States, Canada and Mexico.   93 ed.
     Chicago, 1968.
     258 p.   col.   maps.   38 cm.

3473 American Hotel Register Co.
     Leahy's hotel-motel guide and travel atlas of the
     United States, Canada and Mexico.   94 ed.
     Chicago, 1969.
     258 p.   col.   maps.   38 cm.

3474 American Hotel Register Co.
     Leahy's hotel-motel guide and travel atlas of the
     United States, Canada and Mexico.   95 ed.
     Chicago, 1970.
     258 p.   col.   maps.   38 cm.

3475 American Map Co., Inc.
     Cleartype business control atlas of the United States
     and Canada.   New York, 1968.
     120 p.   28 cm.

3476 American Map Co., Inc.
     Cleartype business control atlas of the United States
     and Canada.   New York, 1969.
     120 p.   29 cm.

3477 American Map Co., Inc.
     Cleartype executive sales control atlas of the United

States and Canada.   New York, [1968].
132 p.   30 cm.

3478 Better Camping Magazine.
Campground atlas of the United States and Canada.
Milwaukee, Wisc., [1970].
314 p.   col. maps.   28 cm.

3479 Canada.   Department of Energy, Mines & Resources.
Atlas and Gazetteer of Canada.   Ottawa, 1970.
50 p.   col. maps.   25 cm.

3480 Canada.   Department of Energy, Mines & Resources.
National atlas of Canada.   4 ed.   Ottawa, 1970—
in parts.   col. maps.   37 cm.

3481 Canada.   Department of Mines and Technical Surveys.
Atlas of Canada.   Ottawa, 1957.
110 p.   col. maps.   52.5 cm.

3482 Canada.   Department of Transport.
Climatological atlas of Canada.   By Morley K.
Thomas.   Ottawa, 1953.
256 p.   31 cm.

3483 Canada.   Surveys and Mapping Branch.
Atlas and gazetteer of Canada.   Ottawa, [1969].
104 p.   col. maps.   38 cm.

3484 Dent, J. M.
Canadian school atlas.   By H. E. Mindak.   Toronto,
[1961].
115 p.   col. maps.   29 cm.

3485 Dent, J. M.
Dent's Canadian school atlas.   Toronto, 1958.
115 p.   col. maps.   29 cm.

3486 Dent, J. M.
Dent's Canadian school atlas.   Toronto, 1965.
115 p.   col. maps.   29 cm.

3487 Dent, J. M.
The Aldine world atlas; geography and history.
1 ed.   By J. W. Hamilton and G. E. Tait.   With
Bartholomew.   Toronto, 1961.
166 p.   col. maps.   29 cm.

3488 Dent, J. M.
        The Aldine world atlas; geography and history.
        2 ed. By J. W. Hamilton and G. E. Tait. With
        Bartholomew. Toronto, [1963].
        166 p. col. maps. 29 cm.

3489 Diversified Map Corporation.
        The complete Abercrombie & Fitch vacation atlas
        for all North America. New York, 1965.
        142 p. col. maps. 34 cm.

3490 Diversified Map Corporation.
        This week magazine's vacation planner and speedy
        flipout road atlas...to all North America. New
        York, [1965].
        142 p. col. maps. 34 cm.

3491 Editions du Renouveau pédagogique.
        Atlas du monde contemporain. By Pierre Gourou.
        Montréal, [1967].
        88 p. col. maps. 36 cm.

3492 Encyclopedia Canadiana.
        Encyclopedia Canadiana atlas of Canada. With
        Hammond. Ottawa, 1965.
        32 p. col. maps. 31 cm.

3493 Farmers Insurance Group.
        Vacation guide and atlas. With Goushá. Los
        Angeles, Calif., [1958].
        64 p. col. maps. 28 cm.

3494 Farmers Insurance Group.
        Vacation guide and atlas. With Goushá. Los
        Angeles, Calif., [1965].
        64 p. col. maps. 28 cm.

3495 Farmers Insurance Group.
        Vacation guide and road atlas. With Goushá. Los
        Angeles, Calif., [1966].
        64 p. col. maps. 28 cm.

3496 Goushá, H. M. Co.
        American highway atlas. Chicago, 1962.
        112 p. col. maps. 43 cm.

3497 Goushá, H. M. Co.
        North American vacation guide and road atlas.

San Jose, Calif., 1967.
64 p. col. maps. 28 cm.

3498 Goushá, H. M. Co.
Trip plan (atlas), Allstate Motor Club travel
service. Skokie, Ill., 1965.
1 vol. col. maps. 29 cm.

3499 Goushá, H. M. Co.
United States, Canada and Mexico. Chicago, 1963.
64 p. col. maps. 26 cm.

3500 Goushá, H. M. Co.
United States, Canada and Mexico. Road atlas.
With National Safety Council. San Jose, Calif.,
1965.
64 p. 28 cm.

3501 Grolier Society.
World atlas; an encyclopedic atlas of the world.
Canadian classics ed. With Hammond. Toronto,
1953.
340 p. col. maps. 32 cm.

3502 Grosset & Dunlap.
The new Grosset road atlas of the United States,
Canada and Mexico. With Diversified Map Corporation. New York, 1967.
144 p. col. maps. 34 cm.

3503 Grosset & Dunlap.
The new Grosset road atlas of the United States,
Canada and Mexico. With Diversified Map Corporation. New York, [1968].
144 p. col. maps. 34 cm.

3504 Grosset & Dunlap.
The new Grosset road atlas of the United States,
Canada and Mexico. With Diversified Map Corporation. New York, [1969].
144 p. col. maps. 34 cm.

3505 Hammond, C. S. & Co., Inc.
Hammond modern world atlas and gazetteer.
Canadian ed. Maplewood, N. J., 1965.
40 p. col. maps. 31 cm.

3506 Hammond, C. S. & Co., Inc.
     Hammond's pictorial travel atlas of scenic America.
     By E. L. Jordan. Maplewood, N. J., [1955].
     256 p. col. maps. 32 cm.

3507 Hammond, C. S. & Co., Inc.
     Hammond road atlas of the United States, Canada,
     Mexico. Maplewood, N. J., [1964].
     48 p. col. maps. 32 cm.

3508 Hammond, C. S. & Co., Inc.
     Hammond road atlas of the United States, Canada,
     Mexico. Maplewood, N. J., 1965.
     48 p. col. maps. 32 cm.

3509 Hammond, C. S. & Co., Inc.
     Hammond's road atlas and city street guide of the
     United States, Canada, Mexico. Maplewood, N. J.,
     1963.
     96 p. col. maps. 31 cm.

3510 Hammond, C. S. & Co., Inc.
     Hammond's sports atlas of America. New York,
     1956.
     40 p. col. maps. 32 cm.

3511 Hammond, C. S. & Co., Inc.
     Hammond universal world atlas. Canadian ed.
     Maplewood, N. J., [1964].
     160 p. col. maps. 32 cm.

3512 Hammond, C. S. & Co., Inc.
     Sales planning atlas of the United States and Canada.
     Maplewood, N. J., [1962].
     160 p. 28 cm.

3513 Hammond, C. S. & Co., Inc.
     Standard world atlas. Canadian ed. New York,
     1955.
     328 p. col. maps. 32 cm.

3514 Hammond, Inc.
     Road atlas of the United States and Canada.
     Maplewood, N. J., 1968.
     48 p. col. maps. 31 cm.

3515 Hammond, Inc.
     Sales planning atlas of the United States and Canada.

Maplewood, N. J., [1968].
160 p. 28 cm.

3516 Kalmbach Publishing Co.
Campground atlas of the United States and Canada.
Milwaukee, Wisc., 1970-71.
314 p. col. maps. 28 cm.

3517 Macmillan & Co., Ltd.
The Macmillan Canada atlas.   By Ronald C. Daly.
Toronto, [1966].
114 p. col. maps. 28 cm.

3518 National Bus Traffic Association.
Atlas of motor bus routes and express blocks no
A-602-B.   Chicago, 1966.
90 p. 40 cm.

3519 Nelson, Thomas & Sons, Ltd.
An historical atlas of Canada.   By D. G. G. Kerr.
Toronto, [1960].
120 p. col. maps. 31 cm.

3520 Nelson, Thomas & Sons, Ltd.
An historical atlas of Canada. 2ed.   By D. G. G.
Kerr.   Don Mills, Ont., [1966].
120 p. col. maps. 31 cm.

3521 Nelson, Thomas & Sons, Ltd.
Nelson's Canadian school atlas.   By J. Wreford
Watson.   Toronto, [1958].
92 p. col. maps. 29 cm.

3522 Nelson, Thomas & Sons, Ltd.
Nelson's Canadian school atlas. 2 ed.   B. J.
Wreford Watson.   Toronto, [1960].
92 p. col. maps. 29 cm.

3523 Nelson, Thomas & Sons, Ltd.
Nelson's Canadian school atlas. 3 ed.   By J.
Wreford Watson.   Toronto, 1963.
92 p. col. maps. 29 cm.

3524 Nelson, Thomas & Sons, Ltd.
Nelson's Canadian school atlas. 4 ed.   By J.
Wreford Watson.   Don Mills, Ont., 1965.
92 p. col. maps. 29 cm.

3525 Oxford University Press.
     Oxford regional economic atlas of the United States
     and Canada. By John D. Chapman and John C.
     Sherman. Oxford, 1967.
     164 p. col. maps. 25.5 cm.

3526 Oxford University Press.
     The Canadian Oxford atlas of the world. 2 ed.
     Toronto, 1957.
     1 vol. col. maps. 39 cm.

3527 Oxford University Press.
     The Canadian Oxford desk atlas of the world.
     Toronto, 1957.
     137 p. col. maps. 26 cm.

3528 Oxford University Press.
     The Canadian Oxford desk atlas of the world. 2 ed.
     Toronto, 1963.
     155 p. col. maps. 26 cm.

3529 Oxford University Press.
     The Canadian Oxford junior atlas. Toronto, 1969.
     64 p. col. maps. 26 cm.

3530 Oxford University Press.
     The Canadian Oxford school atlas. 2 ed. Toronto,
     1966.
     120 p. col. maps. 39 cm.

3531 Petroleum Publishing Co.
     Atlas of crude-oil pipelines of the United States
     and Canada. Tulsa, Okla., 1965.
     22 p. 31 cm.

3532 Petroleum Publishing Co.
     Atlas of natural-gas pipelines of the United States
     and Canada. Tulsa, Okla., 1965.
     24 p. 31 cm.

3533 Philip, George & Son, Ltd.
     Philip's historical atlas of Canada. By J. W.
     Chalmers, W. J. Eccles and H. Fullard, London,
     1966.
     48 p. col. maps. 28 cm.

3534 Philip, George & Son, Ltd.
     Philip's senior atlas for Canada. London, [1966].

80 p.   col.   maps.   29 cm.

3535 Rand McNally & Co.
Rand McNally interstate road atlas: United States,
Canada, Mexico.   Chicago, [1967].
96 p.   col.   maps.   28 cm.

3536 Rand McNally & Co.
Rand McNally interstate road atlas: United States,
Canada, Mexico.   Chicago, 1968.
96 p.   col.   maps.   28 cm.

3537 Rand McNally & Co.
Rand McNally road atlas and travel guide, United
States, Canada, Mexico.   Chicago, 1963.
84 p.   col.   maps.   25 cm.

3538 Rand McNally & Co.
Rand McNally road atlas and travel guide, United
States, Canada, Mexico.   Chicago, 1964.
84 p.   col.   maps.   25 cm.

3539 Rand McNally & Co.
Rand McNally road atlas and travel guide, United
States, Canada, Mexico.   Chicago, 1965.
84 p.   col.   maps.   25 cm.

3540 Rand McNally & Co.
Rand McNally road atlas and travel guide, United
States, Canada, Mexico.   Chicago, 1966.
84 p.   col.   maps.   25 cm.

3541 Rand McNally & Co.
Rand McNally road atlas and travel guide, United
States, Canada, Mexico.   Chicago, 1967.
96 p.   col.   maps.   25 cm.

3542 Rand McNally & Co.
Rand McNally road atlas and travel guide, United
States, Canada, Mexico.   Chicago, 1968.
96 p.   col.   maps.   25 cm.

3543 Rand McNally & Co.
Rand McNally road atlas and travel guide, United
States, Canada, Mexico.   Chicago, 1969.
96 p.   col.   maps.   25 cm.

3544 Rand McNally & Co.
      Rand McNally road atlas and travel guide, United
      States, Canada, Mexico. Chicago, 1970.
      96 p. col. maps. 25 cm.

3545 Rand McNally & Co.
      Rand McNally road atlas, United States, Canada,
      Mexico. Chicago, 1950.
      112 p. col. maps. 40 cm.

3546 Rand McNally & Co.
      Rand McNally road atlas, United States, Canada,
      Mexico. Chicago, 1951.
      112 p. col. maps. 40 cm.

3547 Rand McNally & Co.
      Rand McNally road atlas, United States, Canada,
      Mexico. Chicago, 1952.
      112 p. col. maps. 40 cm.

3548 Rand McNally & Co.
      Rand McNally road atlas, United States, Canada,
      Mexico. Chicago, 1953.
      112 p. col. maps. 40 cm.

3549 Rand McNally & Co.
      Rand McNally road atlas, United States, Canada,
      Mexico. Chicago, 1954.
      112 p. col. maps. 40 cm.

3550 Rand McNally & Co.
      Rand McNally road atlas, United States, Canada,
      Mexico. Chicago, 1955.
      112 p. col. maps. 40 cm.

3551 Rand McNally & Co.
      Rand McNally road atlas, United States, Canada,
      Mexico. Chicago, 1956.
      112 p. col. maps. 40 cm.

3552 Rand McNally & Co.
      Rand McNally road atlas, United States, Canada,
      Mexico. Chicago, 1957.
      112 p. col. maps. 40 cm.

3553 Rand McNally & Co.
      Rand McNally road atlas, United States, Canada,

Mexico. Chicago, 1958.
112 p. col. maps. 40 cm.

3554 Rand McNally & Co.
Rand McNally road atlas, United States, Canada,
Mexico. Chicago, 1959.
112 p. col. maps. 40 cm.

3555 Rand McNally & Co.
Rand McNally road atlas, United States, Canada,
Mexico. Chicago, 1960.
112 p. col. maps. 40 cm.

3556 Rand McNally & Co.
Rand McNally road atlas, United States, Canada,
Mexico. Chicago, 1961.
112 p. col. maps. 40 cm.

3557 Rand McNally & Co.
Rand McNally road atlas, United States, Canada,
Mexico. Chicago, 1962.
112 p. col. maps. 40 cm.

3558 Rand McNally & Co.
Rand McNally road atlas, United States, Canada,
Mexico. Chicago, 1963.
112 p. col. maps. 40 cm.

3559 Rand McNally & Co.
Rand McNally road atlas, United States, Canada,
Mexico. Chicago, 1964.
112 p. col. maps. 40 cm.

3560 Rand McNally & Co.
Rand McNally road atlas, United States, Canada,
Mexico. Chicago, 1965.
112 p. col. maps. 40 cm.

3561 Rand McNally & Co.
Rand McNally road atlas, United States, Canada,
Mexico. Chicago, 1966.
114 p. col. maps. 40 cm.

3562 Rand McNally & Co.
Rand McNally road atlas, United States, Canada,
Mexico. Chicago, 1967.
114 p. col. maps. 40 cm.

3563 Rand McNally & Co.
     Rand McNally road atlas, United States, Canada,
     Mexico. Chicago, 1968.
     114 p. col. maps. 40 cm.

3564 Rand McNally & Co.
     Rand McNally road atlas, United States, Canada,
     Mexico. Chicago, 1969.
     114 p. col. maps. 40 cm.

3565 Rand McNally & Co.
     Rand McNally road atlas, United States, Canada,
     Mexico. Chicago, 1970.
     114 p. col. maps. 40 cm.

3566 Rand McNally & Co.
     Rand McNally vacation atlas guide: Canada, United
     States, Mexico. Chicago, [1965].
     108 p. col. maps. 26 cm.

3567 Rand McNally & Co.
     Rolph McNally Canadian road atlas; travel guide
     with campground information. Toronto, [1969].
     96 p. col. maps. 29 cm.

3568 Rand McNally & Co.
     Texaco touring atlas: United States, Canada, Mexico.
     New York, 1965.
     220 p. col. maps. 38 cm.

3569 Rand McNally & Co.
     Texaco touring atlas: United States, Canada, Mexico.
     New York, 1966.
     220 p. col. maps. 38 cm.

3570 Rand McNally & Co.
     Texaco touring atlas: United States, Canada, Mexico.
     New York, 1967.
     220 p. col. maps. 38 cm.

3571 Rand McNally & Co.
     Texaco touring atlas: United States, Canada, Mexico.
     Chicago, 1968.
     220 p. col. maps. 38 cm.

3572 Rand McNally & Co.
     Texaco touring atlas: United States, Canada, Mexico.

Chicago, [1969].
220 p. co. maps. 38 cm.

3573 Rand McNally & Co.
Texaco travel atlas: United States, Canada, Mexico.
Chicago, [1970].
220 p. col. maps. 38 cm.

3574 Vilas Industries.
Philip's historical atlas of Canada. By J. W.
Chalmers, W. J. Eccles and H. Fullard. Toronto,
1966.
48 p. col. maps. 28 cm.

3575 Wiley, John & Sons.
Lithofacies maps; an atlas of the United States and
southern Canada. By Laurence L. Sloss, E. C.
Dapples and W. C. Krumbein. New York, [1960].
153 p. col. maps. 28 cm.

3576 World Pub. Co.
World's road atlas and vacation guide of North
America for 1966-67. Cleveland, 1966.
64 p. col. maps. 28 cm.

3577 World Pub. Co.
World's road atlas and vacation guide of North
America for 1967-68. Cleveland, 1967.
64 p. col. maps. 28 cm.

3578 World Pub. Co.
World's road atlas and vacation guide of North
America for 1968-69. Cleveland, 1968.
64 p. col. maps. 28 cm.

Costa Rica

3579 Costa Rica. Ministerio de Economia y Hacienda.
Atlas Estadístico de Costa Rica. San José, 1953.
114 p. 27.5 cm.

Cuba

3580 U.S.S.R. Glavnoe upravlenie geodezii i kartografii.
Natsionalnyi atlas kuby. Moskva, 1970.
128 p. col. maps. 32 cm.

Dominican Republic

3581 Editorial Seix Barral, S. A.
Atlas escolar de la República Dominicana. Barcelona,
[1969].
1 vol. col. maps. 29 cm.

3582 Obiols, Alfredo.
Atlas de información básica existente y lineamientos
para la planificación del desarrollo integral de la
República Dominicana. Guatemala, 1966.
45 p. col. maps. 53 cm.

El Salvador

3583 Salvador. Dirección General de Cartografía.
El Salvador 1:100,00: Departamentos. San Salvador,
1964 –
in parts. col. maps. 78 cm.

3584 Salvador. Estadistica y cencos.
Atlas censal de El Salvador. San Salvador, [1955].
110 p. col. maps. 36 cm.

3585 Salvador. Universidade Federal da Bahia, Centro de
Estudos Afro-Orientais.
Atlas histórico regional do mundo árabe. A his-
torical and regional atlas of the Arabic world. San
Salvador, [1969].
204 p. 25 cm.

3586 U.S. Engineer Resources Inventory Center.
El Salvador: análisis regional de recursos físicos.
1 ed. Washington, D. C., 1965.
1 vol. col. maps. 82 cm.

Guatemala

3587 Editorial Escolar "Piedra Santa."
Datos geográficos de Guatemala. Guatemala, [1962].
32 p. 22 cm.

3588 Guatemala. Dirección General de Cartografia.
Atlas preliminar de Guatemala. 2 ed. Guatemala,
1964.
78 p. col. maps. 40 cm.

3589 Guatemala.   Instituto Geográfico Nacional.
        Atlas preliminar de Guatemala.   Guatemala, 1966.
        1 vol.   col.   maps.   39 cm.

3590 Guatemala.   Ministerio de educación pública.
        Atlas político-administrativo de la República de
        Guatemala.   By Clemente Castillo Cordero and
        Juan Alfredo García O.   Guatemala, 1953.
        62 p.   23 cm.

3591 Guatemala.   Observatorio Meteorológico y Estacion
        Sismográfia.
        Atlas climatológico de Guatemala.   Guatemala,
        [1964].
        38 p.   col.   maps.   40 cm.

Honduras

3592 U.S. Engineer Agency of Resources Inventories.
        Honduras: inventario nacional de recursos físicos.
        1 ed.   Washington, D. C., 1966.
        1 vol.   col.   maps.   83 cm.

Jamaica

3593 Kings College School.
        Jamaica.   An Atlas of agricultural production.
        London, [1969].
        1 vol.   25 cm.

Mexico

3594 Abercrombie & Fitch.
        The complete Abercrombie & Fitch vacation atlas
        for all of North America.   New York, 1965.
        142 p.   col.   maps.   34 cm.

3595 American Hotel Register Co.
        Leahy's hotel-motel guide and travel atlas of the
        United States, Canada and Mexico.   75 ed.   Chicago,
        1950.
        256 p.   col.   maps.   38 cm.

3596 American Hotel Register Co.
        Leahy's hotel-motel guide and travel atlas of the
        United States, Canada and Mexico.   76 ed.   Chicago,
        1951.
        256 p.   col.   maps.   38 cm.

3597 American Hotel Register Co.
      Leahy's hotel-motel guide and travel atlas of the
      United States, Canada and Mexico. 77 ed. Chicago,
      1952.
      256 p. col. maps. 38 cm.

3598 American Hotel Register Co.
      Leahy's hotel-motel guide and travel atlas of the
      United States, Canada and Mexico. 78 ed. Chicago,
      1953.
      256 p. col. maps. 38 cm.

3599 American Hotel Register Co.
      Leahy's hotel-motel guide and travel atlas of the
      United States, Canada and Mexico. 79 ed. Chicago,
      1954.
      256 p. col. maps. 38 cm.

3600 American Hotel Register Co.
      Leahy's hotel-motel guide and travel atlas of the
      United States, Canada and Mexico. 80 ed. Chicago,
      1955.
      256 p. col. maps. 38 cm.

3601 American Hotel Register Co.
      Leahy's hotel-motel guide and travel atlas of the
      United States, Canada and Mexico. 81 ed. Chicago,
      1956.
      256 p. col. maps. 38 cm.

3602 American Hotel Register Co.
      Leahy's hotel-motel guide and travel atlas of the
      United States, Canada and Mexico. 82 ed. Chicago,
      1957.
      256 p. col. maps. 38 cm.

3603 American Hotel Register Co.
      Leahy's hotel-motel guide and travel atlas of the
      United States, Canada and Mexico. 83 ed. Chicago,
      1958.
      256 p. col. maps. 38 cm.

3604 American Hotel Register Co.
      Leahy's hotel-motel guide and travel atlas of the
      United States, Canada and Mexico. 84 ed. Chicago,
      1959.
      256 p. col. maps. 38 cm.

3605 American Hotel Register Co.
        Leahy's hotel-motel guide and travel atlas of the
        United States, Canada and Mexico.   85 ed. Chicago,
        1960.
        256 p.   col. maps.   38 cm.

3606 American Hotel Register Co.
        Leahy's hotel-motel guide and travel atlas of the
        United States, Canada and Mexico.   86 ed. Chicago,
        1961.
        256 p.   col. maps.   38 cm.

3607 American Hotel Register Co.
        Leahy's hotel-motel guide and travel atlas of the
        United States, Canada and Mexico.   87 ed. Chicago,
        1962.
        256 p.   col. maps.   38 cm.

3608 American Hotel Register Co.
        Leahy's hotel-motel guide and travel atlas of the
        United States, Canada and Mexico.   88 ed. Chicago,
        1963.
        256 p.   col. maps.   38 cm.

3609 American Hotel Register Co.
        Leahy's hotel-motel guide and travel atlas of the
        United States, Canada and Mexico.   89 ed. Chicago,
        1964.
        257 p.   col. maps.   38 cm.

3610 American Hotel Register Co.
        Leahy's hotel-motel guide and travel atlas of the
        United States, Canada and Mexico.   90 ed. Chicago,
        1965.
        257 p.   col. maps.   38 cm.

3611 American Hotel Register Co.
        Leahy's hotel-motel guide and travel atlas of the
        United States, Canada and Mexico.   91 ed. Chicago,
        1966.
        258 p.   col. maps.   38 cm.

3612 American Hotel Register Co.
        Leahy's hotel-motel guide and travel atlas of the
        United States, Canada and Mexico.   92 ed. Chicago,
        1967.
        258 p.   col. maps.   38 cm.

3613 American Hotel Register Co.
   Leahy's hotel-motel guide and travel atlas of the
   United States, Canada and Mexico. 93 ed. Chicago,
   1968.
   258 p. col. maps. 38 cm.

3614 American Hotel Register Co.
   Leahy's hotel-motel guide and travel atlas of the
   United States, Canada and Mexico. 94 ed. Chicago,
   1969.
   258 p. col. maps. 38 cm.

3615 American Hotel Register Co.
   Leahy's hotel-motel guide and travel atlas of the
   United States, Canada and Mexico. 95 ed. Chicago,
   1970.
   258 p. col. maps. 38 cm.

3616 Asociación Nacional Automovilística.
   Atlas: rutas de México; routes of Mexico. 2 ed.
   Mexico. [1962].
   2 vol. col. maps. 24 cm.

3617 Asociación Nacional Automovilística.
   Atlas: rutas de México; routes of Mexico. 3 ed.
   Mexico, [1965].
   2 vol. col. maps. 24 cm.

3618 Asociación Nacional Automovilística.
   Atlas: rutas de Mexico; routes of Mexico. 4 ed.
   Mexico, 1967.
   2 vol. col. maps. 24 cm.

3619 Camping Maps, U.S.A.
   Private campgrounds U.S.A. and Mexico. By
   Glenn and Dale Rhodes. Upper Montclair, N. J.,
   1964.
   142 p. col. maps. 22 cm.

3620 Compañia Hulera Euzkadi, S.A.
   Caminos de México; atlas Goodrich Euzkadi. 1 ed.
   Mexico, 1964.
   16 p. col. maps. 27 cm.

3621 Compañia Hulera Euzkadi, S.A.
   Caminos de México, atlas B.F. Goodrich Euzkadi.
   2 ed. México, [1966].
   16 p. col. maps. 27 cm.

3622 Compañia Hulera Euzkadi, S.A.
 Caminos de México, atlas B.F. Goodrich Euzkadi.
 3 ed. México, 1967.
 16 p. col. maps. 27 cm.

3623 Diversified Map Corporation.
 The complete Abercrombie & Fitch vacation atlas
 for all North America. New York, 1965.
 142 p. col. maps. 34 cm.

3624 Diversified Map Corporation.
 This week magazine's vacation planner and speedy
 flipout road atlas...to all North America. New
 York, [1965].
 142 p. col. maps. 34 cm.

3625 Ediciones Ateneo.
 Atlas geográfico de la República Mexicano; por
 estados. 1 ed. México, D. F., [1966].
 24 p. col. maps. 40 cm.

3626 Edi-Mapas de México.
 Atlas de la República Mexicana, 1967. México,
 [1966].
 32 p. 60 cm.

3627 Edi-Mapas de México.
 Atlas de México. Mexico, 1966.
 32 p. col. maps. 46 cm.

3628 Edi-Mapas de México.
 Atlas geográfico de communicaciones de la República
 Mexicana. By Roberto Beltrán Frias. México,
 1964.
 32 p. col. maps. 67 cm.

3629 Editorial Patria, S.A.
 Atlas geográfico de Mexico. 2 ed. Mexico, D. F.,
 1957.
 40 p. col. maps. 39 cm.

3630 Editorial Porrúa, S.A.
 Atlas Porrúa de la República Mexicana. México,
 1966.
 127 p. col. maps. 33 cm.

3631 Editorial Progreso.
 Atlas historico universal y de México. 1 ed. By

J. Jesús Carabes Pearoasa and Roberto Torres
Padilla. Mexico, 1963.
48 p. col. maps. 27 cm.

3632 Farmers Insurance Group.
Vacation guide and atlas. With Goushá. Los
Angeles, Calif., [1958].
64 p. col. maps. 28 cm.

3633 Farmers Insurance Group.
Vacation guide and atlas. With Goushá. Los
Angeles, Calif., [1965].
64 p. col. maps. 28 cm.

3634 Farmers Insurance Group.
Vacation guide and road atlas. With Goushá. Los
Angeles, Calif., [1966].
64 p. col. maps. 28 cm.

3635 Goushá, H. M. Co.
North American vacation guide and road atlas. San
Jose, Calif., 1967.
64 p. col. maps. 28 cm.

3636 Goushá, H. M. Co.
Trip plan (atlas), Allstate Motor Club travel service.
Skokie, Ill., 1965.
1 vol. col. maps. 29 cm.

3637 Goushá, H. M. Co.
United States, Canada and Mexico. Chicago, 1963.
64 p. col. maps. 26 cm.

3638 Goushá, H. M. Co.
United States, Canada and Mexico. Road atlas.
With National Safety Council. San Jose, Calif.,
1965.
64 p. 28 cm.

3639 Grosset & Dunlap.
The new Grosset road atlas of the United States,
Canada and Mexico. With Diversified Map Corporation. New York, 1967.
144 p. col. maps. 34 cm.

3640 Grosset & Dunlap.
The new Grosset road atlas of the United States,
Canada and Mexico. With Diversified Map Corpora-

tion. New York, [1968].
144 p. col. maps. 34 cm.

3641 Grosset & Dunlap.
The new Grosset road atlas of the United States,
Canada and Mexico. With Diversified Map Corporation. New York, [1969].
144 p. col. maps. 34 cm.

3642 Hammond, C. S. & Co., Inc.
Atlas internacional. (Atlas mundial). Mexico,
[1963].
224 p. col. maps. 37 cm.

3643 Hammond, C. S. & Co., Inc.
Atlas internacional. (Atlas mundial). Mexico, D. F.,
[1965].
224 p. col. maps. 37 cm.

3644 Hammond, C. S. & Co., Inc.
Hammond road atlas of the United States, Canada,
Mexico. Maplewood, N. J., [1964].
48 p. col. maps. 32 cm.

3645 Hammond, C. S. & Co., Inc.
Hammond road atlas of the United States, Canada,
Mexico. Maplewood, N. J., 1965.
48 p. col. maps. 32 cm.

3646 Hammond, C. S. & Co., Inc.
Hammond's road atlas and city street guide of the
United States, Canada, Mexico. Maplewood, N. J.,
1963.
96 p. col. maps. 31 cm.

3647 Hammond, Inc.
Atlas internacional. (Atlas mundial). México,
[1966].
224 p. col. maps. 37 cm.

3648 México. Comisión Nacional de Caminos Vecinales.
Atlas con la red de caminos vecinales construidos
en el sexenio 1958-1964. Mexico, [1964].
31 p. col. maps. 60 cm.

3649 México. Comisión Nacional de Caminos Vecinales.
Atlas geografico nacional. Mexico, 1964.
29 p. col. maps. 61 cm.

3650 México.   Fondo de cultura economica.
      Atlas mexicano de la conquista, historia geográfica
      en 40 cartas. 1 ed. By Jesus Amaya. Mexico,
      1958.
      42 p. col. maps. 35 cm.

3651 Mexico.   Instituto Mexicano de Investigaciones
      Economicas.
      Atlas geografico general de Mexico; con cartes
      fisicas, biologicas, demografícas, sociales,
      economicas y cartogramas. 2 ed. México, 1962.
      1 vol. col. maps. 54 cm.

3652 Mexico.   Ministerio de Comunicaciones y Obras Públi-
      cas.
      Atlas de la Memoria de labores de la Secretaría
      de Comunicaciones y Obras Públicas, 1955-56, con
      un resumen de los avances logrados de 1953-56.
      México, [1957].
      83 p. col. maps. 48 cm.

3653 Mexico.   Ministerio de Comunicaciones y Obras Públi-
      cas.
      Atlas: resumen de los avances logrados en el
      sexenio 1953-58. México, [1959].
      111 p. col. maps. 48 cm.

3654 Mexico.   Secretaría de Comunicaciones y Transportes.
      México; guía de las vías generales de comunicación.
      México, 1963.
      94 p. col. maps. 21 cm.

3655 Mexico.   Universidad Nacional Autónoma.
      Cartografia de elementos bioclimáticos en la Repúb-
      lica Mexicana. By Consuelo Soto Mora and Ernesto
      Jáuregui O. Mexico, D. F., 1968.
      72 p. 27 cm.

3656 Mexico.   Universidad National Autónoma.
      Mapas y planos contemporáneos de México. By
      Ernesto Jáuregui O. Mexico D. F., 1968.
      1 vol. 27 cm.

3657 National Bus Traffic Association.
      Atlas of motor bus routes and express blocks no.
      A-602-B. Chicago, 1966.
      90 p. 40 cm.

3658 Nelson, Thomas & Sons, Ltd.
     Atlas universal y de Mexico.   London, 1966.
     33 p.   col. maps.   28 cm.

3659 Nelson, Thomas & Sons, Ltd.
     Atlas universal y de Mexico.   London, [1968].
     30 p.   col. maps.   28 cm.

3660 Pan American Union.
     Atlas of Mexico.   Washington, D. C., 1967.
     1 vol.   col. maps.   28 cm.

3661 Rand McNally & Co.
     Rand McNally interstate road atlas: United States,
     Canada, Mexico.   Chicago, [1967].
     96 p.   col. maps.   28 cm.

3662 Rand McNally & Co.
     Rand McNally interstate road atlas: United States,
     Canada, Mexico.   Chicago, 1968.
     96 p.   col. maps.   28 cm.

3663 Rand McNally & Co.
     Rand McNally road atlas and travel guide, United
     States, Canada, Mexico.   Chicago, 1963.
     84 p.   col. maps.   25 cm.

3664 Rand McNally & Co.
     Rand McNally road atlas and travel guide, United
     States, Canada, Mexico.   Chicago, 1964.
     84 p.   col. maps.   25 cm.

3665 Rand McNally & Co.
     Rand McNally road atlas and travel guide, United
     States, Canada, Mexico.   Chicago, 1965.
     84 p.   col. maps.   25 cm.

3666 Rand McNally & Co.
     Rand McNally road atlas and travel guide, United
     States, Canada, Mexico.   Chicago, 1966.
     84 p.   col. maps.   25 cm.

3667 Rand McNally & Co.
     Rand McNally road atlas and travel guide, United
     States, Canada, Mexico.   Chicago, 1967.
     96 p.   col. maps.   25 cm.

3668 Rand McNally & Co.
      Rand McNally road atlas and travel guide, United
      States, Canada, Mexico. Chicago, 1968.
      96 p. col. maps. 25 cm.

3669 Rand McNally & Co.
      Rand McNally road atlas and travel guide, United
      States, Canada, Mexico. Chicago, 1969.
      96 p. col. maps. 25 cm.

3670 Rand McNally & Co.
      Rand McNally road atlas and travel guide, United
      States, Canada, Mexico. Chicago, 1970.
      96 p. col. maps. 25 cm.

3671 Rand McNally & Co.
      Rand McNally road atlas, United States, Canada,
      Mexico. Chicago, 1950.
      112 p. col. maps. 40 cm.

3672 Rand McNally & Co.
      Rand McNally road atlas, United States, Canada,
      Mexico. Chicago, 1951.
      112 p. col. maps. 40 cm.

3673 Rand McNally & Co.
      Rand McNally road atlas, United States, Canada,
      Mexico. Chicago, 1952.
      112 p. col. maps. 40 cm.

3674 Rand McNally & Co.
      Rand McNally road atlas, United States, Canada,
      Mexico. Chicago, 1953.
      112 p. col. maps. 40 cm.

3675 Rand McNally & Co.
      Rand McNally road atlas, United States, Canada,
      Mexico. Chicago, 1954.
      112 p. col. maps. 40 cm.

3676 Rand McNally & Co.
      Rand McNally road atlas, United States, Canada,
      Mexico. Chicago, 1955.
      112 p. col. maps. 40 cm.

3677 Rand McNally & Co.
      Rand McNally road atlas, United States, Canada,

Mexico. Chicago, 1956.
112 p. col. maps. 40 cm.

3678 Rand McNally & Co.
Rand McNally road atlas, United States, Canada,
Mexico. Chicago, 1957.
112 p. col. maps. 40 cm.

3679 Rand McNally & Co.
Rand McNally road atlas, United States, Canada,
Mexico. Chicago, 1958.
112 p. col. maps. 40 cm.

3680 Rand McNally & Co.
Rand McNally road atlas, United States, Canada,
Mexico. Chicago, 1959.
112 p. col. maps. 40 cm.

3681 Rand McNally & Co.
Rand McNally road atlas, United States, Canada,
Mexico. Chicago, 1960.
112 p. col. maps. 40 cm.

3682 Rand McNally & Co.
Rand McNally road atlas, United States, Canada,
Mexico. Chicago, 1961.
112 p. col. maps. 40 cm.

3683 Rand McNally & Co.
Rand McNally road atlas, United States, Canada,
Mexico. Chicago, 1962.
112 p. col. maps. 40 cm.

3684 Rand McNally & Co.
Rand McNally road atlas, United States, Canada,
Mexico. Chicago, 1963.
112 p. col. maps. 40 cm.

3685 Rand McNally & Co.
Rand McNally road atlas, United States, Canada,
Mexico. Chicago, 1964.
112 p. col. maps. 40 cm.

3686 Rand McNally & Co.
Rand McNally road atlas, United States, Canada,
Mexico. Chicago, 1965.
112 p. col. maps. 40 cm.

3687 Rand McNally & Co.
      Rand McNally road atlas, United States, Canada,
      Mexico. Chicago, 1966.
      114 p. col. maps. 40 cm.

3688 Rand McNally & Co.
      Rand McNally road atlas, United States, Canada,
      Mexico. Chicago, 1967.
      114 p. col. maps. 40 cm.

3689 Rand McNally & Co.
      Rand McNally road atlas, United States, Canada,
      Mexico. Chicago, 1968.
      114 p. col. maps. 40 cm.

3690 Rand McNally & Co.
      Rand McNally road atlas, United States, Canada,
      Mexico. Chicago, 1969.
      114 p. col. maps. 40 cm.

3691 Rand McNally & Co.
      Rand McNally road atlas, United States, Canada,
      Mexico. Chicago, 1970.
      114 p. col. maps. 40 cm.

3692 Rand McNally & Co.
      Rand McNally vacation atlas guide: Canada, United
      States, Mexico. Chicago, [1965].
      108 p. col. maps. 26 cm.

3693 Rand McNally & Co.
      Texaco touring atlas: United States, Canada, Mexico.
      New York, 1965.
      220 p. col. maps. 38 cm.

3694 Rand McNally & Co.
      Texaco touring atlas: United States, Canada, Mexico.
      New York, 1966.
      220 p. col. maps. 38 cm.

3695 Rand McNally & Co.
      Texaco touring atlas: United States, Canada, Mexico.
      New York, 1967.
      220 p. col. maps. 38 cm.

3696 Rand McNally & Co.
      Texaco touring atlas: United States, Canada, Mexico.

Chicago, 1968.
220 p. col. maps. 38 cm.

3697 Rand McNally & Co.
Texaco touring atlas. United States, Canada, Mexico.
Chicago, [1969].
220 p. col. maps. 38 cm.

3698 Rand McNally & Co.
Texaco travel atlas: United States, Canada, Mexico.
Chicago, [1970].
220 p. col. maps. 38 cm.

3699 Reader's Digest Mexico, S. A.
El atlas de nuestro tiempo de selecciones del
Reader's Digest. Mexico, [1964].
207 p. col. maps. 40 cm.

3700 University of Texas.
Atlas of Mexico. Austin, Texas, 1970.
127 p. col. maps. 36 cm.

3701 World Pub. Co.
World's road atlas and vacation guide of North
America for 1966-67. Cleveland, 1966.
64 p. col. maps. 28 cm.

3702 World Pub. Co.
World's road atlas and vacation guide of North
America for 1967-68. Cleveland, 1967.
64 p. col. maps. 28 cm.

3703 World Pub. Co.
World's road atlas and vacation guide of North
America for 1968-69. Cleveland, 1968.
64 p. col. maps. 28 cm.

Nicaragua

3704 Castillo, Guillermo J.
Atlas de Centro América y especial de Nicaragua.
3 ed. Managua, 1961.
51 p. col. maps. 28 cm.

Panama

3705 Ediciones Oasis.
Pequeño atlas geográfico de Panamá. 5 ed.

[Panamá], 1959.
63 p. col. maps. 23 cm.

3706 Panama. Comisión del Atlas de Panamá.
     Atlas de Panamá. 1 ed. [Panamá], 1965.
     191 p. col. maps. 45.5 cm.

3707 Pan American Union.
     Atlas of Central America and Panama. Washington,
     D. C., 1968.
     1 vol. col. maps. 28 cm.

3708 U.S. Engineer Agency of Resources Inventories.
     Panamá: inventario nacional de recursos físicos.
     1 ed. Washington, D. C., 1967.
     1 vol. col. maps. 77 cm.

Puerto Rico

3709 Puerto Rico. Dept. of Education.
     Atlas escolar. With Hammond. San Juan, 1959.
     48 p. col. maps. 32 cm.

3710 Puerto Rico. Dept. of Education.
     Atlas escolar. With Hammond. San Juan, 1966.
     48 p. col. maps. 32 cm.

U. S. A.

3711 Abercrombie & Fitch.
     The complete Abercrombie & Fitch vacation atlas
     for all of North America. New York, 1965.
     142 p. col. maps. 34 cm.

3712 Alpine Geographical Press.
     Campground atlas of the United States and Canada.
     Champaign, Ill., [1960].
     176 p. col. maps. 28 cm.

3713 Alpine Geographical Press.
     Campground atlas of the United States and Canada.
     Champaign, Ill., [1962].
     182 p. col. maps. 28 cm.

3714 Alpine Geographical Press.
     Campground atlas of the United States and Canada.
     Champaign, Ill., [1964].
     186 p. col. maps. 28 cm.

3715 Alpine Geographical Press.
      Campground atlas of the United States and Canada.
      Champaign, Ill., 1966.
      204 p. col. maps. 28 cm.

3716 Alpine Geographical Press.
      Campground atlas of the United States and Canada.
      Champaign, Ill., 1966-67.
      157 p. col. maps. 28 cm.

3717 Alpine Geographical Press.
      Campground atlas of the United States and Canada.
      Champaign, Ill., 1967-68.
      260 p. col. maps. 28 cm.

3718 Alpine Geographical Press.
      Campground atlas of the United States and Canada.
      Champaign, Ill., 1968-69.
      260 p. col. maps. 28 cm.

3719 Alpine Geographical Press.
      Campground atlas of the United States and Canada.
      Champaign, Ill., 1969-70.
      260 p. col. maps. 28 cm.

3720 American Heritage.
      The American heritage pictorial atlas of United
      States history. New York, [1966].
      424 p. col. maps. 29 cm.

3721 American Hotel Register Co.
      Leahy's hotel-motel guide and travel atlas of the
      United States, Canada and Mexico. 75 ed.
      Chicago, 1950.
      256 p. col. maps. 38 cm.

3722 American Hotel Register Co.
      Leahy's hotel-motel guide and travel atlas of the
      United States, Canada and Mexico. 76 ed.
      Chicago, 1951.
      256 p. col. maps. 38 cm.

3723 American Hotel Register Co.
      Leahy's hotel-motel guide and travel atlas of the
      United States, Canada and Mexico. 77 ed.
      Chicago, 1952.
      256 p. col. maps. 38 cm.

3724 American Hotel Register Co.
       Leahy's hotel-motel guide and travel atlas of the
       United States, Canada and Mexico. 78 ed. Chicago,
       1953.
       256 p.   col. maps.   38 cm.

3725 American Hotel Register Co.
       Leahy's hotel-motel guide and travel atlas of the
       United States, Canada and Mexico. 79 ed. Chicago,
       1954.
       256 p.   col. maps.   38 cm.

3726 American Hotel Register Co.
       Leahy's hotel-motel guide and travel atlas of the
       United States, Canada and Mexico. 80 ed. Chicago,
       1955.
       256 p.   col. maps.   38 cm.

3727 American Hotel Register Co.
       Leahy's hotel-motel guide and travel atlas of the
       United States, Canada and Mexico. 81 ed. Chicago,
       1956.
       256 p.   col. maps.   38 cm.

3728 American Hotel Register Co.
       Leahy's hotel-motel guide and travel atlas of the
       United States, Canada and Mexico. 82 ed. Chicago,
       1957.
       256 p.   col. maps.   38 cm.

3729 American Hotel Register Co.
       Leahy's hotel-motel guide and travel atlas of the
       United States, Canada and Mexico. 83 ed. Chicago,
       1958.
       256 p.   col. maps.   38 cm.

3730 American Hotel Register Co.
       Leahy's hotel-motel guide and travel atlas of the
       United States, Canada and Mexico. 84 ed. Chicago,
       1959.
       256 p.   col. maps.   38 cm.

3731 American Hotel Register Co.
       Leahy's hotel-motel guide and travel atlas of the
       United States, Canada and Mexico. 85 ed. Chicago,
       1960.
       256 p.   col. maps.   38 cm.

3732 American Hotel Register Co.
Leahy's hotel-motel guide and travel atlas of the
United States, Canada and Mexico. 86 ed. Chicago,
1961.
256 p. col. maps. 38 cm.

3733 American Hotel Register Co.
Leahy's hotel-motel guide and travel atlas of the
United States, Canada and Mexico. 87 ed. Chicago,
1962.
256 p. col. maps. 38 cm.

3734 American Hotel Register Co.
Leahy's hotel-motel guide and travel atlas of the
United States, Canada and Mexico. 88 ed. Chicago,
1963.
256 p. col. maps. 38 cm.

3735 American Hotel Register Co.
Leahy's hotel-motel guide and travel atlas of the
United States, Canada and Mexico. 89 ed. Chicago,
1964.
257 p. col. maps. 38 cm.

3736 American Hotel Register Co.
Leahy's hotel-motel guide and travel atlas of the
United States, Canada and Mexico. 90 ed. Chicago,
1965.
257 p. col. maps. 38 cm.

3737 American Hotel Register Co.
Leahy's hotel-motel guide and travel atlas of the
United States, Canada and Mexico. 91 ed. Chicago,
1966.
258 p. col. maps. 38 cm.

3738 American Hotel Register Co.
Leahy's hotel-motel guide and travel atlas of the
United States, Canada and Mexico. 92 ed. Chicago,
1967.
258 p. col. maps. 38 cm.

3739 American Hotel Register Co.
Leahy's hotel-motel guide and travel atlas of the
United States, Canada and Mexico. 93 ed. Chicago,
1968.
258 p. col. maps. 38 cm.

3740 American Hotel Register Co.
Leahy's hotel-motel guide and travel atlas of the United
States, Canada and Mexico. 94 ed. Chicago, 1969.
258 p. col. maps. 38 cm.

3741 American Hotel Register Co.
Leahy's hotel-motel guide and travel atlas of the
United States, Canada and Mexico. 95 ed. Chicago,
1970.
258 p. col. maps. 38 cm.

3742 American Map Co., Inc.
Cleartype business control atlas of the United
States and Canada. New York, 1968.
120 p. 28 cm.

3743 American Map Co., Inc.
Cleartype business control atlas of the United States
and Canada. New York, 1969.
120 p. 29 cm.

3744 American Map Co., Inc.
Cleartype executive sales control atlas of the
United States and Canada. New York, [1968].
132 p. 30 cm.

3745 Better Camping Magazine.
Campground atlas of the United States and Canada.
Milwaukee, Wisc., [1970].
314 p. col. maps. 28 cm.

3746 Boy Scouts of America.
Road atlas and guide to overnight camping. With
Hammond. New Brunswick, N. J., 1964.
80 p. col. maps. 32 cm.

3747 Brown, W. C. Co.
Workbook of weather maps. By John J. Hidore.
Dubuque, Iowa, [1968].
64 p. 28 cm.

3748 Camping Maps, U.S.A.
Private campgrounds and overnight trailer parks.
Palos Verdes Peninsula, Calif., 1965.
204 p. 22 cm.

3749 Camping Maps, U.S.A.
Private campgrounds USA and Mexico. By Glenn

and Dale Rhodes. Upper Montclair, N. J., 1964.
142 p. col. maps. 22 cm.

3750 Denoyer-Geppert Co.
Our United States: its history in cartovues. By
Edgar Bruce Wesley. Chicago, [1965].
2 vol. col. maps. 28 cm.

3751 Denoyer-Geppert Co.
Our United States; its history in maps. 1 ed. By
Edgar Bruce Wesley. Chicago, [1956].
96 p. col. maps. 28 cm.

3752 Diversified Map Corporation.
Diversified Map Corporation road atlas. St. Louis,
1967.
84 p. col. maps. 23 cm.

3753 Diversified Map Corporation.
The complete Abercrombie & Fitch vacation atlas
for all North America. New York, 1965.
142 p. col. maps. 34 cm.

3754 Diversified Map Corporation.
This week magazine's vacation planner and speedy
flipout road atlas...to all North America. New
York, [1965].
142 p. col. maps. 34 cm.

3755 Dorsey Press.
American expansion; a book of maps. By Randall
D. Sale and Edwin D. Karn. Homewood, Ill., 1962.
27 p. col. maps. 28 cm.

3756 Everton Publishers.
Genealogical atlas of the United States. By George
B. Everton, Jr. Logan, Utah, 1966.
120 p. 28 cm.

3757 Farmers Insurance Group.
Vacation guide and atlas. With Goushá. Los
Angeles, Calif., [1958].
64 p. col. maps. 28 cm.

3758 Farmers Insurance Group.
Vacation guide and atlas. With Goushá. Los
Angeles, Calif., [1965].
64 p. col. maps. 28 cm.

3759 Farmers Insurance Group.
    Vacation guide and road atlas.
    With Goushá. Los Angeles, Calif., [1966].
    64 p. col. maps. 28 cm.

3760 General Drafting Co.
    Family travel atlas. With Humble Travel Club.
    Houston, Tex., 1965.
    96 p. col. maps. 32.5 cm.

3761 General Drafting Co.
    Family travel atlas. Houston, Tex., [1967].
    96 p. col. maps. 29 cm.

3762 General Drafting Co.
    Pocket atlas of the United States. Convent Station,
    N. J., 1962.
    35 p. col. maps. 21 cm.

3763 Geographia Map Co.
    Geographia atlas of the United States. New York,
    [1962].
    40 p. col. maps. 26 cm.

3764 Ginn & Co.
    Atlas of American History. By D. B. Cole.
    Boston, [1963].
    150 p. col. maps. 24 cm.

3765 Ginn & Co.
    Atlas of American History. By D. B. Cole.
    Boston, [1968].
    150 p. col. maps. 24 cm.

3766 Goushá, H. M., Co.
    American highway atlas. Chicago, 1962.
    112 p. col. maps. 43 cm.

3767 Goushá, H. M., Co.
    Conoco deluxe touraide. With Continental Oil Co.
    Chicago, 1963.
    128 p. col. maps. 31.5 cm.

3768 Goushá, H. M., Co.
    Conoco deluxe touraide travel guide. With Conti-
    nental Oil Co. Chicago, 1964.
    128 p. col. maps. 31 cm.

3769 Goushá, H. M., Co.
Conoco pocket touraide travel guide. Chicago, 1964.
15 p. col. maps. 23 cm.

3770 Goushá, H. M., Co.
Conoco pocket touraide travel guide. Chicago, 1965.
15 p. col. maps. 23 cm.

3771 Goushá, H. M., Co.
Discover America road atlas. San Jose, Calif.,
[1968].
64 p. col. maps. 28 cm.

3772 Goushá, H. M., Co.
Discover America road atlas. San Jose, Calif.,
[1969].
64 p. col. maps. 28 cm.

3773 Goushá, H. M., Co.
National Safety Council road atlas. Chicago, 1964.
64 p. 28 cm.

3774 Goushá, H. M., Co.
North American vacation guide and road atlas.
San Jose, Calif., 1967.
64 p. col. maps. 28 cm.

3775 Goushá, H. M., Co.
Shell USA travel guide. San Jose, Calif., [1968].
31 p. col. maps. 28 cm.

3776 Goushá, H. M., Co.
Trip plan (atlas), Allstate Motor Club travel
service. Skokie, Ill., 1965.
1 vol. col. maps. 29 cm.

3777 Goushá, H. M., Co.
United States, Canada and Mexico. Chicago, 1963.
64 p. col. maps. 26 cm.

3778 Goushá, H. M., Co.
United States, Canada and Mexico. Road atlas.
With National Safety Council. San Jose, Calif.,
1965.
64 p. 28 cm.

3779 Grosset & Dunlap.
The new Grosset road atlas of the United States,

Canada and Mexico. With Diversified Map Corporation. New York, 1967.
144 p. col. maps. 34 cm.

3780 Grosset & Dunlap.
The new Grosset road atlas of the United States,
Canada and Mexico. With Diversified Map Corporation. New York, [1968].
144 p. col. maps. 34 cm.

3781 Grosset & Dunlap.
The new Grosset road atlas of the United States,
Canada and Mexico. With Diversified Map Corporation. New York, [1969].
144 p. col. maps. 34 cm.

3782 Hammond, C. S. & Co., Inc.
American history atlas. Maplewood, N. J., 1963.
40 p. col. maps. 31 cm.

3783 Hammond, C. S. & Co., Inc.
American history atlas. Maplewood, N. J., 1965.
40 p. col. maps. 31 cm.

3784 Hammond, C. S. & Co., Inc.
Hammond road atlas of the United States, Canada,
Mexico. Maplewood, N. J., [1964].
48 p. col. maps. 32 cm.

3785 Hammond, C. S. & Co., Inc.
Hammond road atlas of the United States, Canada,
Mexico. Maplewood, N. J., 1965.
48 p. col. maps. 32 cm.

3786 Hammond, C. S. & Co., Inc.
Hammond's pictorial travel atlas of scenic America.
By E. L. Jordan. Maplewood, N. J., [1955].
256 p. col. maps. 32 cm.

3787 Hammond, C. S. & Co., Inc.
Hammond's road atlas and city street guide of the
United States, Canada, Mexico. Maplewood, N. J.,
1963.
96 p. col. maps. 31 cm.

3788 Hammond, C. S. & Co., Inc.
Hammond's sports atlas of America. By E. L.

Jordan. New York, 1956.
40 p. col. maps. 32 cm.

3789 Hammond, C. S. & Co., Inc.
Sales planning atlas of the United States and Canada.
Maplewood, N. J., [1962].
160 p.   28 cm.

3790 Hammond, Inc.
American history atlas. Maplewood, N. J., 1968.
40 p. col. maps. 31 cm.

3791 Hammond, Inc.
Hammond road atlas. Maplewood, N. J., 1967.
48 p. col. maps. 31 cm.

3792 Hammond, Inc.
Hammond road atlas. Maplewood, N. J., 1969.
48 p. col. maps. 31 cm.

3793 Hammond, Inc.
History atlas of America. Maplewood, N. J., [1969].
31 p. col. maps. 28 cm.

3794 Hammond, Inc.
North American bicycle atlas. Maplewood, N. J.,
1969.
128 p. 24 cm.

3795 Hammond, Inc.
Road atlas of the United States and Canada. Maplewood, N. J., 1968.
48 p. col. maps. 31 cm.

3796 Hammond, Inc.
Sales planning atlas of the United States and Canada.
Maplewood, N. J., [1968].
160 p. 28 cm.

3797 Hammond, Inc.
United States history atlas. Maplewood, N. J.,
[1968].
64 p. col. maps. 31 cm.

3798 Harvard University Press.
Climatic atlas of the United States. By Stephen
Sargent Visher. Cambridge, Mass., 1954.
403 p. 30 cm.

3799 Harvard University Press.
      Climatic atlas of the United States.   By Stephen
      Sargent Visher.   Cambridge, Mass., 1966.
      403 p.   30 cm.

3800 Hearst Magazines, Inc.
      Marketing maps of the individual states of the
      United States, and maps of 10 multiple markets.
      New York, [1952].
      58 p.   col. maps.   28 cm.

3801 Holt.
      Historical atlas of the United States.   By Clifford
      L. Lord.   New York, [1953].
      258 p.   col. maps.   28 cm.

3802 Household Goods Carrier's Bureau.
      Mileage guide No. 8, containing maps and charts for
      determining distances in highway miles between
      points in the United States.   Washington, D. C.,
      1966.
      338 p.   col. maps.   45 cm.

3803 Industrial Atlas Corporation.
      Industrial atlas mining guide.   New York, 1967.
      103 p.   23.5 cm.

3804 Kalmbach Publishing Co.
      Campground atlas of the United States and Canada.
      Milwaukee, Wisc., 1970-71.
      314 p.   col. maps.   28 cm.

3805 Macmillan & Co., Ltd.
      Camping maps U.S.A.   By Glenn and Dale Rhodes.
      New York, 1963.
      297 p.   25 cm.

3806 Macmillan & Co., Ltd.
      Camping maps U.S.A.   By Glenn and Dale Rhodes.
      New York, 1964.
      352 p.   26 cm.

3807 Macmillan Co.
      American history atlas.   By Martin Gilbert.   New
      York, 1968.
      112 p.   24 cm.

3808 Macmillan Co.
American history atlas. By Martin Gilbert. New
York, 1969.
112 p. 24 cm.

3809 National Bus Traffic Association.
Atlas of motor bus routes and express blocks no
A-602-B. Chicago, 1966.
90 p. 40 cm.

3810 National Geographic Society.
Atlas of the United States. Washington, D. C., 1964.
1 vol. col. maps. 31 cm.

3811 National Geographic Society.
National Geographic atlas of the fifty United States.
Washington, D. C., 1960.
72 p. col. maps. 31 cm.

3812 Oxford University Press.
Atlas of American history. By Edward Whiting Fox.
New York, 1964.
48 p. col. maps. 26 cm.

3813 Oxford University Press.
Atlas of American history. By J. T. Adams and
R. V. Coleman. London, 1967.
372 p. col. maps. 23.5 cm.

3814 Oxford University Press.
Oxford regional economic atlas of the United States
& Canada. By John D. Chapman and John C.
Sherman. Oxford, 1967.
164 p. col. maps. 25.5 cm.

3815 Petroleum Publishing Co.
Atlas of crude-oil pipeline of the United States and
Canada. Tulsa, Okla., 1965.
22 p. 31 cm.

3816 Petroleum Publishing Co.
Atlas of natural gas pipelines of the United States
and Canada. Tulsa, Okla., 1965.
24 p. 31 cm.

3817 Philip, George & Son, Ltd.
Wesley's historical atlas of the United States. 3 ed.

By Edgar Bruce Wesley. London, 1965.
96 p. col. maps. 28 cm.

3818 Philip, George & Son, Ltd.
Wesley's historical atlas of the United States. By
Edgar Bruce Wesley. London, 1966.
96 p. col. maps. 28 cm.

3819 Praeger, Frederick A.
The West Point atlas of American Wars. By Vincent
J. Esposito. New York, [1959].
2 vol. col. maps. 37 cm.

3820 Praeger, Frederick A.
The West Point atlas of the Civil War. By Vincent
J. Esposito. New York, [1962].
1 vol. col. maps. 37 cm.

3821 Rand McNally & Co.
Chevrolet's family travel guide. Chicago, 1967.
122 p. col. maps. 28 cm.

3822 Rand McNally & Co.
Gulf travel atlas and vacation planning guide.
Chicago, 1968.
248 p. col. maps. 28 cm.

3823 Rand McNally & Co.
Rand McNally commercial atlas and marketing guide.
81 ed. New York, [1950].
584 p. col. maps. 53 cm.

3824 Rand McNally & Co.
Rand McNally commercial atlas and marketing guide.
82 ed. New York, 1951.
584 p. col. maps. 53 cm.

3825 Rand McNally & Co.
Rand McNally commercial atlas and marketing guide.
83 ed. New York, 1952.
584 p. col. maps. 53 cm.

3826 Rand McNally & Co.
Rand McNally commercial atlas and marketing guide.
84 ed. New York, 1953.
562 p. col. maps. 53 cm.

3827 Rand McNally & Co.
Rand McNally commercial atlas and marketing guide.
85 ed.   New York, 1954.
584 p.   col. maps.   53 cm.

3828 Rand McNally & Co.
Rand McNally commercial atlas and marketing guide.
86 ed.   Chicago, 1955.
584 p.   col. maps.   53 cm.

3829 Rand McNally & Co.
Rand McNally commercial atlas and marketing guide.
87 ed.   Chicago, 1956.
566 p.   col. maps.   53 cm.

3830 Rand McNally & Co.
Rand McNally commercial atlas and marketing guide.
88 ed.   Chicago, 1957.
566 p.   col. maps.   53 cm.

3831 Rand McNally & Co.
Rand McNally commercial atlas and marketing guide.
89 ed.   Chicago, 1958.
566 p.   col. maps.   53 cm.

3832 Rand McNally & Co.
Rand McNally commercial atlas and marketing guide.
90 ed.   Chicago, 1959.
566 p.   col. maps.   53 cm.

3833 Rand McNally & Co.
Rand McNally commercial atlas and marketing guide.
91 ed.   Chicago, 1960.
566 p.   col. maps.   53 cm.

3834 Rand McNally & Co.
Rand McNally commercial atlas and marketing guide.
92 ed.   Chicago, 1961.
566 p.   col. maps.   53 cm.

3835 Rand McNally & Co.
Rand McNally commercial atlas and marketing guide.
93 ed.   Chicago, 1962.
566 p.   col. maps.   53 cm.

3836 Rand McNally & Co.
Rand McNally commercial atlas and marketing guide.

94 ed.   Chicago, 1963.
566 p.   col. maps.   53 cm.

3837 Rand McNally & Co.
Rand McNally commercial atlas and marketing guide.
95 ed.   Chicago, 1964.
566 p.   col. maps.   53 cm.

3838 Rand McNally & Co.
Rand McNally commercial atlas and marketing guide.
96 ed.   Chicago, 1965.
572 p.   col. maps.   53 cm.

3839 Rand McNally & Co.
Rand McNally commercial atlas and marketing guide.
97 ed.   Chicago, 1966.
572 p.   col. maps.   53 cm.

3840 Rand McNally & Co.
Rand McNally commercial atlas and marketing guide.
98 ed.   Chicago, 1967.
572 p.   col. maps.   53 cm.

3841 Rand McNally & Co.
Rand McNally commercial atlas and marketing guide.
99 ed.   Chicago, 1968.
572 p.   col. maps.   53 cm.

3842 Rand McNally & Co.
Rand McNally commercial atlas and marketing guide.
100 ed.   Chicago, 1969.
572 p.   col. maps.   53 cm.

3843 Rand McNally & Co.
Rand McNally commercial atlas and marketing guide.
101 ed.   Chicago, 1970.
657 p.   col. maps.   53 cm.

3844 Rand McNally & Co.
Rand McNally handy railroad atlas of the United
States.   Chicago, [1952].
48 p.   31 cm.

3845 Rand McNally & Co.
Rand McNally handy railroad atlas of the United
States.   Chicago, 1965.
64 p.   31 cm.

3846 Rand McNally & Co.
    Rand McNally interstate road atlas: United States,
    Canada, Mexico. Chicago, [1967].
    96 p. col. maps. 28 cm.

3847 Rand McNally & Co.
    Rand McNally interstate road atlas: United States,
    Canada, Mexico. Chicago, 1968.
    96 p. col. maps. 28 cm.

3848 Rand McNally & Co.
    Rand McNally road atlas and travel guide, United
    States, Canada, Mexico. Chicago, 1963.
    84 p. col. maps. 25 cm.

3849 Rand McNally & Co.
    Rand McNally road atlas and travel guide, United
    States, Canada, Mexico. Chicago, 1964.
    84 p. col. maps. 25 cm.

3850 Rand McNally & Co.
    Rand McNally road atlas and travel guide, United
    States, Canada, Mexico. Chicago, 1965.
    84 p. col. maps. 25 cm.

3851 Rand McNally & Co.
    Rand McNally road atlas and travel guide, United
    States, Canada, Mexico. Chicago, 1966.
    84 p. col. maps. 25 cm.

3852 Rand McNally & Co.
    Rand McNally road atlas and travel guide, United
    States, Canada, Mexico. Chicago, 1967.
    96 p. col. maps. 25 cm.

3853 Rand McNally & Co.
    Rand McNally road atlas and travel guide, United
    States, Canada, Mexico. Chicago, 1968.
    96 p. col. maps. 25 cm.

3854 Rand McNally & Co.
    Rand McNally road atlas and travel guide, United
    States, Canada, Mexico. Chicago, 1969.
    96 p. col. maps. 25 cm.

3855 Rand McNally & Co.
    Rand McNally road atlas and travel guide, United

States, Canada, Mexico.   Chicago, 1970.
96 p. col. maps. 25 cm.

3856 Rand McNally & Co.
Rand McNally road atlas, United States, Canada,
Mexico.   Chicago, 1950.
112 p.   col. maps.   40 cm.

3857 Rand McNally & Co.
Rand McNally road atlas, United States, Canada,
Mexico.   Chicago, 1951.
112 p.   col. maps.   40 cm.

3858 Rand McNally & Co.
Rand McNally road atlas, United States, Canada,
Mexico.   Chicago, 1952.
112 p.   col. maps.   40 cm.

3859 Rand McNally & Co.
Rand McNally road atlas, United States, Canada,
Mexico.   Chicago, 1953.
112 p.   col. maps.   40 cm.

3860 Rand McNally & Co.
Rand McNally road atlas, United States, Canada,
Mexico.   Chicago, 1954.
112 p.   col. maps.   40 cm.

3861 Rand McNally & Co.
Rand McNally road atlas, United States, Canada,
Mexico.   Chicago, 1955.
112 p.   col. maps.   40 cm.

3862 Rand McNally & Co.
Rand McNally road atlas, United States, Canada,
Mexico.   Chicago, 1956.
112 p.   col. maps.   40 cm.

3863 Rand McNally & Co.
Rand McNally road atlas, United States, Canada,
Mexico.   Chicago, 1957.
112 p.   col. maps.   40 cm.

3864 Rand McNally & Co.
Rand McNally road atlas, United States, Canada,
Mexico.   Chicago, 1958.
112 p.   col. maps.   40 cm.

3865 Rand McNally & Co.
    Rand McNally road atlas, United States, Canada,
    Mexico. Chicago, 1959.
    112 p. col. maps. 40 cm.

3866 Rand McNally & Co.
    Rand McNally road atlas, United States, Canada,
    Mexico. Chicago, 1960.
    112 p. col. maps. 40 cm.

3867 Rand McNally & Co.
    Rand McNally road atlas, United States, Canada,
    Mexico. Chicago, 1961.
    112 p. col. maps. 40 cm.

3868 Rand McNally & Co.
    Rand McNally road atlas, United States, Canada,
    Mexico. Chicago, 1962.
    112 p. col. maps. 40 cm.

3869 Rand McNally & Co.
    Rand McNally road atlas, United States, Canada,
    Mexico. Chicago, 1963.
    112 p. col. maps. 40 cm.

3870 Rand McNally & Co.
    Rand McNally road atlas: United States, Canada,
    Mexico. Chicago, 1964.
    112 p. col. maps. 40 cm.

3871 Rand McNally & Co.
    Rand McNally road atlas, United States, Canada,
    Mexico. Chicago, 1965.
    112 p. col. maps. 40 cm.

3872 Rand McNally & Co.
    Rand McNally road atlas, United States, Canada,
    Mexico. Chicago, 1966.
    114 p. col. maps. 40 cm.

3873 Rand McNally & Co.
    Rand McNally road atlas, United States, Canada,
    Mexico. Chicago, 1967.
    114 p. col. maps. 40 cm.

3874 Rand McNally & Co.
    Rand McNally road atlas, United States, Canada,

Mexico. Chicago, 1968.
114 p. col. maps. 40 cm.

3875 Rand McNally & Co.
Rand McNally road atlas, United States, Canada,
Mexico. Chicago, 1969.
114 p. col. maps. 40 cm.

3876 Rand McNally & Co.
Rand McNally road atlas, United States, Canada,
Mexico. Chicago, 1970.
114 p. col. maps. 40 cm.

3877 Rand McNally & Co.
Rand McNally vacation atlas guide: Canada, United
States, Mexico. Chicago, [1965].
108 p. col. maps. 26 cm.

3878 Rand McNally & Co.
Texaco touring atlas: United States, Canada, Mexico.
New York, 1965.
220 p. col. maps. 38 cm.

3879 Rand McNally & Co.
Texaco touring atlas: United States, Canada, Mexico.
New York, 1966.
220 p. col. maps. 38 cm.

3880 Rand McNally & Co.
Texaco touring atlas: United States, Canada, Mexico.
New York, 1967.
220 p. col. maps. 38 cm.

3881 Rand McNally & Co.
Texaco touring atlas: United States, Canada, Mexico.
Chicago, 1968.
220 p. col. maps. 38 cm.

3882 Rand McNally & Co.
Texaco touring atlas: United States, Canada, Mexico.
Chicago, [1969].
220 p. col. maps. 38 cm.

3883 Rand McNally & Co.
Texaco travel atlas: United States, Canada, Mexico.
Chicago, [1970].
220 p. col. maps. 38 cm.

3884 Reader's Digest Association, Ltd.
These United States; our nation's geography, history,
and people. Pleasantville, N. Y., [1968].
236 p. col. maps. 41 cm.

3885 Scribner, C.
Atlas of American history. By James T. Adams.
New York, [1966].
360 p. 26 cm.

3886 U. S. Department of Agriculture.
Agricultural conservation program - Maps. Washington, D. C., 1964.
51 p. 28 cm.

3887 U. S. Department of Commerce.
Climatic atlas of the United States. Washington,
D. C., 1968.
80 p. 55 cm.

3888 U. S. Department of Commerce.
Congressional district atlas. Washington, D. C.,
1964.
1 vol. 29 cm.

3889 U. S. Department of Commerce.
Congressional district atlas. Washington, D. C.,
1966.
1 vol. 29 cm.

3890 U. S. Department of Commerce.
Congressional district atlas. Washington, D. C.,
[1968].
203 p. 29 cm.

3891 U. S. Department of Commerce.
National atlas of the United States. Washington,
D. C., 1955—
in parts. col. maps. 58 cm.

3892 U. S. Economic Development Administration.
Atlas of planning jurisdiction; maps and information.
Washington, D. C., 1968.
1 vol. col. maps. 30 cm.

3893 U. S. Geological Survey.
The National atlas of the United States. Washington,

D. C., 1970.
417 p. col. maps. 49 cm.

3894 U.S.S.R. Glavnoe upravlenie geodezii i kartografii.
Atlas S.S.A. Moskva, 1966.
81 p. col. maps. 34 cm.

3895 Water Information Center, Inc.
Water atlas of the United States. By David M.
Miller, James J. Geraghty and Robert S. Collins.
Port Washington, N. Y., [1962].
48 p. col. maps. 34 cm.

3896 Water Information Center, Inc.
Water atlas of the United States. 2 ed. By David
M. Miller, James J. Geraghty and Robert S.
Collins. Port Washington, N. Y., [1963].
48 p. col. maps. 34 cm.

3897 Weidenfeld & Nicolson.
American history atlas. By Martin Gilbert.
London, 1968.
119 p. 26 cm.

3898 Wiley, John & Sons.
Graphic history of the Americas. A historical
atlas. By Theodore R. Miller. New York, 1969.
61 p. col. maps. 38 cm.

3899 Wiley, John & Sons.
Landforms and topographic maps illustrating landforms of the continental United States. By William
Bayly Upton. New York, [1970].
134 p. col. maps. 31 cm.

3900 Wiley, John & Sons.
Lithofacies maps; an atlas of the United States and
southern Canada. By Laurence L. Sloss, E. C.
Dapples and W. C. Krumbein. New York, [1960].
153 p. col. maps. 28 cm.

3901 World Pub. Co.
World's road atlas and vacation guide of North
America for 1966-67. Cleveland, 1966.
64 p. col. maps. 28 cm.

3902 World Pub. Co.
World's road atlas and vacation guide of North

America for 1967-68. Cleveland, 1967.
64 p. col. maps. 28 cm.

3903 World Pub. Co.
World's road atlas and vacation guide of North
America for 1968-69. Cleveland, 1968.
64 p. col. maps. 28 cm.

Argentina

3904 Aguilar, S. A. de Ediciones.
Atlas medio universal y de la República Argentina.
Madrid, [1959].
140 p. col. maps. 31 cm.

3905 Antonio, Roberta O.
Compendio geográfico y atlas Argentina. Buenos
Aires, 1965.
70 p. col. maps. 26 cm.

3906 Argentina. Instituto Geográfico Militar.
Atlas Argentina y Americano. By Roberto Manuel
Cayo. Buenos Aires, [1966].
78 p. col. maps. 32 cm.

3907 Argentina. Instituto Geográfico Militar.
Atlas de la República Argentina. Fisico, politico y
estadistico. 2 ed. Buenos Aires, 1954.
101 p. col. maps. 31 cm.

3908 Argentina. Instituto Geográfico Militar.
Atlas de la República Argentina. Buenos Aires,
1956 —
in 3 vol. col. maps. 31.5 cm.

3909 Argentina. Instituto Geográfico Militar.
Atlas de la República Argentina. 3 ed. Buenos
Aires, 1962.
20 p. col. maps. 40 cm.

3910 Argentina. Instituto Geográfico Militar.
Atlas de la República Argentina. 1 ed. Buenos
Aires, 1965.
122 p. col. maps. 31 cm.

3911 Argentina. Instituto Geográfico Militar.
Atlas de ruta. 2 ed. Buenos Aires, 1967.
27 p. col. maps. 32 cm.

3912 Automóvil Club Argentino.
Hojas de ruta. Buenos Aires, 1950—
29 p. col. maps. 23 cm.

3913 Editorial Mapa.
Atlas argentina; geografía general. 1 ed. By
Mario Borio. Buenos Aires, [1967].
48 p. col. maps. 26 cm.

3914 Editorial Mapa.
Atlas de la Republica Argentina y sus caminos.
Buenos Aires, [1964].
47 p. col. maps. 24 cm.

3915 Editorial Mapa.
Atlas de ruta. Buenos Aires, 1967.
19 p. col. maps. 33 cm.

3916 Ford Motor Argentina.
Atlas de los camínos argentinos. 2 ed. By
Enrique C. Pugliese. Buenos Aires, [1967].
77 p. col. maps. 24 cm.

3917 Peuser, Ediciones Geográficas.
Mapa general de la República Argentina. By J.
Anesi. Buenos Aires, [1967].
1 vol. col. maps. 29 cm.

3918 Peuser, Ediciones Geográficas.
Nuevo atlas geográfico de la Argentina. 6 ed. By
José Anesi. Buenos Aires, 1962.
28 p. col. maps. 37 cm.

3919 Peuser, Ediciones Geográficas.
Nuevo atlas geográfico de la Argentina. 7 ed. By
José Anesi. Buenos Aires, 1966.
29 p. col. maps. 37 cm.

3920 Peuser, Ediciones Geográficas.
Nuevo atlas geográfico metódico universal. 13 ed.
By José Anesi. Buenos Aires, 1955.
76 p. col. maps. 37 cm.

3921 Peuser, Ediciones Geográficas.
Nuevo atlas geográfico metódico universal. 32 ed.
By José Anesi. Buenos Aires, 1969.
96 p. col. maps. 38 cm.

Bolivia

3922 Camacho Lara, René R.
Atlas de Bolivia. La Paz, 1958.
2 vol. col. maps. 31 cm.

Brazil

3923 Brazil. Conselho Nacional de Geografia.
Atlas geográfico escolar. 2 ed. Rio de Janeiro,
[1962].
60 p. col. maps. 32 cm.

3924 Brasil. Conselho Nacional de Geografia.
Atlas nacional do Brasil. Rio de Janeiro, 1966.
50 p. col. maps. 54 cm.

3925 Brazil. Instituto brasileiro de geografia e estatística.
Atlas do Brasil, geral e regional. Rio de Janeiro,
1959.
132 p. col. maps. 52 cm.

3926 Brazil. Instituto brasileiro de geografia e estatística.
Atlas do Brasil. 2 ed. Rio de Janeiro, 1960.
1 vol. col. maps. 52 cm.

3927 Brazil. Instituto brasileiro de geografia e estatística.
Atlas geográfico escolar. 3 ed. Rio de Janeiro,
[1965].
58 p. col. maps. 31 cm.

3928 Brazil. Instituto brasileiro de geografia e estatística.
Atlas geográfico escolar. Rio de Janeiro, 1968.
58 p. col. maps. 31 cm.

3929 Brazil. Ministerio de Agricultura.
Atlas florestal do Brasil. By Henrique Pimenta
Veloso. Rio de Janeiro, 1966.
82 p. col. maps. 44 cm.

3930 Brazil. Ministério da educação e cultura.
Atlas histórico e geográfico brasileiro. Rio de
Janeiro, [1962].
47 p. col. maps. 31 cm.

3931 Brazil. Ministério da educação e cultura.
Atlas histórico e geográfico brasileiro. [Brasilia,

1963].
47 p. col. maps. 31 cm.

3932 Brazil. Ministério da educação e cultura.
Atlas histórico e geográfico brasileiro. 1 ed. Rio
de Janeiro, 1966.
63 p. col. maps. 31 cm.

3933 Brazil. Serviço de Meterologia.
Atlas climatológico do Brasil. By Adalberto B.
Serra. Rio de Janeiro, 1955-1960.
3 pts in 5 vol. col. maps. 39 cm.

3934 Brazil. Serviço de Meterologia.
Atlas climatológico do Brasil. Rio de Janeiro, 1969.
100 p. col. maps. 36 cm.

3935 Brazil. Serviço nacional de recensamento.
Atlas censitário industrial do Brasil. Rio de
Janeiro, 1965.
104 p. col. maps. 41 cm.

3936 Edições Melhoramentos.
Atlas geográfico Melhoramentos. 8 ed. São Paulo,
1950.
61 p. col. maps. 35 cm.

3937 Edições Melhoramentos.
Atlas geográfico Melhoramentos. 12 ed. São Paulo,
1954.
95 p. col. maps. 35 cm.

3938 Edições Melhoramentos.
Atlas geográfico Melhoramentos. 15 ed. São
Paulo, 1957.
67 p. col. maps. 35 cm.

3939 Edições Melhoramentos.
Atlas geográfico Melhoramentos. 20 ed. São
Paulo, 1962.
95 p. col. maps. 35 cm.

3940 Edições Melhoramentos.
Atlas geográfico Melhoramentos. São Paulo, 1964.
89 p. col. maps. 35 cm.

3941 Edições Melhoramentos.
Atlas geográfico Melhoramentos. 24 ed. São Paulo,

1966.
89 p.   col.   maps.   35 cm.

3942 Edições Melhoramentos.
     Atlas geográfico Melhoramentos.   28 ed.   São Paulo,
     1968.
     95 p.   col.   maps.   35 cm.

3943 Editôra do Brasil.
     Geografia e atlas do Brasil.   By Guaracy Ribeiro.
     São Paulo, [1966].
     105 p.   col.   maps.   29 cm.

3944 Editôra Globo.
     Atlas do Brazil.   Rio de Janeiro, [1960].
     98 p.   col.   maps.   45 cm.

3945 Editôra Globo.
     Atlas do Brasil.   Rio de Janeiro, 1966.
     128 p.   col.   maps.   45 cm.

Chile

3946 Chile.   Instituto Geográfico Militar.
     Atlas de la república de Chile.   Santiago de Chile,
     1966.
     125 p.   col.   maps.   61 cm.

3947 Chile.   Instituto Geográfico Militar.
     Atlas de la república de Chile.   2 ed.   Santiago de
     Chile, [1970].
     246 p.   col.   maps.   61 cm.

3948 Chile.   Instituto Geográfico Militar.
     Carta preliminar.   Santiago de Chile, [1967].
     100 p.   col.   maps.   56 cm.

3949 Empresa Editora Zig Zag.
     Atlas universal, edición escolar.   4 ed.   [con
     nuevos mapas de Chile].   By Alejandro Ríos Valdavia
     Santiago de Chile, 1957.
     43 p.   col.   maps.   29 cm.

3950 Liga Chileno-Alemana.
     Atlas historico de Chile.   By Pedro Cunill Grau.
     Santiago de Chile, 1961.
     34 p.   col.   maps.   30 cm.

3951 Liga Chileno-Alemana.
    Atlas historico de Chile. 2 ed. By Pedro Cunill
    Grau. Santiago de Chile, [1961].
    34 p. col. maps. 30 cm.

Colombia

3952 Aguilar, S. A. de Ediciones.
    Atlas medio universal y de Colombia. Madrid, 1959.
    140 p. col. maps. 31 cm.

3953 Codazzi, Instituto Geográfico.
    Atlas de Colombia. By Alfredo Diaz. Bogotá, 1967.
    203 p. col. maps. 45 cm.

3954 Codazzi, Instituto Geográfico.
    Atlas escolar de Colombia. 1 ed. Bogotá, [1969].
    97 p. col. maps. 28 cm.

3955 Colombia. Banco de la Republica. Departmento de
    investigaciones economicas.
    Atlas de Economica Colombiana. Bogotá, 1959-1965.
    in parts. col. maps. 39 cm.

3956 Colombia. Ministerio de Obras Publicas.
    Atlas vial. Bogotá, [1950].
    24 p. col. maps. 56 cm.

3957 Compañia Suramericana de Seguros.
    Atlas de Colombia; una contribución al mejor cono-
    cimiento de nuestro país. Medellin, [1965].
    72 p. col. maps. 18 cm.

3958 Editorial Seix Barral, S. A.
    Atlas universal y de Colombia. Barcelona, 1953.
    20 p. col. maps. 29 cm.

Ecuador

3959 Ecuador. Ministerio de Relaciones Exteriores.
    Ecuador. Atlas histórico-geográfico. By Juan
    Morales y Eloy. Quito, 1952.
    1 vol. col. maps. 18 cm.

3960 Publicaciones Educativas Ariel.
    Atlas del Ecuador. Guayaquil, [1965].
    17 p. col. maps. 25 cm.

3961 SAM.
 Atlas geográfico escolar del Ecuador "Sam"; con
 las básicas nociones históricas de la nacionalidad.
 By Francisco Sampedro V. Quito, 1963-64.
 39 p. col. maps. 31 cm.

3962 SAM.
 Atlas histórico-geográfico del Ecuador.   By
 Francisco Sampedro V. Quito, 1960.
 78 p. col. maps. 32 cm.

Paraguay

3963 Machuca Martinez, Marcelino.
 Mapas históricos del Paraguay gigante.   Asunción,
 [1951].
 44 p. col. maps. 27 cm.

Peru

3964 Editorial F. T. D.
 Atlas universal y del Perú. Lima, [1967].
 88 p. col. maps. 32 cm.

3965 Editorial Seix Barral, S. A.
 Atlas escolar universal y del Perú.   Barcelona,
 1954.
 20 p. col. maps. 29 cm.

3966 Librería e Imprenta "Guía Lascano."
 Atlas del Perú. 22 ed. Lima, 1960.
 68 p. col. maps. 27 cm.

3967 Librería e Imprenta "Guía Lascano."
 Atlas del Perú. 23 ed. Lima, [1961].
 68 p. col. maps. 27 cm.

3968 Librería e Imprenta "Guía Lascano."
 Atlas del Perú. 24 ed. Lima, [1962].
 68 p. col. maps. 27 cm.

3969 Librería e Imprenta "Guía Lascano."
 Atlas del Perú. 25 ed. Lima, 1964.
 68 p. col. maps. 27 cm.

3970 Librería e Imprenta "Guía Lascano."
 Atlas del Perú. 26 ed. Lima, 1965.
 68 p. col. maps. 27 cm.

3971 Librería e Imprenta "Guia Lascano. "
Atlas del Perú. Lima, 1969.
68 p. col. maps. 27 cm.

3972 Nelson, Thomas & Sons, Ltd.
Atlas universal y del Perú. London, 1968.
25 p. col. maps. 28 cm.

3973 Peru. Dirección de Caminos.
Mapa vial de los Departamentos del Perú. Lima,
1956 —
in parts. col. maps. 77 cm.

Surinam

3974 Duif.
Atlas van Suriname. 1 ed. Paramaribo, [1968].
24 p. col. maps. 28 cm.

3975 Wolters, J. B.
Atlas de Nederlandse Antilen, Suriname, Nederland,
en de wereld. Groningen, 1956.
40 p. col. maps. 31 cm.

Venezuela

3976 American Map Co., Inc.
Atlas de Venezuela y del mundo. New York, [1964].
23 p. col. maps. 31 cm.

3977 Discolar.
Atlas de Venezuela y del mundo. With American
Map Co. Caracas, [196-].
23 p. col. maps. 31 cm.

3978 Ediciones Nueva Cadiz.
Atlas de bolsillo de Venezuela; datos geograficos,
division política, vías de comunicación. 5 ed.
Caracas, 1951.
54 p. col. maps. 14 cm.

3979 Istituto Geografico De Agostini.
Atlas mundial y de Venezuela. By Marco Aureilo
Vila. Caracas, [1956].
80 p. col. maps. 28 cm.

3980 Minerva Books.
Atlas de Venezuela y del mundo. With American

Map Co.   Caracas, [1964].
23 p.   col. maps.   31 cm.

3981 Pensamiento Vivo.
Atlas de bolsillo de Venezuela.   8 ed.   By Juan
Jones Parra.   Caracas, 1954.
145 p.   col. maps.   14.5 cm.

3982 Societa Cartografica G. De Agostini.
Atlas escolar de Venezuela.   2 ed.   By Pedro Arnal.
Caracas, [1956].
97 p.   col. maps.   24 cm.

3983 U. S. Engineer Agency of Resources Inventories.
Venezuela: inventario nacional de recursos.   1 ed.
Washington, 1968.
1 vol.   col. maps.   75 cm.

3984 Venezuela.   Consejo nacional de vialidad.
Atlas de las carreteras de Venezuela.   Caracas,
1954.
24 p.   col. maps.   24 cm.

3985 Venezuela.   Direccion de plantificacion agropecuaria.
Atlas agricole de Venezuela.   Caracas, 1960.
107 p.   col. maps.   44 cm.

3986 Venezuela.   Ministerio de Agricultura.
Atlas Forestal de Venezuela.   Caracas, 1961.
39 p.   42.5 cm.

3987 Venezuela.   Ministerio de la Defensa.
Atlas climatológico provisional.   Período 1951/55.
Caracas, 1957.
40 p.   col. maps.   87.5 cm.

3988 Venezuela.   Ministerio de obras públicas.
Atlas de Venezuela.   Caracas, 1969.
216 p.   col. maps.   45 cm.

THEMATIC ATLASES

AGRICULTURE

3989 Afrika Instituut.
  Africa; maps and statistics. Pretoria, 1962-65.
  10 vol. col. maps. 35 cm.

3990 BLV Verlagsgesellschaft.
  BLV-Atlas. Die Landwirtschaft der Bundesrepublik
  Deutschland. By Inge Kloppenburg. München,
  Basel, Wien, [1968-].
  1 vol. col. maps. 44 cm.

3991 British Sulphur Corp. Ltd.
  World fertilizer atlas, 1964. London, [1965].
  82 p. 28 cm.

3992 British Sulphur Corporation, Ltd.
  World fertilizer atlas. 3 ed. London, 1969.
  82 p. 28 cm.

3993 Buchverlag Verlandsdruckerei.
  Atlas der schweizerischen Landwirtschaft. By W.
  Baggli. Bern, 1954.
  92 p. col. maps. 24 cm.

3994 Colombia. Banco de la Republica. Departmento de
  investigaciones economicas.
  Atlas de Economica Colombiana. Bogotá, 1959-
  1965.
  in parts. col. maps. 39 cm.

3995 Elsevier.
  Agro-Climatic atlas of Europe. By P. Thran and
  S. Broekhuizen. Amsterdam, 1965.
  in parts. col. maps. 44 cm.

3996 Elsevier.
  Agro-ecological atlas of cereal growing in Europe.
  New York, 1965--
  1 vol. col. maps. 46 cm.

3997 Elsevier.
 Atlas of the cereal growing areas in Europe.
 Amsterdam, London, New York, 1969.
 1 vol. col. maps. 46 cm.

3998 Faber & Faber.
 An agricultural atlas of England and Wales. By
 J. T. Coppock. London, 1964.
 255 p. 25 cm.

3999 Haack, Hermann.
 Agraratlas über das Gebiet der Deutschen Demokratischen Republik. By R. Matz. Gotha, 1956.
 1 vol. col. maps. 63 cm.

4000 Haack, Hermann.
 Agrarwirtschaftsatlas der Erde. Gotha, 1958.
 248 p. col. maps. 41 cm.

4001 India. Directorate of Economics and Statistics.
 Indian agricultural atlas. [Delhi], 1952.
 55 p. col. maps. 30 cm.

4002 India. Directorate of Economics and Statistics.
 Indian agricultural atlas. 2 ed. [New Delhi], 1958.
 59 p. col. maps. 31 cm.

4003 Istituto Geografico De Agostini.
 World atlas of agriculture. Novara, 1969—
 in parts. col. maps. 69 cm.

4004 Kings College School.
 Jamaica. An atlas of agricultural production.
 London, [1969].
 1 vol. 25 cm.

4005 Lantbruksförbundets Tidskriftsaktiebolag.
 Jordbruksatlas över Sverige. Stockholm, 1952.
 183 p. 26 cm.

4006 L'Institut National Pour L'Étude Agronomique du Congo.
 Atlas des sols et de la végétation du Congo, du
 Rwanda et du Burundi. Bruxelles, 1954—
 in parts. col. maps. 46 cm.

4007 Malagasy. Bureau pour le developpement de la production agricole.

Atlas de Madagascar.   Tananarive, 1969.
1 vol.   40 cm.

4008 Marco Surveys, Ltd.
Marketing maps: East Africa; cash crops and
harvest times.   Nairobi, 1962.
1 vol.   37 cm.

4009 Netherlands.   Department van landbouw en visscherij.
Landbouwatlas van Nederland.   Zwolle, [1959].
79 p.   col. maps.   36 cm.

4010 Philippines.   Agriculture and natural resources dept.
Philippine agricultural atlas, 1957.   Quezon City,
[1960].
108 p.   38 cm.

4011 Prentice-Hall.
Atlas of the world's resources.   Vol. 1: The
agricultural resources of the world.   By William
Van Royen.   New York, 1954.
258 p.   40 cm.

4012 Reitzels, C. A. Forlag.
Atlas over Denmark.   København, 1950-
in 5 vols.   col. maps.   55 cm.

4013 Ruhr-Stickstoff, A. G.
Landwirtschaftsatlas.   Bochum, [1955].
62 p.   col. maps.   43 cm.

4014 Steiner Verlag.
Atlas der Deutschen Agrarlandschaft.   By Erich
Otremba.   Wiesbaden, 1962-
in parts.   col. maps.   57 cm.

4015 Taiwan.   National University.
Atlas of the land utilization in Taiwan.   By Chêng-
hsiang Ch'en.   Taipei, 1950.
121 p.   col. maps.   38 cm.

4016 Thailand.   Department of Commercial Intelligence.
An atlas of Thailand's agricultural resources.
Bangkok, [1959].
73 p.   25 cm.

4017 United Nations.   Food and Agricultural Organization.
Crop ecological survey in West Africa.   By J.

Papadakis. Roma, 1965.
1 vol. col. maps. 58 cm.

4018 United Nations. Food and Agricultural Organization.
East African livestock survey. Regional-Kenya,
Tanzania, Uganda. Firenze, 1967.
1 vol. col. maps. 58 cm.

4019 U. S. Department of Agriculture.
Agricultural conservation program - maps. Washington, D. C., 1964.
51 p. 28 cm.

4020 U.S.S.R. Gidronet.
Agroklimatocheski atlas mira. Leningrad, 1970.
512 p. col. maps. 32 cm.

4021 U.S.S.R. Glavnoe upravlenie geodezii i kartografii.
Atlas sel'skovo khozyaystva SSSR. Moskva, 1960.
308 p. col. maps. 35 cm.

4022 Venezuela. Direccion de plantificacion agropecuaria.
Atlas agricole de Venezuela. Caracas, 1960.
107 p. col. maps. 44 cm.

4023 Verlag Enzyklopädie.
Indien. Entwicklung seiner Wirtschaft und Kultur.
Historisch-geographisches Kartenwerk. Leipzig,
1958.
1 vol. col. maps. 42.5 cm.

AIRWAYS - SEE TRANSPORTATION

ANTHROPOLOGY

4024 Brown, W. C. Co.
Atlas for anthropology. By Robert F. Spencer and
Elden Johnson. Dubuque, Iowa, [1960].
1 vol. 28 cm.

4025 Brown, W. C. Co.
Atlas for anthropology. By Robert F. Spencer and
Elden Johnson. Dubuque, Iowa, 1969.
61 p. 28 cm.

4026 East African institute of social research.
Tribal maps of East Africa and Zanzibar. By

E. J. Goldthorpe and F. B. Wilson. Kampala,
Uganda, 1960.
14 p. col. maps. 25 cm.

ARCHAEOLOGY

4027 Codex Verlag.
Kulturatlas der Türkei. Gundholzen, [1967].
in 12 parts. col. maps. 43 cm.

4028 Codex Verlag.
Kulturatlas von Ägypten. Gundholzen, [1970-].
in 10 parts. col. maps. 43 cm.

4029 Codex Verlag.
Kulturatlas von Griechenland. Gundholzen, [1970-].
in 6 parts. col. maps. 43 cm.

4030 Codex Verlag.
Kulturatlas von Lybien. Gundholzen, [1970-].
in 3 parts. col. maps. 43 cm.

4031 Codex Verlag.
Kulturatlas von Palästina. Gundholzen, [1970-].
in 4 parts. col. maps. 43 cm.

4032 Codex Verlag.
Kulturatlas von Syrien. Gundholzen, [1970-].
in 4 parts. col. maps. 43 cm.

4033 Elsevier.
Atlas de la civilisation occidentale. By Frederik
van der Meer. Paris, 1952.
227 p. col. maps. 36 cm.

4034 Elsevier.
Atlas van de Westerse beschaving. By Frederik
van der Meer. Amsterdam, 1951.
228 p. col. maps. 36 cm.

4035 Elsevier.
Atlas van het tweestromen land. By M. A. Beek.
Amsterdam, 1960.
163 p. col. maps. 36 cm.

4036 Institut français d'archéologie orientale.
Atlas of Christian sites in Egypt. By Otto

Meinardus.   Cairo, 1962.
13 p.   28 cm.

4037 Nelson, Thomas & Sons, Ltd.
Atlas of Mesopotamia.   By D. R. Welsh and H. H.
Rowley.   London, 1962.
164 p.   col. maps.   36 cm.

ASTRONOMY

4038 Czechoslovakia.   Akademie věd.
Atlas australis 1950. 0.   1 ed.   By Antonin Bečvář.
Praha, 1964.
24 p.   col. maps.   64 cm.

4039 Czechoslovakia.   Akademie věd.
Atlas borealis 1950. 0.   1 ed.   By Antonin Bečvář.
Praha, 1962.
24 p.   col. maps.   64 cm.

4040 Czechoslovakia.   Akademie věd.
Atlas eclipticalis 1950. 0.   1 ed.   By Antonin Bečvář.
Praha, 1958.
32 p.   col. maps.   66 cm.

4041 Houghton, Mifflin Co.
The Stars.   A new way to see them.   Worldwide
ed.   Boston, 1967.
160 p.   col. maps.   32 cm.

4042 Kapelusz y Cía.
Atlas mundi, astronómico-general: Asia, Africa,
Europa, Oceania, América; físico, político,
económico.   Buenos Aires, [1964].
40 p.   col. maps.   27 cm.

4043 Meyer.   Kartographisches Institut.
Meyers grosser physischer Weltatlas.   Mannheim,
1965—
in 8 vol.   col. maps.   30 cm.

4044 U.S.S.R.   Akademia nauk.
Zvezdnyi atlas.   By A. A. Mikhailov.   Moskva, 1965.
12 p.   col. maps.   34 cm.

4045 U.S.S.R.   Glavnoe upravlenie geodezii i kartografii.
Uchebnyi zvezdnyi atlas.   By A. D. Mogilko.

Moskva, 1958.
15 p. col. maps. 33 cm.

4046 U.S.S.R. Glavnoe upravlenie geodezii i kartografii.
Zvezdnyi atlas. By A. A. Mikhailov. Moskva, 1969.
60 p. col. maps. 49 cm.

BIBLE

4047 Association Press.
The modern reader's Bible atlas. By Harold Henry
Rowley. New York, [1960].
88 p. col. maps. 18 cm.

4048 Augsburg Publishing House.
Augsburg historical atlas of Christianity in the
Middle Ages and Reformation. By Charles S.
Anderson. Minneapolis, Minn., 1967.
61 p. col. maps. 29 cm.

4049 Ben-Eliyahu, Ephraim.
Atlas li-yedi'at Erets-Yisrael veha-TaNaKH.
Jerusalem, [1957/58].
136 p. 34 cm.

4050 Benziger & Co.
Die zwanzig jahrhunderte der kirche. Geohistorischer atlas mit kirchengeschichtlichem Begleittext.
By Frederico de Agostini. Einsiedeln, 1950.
42 p. col. maps. 32 cm.

4051 Burns & Oates, Ltd.
The twentieth century atlas of the Christian world.
1 ed. By Anton Freitag. London, [1963].
199 p. col. maps. 35 cm.

4052 Burns & Oates, Ltd.
The universe atlas of the Christian world. 1 ed
(rev.). By Anton Freitag. London, [1963].
199 p. col. maps. 35 cm.

4053 Carta.
Carta's atlas of the Bible. By Yohanan Aharoni.
Jerusalem, 1964.
1 vol. col. maps. 30 cm.

4054 Carta.
Carta's atlas of the period of the Second Temple

the Mishnah and the Talmud. By Michael Avi-Jonah
and Shmuel Safrai. Jerusalem, 1966.
162 p. col. maps. 30 cm.

4055 Catholic War Veterans.
     Twenty centuries of Catholicism; a Catholic historical
     atlas with commentary. By Federico de Agostini.
     Washington, D. C., 1950.
     42 p. col. maps. 31 cm.

4056 Collins, William Sons & Co., Ltd.
     New atlas of the Bible. By Jan H. Negenman.
     London, 1969.
     208 p. col. maps. 32 cm.

4057 Cram, George F. Co.
     Maps of the Bible lands. Indianapolis, 1950.
     19 p. col. maps. 28 cm.

4058 Djambatan.
     Historical atlas of the Muslim people. By R.
     Roolvink. Amsterdam, 1957.
     40 p. col. maps. 30 cm.

4059 Dom Verlag.
     Kirchenhistorischer atlas von Österreich. By E.
     Bernleithner. Wien, 1966 —
     in parts. col. maps. 63 cm.

4060 Doubleday.
     New atlas of the Bible. By Jan H. Negenman.
     New York, [1969].
     208 p. col. maps. 32 cm.

4061 Dreyers Forlag.
     Bibelatlas for hjem og skole. Oslo, 1964.
     32 p. col. maps. 25 cm.

4062 Editions du Centurion.
     Atlas de la Bible, histoire, géographie, chronologie.
     By H. H. Rowley. Paris, 1969.
     63 p. col. maps. 25 cm.

4063 Elsevier.
     Atlas van de Bijbel. By L. Grollenberg and A. van
     Deursen. Amsterdam, [1956].
     158 p. col. maps. 36 cm.

4064 Elsevier.
        Atlas van de oudchristelijke wereld. By Frederik
        van der Meer and Christine Mohrmann. Amsterdam,
        1958.
        215 p. col. maps. 36 cm.

4065 Hammond, C. S. & Co. , Inc.
        Atlas of the Bible lands. New York, 1950.
        32 p. col. maps. 32 cm.

4066 Hammond, C. S. & Co. , Inc.
        Story of the Bible world; in map, word and picture.
        New York, [1959].
        192 p. col. maps. 26 cm.

4067 Hammond, Inc.
        Pictorial atlas of the Bible world. Maplewood,
        N. J., [1969].
        32 p. col. maps. 31 cm.

4068 Harper & Row.
        Historical atlas of religion in America. 1 ed. By
        Edwin Scott Gaustad. New York, [1962].
        179 p. col. maps. 31 cm.

4069 Harvard University Press.
        Historical atlas of the Muslim people. By R.
        Roolvink. Cambridge, Mass. , 1957.
        40 p. col. maps. 30 cm.

4070 Hawthorne Books.
        The twentieth century atlas of the Christian world.
        1 ed. By Anton Freitag. New York, [1963].
        199 p. col. maps. 35 cm.

4071 Humphrey, H. A. , Ltd.
        The new Israel atlas. By Zev Vilnay. London,
        1968.
        114 p. col. maps. 30 cm.

4072 Institut français d'archéologie orientale.
        Atlas of Christian sites in Egypt. By Otto
        Meinardus. Cairo, 1962.
        13 p. 28 cm.

4073 Israel University Press.
        The new Israel atlas; Bible to present. By Zev

Vilnay. Jerusalem, 1968.
112 p. col. maps. 30 cm.

4074 L'Oeuvre de la propagation de la foi.
Nouvel atlas des missions. By J. Despont. Paris,
Lyon, 1951—
59 p. col. maps. 33 cm.

4075 Lutterworth Press.
Student's Bible atlas. By Harold Henry Rowley.
London, 1965.
48 p. col. maps. 26 cm.

4076 Macmillan Co.
The Macmillan Bible atlas. By Yohanan Aharoni
and Michael Avi-Yonah. With Carta. New York,
Jerusalem, [1968].
184 p. col. maps. 30 cm.

4077 McGraw Hill Book Co.
The new Israel atlas, Bible to present. By Zev
Vilnay. New York, 1969.
112 p. col. maps. 30 cm.

4078 Nelson, Thomas & Sons, Ltd.
Atlas of the Bible. By Joyce M. H. Reid and
H. H. Rowley. London, 1957.
165 p. col. maps. 36 cm.

4079 Nelson, Thomas & Sons, Ltd.
Atlas of the Bible. By L. H. Grollenberg. London,
1959.
166 p. col. maps. 36 cm.

4080 Nelson, Thomas & Sons, Ltd.
Atlas of the early Christian world. By F. van der
Meer and Christine Mohrmann. London, 1958.
215 p. col. maps. 36 cm.

4081 Nelson, Thomas & Sons, Ltd.
Shorter atlas of the Bible. By L. H. Grollenberg.
New York, 1959.
1 vol. col. maps. 36 cm.

4082 Oxford University Press.
Oxford Bible atlas. By Herbert G. May. London,
1962.
144 p. col. maps. 26 cm.

4083 Philip, George & Son, Ltd.
An atlas illustrating the Acts of the Apostles and
the Epistles. London, 1954.
1 vol. col. maps. 23 cm.

4084 Philip, George & Son, Ltd.
An atlas of the Acts. 3 ed. By John F. Stirling.
London, 1966.
29 p. col. maps. 22.5 cm.

4085 Philip, George & Son, Ltd.
An atlas of the life of Christ. 4 ed. By John F.
Stirling. London, 1966.
27 p. col. maps. 22.5 cm.

4086 Philip, George & Son, Ltd.
An atlas of the New Testament; comprising an atlas
of the life of Christ, and an atlas of the Acts. By
John F. Stirling. London, [1966].
64 p. col. maps. 22.5 cm.

4087 Philip, George & Son, Ltd.
Philip's new scripture atlas. By George Goodall.
London, [1954].
16 p. col. maps. 29 cm.

4088 Portugal. Junta de Investigações do Ultramar.
Atlas missionário português. Lisboa, 1962.
175 p. col. maps. 33 cm.

4089 Portugal. Junta de Investigações do Ultramar.
Atlas missionário português. 2 ed. Lisboa, 1964.
198 p. col. maps. 33 cm.

4090 Princeton University Press.
Atlas of Islamic history. 1 ed. By Harry W.
Hazard. Princeton, N. J., 1951.
49 p. col. maps. 38 cm.

4091 Princeton University Press.
Atlas of Islamic history. 2 ed. By Harry W.
Hazard. Princeton, N. J., 1952.
49 p. col. maps. 38 cm.

4092 Princeton University Press.
Atlas of Islamic history. 3 ed. By Harry W.
Hazard. Princeton, N. J., 1954.
49 p. col. maps. 38 cm.

4093 Rand McNally & Co.
     Historical atlas of the Holy Land. By Emil G.
     Kraeling. Chicago, 1959.
     88 p. col. maps. 26 cm.

4094 Society of the Divine Word.
     A statistical and geographical survey of all the
     activities of the Society of the Divine Word.
     Mödling, 1952.
     33 p. 32 cm.

4095 Stein, Jack.
     Great events in the Bible recorded on maps.
     Dayton, Ohio, 1963.
     14 p. 29 cm.

4096 St. Gabriel Verlag.
     Atlas hierarchicus. By Heinrich Emmerich.
     Mödling, 1968.
     71 p. col. maps. 45 cm.

4097 Westminster Press.
     The Westminster historical atlas of the Bible. By
     George Ernest Wright. Philadelphia, [1956].
     130 p. col. maps. 37 cm.

4098 Westminster Press.
     Westminster historical maps of Bible lands. By
     G. E. Wright. Philadelphia, [1952].
     24 p. col. maps. 24 cm.

4099 Whittemore Associates.
     A map book for Bible students. By Frederic L.
     Fay. Needham Heights, Mass., [1966].
     64 p. 19 cm.

4100 World Pub. Co.
     Student's Bible atlas. By Harold Henry Rowley.
     Cleveland, Ohio, [1965].
     48 p. col. maps. 26 cm.

4101 Zondervan Pub. House.
     Pictorial Bible atlas. Grand Rapids, Mich., 1969.
     491 p. col. maps. 27 cm.

BIOGEOGRAPHY

4102 Meyer, Kartographisches Institut.
Meyers grosser physischer Weltatlas. Mannheim,
1965—
in 8 vol. col. maps. 30 cm.

BIOLOGY

4103 Elsevier.
Agro-ecological atlas of cereal growing in Europe.
New York, 1965—
1 vol. col. maps. 46 cm.

4104 Mexico. Instituto Mexicano de Investigaciones
Economicas.
Atlas geografico general de Mexico, con cartes
fisicas, biologicas, demograficas, sociales,
economicas y cartogramas. 2 ed. México, 1962.
1 vol. col. maps. 54 cm.

BOTANY

4105 Kümmerly & Frey.
Pflanzengeographischer Welt Atlas. Bern, 1941 -
[52].
1 vol. col. maps. 33 cm.

4106 Nelson, Thomas & Sons, Ltd.
Atlas of the British flora. By F. H. Perring and
S. M. Walters. London, 1962.
432 p. 34 cm.

4107 Poland. Akademia nauk.
Atlas flory polskiej i ziem osciennych. Warszawa,
1965.
in parts. col. maps. 34 cm.

4108 Poland. Akademia nauk.
Atlas rozmieszczenia drzew i krzewów w Polsce.
Poznań, 1963—
in parts. col. maps. 33 cm.

4109 Poland. Państwowe Wydawnictw naukowe.
Atlas rozmieszcenia roslin zarodnikowych w Polsce.
Poznan, 1964.
23 p. 34 cm.

CAMPING

4110 Alpine Geographical Press.
      Campground atlas of the United States and Canada.
      Champaign, Ill., [1960].
      176 p. col. maps. 28 cm.

4111 Alpine Geographical Press.
      Campground atlas of the United States and Canada.
      Champaign, Ill., [1962].
      182 p. col. maps. 28 cm.

4112 Alpine Geographical Press.
      Campground atlas of the United States and Canada.
      Champaign, Ill., [1964].
      186 p. col. maps. 28 cm.

4113 Alpine Geographical Press.
      Campground atlas of the United States and Canada.
      Champaign, Ill., 1966.
      204 p. col. maps. 28 cm.

4114 Alpine Geographical Press.
      Campground atlas of the United States and Canada.
      Champaign, Ill., 1966-67.
      157 p. col. maps. 28 cm.

4115 Alpine Geographical Press.
      Campground atlas of the United States and Canada.
      Champaign, Ill., 1967-68.
      260 p. col. maps. 28 cm.

4116 Alpine Geographical Press.
      Campground atlas of the United States and Canada.
      Champaign, Ill., 1968-69.
      260 p. col. maps. 28 cm.

4117 Alpine Geographical Press.
      Campground atlas of the United States and Canada.
      Champaign, Ill., 1969-70.
      260 p. col. maps. 28 cm.

4118 Better Camping Magazine.
      Campground atlas of the United States and Canada.
      Milwaukee, Wisc., [1970].
      314 p. col. maps. 28 cm.

4119 Boy Scouts of America.
   Road atlas and guide to overnight camping.   With
   Hammond. New Brunswick, N. J., 1964.
   80 p.   col. maps.   32 cm.

4120 Camping Maps, U. S. A.
   Private campgrounds and overnight trailer parks.
   Palos Verdes Peninsula, Calif., 1965.
   204 p.   22 cm.

4121 Camping Maps, U. S. A.
   Private campgrounds USA and Mexico.   By Glenn
   and Dale Rhodes.   Upper Montclair, N. J., 1964.
   142 p.   col. maps.   22 cm.

4122 Fédération internationale de l'automobile.
   Atlas camping and caravaning.   Roma, 1966.
   66 p.   col. maps.   30 cm.

4123 Kalmbach Publishing Co.
   Campground atlas of the United States and Canada.
   Milwaukee, Wisc., 1970-71.
   314 p.   col. maps.   28 cm.

4124 Macmillan & Co., Ltd.
   Camping maps U.S.A.   By Glenn and Dale Rhodes.
   New York, 1963.
   297 p.   25 cm.

4125 Macmillan & Co., Ltd.
   Camping maps U.S.A.   By Glenn and Dale Rhodes.
   New York, 1964.
   352 p.   26 cm.

4126 Michelin et Cie.
   Camping en France.   [Atlas].   Paris, 1957.
   85 p.   25 cm.

4127 Rand McNally & Co.
   Rolph McNally Canadian road atlas; travel guide
   with campground information.   Toronto, [1969].
   96 p.   col. maps.   29 cm.

4128 Ravenstein Geographische Verlagsanstalt.
   Jugendherbergs-Taschenatlas der Bundesrepublik.
   Frankfurt, [1953].
   10 p.   col. maps.   15 cm.

4129 Royal Automobile Club.
Camping and caravaning guide and atlas of Europe.
3 ed.　London, 1966.
66 p.　col. maps.　30 cm.

4130 Royal Automobile Club.
Camping and caravaning guide and atlas of Europe.
4 ed.　London, 1967.
66 p.　col. maps.　30 cm.

4131 Royal Automobile Club.
Camping and caravaning guide and atlas of Europe.
5 ed.　London, 1968.
66 p.　col. maps.　30 cm.

4132 Royal Automobile Club.
Camping and caravaning guide and atlas of Europe.
6 ed.　London, 1969.
66 p.　col. maps.　30 cm.

4133 Tourist Publications.
South Africa in maps, and a guide to the caravan
parks.　By Denis Conolly.　Cape Town, 1966.
51 p.　25 cm.

CAVE

4134 Belgium.　Centre national de recherches scientifiques
souterraines.
Atlas de grottes de Belgique.　Liège, [1961-].
1 vol.　30 cm.

CLIMATE

4135 Akademie Verlag.
Klima atlas für das Gebiet der Deutschen Demokratischen Republik.　Berlin, 1953 –
in parts.　col. maps.　67 cm.

4136 Brazil.　Serviçio de Meterologia.
Atlas climatológico do Brasil.　By Adalberto B.
Serra.　Rio de Janeiro, 1955-1960.
3 pts in 5 vol.　col. maps.　39 cm.

4137 Brazil.　Serviçio de Meteorologia.
Atlas climatológico do Brasil.　Rio de Janeiro, 1969.
100 p.　col. maps.　36 cm.

4138 Brown, W. C. Co.
Workbook of weather maps. By John J. Hidore.
Dubuque, Iowa, [1968].
64 p. 28 cm.

4139 Canada. Department of Transport.
Climatological atlas of Canada. By Morley K.
Thomas. Ottawa, 1953.
256 p. 31 cm.

4140 Commission for Technical Cooperation in Africa South
of the Sahara.
Climatological atlas of Africa. Lagos, 1961.
55 p. col. maps. 60 cm.

4141 Czechoslovakia. Ústřední správa geodézie a kartografie.
Atlas podnebí Československé republiky. Praha,
1958.
1 vol. col. maps. 45 cm.

4142 Elsevier.
Agro-climatic atlas of Europe. By P. Thran and
S. Broekhuizen. Amsterdam, 1965.
in parts. col. maps. 44 cm.

4143 Falk Verlag.
Niederschlag und Temperatur in Europa. [Atlas].
Hamburg, [1956].
1 vol. col. maps. 48 cm.

4144 Falk Verlag.
Niederschlag, Temperatur und Schwule in Afrika
[Atlas]. Hamburg, 1955.
15 p. col. maps. 47.5 cm.

4145 Fischer, G.
Klimadiagramm-Weltatlas. By Heinrich Walter and
Helmut Lieth. Jena, 1960—
in 3 pts. col. maps. 62 cm.

4146 France. Ministère de L'Équipment.
Cartes annuelle et mensuelles de la Hauteur Moyenne
Des Précipitations. Extraites de l'Atlas Climatique
de la France. Paris, 1966.
14 p. col. maps. 52 cm.

4147 Germany. Deutscher Wetterdienst.
World weather maps. Hamburg, 1958—

in parts.   col. maps.   58 cm.

4148 Gt. Britain.   Meteorological Office.
     Climatological atlas of the British Isles.   London,
     1952.
     139 p.   col. maps.   31 cm.

4149 Guatemala.   Observatorio Meteorológico y Estacion
     Sismográfia.
     Atlas climatológico de Guatemala.   Guatemala,
     [1964].
     38 p.   col. maps.   40 cm.

4150 Guruhi Jughrafiya.
     Atlas-i Iglimi-yi Iran.   By Ahmad Mustaufi.
     Teheran, [1969].
     1 vol.   col. maps.   30 cm.

4151 Harvard University Press.
     Climatic atlas of the United States.   By Stephen
     Sargent Visher.   Cambridge, Mass., 1954.
     403 p.   30 cm.

4152 Harvard University Press.
     Climatic atlas of the United States.   By Stephen
     Sargent Visher.   Cambridge, Mass., 1966.
     403 p.   30 cm.

4153 Hilâl.
     [Atlas of climates, politics, and economics of the
     earth].   In Arabic.   By Ahmad Hafiz.   Cairo,
     [1962].
     84 p.   col. maps.   29 cm.

4154 International Publications Service.
     Climatological atlas of Africa.   New York, 1963.
     55 p.   col. maps.   60 cm.

4155 Kishô Kyôkai.
     Nihon no kikōzu; me de mirn Nihon no shiki. [Me-
     teorological atlas of Japan].   Tokyo, [1957].
     75 p.   col. maps.   27 cm.

4156 Lebanon.   Service météorologique.
     Atlas climatique du Liban.   Beyrouth, 1966 —
     in parts.   col. maps.   33 cm.

4157 Macmillan & Co., Ltd.
British weather in maps. By James A. Taylor and
R. A. Yates. London, 1958.
256 p. col. maps. 23 cm.

4158 Mexico. Universidad Nacional Autónoma.
Cartografia de elementos bioclimáticos en la República Mexicana. By Consuelo Soto Mora and
Ernesto Jáuregui O. Mexico, D. F., 1968.
72 p. 27 cm.

4159 Meyer, Kartographisches Institut.
Meyers grosser physischer Weltatlas. Mannheim,
1965—
in 8 vol. col. maps. 30 cm.

4160 Netherlands. Ministerie van Marine.
Meteorologie Nederlands Nieuw Guinea. Voorlopige
atlas. 's Gravenhage, 1959.
1 vol. 34 cm.

4161 Netherlands. Staatsdrukkerij-en Uitgeverijbedrijf.
Stroomatlas Nederland. 2 ed. 's Gravenhage, 1963—
1 vol. col. maps. 37 cm.

4162 Országos Meteorológiai Intézet.
Magyarórszág éghajlati atlasza. Klima-Atlas von
Ungarn. By J. Kakas. Budapest, 1960-67.
2 vol. col. maps. 50 cm.

4163 Oxford University Press.
The climate of Africa. [Atlas]. By B. W. Thompson. Nairobi, New York, 1965.
132 p. col. maps. 52 cm.

4164 Romania. Institutul Meteorologie.
Atlasul climatologic al Republicii Socialiste
România. Bucuresti, 1966.
180 p. col. maps. 58 cm.

4165 South Africa. Government Printer Office.
Climatological atlas of Africa. By Stanley P. Jackson. Pretoria, 1962.
56 p. col. maps. 60 cm.

4166 South Africa. Government Printer Office.
Climatological atlas of Africa. By Stanley P.

Jackson. Pretoria, 1964.
56 p. col. maps. 60 cm.

4167 Springer Verlag.
Weltkarte zur Klimakunde. By H. E. Landsberg.
Berlin, 1963.
28 p. col. maps. 30 cm.

4168 U. S. Army Natick Laboratories.
Climatic atlas of Southeast Asia. Natick, Mass.
1967.
1 vol. col. maps. 46 cm.

4169 U. S. Department of Commerce.
Climatic atlas of the United States. Washington,
D. C., 1968.
80 p. 55 cm.

4170 U. S. Weather Bureau.
Climatological and oceanographic atlas for mariners.
Washington, D. C., 1959—
in parts. col. maps. 39 cm.

4171 U. S. Weather Bureau.
U. S. Navy Marine climatic atlas of the world.
Washington, D. C., 1955—68.
8 vol. col. maps. 50 cm.

4172 U. S. S. R. Gidronet.
Agroklimatocheski atlas mira. Leningrad, 1970.
512 p. col. maps. 32 cm.

4173 Venezuela. Ministerio de la Defensa.
Atlas climatológico provisional. Período 1951/55.
Caracas, 1957.
40 p. col. maps. 87.5 cm.

4174 Vietnam. Nha g'ám-dôc khí-tu'o'ng.
Gian-dô khi-hâu; cao dô mu'a trung-bính tai Vietnam,
Ailao và Cambodge. Saigon, 1958.
13 p. col. maps. 33 cm.

COAL

4175 U. S. S. R. Glavnoe upravlenie geodezii i kartografii.
Atlas uglenakoplenia na territorii SSSR. Moskva,
1962.
528 p. col. maps. 60 cm.

COMMERCE - SEE ECONOMIC

COMMUNICATION

4176 France.   Ministère des postes et télécommunications.
     Mémento de nomenclature géographique.   Paris, 1964.
     81 p.   31 cm.

4177 International Telecommunication Union.
     Atlas des circuits internationaux d'Europe sous
     câble.   Geneva, 1953.
     1 portf.   col.   maps.   31 cm.

4178 International Telecommunication Union.
     Cartes de stations côtières ouvertes à la corres-
     pondance publique.   6 ed.   Geneva, 1952.
     12 p.   col.   maps.   34 cm.

4179 Mexico.   Ministerio de Comunicaciones y Obras Públicas.
     Atlas de la Memoría de labores de la Secretaría de
     Comunicaciones y Obras Públicas, 1955-56, con un
     resumen de los avances logrades de 1953-56.
     México, [1957].
     83 p.   col.   maps.   48 cm.

4180 Mexico.   Ministerio de Comunicaciones y Obras Públicas.
     Atlas: resumen de los avances logrados en el
     sexenio 1953-58.   México, [1959].
     111 p.   col.   maps.   48 cm.

4181 Mexico.   Secretaría de Comunicaciones y Transportes.
     México; guía de las vías generales de comunicación.
     México, 1963.
     94 p.   col.   maps.   21 cm.

4182 Norway.   Poststyret.
     Postkart over Norge, 1:400,000.   Oslo, [1952].
     10 p.   col.   maps.   49 cm.

4183 Poståpnernes Landsforbund.
     Post-, vej - og fylkeskarte.   Oslo, [1950].
     43 p.   col.   maps.   23 cm.

4184 Radio Amateur Callbook, Inc.
     Radio amateurs' world atlas.   Chicago, 1968.
     16 p.   col.   maps.   31 cm.

4185 Verlag Sport & Technik.
    Funkatlas. Radioatlas. By Ernst Georg Berends.
    Berlin, 1959.
    198 p. col. maps. 31 cm.

4186 Villarroya San Mateo, Antonio.
    Atlas de geografía postal de España.   Madrid, [1961].
    57 p. 28 cm.

4187 Villarroya San Mateo, Antonio.
    Atlas de geografía postal de España.   [Madrid], 1962.
    55 p. 35 cm.

DISCOVERY - SEE HISTORY

EARTHQUAKE

4188 U.S.S.R. Glavnoe upravlenie geodezii i kartografii.
    Atlas zemletriasenii SSSR. Moskva, 1962.
    337 p. col. maps. 34 cm.

ECONOMIC

4189 Afrika Instituut.
    Africa; maps and statistics.   Pretoria, 1962-65.
    10 vol. col. maps. 35 cm.

4190 Aguilar, S. A. de Ediciones.
    Atlas bachillerato universal y de España.   1 ed.
    By A. L. Gómez. Madrid, 1962.
    132 p. col. maps. 35 cm.

4191 Aguilar, S. A. de Ediciones.
    Atlas bachillerato, universal y de España.   2 ed.
    By A. L. Gómez. Madrid, 1963.
    132 p. col. maps. 35 cm.

4192 Aguilar, S. A. de Ediciones.
    Atlas bachillerato universal y de España.   3 ed.
    By A. L. Gómez. Madrid, 1963.
    132 p. col. maps. 35 cm.

4193 Aguilar, S. A. de Ediciones.
    Atlas bachillerato universal y de España.   4 ed.
    By A. L. Gómez. Madrid, 1964.
    132 p. col. maps. 35 cm.

4194 Aguilar, S. A. de Ediciones.
     Atlas bachillerato universal y de España.   5 ed.
     By A. L. Gómez.   Madrid, 1964.
     132 p.   col. maps.   35 cm.

4195 Aguilar, S. A. de Ediciones.
     Atlas bachillerato universal y de España.   6 ed.
     By A. L. Gómez.   Madrid, 1964.
     132 p.   col. maps.   35 cm.

4196 Aguilar, S. A. de Ediciones.
     Atlas bachillerato universal y de España.   7 ed.
     By A. L. Gómez.   Madrid, 1965.
     132 p.   col. maps.   35 cm.

4197 Aguilar, S. A. de Ediciones.
     Atlas bachillerato universal y de España.   8 ed.
     By A. L. Gómez.   Madrid, 1965.
     132 p.   col. maps.   35 cm.

4198 Aguilar, S. A. de Ediciones.
     Atlas bachillerato universal y de España.   9 ed.
     By A. L. Gómez.   Madrid, 1966.
     132 p.   col. maps.   35 cm.

4199 Aguilar, S. A. de Ediciones.
     Atlas bachillerato universal y de España.   10 ed.
     By A. L. Gómez.   Madrid, 1966.
     132 p.   col. maps.   35 cm.

4200 Aguilar, S. A. de Ediciones.
     Atlas bachillerato universal y de España.   11 ed.
     By A. L. Gómez.   Madrid, 1966.
     132 p.   col. maps.   35 cm.

4201 Aguilar, S. A. de Ediciones.
     Atlas bachillerato universal y de España.   12 ed.
     By A. L. Gómez.   Madrid, 1967.
     117 p.   col. maps.   35 cm.

4202 Aguilar, S. A. de Ediciones.
     Atlas bachillerato universal y de España.   13 ed.
     By A. L. Gómez.   Madrid, 1967.
     117 p.   col. maps.   35 cm.

4203 Aguilar, S. A. de Ediciones.
     Atlas bachillerato universal y de España.   14 ed.

By A. L. Gómez. Madrid, 1967.
117 p. col. maps. 35 cm.

4204 Aguilar, S. A. de Ediciones.
Atlas bachillerato universal y de España.   15 ed.
By A. L. Gómez. Madrid, 1968.
117 p. col. maps. 35 cm.

4205 Aguilar, S. A. de Ediciones.
Atlas bachillerato universal y de España.   16 ed.
By A. L. Gómez. Madrid, 1968.
117 p. col. maps. 35 cm.

4206 Aguilar, S. A. de Ediciones.
Atlas bachillerato universal y de España.   17 ed.
By A. L. Gómez. Madrid, 1968.
117 p. col. maps. 35 cm.

4207 Aguilar, S. A. de Ediciones.
Atlas bachillerato universal y de España.   18 ed.
By A. L. Gómez. Madrid, 1968.
117 p. col. maps. 35 cm.

4208 Aguilar, S. A. de Ediciones.
Atlas bachillerato universal y de España.   19 ed.
By A. L. Gómez. Madrid, 1969.
117 p. col. maps. 35 cm.

4209 Aguilar, S. A. de Ediciones.
Atlas bachillerato universal y de España.   20 ed.
By A. L. Gómez. Madrid, 1969.
117 p. col. maps. 35 cm.

4210 Aguilar, S. A. de Ediciones.
Atlas bachillerato universal y de España.   21 ed.
By A. L. Gómez. Madrid, 1969.
117 p. col. maps. 35 cm.

4211 Aguilar, S. A. de Ediciones.
Atlas bachillerato universal y de España.   22 ed.
By A. L. Gómez. Madrid, 1969.
117 p. col. maps. 35 cm.

4212 Aguilar, S. A. de Ediciones.
Atlas bachillerato universal y de España.   23 ed.
By A. L. Gómez. Madrid, 1970.
117 p. col. maps. 35 cm.

4213 Akademiförlaget.
Atlas of the world commodities; production, trade
and consumption. By Olof Jonasson. Göteborg,
[1961].
81 p. col. maps. 22 cm.

4214 American Map Co., Inc.
Cleartype business control atlas of the United States
and Canada. New York, 1968.
120 p. 28 cm.

4215 American Map Co., Inc.
Cleartype business control atlas of the United States
and Canada. New York, 1969.
120 p. 29 cm.

4216 American Map Co., Inc.
Cleartype executive sales control atlas of the United
States and Canada. New York, [1968].
132 p. 30 cm.

4217 Argentina. Instituto Geográfico Militar.
Atlas de la República Argentina. Fisico, politico y
estadistico. 2 ed. Buenos Aires, 1954.
101 p. col. maps. 31 cm.

4218 Atlantik Verlag.
Handelschulatlas. Atlas für Wirtschaftsschulen.
By Willy Eggers. Frankfurt, [1956].
61 p. col. maps. 34 cm.

4219 Australia. Department of National Development.
Atlas of Australian resources. First series.
Canberra, 1952-60.
in parts. col. maps. 71 cm.

4220 Australia. Department of National Development.
Atlas of Australian resources. Second series.
Canberra, 1962—
in parts. col. maps. 71 cm.

4221 Barnes & Noble, Inc.
An atlas of North American affairs. By D. K.
Adams and H. B. Rodgers. New York, 1969.
135 p. 22 cm.

4222 Belgium. Ministère des travaux publics et de la
reconstruction.

Atlas du survey national.   Bruxelles, 1954—
in parts.   col. maps.   38 cm.

4223 Bosch.
Atlas elemental de España, geográfico y estadístico.
Barcelona, [1950].
13 p.   col. maps.   22 cm.

4224 Brazil.   Conselho Nacional de Geografia.
Atlas geográfico escolar.   2 ed.   Rio de Janeiro,
[1962].
60 p.   col. maps.   32 cm.

4225 Brazil.   Serviço nacional de recensamento.
Atlas censitário industrial do Brasil.   Rio de
Janeiro, 1965.
104 p.   col. maps.   41 cm.

4226 Cassell.
Cassell's new atlas of the world, the world in physical, political, and economic maps.   By Harold
Fullard.   London, [1961].
233 p.   col. maps.   35 cm.

4227 Collier, P. F. & Son, Corp.
World atlas and gazetteer, presenting the world in
its geographical, physical, and commercial aspects.
New York, [1955].
480 p.   col. maps.   37 cm.

4228 Collier, P. F. & Son, Corp.
World atlas and gazetteer, presenting the world in
its geographical, physical and commercial aspects.
New York, [1957].
472 p.   col. maps.   37 cm.

4229 Collins, M. O. (pvt), Ltd.
Rhodesia.   [Atlas].   Its natural resources and
economic development.   Salisbury, 1965.
52 p.   col. maps.   33 cm.

4230 Colombia.   Banco de la Republica.   Departmento de
investigaciones economicas.
Atlas de economica Colombiana.   Bogotá, 1959-
1965.
in parts.   col. maps.   39 cm.

4231 Consociazione Turistica Italiana.
Atlante fisico economico d'Italia.   Milano, 1950.
1 vol.   col.   maps.   40 cm.

4232 Cooper Square Publishers.
Historical atlas of Latin America.   Political,
geographic, economic, cultural.   By A. Curtis
Wilgus.   New York, 1967.
365 p.   24 cm.

4233 Costa Rica.   Ministerio de Economia y Hacienda.
Atlas Estadístico de Costa Rica.   San José, 1953.
114 p.   27.5 cm.

4234 Czechoslovakia.   Ústřední správa geodesie a kartografie.
Politicko-hospodářský atlas světa.   Praha, 1951-56.
in parts.   col.   maps.   37 cm.

4235 Dijkstra.
Ons eigen land.   Eenvoudige atlas van Nederland.
By W. Bakker and H. Rusch.   Zeist, [1966].
1 vol.   col.   maps.   26 cm.

4236 Djambatan.
Atlas of South-east Asia.   By D. G. E. Hall.
Amsterdam, [1964].
84 p.   col.   maps.   35 cm.

4237 Droemer.
Knaurs Welt Atlas.   By Günter Pahl.   München,
[1950].
463 p.   col.   maps.   29 cm.

4238 Droemer.
Knaurs Welt Atlas.   Ausführlicher geographischer
bevölkerungs- und wirtschaftlicher Text.   München,
[1957].
537 p.   col.   maps.   25 cm.

4239 Državana založba slovenije.
Gospodarski atlas sveta.   By Stane Zrimec.
Lujbljana, 1952.
120 p.   35 cm.

4240 E. D. A. F.
El Universo en color: Gran atlas y geografia EDAF;
fisico-politico-económico.   Madrid, [1968].
395 p.   col.   maps.   40 cm.

4241 Editions Bordas.
      Petit atlas politique et économique de la France et
      du monde. Paris, [1966].
      32 p. col. maps. 27 cm.

4242 Editions de Lyon.
      Atlas de l'Europe occidentale. By Jean Chardonnet.
      Lyon, [1953].
      50 p. col. maps. 31 cm.

4243 Éditions Rencontre.
      Nouvel atlas mondial géographique et économique de
      tous les pays. By Eugen Theodor Rimli. Lausanne,
      [1956-].
      1 vol. in parts. col. maps. 28 cm.

4244 Editorial Seix Barral, S. A.
      Atlas geográfico de España, físico, político y
      estadístico. Barcelona, 1950.
      64 p. col. maps. 34 cm.

4245 Editorial Seix Barral, S. A.
      Atlas geográfico de España, físico, político y
      estadístico. Barcelona, 1953.
      64 p. col. maps. 34 cm.

4246 Editorial Seix Barral, S. A.
      Atlas geográfico de España, fisico, político y
      estadístico. Barcelona, 1957.
      64 p. col. maps. 34 cm.

4247 Editorial Teide.
      Atlas universal Teide: geográfico, estadístico,
      illustrado. By Luigi Visintin. With Istituto Geo-
      grafico De Agostini. Barcelona, [1964].
      120 p. col. maps. 34 cm.

4248 Elsevier.
      Grote Elsevier atlas voor buitenlandse handel.
      Amsterdam, 1950—
      2 vol. col. maps. 36 cm.

4249 European Communities. Press and Information Service.
      Die Europäische Gemeinschaft in Karten. Bruxelles,
      [1962].
      12 p. col. maps. 28 cm.

4250 European Communities.   Press and Information Service.
The European community in maps.   Bruxelles,
[1962].
16 p.   col.   maps.   28 cm.

4251 European Communities.   Press and Information Service.
The European community in maps.   Bruxelles, [1967].
12 p.   col.   maps.   28 cm.

4252 France.   Commissariat général à la productivité.
Atlas de la productivité.   Paris, [1958].
1 vol.   col.   maps.   43 cm.

4253 France.   Conseil national du patronat français.
Atlas de l'industrie française.   Paris, 1959.
354 p.   col.   maps.   38 cm.

4254 France.   La Documentation Française.
Atlas économique et social pour l'aménagement du
territoire.   By T. Hautreux.   Paris, 1966—
in parts.   col.   maps.   56 cm.

4255 France.   La Documentation Française.
Atlas industriel de la France.   By Robert Giry.
Paris, 1959.
201 p.   col.   maps.   39 cm.

4256 Generalstabens litografiska anstalt.
Ekonomisk karta över Europa.   Stockholm, 1953.
33 p.   col.   maps.   35 cm.

4257 Generalstabens litografiska anstalt.
Vår värld.   Politisk-ekonomisk atlas.   Stockholm,
1968—
in 6 vol.   col.   maps.   31 cm.

4258 Generalstabens litografiska anstalt.
Vår värld Europa.   Politisk-ekonomisk atlas.   By
Leif Söderström and Gunnar Schalin.   Stockholm,
1968.
72 p.   col.   maps.   22 cm.

4259 Geokarta.
Atlas Federativne Narodne Republike Jugoslavije.
By Josip J. Uhlik.   Beograd, 1952.
63 p.   col.   maps.   18 cm.

4260 Greece.   National Statistical Service.
      Industrial atlas of Greece.   (in Greek).   Athens,
      1966.
      46 p.   col.   maps.   58 cm.

4261 Greece.   Statistikon graphelon.
      Economic and social atlas of Greece.   (in Greek).
      Athens, 1964.
      508 p.   col.   maps.   48 cm.

4262 Gumperts Förlag.
      Atlas of the world commodities: production, trade
      and consumption.   By Olof Jonasson.   Göteborg,
      1961.
      82 p.   col.   maps.   21 cm.

4263 Gyldendal.
      Kulturgeografisk atlas.   3 ed.   By Johannes Hum-
      lum.   København, 1963.
      2 vol.   col.   maps.   27 cm.

4264 Gyldendal.
      Kulturgeografisk atlas.   4 ed.   By Johannes Hum-
      lum.   København, 1964.
      2 vol.   col.   maps.   27 cm.

4265 Gyldendal.
      Kulturgeografisk atlas.   5 ed.   By Johannes Hum-
      lum.   Atlas of economic geography.   København,
      [1965-67].
      2 vol.   col.   maps.   27 cm.

4266 Gyldendal.
      Kulturgeografisk atlas.   6 ed.   By Johannes Hum-
      lum.   København, 1967.
      2 vol.   col.   maps.   27 cm.

4267 Gyldendal.
      Kulturgeografisk atlas.   6 ed.   By Johannes Hum-
      lum.   København, 1969.
      2 vol.   col.   maps.   27 cm.

4268 Haack, Hermann.
      Agrarwirtschaftsatlas der Erde.   Gotha, 1958.
      248 p.   col.   maps.   41 cm.

4269 Haack, Hermann.
      Taschenatlas Staaten und Wirtschaft.   1 ed.   Gotha,

1963.
400 p.   col.   maps.   16.5 cm.

4270 Haack, Herman.
Weltatlas; die Staaten der Erde und ihre Wirtschaft.
1 ed.   Gotha, 1952 —
in parts.   col.   maps.   35 cm.

4271 Haack, Hermann.
Weltatlas die Staaten der Erde und ihre Wirtschaft.
Leipzig, 1961.
105 p.   col.   maps.   34 cm.

4272 Haack, Hermann.
Weltatlas.   Die Staaten der Erde und ihre Wirtschaft.
7 ed.   By E. Lehmann.   Gotha, 1963.
181 p.   col.   maps.   34 cm.

4273 Haack, Hermann.
Weltatlas.   Die Staaten der Erde und ihre Wirtschaft.
8 ed.   Gotha, [1964].
172 p.   col.   maps.   35 cm.

4274 Hammond, C. S. & Co., Inc.
Sales planning atlas of the United States and Canada.
Maplewood, N. J., [1962].
160 p.   28 cm.

4275 Hammond, Inc.
Sales planning atlas of the United States and Canada.
Maplewood, N. J., [1968].
160 p.   28 cm.

4276 Hearst Magazines, Inc.
Marketing maps of the individual states of the United
States, and maps of the 10 multiple markets.   New
York, [1952].
58 p.   col.   maps.   28 cm.

4277 Hilâl.
[Atlas of climates, politics, and economics of the
earth].   In Arabic.   By Ahmad Hafiz.   Cairo, [1962].
84 p.   col.   maps.   29 cm.

4278 India.   Information and broadcasting ministry.
India in maps.   Calcutta, [1950].
81 p.   32 cm.

4279 India University.   Department of Geography.
      An atlas of the European economic council.   Bloom-
      ington, Ind. , 1964.
      45 p.   28 cm.

4280 Indonesia.   Army Topographical Directorate.
      Atlas of Indonesian resources.   Djakarta, 1963.
      1 vol.   col. maps.   112 cm.

4281 Indonesia.   Badan Atlas Nacional.
      Atlas sumber2 kemakmuran Indonesia.   [Atlas of
      Indonesian resources].   Djakarta, 1965—
      in parts.   col. maps.   112 cm.

4282 International Bank for Reconstruction and Development.
      World bank atlas of per capita product and popula-
      tion.   Washington, D. C. , 1966.
      14 p.   col. maps.   28 cm.

4283 International Bank for Reconstruction and Development.
      World bank atlas; per capita product, population,
      main urban centers.   Washington, D. C. , 1967.
      7 p.   col. maps.   28 cm.

4284 International Bank for Reconstruction and Development.
      World bank atlas; population and per capita product.
      3 ed.   Washington, D. C. , 1968.
      16 p.   col. maps.   28 cm.

4285 International Bank for Reconstruction and Development.
      World bank atlas; population, per capita product and
      growth rate.   4 ed.   Washington, D. C. , 1969.
      16 p.   col. maps.   28 cm.

4286 Israel.   Department of Surveys.
      Atlas of Israel.   (in Hebrew).   Jerusalem, 1956-1964.
      1 vol.   col. maps.   47. 5 cm.

4287 Istituto Geografico De Agostini.
      Atlante geografico commerciale.   By Luigi Visintin.
      Novara, [1954].
      64 p.   col. maps.   33 cm.

4288 Istituto Geografico De Agostini.
      Grande atlante geografico economico.   Novara, 1966.
      351 p.   col. maps.   25 cm.

4289 Istituto Geografico De Agostini.
Grande atlante geografico, economico, storico.
Novara, 1965.
1 vol. col. maps. 42 cm.

4290 Istituto Geografico De Agostini.
Piccolo atlante della produzione e dei commerci.
By L. Visintin. Novara, [1953].
86 p. col. maps. 26 cm.

4291 Istituto Geografico De Agostini.
Piccolo atlante della produzione e dei commerci.
By L. Visintin. Novara, [1963].
90 p. col. maps. 26 cm.

4292 Istituto Geografico De Agostini.
Piccolo atlante della produzione e dei commerci.
Novara, 1964.
86 p. col. maps. 26 cm.

4293 Italy. Direzione generale della statistica.
Atlante dei comuni d'Italia. Roma, 1951.
1 vol. 35 cm.

4294 JRO Verlag.
JRO Deutschland Spezialatlas für Organisation,
Handel und Verkehr. München, [1950].
38 p. col. maps. 45 cm.

4295 JRO Verlag.
Weltwirtschafts Atlas: Atlas für Politik und Zeit-
geschichte. By Ernst Kremling. München, 1957—
in parts. col. maps. 30 cm.

4296 JRO Verlag.
Weltwirtschafts-Atlas. Atlas für Politik und Zeit-
geschichte. Permanente Ausgabe. München, 1961.
2 vol. col. maps. 30 cm.

4297 Kapelusz y Cía.
Atlas mundi, astronómico-general: Asia, Africa,
Europa, Oceanía, América; físico, político,
económico. Buenos Aires, [1964].
40 p. col. maps. 27 cm.

4298 Kartográfiai Vállalat.
Gazdasági és politikai világatlasz. Budapest, 1962.
353 p. col. maps. 35 cm.

4299 Kartográfiai Vállalat.
Képes politikai és gazdasági, világatlasz.   By Radó
Sándor.   Budapest, 1966.
1 vol.   col.   maps.   34 cm.

4300 Kartográfiai Vállalat.
Képes politikai és gazdasági, világatlasz.   Budapest, 1968.
1 vol.   col.   maps.   34 cm.

4301 Kartográfiai Vállalat.
Politikai és gazdasági világatlasz.   By Radó Sándor.
Budapest, 1961.
353 p.   col.   maps.   35 cm.

4302 Katholiek Sociaal-Kerkelijk Instituut.
Étude cartographique de la structure économique et
démographique de l'Europe occidentale. 's Gravenhage, [1959].
10 p.   col.   maps.   29 cm.

4303 Książnica-Atlas.
Atlas Polski wspólczesnej.   4 ed.   By E. Romer
and J. Wąsowicz.   Wrocław, 1950.
16 p.   col.   maps.   23 cm.

4304 Książnica-Atlas.
Atlas Polski wspólczesnej.   By E. Romer and J.
Wąsowicz.   Wrocław, 1951.
16 p.   col.   maps.   23 cm.

4305 Książnica-Atlas.
Atlas Polski wspólszesnej.   5 ed.   By E. Romer
and J. Wąsowicz.   Wrocław, 1952.
16 p.   col.   maps.   23 cm.

4306 Kümmerly & Frey.
Wirtschaftsgeographischer Atlas der Welt.   By Hans
Boesch.   Bern, 1951.
87 p.   col.   maps.   30 cm.

4307 Kümmerly & Frey.
Wirtschaftsgeographischer Weltatlas.   By Hans
Boesch.   Zürich, 1968.
90 p.   col.   maps.   34 cm.

4308 Larousse.
Atlas international Larousse, politico y economico.

Paris, 1966.
272 p. col. maps. 50 cm.

4309 Larousse.
Atlas international Larousse; politique et économique.
Paris, [1950].
172 p. col. maps. 50 cm.

4310 Larousse.
Atlas international Larousse, politique et économique.
Paris [1951].
170 p. col. maps. 50 cm.

4311 Larousse.
Atlas international Larousse, politique et économique.
By Jean Chardonnet and Ivan Du Jonchay. Paris,
[1957].
239 p. col. maps. 50 cm.

4312 Larousse.
Atlas international Larousse politique et économique.
2 ed. Paris, 1965.
272 p. col. maps. 50 cm.

4313 Larousse.
Atlas international Larousse. Paris, 1966.
272 p. col. maps. 50 cm.

4314 List, P.
Harms Wirtschaftsatlas. By W. Eggers. München,
[1963].
73 p. col. maps. 33 cm.

4315 List, P.
Wirtschaftsgeographischer Weltatlas. By Hans
Boesch. With Kümmerly & Frey. München, 1968.
89 p. col. maps. 34 cm.

4316 Livravia popular de F. Franco.
Atlas do mundo commercial e politico. By J. R.
Silva. Lisboa, [1950].
24 p. col. maps. 27 cm.

4317 Macmillan & Co., Ltd.
A map book of Australasia. 2 ed. By Alan Ferriday. London, 1959.
48 p. 25 cm.

4318 Macmillan & Co. , Ltd.
     A map book of Australasia. 3 ed. By Alan Ferri-
     day. London, Melbourne, 1966.
     52 p. 25 cm.

4319 Macmillan & Co. , Ltd.
     A map book of Australasia. 4 ed. By Alan Ferri-
     day. London, Melbourne, 1969.
     52 p. 25 cm.

4320 Mariam, Mesfin Wolde.
     A preliminary atlas of Ethiopia. Addis Ababa,
     [1962].
     34 p. col. maps. 28 cm.

4321 Martins Forlag.
     Martin Verdensatlas. 2 ed. København, 1963.
     342 p. col. maps. 30.5 cm.

4322 Methuen.
     An atlas of North American affairs. By David Keith
     Adams and H. B. Rodgers. London, 1969.
     135 p. 22 cm.

4323 Mexico. Instituto Mexicano de Investigaciones
     Economicas.
     Atlas geografico general de Mexico, con cartes
     fisicas, biologicas, demograficas, sociales,
     economicas y cartogramas. 2 ed. México, 1962.
     1 vol. col. maps. 54 cm.

4324 New Zealand. Town and Country Planning Branch.
     Atlas of New Zealand regional statistics. Welling-
     ton, [1968].
     62 p. 37 cm.

4325 Nomos Verlagsgesellschaft.
     Atlas sozialökonomischer Regionen Europas. With
     Soziographisches Institut der Universität Frankfurt.
     By L. Neundörfer. Baden-Baden, 1964—
     in parts. col. maps. 60 cm.

4326 Nouvelles de l'Enseignement.
     Synthèse de la vie économique en France. Petit
     atlas de la France et de l'Union Française. By
     Robert Poirier. Paris, [1956].
     92 p. 27 cm.

4327 Orbis.
    Politicko-hospodářský atlas světa. 1 ed. Praha,
    [1952-54].
    in parts. col. maps. 33 cm.

4328 Orbis.
    Politicko-hospodářský atlas světa. 4 ed. Praha,
    1953 —
    in parts. col. maps. 33 cm.

4329 Oxford University Press.
    Oxford economic atlas for Pakistan. By C. F. W. R.
    Gullick. Oxford, 1955.
    131 p. col. maps. 26 cm.

4330 Oxford University Press.
    Oxford economic atlas for Pakistan. By C. F. W. R.
    Gullick. New York, 1958.
    131 p. col. maps. 26 cm.

4331 Oxford University Press.
    Oxford economic atlas of India and Ceylon. London,
    1953.
    97 p. col. maps. 25. 5 cm.

4332 Oxford University Press.
    Oxford economic atlas of the world. 1 ed. London,
    1954.
    279 p. col. maps. 27 cm.

4333 Oxford University Press.
    Oxford economic atlas of the world. London, 1955.
    279 p. col. maps. 27 cm.

4334 Oxford University Press.
    Oxford economic atlas of the world. London, 1956.
    279 p. col. maps. 27 cm.

4335 Oxford University Press.
    Oxford economic atlas of the world. 2 ed. London,
    1959.
    279 p. col. maps. 27 cm.

4336 Oxford University Press.
    Oxford economic atlas of the world. London, 1960.
    279 p. col. maps. 27 cm.

4337 Oxford University Press.
     Oxford economic atlas of the world.   3 ed. London,
     New York, 1965.
     286 p. col. maps. 27 cm.

4338 Oxford University Press.
     Oxford regional economic atlas of the Middle East.
     Oxford, 1956.
     1 vol. col. maps. 26 cm.

4339 Oxford University Press.
     Oxford regional economic atlas of the United States
     and Canada. By John D. Chapman and John C.
     Sherman. Oxford, 1967.
     164 p. col. maps. 25.5 cm.

4340 Oxford University Press.
     Oxford regional economic atlas of the U.S.S.R. and
     Eastern Europe. Oxford, 1956.
     140 p. col. maps. 26 cm.

4341 Oxford University Press.
     Oxford regional economic atlas of the U.S.S.R. and
     Eastern Europe. Oxford, [1963].
     1 vol. col. maps. 26 cm.

4342 Oxford University Press.
     The Australasian school atlas, physical, political,
     economic and historical. With Bartholomew. 4 ed.
     Melbourne, [1954].
     84 p. col. maps. 28 cm.

4343 Oxford University Press.
     The Australasian school atlas, physical, political,
     economic, and historical. 4 ed. With Bartholomew.
     Melbourne, [1959].
     68 p. col. maps. 28 cm.

4344 Oxford University Press.
     The Middle East and North Africa.   London, [1960].
     135 p. col. maps. 27 cm.

4345 Oxford University Press.
     The Middle East and North Africa.   London, [1964].
     135 p. col. maps. 27 cm.

4346 Oxford University Press.
     The Oxford regional economic atlas of Africa.   By

P. H. Andy and A. H. Hazlewood.   London, 1965.
244 p. col. maps. 26 cm.

4347 Oxford University Press.
The shorter Oxford economic atlas of the world.
3 ed. London, New York, 1965.
128 p. col. maps. 26 cm.

4348 Pensamiento Vivo.
Atlas de bolsillo de Venezuela.   8 ed.   By Juan
Jones Parra. Caracas, 1954.
145 p. col. maps. 14.5 cm.

4349 Pfahl Verlag.
Hansa Universal atlas.   1 ed.   By Oswald Muris.
Baden-Baden, 1957.
480 p. col. maps. 24 cm.

4350 Pfahl Verlag.
Hansa Weltatlas.   6 ed.   Laupheim, 1951.
293 p. 22 cm.

4351 Pfahl Verlag.
Hansa Weltatlas.   9 ed.   Laupheim, 1955.
446 p. col. maps. 24 cm.

4352 Philip, George & Son, Ltd.
Philips commercial course atlas.   By Harold
Fullard.   London, [1965].
117 p. col. maps. 29 cm.

4353 Philippines. Office of the President.
The Philippine economic atlas.   Manila, [1965].
163 p. col. maps. 37 cm.

4354 Praeger, Frederick A.
An atlas of Soviet affairs.   By Robert N. Taafee.
New York, [1965].
143 p. 21 cm.

4355 Quillet, A.
Atlas universal Quillet, physique, economique,
politique.   By Maurice Allain.   Paris, 1951—
in parts. col. maps. 46 cm.

4356 Rand McNally & Co.
Goode school atlas; physical, political and economic.

8 ed. By Edward B. Espenshade, Jr. Chicago,
[1950].
272 p. col. maps. 29 cm.

4357 Rand McNally & Co.
Goode's world atlas. By Edward B. Espenshade,
Jr. Chicago, 1961.
207 p. col. maps. 29 cm.

4358 Rand McNally & Co.
Goode's world atlas. 12 ed. By Edward B.
Espenshade, Jr. Chicago, 1964.
288 p. col. maps. 29 cm.

4359 Rand McNally & Co.
Goode's world atlas. 12 ed. By Edward B.
Espenshade, Jr. Chicago, 1966.
310 p. col. maps. 29 cm.

4360 Rand McNally & Co.
Goode's world atlas. 13 ed. By Edward B.
Espenshade, Jr. Chicago, [1969].
315 p. col. maps. 29 cm.

4361 Rand McNally & Co.
Rand McNally commercial atlas and marketing guide.
81 ed. New York, [1950].
584 p. col. maps. 53 cm.

4362 Rand McNally & Co.
Rand McNally commercial atlas and marketing guide.
82 ed. New York, 1951.
584 p. col. maps. 53 cm.

4363 Rand McNally & Co.
Rand McNally commercial atlas and marketing guide.
83 ed. New York, 1952.
584 p. col. maps. 53 cm.

4364 Rand McNally & Co.
Rand McNally commercial atlas and marketing guide.
84 ed. New York, 1953.
562 p. col. maps. 53 cm.

4365 Rand McNally & Co.
Rand McNally commercial atlas and marketing guide.
85 ed. New York, 1954.
584 p. col. maps. 53 cm.

4366 Rand McNally & Co.
    Rand McNally commercial atlas and marketing guide.
    86 ed.   Chicago, 1955.
    584 p.   col. maps.   53 cm.

4367 Rand McNally & Co.
    Rand McNally commercial atlas and marketing guide.
    87 ed.   Chicago, 1956.
    566 p.   col. maps.   53 cm.

4368 Rand McNally & Co.
    Rand McNally commercial atlas and marketing guide.
    88 ed.   Chicago, 1957.
    566 p.   col. maps.   53 cm.

4369 Rand McNally & Co.
    Rand McNally commercial atlas and marketing guide.
    89 ed.   Chicago, 1958.
    566 p.   col. maps.   53 cm.

4370 Rand McNally & Co.
    Rand McNally commercial atlas and marketing guide.
    90 ed.   Chicago, 1959.
    566 p.   col. maps.   53 cm.

4371 Rand McNally & Co.
    Rand McNally commercial atlas and marketing guide.
    91 ed.   Chicago, 1960.
    566 p.   col. maps.   53 cm.

4372 Rand McNally & Co.
    Rand McNally commercial atlas and marketing guide.
    92 ed.   Chicago, 1961.
    566 p.   col. maps.   53 cm.

4373 Rand McNally & Co.
    Rand McNally commercial atlas and marketing guide.
    93 ed.   Chicago, 1962.
    566 p.   col. maps.   53 cm.

4374 Rand McNally & Co.
    Rand McNally commercial atlas and marketing guide.
    94 ed.   Chicago, 1963.
    566 p.   col. maps.   53 cm.

4375 Rand McNally & Co.
    Rand McNally commercial atlas and marketing guide.

95 ed.   Chicago, 1964.
566 p.   col. maps.   53 cm.

4376 Rand McNally & Co.
Rand McNally commercial atlas and marketing guide.
96 ed.   Chicago, 1965.
572 p.   col. maps.   53 cm.

4377 Rand McNally & Co.
Rand McNally commercial atlas and marketing guide.
97 ed.   Chicago, 1966.
572 p.   col. maps.   53 cm.

4378 Rand McNally & Co.
Rand McNally commercial atlas and marketing guide.
98 ed.   Chicago, 1967.
572 p.   col. maps.   53 cm.

4379 Rand McNally & Co.
Rand McNally commercial atlas and marketing guide.
99 ed.   Chicago, 1968.
572 p.   col. maps.   53 cm.

4380 Rand McNally & Co.
Rand McNally commercial atlas and marketing guide.
100 ed.   Chicago, 1969.
572 p.   col. maps.   53 cm.

4381 Rand McNally & Co.
Rand McNally commercial atlas and marketing guide.
101 ed.   Chicago, 1970.
657 p.   col. maps.   53 cm.

4382 Rand McNally & Co.
World atlas; physical, political and economic.   9 ed.
By Edward B. Espenshade, Jr.   Chicago, [1953].
272 p.   col. maps.   29 cm.

4383 Rand McNally & Co.
World atlas; physical, political and economic.   9 ed.
By Edward B. Espenshade, Jr.   New York, [1955].
272 p.   col. maps.   29 cm.

4384 Rand McNally & Co.
World atlas; physical, political and economic.   10 ed.
By Edward B. Espenshade, Jr.   Chicago, [1957].
272 p.   col. maps.   29 cm.

4385 Rand McNally & Co.
     World atlas. 13 ed. By Edward B. Espenshade,
     Jr. Chicago, 1970.
     315 p. col. maps. 29 cm.

4386 Reitzels, C. A. Forlag.
     Atlas over Denmark. København, 1950–
     in 5 vols. col. maps. 55 cm.

4387 Romania. Editura Didactică si Pedagogică.
     Atlas geografic pentru clasele III-IV ale scolii
     generale de 8 ani. By Elena Papatănese and Florica
     Vornicescu. Bucuresti, 1964.
     51 p. col. maps. 34 cm.

4388 Romania. Editura Didactică si Pedagogică.
     Atlas geografic: Republica Socialistă România. By
     Victor Tufescu. Bucuresti, 1965.
     144 p. col. maps. 34 cm.

4389 Salvador. Estadistica y cencos.
     Atlas censal de El Salvador. San Salvador, [1955].
     110 p. col. maps. 36 cm.

4390 Siemens & Halske, A. G.
     Welt-Telex-Atlas. München, 1961.
     119 p. col. maps. 30 cm.

4391 Silva, J. R.
     Atlas do mundo comercial e politico. 3 ed. Lisboa,
     1958.
     24 p. col. maps. 27 cm.

4392 Société européenne d'études et d'informations.
     Atlante dell 'Europa occidentale. By Jean Dollfus.
     Paris, [1961].
     46 p. col. maps. 34 cm.

4393 Société européenne d'études et d'informations.
     Atlas de l'Europe de l'Ouest. By Jean Dollfus.
     Paris, 1961.
     46 p. col. maps. 34 cm.

4394 Société européenne d'études et d'informations.
     Atlas of western Europe. By Jean Dollfus. Paris,
     1963.
     46 p. col. maps. 34 cm.

4395 South Africa.　Department of Planning.
　　　Ontwikkelingsatlas.　Pretoria, 1966—
　　　1 vol.　col.　maps.　57 cm.

4396 Spain.　Cámeras Oficiales de Comercio, Industria y
　　　Navegación.
　　　Atlas comercial de España.　Madrid, 1963.
　　　182 p.　col.　maps.　49 cm.

4397 Spain.　Cámeras Oficiales de Comercio, Industria y
　　　Navegación.
　　　Atlas industrial de España.　Madrid, 1964-66.
　　　2 vol.　col.　maps.　44, 32 cm.

4398 St. Martin's Press.
　　　A map book of Australasia.　3 ed.　By A. Ferri-
　　　day.　New York, 1966.
　　　52 p.　25 cm.

4399 St. Martin's Press.
　　　A map book of Australasia.　4 ed.　By Alan Ferri-
　　　day.　New York, 1969.
　　　52 p.　25 cm.

4400 St. Martin's Press.
　　　Atlas of South-east Asia.　By D. G. E. Hall.　With
　　　Djambatan.　New York, 1964.
　　　84 p.　col.　maps.　35 cm.

4401 St. Martin's Press.
　　　Atlas of South-east Asia.　By D. G. E. Hall.　With
　　　Djambatan.　New York, 1965.
　　　84 p.　col.　maps.　35 cm.

4402 Studi geo-cartografici.
　　　Atlante econometrico delle regioni d'Italia.　By
　　　Frederico de Agostini.　Milano, [196-].
　　　1 vol.　col.　maps.　41 cm.

4403 Südwest Verlag.
　　　Neuer Taschenatlas.　Die Erde und ihre Länder in
　　　polit. und wirtschaftl. Darstellung.　By Hans R.
　　　Fischer.　München, [1963].
　　　156 p.　col.　maps.　32 cm.

4404 Südwest Verlag.
　　　Neuer Taschenatlas.　Die Erde und ihre Länder in
　　　politischer und wirtschaftlicher Darstellung.　By

H. R. Fischer. München, 1964.
156 p. col. maps. 32 cm.

4405 Svenska bokförlaget.
Ekonomisk geografi. Statistik atlas för den ekonomiska geografin. 4 ed. By Sven Olof Garland.
Stockholm, [1963].
32 p. col. maps. 27 cm.

4406 Sveriges köpmannaförbund.
Handelsmoräden i Sverige. Ekonomisk-geografisk
atlas. By Sven Dahl and Hans Jalinder. Stockholm, 1966.
43 p. col. maps. 40 cm.

4407 Thailand. Royal Thai Survey Department.
Natural resources atlas. Bangkok, 1966.
in parts. 34 cm.

4408 Thailand. Royal Thai Survey Department.
Natural resources atlas. Bangkok, 1970.
1 vol. 34 cm.

4409 University of Chicago Press.
Atlas of economic development. By Norton S.
Ginsburg. Chicago, [1961].
119 p. col. maps. 36 cm.

4410 University of Michigan Press.
Economic atlas of the Soviet Union. By George
Kish. Ann Arbor, Mich., [1960].
96 p. col. maps. 27 cm.

4411 University of Texas.
Atlas of Mexico. Austin, Texas, 1970.
127 p. col. maps. 36 cm.

4412 U. S. Aid Mission to Laos.
Laos. [Washington, D. C., 1965].
11 p. 97 cm.

4413 U. S. Economic Development Administration.
Atlas of planning jurisdiction, maps and information. Washington, D. C., 1968.
1 vol. col. maps. 30 cm.

4414 U. S. Engineer Agency of Resources Inventories.
Honduras: inventario nacional de recursos físicos.

1 ed.   Washington, D. C., 1966.
1 vol.   col. maps.   83 cm.

4415 U. S. Engineer Agency of Resources Inventories.
Panamá: inventario nacional de recursos físicos.
1 ed.   Washington, D. C., 1967.
1 vol.   col. maps.   77 cm.

4416 U. S. Engineer Agency of Resources Inventories.
Venezuela: inventario nacional de recursos.   1 ed.
Washington, 1968.
1 vol.   col. maps.   75 cm.

4417 U. S. Engineer Resources Inventory Center.
El Salvador: análisis regional de recursos físicos.
1 ed.   Washington, D. C., 1965.
1 vol.   col. maps.   82 cm.

4418 U. S. S. R. Glavnoe upravlenie geodezii i kartografii.
Atlas Frantsii.   Moskva, 1970-71.
1 vol.   col. maps.   32 cm.

4419 U. S. S. R. Glavnoe upravlenie geodezii i kartografii.
Atlas Latinskoi Ameriki.   Moskva, 1967.
54 p.   col. maps.   32 cm.

4420 U. S. S. R. Glavnoe upravlenie geodezii i kartografii.
Atlas Latinskoi Ameriki.   Moskva, 1968.
54 p.   col. maps.   32 cm.

4421 U. S. S. R. Glavnoe upravlenie geodezii i kartografii.
Atlas razvitia khoziaistva i kultury SSSR.   Moskva,
1967.
172 p.   col. maps.   34 cm.

4422 U. S. S. R. Glavnoe upravlenie geodezii i kartografii.
Atlas S. S. A.   Moskva, 1966.
81 p.   col. maps.   34 cm.

4423 U. S. S. R. Glavnoe upravlenie geodezii i kartografii.
Atlas SSSR dlya srednei shkoly.   Moskva, 1960.
50 p.   col. maps.   28 cm.

4424 U. S. S. R. Glavnoe upravlenie geodezii i kartografii.
Atlas SSSR dlya srednei shkoly.   Moskva, [1961].
50 p.   col. maps.   28 cm.

4425 U.S.S.R. Glavnoe upravlenie geodezii i kartografii.
Atlas SSSR dlya srednei shkoly. 3 ed. Moskva,
[1967].
50 p. col. maps. 28 cm.

4426 U.S.S.R. Glavnoe upravlenie geodezii i kartografii.
Atlas SSSR dlya srednei shkoly. Moskva, 1968.
48 p. col. maps. 28 cm.

4427 U.S.S.R. Glavnoe upravlenie geodezii i kartografii.
Atlas Yaponii. Moskva, 1970-71.
1 vol. col. maps. 32 cm.

4428 U.S.S.R. Glavnoe upravlenie geodezii i kartografii.
Atlas zarubezhnykh stran dlya srednei shkoly; kurs
ekonomicheskoi geografii. Moskva, [1965].
40 p. col. maps. 28 cm.

4429 U.S.S.R. Glavnoe upravlenie geodezii i kartografii.
Atlas zarubezhnykh stran dlya srednei shkoly; kurs
ekonomicheskoi geografii. Moskva, [1966].
40 p. col. maps. 28 cm.

4430 U.S.S.R. Glavnoe upravlenie geodezii i kartografii.
Atlas zarubezhnykh stran dlya strednei shkoly.
Moskva, 1968.
48 p. col. maps. 29 cm.

4431 U.S.S.R. Glavnoe upravlenie geodezii i kartografii.
Ekonomicheskii atlas mira. Moskva, 1970-1.
1 vol. col. maps. 50 cm.

4432 Vallardi, A.
Atlante geografico illustrato fisico politico economico.
By Cesare Saibene. Milano, 1968.
282 p. col. maps. 32 cm.

4433 VEB Bibliographisches Institut.
Weltatlas; die Staaten der Erde und ihre Wirtschaft.
Leipzig, [1952].
166 p. col. maps. 33 cm.

4434 Verlag Enzyklopädie.
Historisch-geographisches Kartenwerk. Wirtschafts-
historische Entwicklung. By Edgar Lehmann.
Leipzig, 1960.
81 p. col. maps. 41 cm.

4435 Verlag Enzyklopädie.
     Indien. Entwicklung seiner Wirtschaft und Kultur.
     Historisch-geographisches Kartenwerk. Leipzig,
     1958.
     1 vol. col. maps. 42.5 cm.

4436 Verlag Enzyklopädie.
     Weltatlas; die Staaten der Erde und ihre Wirtschaft.
     2 ed. By Edgar Lehmann. Leipzig, 1957.
     170 p. col. maps. 35 cm.

4437 Verlag Enzyklopädie.
     Weltatlas; die Staaten der Erde und ihre Wirtschaft.
     3 ed. By Edgar Lehmann. Leipzig, 1958.
     170 p. col. maps. 35 cm.

4438 Walker, Gerlad E.
     A short atlas of European economic history.
     Berkeley, Calif., [1963].
     1 vol. 28 cm.

4439 Walker, Gerald E.
     A short atlas of European economic history.
     Berkeley, Calif., 1964.
     41 p. 28 cm.

4440 Westermann, Georg.
     Westermanns Hausatlas. By Carl Diercke and R.
     Dehmel. Braunschweig, [1958].
     238 p. col. maps. 34 cm.

4441 Weststadt Verlag.
     The world shipping scene; atlas of shipping, ship-
     building, seaports, and sea-borne trade. By G. A.
     Theel. München, 1963.
     1 vol. col. maps. 31 cm.

4442 Yavneh.
     Atlas fisi, medini ve-kalkali. (In Hebrew). By
     Moshe Brawer. Tel Aviv, 1958.
     80 p. col. maps. 31 cm.

4443 Yavneh.
     Atlas fisi, medini ve-kalkali. (In Hebrew). By
     Moshe Brawer. Tel Aviv, 1960.
     80 p. col. maps. 31 cm.

4444 Yavneh.
   Atlas fisi, medini ve kalkali. (In Hebrew). By
   Moshe Brawer. Tel Aviv, 1962.
   128 p. col. maps. 31 cm.

4445 Yavneh.
   Atlas kis, entsiklopedia geo-grafit, kalkalit,
   u-medinit. By Moshe Brawer. Tel Aviv, [1960].
   630 p. col. maps. 17 cm.

4446 Yavneh.
   Atlas kis, entsiklopedia geo-grafit, kalkalit,
   u-medinit. 2 ed. By Moshe Brawer. Tel Aviv,
   [1960].
   633 p. col. maps. 17 cm.

4447 Zenkoku Kyóiku tocho.
   Nippon keizai chizu. (The economic atlas of Japan).
   By Kóichi Aki. Tokyo, 1954.
   186 p. col. maps. 37 cm.

4448 Znanje.
   Geografski atlas i statisticko-geografski pregled
   svijeta. 7 ed. By Petar Mardesić, Zvonimir
   Dugački and Josip Zoricić. Zagreb, 1962.
   533 p. col. maps. 22 cm.

4449 Znanje.
   Geografski atlas Jugoslavije. By Petar Mardesić
   and Zvonimir Dugački. Zagreb, 1961.
   256 p. col. maps. 22 cm.

ETHNOGRAPHY

4450 Poland. Akademia nauk.
   Polski atlas etnograficzny. Warszawa, 1964—
   in parts. col. maps. 49 cm.

EXPLORATION - SEE HISTORY

FOLK LORE

4451 Austria. Akademie der Wissenschaften.
   Österreichischer Volkskundeatlas. Wien, 1959—
   in parts. col. maps. 60 cm.

4452 Elwert Verlag.
   Atlas der Deutschen Volkskunde. Neue Folge. By

Matthias Zender.   Marburg, 1958—
in parts. col. maps. 72 cm.

4453 Netherlands.   Volkskundecommissie der Koninklijke
Nederlandse Akademie van Wetenschappen.
Volkskunde-atlas. By Pieter Jacobus Meertens.
's Gravenhage, 1959—
in parts. col. maps. 50 cm.

4454 Schweizerische Gesellschaft für Volkskunde.
Atlas der Schweizerischen Volkskunde.   Basle,
[1950-].
in parts. col. maps. 40 cm.

FORESTRY

4455 Afrika Instituut.
Africa; maps and statistics.   Pretoria, 1962-65.
10 vol. col. maps. 35 cm.

4456 Brazil.   Ministerio de Agricultura.
Atlas florestal do Brasil.   By Henrique Pimenta
Veloso.   Rio de Janeiro, 1966.
82 p. col. maps. 44 cm.

4457 Czechoslovakia.   Ústřední správa geodesie a kartografie.
Lesnický a myslivecký atlas.   1 ed.   Praha, 1955.
120 p. col. maps. 33 cm.

4458 France.   Service de l'économie forestière.
Atlas forestièr, année 1963.   Paris, [1964].
65 p. col. maps. 32 cm.

4459 Haller Verlag.
Weltforst atlas.   Berlin, 1951—
in parts. col. maps. 61 cm.

4460 Internationaler Holzmarkt.
Österreichischer Sägewerksatlas.   1 ed.   Wien,
[1951].
1 vol. col. maps. 26 cm.

4461 Internationaler Holzmarkt.
Österreichischer Sägewerksatlas.   2 ed.   Wien,
[1960].
1 vol. col. maps. 26 cm.

4462 Spain.   Direción General de Montes, Caza y Pesca
Fluvid.
Mapa forestal de España.   Madrid, 1966.
50 p.   col. maps.   54 cm.

4463 U. S. S. R.   Glavnoe upravlenie geodezii i kartografii.
Atlas lesov SSSR.   Moskva, 1970-71.
1 vol.   col. maps.   34 cm.

4464 Venezuela.   Ministerio de Agricultura.
Atlas forestal de Venezuela.   Caracas, 1961.
39 p.   42. 5 cm.

GENEALOGY

4465 Bookcraft.
A genealogical atlas of Scotland.   By David E.
Gardner, Derek Harland, and Frank Smith.   Salt
Lake City, Utah, [1962].
32 p.   27 cm.

4466 Deseret Book Co.
A genealogical atlas of England and Wales.   By
David E. Gardner, Derek Harland and Frank Smith.
Salt Lake City, Utah, [1960].
88 p.   27 cm.

4467 Deseret Book Co.
A genealogical atlas of Ireland.   By David E.
Gardner, Derek Harland and Frank Smith.   Salt
Lake City, Utah, 1964.
41 p.   26 cm.

4468 Everton Publishers.
Genealogical atlas of the United States.   By George
B. Everton, Jr.   Logan, Utah, 1966.
120 p.   28 cm.

GEOLOGY

4469 Afrika Instituut.
Africa; maps and statistics.   Pretoria, 1962-65.
10 vol.   col. maps.   35 cm.

4470 Australia.   Bureau of Mineral Resources, Geology and
Geophysics.
South Australia geological atlas series.   Adelaide,

1962—
in parts. col. maps. 31 cm.

4471 Czechoslovakia. Ústřední správa geodézie a kartografie.
Geological atlas. Regional geology of Czechoslovakia.
Praha, 1967.
15 p. col. maps. 24 cm.

4472 Czechoslovakia. Ústřední ústav geologický.
Geologický atlas ČSSR. 1 ed. Praha, 1966.
1 vol. col. maps. 51 cm.

4473 Industrial Atlas Corporation.
Industrial atlas mining guide. New York, 1967.
103 p. 23.5 cm.

4474 Informations et Conjoncture.
Atlas Mondial du Pétrole et du Gaz Naturel. By
Jacques Bloch-Morhange. Paris, 1962.
1 vol. col. maps. 45 cm.

4475 Kümmerly & Frey.
Geologischer atlas der Schweiz. Bern, 1962—
in parts. col. maps. 70 cm.

4476 Meyer, Kartographisches Institut.
Meyers grosser physischer Weltatlas. Mannheim,
1965—
in 8 vol. col. maps. 30 cm.

4477 Munger Oil Information Service.
Munger map book: petroleum developments and
generalized geology of Africa and Middle East. Los
Angeles, Calif., 1960.
115 p. 45 cm.

4478 Petroleum Publishing Co.
Atlas of crude-oil pipelines of the United States and
Canada. Tulsa, Okla., 1965.
22 p. 31 cm.

4479 Petroleum Publishing Co.
Atlas of natural-gas pipelines of the United States
and Canada. Tulsa, Okla., 1965.
24 p. 31 cm.

4480 Poland. Instytut geologiczny.
Atlas geologiczny Polski. Warszawa, 1957—

in parts.   col.   maps.   43 cm.

4481 Poland.   Instytut geologiczny.
    Atlas geologiczny Polski.   Warszawa, 1968.
    11 p.   col.   maps.   59 cm.

4482 Poland.   Instytut geologiczny.
    Atlas géologique de Pologne [1:2,000,000).   Text in
    French.   Prepared for the Geological Congress in
    Mexico City.   Warszawa, 1956.
    1 portfolio.   col.   maps.   37 cm.

4483 Poland.   Instytut geologiczny.
    Geological atlas of Poland.   By Jerzy Znosko.
    Warszawa, 1968.
    7 p.   col.   maps.   31 cm.

4484 Poland.   Instytut geologiczny.
    Mineralogenic atlas of Poland.   (In English).
    Warszawa, 1970.
    1 vol.   col.   maps.   30 cm.

4485 Prentice-Hall.
    Atlas of the world's resources.   Vol. II.   The
    mineral resources of the world.   By William Van
    Royen, Oliver Bowles, Elmer W. Pehrson.   New
    York, 1952.
    181 p.   40 cm.

4486 Stanford, Edward.
    Stanford's geological atlas of Great Britain.   By T.
    Eastwood.   London, 1964.
    288 p.   25 cm.

4487 Technical Press, Ltd.
    Oil-field atlas.   By Arthur Beeby-Thompson.
    London, 1952.
    15 p.   27 cm.

4488 U. S. Geological Survey.
    Geological atlas of the moon.   Washington, D. C.,
    1967.
    in parts.   col.   maps.   47 cm.

4489 Westermann, Georg.
    Erdöl Weltatlas.   By F. Mayer.   Braunschweig, 1966.
    152 p.   col.   maps.   31 cm.

4490 Wiley, John & Sons.
   Lithofacies maps; an atlas of the United States and
   southern Canada. By Lawrence L. Sloss, E. C.
   Dapples and W. C. Krumbein. New York, [1960].
   153 p. col. maps. 28 cm.

GEOMORPHOLOGY

4491 Meyer, Kartographisches Institut.
   Meyers grosser physischer Weltatlas.   Mannheim,
   1965—
   in 8 vol. col. maps. 30 cm.

HISTORY

4492 Ahiever.
      The Hebrew maps of the Holy Land. 2 ed. By
      Zev Vilnay. Jerusalem, 1968.
      30 p. col. maps. 40 cm.

4493 Aldine Pub. Co.
      An historical atlas of China. By Albert Herrmann
      and Norton Ginsburg. With Djambatan. Chicago,
      [1966].
      88 p. col. maps. 30 cm.

4494 American Heritage.
      The American heritage pictorial atlas of United
      States history. New York, [1966].
      424 p. col. maps. 29 cm.

4495 Arnold, E.
      A historical atlas 1789-1962 for first examinations.
      By R. R. Sellman. London, 1964.
      68 p. 26 cm.

4496 Arnold, E.
      A student's atlas of modern history. By R. R.
      Sellman. London, [1952].
      95 p. 28 cm.

4497 Arnold, E.
      An atlas of African history. By J. D. Fage.
      London, [1958].
      64 p. 29 cm.

4498 Arnold, E.
      An outline atlas of eastern history. By R. R.

Sellman. London, [1954].
63 p. 28 cm.

4499 Arnold, E.
An outline atlas of world history. London, 1970.
1 vol. 28 cm.

4500 Aschehoug & Co.
Kartbok historie folkeskolen. Oslo, 1965.
22 p. col. maps. 32 cm.

4501 Atlantik Verlag.
Harms Geschichts- und Kulturatlas. 52 ed. By
Hans Zeissig. Frankfurt, 1959.
120 p. col. maps. 27 cm.

4502 Atlantik Verlag.
Neuer Geschichts- und Kulturatlas; von der Urzeit
zur Gegenwart. By Hans Zeissig. Frankfurt, [1950].
120 p. col. maps. 27 cm.

4503 Atlantik Verlag.
Neuer Geschichts-und Kulturatlas; von der Urzeit zur
Gegenwart. By Hans Zeissig. Frankfurt, [1954].
120 p. col. maps. 27 cm.

4504 Augsburg Publishing House.
Augsburg historical atlas of Christianity in the
Middle Ages and Reformation. By Charles S.
Anderson. Minneapolis, Minn., 1967.
61 p. col. maps. 29 cm.

4505 Barnes & Noble, Inc.
Atlas of ancient and classical history. 2 ed. By
George Goodall and R. F. Treharne. New York,
1960.
35 p. col. maps. 28 cm.

4506 Barnes & Noble, Inc.
Historical atlas. 8 ed. By William R. Shepherd.
New York, 1956.
226 p. col. maps. 27 cm.

4507 Barnes & Noble, Inc.
Historical atlas. 8 ed. By William R. Shepherd.
New York, 1962.
226 p. col. maps. 27 cm.

4508 Barnes & Noble, Inc.
     Historical atlas. 9 ed.   By William R. Shepherd.
     New York, 1964.
     226 p. col. maps. 27 cm.

4509 Barnes & Noble, Inc.
     Historical atlas. 9 ed.   By William R. Shepherd.
     New York, 1966.
     226 p. col. maps. 27 cm.

4510 Barnes & Noble, Inc.
     Historical atlas. By William R. Shepherd.   New
     York, 1967.
     227 p. col. maps. 27 cm.

4511 Barnes & Noble, Inc.
     Historical atlas, medieval and modern. 8 ed.   By
     George Goodall and R. F. Treharne. New York,
     [1952].
     127 p. col. maps. 29 cm.

4512 Barnes & Noble, Inc.
     Historical atlas, medieval and modern. 9 ed.   By
     R. F. Treharne and Harold Fullard. New York,
     1962.
     120 p. col. maps. 29 cm.

4513 Barnes & Noble, Inc.
     Historical atlas, medieval and modern. 9 ed. By
     R. F. Treharne and Harold Fullard. New York,
     [1963].
     120 p. col. maps. 29 cm.

4514 Barnes & Noble, Inc.
     Historical atlas of the world. By Oddvar Bjørklund.
     New York, 1970.
     108 p. col. maps. 21 cm.

4515 Barnes & Noble, Inc.
     Muir's historical atlas, medieval and modern.
     10 ed. By R. F. Treharne and Harold Fullard.
     New York, 1964.
     112 p. col. maps. 29 cm.

4516 Barnes & Noble, Inc.
     Muir's historical atlas, medieval and modern. By
     R. F. Treharne and Harold Fullard. New York,
     [1965].
     112 p. col. maps. 29 cm.

4517 Barnes & Noble, Inc.
Ramsey Muir's historical atlas, ancient, medieval
and modern. By R. F. Treharne and Harold
Fullard. New York, 1963.
127 p. col. maps. 29 cm.

4518 Bartholomew, John & Son, Ltd.
The Aldine atlas; geography and history. 3 ed.
Toronto, Vancouver, [1968].
166 p. col. maps. 29 cm.

4519 Bayerischer Schulbuch Verlag.
Die Welt im Spiegel der Geschichte. 4 ed.
München, [1952].
33 p. col. maps. 34 cm.

4520 Bayerischer Schulbuch Verlag.
Die Welt im Spiegel der Geschichte. 5 ed.
München, [1952].
33 p. col. maps. 34 cm.

4521 Bayerischer Schulbuch Verlag.
Die Welt im Spiegel der Geschichte. 15 ed.
München, 1965.
43 p. 34 cm.

4522 Bayerischer Schulbuch Verlag.
Grosser Historischer Weltatlas. München, 1953.
1 vol. col. maps. 34 cm.

4523 Bayerischer Schulbuch Verlag.
Grosser Historischer Weltatlas. München, 1954-57.
in parts. col. maps. 34 cm.

4524 Bayerischer Schulbuch Verlag.
Grosser Historischer Weltatlas. II Teil: Mittelalter.
By Josef Engel. München, 1970.
191 p. col. maps. 34 cm.

4525 Benziger & Co.
Die zwanzig Jahrhunderte der Kirche. Geohistorischer
Atlas mit Kirchengeschichtlichem Begleittext. By
Frederico de Agostini. Einsiedeln, 1950.
42 p. col. maps. 32 cm.

4526 BLV Verlagsgesellschaft.
Bildatlas der Kultur und Geschichte der slawischen

Welt.   By P. Kovalewsky.   München, [1964].
215 p.   col. maps.   35 cm.

4527 Bosch & Keuning.
Sesam atlas bij de wereldgeschieddenis.   Part 1.
Baarn, 1965.
287 p.   col. maps.   27 cm.

4528 Brazil.   Instituto Brasileiro de Geografia e Estatistica.
Atlas de relaçoes internacionais.   Rio de Janeiro,
1960.
160 p.   col. maps.   32 cm.

4529 Brazil.   Ministério da educação e cultura.
Atlas histórico e geográfico brasileiro.   Rio de
Janeiro, [1962].
47 p.   col. maps.   31 cm.

4530 Brazil.   Ministério da educação e cultura.
Atlas histórico e geográfico brasileiro.   [Brasilia,
1963].
47 p.   col. maps.   31 cm.

4531 Brazil.   Ministério da educação e cultura.
Atlas histórico e geográfico brasileiro.   1 ed.   Rio
de Janeiro, 1966.
63 p.   col. maps.   31 cm.

4532 Brazil.   Ministério da educação e cultura.
Atlas historico escolar.   2 ed.   Rio de Janeiro,
1965.
124 p.   col. maps.   31 cm.

4533 Bulgaria.   Akademiya na naukite.
Atlas po bŭlgarska istoriya.   Sofia, 1963.
87 p.   col. maps.   32 cm.

4534 Bulgaria.   Muzei na revoliutsionnoto dvizhenie v
Bŭlgariiá.
Atlas na partizanskoto dvizhenie v Bulgariiá.   Sofia,
[1968].
96 p.   col. maps.   34 cm.

4535 Cappelens, J. W. Forlag, A. S.
Cappelens historiske atlas.   By Oddvar Bjørklund.
Oslo, [1962].
1 vol.   col. maps.   21 cm.

4536 Catholic War Veterans.
Twenty centuries of Catholicism; a Catholic historical
atlas with commentary. By Federico de Agostini.
Washington, D. C., 1950.
42 p. col. maps. 31 cm.

4537 Colin.
Atlas d'histoire universelle de 4000 avant J. -C. a
1963. By Franz Hayt. Paris, 1965.
126 p. col. maps. 23 cm.

4538 Colin.
Atlas historique. Paris, 1969.
258 p. col. maps. 32 cm.

4539 Colin.
Atlas historique. Paris, [1970].
326 p. col. maps. 32 cm.

4540 Colin.
Atlas historique de la France contemporaine, 1800-
1965. Paris, 1966.
235 p. col. maps. 23 cm.

4541 Colin.
Atlas historique et géographique Vidal-Lablache.
Paris, [1951].
164 p. col. maps. 40 cm.

4542 Colin.
Atlas historique et géographique Vidal-Lablache.
Paris, [1952].
160 p. col. maps. 40 cm.

4543 Colin.
Atlas historique et géographique Vidal-Lablache.
Paris, 1955—
1 vol. col. maps. 40 cm.

4544 Colin.
Atlas historique et géographique Vidal-Lablache.
Paris, [1960].
187 p. col. maps. 40 cm.

4545 Collins, William Sons & Co., Ltd.
Our changing Commonwealth: where, how and why.
[Atlas]. By Allan Murray. London, [1960].
96 p. col. maps. 26 cm.

4546 Cooper Square Publishers.
Historical atlas of Latin America. Political, geographic, economic, cultural. By A. Curtis Wilgus.
New York, 1967.
365 p. 24 cm.

4547 Czechoslovakia. Kartografické nakladatelství.
Školní atlas Československých dějin. Praha, 1967.
1 vol. col. maps. 30 cm.

4548 Czechoslovakia. Ústřední správa geodezie a kartografie.
Atlas Československých dějin. 1 ed. Praha, [1965].
58 p. col. maps. 52 cm.

4549 Czechoslovakia. Ústřední správa geodesie a kartografie.
Historický atlas revolučního hnutí. Praha, 1956.
180 p. col. maps. 33 cm.

4550 Czechoslovakia. Ústřední správa geodézie a kartografie.
Školní atlas Československých dějin. 2 ed. By
Ivan Beneš. Praha, 1964.
63 p. col. maps. 31 cm.

4551 Czechoslovakia. Ústřední správa geodézie a kartografie.
Školni atlas Československých dějin. Praha, 1965.
45 p. col. maps. 42.5 cm.

4552 Czechoslovakia. Ústřední správa geodézie a kartografie.
Školní atlas světových dějin. Praha, 1965.
92 p. col. maps. 30 cm.

4553 Czechoslovakia. Ústřední správa geodézie a kartografie.
Školní atlas světových dějin. 2 ed. Praha, 1966.
52 p. col. maps. 30 cm.

4554 Czechoslovakia. Ústřední správa geodesie a kartografie.
Školni atlas světových dějin. 3 ed. Praha, 1967.
87 p. col. maps. 30 cm.

4555 Czechoslovakia. Ústřední správa geodesie a kartografie.
Školní atlas světových dějin. Praha, 1968.
90 p. col. maps. 30 cm.

4556 Czechoslovakia. Ústřední správa geodésie a kartografie.
Školský atlas světových dejín. 1 ed. By Jan
Musílek. Praha, 1962.
76 p. col. maps. 30 cm.

4557 Denoyer-Geppert Co.
      European history atlas; ancient, medieval, and
      modern European and world history. 9 ed. By
      J. H. Breasted. Chicago, 1951.
      62 p. col. maps. 28 cm.

4558 Denoyer-Geppert Co.
      European history atlas; ancient, medieval and
      modern European and world history. 10 ed. By
      J. H. Breasted. Chicago, 1954.
      1 vol. col. maps. 28 cm.

4559 Denoyer-Geppert Co.
      European history atlas: ancient, medieval, and
      modern European and world history. 11 ed. By
      J. H. Breasted. Chicago, 1961.
      1 vol. col. maps. 28 cm.

4560 Denoyer-Geppert Co.
      European history atlas. Student edition. Ancient,
      medieval and modern European and world history.
      1 ed. By J. H. Breasted. Chicago, [1951].
      62 p. col. maps. 28 cm.

4561 Denoyer-Geppert Co.
      Historical atlas of the Far East in modern times.
      By Michael P. Onorato. Chicago, [1967].
      32 p. 28 cm.

4562 Denoyer-Geppert Co.
      Our United States; its history in cartovues. By
      Edgar Bruce Wesley. Chicago, [1965].
      2 vol. col. maps. 28 cm.

4563 Denoyer-Geppert Co.
      Our United States; its history in maps. 1 ed. By
      Edgar Bruce Wesley. Chicago, [1956].
      96 p. col. maps. 28 cm.

4564 Denoyer-Geppert Co.
      The history of Africa in maps. By Harry A. Gailey,
      Jr. Chicago, [1967].
      96 p. 28 cm.

4565 Denoyer-Geppert Co.
      The world; its history in maps. Chicago, [1963].
      96 p. col. maps. 28 cm.

4566 Denoyer-Geppert Co.
       The world, its history in maps.   By William H.
       McNeill.   Chicago, 1968.
       96 p.   col. maps.   28 cm.

4567 Denoyer-Geppert Co.
       The world-its history in maps.   2 ed.   By William
       H. McNeill.   Chicago, [1969].
       96 p.   col. maps.   28 cm.

4568 Dent, J. M.
       Everyman's atlas of ancient and classical geography.
       London, [1952].
       256 p.   col. maps.   20 cm.

4569 Dent, J. M.
       Everyman's classical atlas; with an essay on the
       development of ancient geographical knowledge and
       theory.   3 ed.   By J. Oliver Thomson.   London,
       [1961].
       125 p.   col. maps.   20 cm.

4570 Dent, J. M.
       Historical and geographical atlas.   Toronto, [1958].
       148 p.   col. maps.   29 cm.

4571 Dent, J. M.
       The Aldine world atlas, geography and history.
       1 ed.   By J. W. Hamilton and G. E. Tait.   With
       Bartholomew.   Toronto, 1961.
       166 p.   col. maps.   29 cm.

4572 Dent, J. M.
       The Aldine world atlas; geography and history.
       2 ed.   By J. W. Hamilton and G. E. Tait.   With
       Bartholomew.   Toronto, [1963].
       166 p.   col. maps.   29 cm.

4573 Deutscher Bücherbund.
       Handatlas für Geographie und Geschichte.   By Hans
       Prechtl.   With Hölzel.   Stuttgart, Hamburg, [1968].
       96 p.   col. maps.   32 cm.

4574 Deutscher Taschenbuch Verlag.
       Atlas historique.   München, 1964.
       601 p.   col. maps.   18 cm.

4575 Deutscher Taschenbuch Verlag.
      DTV Atlas zur Weltgeschichte. München, 1964-66.
      2 vol. col. maps. 18 cm.

4576 Deutscher Taschenbuch Verlag.
      DTV Atlas zur Weltgeschichte. München, 1965.
      1 vol. col. maps. 18 cm.

4577 Deutscher Taschenbuch Verlag.
      DTV Atlas zur Weltgeschichte. München, [1966].
      1 vol. col. maps. 18 cm.

4578 Djambatan.
      An historical atlas of China. By Albert Herrmann.
      Amsterdam, 1966.
      88 p. col. maps. 30 cm.

4579 Djambatan.
      Atlas of the Arab world and the Middle East.
      Amsterdam, [1960].
      55 p. col. maps. 35 cm.

4580 Djambatan.
      Atlas of the Arab world and the Middle East.
      Amsterdam, [1966].
      55 p. col. maps. 35 cm.

4581 Djambatan.
      Atlas sedjarah. By Muhammad Yamin. Amster-
      dam, 1956.
      88 p. col. maps. 29 cm.

4582 Djambatan.
      Historical atlas of the Muslim people. By R.
      Roolvink. Amsterdam, 1957.
      40 p. col. maps. 30 cm.

4583 Dom Verlag.
      Kirchenhistorischer atlas von Österreich. By E.
      Bernleithner. Wien, 1966—
      in parts. col. maps. 63 cm.

4584 Dorsey Press.
      American expansion; a book of maps. By Randall
      D. Sale and Edwin D. Karn. Homewood, Ill., 1962.
      27 p. col. maps. 28 cm.

4585 Doubleday.
Discovery and Exploration; an atlas-history of man's
wanderings. By Frank Debenham. New York, 1960.
272 p. col. maps. 32 cm.

4586 Dutton, E. P. & Co.
Classical atlas. By J. O. Thomson. New York,
[1965].
61 p. col. maps. 20 cm.

4587 Dutton, E. P. & Co.
Everyman's classical atlas, with an essay on the
development of ancient geographical knowledge and
theory. By J. Oliver Thomson. 3 ed. New York,
[1961].
125 p. col. maps. 20 cm.

4588 Ecuador. Ministerio de Relaciones Exteriores.
Ecuador. Atlas histórico-geográfico. By Juan
Morales y Eloy. Quito, 1952.
1 vol. col. maps. 18 cm.

4589 Ediciones Condarco.
Atlas histórico de América. La Paz, 1968.
186 p. col. maps. 26 cm.

4590 Edinburgh University Press.
An historical atlas of China. By Albert Herrmann.
Edinburgh, [1966].
88 p. col. maps. 30 cm.

4591 Editions Bordas.
Atlas général Bordas historique et géographique.
Paris, 1964.
164 p. col. maps. 30.5 cm.

4592 Editions Bordas.
Atlas général Bordas; historique et géographique.
Paris, [1966].
208 p. col. maps. 33 cm.

4593 Editions Bordas.
Nouvel atlas historique. By Pierre Serryn and
René Blasselle. Paris, [1957].
72 p. col. maps. 33 cm.

4594 Editions Meddens.
Atlas historique et culturel del l'Europe. By

Fernand Vercauteren. Bruxelles, [1962].
245 p. col. maps. 35 cm.

4595 Editions R. de Rouck.
Atlas géographique et historique du Congo Belge et
des territoires sous mandat du Ruanda-Urundi. 4 ed.
Bruxelles, [1951].
11 p. col. maps. 36 cm.

4596 Éditions Sequoia.
Atlas de la grande armée. By J. C. Quennevat.
Paris, [1969].
304 p. col. maps. 27.5 cm.

4597 Éditions Sequoia.
Atlas de l'antiquité classique. By A. A. M. van
der Heyden. Paris, [1961].
218 p. col. maps. 36 cm.

4598 Editôra F. T. D.
Atlas histórico para o estudo da história universal.
By José A. de Carvalho Batalha-Marista. São
Paulo, [1966].
67 p. col. maps. 29 cm.

4599 Editorial Luis Vives, S. A.
Atlas historico Edelvives. Zaragoza, [1962].
68 p. col. maps. 21 cm.

4600 Editorial Progreso.
Atlas historico universal y de México. 1 ed. By
J. Jesús Carabes Pedroasa and Roberto Torres
Padilla. Mexico, 1963.
48 p. col. maps. 27 cm.

4601 Editorial Teide.
Atlas de historia de España. 3 ed. By Jaime
Vicéns Vives. Barcelona, [1963].
74 p. col. maps. 26 cm.

4602 Editorial Teide.
Atlas de historia universal. By Jaime Vicéns Vives.
Barcelona, [1954].
2 vol. in 1. col. maps. 28 cm.

4603 Elsevier.
Atlas culturel et historique de Belgique. By Theo

Luykx. New York, 1954.
192 p. col. maps. 35 cm.

4604 Elsevier.
Atlas de la civilisation occidentale. By Frederik
van der Meer. Paris, 1952.
227 p. col. maps. 36 cm.

4605 Elsevier.
Atlas historique et culturel de la France. By
Jacques Boussard. Paris, [1957].
214 p. col. maps. 35 cm.

4606 Elsevier.
Atlas historique et culturel de la Russie et du
monde slave. By Pierre Kovalewsky. Paris, [1961].
216 p. col. maps. 35 cm.

4607 Elsevier.
Atlas historique et culturel de l'Europe. By
Fernand Vercauteren. Paris, [1962].
245 p. col. maps. 35 cm.

4608 Elsevier.
Atlas van de oudchristelijke wereld. By Frederik
van der Meer and Christine Mohrmann. Amsterdam, 1958.
215 p. col. maps. 36 cm.

4609 Elsevier.
Atlas van de Westerse beschaving. By Frederik van
der Meer. Amsterdam, 1951.
228 p. col. maps. 36 cm.

4610 Elsevier.
Atlas van het tweestromenland. By M. A. Beek.
Amsterdam, 1960.
163 p. col. maps. 36 cm.

4611 Elsevier.
Culturhistorische atlas van Belgie. By Theo Luykx.
Amsterdam, [1954].
226 p. col. maps. 36 cm.

4612 Elsevier.
Elseviers historische atlas. Amsterdam, Brussels,
1963.
278 p. col. maps. 28 cm.

4613 Elsevier.
    <u>Elseviers historische atlas.</u> 2 ed. By Sjoerd de
    Vries. Amsterdam, 1964.
    278 p. col. maps. 28 cm.

4614 Elsevier.
    <u>Elseviers historische schoolatlas.</u> Amsterdam, 1963.
    176 p. col. maps. 27 cm.

4615 Elsevier.
    <u>Kleine atlas van de antieke wereld.</u> By H. H.
    Scullard and A. A. M. van der Heyden. Amster-
    dam, 1962.
    239 p. col. maps. 21 cm.

4616 Faber & Faber.
    <u>An historical atlas of Wales.</u> 2 ed. By William
    Rees. Cardiff, 1951.
    70 p. 26 cm.

4617 Faber & Faber.
    <u>An historical atlas of Wales.</u> By William Rees.
    London, [1959].
    71 p. 26 cm.

4618 Faber & Faber.
    <u>An historical atlas of Wales from early to modern</u>
    <u>times.</u> London, 1966.
    73 p. 26 cm.

4619 Faber & Faber.
    <u>An historical atlas of Wales from early to modern</u>
    <u>times.</u> 3 ed. London, 1967.
    73 p. 26 cm.

4620 Flemmings Verlag.
    <u>2000 Jahre Europäische Geschichte.</u> Geschichtsatlas.
    By A. Koselleck. Hamburg, 1957.
    35 p. col. maps. 31 cm.

4621 Generalstabens litografiska anstalt.
    <u>En delad värld; världspolitisk atlas.</u> By Tor S.
    Åhman and Gunnar Schalin. Stockholm, [1963].
    64 p. col. maps. 22 cm.

4622 Generalstabens litografiska anstalt.
    <u>En delad värld; världspolitisk atlas.</u> By Tor S.

Ahman.   Stockholm, [1965].
80 p.   col. maps.   22 cm.

4623 Generalstabens litografiska anstalt.
En delad värld.   Världspolitisk atlas.   3 ed.   By
Tor S. Ahman.   Stockholm, [1966].
96 p.   col. maps.   22 cm.

4624 Generalstabens litografiska anstalt.
Tid och rum; världhistorisk atlas.   By Alf Aberg.
Stockholm, [1963].
126 p.   col. maps.   23 cm.

4625 Generalstabens litografiska anstalt.
Tid och rum.   Världshistorisk atlas.   2 ed.   By
Alf Aberg.   Stockholm, 1967.
126 p.   col. maps.   23 cm.

4626 Ginn & Co.
Atlas of American history.   By D. B. Cole.   Boston,
[1963].
150 p.   col. maps.   24 cm.

4627 Ginn & Co.
Atlas of American history.   By D. B. Cole.   Boston,
[1968].
150 p.   col. maps.   24 cm.

4628 Ginn & Co.
Atlas of world history.   By Edward H. Merrill and
John L. Teall.   Boston, [1965].
173 p.   col. maps.   24 cm.

4629 Gjellerups Forlag.
Historisk verdensatlas.   By H. C. Eskildsen.
København, 1969.
51 p.   col. maps.   33 cm.

4630 Gwasg Prifysgol Cymru.
Atlas hanesyddol o Gymru.   By James Idwal Jones.
Caerdydd, 1952.
99 p.   25 cm.

4631 Haack, Hermann.
Orbis terrarum antiquus in scholarum usum
descriptus.   Gotha, 1964.
16 p.   col. maps.   30 cm.

4632 Hachette.
   Atlas classique de géographie ancienne et moderne.
   By F. Schrader and L. Gallouédec. Paris, [1953].
   110 p. col. maps. 32 cm.

4633 Hachette.
   Atlas classique de géographie ancienne et moderne.
   By F. Schrader and L. Gallouédec. Paris, [1957].
   126 p. col. maps. 32 cm.

4634 Hammond, C. S. & Co., Inc.
   Advanced reference atlas, the modern, medieval and
   ancient world. New York, 1950.
   1 vol. col. maps. 32 cm.

4635 Hammond, C. S. & Co., Inc.
   American history atlas. Maplewood, N. J., 1963.
   40 p. col. maps. 31 cm.

4636 Hammond, C. S. & Co., Inc.
   American history atlas. Maplewood, N. J., 1965.
   40 p. col. maps. 31 cm.

4637 Hammond, C. S. & Co., Inc.
   Atlas of world war II. 20th commemorative ed.
   Maplewood, N. J., [1965].
   16 p. col. maps. 22 cm.

4638 Hammond, C. S. & Co., Inc.
   Hammond's historical atlas. New York, 1950.
   40 p. col. maps. 31 cm.

4639 Hammond, C. S. & Co., Inc.
   Hammond's historical atlas. New York, 1951.
   40 p. col. maps. 31 cm.

4640 Hammond, C. S. & Co., Inc.
   Hammond's historical atlas. New York, 1953.
   40 p. col. maps. 31 cm.

4641 Hammond, C. S. & Co., Inc.
   Hammond's historical atlas. New York, 1954.
   40 p. col. maps. 31 cm.

4642 Hammond, C. S. & Co., Inc.
   Hammond historical atlas. Maplewood, N. J., 1960.
   48 p. col. maps. 31 cm.

4643 Hammond, C. S. & Co., Inc.
     Hammond historical atlas.   Maplewood, N. J., 1963.
     48 p. col. maps. 31 cm.

4644 Hammond, C. S. & Co., Inc.
     Hammond historical atlas.   Maplewood, N. J., 1965.
     48 p. col. maps. 31 cm.

4645 Hammond, C. S. & Co., Inc.
     Hammond's historical atlas.   U. S. Air Force
     Academy ed. New York, 1955.
     79 p. col. maps. 31 cm.

4646 Hammond, C. S. & Co., Inc.
     Hammond's historical atlas.   U. S. Naval Academy
     ed. New York, 1955.
     97 p. col. maps. 31 cm.

4647 Hammond, C. S. & Co., Inc.
     Hammond's historical atlas.   U. S. Naval Academy
     ed. Maplewood, N. J., 1964.
     90 p. col. maps. 31 cm.

4648 Hammond, C. S. & Co., Inc.
     Hammond's world history wall atlas.   New York,
     1953.
     24 p. col. maps. 73 cm.

4649 Hammond, C. S. & Co., Inc.
     New international world atlas; the modern, medieval
     and ancient world. New York, [1950].
     124 p. col. maps. 32 cm.

4650 Hammond, C. S. & Co., Inc.
     New international world atlas; the modern, medieval
     and ancient world. New York, [1952].
     120 p. col. maps. 32 cm.

4651 Hammond, C. S. & Co., Inc.
     New international world atlas; the modern, medieval
     and ancient world. New York, [1953].
     120 p. col. maps. 32 cm.

4652 Hammond, C. S. & Co., Inc.
     New international world atlas; the modern, medieval
     and ancient world. Maplewood, N. J., [1956].
     1 vol. col. maps. 32 cm.

4653 Hammond, C. S. & Co., Inc.
   The march of civilization in maps and pictures.
   New York, 1950.
   102 p.   col. maps.   31 cm.

4654 Hammond, C. S. & Co., Inc.
   The march of civilization in maps and pictures.
   Maplewood, N. J., 1962.
   280 p.   col. maps.   32 cm.

4655 Hammond, C. S. & Co., Inc.
   The march of civilization in maps and pictures.
   Maplewood, N. J., 1963.
   280 p.   col. maps.   32 cm.

4656 Hammond, Inc.
   American history atlas.   Maplewood, N. J., 1968.
   40 p.   col. maps.   31 cm.

4657 Hammond, Inc.
   History atlas of America.   Maplewood, N. J., [1969].
   31 p.   col. maps.   28 cm.

4658 Hammond, Inc.
   Historical atlas of the world.   Maplewood, N. J.,
   1968.
   48 p.   col. maps.   31 cm.

4659 Hammond, Inc.
   United States history atlas.   Maplewood, N. J.,
   [1968].
   64 p.   col. maps.   31 cm.

4660 Harper & Row.
   Historical atlas of religion in America.   1 ed.   By
   Edwin Scott Gaustad.   New York, [1962].
   179 p.   col. maps.   31 cm.

4661 Harvard University Press.
   Historical atlas of the Muslim people.   By R. Rool-
   vink.   Cambridge, Mass., 1957.
   40 p.   col. maps.   30 cm.

4662 Heinemann.
   An atlas of Russian and East European history.   By
   Arthur E. Adams and William O. McCagg.   London,
   1966.
   204 p.   21 cm.

4663 Heinemann.
       An atlas of Russian and East European history. By
       Arthur E. Adams.   London, 1967.
       204 p.   21 cm.

4664 Hölder, Pichler, Tempsky.
       Atlas zur allgemeinen und Österreichischen
       Geschichte. By Wilhem Franz Schier. Wien, [1951].
       68 p. col. maps. 28 cm.

4665 Hölder, Pichler, Tempsky.
       Atlas zur allgemeinen und Österreichischen
       Geschichte. By Wilhelm Franz Schier. Wien,
       [1958].
       63 p. col. maps. 28 cm.

4666 Hölder, Pichler, Tempsky.
       Atlas zur allgemeinen und Österreichischen
       Geschichte. 7 ed. By Wilhelm Franz Schier.
       Wien, 1964.
       63 p. col. maps. 28 cm.

4667 Hölder, Pichler, Tempsky.
       Atlas zur allgemeinen und Österreichischen
       Geschichte. 8 ed. By Wilhem Franz Schier.
       Wien, [1966].
       68 p. col. maps. 28 cm.

4668 Hölder, Pichler, Tempsky.
       Historischer Schul-Atlas zur allgemeinen und
       Österreichischen Geschichte. By F. W. Putzger.
       Wien, [1961].
       146 p. col. maps. 27 cm.

4669 Hölder, Pichler, Tempsky.
       Historischer Schul-Atlas zur allgemeinen und
       Österreichischen Geschichte. 43 ed. By F. W.
       Putzger. Wien, 1963.
       146 p. col. maps. 27 cm.

4670 Holt.
       Historical atlas of the United States.   By Clifford
       L. Lord. New York, [1953].
       258 p. col. maps. 28 cm.

4671 Hölzel, Ed. Verlag.
       Tarih atlasi, Faik Hesit Unat. Wien, 1964. (In

Turkish).
62 p. col. maps. 24.5 cm.

4672 Hsin ya shu tien.
Chung-kuo li shih ti t'u. [Historical atlas of China].
By Shu-shih Wang. Shanghai, 1953.
6 p. col. maps. 40 cm.

4673 Hughes & Son.
An atlas of Wales. By J. Idwal Jones. Wrexham,
[1957].
2 vol. 29 cm.

4674 Hulton Educational Publications, Ltd.
A sketch-map history of West Africa. By Norah
Latham. London, [1959].
80 p. 25 cm.

4675 Humphrey, H. A., Ltd.
The New Israel atlas. By Zev Vilnay. London,
1968.
114 p. col. maps. 30 cm.

4676 Indian Book Depot & Map House.
The new rashtriya atlas, geographical and historical.
By Biba Singh Kaushal. Delhi, [1951].
120 p. col. maps. 28 cm.

4677 Israel. Department of Surveys.
Atlas of Israel. (In Hebrew). Jerusalem, 1956-
1964.
1 vol. col. maps. 47.5 cm.

4678 Israel. Ministry of Labour.
Atlas of Israel; cartography, physical geography,
human and economic geography, history. 2 ed.
Jerusalem, 1970.
296 p. col. maps. 49 cm.

4679 Israel. Tseva haganah le-Yisrael.
Atlas geografi-histori shel Erets-Yisrael. By
Michael Ari-Yonah. Jerusalem, [195-].
60 p. col. maps. 36 cm.

4680 Israel University Press.
The new Israel atlas; Bible to present. By Zev
Vilnay. Jerusalem, 1968.
112 p. col. maps. 30 cm.

4681 Istituto Geografico De Agostini.
     Atlante storico. Novara, [1942-54].
     3 vol. col. maps. 33 cm.

4682 Istituto Geografico De Agostini.
     Atlante storico. Novara, 1963.
     294 p. col. maps. 30 cm.

4683 Istituto Geografico De Agostini.
     Atlante storico per la scuola media. By Ugo
     Dèttore. Novara, [1964-1966].
     3 vol. col. maps. 30 cm.

4684 Istituto Geografico De Agostini.
     Grande atlante geografico, economico, storico.
     Novara, 1965.
     1 vol. col. maps. 42 cm.

4685 Istituto Geografico De Agostini.
     Piccolo atlante storico. Novara, 1963.
     137 p. col. maps. 26 cm.

4686 Istituto geografico editoriale italiano.
     Atlante storico e geografico elementare. By
     Riccardo Riccardi. Roma, [1954].
     16 p. col. maps. 26 cm.

4687 Istituto italiano per l'Africa.
     L'Africa nei suoi aspetti geografici, storici ed
     umani. By Luchino Franciosa. Roma, [1953].
     149 p. col. maps. 30 cm.

4688 Italgeo.
     Via maestra atlante storico ad uso della scuola
     media e avviamento al lavoro. By G. Mori.
     Milano, 1951.
     50 p. col. maps. 29 cm.

4689 Johnston, W. & A. K.
     Atlas of world history. Edinburgh, 1950.
     40 p. col. maps. 25 cm.

4690 Juta & Co., Ltd.
     An historical atlas for South African schools. By
     W. Dale and T. A. Rennard. Cape Town, Johannes-
     burg, [195-].
     47 p. col. maps. 18 cm.

4691 Kanaat Yayinlari.
Tarih atlasi. By Faik Reşit Unat. Istanbul, [1958].
56 p. col. maps. 25 cm.

4692 Kanaat Yayinlari.
Tarih atlasi. Genişletilmis basim. By Farik Reşit
Unat. Istanbul, [1967].
56 p. col. maps. 25 cm.

4693 Kartografiai Vallalat.
Tórténelmi atlasz. By Radó Sandor. Budapest,
1963.
32 p. col. maps. 29 cm.

4694 Kartográfiai Vállalat.
Tórténelmi atlasz. 6 ed. Budapest, [1965].
32 p. col. maps. 29 cm.

4695 Keysersche Verlagsbuchhandlung, G. M. B. H.
Keysers Handatlas für Geographie und Geschichte.
With Hölzel. München, [1967].
96 p. col. maps. 31 cm.

4696 Ksiaznica-Atlas.
Maly atlas historiczny. By Czestaw Nanke.
Wroclaw, 1950.
12 p. col. maps. 30 cm.

4697 Ksiaznica-Atlas.
Maly atlas historicny. By Czestaw Nanke.
Wroclaw, 1951.
12 p. col. maps. 30 cm.

4698 Lehrmittel Verlag.
Atlas zur Weltgeschichte. By Karl Leonhardt.
Offenburg, 1951.
34 p. col. maps. 35 cm.

4699 Liga Chileno-Alemana.
Atlas historico de Chile. By Pedro Cunill Grau.
Santiago de Chile, 1961.
34 p. col. maps. 30 cm.

4700 Liga Chileno-Alemana.
Atlas historico de Chile. 2 ed. By Pedro Cunill
Grau. Santiago de Chile, [1961].
34 p. col. maps. 30 cm.

4701 List, P.
      Harms Geschichts-und Kulturatlas.   56-59 ed.   By
      Hans Zeissig. München, 1964.
      128 p. col. maps. 27 cm.

4702 List, P.
      Harms Geschichts-und Kulturatlas.   By Hanz Zeissig.
      München, [1968].
      120 p. col. maps. 27 cm.

4703 List, P.
      Harms kleiner Geschichtsatlas.   München, 1963.
      72 p. col. maps. 27 cm.

4704 List, P.
      Harms kleiner Geschichtatlas.   München, 1965.
      1 vol. col. maps. 27 cm.

4705 List, P.
      List Geschichte unserer Welt in Karten und
      Dokumenten. München, [1965].
      196 p. col. maps. 29 cm.

4706 Livraria Sá da Costa.
      Novo atlas escolar português, histórico-geográfico.
      5 ed. By João Soares. Lisboa, [1954].
      80 p. col. maps. 34 cm.

4707 Livravia Sá da Costa.
      Novo atlas escolar português; histórico-geográfico.
      7 ed. By João Soares. Lisboa, [1959].
      83 p. col. maps. 34 cm.

4708 Lux Verlag.
      Lux historischer Bildatlas.   Murnau, München,
      [1955].
      72 p. col. maps. 26 cm.

4709 Lux Verlag.
      Lux historischer Bildatlas.   Murnau, München,
      [1959].
      240 p. col. maps. 19 cm.

4710 Machuca Martinez, Marcelino.
      Mapas históricos del Paraguay gigante.   Asunción,
      [1951].
      44 p. col. maps. 27 cm.

4711 Macmillan & Co., Ltd.
     Atlas of the Arab World and Middle East.   London,
     1960.
     68 p.   col. maps.   35 cm.

4712 Macmillan Co.
     American history atlas.   By Martin Gilbert.   New
     York, 1968.
     112 p.   24 cm.

4713 Macmillan Co.
     American history atlas.   By Martin Gilbert.   New
     York, 1969.
     112 p.   24 cm.

4714 Macmillan Co.
     British history atlas.   By Martin Gilbert.   New
     York, [1969].
     118 p.   24 cm.

4715 Macmillan Co.
     Jewish history atlas.   By Martin Gilbert.   New
     York, [1969].
     126 p.   24 cm.

4716 Macmillan Co.
     Recent history atlas: 1870 to the present day.   By
     Martin Gilbert.   New York, 1966.
     130 p.   24 cm.

4717 Macmillan Co.
     Recent history atlas: 1870 to the present day.   By
     Martin Gilbert.   New York, 1969.
     130 p.   24 cm.

4718 Martindale Press.
     Map guide to modern history; 1789 to the present.
     By B. J. Price.   Sydney, 1967.
     96 p.   25 cm.

4719 McGraw-Hill Book Co.
     The New Israel atlas: Bible to present.   By Zev
     Vilnay.   New York, 1969.
     112 p.   col. maps.   30 cm.

4720 Methuen.
     An atlas of Latin American affairs.   By Ronald M.

Schneider.   London, 1966.
136 p.   20.5 cm.

4721 Methuen.
    An atlas of world affairs.   1 ed.   By Andrew Boyd.
    London, 1957.
    160 p.   21 cm.

4722 Methuen.
    An atlas of world affairs.   2 ed.   By Andrew Boyd.
    London, 1959.
    160 p.   21 cm.

4723 Methuen.
    An atlas of world affairs. 3 ed.   By Andrew Boyd.
    London, 1960.
    160 p.   21 cm.

4724 Methuen.
    An atlas of world affairs.   4 ed.   By Andrew Boyd.
    London, 1962.
    160 p.   21 cm.

4725 Methuen.
    An atlas of world affairs.   5 ed.   By Andrew Boyd.
    London, 1964.
    160 p.   21 cm.

4726 Methuen.
    An atlas of world affairs.   6 ed.   By Andrew Boyd.
    London, 1970.
    176 p.   21 cm.

4727 México.   Fondo de cultura economica.
    Atlas mexicano de la conquista, historia geográfica
    en 40 cartas.   1 ed.   By Jesus Amaya.   Mexico,
    1958.
    42 p.   col. maps.   35 cm.

4728 Minerva italica.
    Atlante storico.   By Tiberio Menin.   Bergamo, 1968.
    3 vol.   col. maps.   24 cm.

4729 Mohn.
    Bildatlas der klassichen Welt.   1 ed.   By A. A. M.
    van der Heyden.   Gütersloh, 1960.
    222 p.   col. maps.   36 cm.

4730 National Trust.
  The National Trust atlas showing places of historic,
  architectual & scenic interest in England, Wales and
  Northern Ireland. With Bartholomew. London, 1964.
  80 p. col. maps. 25 cm.

4731 National Trust.
  The National Trust maps. London, 1957.
  48 p. 22 cm.

4732 Nationale boekhandel.
  Geskiedenis atlas vir Suid-Afrika. 2 ed. By A. J.
  Böeseken. Kaapstad, [1953].
  92 p. 31 cm.

4733 Nelson, Thomas & Sons, Ltd.
  An atlas of world history. By S. de Vries, T.
  Luykx and W. O. Henderson. London, 1965.
  183 p. col. maps. 28 cm.

4734 Nelson, Thomas & Sons, Ltd.
  An historical atlas of Canada. By D. G. G. Kerr.
  Toronto, [1960].
  120 p. col. maps. 31 cm.

4735 Nelson, Thomas & Sons, Ltd.
  An historical atlas of Canada. 2 ed. By D. G. G.
  Kerr. Don Mills, Ont., [1966].
  120 p. col. maps. 31 cm.

4736 Nelson, Thomas & Sons, Ltd.
  Atlas of Mesopotamia. By D. R. Welsh and H. H.
  Rowley. London, 1962.
  164 p. col. maps. 36 cm.

4737 Nelson, Thomas & Sons, Ltd.
  Atlas of the classical world. By A. A. M. van der
  Heyden and H. H. Scullard. London, New York,
  1959.
  221 p. col. maps. 36 cm.

4738 Nelson, Thomas & Sons, Ltd.
  Atlas of the early Christian world. By F. van der
  Meer and Christine Mohrmann. London, 1958.
  215 p. col. maps. 36 cm.

4739 Nelson, Thomas & Sons, Ltd.
  Shorter atlas of the classical world. By H. H.

Scullard and A. A. M. van der Heyden.   London,
[1962].
239 p.   col. maps.   21 cm.

4740 N. I. Sh. Mjete Mesimore e Sportive "Hamid Shijaku."
Atlas i luftes nacional çlirimtare.   Tiranë, 1969.
38 p.   col. maps.   32 cm.

4741 Noordhoff, P.
Atlas algemene en vaderlandse geschiedenis.   17 ed.
Groningen, 1963.
96 p.   col. maps.   29.5 cm.

4742 Normanns forlag.
Normanns historiske atlas.   Odense, 1965.
36 p.   col. maps.   28.5 cm.

4743 Oceana Publications.
Focus on maps of world crisis.   By Jack Bloomfield
and Leo Martin.   Dobbs Ferry, N. Y., 1963.
90 p.   29 cm.

4744 Oldenburger Verlagshaus.
Kleiner Geschichtsatlas.   By Renate Riemeck.
Oldenburg, [1950].
32 p.   22 cm.

4745 Oxford University Press.
A map history of Australia.   By Ian Wynd and Joyce
Wood.   Melbourne, [1963].
60 p.   col. maps.   25 cm.

4746 Oxford University Press.
An historical atlas of the Indian peninsula.   Madras,
New York, [1953].
141 p.   col. maps.   25 cm.

4747 Oxford University Press.
An historical atlas of the Indian peninsula.   2 ed.
Madras, New York, 1959.
141 p.   col. maps.   25 cm.

4748 Oxford University Press.
Atlas of American history.   By Edward Whiting Fox.
New York, 1964.
48 p.   col. maps.   26 cm.

4749 Oxford University Press.
    Atlas of American history. By J. T. Adams and
    R. V. Coleman. London, 1967.
    372 p. col. maps. 23.5 cm.

4750 Oxford University Press.
    Atlas of European history. By Edward Whiting Fox.
    London, 1957.
    64 p. col. maps. 26 cm.

4751 Oxford University Press.
    Atlas of European history. By Edward Whiting Fox.
    London, [1964].
    64 p. col. maps. 26 cm.

4752 Oxford University Press.
    Atlas of European history. By Edward Whiting Fox.
    New York, 1968.
    76 p. col. maps. 26 cm.

4753 Oxford University Press.
    Atlas of European history. By E. W. Fox and H. S.
    Deighton. London, 1969.
    96 p. col. maps. 26 cm.

4754 Oxford University Press.
    Historical atlas and gazetteer. By Arnold J. Toyn-
    bee and Edward D. Myers. London, New York,
    Toronto, 1959.
    257 p. col. maps. 26 cm.

4755 Oxford University Press.
    The Australasian school atlas, physical, political,
    economic and historical. 4 ed. With Bartholomew.
    Melbourne, [1954].
    84 p. col. maps. 28 cm.

4756 Oxford University Press.
    The Australasian school atlas, physical, political,
    economic and historical. 4 ed. With Bartholomew.
    Melbourne, [1959].
    68 p. col. maps. 28 cm.

4757 Penguin Books.
    The Penguin atlas of medieval history. By Colin
    McEvedy. Harmondsworth, Middlesex, [1961].
    96 p. col. maps. 23 cm.

4758 Pfahl Verlag.
    Hansa Universal atlas. 1 ed. By Oswald Muris.
    Baden-Baden, 1957.
    480 p. col. maps. 24 cm.

4759 Pfahl Verlag.
    Hansa Weltatlas. 8 ed. By Oswald Muris and Hans
    Kleinert. Laupheim, 1954.
    446 p. col. maps. 24 cm.

4760 Phil-Asian Publishers, Inc.
    Atlas of the Philippines. By Robert S. Hendry.
    Manila, 1959.
    228 p. col. maps. 48 cm.

4761 Philip, George & Son, Ltd.
    Muir's historical atlas. London, 1964.
    1 vol. col. maps. 29 cm.

4762 Philip, George & Son, Ltd.
    Muir's historical atlas: ancient, medieval and
    modern. By George Goodall and R. F. Treharne.
    London, [195-].
    1 vol. col. maps. 29 cm.

4763 Philip, George & Son, Ltd.
    Muir's historical atlas: ancient, medieval and
    modern. By R. F. Treharne and Harold Fullard.
    London, [1962].
    1 vol. col. maps. 29 cm.

4764 Philip, George & Son, Ltd.
    Muir's historical atlas, ancient, medieval, and
    modern. By R. F. Treharne and Harold Fullard.
    London, 1963.
    127 p. col. maps. 28 cm.

4765 Philip, George & Son, Ltd.
    Muir's historical atlas, medieval and modern. By
    George Goodall and R. F. Treharne. London, 1952.
    68 p. col. maps. 29 cm.

4766 Philip, George & Son, Ltd.
    Muir's historical atlas, mediaeval & modern. By
    George Goodall and R. F. Treharne. London, 1956.
    68 p. col. maps. 29 cm.

4767 Philip, George & Son, Ltd.
 Muir's historical atlas, mediaeval & modern. 8 ed.
 By George Goodall and R. F. Treharne. London,
 1959.
 68 p. col. maps. 29 cm.

4768 Philip, George & Son, Ltd.
 Muir's historical atlas, medieval & modern. 11 ed.
 London, 1969.
 1 vol. col. maps. 29 cm.

4769 Philip, George & Son, Ltd.
 Muir's new school historical atlas. 22 ed. By
 R. F. Treharne and Harold Fullard. London, [1966].
 68 p. col. maps. 29 cm.

4770 Philip, George & Son, Ltd.
 New school atlas of universal history. 21 ed. By
 R. F. Treharne and Harold Fullard. London, [1961].
 68 p. col. maps. 29 cm.

4771 Philip, George & Son, Ltd.
 Philip's historical atlas of Canada. By J. W.
 Chalmers, W. J. Eccles and H. Fullard. London,
 1966.
 48 p. col. maps. 28 cm.

4772 Philip, George & Son, Ltd.
 Philip's atlas of modern history. London, [1964].
 48 p. col. maps. 28 cm.

4773 Philip, George & Son, Ltd.
 Philip's atlas of modern history. 3 ed. London,
 [1967].
 48 p. col. maps. 28 cm.

4774 Philip, George & Son, Ltd.
 Philip's intermediate historical atlas for schools.
 21 ed. London, 1964.
 41 p. col. maps. 23 cm.

4775 Philip, George & Son, Ltd.
 Philip's intermediate historical atlas for schools.
 22 ed. London, 1969.
 41 p. col. maps. 23 cm.

4776 Philip, George & Son, Ltd.
 Shepherd's historical atlas. 9 ed. London, 1967.

227 p.   col.   maps.   26.5 cm.

4777 Philip, George & Son, Ltd.
      Wesley's historical atlas of the United States.   3 ed.
      By Edgar Bruce Wesley.   London, 1965.
      96 p.   col.   maps.   28 cm.

4778 Philip, George & Son, Ltd.
      Wesley's historical atlas of the United States.   By
      Edgar Bruce Wesley.   London, 1966.
      96 p.   col.   maps.   28 cm.

4779 Poland.   Akademia nauk.
      Atlas historyczny Polski.   Warszawa, [1958].
      2 vol.   col.   maps.   31 cm.

4780 Poland.   Akademia nauk.
      Historia Polski.   1 ed.   Warszawa, [1955]-63.
      3 vol.   col.   maps.   25 cm.

4781 Poland.   Centralny urzad geodezii i kartografii.
      Maly atlas historiczny.   Warszawa, 1955.
      12 p.   col.   maps.   30 cm.

4782 Poland.   Państwowe przedsiębiorstwo wydawnictw
      kartograficznych.
      Atlas do historii starozytnej.   Warszawa, 1963.
      1 vol.   col.   maps.   30 cm.

4783 Poland.   Państwowe przedsiębiorstwo wydawnictw
      kartograficznych.
      Atlas historyczny Polski.   Warszawa, 1967.
      105 p.   col.   maps.   31 cm.

4784 Poland.   Państwowe przedsiębiorstwo wydawnictw
      kartograficznych.
      Maly atlas historyczny.   Warszawa, 1963.
      1 vol.   col.   maps.   30 cm.

4785 Poland.   Państwowe przedsiębiorstwo wydawnictw
      kartograficznych.
      Maly atlas historyczny.   Warszawa, 1964.
      1 vol.   col.   maps.   30 cm.

4786 Poland.   Państwowe przedsiębiorstwo wydawnictw
      kartograficznych.
      Maly atlas historyczny.   Warszawa, 1965.
      1 vol.   col.   maps.   30 cm.

4787 Politikens forlag.
      Politikens historiske atlas. København, 1965.
      247 p. col. maps. 20.5 cm.

4788 Praeger, Frederick A.
      A military history and atlas of the Napoleonic Wars.
      By Vincent J. Esposito and John Robert Elting.
      New York, [1964].
      1 vol. col. maps. 37 cm.

4789 Praeger, Frederick A.
      An atlas of Africa. By J. F. Horrabin. New York,
      [1960].
      126 p. 21 cm.

4790 Praeger, Frederick A.
      An atlas of Africa. 2 ed. By J. F. Horrabin.
      New York, 1961.
      126 p. 21 cm.

4791 Praeger, Frederick A.
      An atlas of European affairs. By Norman J. G.
      Pounds. New York, 1964.
      142 p. 22 cm.

4792 Praeger, Frederick A.
      An atlas of Latin American affairs. By Ronald M.
      Schneider, New York, 1965.
      136 p. 22 cm.

4793 Praeger, Frederick A.
      An atlas of Middle Eastern affairs. By Norman J.
      G. Pounds and Robert C. Kingsbury. New York,
      London, 1963.
      117 p. 21 cm.

4794 Praeger, Frederick A.
      An atlas of Middle Eastern affairs. By Norman J.
      G. Pounds and Robert C. Kingsbury. New York,
      London, 1966.
      117 p. 21 cm.

4795 Praeger, Frederick A.
      An atlas of Russian and East European history. By
      Arthur E. Adams, Ian M. Matley, William O.
      McCagg. New York, 1966.
      204 p. 21 cm.

4796 Praeger, Frederick A.
     An atlas of world affairs. 1 ed. By Andrew Boyd.
     New York, [1957].
     160 p. 21 cm.

4797 Praeger, Frederick A.
     An atlas of world affairs. 2 ed. By Andrew Boyd.
     New York, 1959.
     160 p. 21 cm.

4798 Praeger, Frederick A.
     An atlas of world affairs. 3 ed. By Andrew Boyd.
     New York, 1960.
     160 p. 21 cm.

4799 Praeger, Frederick A.
     An atlas of world affairs. By Andrew Boyd. New
     York, [1962].
     160 p. 21 cm.

4800 Praeger, Frederick A.
     An atlas of world affairs. 4 ed. By Andrew Boyd.
     New York, 1963.
     160 p. 21 cm.

4801 Praeger, Frederick A.
     An atlas of world affairs. 5 ed. By Andrew Boyd.
     New York, 1964.
     160 p. 21 cm.

4802 Praeger, Frederick A.
     The West Point atlas of American wars. By Vincent
     J. Esposito. New York, [1959].
     2 vol. col. maps. 37 cm.

4803 Praeger, Frederick A.
     The West Point atlas of the Civil War. By Vincent
     J. Esposito. New York, [1962].
     1 vol. col. maps. 37 cm.

4804 Princeton University Press.
     Atlas of Islamic history. 1 ed. By Harry W.
     Hazard. Princeton, N. J., 1951.
     49 p. col. maps. 38 cm.

4805 Princeton University Press.
     Atlas of Islamic history. 2 ed. By Harry W.

Hazard. Princeton, N. J., 1952.
49 p. col. maps. 38 cm.

4806 Princeton University Press.
Atlas of Islamic history. 3 ed. By Harry W.
Hazard. Princeton, N. J., 1954.
49 p. col. maps. 38 cm.

4807 Rand McNally & Co.
Historical atlas of the Holy Land. By Emil G.
Kraeling. Chicago, 1959.
88 p. col. maps. 26 cm.

4808 Rand McNally & Co.
Historical atlas of the world. By R. R. Palmer.
Chicago, 1961.
40 p. col. maps. 35 cm.

4809 Rand McNally & Co.
Rand McNally atlas of world history. By R. R.
Palmer. Chicago, [1957].
216 p. col. maps. 27.5 cm.

4810 Rand McNally & Co.
Rand McNally atlas of world history. By R. R.
Palmer. Chicago, 1965.
216 p. col. maps. 27.5 cm.

4811 Ryerson Press.
The world crisis in maps. By Dimitri J. Tosević.
Toronto, [1954].
127 p. col. maps. 25 cm.

4812 Salvador. Universidade Federal da Bahia, Centro de
Estudos Afro-Orientais.
Atlas histórico regional do mundo árabe. A
historical and regional atlas of the Arabic world.
San Salvador, [1969].
204 p. 25 cm.

4813 SAM.
Atlas geográfico escolar del Ecuador "SAM"; con las
básicas nociones historicas de la nacionalidad. By
Francisco Sampedro V. Quito, 1963-64.
39 p. col. maps. 31 cm.

4814 SAM.
Atlas histórico-geográfico del Ecuador. By Francisco

Sampedro V.   Quito, 1960.
78 p.   col. maps.   32 cm.

4815 Sauerländer, H. R.
Historischer atlas der Schweiz.   By Hektor Ammann
and Karl Schib.   Aarau, 1951.
95 p.   col. maps.   35 cm.

4816 Sauerländer, H. R.
Historischer atlas der Schweiz.   2 ed.   By Hektor
Ammann and Karl Schib.   Aarau, 1958.
103 p.   col. maps.   35 cm.

4817 Sauerländer, H. R.
Historischer atlas zur Welt-und Schweizer Geschichte.
6 ed.   By F. W. Putzger.   Aarau, [1965].
158 p.   col. maps.   27 cm.

4818 Scribner, C.
Atlas of American history.   By James T. Adams.
New York, [1966].
360 p.   26 cm.

4819 Siemens & Halske, A. G.
Welt- Texlex - Atlas.   München, 1963.
205 p.   col. maps.   30 cm.

4820 Söderström, Werner.
Historian kartasto.   1 ed.   By J. Gustafson.
Helsinki, 1961.
48 p.   col. maps.   29 cm.

4821 Söderström, Werner.
Historian kartasto.   2 ed.   By J. Gustafson.
Helsinki, 1963.
48 p.   col. maps.   29 cm.

4822 Spain.   Dirreción general de Marruecos y Colonias e
instituto de estudios Africanos.
Atlas histórico y geográfico de Africa Española.
Madrid, 1955.
197 p.   col. maps.   42 cm.

4823 Spencer Press, Inc.
5000 years of history; excerpts from the new 64 page
section of full color historical maps appearing in the
American Peoples Encyclopedia.   With Hammond.

Chicago, [1955].
32 p. col. maps. 25 cm.

4824 St. Martin's Press.
An outline atlas of world history. By R. R. Sellman. New York, [1970].
127 p. 28 cm.

4825 St. Martin's Press.
Atlas of the Arab World and Middle East. New
York, 1960.
68 p. col. maps. 35 cm.

4826 Stock.
Atlas historique. By H. Kinder and Pierre
Mougenot. Paris, 1968.
608 p. col. maps. 18 cm.

4827 Svenska bokförlaget.
Atlas till världhistorien. 3 ed. With Westermann.
Stockholm, 1967.
170 p. col. maps. 30 cm.

4828 Szapiro, J.
Atlas histori shel 'am Yisrael. Tel Aviv, 1960.
71 p. col. maps. 28 cm.

4829 T'ai-wan ta hsüeh.
Chien ming Chung-kuo yen ko ti t'u. [Simplified
historical atlas of China]. Taipei, [1952].
27 p. 26 cm.

4830 Teikoku-Shoin Co., Ltd.
Saishin Nihon shi seizu. Kaiteiban. [New detailed
historical atlas of Japan]. Tokyo, [1954].
51 p. col. maps. 26 cm.

4831 Učila.
Istorijski atlas za niže razrede srednijih škol.
Zagreb, 1954.
36 p. col. maps. 22 cm.

4832 University of Chicago Press.
Atlas of African prehistory. By J. Desmond Clark.
Chicago, 1967.
112 p. col. overlays. 61 cm.

4833 University Tutorial Press.
The map approach to African history. By A. M.
Healy and E. R. Vere-Hodge. London, [1959].
64 p. 21 cm.

4834 U. S. S. R. Glavnoe upravlenie geodezii i kartografii.
Atlas istorii geograficheskich otkrytii i issledovanii.
By K. B. Martova. Moskva, 1959.
109 p. col. maps. 34 cm.

4835 U. S. S. R. Glavnoe upravlenie geodezii i kartografii.
Atlas istorii srednich shkol. Moskva, 1966.
16 p. col. maps. 27 cm.

4836 U. S. S. R. Glavnoe upravlenie geodezii i kartografii.
Atlas istorii srednich vekov. Moskva, 1951.
65 p. col. maps. 31 cm.

4837 U. S. S. R. Glavnoe upravlenie geodezii i kartografii.
Atlas istorii srednich vekov. Moskva, 1953.
65 p. col. maps. 31 cm.

4838 U. S. S. R. Glavnoe upravlenie geodezii i kartografii.
Atlas istorii srednich vekov dlya VI klassa srednei
shkoly. Moskva, 1968.
16 p. col. maps. 26 cm.

4839 U. S. S. R. Glavnoe upravlenie geodezii i kartografii.
Atlas istorii srednich vekov dlya vosmilet shkoly.
Moskva, 1964.
16 p. col. maps. 27 cm.

4840 U. S. S. R. Glavnoe upravlenie geodezii i kartografii.
Atlas istorii SSSR. Moskva, 1968.
38 p. col. maps. 26 cm.

4841 U. S. S. R. Glavnoe upravlenie geodezii i kartografii.
Atlas istorii SSSR dlya IV klassa. Moskva, 1967.
12 p. col. maps. 26 cm.

4842 U. S. S. R. Glavnoe upravlenie geodezii i kartografii.
Atlas istorii SSSR dlya IV klassa. Moskva, 1968.
12 p. col. maps. 26 cm.

4843 U. S. S. R. Glavnoe upravlenie geodezii i kartografii.
Atlas istorii SSSR dlya VII klassa. Moskva, 1967.
18 p. col. maps. 26 cm.

4844 U. S. S. R. Glavnoe upravlenie geodezii i kartografii.
Atlas istorii SSSR dlya VII klassa. Moskva, 1968.
16 p. col. maps. 26 cm.

4845 U. S. S. R. Glavnoe upravlenie geodezii i kartografii.
Atlas istorii SSSR dlya VIII klassa. Moskva, 1967.
12 p. col. maps. 26 cm.

4846 U. S. S. R. Glavnoe upravlenie geodezii i kartografii.
Atlas istorii SSSR dlya VIII klassa. Moskva, 1968.
11 p. col. maps. 26 cm.

4847 U. S. S. R. Glavnoe upravlenie geodezii i kartografii.
Atlas istorii SSSR dlya IX klassa. Moskva, 1967.
20 p. col. maps. 26 cm.

4848 U. S. S. R. Glavnoe upravlenie geodezii i kartografii.
Atlas istorii SSSR dlya IX klassa. Moskva, 1968.
20 p. col. maps. 26 cm.

4849 U. S. S. R. Glavnoe upravlenie geodezii i kartografii.
Atlas istorii SSSR dlya 7go i 8go klassov. Moskva,
1964.
40 p. col. maps. 26 cm.

4850 U. S. S. R. Glavnoe upravlenie geodezii i kartografii.
Atlas istorii SSSR dlya 7go i 8go klassov. Moskva,
1967.
40 p. col. maps. 26 cm.

4851 U. S. S. R. Glavnoe upravlenie geodezii i kartografii.
Atlas istorii SSSR dlya V klassa srednei shkoly.
Moskva, 1968.
12 p. col. maps. 26 cm.

4852 U. S. S. R. Glavnoe upravlenie geodezii i kartografii.
Atlas istorii SSSR dlya srednei shkoly. Moskva,
1950.
1 vol. col. maps. 30 cm.

4853 U. S. S. R. Glavnoe upravlenie geodezii i kartografii.
Atlas istorii SSSR dlya srednei shkoly. Moskva,
1951.
1 vol. col. maps. 30 cm.

4854 U. S. S. R. Glavnoe upravlenie geodezii i kartografii.
Atlas istorii SSSR dlya srednei shkoly. Moskva, 1953.
2 vol. col. maps. 30 cm.

4855 U. S. S. R. Glavnoe upravlenie geodezii i kartografii.
     Atlas istorii SSSR dlya srednei shkoly. Moskva,
     1954.
     3 vol. col. maps. 30 cm.

4856 U. S. S. R. Glavnoe upravlenie geodezii i kartografii.
     Atlas istorii SSSR dlya srednei shkoly. Moskva,
     1955.
     2 vol. col. maps. 30 cm.

4857 U. S. S. R. Glavnoe upravlenie geodezii i kartografii.
     Atlas istorii SSSR dlya srednei shkoly. Moskva,
     1964.
     20 p. col. maps. 27 cm.

4858 U. S. S. R. Glavnoe upravlenie geodezii kartografii.
     Atlas istorii SSSR dlya srednei shkoly. Part I.
     Moskva, 1964.
     16 p. col. maps. 27 cm.

4859 U. S. S. R. Glavnoe upravlenie geodezii i kartografii.
     Atlas istorii SSSR dlya srednei shkoly. Part II.
     Moskva, 1964.
     12 p. col. maps. 27 cm.

4860 U. S. S. R. Glavnoe upravlenie geodezii i kartografii.
     Atlas Latinskoi Ameriki. Moskva, 1967.
     54 p. col. maps. 32 cm.

4861 U. S. S. R. Glavnoe upravlenie geodezii i kartografii.
     Atlas Latinskoi Ameriki. Moskva, 1968.
     54 p. col. maps. 32 cm.

4862 U. S. S. R. Glavnoe upravlenie geodezii i kartografii.
     Atlas noveishei istorii zarubezhnykh stran dlya
     srednei shkoly. Moskva, [1966].
     20 p. col. maps. 27 cm.

4863 U. S. S. R. Glavnoe upravlenie geodezii i kartografii.
     Atlas novoi istorii. By A. V. Yefimov. Moskva,
     1952-54.
     2 vol. col. maps. 30 cm.

4864 U. S. S. R. Glavnoe upravlenie geodezii i kartografii.
     Atlas novoi istorii. Part 1. Moskva, 1966.
     16 p. col. maps. 26 cm.

4865 U.S.S.R. Glavnoe upravlenie geodezii i kartografii.
Atlas novoi istorii. Part 2. Moskva, 1966.
16 p. col. maps. 26 cm.

4866 U.S.S.R. Glavnoe upravlenie geodezii i kartografii.
Atlas novoi istorii. Moskva, 1967.
16 p. col. maps. 26 cm.

4867 U.S.S.R. Glavnoe upravlenie geodezii i kartografii.
Atlas novoi istorii. Moskva, 1968.
16 p. col. maps. 26 cm.

4868 U.S.S.R. Glavnoe upravlenie geodezii i kartografii.
Atlas novoi istorii dlya IXgo klassa srednei shkoly.
Moskva, 1964.
16 p. col. maps. 27 cm.

4869 U.S.S.R. Glavnoe upravlenie geodezii i kartografii.
Atlas novoi istorii dlya X go klassa srednei shkoly.
Moskva, 1964.
16 p. col. maps. 27 cm.

4870 U.S.S.R. Glavnoe upravlenie geodezii i kartografii.
Atlas po istorii drevnego mira. 3 ed. Moskva,
1953.
20 p. col. maps. 30 cm.

4871 U.S.S.R. Glavnoe upravlenie geodezii i kartografii.
Atlas po istorii drevnego mira. 3 ed. Moskva,
[1954].
20 p. col. maps. 30 cm.

4872 U.S.S.R. Glavnoe upravlenie geodezii i kartografii.
Atlas po istorii drevnego mira. Moskva, 1964.
12 p. col. maps. 27 cm.

4873 U.S.S.R. Glavnoe upravlenie geodezii i kartografii.
Atlas po istorii drevnego mira. Moskva, 1965.
1 vol. col. maps. 27 cm.

4874 U.S.S.R. Glavnoe upravlenie geodezii i kartografii.
Atlas vsemirnoi istorii. Moskva, 1969-70.
400 p. col. maps. 50 cm.

4875 Vallardi, A.
Atlante storico. Milano, 1967−
in parts. col. maps. 24 cm.

4876 Vallardi, A.
      Testo-atlante storico per le scuola.   By Alfredo
      Bosisio. Milano, [1959].
      32 p. col. maps. 35 cm.

4877 Van Nostrand Co.
      Atlas of Western Civilization.   By Frederik van der
      Meer. With Elsevier. Princeton, N. J., 1960.
      1 vol. col. maps. 26 cm.

4878 Velhagen & Klasing.
      Atlas zur Geschichte der deutschen Ostsiedlung.
      2 ed. By Wilfried Krallert. Biclcfeld, [1958].
      56 p. col. maps. 27 cm.

4879 Velhagen & Klasing.
      Putzger Historischer Schulatlas, von der Altsteinzeit
      bis zur Gegenwart.   63 ed. Bielefeld, [1954].
      144 p. col. maps. 26 cm.

4880 Velhagen & Klasing.
      Putzger Historischer Schulatlas, von der Altsteinzeit
      bis zur Gegenwart.   64 ed. Bielefeld, [1954].
      144 p. col. maps. 26 cm.

4881 Velhagen & Klasing.
      Putzger Historischer Schulatlas, von der Altsteinzeit
      bis zur Gegenwart.   67 ed. Bielefeld, [1954].
      144 p. col. maps. 26 cm.

4882 Velhagen & Klasing.
      Putzger Historischer Schulatlas, von der Altsteinzeit
      bis zur Gegenwart.   70 ed. Biclefeld, [1957].
      144 p. col. maps. 26 cm.

4883 Velhagen & Klasing.
      Putzger Historischer Schul-Atlas zur allgemeinen und
      Österreichischen Geschichte.   43 ed.   Berlin,
      Bielefeld, 1964.
      190 p. col. maps. 26.5 cm.

4884 Velhagen & Klasing.
      Putzger Historischer Weltatlas.   80 ed. Bielefeld,
      [1961].
      146 p. col. maps. 27 cm.

4885 Velhagen & Klasing.
      Putzger Historischer Weltatlas.   83 ed.   Bielefeld,

1963.
160 p.   col. maps.   27 cm.

4886 Velhagen & Klasing.
Putzger Historischer Weltatlas.   84 ed.   Bielefeld,
1964.
194 p.   col. maps.   27 cm.

4887 Verlag Enzyklopädie.
Historisch-geographisches Kartenwerk.   Wirtschafts-
historische Entwicklung.   By Edgar Lehmann.
Leipzig, 1960.
81 p.   col. maps.   41 cm.

4888 Verlag Enzyklopädie.
Indien.   Entwicklung seiner Wirtschaft und Kultur.
Historisch-geographisches Kartenwerk.   Leipzig,
1958.
1 vol.   col. maps.   42.5 cm.

4889 Vilas Industries.
Philip's historical atlas of Canada.   By J. W.
Chalmers, W. J. Eccles and H. Fullard.   Toronto,
1966.
48 p.   col. maps.   28 cm.

4890 Volk und Wissen Verlag.
Karten für den Geschichtsunterricht.   By Gerhard
Ziegler.   Berlin, 1953.
80 p.   col. maps.   31 cm.

4891 Walker, Gerald E.
A short atlas of European economic history.
Berkeley, Calif., [1963].
1 vol.   28 cm.

4892 Walker, Gerald E.
A short atlas of European economic history.
Berkeley, Calif., 1964.
41 p.   28 cm.

4893 Weidenfeld & Nicolson.
American history atlas.   By Martin Gilbert.   London,
1968.
119 p.   26 cm.

4894 Weidenfeld & Nicolson.
British history atlas.   London, 1968.

118 p.   26 cm.

4895 Weidenfeld & Nicolson.
     Jewish history atlas.   By Martin Gilbert.   London,
     1969.
     112 p.   25.5 cm.

4896 Weidenfeld & Nicolson.
     Recent history atlas.   1870 to the present.   By
     Martin Gilbert.   London, 1966.
     121 p.   25 cm.

4897 Wesmael-Charlier.
     Atlas der algemene geschiedenis.   By F. Hayt.
     Namur, 1968.
     144 p.   col. maps.   26 cm.

4898 Wesmael-Charlier.
     Atlas d'histoire.   By L. Th. Maes, L. Piérard
     and E. Tellier.   Namur, 1966.
     54 p.   col. maps.   32 cm.

4899 Wesmael-Charlier.
     Atlas d'histoire universelle.   By Paul Schmets.
     Namur, [1962].
     126 p.   col. maps.   26 cm.

4900 Wesmael-Charlier.
     Atlas d'histoire universelle.   By Paul Schmets and
     Franz Hayt.   Namur, [1965].
     126 p.   col. maps.   26 cm.

4901 Wesmael-Charlier.
     Atlas d'histoire universelle (et d'histoire de Belgique).
     By Franz Hayt.   Namur, 1967.
     144 p.   col. maps.   26 cm.

4902 Wesmael-Charlier.
     Atlas d'histoire universelle.   By F. Hayt.   Namur,
     1968.
     132 p.   col. maps.   26 cm.

4903 Westermann, Georg.
     Atlas zur Weltgeschichte.   Berlin, 1953-56.
     3 vol.   col. maps.   30 cm.

4904 Westermann, Georg.
     Atlas zur Weltgeschichte: Vorzeit, Altertum,

Mittelalter, Neuzeit. Braunschweig, 1956.
160 p. col. maps. 30 cm.

4905 Westermann, Georg.
Grosser Atlas zur Weltgeschichte: Vorzeit, Altertum,
Mittelalter. Braunschweig, [1965].
171 p. col. maps. 30 cm.

4906 Westermann, Georg.
Grosser Atlas zur Weltgeschichte. Vorzeit, Altertum, Mittelalter, Neuzeit. By Hans-Erich Stier.
Braunschweig, Berlin, Hamburg, München, [1968].
270 p. col. maps. 30 cm.

4907 Westermann, Georg.
Grosser Atlas zur Weltgeschichte. Vorzeit, Altertum, Mittelalter, Neuzeit. By Hans-Erich Stier.
Braunschweig, 1969.
2 vol. col. maps. 30 cm.

4908 Westermann, Georg.
Völker, Staaten und Kulturen. Ein Kartenwerk zur
Geschichte. Braunschweig, [1956].
89 p. col. maps. 30 cm.

4909 Westermann, Georg.
Völker, Staaten und Kulturen. Ein Kartenwerk zur
Geschichte. Braunschweig, 1963.
98 p. col. maps. 30 cm.

4910 Westermann, Georg.
Völker, Staaten und Kulturen. Ein Kartenwerk zur
Geschichte. By Hans-Erich Stier. Braunschweig,
[1965].
98 p. col. maps. 30 cm.

4911 Westermann, Georg.
Völker, Staaten und Kulturen. Ein Kartenwerk zur
Geschichte. Braunschweig, [1966].
146 p. col. maps. 30 cm.

4912 Westermann, Georg.
Völker, Staaten und Kulturen. Ein Kartenwerk zur
Geschichte. Braunschweig, 1968.
146 p. col. maps. 30 cm.

4913 Westermann, Georg.
Westermanns Atlas zur Weltgeschichte. 4 ed.

Braunschweig, 1963.
170 p. col. maps. 30 cm.

4914 Westermann, Georg.
Westermanns Atlas zur Weltgeschichte. Braunschweig, 1967.
1 vol. col. maps. 30 cm.

4915 Westminster Press.
The Westminster historical atlas of the Bible. By
George Ernest Wright. Philadelphia, [1956].
130 p. col. maps. 37 cm.

4916 Westminster Press.
Westminster historical maps of Bible lands. By
G. E. Wright. Philadelphia, [1952].
24 p. col. maps. 24 cm.

4917 Wheaton & Co., Ltd.
History teaching atlas and notebook of British and
world history from the earliest times to 1960.
Exeter, 1968.
88 p. col. maps. 28 cm.

4918 Wiley, John & Sons.
Graphic history of the Americas. A historical
atlas. By Theodore R. Miller. New York, 1969.
61 p. col. maps. 38 cm.

4919 Wolters, J. B.
Atlas algemene en vaderlandse geschiedenis. By
B. A. Vermaseren. Groningen, 1966.
96 p. col. maps. 31 cm.

4920 Yale University Press.
An atlas of Russian history. By Allen F. Chew.
New Haven, Conn., 1967.
111 p. 27.5 cm.

4921 Yale University Press.
An atlas of Russian history. 2 ed. By Allen F.
Chew. New Haven, Conn., 1970.
111 p. 27.5 cm.

4922 Yugoslavia. Vojno-istoriski institut.
Historical atlas of the liberation war of the peoples
of Yugoslavia, 1941-1945. Beograd, 1957.
41 p. col. maps. 41 cm.

4923 Yugoslavia. Vojno-istoriski institut.
Istoriski atlas oslobodilačkog rata naroda Jugoslavije 1941-1945. Beograd, 1952.
41 p. col. maps. 41 cm.

4924 Znanje.
Istoricki atlas nacionalni istorii. Beograd, 1953.
18 p. col. maps. 34 cm.

4925 Znanje.
Istoricki atlas nacionalni istorii. Beograd, 1956.
18 p. col. maps. 34 cm.

4926 Znanje.
Istoricki atlas za III i IV razred osnovne shkole.
By Slobadan Dukič. Beograd, 1953.
1 vol. col. maps. 31 cm.

HYDROGRAPHY

4927 Cranfield & Bonfiel Books.
Waterways atlas of the British Isles. London, 1966.
54 p. col. maps. 24 cm.

4928 France. La Documentation Française.
Atlas de la polution des eaux en France métropoli-
taine. By Louis Coin. Paris, 1963.
126 p. col. maps. 27 cm.

4929 France. La Documentation Française.
Atlas des eaux souterraines de la France. Paris,
[1970].
360 p. col. maps. 28 cm.

4930 Instituto de Estudos Geograficos.
Mapa-oro-hidrográfico de Portugal. Lisboa, 1965.
37 p. 46 cm.

4931 Netherlands. Staatsdrukkerij-en Uitgeverijbedrijf.
Stroomatlas Nederland. 2 ed. 's Gravenhage, 1963-
1 vol. col. maps. 37 cm.

4932 Ronai, Andras.
Az alföld talajvizterkepe. Magyarazö a talajviztükör
felszínalatti mélységének 1:200,000-es méretü
térkékéhez. Budapest, 1961.
102 p. col. maps. 25 cm.

4933 Spain.   Comité Español de Riegos y Drenajes.
      Los riegos en España, datos para su estudio.
      Madrid, 1956.
      1 vol.   col. maps.   31 cm.

4934 U. S. Navy Hydrographic Office.
      Oceanographic atlas of the Polar Seas.   Antarctic.
      Arctic.   Washington, D. C., 1957-58.
      2 vol.   col. maps.   40 cm.

4935 Water Information Center, Inc.
      Water atlas of the United States.   By David M.
      Miller, James J. Geraghty and Robert S. Collins.
      Port Washington, N. Y., [1962].
      48 p.   col. maps.   34 cm.

4936 Water Information Center, Inc.
      Water atlas of the United States.   2 ed.   By David
      M. Miller, James J. Geraghty and Robert S. Collins.
      Port Washington, N. Y., [1963].
      48 p.   col. maps.   34 cm.

INDUSTRIAL - SEE ECONOMIC

IRRIGATION

4937 Gt. Britain.   Ministry of Agriculture, Fisheries & Food.
      Atlas of long-term irrigation needs for England and
      Wales.   London, 1967.
      1 vol.   32 cm.

LANGUAGE

4938 Dublin Institute for Advanced Studies.
      Linguistic atlas and survey of Irish dialects.   By
      Heinrich Wagner.   Dublin, 1958.
      300 p.   col. maps.   43 cm.

4939 Elwert Verlag.
      Deutscher Sprachatlas.   Marburg, —1967.
      in parts.   col. maps.   69 cm.

4940 Elwert Verlag.
      Luxemburgischer Sprachatlas.   By R. Bruch.
      Marburg, 1963.
      174 p.   col. maps.   50 cm.

4941 Poland. Akademia nauk.
Maly atlas gwar polskich. 1 ed. Wrocław, 1957—
in parts. col. maps. 50 cm.

4942 Romania. Academia Republicii Socialiste.
Noul atlas lingvistic român pe reguini. By Boris
Cazacu. Bucuresti, 1967—
in parts. col. maps. 53 cm.

4943 Romania. Editura Academici Republicii Populare
Romîne.
Micul atlas lingvistic romîn. By Ioan Patrut.
Bucuresti, 1956—
in parts. col. maps. 25 cm.

4944 Spain. Consejo Superior de Investigaciones Científicas.
Atlas linguístico de la península Ibérica. Madrid,
1962—
1 vol. col. maps. 62 cm.

MARINE

4945 American Geographical Society.
Serial atlas of the marine environment. New York,
1962—
in folios. col. maps. 41 cm.

4946 Lloyd's Corp. of.
Lloyd's maritime atlas. 1 ed. London, 1951.
1 vol. col. maps. 25 cm.

4947 Lloyd's Corp. of.
Lloyd's maritime atlas. 2 ed. London, 1953.
1 vol. col. maps. 25 cm.

4948 Lloyd's Corp. of.
Lloyd's maritime atlas. 3 ed. London, 1958.
1 vol. col. maps. 25 cm.

4949 Lloyd's Corp. of.
Lloyd's maritime atlas. 4 ed. London, 1961.
1 vol. col. maps. 25 cm.

4950 Lloyd's Corp. of.
Lloyd's maritime atlas. 5 ed. London, 1964.
1 vol. col. maps. 25 cm.

4951 Lloyd's Corp. of.
      Lloyd's maritime atlas.   6 ed.   London, 1966.
      1 vol.   col.   maps.   25 cm.

4952 Netherlands.   Staatsdrukkerij-en Uitgeverijbedrijf.
      Stroomatlas Nederland.   2 ed.   's Gravenhage, 1963-
      1 vol.   col.   maps.   37 cm.

4953 Philip, George & Son, Ltd.
      Philips mercantile marine atlas.   14 ed.   By Harold
      Fuller.   London, 1952.
      96 p.   col.   maps.   53 cm.

4954 Philip, George & Son, Ltd.
      Philips mercantile marine atlas.   15 ed.   By Harold
      Fuller.   London, 1955.
      96 p.   col.   maps.   53 cm.

4955 Philip, George & Son, Ltd.
      Philips mercantile marine atlas.   16 ed.   By Harold
      Fullard.   London, 1959.
      96 p.   col.   maps.   53 cm.

4956 U. S. Navy Hydrographic Office.
      Oceanographic atlas of the Polar seas.   Antarctic.
      Arctic.   Washington, D. C., 1957-58.
      2 vol.   col.   maps.   40 cm.

4957 U.S.S.R. Voyenno-morskoe ministerstvo.
      Morskoi atlas.   Moskva, 1950-1958.
      3 vol.   col.   maps.   35 cm.

4958 Weststadt Verlag.
      The world shipping scene; atlas of shipping, ship-
      building, seaports, and sea-borne trade.   By G. A.
      Theel.   München, 1963.
      1 vol.   col.   maps.   31 cm.

MEDICAL

4959 American Geographical Society.
      Atlas of diseases.   New York, 1950-1955.
      17 p.   col.   maps.   90 cm.

4960 Falk Verlag.
      Welt-Seuchen-Atlas.   [World atlas of epidemic
      diseases].   Hamburg, 1952-61.
      3 vol.   col.   maps.   48 cm.

4961 India.   Directorate General of Health Services.
      Health atlas of India. Delhi, [1953].
      54 p.   36 cm.

4962 Nelson, Thomas & Sons, Ltd.
      National atlas of the disease mortality in the United
      Kingdom. By G. M. Howe. London, Edinburgh,
      1963.
      111 p.   col. maps.   29 cm.

4963 Nelson, Thomas & Sons, Ltd.
      National atlas of disease mortality in the United
      Kingdom. 2 ed. By G. M. Howe. London, Edin-
      burgh, 1968.
      120 p.   col. maps.   29 cm.

4964 Nelson, Thomas & Sons, Ltd.
      National atlas of disease mortality in the United
      Kingdom. 2 ed. By G. M. Howe. London, 1970.
      197 p.   col. maps.   29 cm.

4965 U.S.S.R. Glavnoe upravlenie geodezii i kartografii.
      Atlas zdravookhranenia SSSR. Moskva, 1970-71.
      1 vol.   col. maps.   34 cm.

MILITARY - SEE HISTORY

MINERAL - SEE GEOLOGY

MINING - SEE GEOLOGY

OCEANOGRAPHY

4966 Meyer, Kartographisches Institut.
      Meyers grosser physischer Weltatlas.   Mannheim,
      1965 –
      in 8 vol.   col. maps.   30 cm.

4967 U. S. Navy Hydrographic Office.
      Oceanographic atlas of the Polar seas.   Antarctic.
      Arctic.   Washington, D. C., 1957-58.
      2 vol.   col. maps.   40 cm.

4968 U. S. Weather Bureau.
      Climatological and Oceanographic atlas for mariners.
      Washington, D. C., 1959 –
      in parts.   col. maps.   39 cm.

OIL - SEE GEOLOGY

OREOGRAPHY

4969 Meyer, Kartographisches Institut.
     Meyers grosser physischer Weltatlas.   Mannheim,
     1965—
     in 8 vols.   col. maps.   30 cm.

PALEOGEOGRAPHY

4970 Blackie & Son, Ltd.
     A paleogeographical atlas of the British Isles and
     adjacent parts of Europe.   By Leonard J. Wills.
     London, 1951.
     64 p.   col. maps.   22 cm.

4971 Blackie & Son, Ltd.
     A paleogeographical atlas of the British Isles and
     adjacent parts of Europe.   By Leonard J. Wills.
     London, 1952.
     64 p.   col. maps.   22 cm.

4972 Blackie & Son, Ltd.
     A paleogeographical atlas of the British Isles and
     adjacent parts of Europe.   4 ed.   By Leonard J.
     Wills.   London, 1962.
     64 p.   col. maps.   22 cm.

4973 China.   Academy of Sciences.
     [Paleogeographic maps of China].   In Chinese.   Peking,
     1955.
     21 p.   col. maps.   37 cm.

4974 U. S. S. R.   Akademiia nauk.
     Atlas paleogeograficheskikh kart SSSR.   Kiev, 1965—
     in parts.   col. maps.   66 cm.

4975 U. S. S. R.   Glavnoe upravlenie geodezii i kartografii.
     Litologo-paleogeograficheskii atlas SSSR.   Moskva,
     1967-68.
     2 vol.   col. maps.   66 cm.

PETROLEUM - SEE GEOLOGY

POLLUTION

4976 France. La Documentation Française.
Atlas de la pollution des eaux en France métropoli-
taine. By Louis Coin. Paris, 1963.
126 p. col. maps. 27 cm.

POPULATION

4977 Africa Instituut.
Africa; maps and statistics. Pretoria, 1962-65.
10 vol. col. maps. 35 cm.

4978 Czechoslovakia. Ústřední správa geodesie a kartografie.
Atlas obyvatelstva ČSSR. 1 ed. By Jindřich
Svoboda. Praha, [1962].
91 p. col. maps. 22 cm.

4979 Droemer.
Knaurs Welt Atlas. Ausführlicher geographischer,
bevölkerungs-und wirtschaftlicher Text. München,
[1957].
537 p. col. maps. 25 cm.

4980 East African institute of social research.
Tribal maps of East Africa and Zanzibar. By E.
J. Goldthorpe and F. B. Wilson. Kampala, Uganda,
1960.
14 p. col. maps. 25 cm.

4981 Falk Verlag.
Welt-Bevölkerungs-Atlas. Hamburg, 1954-[1957].
in parts. col. maps. 47.5 cm.

4982 Ghana. Census Office.
1960 population census of Ghana; atlas of population
characteristics. Accra, 1964.
29 p. col. maps. 43 cm.

4983 Institut Français d'Afrique Noire.
Cartes ethno-demographique de l'Afrique Occidentale.
Dakar, 1952.
12 p. col. maps. 28 cm.

4984 International Bank for Reconstruction and Development.
World bank atlas of per capita product and population. Washington, D. C., 1966.
14 p. col. maps. 28 cm.

4985 International Bank for Reconstruction and Development.
World bank atlas; per capita product; population;
main urban centers.   Washington, D. C., 1967.
7 p.   col. maps.   28 cm.

4986 International Bank for Reconstruction and Development.
World bank atlas; population and per capita product.
3 ed.   Washington, D. C., 1968.
16 p.   col. maps.   28 cm.

4987 International Bank for Reconstruction and Development.
World bank atlas; population, per capita product and
growth rate.   4 ed.   Washington, D. C., 1969.
16 p.   col. maps.   28 cm.

4988 Israel.   Department of Surveys.
Atlas of Israel.   (in Hebrew).   Jerusalem, 1956-
1964.
1 vol.   col. maps.   47. 5 cm.

4989 Katholiek Sociaal-Kerkelijk Instituut.
Étude cartographique de la structure économique et
démographique de l'Europe occidentale.   's Gravenhage, [1959].
10 p.   col. maps.   29 cm.

4990 Mexico.   Instituto Mexicano de Investigaciones Econo-
micos.
Atlas geografico general de Mexico, con cartes
fisicas, biologicas, demograficas, sociales, economicas y cartogramas.   2 ed.   Mexico, 1962.
1 vol.   col. maps.   54 cm.

4991 Nelson, Thomas & Sons, Ltd.
Ghana population atlas.   By T. E. Hilton.   Edinburgh, 1960.
40 p.   col. maps.   40 cm.

4992 Norway.   Statistik Sentrabyrå.
Bosettingskart over Norge, 1:400,000.   Oslo, [1955].
15 p.   col. maps.   25 cm.

4993 Poland.   Akademia nauk.
Polski atlas etnograficzny.   Warszawa, 1964—
in parts.   col. maps.   49 cm.

4994 Reitzels, C. A. Forlag.
     Atlas over Denmark, København, 1950—
     in 5 vols.   col. maps.   55 cm.

4995 Surveys Press.
     Atlas of Iraq, showing administrative boundaries,
     areas & population.   1 ed.   By Ahmed Sousa.   Bagh-
     dad, 1953.
     40 p.   col. maps.   35 cm.

4996 U. S. S. R.   Glavnoe upravlenie geodezii i kartografii.
     Atlas narodov mira.   Moskva, 1962.
     112 p.   col. maps.   34 cm.

4997 U. S. S. R.   Glavnoe upravlenie geodezii i kartografii.
     Atlas narodov mira.   Moskva, 1964.
     184 p.   col. maps.   34. 5 cm.

4998 U. S. S. R.   Glavnoe upravlenie geodezii i kartografii.
     Atlas narodov SSSR.   Moskva, 1969-70.
     1 vol.   col. maps.   37 cm.

4999 U. S. S. R.   Glavnoe upravlenie geodezii i kartografii.
     Atlas naselenia mira.   Moskva, 1967.
     1 vol.   col. maps.   37 cm.

5000 U. S. S. R.   Glavnoe upravlenie geodezii i kartografii.
     Atlas naselenia mira.   Moskva, 1969-70.
     160 p.   col. maps.   37 cm.

RADIO - SEE COMMUNICATION

RAILROADS - SEE TRANSPORTATION

ROAD

5001 Abercrombie & Fitch.
     The complete Abercrombie & Fitch vacation atlas for
     all of North America.   New York, 1965.
     142 p.   col. maps.   34 cm.

5002 Accumulatoren-Fabrik, A. G.
     Varta Auto-atlas.   Hannover, [1950].
     174 p.   col. maps.   30 cm.

5003 Accumulatoren-Fabrik, A. G.
     Varta Auto-atlas.   3 ed.   Frankfurt, 1952.
     164 p.   col. maps.   30 cm.

5004 AGIP.
    Carta automobitistica d'Italia.   By Giuseppe Vallardi.
    Milano, [1963].
    32 p.   col. maps.   24 cm.

5005 Allgemeiner Deutscher Automobil-Club.
    ADAC Auto-atlas.   Kiel, [1950-51].
    2 vol.   col. maps.   28 cm.

5006 Alpine Geographical Press.
    Campground atlas of the United States and Canada.
    Champaign, Ill., [1960].
    176 p.   col. maps.   28 cm.

5007 Alpine Geographical Press.
    Campground atlas of the United States and Canada.
    Champaign, Ill., [1962].
    182 p.   col. maps.   28 cm.

5008 Alpine Geographical Press.
    Campground atlas of the United States and Canada.
    Champaign, Ill., [1964].
    186 p.   col. maps.   28 cm.

5009 Alpine Geographical Press.
    Campground atlas of the United States and Canada.
    Champaign, Ill., 1966.
    204 p.   col. maps.   28 cm.

5010 Alpine Geographical Press.
    Campground atlas of the United States and Canada.
    Champaign, Ill., 1966-67.
    157 p.   col. maps.   28 cm.

5011 Alpine Geographical Press.
    Campground atlas of the United States and Canada.
    Champaign, Ill., 1967-68.
    260 p.   col. maps.   28 cm.

5012 Alpine Geographical Press.
    Campground atlas of the United States and Canada.
    Champaign, Ill., 1968-69.
    260 p.   col. maps.   28 cm.

5013 Alpine Geographical Press.
    Campground atlas of the United States and Canada.
    Champaign, Ill., 1969-70.
    260 p.   col. maps.   28 cm.

5014 American Hotel Register Co.
Leahy's hotel-motel guide and travel atlas of the
United States, Canada and Mexico.   75 ed.   Chicago,
1950.
256 p.   col. maps.   38 cm.

5015 American Hotel Register Co.
Leahy's hotel-motel guide and travel atlas of the
United States, Canada and Mexico.   76 ed.   Chicago,
1951.
256 p.   col. maps.   38 cm.

5016 American Hotel Register Co.
Leahy's hotel-motel guide and travel atlas of the
United States, Canada and Mexico.   77 ed.   Chicago,
1952.
256 p.   col. maps.   38 cm.

5017 American Hotel Register Co.
Leahy's hotel-motel guide and travel atlas of the
United States, Canada and Mexico.   78 ed.   Chicago,
1953.
256 p.   col. maps.   38 cm.

5018 American Hotel Register Co.
Leahy's hotel-motel guide and travel atlas of the
United States, Canada and Mexico.   79 ed.   Chicago,
1954.
256 p.   col. maps.   38 cm.

5019 American Hotel Register Co.
Leahy's hotel-motel guide and travel atlas of the
United States, Canada and Mexico.   80 ed.   Chicago,
1955.
256 p.   col. maps.   38 cm.

5020 American Hotel Register Co.
Leahy's hotel-motel guide and travel atlas of the
United States, Canada and Mexico.   81 ed.   Chicago,
1956.
256 p.   col. maps.   38 cm.

5021 American Hotel Register Co.
Leahy's hotel-motel guide and travel atlas of the
United States, Canada and Mexico.   82 ed.   Chicago,
1957.
256 p.   col. maps.   38 cm.

5022 American Hotel Register Co.
          Leahy's hotel-motel guide and travel atlas of the
          United States, Canada and Mexico.   83 ed.   Chicago,
          1958.
          256 p.   col. maps.   38 cm.

5023 American Hotel Register Co.
          Leahy's hotel-motel guide and travel atlas of the
          United States, Canada and Mexico.   84 ed.   Chicago,
          1959.
          256 p.   col. maps.   38 cm.

5024 American Hotel Register Co.
          Leahy's hotel-motel guide and travel atlas of the
          United States, Canada and Mexico.   85 ed.   Chicago,
          1960.
          256 p.   col. maps.   38 cm.

5025 American Hotel Register Co.
          Leahy's hotel-motel guide and travel atlas of the
          United States, Canada and Mexico.   86 ed.   Chicago,
          1961.
          256 p.   col. maps.   38 cm.

5026 American Hotel Register Co.
          Leahy's hotel-motel guide and travel atlas of the
          United States, Canada and Mexico.   87 ed.   Chicago,
          1962.
          256 p.   col. maps.   38 cm.

5027 American Hotel Register Co.
          Leahy's hotel-motel guide and travel atlas of the
          United States, Canada and Mexico.   88 ed.   Chicago,
          1963.
          256 p.   col. maps.   38 cm.

5028 American Hotel Register Co.
          Leahy's hotel-motel guide and travel atlas of the
          United States, Canada and Mexico.   89 ed.   Chicago,
          1964.
          257 p.   col. maps.   38 cm.

5029 American Hotel Register Co.
          Leahy's hotel-motel guide and travel atlas of the
          United States, Canada and Mexico.   90 ed.   Chicago,
          1965.
          257 p.   col. maps.   38 cm.

5030 American Hotel Register Co.
Leahy's hotel-motel guide and travel atlas of the
United States, Canada and Mexico. 91 ed. Chicago,
258 p. col. maps. 38 cm.

5031 American Hotel Register Co.
Leahy's hotel-motel guide and travel atlas of the
United States, Canada and Mexico. 92 ed. Chicago,
1967.
258 p. col. maps. 38 cm.

5032 American Hotel Register Co.
Leahy's hotel-motel guide and travel atlas of the
United States, Canada and Mexico. 93 ed. Chicago,
1968.
258 p. col. maps. 38 cm.

5033 American Hotel Register Co.
Leahy's hotel-motel guide and travel atlas of the
United States, Canada and Mexico. 94 ed. Chicago,
1969.
258 p. col. maps. 38 cm.

5034 American Hotel Register Co.
Leahy's hotel-motel guide and travel atlas of the
United States, Canada and Mexico. 95 ed. Chicago,
1970.
258 p. col. maps. 38 cm.

5035 Ampol Petroleum, Ltd.
The Ampol touring atlas of Australia. Sydney, [1969].
93 p. col. maps. 32 cm.

5036 Argentina. Instituto Geográfico Militar.
Atlas de ruta. 2 ed. Buenos Aires, 1967.
27 p. col. maps. 32 cm.

5037 Asociación Nacional Automovilística.
Atlas: rutas de Mexico; routes of Mexico. 2 ed.
Mexico, [1962].
2 vol. col. maps. 24 cm.

5038 Asociación Nacional Automovilística.
Atlas: rutas de México; routes of Mexico. 3 ed.
Mexico, [1965].
2 vol. col. maps. 24 cm.

5039 Asociación Nacional Automovilística.
      Atlas: rutas de Mexico; routes of Mexico.   4 ed.
      Mexico, 1967.
      2 vol.   col.   maps.   24 cm.

5040 Atlantik Refining Company of Africa.
      Union of South Africa, South-West Africa and
      Rhodesia road maps.   Cape Town, [195-].
      24 p.   col.   maps.   29 cm.

5041 Austin Motor Co., Ltd.
      Austin road atlas of Great Britain.   Birmingham,
      [1955].
      72 p.   col.   maps.   27. 5 cm.

5042 Austin Motor Co., Ltd.
      Austin road atlas of Great Britain.   3 ed.   Birming-
      ham, [1956].
      75 p.   col.   maps.   27. 5 cm.

5043 Austin Motor Co., Ltd.
      Austin road atlas of Great Britain.   4 ed.   Birming-
      ham, [1957].
      75 p.   col.   maps.   27. 5 cm.

5044 Austin Motor Co., Ltd.
      Austin road atlas of Great Britain.   6 ed.   Birming-
      ham, 1963.
      31 p.   col.   maps.   27. 5 cm.

5045 Austin Motor Co., Ltd.
      Great Britain road atlas and touring guide.   With
      Geographia, Ltd.   Birmingham, [1967].
      1 vol.   col.   maps.   27. 5 cm.

5046 Austin Motor Co., Ltd.
      Motoring through Britain.   2 ed.   With Geographia,
      Ltd.   London, 1964.
      93 p.   col.   maps.   27. 5 cm.

5047 Austin Motor Co., Ltd.
      Road atlas of Great Britain.   With Geographia, Ltd.
      London, 1964.
      93 p.   col.   maps.   27. 5 cm.

5048 Autokarten und Reiseführer Verlag.
      Der neue Auto-Strassen Atlas.   Kiel, [1952].
      3 vol. in 1.   col.   maps.   28 cm.

5049 Automobile Association.
 The automobile association atlas of Ireland. London,
 1963.
 31 p. col. maps. 26 cm.

5050 Automobile Association of Malaya.
 Malaysia road atlas. Penang, [1967].
 16 p. col. maps. 25 cm.

5051 Automobile Association of South Africa.
 Road atlas and touring guide of Southern Africa.
 2 ed. Johannesburg, [1963].
 200 p. col. maps. 25 cm.

5052 Automobile Association of South Africa.
 Trans-African highways; a route book of the main
 trunk roads in Africa. 5 ed. Johannesburg, 1963.
 352 p. col. maps. 28 cm.

5053 Automobile Club d'Italia.
 Atlante automobilistico d'Europa. Roma, [1958].
 90 p. col. maps. 27 cm.

5054 Automobile Club d'Italia.
 Atlante automobilistico d'Europa. Roma, [1965].
 51 p. col. maps. 26 cm.

5055 Automobile Club d'Italia.
 Autostrade d'Italia. Roma, 1965.
 12 p. col. maps. 27 cm.

5056 Automobile Club d'Italia.
 Italia; atlante automobilistico. Roma, [1957].
 72 p. col. maps. 27 cm.

5057 Auto-Motor-und Radfahrerbund Österreichs.
 Auto-atlas Europa. With Ravenstein. Wien, 1966.
 80 p. col. maps. 38 cm.

5058 Auto-Motor-und Radfahrerbund Österreichs.
 Auto-atlas Europa. With Ravenstein. Wien, 1967.
 80 p. col. maps. 38 cm.

5059 Automóvil Club Argentino.
 Hojas de ruta. Buenos Aires, 1950-
 29 p. col. maps. 23 cm.

5060 Bartholomew, John & Son, Ltd.
    <u>Bartholomew road atlas Europe.</u> Edinburgh, [1969].
    40 p. col. maps. 25 cm.

5061 Bartholomew, John & Son, Ltd.
    <u>Bartholomew road atlas Europe.</u> Edinburgh, 1970.
    49 p. col. maps. 25 cm.

5062 Bartholomew, John & Son, Ltd.
    <u>Bartholomew's road atlas of England and Wales.</u>
    London, 1963.
    59 p. col. maps. 25 cm.

5063 Bartholomew, John & Son, Ltd.
    <u>Road atlas of Great Britain.</u> 9 ed. Edinburgh, 1952.
    112 p. col. maps. 25 cm.

5064 Bartholomew, John & Son, Ltd.
    <u>Road atlas of Great Britain.</u> 16 ed. Edinburgh,
    1963.
    95 p. col. maps. 25 cm.

5065 Bartholomew, John & Son, Ltd.
    <u>Road atlas of Great Britain.</u> 17 ed. Edinburgh,
    1964.
    95 p. col. maps. 25 cm.

5066 Bartholomew, John & Son, Ltd.
    <u>Road atlas of Great Britain.</u> 18 ed. Edinburgh,
    1965.
    112 p. col. maps. 25 cm.

5067 Bartholomew, John & Son, Ltd.
    <u>Road atlas of Great Britain.</u> 19 ed. Edinburgh,
    1966.
    112 p. col. maps. 25 cm.

5068 Bartholomew, John & Son, Ltd.
    <u>Road atlas of Great Britain.</u> 20 ed. Edinburgh,
    1967.
    112 p. col. maps. 25. 5 cm.

5069 Bartholomew, John & Son, Ltd.
    <u>Road atlas of Great Britain.</u> 21 ed. Edinburgh,
    1968.
    112 p. col. maps. 25. 5 cm.

5070 Bartholomew, John & Son, Ltd.
     <u>Road atlas of Great Britain.</u>   Edinburgh, 1970.
     112 p.   col. maps.   25 cm.

5071 Bartholomew, John & Son, Ltd.
     <u>Roadmaster atlas of Great Britain.</u>   3 ed.   Edin-
     burgh, 1964.
     72 p.   col. maps.   25 cm.

5072 Bartholomew, John & Son, Ltd.   .
     <u>Roadmaster motoring atlas of Great Britain.</u>   Edin-
     burgh, 1958.
     38 p.   col. maps.   25 cm.

5073 Bartholomew, John & Son, Ltd.
     <u>Roadmaster travel maps of Britain.</u>   Edinburgh, 1970.
     1 vol.   col. maps.   25 cm.

5074 Bartholomew, John & Son, Ltd.
     The British Isles pocket atlas for touring.   14 ed.
     <u>Edinburgh, 1952.</u>
     120 p.   col. maps.   16 cm.

5075 Bertelsmann, C.
     <u>Autoatlas Bertelsmann.</u>   Deutschland-Europa.
     Gütersloh, [1964].
     388 p.   col. maps.   27 cm.

5076 Bertelsmann, C.
     <u>Autoatlas Bertelsmann.</u>   Deutschland-Europa.
     Gütersloh, 1965.
     388 p.   col. maps.   27 cm.

5077 Bertelsmann, C.
     <u>Autoatlas Bertelsmann.</u>   Deutschland-Europa.
     Gütersloh, 1966.
     388 p.   col. maps.   27 cm.

5078 Blondel La Rougery.
     <u>Atlas des routes de France.</u>   Paris, 1967.
     31 p.   col. maps.   24 cm.

5079 Blondel La Rougery.
     <u>Atlas Simca des routes de France.</u>   Paris, [1950].
     32 p.   col. maps.   23 cm.

5080 Blondel La Rougery.
      Atlas Simca des routes de France.   Paris, [1952].
      32 p.   col. maps.   23 cm.

5081 Blondel La Rougery.
      Europe, routes, highways.   Paris, [1952].
      215 p.   col. maps.   15 cm.

5082 Bootsma.
      Autokaart Nederland.   1 ed.   's Gravenhage, [1952].
      48 p.   col. maps.   29 cm.

5083 Boy Scouts of America.
      Road atlas and guide to overnight camping.   With
      Hammond.   New Brunswick, N. J. , 1964.
      80 p.   col. maps.   32 cm.

5084 B. P. Australia, Ltd.
      Roads of Australia, with insets of main towns.
      Melbourne, 1966.
      76 p.   col. maps.   22 cm.

5085 BP Benzin & Petroleum Gesellschaft.
      BP Dieselatlas Deutschland.   Hamburg, [195-].
      39 p.   col. maps.   21 cm.

5086 B. P. Southern Africa Pty, Ltd.
      Padkaarte.   Road maps.   Union of South Africa,
      South West Africa. Cape Town, [196-].
      10 p.   col. maps.   29 cm.

5087 British Motor Corp. Ltd.
      B. M. C. route planner, including motorways.   London,
      [1968].
      50 p.   col. maps.   28 cm.

5088 Buchgemeinschaft Donauland.
      Donauland autoatlas.   Wien, [1965].
      1 vol.   col. maps.   27 cm.

5089 Bulgaria.   Glavno upravlenie po geodeziå i kartografiå.
      Automobilei atlas Bulgaria.   Sofia, 1967.
      56 p.   col. maps.   20. 5 cm.

5090 Caltex (Philippines).
      Road map of the Philippines.   Manila, 1957.
      60 p.   col. maps.   25 cm.

5091 Cappelens, J. W. Forlag, A. S.
      Cappelen Bilkartbok.   Oslo, 1967.
      56 p.   col. maps.   27. 5 cm.

5092 Carta.
      Carta's Israel road guide.   Jerusalem, 1963.
      68 p.   col. maps.   24 cm.

5093 Carta.
      Carta's Israel road guide.   Jerusalem, 1969.
      68 p.   col. maps.   24 cm.

5094 Chile.   Instituto Geográfico Militar.
      Carta preliminar.   Santiago de Chile, [1967].
      100 p.   col. maps.   56 cm.

5095 Collins, William, Sons & Co. , Ltd.
      Collins road atlas, Europe.   London, [1965].
      232 p.   col. maps.   25 cm.

5096 Colombia.   Ministerio de Obras Publicas.
      Atlas vial.   Bogotá, [1950].
      24 p.   col. maps.   56 cm.

5097 Columbus Verlag Oestergaard.
      Columbus Auto-atlas für Reise, Verkehr und Handel.
      Berlin, [1950].
      40 p.   col. maps.   28 cm.

5098 Compania Hulera Euzkadi, S. A.
      Caminos de México; atlas Goodrich Euzkadi.   1 ed.
      México, 1964.
      16 p.   col. maps.   27 cm.

5099 Compania Hulera Euzkadi, S. A.
      Caminos de México, atlas B. F. Goodrich Euzkadi.
      2 ed.   México, [1966].
      16 p.   col. maps.   27 cm.

5100 Compania Hulera Euzkadi, S. A.
      Caminos de México; atlas B. F. Goodrich Euzkadi.
      3 ed.   México, 1967.
      16 p.   col. maps.   27 cm.

5101 Continental Gummiwerke Kartographischer Verlag.
      Continental atlas.   27 ed.   Hannover, [1957].
      485 p.   col. maps.   26 cm.

5102 Continental Gummiwerke Kartographischer Verlag.
      Continental atlas. 28 ed. Hannover, [1958].
      489 p. col. maps. 26 cm.

5103 Continental Gummiwerke Kartographischer Verlag.
      Continental atlas. 32 ed. Hannover, 1963.
      757 p. col. maps. 26 cm.

5104 Continental Gummiwerke Kartographischer Verlag.
      Continental atlas. 35 ed. Hannover, 1964.
      644 p. col. maps. 26 cm.

5105 Continental Gummiwerke Kartographischer Verlag.
      Continental atlas. Hannover, 1966/67.
      531 p. col. maps. 26 cm.

5106 Continental Gummiwerke Kartographischer Verlag.
      Continental atlas. Hannover, 1968-69.
      531 p. col. maps. 26 cm.

5107 Continental Gummiwerke Kartographischer Verlag.
      Continental atlas. Deutschland, Benelux, Alpen-
      länder. 26 ed. Hannover, [1956].
      453 p. col. maps. 26 cm.

5108 Continental Gummiwerke Kartographischer Verlag.
      Continental atlas. Deutschland, Benelux, Schweiz,
      Österreich, Norditalien. 33 ed. Hannover, 1964.
      635 p. col. maps. 26 cm.

5109 Continental Gummiwerke Kartographischer Verlag.
      Continental atlas. Deutschland, Europa. 34 ed.
      Hannover, [1966].
      531 p. col. maps. 26 cm.

5110 Continental Gummiwerke Kartographischer Verlag.
      Continental atlas. Deutschland, Europa. 35 ed.
      Hannover, 1968-69.
      531 p. col. maps. 26 cm.

5111 Continental Gummiwerke Kartographsicher Verlag.
      Der grosse Continental Atlas. 21 ed. Hannover,
      [1951].
      212 p. col. maps. 26 cm.

5112 Continental Gummiwerke Kartographischer Verlag.
      Der gross Continental Atlas. 22 ed. Hannover, [1951].
      212 p. col. maps. 26 cm.

5113 Continental Gummiwerke Kartographischer Verlag.
Der grosse Continental atlas. 23 ed. Hannover,
[1952].
212 p. col. maps. 26 cm.

5114 Continental Gummiwerke Kartographischer Verlag.
Der grosse Continental atlas. 24 ed. Hannover,
[1953].
269 p. col. maps. 26 cm.

5115 Continental Gummiwerke Kartographischer Verlag.
Der grosse Continental atlas. 25 ed. Hannover,
[1955].
318 p. col. maps. 26 cm.

5116 Continental Gummiwerke Kartographischer Verlag.
Der grosse Continental atlas für Kraftfahrer. 20 ed.
Hannover, [1950].
61 p. col. maps. 26 cm.

5117 Czechoslovakia. Kartografické nakladatelstvi.
Autoatlas ČSSR. Praha, 1963.
163 p. col. maps. 31 cm.

5118 Czechoslovakia. Kartografické nakladatelstvi.
Autoatlas ČSSR. Praha, 1966.
163 p. col. maps. 31 cm.

5119 Czechoslovakia. Kartografické nakladatelstvi.
Autoatlas ČSSR. Praha, [1967].
163 p. col. maps. 31 cm.

5120 Czechoslovakia. Ústřední správa geodesie a kartografie.
Autoatlas ČSSR. Praha, 1963.
165 p. col. maps. 25 cm.

5121 Czechoslovakia, Ústřední správa geodesie a kartografie.
Autoatlas ČSSR. Praha, 1965.
163 p. col. maps. 25 cm.

5122 Czechoslovakia. Ústřední správa geodesie a kartografie.
Automapa ČSR. 1 ed. Praha, 1957.
98 p. col. maps. 22 cm.

5123 Czechoslovakia. Ústřední správa geodesie a kartografie.
Automapa ČSR. 2 ed. Praha, 1958.
98 p. col. maps. 22 cm.

5124 Czechoslovakia, Ústřední správa geodesie a kartografie.
     Automapa ČSR. 3 ed. Praha, 1959.
     98 p. col. maps. 22 cm.

5125 Daily Express.
     Daily Express road book and gazetteer of Great
     Britain. London, [1950].
     128 p. col. maps. 25 cm.

5126 Denmark. Geodaetisk Institut.
     FDM Kortbog. Denmark. 25 ed. Kφbenhavn, 1964.
     208 p. col. maps. 24 cm.

5127 Deutsche Viscobil Öl Gesellschaft.
     Viscobil Auto Tourenkarte. Hamburg, 1953.
     49 p. col. maps. 22 cm.

5128 Deutscher Zentralverlag VEB.
     Strassen Atlas von Deutschland. 3 ed. Berlin,
     [1952].
     26 p. col. maps. 22 cm.

5129 Diversified Map Corporation.
     Diversified Map Corporation road atlas. St. Louis,
     Mo. , 1967.
     84 p. col. maps. 23 cm.

5130 Diversified Map Corporation.
     The complete Abercrombie & Fitch vacation atlas for
     all North America. New York, 1965.
     142 p. col. maps. 34 cm.

5131 Diversified Map Corporation.
     This week magazine's vacation planner and speedy
     flipout road atlas... to all North America. New
     York, [1965].
     142 p. col. maps. 34 cm.

5132 Ebury Press.
     The Shell guide to Scotland. By Moray McLaren.
     London, 1967.
     496 p. col. maps. 26 cm.

5133 Edi-Mapas de México.
     Atlas de México. Mexico, 1966.
     32 p. col. maps. 46 cm.

5134 Editorial Mapa.
     Atlas argentina; geografía general.   1 ed.   By Mario
     Borio. Buenos Aires, [1967].
     48 p.   col. maps.   26 cm.

5135 Editorial Mapa.
     Atlas de la Republica Argentina y sus caminos.
     Buenos Aires, [1964].
     47 p.   col. maps.   24 cm.

5136 Editorial Mapa.
     Atlas de ruta. Buenos Aires, 1967.
     19 p.   col. maps.   33 cm.

5137 Esso, A. G.
     Esso Europa atlas.   Hamburg, 1965.
     204 p.   col. maps.   27 cm.

5138 Esso, A. G.
     Esso Reise-Atlas für Kraftfahrer.   München, [1956].
     164 p.   col. maps.   24 cm.

5139 Esso, A. G.
     Esso Reise-Atlas von Deutschland.   München, [1955].
     156 p.   col. maps.   24 cm.

5140 Esso, A. G.
     Europa Atlas. Hamburg, 1967.
     96 p.   col. maps.   30 cm.

5141 Europa im Automobile, A. G.
     Reiseführer und Atlas.   Zürich, 1966.
     584 p.   col. maps.   27 cm.

5142 European Road Guide, Inc.
     European motoring atlas, 1967-68.   Larchmont,
     N. Y., 1967.
     23 p.   col. maps.   28 cm.

5143 European Road Guide, Inc.
     Motoring atlas: Europe and Israel 1968/69.   Larch-
     mont, N. Y., 1968.
     48 p.   col. maps.   28 cm.

5144 European Road Guide, Inc.
     Motoring atlas of Europe and Israel.   1969-70 ed.
     Larchmont, N. Y., 1969.
     68 p.   col. maps.   28 cm.

5145 Falk Verlag.
Autoatlas der Bundesrepublik Deutschland. 15 ed.
Hamburg, [1952].
57 p. col. maps. 25 cm.

5146 Falk Verlag.
Autoatlas der Bundesrepublik Deutschland. 51 and
53 ed. Hamburg, 1963.
68 p. col. maps. 24. 5 cm.

5147 Falk Verlag.
Autoatlas der Bundesrepublik Deutschland. 54 and
55 ed. Hamburg, 1964.
68 p. col. maps. 24. 5 cm.

5148 Falk Verlag.
Autoatlas der Bundesrepublik Deutschland. Hamburg,
1968.
68 p. col. maps. 24. 5 cm.

5149 Falk Verlag.
Autostrassen Atlas der Bundesrepublik Deutschland.
Hamburg, [1955].
51 p. col. maps. 25 cm.

5150 Falk Verlag.
Falk Auto-Atlas, Bundesrepublik Deutschland. 2 ed.
Köln, 1953.
52 p. col. maps. 25 cm.

5151 Falk Verlag.
Falk Autoatlas Nr. 355. Von Kopenhagen bis
Mailand. 19 ed. Hamburg, 1963.
70 p. col. maps. 27 cm.

5152 Falk Verlag.
Falk Auto-Atlas Österreich. Hamburg, [1959].
32 p. col. maps. 25 cm.

5153 Falk Verlag.
Falk Plan Österreich; Auto-Atlas Österreich. 4 ed.
Hamburg, [1964].
32 p. col. maps. 25 cm.

5154 Falk Verlag.
Ford Auto-Atlas. Bundesrepublik Deutschland. 2 ed.
Köln, [1953].
52 p. col. maps. 25 cm.

5155 Farmers Insurance Group.
       Vacation guide and atlas.   With Goushá.   Los
       Angeles, Calif. , [1958].
       64 p.   col. maps.   28 cm.

5156 Farmers Insurance Group.
       Vacation guide and atlas.   With Goushá.   Los
       Angeles, Calif. , [1965].
       64 p.   col. maps.   28 cm.

5157 Farmers Insurance Group.
       Vacation guide and road atlas.   With Goushá.   Los
       Angeles, Calif. , [1966].
       64 p.   col. maps.   28 cm.

5158 Fédération internationale de l'automobile.
       Atlas camping and caravaning.   Roma, 1966.
       66 p.   col. maps.   30 cm.

5159 Firestone-Hispania, S. A.
       Atlas de España y Portugal.   3 ed.   Bilbao, [1964].
       79 p.   col. maps.   28 cm.

5160 Firestone-Hispania, S. A.
       Atlas de España y Portugal.   Bilbao, 1969.
       1 vol.   col. maps.   28 cm.

5161 Firestone-Hispania, S. A.
       Firestone- Hispania nuevo atlas de España y Portugal.
       Bilbao, [1961].
       79 p.   col. maps.   28 cm.

5162 Foldex (France), Ltd.
       France: atlas des grandes routes.   Paris, [1966].
       32 p.   col. maps.   19 cm.

5163 Ford Motor Argentina.
       Atlas de los camĭnos argentinos.   2 ed.   By Enrique
       C. Pugliese.   Buenos Aires, [1967].
       77 p.   col. maps.   24 cm.

5164 Freytag-Berndt & Artaria.
       Autoatlas von Österreich.   Wien, [1950].
       85 p.   col. maps.   26 cm.

5165 Freytag-Berndt & Artaria.
       Autoatlas von Österreich.   Wien, [1954].
       87 p.   col. maps.   26 cm.

5166 Freytag-Berndt & Artaria.
      Autoatlas von Österreich.   Wien, [1956].
      87 p.   col.   maps.   26 cm.

5167 Freytag-Berndt & Artaria.
      Autoatlas von Österreich.   Wien, [1958].
      67 p.   col.   maps.   26 cm.

5168 Freytag-Berndt & Artaria.
      Autoatlas von Österreich.   Wien, [1962].
      67 p.   col.   maps.   26 cm.

5169 Freytag-Berndt & Artaria.
      Autoatlas von Österreich.   Wien, 1964.
      105 p.   col.   maps.   26 cm.

5170 Freytag-Berndt & Artaria.
      Autoatlas von Österreich.   Wien, [1966].
      67 p.   col.   maps.   26 cm.

5171 Freytag-Berndt & Artaria.
      Autoatlas von Österreich.   Wien, 1968.
      105 p.   col.   maps.   26 cm.

5172 General Drafting Co.
      Family travel atlas.   With Humble Travel Club.
      Houston, Tex. , 1965.
      96 p.   col.   maps.   32. 5 cm.

5173 General Drafting Co.
      Family travel atlas.   Houston, Tex. , [1967].
      96 p.   col.   maps.   29 cm.

5174 Generalstabens litografiska anstalt.
      KAKs Bilatlas över Sverige.   Stockholm, 1955.
      297 p.   col.   maps.   26 cm.

5175 Generalstabens litografiska anstalt.
      KAK Bilatlas.   Stockholm, 1966.
      202 p.   col.   maps.   31 cm.

5176 Generalstabens litografiska anstalt.
      KAK Bilatlas.   Stockholm, [1967].
      202 p.   col.   maps.   31 cm.

5177 Generalstabens litografiska anstalt.
      KAK bilartor.   Stockholm, 1968.
      92 p.   col.   maps.   31 cm.

5178 Generalstabens litografiska anstalt.
     S-N bilatlas över Sverige.   Stockholm, 1964.
     123 p.   col. maps.   24 cm.

5179 Generalstabens litografiska anstalt.
     S-N bilkarta över Sverige.   Stockholm, 1957.
     104 p.   col. maps.   24 cm.

5180 Geographers' Map Co.
     Geographers' road atlas: Great Britain and Northern
     Ireland.   By Phyllis Pearsall.   Sevenoaks, Kent,
     [1964].
     158 p.   col. maps.   28 cm.

5181 Geographia, Ltd.
     Austin Great-Britain road atlas and touring guide.
     7 ed.   London, [1970].
     1 vol.   col. maps.   28 cm.

5182 Geographia, Ltd.
     Geographia European motoring atlas and guide.
     London, [1969].
     1 vol.   col. maps.   26 cm.

5183 Geographia, Ltd.
     Geographia road atlas of Great Britain.   London,
     [1969].
     1 vol.   col. maps.   26 cm.

5184 Geographia, Ltd.
     Great Britain road atlas; showing new and projected
     pass roads and motorways.   London, [1960].
     30 p.   col. maps.   26 cm.

5185 Geographia, Ltd.
     Pocket road map of the British Isles.   London, [1966].
     64 p.   col. maps.   14 cm.

5186 Geographia, Ltd.
     Road atlas and route guide.   London, [195-].
     6 vol.   16 cm.

5187 Geographia, Ltd.
     Road atlas and route guide.   London, [1951].
     6 vol.   16 cm.

5188 Goushá, H. M. Co.
     American highway atlas.   Chicago, 1962.
     112 p.   col. maps.   43 cm.

5189 Goushá, H. M. Co.
     Conoco deluxe touraide.   With Continental Oil Co.
     Chicago, 1963.
     128 p.   col. maps.   31.5 cm.

5190 Goushá, H. M. Co.
     Conoco deluxe touraide travel guide.   With Conti-
     nental Oil Co.   Chicago, 1964.
     128 p.   col. maps.   31 cm.

5191 Goushá, H. M. Co.
     Conoco pocket touraide travel guide.   Chicago, 1964.
     15 p.   col. maps.   23 cm.

5192 Goushá, H. M. Co.
     Conoco pocket touraide travel guide.   Chicago, 1965.
     15 p.   col. maps.   23 cm.

5193 Goushá, H. M. Co.
     Discover America road atlas.   San Jose, Calif.,
     [1968].
     64 p.   col. maps.   28 cm.

5194 Goushá, H. M. Co.
     Discover America road atlas.   San Jose, Calif.,
     [1969].
     64 p.   col. maps.   28 cm.

5195 Goushá, H. M. Co.
     National Safety Council road atlas.   Chicago, 1964.
     64 p.   28 cm.

5196 Goushá, H. M. Co.
     North American vacation guide and road atlas.   San
     Jose, Calif., 1967.
     64 p.   col. maps.   28 cm.

5197 Goushá, H. M. Co.
     Shell USA travel guide.   San Jose, Calif., [1968].
     31 p.   col. maps.   28 cm.

5198 Goushá, H. M. Co.
     Trip plan (atlas), Allstate Motor Club travel service.

Skokie, Ill. , 1965.
1 vol.   col.   maps.   29 cm.

5199 Goushá, H. M. Co.
United States, Canada and Mexico.   Chicago, 1963.
64 p.   col.   maps.   26 cm.

5200 Goushá, H. M. Co.
United States, Canada and Mexico.   Road atlas.
With National Safety Council.   San Jose, Calif. , 1965.
64 p.   28 cm.

5201 Grosset & Dunlap.
The new Grosset road atlas of the United States,
Canada and Mexico.   With Diversified Map Corporation.   New York, 1967.
144 p.   col.   maps.   34 cm.

5202 Grosset & Dunlap.
The new Grosset road atlas of the United States,
Canada and Mexico.   With Diversified Map Corporation.   New York, [1968].
144 p.   col.   maps.   34 cm.

5203 Grosset & Dunlap.
The new Grosset road atlas of the United States,
Canada and Mexico.   With Diversified Map Corporation.   New York, [1969].
144 p.   col.   maps.   34 cm.

5204 Haack, Hermann.
Autoatlas der Deutschen Demokratischen Republik.
1 ed.   Gotha, 1962.
80 p.   col.   maps.   27 cm.

5205 Haack, Hermann.
Autoatlas der Deutschen Demokratischen Republik.
2 ed.   Gotha, 1963.
97 p.   col.   maps.   27 cm.

5206 Haack, Hermann.
Verkehrsatlas.   Deutsche Demokratische Republik.
1 ed.   Gotha, 1959.
115 p.   col.   maps.   18 cm.

5207 Haack, Hermann.
Verkehrsatlas.   Deutsche Demokratische Republik.

2 ed.   Gotha, 1960.
115 p.   col. maps.   18 cm.

5208 Haack, Hermann.
    <u>Verkehrsatlas.</u>   Deutsche Demokratische Republik.
    3 ed.   Gotha, 1961.
    83 p.   col. maps.   18 cm.

5209 Haack, Hermann.
    <u>Verkehrsatlas.</u>   Deutsche Demokratische Republik.
    4 ed.   Gotha, 1962.
    87 p.   col. maps.   18 cm.

5210 Haack, Hermann.
    <u>Verkehrsatlas.</u>   Deutsche Demokratische Republik.
    5 ed.   Gotha, 1963.
    111 p.   col. maps.   18 cm.

5211 Haack, Hermann.
    <u>Verkehrsatlas.</u>   Deutsche Demokratische Republik.
    6 ed.   Gotha, 1966.
    220 p.   col. maps.   18 cm.

5212 Hallwag, A. G.
    <u>Europa Auto Atlas.</u>   Bern, [1967].
    124 p.   col. maps.   26 cm.

5213 Hallwag, A. G.
    <u>Europa touring; motoring guide of Europe.</u>   Bern,
    1962.
    740 p.   col. maps.   26 cm.

5214 Hallwag, A. G.
    <u>Europa touring; motoring guide to Europe.</u>   Bern,
    1966.
    788 p.   col. maps.   26 cm.

5215 Hallwag, A. G.
    <u>Europa touring; motoring guide to Europe.</u>   Bern,
    1967.
    788 p.   col. maps.   26 cm.

5216 Hallwag, A. G.
    <u>Europa touring; motoring guide to Europe.</u>   Bern,
    1968.
    788 p.   col. maps.   26 cm.

5217 Hallwag, A. G.
   Europa touring; motoring guide to Europe. Bern,
   1969.
   788 p.   col. maps.   26 cm.

5218 Hammond, C. S. & Co., Inc.
   Hammond road atlas of the United States, Canada,
   Mexico. Maplewood, N. J., [1964].
   48 p.   col. maps.   32 cm.

5219 Hammond, C. S. & Co., Inc.
   Hammond road atlas of the United States, Canada,
   Mexico. Maplewood, N. J., 1965.
   48 p.   col. maps.   32 cm.

5220 Hammond, C. S. & Co., Inc.
   Hammond's road atlas and city street guide of the
   United States, Canada, Mexico. Maplewood, N. J.,
   1963.
   96 p.   col. maps.   31 cm.

5221 Hammond, Inc.
   Hammond road atlas. Maplewood, N. J., 1967.
   48 p.   col. maps.   31 cm.

5222 Hammond, Inc.
   Hammond road atlas. Maplewood, N. J., 1969.
   48 p.   col. maps.   31 cm.

5223 Hammond, Inc.
   Road atlas of the United States and Canada. Maplewood, N. J., 1968.
   48 p.   col. maps.   31 cm.

5224 Hellēnikē Leschē Autokiñetou Kai Periēgēséon.
   Road maps and tourist guide of Greece.   (in Greek).
   Athens, 1959.
   42 p.   col. maps.   22 cm.

5225 Hellēnikē Leschē Autokinētou Kai Periēgēséon.
   Road maps and tourist guide of Greece.   (in Greek).
   7 ed.   Athens, [1965].
   44 p.   col. maps.   22 cm.

5226 Hellēnikē Leschē Autokinētou Kai Periēgēséon.
   Road maps and tourist guide of Greece.   (in Greek).
   Athens, [1967].
   44 p.   col. maps.   22 cm.

5227 Hong Kong.   Govt. Printer.
      Road maps of Hong Kong.   Hong Kong, 1953.
      1 vol.   29 cm.

5228 Household Goods Carriers' Bureau.
      Mileage guide No. 8, containing maps and charts
      for determining distances in highway miles between
      points in the United States.   Washington, D. C. ,
      1966.
      338 p.   col. maps.   45 cm.

5229 Imperial Press.
      Atlas guide Denmark.   København, [1963].
      40 p.   col. maps.   24 cm.

5230 Imperial Press.
      Atlas guide Denmark.   København, 1964.
      1 vol.   col. maps.   24 cm.

5231 Istituto Geografico De Agostini.
      Atlante stradale d'Italia.   Novara, 1964.
      1 vol.   col. maps.   24 cm.

5232 Italatlas.
      Atlas.   Guida atlante delle strade d'Italia.   Roma,
      [1956].
      84 p.   col. maps.   25 cm.

5233 Johnston, W. & A. K. & G. W. Bacon, Ltd.
      Autoway atlas.   Great Britain and Ireland.   London,
      1967.
      1 vol.   col. maps.   26 cm.

5234 Johnston, W. & A. K. & G. W. Bacon, Ltd.
      Johnston's A and B roads motoring atlas of Great
      Britain.   Edinburgh, [1958].
      48 p.   col. maps.   34 cm.

5235 Johnston, W. & A. K. & G. W. Bacon, Ltd.
      Johnston's A and B roads motoring atlas of Great
      Britain.   Edinburgh, 1968.
      1 vol.   col. maps.   34 cm.

5236 Johnston, W. & A. K. & G. W. Bacon, Ltd.
      Johnston's county motoring atlas of Great Britain and
      Ireland.   Edinburgh, [1965].
      64 p.   col. maps.   28 cm.

5237 Johnston, W. & A. K. & G. W. Bacon, Ltd.
     Johnston's handy road atlas of Great Britain and
     Ireland. Edinburgh, [1953].
     72 p. col. maps. 19 cm.

5238 Johnston, W. & A. K. & G. W. Bacon, Ltd.
     Johnston's pocket road atlas of Great Britain and
     Ireland. London, [1969].
     64 p. col. maps. 13. 5 cm.

5239 Johnston, W. & A. K. & G. W. Bacon, Ltd.
     Johnston's road atlas of Great Britain. Edinburgh,
     [1964].
     16 p. col. maps. 25 cm.

5240 Johnston, W. & A. K. & G. W. Bacon, Ltd.
     Pocket road atlas of Ireland. London, 1966.
     1 vol. col. maps. 18 cm.

5241 Johnston, W. & A. K. & G. W. Bacon, Ltd.
     Road atlas of Great Britain. 3 miles to 1 inch.
     Edinburgh, [1954].
     370 p. col. maps. 22 cm.

5242 Johnston, W. & A. K. & G. W. Bacon, Ltd.
     Road atlas of Great Britain. 4 ed. Edinburgh,
     [1957].
     370 p. col. maps. 22 cm.

5243 Johnston, W. & A. K. & G. W. Bacon, Ltd.
     3 mile to 1 inch road atlas of Great Britain. 5 ed.
     Edinburgh, London, 1965.
     1 vol. col. maps. 28 cm.

5244 JRO Verlag.
     Der Grosse JRO Europa Autoatlas. München, [1965].
     630 p. col. maps. 24. 5 cm.

5245 JRO Verlag.
     JRO Atlas für Kraftfahrer und alle Reisenden.
     München, [1950].
     344 p. col. maps. 25 cm.

5246 JRO Verlag.
     JRO Autoatlas. Deutschland, Europäische Reise-
     länder. München, [1954].
     514 p. col. maps. 25 cm.

5247 JRO Verlag.
  JRO Autoatlas. Deutschland, Europäische Reise-
  länder. München, [1955].
  515 p. col. maps. 25 cm.

5248 JRO Verlag.
  JRO Autoatlas. Deutschland, Schweiz, Westöster-
  reich. München, [1953].
  468 p. col. maps. 25 cm.

5249 JRO Verlag.
  JRO Autoatlas Italien, Französische Riviera, West-
  österreich. München, [1955].
  260 p. col. maps. 25 cm.

5250 JRO Verlag.
  JRO Autoatlas Österreich, Südostdeutschland,
  Oberitalien, Nordwest Jugoslawien, Ostschweiz.
  München, [1956].
  239 p. col. maps. 25 cm.

5251 JRO Verlag.
  JRO Strassen atlas. Deutschland. Europa.
  München, [1968].
  78 p. col. maps. 29. 5 cm.

5252 JRO Verlag.
  JRO Strassen Taschenatlas. München, [1951].
  160 p. col. maps. 21 cm.

5253 JRO Verlag.
  JRO Strassen Taschenatlas. 2 ed. München, [1954].
  162 p. col. maps. 21 cm.

5254 Jugoslavenski leksikografski zavod.
  Jugoslavija; auto atlas. Zagreb, [1967].
  1 vol. col. maps. 28 cm.

5255 Jugoslavenski leksikografski zavod.
  Jugoslavija; auto atlas. Zagreb, [1968].
  1 vol. col. maps. 28 cm.

5256 Kalmbach Publishing Co.
  Campground atlas of the United States and Canada.
  Milwaukee, Wisc., 1970-71.
  314 p. col. maps. 28 cm.

5257 Kartografiai Vállalat.
Európa autóatlasza. Budapest, [1968].
192 p. col. maps. 26 cm.

5258 Kartográfiai Vállalat.
Magyarország autóatlasza. Budapest, 1960.
39 p. col. maps. 20. 5 cm.

5259 Kartográfiai Vállalat.
Magyarország autóatlasza. Budapest, 1962.
39 p. col. maps. 20. 5 cm.

5260 Kartográfiai Vállalat.
Magyarország autóatlasza. Budapest, 1966.
135 p. col. maps. 28 cm.

5261 Kartográfiai Vállalat.
Magyarország autóatlasza. Budapest, 1968.
135 p. col. maps. 28 cm.

5262 Kartográfiai Vállalat.
Magyarország autóatlasza. By Sándor Radó. Budapest, 1963.
39 p. col. maps. 20. 5 cm.

5263 Kartográfiai Vállalat.
Magyarország autóatlasza. By Sándor Radó. Budapest, 1968.
40 p. col. maps. 20. 5 cm.

5264 Kartografiai Vállalat.
Magyarországi autóutak térképe. Budapest, 1955.
75 p. col. maps. 22 cm.

5265 Kartográfiai Vállalat.
Magyarországi autóutak térképe. 2 ed. Budapest, 1956.
75 p. col. maps. 22 cm.

5266 Kongelik Norsk automobilklub.
Kartbok for Norge. 2 ed. Oslo, 1954.
103 p. col. maps. 26 cm.

5267 Kongelig Norsk automobilklub.
KNA Kart-og reisehändbok. Oslo, [1967].
1 vol. col. maps. 26 cm.

5268 König, Hans, Verlag.
    Caltex Städte und Reiseatlas der Bundesrepublik
    Deutschland. 4 ed. Bergen-Enkheim, 1964.
    273 p. col. maps. 29 cm.

5269 König, Hans, Verlag.
    Deutscher Ferien Atlas. Frankfurt am Main, [1960].
    84 p. col. maps. 24 cm.

5270 König, Hans, Verlag.
    Fina Europa Atlas. 1 ed. Frankfurt am Main,
    [1963].
    114 p. col. maps. 25 cm.

5271 König, Hans, Verlag.
    Reiseatlas Deutschland, Europa. Enkheim, 1965.
    61 p. col. maps. 29 cm.

5272 König, Hans, Verlag.
    Reiseatlas Deutschland, Europa. Frankfurt am
    Main, [1966].
    64 p. col. maps. 29 cm.

5273 Kümmerly & Frey.
    All about Switzerland. [Atlas]. Bern, [1957].
    24 p. col. maps. 13 cm.

5274 Kümmerly & Frey.
    Autoatlas Schweiz. Bern, [1952].
    48 p. col. maps. 23 cm.

5275 Kümmerly & Frey.
    Autoatlas Schweiz. Bern, [1954].
    48 p. col. maps. 23 cm.

5276 Kümmerly & Frey.
    Autoatlas Schweiz, Mitteleuropa. Bern, [1955].
    48 p. col. maps. 24 cm.

5277 Kümmerly & Frey.
    Autoatlas Schweiz, Mitteleuropa. Bern, [1956].
    48 p. col. maps. 24 cm.

5278 Kümmerly & Frey.
    Auto-Europa. Bern, 1965.
    216 p. col. maps. 26 cm.

5279 Kümmerly & Frey.
Auto Europa. Bern, 1966.
216 p. col. maps. 26 cm.

5280 Kümmerly & Frey.
Autokarte Schweiz und angrenzende Gebiete. Zürich,
[1955].
48 p. col. maps. 22 cm.

5281 Kümmerly & Frey.
Euroatlas; Strassen-und Reise Atlas. Bern, 1961.
152 p. col. maps. 30 cm.

5282 Kümmerly & Frey.
Euroatlas; Strassen-und Reise Atlas. Bern, [1963].
150 p. col. maps. 30 cm.

5283 Kümmerly & Frey.
Euroatlas; Strassen-und Reise Atlas. Bern, 1966.
150 p. col. maps. 30 cm.

5284 Kümmerly & Frey.
Europa, Europe. Strassenatlas. Bern, 1962.
218 p. col. maps. 26 cm.

5285 Kümmerly & Frey.
Europa, Europe, Strassenatlas. Bern, [1965].
140 p. col. maps. 26 cm.

5286 Kümmerly & Frey.
Europa, Europe, Strassenatlas. 4 ed. Bern, 1967.
218 p. col. maps. 26 cm.

5287 Kümmerly & Frey.
Europa. Strassenatlas. 19 ed. Bern, [1965].
43 p. col. maps. 26 cm.

5288 Kümmerly & Frey.
Europe, atlas routier. Bern, [1955].
140 p. col. maps. 23 cm.

5289 Kümmerly & Frey.
Europe, atlas routier. Bern, [1957].
140 p. col. maps. 23 cm.

5290 Kümmerly & Frey.
Schweiz. [Atlas]. Bern, [1956].
28 p. col. maps. 15 cm.

5291 Kümmerly & Frey.
      Schweiz und angrenzende Länder; Strassenatlas.
      Bern, [1961].
      60 p.   col. maps.   23 cm.

5292 Kümmerly & Frey.
      Schweiz, angrenzende Länder und Stadtpläne.   Bern,
      [1962].
      60 p.   col. maps.   23 cm.

5293 Kümmerly & Frey.
      Schweiz, angrenzende Länder und Stadtpläne.   Bern,
      [1965].
      60 p.   col. maps.   23 cm.

5294 Kümmerly & Frey.
      Schweiz, angrenzende Länder und Stadtpläne.   Bern,
      [1966].
      60 p.   col. maps.   23 cm.

5295 Kungliga Automobil Klubben.
      Kungl.   Automobilklubbens Karta över Sverige.
      Stockholm, 1954.
      15 p.   col. maps.   26 cm.

5296 Kungliga Automobil Klubben.
      Road atlas, Sweden.   With Generalstabens litografiska
      anstalt.   Stockholm, 1961.
      128 p.   col. maps.   26 cm.

5297 Landkartenverlag VEB.
      Atlas für Motortouristik der Deutschen Demokratischen
      Republik.   1 ed.   Berlin, 1963.
      228 p.   col. maps.   23 cm.

5298 Landkartenverlag VEB.
      Atlas für Motortouristik der Deutschen Demokratischen
      Republik.   2 ed.   Berlin, 1964.
      228 p.   col. maps.   23 cm.

5299 Landkartenverlag VEB.
      Autoatlas der Deutschen Demokratischen Republik.
      4 ed.   Berlin, [1966].
      133 p.   col. maps.   25. 5 cm.

5300 Landkartenverlag VEB.
      Reiseatlas der Deutschen Demokratischen Republik.

Berlin, 1967.
100 p.   col. maps.   26 cm.

5301 Landkartenverlag VEB.
Reiseatlas der Deutschen Demokratischen Republik.
Berlin, [1969].
100 p.   col. maps.   26 cm.

5302 Lebanon.   Direction des affaires géographiques.
Liban: carte routière.   Beyrouth, [1967].
21 p.   col. maps.   30 cm.

5303 Le Carrousel Publicité.
Gastronomical roads (atlas) of the French provinces.
Tours, 1967.
36 p.   col. maps.   27 cm.

5304 Librairie Mellottée.
Atlas de route Mellottée.   Paris, [1950].
157 p.   col. maps.   19 cm.

5305 Maanmittaushallitus.
Suomi.   Finland.   Yleiskartta 1:400,000 general
karta.   Helsinski, 1950.
166 p.   col. maps.   25 cm.

5306 Macmillan & Co., Ltd.
Camping maps U.S.A.   By Glenn and Dale Rhodes.
New York, 1963.
297 p.   25 cm.

5307 Macmillan & Co., Ltd.
Camping maps U.S.A.   By Glenn and Dale Rhodes.
New York, 1964.
352 p.   26 cm.

5308 Mairs Geographischer Verlag.
Der Grosse Shell Atlas.   1 ed.   Stuttgart, [1960].
419 p.   col. maps.   27 cm.

5309 Mairs Geographischer Verlag.
Der Grosse Shell Atlas.   8 ed.   Stuttgart, 1963.
335 p.   col. maps.   26.5 cm.

5310 Mairs Geographischer Verlag.
Der Grosse Shell Atlas.   11 ed.   Stuttgart, 1965.
460 p.   col. maps.   26.5 cm.

5311 Mairs Geographischer Verlag.
      Der Grosse Shell Atlas.   12 ed.   Stuttgart, 1966.
      460 p.   col.   maps.   26. 5 cm.

5312 Mairs Geographischer Verlag.
      Der Grosse Shell Atlas.   Stuttgart, 1969/70.
      460 p.   col.   maps.   26. 5 cm.

5313 Mairs Geographischer Verlag.
      Der Grosse Shell Atlas.   Deutschland und Europa.
      10 ed.   Stuttgart, [1965].
      259 p.   col.   maps.   27 cm.

5314 Mairs Geographischer Verlag.
      Der Grosse Shell Atlas.   Deutschland und Europa.
      11 ed.   Stuttgart, [1966].
      283 p.   col.   maps.   27 cm.

5315 Mairs Geographischer Verlag.
      Der Grosse Shell Atlas.   Deutschland und Europa.
      12 ed.   Stuttgart, [1967].
      283 p.   col.   maps.   27 cm.

5316 Mairs Geographischer Verlag.
      Der Grosse Shell Atlas.   Deutschland und Europa.
      13 ed.   Stuttgart, [1968].
      283 p.   col.   maps.   27 cm.

5317 Mairs Geographischer Verlag.
      Der Grosse Shell Atlas.   Deutschland und Europa.
      14 ed.   Stuttgart, 1969.
      283 p.   col.   maps.   27 cm.

5318 Mairs Geographischer Verlag.
      Europa.   Shell Atlas.   Stuttgart, 1964.
      178 p.   col.   maps.   27 cm.

5319 Mairs Geographischer Verlag.
      Shell Atlas.   20 ed.   Stuttgart, [1957].
      272 p.   col.   maps.   27 cm.

5320 Mairs Geographischer Verlag.
      Shell-Atlas.   Stuttgart, [1961].
      1 vol.   col.   maps.   27 cm.

5321 Mairs Geographischer Verlag.
      Shell Autoatlas.   10 ed.   Stuttgart, [1952].
      206 p.   col.   maps.   27 cm.

5322 Mairs Geographischer Verlag.
    Shell Autoatlas. 11 ed. Stuttgart, [1952].
    206 p. col. maps. 27 cm.

5323 Mairs Geographischer Verlag.
    Shell Autoatlas. 12 ed. Stuttgart, [1954].
    266 p. col. maps. 27 cm.

5324 Mairs Geographischer Verlag.
    Shell Autoatlas. 14 ed. Stuttgart, [1954].
    266 p. col. maps. 27 cm.

5325 Mairs Geographischer Verlag.
    Shell Autoatlas. 15 ed. Stuttgart, [1955].
    268 p. col. maps. 27 cm.

5326 Mairs Geographischer Verlag.
    Shell Autoatlas. A new atlas of Germany. Stuttgart,
    [1951].
    109 p. col. maps. 27 cm.

5327 Mairs Geographischer Verlag.
    Shell Autoatlas, ein neues Kartenwerk von Deutsch-
    land. Stuttgart, [1950].
    109 p. col. maps. 27 cm.

5328 Mairs Geographischer Verlag.
    Shell Autoatlas; ein neues Kartenwerk von Deutsch-
    land. 5 ed. Stuttgart, [1951].
    129 p. col. maps. 27 cm.

5329 Mairs Geographischer Verlag.
    Shell Autoatlas; ein neues Kartenwerk von Deutsch-
    land. Stuttgart, [1952].
    129 p. col. maps. 27 cm.

5330 Mairs Geographischer Verlag.
    Shell Autoatlas. Maps of Germany, maps of Euro-
    pean countries. Stuttgart, [1954].
    266 p. col. maps. 27 cm.

5331 Mairs Geographischer Verlag.
    Shell Autoatlas. Maps of Germany, maps of Euro-
    pean countries. Stuttgart, [1956].
    268 p. col. maps. 27 cm.

5332 Mairs Geographischer Verlag.
    Varta Autoatlas. Deutschland. Stuttgart, 1963.

166 p.   col. maps.   29 cm.

5333 Malaysia.   Directorate of National Mapping.
Caltex motorist's guide & map book.   Singapore,
[1969].
24 p.   col. maps.   23 cm.

5334 Map Productions, Ltd.
Motorways: A new atlas to illustrate the motorway
system of Great Britain.   London, [1969].
1 vol.   col. maps.   27 cm.

5335 Map Studio Productions, pty. , Ltd.
BP Padkaarte.   Road maps.   Cape Town, [1963].
22 p.   col. maps.   28 cm.

5336 México.   Comisión Nacional de Caminos Vecinales.
Atlas con la red de caminos vecinales construidos
en el sexenio 1958-1964.   Mexico, [1964].
31 p.   col. maps.   60 cm.

5337 México.   Comisión Nacional de Caminos Vecinales.
Atlas Geografico Nacional.   Mexico, 1964.
29 p.   col. maps.   61 cm.

5338 Michelin et Cie.
Atlas des routes de France.   Paris, 1951-52.
40 p.   col. maps.   26 cm.

5339 Michelin et Cie.
Atlas des routes de France.   Paris, 1953-54.
40 p.   col. maps.   26 cm.

5340 Michelin et Cie.
Atlas des routes de France.   Paris, [1955].
40 p.   col. maps.   26 cm.

5341 Michelin et Cie.
Atlas des routes de France.   Paris, [1956].
40 p.   col. maps.   26 cm.

5342 Michelin et Cie.
Atlas des routes de France.   Paris, [1958].
40 p.   col. maps.   26 cm.

5343 Michelin et Cie.
Camping en France [Atlas].   Paris, 1957.
85 p.   25 cm.

5344 Michelin Tyre Co.
Michelin motoring atlas [of Great Britain].   Stoke-
on-Trent, [1954].
37 p.   col. maps.   25 cm.

5345 Motormännens riksförbund.
M:s vägvisare; Sverige.   Stockholm, 1957.
352 p.   col. maps. 25 cm.

5346 Motormännens riksförbund.
M:s vägvisare: Sverige.   Stockholm, [1961].
1 vol.   col. maps. 25 cm.

5347 Motormännens riksförbund.
M:s vägvisara: Sverige.   Stockholm, [1963].
1 vol.   col. maps.   25 cm.

5348 Motormännens riksförbund.
M:s vägvisare: Sverige.   7 ed.   Stockholm, [1965].
1 vol.   col. maps.   25 cm.

5349 Motormännens riksförbund.
M:s vägvisare: Sverige.   8 ed.   Stockholm, 1968.
1 vol.   col. maps.   25 cm.

5350 Motor Manual.
Highways of Australia.   Melbourne, [1949-50].
208 p.   25 cm.

5351 Motor Manual.
Highways of Australia.   4 ed.   By Keith Winser.
Melbourne, 1954.
240 p.   25 cm.

5352 Motor Manual.
Highways of Australia.   5 ed.   By Keith Winser.
Melbourne, [1956].
248 p.   25 cm.

5353 Motor Manual.
Highways of Australia, road atlas.   6 ed.   By Keith
Winser.   Melbourne, [1958].
250 p.   25 cm.

5354 Motor Manual.
Highways of Australia, road atlas.   6 ed.   By Keith
Winser.   Melbourne, [1959].
248 p.   25 cm.

5355 Motor Manual.
    Highways of Australia, road atlas.   7 ed.   By Keith
    Winser.   Melbourne, 1960/61.
    205 p.   25 cm.

5356 Motor Manual.
    Highways of Australia, road atlas.   8 ed.   By Keith
    Winser.   Melbourne, 1966.
    248 p.   25 cm.

5357 National Bus Traffic Association.
    Atlas of motor bus routes and express blocks no
    A-602-B.   Chicago, 1966.
    90 p.   40 cm.

5358 Nelson, Thomas & Sons, Ltd.
    The Sunday Times road atlas.   London, 1968.
    188 p.   col. maps.   29 cm.

5359 Netherlands.   Bureau voor Wegen en Verkeersstatistiek.
    Atlas van de rijkswegen, 1949.   's Gravenhage,
    [1950].
    39 p.   col. maps.   30 cm.

5360 Netherlands.   Dienst Verkeersonderzoek.
    Atlas van de rijkswegen, 1954.   3 ed.   's Graven-
    hage, [1954].
    14 p.   col. maps.   30 cm.

5361 Netherlands.   Staatsdrukkerij en Uitgeverijbedrijf.
    Atlas rijkswegen, 1960.   's Gravenhage, 1962.
    15 p.   col. maps.   29 cm.

5362 Netherlands.   Staatsdrukkerij en Uitgeverijbedrijf.
    Atlas van de rijkswegen.   's Gravenhage, 1955.
    56 p.   col. maps.   29 cm.

5363 Newnes, George, Ltd.
    Newnes motorists touring maps and gazetteer.   With
    Bartholomew.   London, [1950].
    160 p.   col. maps.   29 cm.

5364 Newnes, George, Ltd.
    Newnes' motorists' touring maps and gazetteer.
    London, [1965].
    48 p.   col. maps.   29 cm.

5365 Newnes, George, Ltd.
     Newnes' motorists' touring maps and gazetteer of
     Scotland. 1 ed. With Bartholomew. London, [1965].
     74 p. col. maps. 29 cm.

5366 Newnes, George, Ltd.
     Newnes' motorists' touring maps and gazetteer of
     Western Europe. London, [1963].
     51 p. col. maps. 29 cm.

5367 Nuffield Organization.
     Great Britain road atlas and touring guide. 7 ed.
     Oxford, [196-].
     1 vol. col. maps. 29 cm.

5368 Nuffield Organization.
     Motoring atlas and touring guide to the Continent.
     2 ed. By K. G. Cleveley. Oxford, [1964].
     88 p. col. maps. 28 cm.

5369 Nuffield Organization.
     Nuffield road atlas of Great Britain. 4 ed. Oxford,
     [1957].
     75 p. col. maps. 28 cm.

5370 Odhams Press, Ltd.
     Odhams new road atlas of Great Britain, Ireland and
     Western Europe. London, [1963].
     239 p. col. maps. 24 cm.

5371 Oxford University Press.
     Oxford travel atlas of Britain. London, New York,
     1953.
     33 p. col. maps. 20 cm.

5372 Peru. Dirección de Caminos.
     Mapa vial de los Departmentos del Perú. Lima,
     1956-
     in parts. col. maps. 77 cm.

5373 Peugeot.
     Atlas routier Peugeot. Paris, [1954].
     19 p. col. maps. 29 cm.

5374 Philip, George & Son, Ltd.
     National road atlas of Great Britain. London, [1963].
     103 p. col. maps. 28 cm.

5375 Philip, George & Son, Ltd.
National road atlas of Great Britain.   London, 1967.
103 p.   col.   maps.   28 cm.

5376 Philip, George & Son, Ltd.
Philip's road atlas of Great Britain.   London, 1963.
47 p.   col.   maps.   28 cm.

5377 Philip, George & Son, Ltd.
Road atlas of Great Britain.   With Shell-Mex and
BP Ltd.   London, 1964.
143 p.   col.   maps.   28 cm.

5378 Philip, George & Son, Ltd.
Road atlas of Great Britain.   With Shell-Mex and
BP Ltd.   London, 1965.
143 p.   col.   maps.   28 cm.

5379 Philip, George & Son, Ltd.
Road atlas of Great Britain.   With Shell-Mex and
BP Ltd.   London, 1966.
144 p.   col.   maps.   28. 5 cm.

5380 Philip, George & Son, Ltd.
Road atlas of Great Britain.   With Shell-Mex and
BP Ltd.   London, [1968].
144 p.   col.   maps.   28 cm.

5381 Philip, George & Son, Ltd.
Road atlas of Great Britain.   With special London
section & town plans.   London, [1968].
176 p.   col.   maps.   29 cm.

5382 Philippines.   Bureau of Public Works.
Official road map of the Philippines.   Manila, [1952].
15 p.   52 cm.

5383 Poland.   Państwowe przedsiębiorstwo wydawnictw
kartograficznych.
Atlas samochodowy Polski.   1 ed.   Warszawa, 1958.
155 p.   col.   maps.   23 cm.

5384 Poland.   Państwowe przedsiębiorstwo wydawnictw
kartograficznych.
Atlas samochodowy Polski.   3 ed.   Warszawa, 1964.
155 p.   col.   maps.   23 cm.

5385 Poland. Państwowe przedsiębiorstwo wydawnictw
kartograficznych.
Atlas samochodowy Polski. 4 ed. Warszawa, 1965.
155 p. col. maps. 23 cm.

5386 Poland. Państwowe przedsiębiorstwo wydawnictw
kartograficznych.
Atlas samochodowy Polski. 5 ed. Warszawa, 1967.
155 p. col. maps. 23 cm.

5387 Poland. Państwowe przedsiębiorstwo wydawnictw
kartograficznych.
Atlas samochodowy Polski. 6 ed. Warszawa, 1968.
155 p. col. maps. 23 cm.

5388 Poland. Państwowe przedsiębiorstwo wydawnictw
kartograficznych.
Atlas samochodowy Polski. Warszawa, 1969.
155 p. col. maps. 23 cm.

5389 Rabén & Sjögren.
Europa guide. With Royal Automobile Club. Stockholm, [1964].
484 p. col. maps. 25 cm.

5390 Rand McNally & Co.
Chevrolet's family travel guide. Chicago, 1967.
122 p. col. maps. 28 cm.

5391 Rand McNally & Co.
Gulf travel atlas and vacation planning guide.
Chicago, 1968.
248 p. col. maps. 28 cm.

5392 Rand McNally & Co.
Rand McNally interstate road atlas: United States,
Canada, Mexico. Chicago, [1967].
96 p. col. maps. 28 cm.

5393 Rand McNally & Co.
Rand McNally interstate road atlas: United States,
Canada, Mexico. Chicago, 1968.
96 p. col. maps. 28 cm.

5394 Rand McNally & Co.
Rand McNally road atlas and travel guide, United
States, Canada, Mexico. Chicago, 1963.
84 p. col. maps. 25 cm.

5395 Rand McNally & Co.
    Rand McNally road atlas and travel guide, United
    States, Canada, Mexico. Chicago, 1964.
    84 p. col. maps. 25 cm.

5396 Rand McNally & Co.
    Rand McNally road atlas and travel guide, United
    States, Canada, Mexico. Chicago, 1965.
    84 p. col. maps. 25 cm.

5397 Rand McNally & Co.
    Rand McNally road atlas and travel guide, United
    States, Canada, Mexico. Chicago, 1966.
    84 p. col. maps. 25 cm.

5398 Rand McNally & Co.
    Rand McNally road atlas and travel guide, United
    States, Canada, Mexico. Chicago, 1967.
    96 p. col. maps. 25 cm.

5399 Rand McNally & Co.
    Rand McNally road atlas and travel guide, United
    States, Canada, Mexico. Chicago, 1968.
    96 p. col. maps. 25 cm.

5400 Rand McNally & Co.
    Rand McNally road atlas and travel guide, United
    States, Canada, Mexico. Chicago, 1969.
    96 p. col. maps. 25 cm.

5401 Rand McNally & Co.
    Rand McNally road atlas and travel guide, United
    States, Canada, Mexico. Chicago, 1970.
    96 p. col. maps. 25 cm.

5402 Rand McNally & Co.
    Rand McNally road atlas, United States, Canada,
    Mexico. Chicago, 1950.
    112 p. col. maps. 40 cm.

5403 Rand McNally & Co.
    Rand McNally road atlas, United States, Canada,
    Mexico. Chicago, 1951.
    112 p. col. maps. 40 cm.

5404 Rand McNally & Co.
    Rand McNally road atlas, United States, Canada,

      Mexico.   Chicago, 1952.
      <u>112 p.</u> col. maps.   40 cm.

5405 Rand McNally & Co.
      <u>Rand McNally road atlas, United States, Canada,</u>
      <u>Mexico.</u>   Chicago, 1953.
      112 p. col. maps.   40 cm.

5406 Rand McNally & Co.
      <u>Rand McNally road atlas, United States, Canada,</u>
      <u>Mexico.</u>   Chicago, 1954.
      112 p. col. maps.   40 cm.

5407 Rand McNally & Co.
      <u>Rand McNally road atlas, United States, Canada,</u>
      <u>Mexico.</u>   Chicago, 1955.
      112 p. col. maps.   40 cm.

5408 Rand McNally & Co.
      <u>Rand McNally road atlas, United States, Canada,</u>
      <u>Mexico.</u>   Chicago, 1956.
      112 p. col. maps.   40 cm.

5409 Rand McNally & Co.
      <u>Rand McNally road atlas, United States, Canada,</u>
      <u>Mexico.</u>   Chicago, 1957.
      112 p. col. maps.   40 cm.

5410 Rand McNally & Co.
      <u>Rand McNally road atlas, United States, Canada,</u>
      <u>Mexico.</u>   Chicago, 1958.
      112 p. col. maps.   40 cm.

5411 Rand McNally & Co.
      <u>Rand McNally road atlas, United States, Canada,</u>
      <u>Mexico.</u>   Chicago, 1959.
      112 p. col. maps.   40 cm.

5412 Rand McNally & Co.
      <u>Rand McNally road atlas, United States, Canada,</u>
      <u>Mexico.</u>   Chicago, 1960.
      112 p. col. maps.   40 cm.

5413 Rand McNally & Co.
      <u>Rand McNally road atlas, United States, Canada,</u>
      <u>Mexico.</u>   Chicago, 1961.
      112 p. col. maps.   40 cm.

5414 Rand McNally & Co.
  Rand McNally road atlas, United States, Canada,
  Mexico. Chicago, 1962.
  112 p. col. maps. 40 cm.

5415 Rand McNally & Co.
  Rand McNally road atlas, United States, Canada,
  Mexico. Chicago, 1963.
  112 p. col. maps. 40 cm.

5416 Rand McNally & Co.
  Rand McNally road atlas, United States, Canada,
  Mexico. Chicago, 1964.
  112 p. col. maps. 38 cm.

5417 Rand McNally & Co.
  Rand McNally road atlas, United States, Canada,
  Mexico. Chicago, 1965.
  112 p. col. maps. 40 cm.

5418 Rand McNally & Co.
  Rand McNally road atlas, United States, Canada,
  Mexico. Chicago, 1966.
  114 p. col. maps. 40 cm.

5419 Rand McNally & Co.
  Rand McNally road atlas, United States, Canada,
  Mexico. Chicago, 1967.
  114 p. col. maps. 40 cm.

5420 Rand McNally & Co.
  Rand McNally road atlas, United States, Canada,
  Mexico. Chicago, 1968.
  114 p. col. maps. 40 cm.

5421 Rand McNally & Co.
  Rand McNally road atlas, United States, Canada,
  Mexico. Chicago, 1969.
  114 p. col. maps. 40 cm.

5422 Rand McNally & Co.
  Rand McNally road atlas, United States, Canada,
  Mexico. Chicago, 1970.
  114 p. col. maps. 40 cm.

5423 Rand McNally & Co.
  Rand McNally vacation atlas guide: Canada, United

States, Mexico. Chicago, [1965].
108 p. col. maps. 26 cm.

5424 Rand McNally & Co.
Rolph McNally Canadian road atlas; travel guide with
campground information. Toronto, [1969].
96 p. col. maps. 29 cm.

5425 Rand McNally & Co.
Texaco touring atlas: United States, Canada, Mexico.
New York, 1965.
220 p. col. maps. 38 cm.

5426 Rand McNally & Co.
Texaco touring atlas: United States, Canada, Mexico.
New York, 1966.
220 p. col. maps. 38 cm.

5427 Rand McNally & Co.
Texaco touring atlas: United States, Canada, Mexico.
New York, 1967.
220 p. col. maps. 38 cm.

5428 Rand McNally & Co.
Texaco touring atlas: United States, Canada, Mexico.
Chicago, 1968.
220 p. col. maps. 38 cm.

5429 Rand McNally & Co.
Texaco touring atlas: United States, Canada, Mexico.
Chicago, [1969].
220 p. col. maps. 38 cm.

5430 Rand McNally & Co.
Texaco travel atlas: United States, Canada, Mexico.
Chicago, [1970].
220 p. col. maps. 38 cm.

5431 Ravenstein Geographische Verlagsanstalt.
Autoatlas Benelux und Europa. Frankfurt am Main,
1964.
36 p. col. maps. 29 cm.

5432 Ravenstein Geographische Verlagsanstalt.
Autoatlas Benelux und Europa. Frankfurt am Main,
[1965].
56 p. col. maps. 29 cm.

5433 Ravenstein Geographische Verlagsanstalt.
     Auto-Atlas Europa.   Frankfurt am Main, [1966].
     80 p.   col. maps.   38 cm.

5434 Ravenstein Geographische Verlagsanstalt.
     Frisia Reise Atlas.   Deutschland und Europa.
     Frankfurt, 1967.
     66 p.   col. maps.   29 cm.

5435 Ravenstein Geographische Verlagsanstalt.
     Strassen Atlas Bundesrepublik Deutschland.   Frank-
     furt, [1955].
     128 p.   col. maps.   25 cm.

5436 Ravenstein Geographische Verlagsanstalt.
     Strassen Atlas Bundesrepublik Deutschland.   Frank-
     furt, [1957].
     128 p.   col. maps.   25 cm.

5437 Ravenstein Geographische Verlagsanstalt.
     Strassen; der aktuelle Auto-Atlas Deutschland und
     Europa.   Frankfurt am Main, [1966].
     1 vol.   col. maps.   29 cm.

5438 Ravenstein Geographische Verlagsanstalt.
     Strassen; der aktuelle Auto-Atlas Deutschland und
     Europa.   Frankfurt am Main, [1969].
     66 p.   col. maps.   29 cm.

5439 Ravenstein Geographische Verlagsanstalt.
     Strassen Deutschland und Europa.   2 ed.   Frankfurt
     am Main, [1962].
     51 p.   col. maps.   29 cm.

5440 Ravenstein Geographische Verlagsanstalt.
     Strassen Deutschland und Europa.   3 ed.   Frankfurt
     am Main, 1963.
     55 p.   col. maps.   29 cm.

5441 Ravenstein Geographische Verlagsanstalt.
     Strassen Deutschland und Europa.   5 ed.   Frankfurt
     am Main, 1964.
     57 p.   col. maps.   29 cm.

5442 Ravenstein Geographische Verlagsanstalt.
     Strassen Deutschland und Europa.   Frankfurt am
     Main, [1966].
     1 vol.   col. maps.   29 cm.

5443 Reader's Digest Association, Ltd.
The Reader's Digest A. A. Book of the road. London, 1966.
1 vol. col. maps. 28 cm.

5444 Reader's Digest Association, Ltd.
The Reader's Digest A. A. Book of the road. 2 ed.
London, 1968.
1 vol. col. maps. 28 cm.

5445 Reise und Verkehrsverlag.
Atlas & Führer Italien. Stuttgart, [1957].
216 p. col. maps. 26 cm.

5446 Romania. Asociatia Automobiliştilor din R. P. R.
Republica Populară Romînă. Hartă automobilistica.
Bucuresti, 1965.
32 p. col. maps. 19 cm.

5447 Royal Automobile Club.
Camping and caravaning guide and atlas of Europe.
3 ed. London, 1966.
66 p. col. maps. 30 cm.

5448 Royal Automobile Club.
Camping and caravaning guide and atlas of Europe.
4 ed. London, 1967.
66 p. col. maps. 30 cm.

5449 Royal Automobile Club.
Camping and caravaning guide and atlas of Europe.
5 ed. London, 1968.
66 p. col. maps. 30 cm.

5450 Royal Automobile Club.
Camping and caravaning guide and atlas of Europe.
6 ed. London, 1969.
66 p. col. maps. 30 cm.

5451 Royal East African Automobile Assoc.
Road book of East Africa. Nairobi, 1952.
227 p. col. maps. 24 cm.

5452 Schweizer Reisekasse.
Reiseatlas Schweiz und Ausland. Bern, [1957].
72 p. col. maps. 21 cm.

5453 Shell Company of South Africa, Ltd.
      Shell road map of southern Africa.   Cape Town, 1953.
      48 p.   col. maps.   28 cm.

5454 Shell Moçambique, Ltd.
      Estados de Moçambique.   Laurenço Marques, [1968].
      12 p.   col. maps.   23 cm.

5455 Shell Oil New Zealand, Ltd.
      New Zealand road maps.   Wellington, 1953.
      22 p.   col. maps.   24 cm.

5456 Shell Oil New Zealand, Ltd.
      Shell road maps, New Zealand.   Wellington, [1956].
      32 p.   col. maps.   25 cm.

5457 Shell Oil New Zealand, Ltd.
      Shell road maps of New Zealand.   Wellington,
      [1950-].
      1 vol.   col. maps.   27 cm.

5458 Societá cartografica G. De Agostini.
      Atlante turistico d'Italia.   Milano, [1960].
      114 p.   col. maps.   15 cm.

5459 Società cartografica G. De Agostini.
      Italia, carta stradale 1:650,000.   Milano, [1957].
      13 p.   col. maps.   28 cm.

5460 Société des pétroles Shell Berre.
      Cartoguide Shell Berre: France.   Paris, 1962-64.
      14 p.   col. maps.   24 cm.

5461 Société française des pétroles BP.
      France B. P.   Courbevoie, Seine, [1964].
      20 p.   col. maps.   28 cm.

5462 Spain.   Ejercito.   Servicio Geografico.
      Agenda.   Madrid, 1964.
      122 p.   col. maps.   11 cm.

5463 Spain.   Ministerio de Obras Públicas.
      Mapa oficial de carreteras.   4 ed.   Madrid, 1961.
      104 p.   col. maps.   32 cm.

5464 Spain.   Ministerio de Obras Públicas.
      Mapa oficial de carreteras.   6 ed.   Madrid, 1964.
      118 p.   col. maps.   32 cm.

5465 Stanford, Edward.
      Esso road atlas of Great Britain and Ireland.
      London, 1970.
      1 vol.   col. maps.   25 cm.

5466 Südwest Verlag.
      Neuer Europa Auto Atlas.   München, [1964].
      246 p.   col. maps.   24 cm.

5467 Tammi.
      Europaan autoilukartasto.   With Kümmerly & Frey.
      Helsinki, 1963.
      156 p.   col. maps.   31 cm.

5468 Tammi.
      Euroopan matkaopas.   Helsinki, 1964.
      368 p.   col. maps.   31 cm.

5469 Ten Brink, H.
      Ten Brink's Reiseatlas van Nederland.   Meppel,
      [1954].
      23 p.   col. maps.   25 cm.

5470 The Age.
      Highways of Australia road atlas to every town in
      Australia.   9 ed.   By Keith Winser.   Melbourne,
      1968.
      190 p.   25 cm.

5471 Thomas, A.
      National road atlas of Great Britain.   Preston,
      [1954].
      370 p.   col. maps.   22 cm.

5472 Tokyo Chizu K. K.
      Zen Nihon Doro Chiaucho.   Tokyo, 1967.
      1 vol.   col. maps.   31 cm.

5473 Touring Club Italiano.
      Atlante automobilistico.   Milano, 1969—
      in parts.   col. maps.   32 cm.

5474 Turistička Stampa.
      Autokarta Jugoslavije.   2 ed.   Beograd, 1956.
      102 p.   col. maps.   29 cm.

5475 Turistička Štampa.
 Road map, Yugoslavia.   Beograd, 1955.
 132 p.   col. maps.   29 cm.

5476 Turistička Štampa.
 Yougoslavie, carte routière.   Beograd, 1954.
 122 p.   col. maps.   29 cm.

5477 Učila.
 Autoatlas Jugoslavije.   Zagreb, 1962.
 29 p.   col. maps.   23 cm.

5478 Učila.
 Autoatlas Jugoslavije.   Zagreb, 1966.
 30 p.   col. maps.   23 cm.

5479 Učila.
 Autoatlas Jugoslavije.   4 ed.   Zagreb, 1967.
 29 p.   col. maps.   23 cm.

5480 Učila.
 Autoatlas Jugoslavije.   Zagreb, 1968.
 29 p.   col. maps.   23 cm.

5481 U. S. S. R.   Glavnoe upravlenie geodezii i kartografii.
 Atlas avtomobilnykh dorog SSSR.   Moskva, 1961.
 130 p.   col. maps.   27 cm.

5482 U. S. S. R.   Glavnoe upravlenie geodezii i kartografii.
 Atlas avtomobilnykh dorog SSSR.   Moskva, 1963.
 130 p.   col. maps.   27 cm.

5483 U. S. S. R.   Glavnoe upravlenie geodezii i kartografii.
 Atlas avtomobilnykh dorog SSSR.   Moskva, 1966.
 166 p.   col. maps.   27 cm.

5484 U. S. S. R.   Glavnoe upravlenie geodezii i kartografii.
 Atlas avtomobilnykh dorog SSSR.   Moskva, 1967.
 166 p.   col. maps.   27 cm.

5485 U. S. S. R.   Glavnoe upravlenie geodezii i kartografii.
 Atlas avtomobilnykh dorog SSSR.   Moskva, 1968.
 168 p.   col. maps.   27 cm.

5486 VEB Bibliographisches Institut.
 Auto-Atlas "Neues Deutschland. "   Leipzig, 1951.
 55 p.   col. maps.   27 cm.

5487 VEB Bibliographisches Institut.
  Auto-Atlas "Neues Deutschland. "   Leipzig, 1953.
  55 p.   col. maps.   27 cm.

5488 VEB Bibliographisches Institut.
  Auto-Atlas "Neues Deutschland. "   Leipzig, 1954.
  56 p.   col. maps.   27 cm.

5489 VEB Bibliographisches Institut.
  Auto-Atlas "Neues Deutschland. "   Leipzig, 1955.
  59 p.   col. maps.   27 cm.

5490 VEB Bibliographisches Institut.
  Auto-Atlas "Neues Deutschland. "   Leipzig, 1956.
  59 p.   col. maps.   27 cm.

5491 VEB Bibliographisches Institut.
  Auto-Atlas "Neues Deutschland. "   Leipzig, 1957.
  59 p.   col. maps.   27 cm.

5492 VEB Bibliographisches Institut.
  Auto-Atlas "Neues Deutschland. "   Leipzig, 1958.
  59 p.   col. maps.   27 cm.

5493 Venezuela.   Consejo nacional de vialidad.
  Atlas de las carreteras de Venezuela.   Caracas,
  1954.
  24 p.   col. maps.   24 cm.

5494 World Pub. Co.
  World's road atlas and vacation guide of North
  America for 1966-67.   Cleveland, 1966.
  64 p.   col. maps.   28 cm.

5495 World Pub. Co.
  World's road atlas and vacation guide of North
  America for 1967-68.   Cleveland, 1967.
  64 p.   col. maps.   28 cm.

5496 World Pub. Co.
  World's road atlas and vacation guide of North
  America for 1968-69.
  Cleveland, 1968.
  64 p.   col. maps.   28 cm.

5497 Yhtyneet Kuvalehdet.
  Suomen kuvalehden karttakiya.   Helsinki, 1965.
  72 p.   col. maps.   25 cm.

5498 Zenkoku ryokaku jidōsha yōran henshūshitsu.
     Zenkoku basu rosenzu sōran. Un'yushō jidōshakyeku
     kanshū. [Atlas of national motor bus routes].
     Tokyo, [1957].
     48 p. col. maps. 37 cm.

SHIPPING - SEE MARINE

SOIL

5499 Australia. Division of Soils, Commonwealth Scientific
     and Industrial Research Organization.
     Atlas of Australian soils. Canberra, 1960-68.
     in parts. col. maps. 77 cm.

5500 L'Institut National Pour L'Étude Agronomique du Congo.
     Atlas des sols et de la végétation du Congo, du
     Rwanda et du Burundi. Bruxelles, 1954—
     in parts. col. maps. 46 cm.

5501 Meyer, Kartographisches Institut.
     Meyers grosser physischer Weltatlas. Mannheim,
     1965—
     in 8 vol. col. maps. 30 cm.

STATISTICAL - SEE ECONOMIC

TERRESTRIAL MAGNETISM

5502 U. S. Army Map Service.
     Atlas of magnetic declination of Europe for 1944-5.
     Washington, D. C., [1951].
     86 p. col. maps. 82 cm.

TRADE - SEE ECONOMIC

TRAFFIC - SEE TRANSPORATION

TRANSPORTATION

5503 Africa Instituut.
     Africa; maps and statistics. Pretoria, 1962-65.
     10 vol. col. maps. 35 cm.

5504 Allan.
     British rail atlas. London, 1967.
     45 p. col. maps. 24 cm.

5505 Argentina. Instituto Geográfico Militar.
Atlas de ruta. 2 ed. Buenos Aires, 1967.
27 p. col. maps. 32 cm.

5506 Compañia Mercantil Anónima Lúneas Aéreas Españolas.
Rutas de España. Madrid, 1960.
16 p. col. maps. 36 cm.

5507 Deutsche Lufthansa.
Lufthansa Streckenatlas. With Mairs. Köln, [1968].
19 p. col. maps. 24 cm.

5508 Edi-Mapas de México.
Atlas geográfico de communicaciones de la República
Mexicana. By Roberto Beltrán Frias. México, 1964.
32 p. col. maps. 67 cm.

5509 Esselte Map Service.
Scandinavian Airline System route atlas. Stockholm,
[1962].
34 p. col. maps. 34 cm.

5510 France. Société nationale des chemins de fer français.
Atlas des lignes ouvertes au trafic marchandises.
Paris, 1964.
14 p. col. maps. 31 cm.

5511 Generalstabens litografiska anstalt.
Post-och järnvägs karta över Sverige. Stockholm,
[1957].
21 p. col. maps. 22. 5 cm.

5512 Generalstabens litografiska anstalt.
Post-och järnvägs karta över Sverige. Stockholm,
1966.
15 p. col. maps. 22. 5 cm.

5513 Haack, Hermann.
Verkehrsatlas. Deutsche Demokratische Republik.
1 ed. Gotha, 1959.
115 p. co. maps. 18 cm.

5514 Haack, Hermann.
Verkehrsatlas. Deutsche Demokratische Republik.
2 ed. Gotha, 1960.
115 p. col. maps. 18 cm.

5515 Haack, Hermann.
      Verkehrsatlas.   Deutsche Demokratische Republik.
      3 ed.   Gotha, 1961.
      83 p.   col. maps.   18 cm.

5516 Haack, Hermann.
      Verkehrsatlas.   Deutsche Demokratische Republik.
      4 ed.   Gotha, 1962.
      87 p.   col. maps.   18 cm.

5517 Haack, Hermann.
      Verkehrsatlas.   Deutsche Demokratische Republik.
      5 ed.   Gotha, 1963.
      111 p.   col. maps.   18 cm.

5518 Haack, Hermann.
      Verkehrsatlas.   Deutsche Demokratische Republik.
      6 ed.   Gotha, 1966.
      220 p.   col. maps.   18 cm.

5519 Hammond, Inc.
      North American bicycle atlas.   Maplewood, N. J.,
      1969.
      128 p.   24 cm.

5520 Imprimeries Oberthur.
      Atlas des départements français.   Rennes, [1961].
      1 vol.   col. maps.   27 cm.

5521 Imprimeries Oberthur.
      Atlas des départements français.   Rennes, 1966.
      1 vol.   col. maps.   27 cm.

5522 Imprimeries Oberthur.
      Atlas des départements français.   Rennes, 1967.
      1 vol.   col. maps.   27 cm.

5523 Imprimeries Oberthur.
      Atlas des départements français et de l'union
      française.   Rennes, 1958.
      114 p.   col. maps.   27 cm.

5524 Imprimeries Oberthur.
      Index-atlas des départements français.   Rennes, 1968.
      210 p.   col. maps.   27 cm.

5525 JRO Verlag.
   JRO Verkehrsatlas für Strasse, Eisenbahn und Büro;
   Deutschland. München, [1953].
   271 p.   col. maps.   25 cm.

5526 Mexico.   Ministerio de Comunicaciones y Obras Públicas.
   Atlas de la memoriá de labores de la secretaría de
   comunicaciones y obras públicas, 1955-56, con un
   resumen de las avances logrados de 1953-56.
   México, [1957].
   83 p.   col. maps.   48 cm.

5527 Mexico.   Ministerio de Comunicaciones y Obras Públicas.
   Atlas: resumen de los avances logrados en el sexenio
   1953-58.   México, [1959].
   111 p.   col. maps.   48 cm.

5528 Mexico.   Secretaría de Comunicaciones y Transportes.
   México; guía de las vías generales de comunicación.
   México, 1963.
   94 p.   col. maps.   21 cm.

5529 National Bus Traffic Association.
   Atlas of motor bus routes and express blocks no
   A-602-B.   Chicago, 1966.
   90 p.   40 cm.

5530 New Zealand.   National Airways Corporation.
   NAC air atlas.   Wellington, [1965].
   15 p.   col. maps.   25. 5 cm.

5531 New Zealand.   National Airways Corporation.
   NAC air atlas of New Zealand.   Wellington, [1968].
   18 p.   col. maps.   25. 5 cm.

5532 Norway.   Veg direktoratet.
   Trafikkart over Norge.   Oslo, [1962].
   19 p.   col. maps.   49 cm.

5533 Orbis Terrarum.
   Atlas skhem zheleznykh dorog SSSR.   New York,
   1964.
   143 p.   16 cm.

5534 Pan American Airways.
      Route maps, PAA.   New York, [1952].
      12 p.   col. maps.   23 cm.

5535 Railway Publications, Ltd.
      British rail atlas and gazetteer.   London, 1965.
      83 p.   col. maps.   25 cm.

5536 Railway Publications, Ltd.
      British rail atlas and gazetteer.   London, 1967.
      1 vol.   col. maps.   25 cm.

5537 Railway Publications, Ltd.
      British railways pre-grouping atlas and gazetteer.
      3 ed.   London, 1963.
      45 p.   col. maps.   25 cm.

5538 Railway Publications, Ltd.
      British railways pre-grouping atlas and gazetteer.
      4 ed.   London, [1965].
      84 p.   col. maps.   25 cm.

5539 Rand McNally & Co.
      Rand McNally handy railroad atlas of the United
      States.   Chicago, [1952].
      48 p.   31 cm.

5540 Rand McNally & Co.
      Rand McNally handy railroad atlas of the United
      States.   Chicago, 1965.
      64 p.   31 cm.

5541 Reitzels, C. A. Forlag.
      Atlas over Denmark.   København, 1950-
      in 5 vols.   col. maps.   55 cm.

5542 United Nations Economic Commission for Europe.
      Census of traffic on main international traffic
      arteries.   [Atlas].   Geneva, 1958.
      1 portf.   col. maps.   28 cm.

5543 U. S. S. R. Glavnoe upravlenie geodezii i kartografii.
      Atlas skhem zheleznykh dorog SSSR.   Moskva, 1963.
      143 p.   col. maps.   16 cm.

5544 U. S. S. R. Glavnoe upravlenie geodezii i kartografii.
      Zheleznye dorogi SSSR.   Moskva, 1965.
      150 p.   col. maps.   16 cm.

5545 U. S. S. R. Glavnoe upravlenie geodezii i kartografii.
Zheleznye dorogi SSSR. Moskva, 1966.
150 p. col. maps. 16 cm.

5546 U. S. S. R. Glavnoe upravlenie geodezii i kartografii.
Zheleznye dorogi SSSR. Moskva, 1967.
148 p. col. maps. 16 cm.

5547 U. S. S. R. Glavnoe upravlenie geodezii i kartografii.
Zheleznye dorogi SSSR. Moskva, 1968.
148 p. col. maps. 16 cm.

UNIVERSE

5548 Dover Publications.
Lunar atlas. New York, 1968.
154 p. col. maps. 28 cm.

5549 Olbers-Gesellschaft.
Mond-atlas. By Philipp Fauth. Bremen, 1964.
56 p. col. maps. 24. 5 cm.

5550 Times of London.
The Times atlas of the moon. With Bartholomew.
London, 1969.
148 p. col. maps. 35 cm.

5551 U. S. Aeronautical Chart and Information Center.
The Times atlas of the moon. By H. A. G. Lewis.
London, 1969.
147 p. col. maps. 35 cm.

5552 U. S. Geological Survey.
Geological atlas of the moon. Washington, D. C.,
1967.
in parts. col. maps. 47 cm.

5553 U. S. S. R. Akademiia nauk.
Atlas obratnoi storony luny. Vol. 2. Moskva, 1967.
236 p. col. maps. 32 cm.

VEGETATION - SEE AGRICULTURE

VOLCANO

5554 U. S. S. R. Glavnoe upravlenie geodezii i kartografii.
      Atlas vulkanov SSSR. Moskva, 1959.
      174 p.   col. maps.   28 cm.

WATERWAYS

5555 Cranfield & Bonfiel Books.
      Waterways atlas of the British Isles.   London, 1966.
      54 p.   col. maps.   24 cm.

5556 Transportikroniek.
      Nijverheids-en handels-atlas der Belgische water-
      wegen.   Antwerpen, 1951.
      257 p.   23 cm.

List of Publishers
by Country

AFRICA

Angola
    Edições Spal   Luanda

Cameroun
    Institut de Recherches Scientifiques
        du Cameroun   Youndé

Ethiopia
    Mariam, Mesfin Wolde   Addis Ababa

Ghana
    Ghana.   Census Office   Accra
    Ghana.   Survey Dept.   Accra

Ivory Coast
    Société pour le Développement de la
        Côte d'Ivoire   Abidjan

Kenya
    Marco Surveys, Ltd.   Nairobi
    Royal East African Automobile Assoc.   Nairobi
    Survey of Kenya   Nairobi

Malagasy
    Malagasy.   Bureau pour le Développement
        de la Production Agricole   Tananarive

Morocco
    Morocco.   Comité National de Géographie   Rabat

Mozambique
    Empresa Moderna   Lourenço
                                     Marques
    Shell Moçambique, Ltd.   Lourenço
                                     Marques

Nigeria
Commission for Technical Cooperation in
    Africa South of the Sahara   Lagos
Nigeria.   Federal Surveys   Lagos
Nigeria.   Survey Dept.   Lagos

Rhodesia
Collins, M. O. (Pvt), Ltd.   Salisbury
Rhodesia. Department of Trigonometrical
    and Topographical Surveys   Salisbury

Senegal
Institut Fondamental d'Afrique Noire   Dakar
Institut Français d'Afrique Noire   Dakar
Senegal.   Ministère du Plan et du
    Développement   Dakar

Sierra Leone
Sierra Leone. Survey and Lands Dept.   Freetown
Sierra Leone. Survey and Lands Division Freetown

South Africa
Afrika Instituut   Pretoria
Atlantik Refining Company of Africa   Cape Town
Automobile Association of South Africa Johannesburg
B. P. Southern Africa Pty, Ltd.   Cape Town
Juta & Co. , Ltd.   Cape Town
Map Studio Productions, Pty, Ltd.   Cape Town
Nationale Boekhandel   Cape Town
Shell Company of South Africa, Ltd.   Cape Town
South Africa. Department of Planning   Pretoria
South Africa. Government Printer Office Pretoria
South Africa. National Council for Social
    Research   Pretoria
Timmins, H. B.   Cape Town
Tourist Publications   Cape Town
Van Schaik's Bookstore   Pretoria

Tanzania
Tanganyika. Department of Lands and
    Surveys   Dar Es Salaam
Tanzania. Ministry of Lands, Housing
    & Urban Development. Survey &
    Mapping Division   Dar Es Salaam
Tanzania. Ministry of Lands, Settle-
    ment and Water Development   Dar Es Salaam

Uganda
    East African Institute of Social Research   Kampala
    Uganda.   Department of Lands and Surveys Kampala

United Arab Republic-Egypt
    Dar Al-Ma'Ārif   Cairo
    Hilâl   Cairo
    Institut Français d'Archéologie Orientale   Cairo

Zambia
    Northern Rhodesia.   Survey Dept.   Lusaka
    Zambia.   Ministry of Lands and Mines   Lusaka

ASIA

China
    China.   Academy of Sciences   Peking
    China.   Geographical Institute   Shanghai
    Chinese Map Publ.   Peking
    Hsin Ya Shu Tien   Shanghai
    Kuang Hua Yü Ti Hsüeh Shê   Peking
    Shih Chieh Yü Ti Hsüeh Shê   Shanghai
    Ta Chung Ti Hsüeh Shê   Shanghai
    Ta Lu Yü Ti Shê   Shanghai
    Ti-Tu Chu-Pan Shê   Shanghai
    Ya Kuang Yü Ti Hsüeh Shê   Shanghai

Hong Kong
    Hai Kuang Ch'u Pan Shê   Hong Kong
    Hong Kong, Govt. Printer   Hong Kong
    Hong Kong University Press   Hong Kong
    Hsin Kuang Yü Ti Hsüeh Shê   Hong Kong
    Liang, Ch'i-Shan   Hong Kong
    Shih Chieh Ch'u Pan Shê   Hong Kong
    Ta Chung Shu Chü   Hong Kong

India
    India.   Directorate General of Health
       Services   Delhi
    India.   Directorate of Economics and
       Statistics   Delhi
    India.   Information and Broadcasting
       Ministry   Calcutta
    India.   Ministry of Education and Scientific
       Research   Calcutta
    India.   National Atlas Organization   Calcutta

India.   Survey of India.   Dehra Dūn
Indian Book Depot & Map House   Delhi
Indian Central Cotton Committee   Bombay
Indian Central Oilseeds Committee   Hyderabad

Indonesia
    Bachtar, A.   Djakarta
    Ganaco, N. V.   Bandung
    Ichtiar   Djakarta
    Indonesia.   Army Topographical Directorate   Djakarta
    Indonesia.   Badan Atlas Nacional   Djakarta
    Noordhoff-Kolff, N. V.   Djakarta
    Pemusatan   Bandung
    Pradnja-Paramita   Djakarta
    Tjempaka, P. T.   Djakarta

Iran
    Guruhi Jughrafiya   Teheran

Iraq
    Sadiq Salih   Baghdad
    Surveys Press   Baghdad

Israel
    Ahiever   Jerusalem
    Anokh, Hanok   Tel Aviv
    Ben-Eliyahu, Ephraim   Jerusalem
    Carta   Jerusalem
    Israel.   Department of Surveys   Jerusalem
    Israel.   Mahleket Ha-Medidot   Jerusalem
    Israel.   Ministry of Labour   Jerusalem
    Israel.   Ministry of Surveys   Tel Aviv
    Israel.   Tseva Haganah Le-Yisrael   Jerusalem
    Israel.   University Press   Jerusalem
    Szapiro, J.   Tel Aviv
    Universitas   Jerusalem
    Yavneh   Tel Aviv

Japan
    Japan.   Un'Yashō Kankōkyoku   Tokyo
    Jimbunsha   Tokyo
    Kishō Kyōkai   Tokyo
    Kokusai Chicaku Kyōkai   Tokyo
    Nihon Kyōzu Kabushiki Kaisha   Tokyo
    Nitchi Shuppan Kabushiki Kaisha   Tokyo
    Reader's Digest of Japan, Ltd.   Tokyo
    Teikoku-Shoin Co. , Ltd.   Tokyo

Tōbunsha	Tokyo
Tokyo Chizu K. K.	Tokyo
Tōsei Shuppan Kabushiki Kaisha	Tokyo
Zenkoko Jichitai Kenkyukai	Tokyo
Zenkoku Kyoiku Tosho	Tokyo
Zenkoku Ryokaku Jidōsha Yōran Henshūshitsu	Tokyo

Korea
Kim, Sang-Jin	Seoul
Sosŏ Publishing Co.	Seoul
Taehan Sŏrim	Seoul

Lebanon
Lebanon. Direction des Affaires Géographiques	Beyrouth
Lebanon. Ministère du Plan	Beyrouth
Lebanon. Service Météorologique	Beyrouth

Malaysia
Automobile Association of Malaya	Penang
Borneo Literature Bureau	Kuching
Malaysia. Directorate of National Mapping	Singapore

Nepal
Nepal. Ministry of Information and Broadcasting	Kathmandu

Pakistan
Pakistan. Dept. of Advertising, Films and Publications	Karachi

Philippines
Caltex (Philippines)	Manila
Phil-Asian Publishers, Inc.	Manila
Philippines. Agriculture and Natural Resources Dept.	Manila
Philippines. Bureau of Public Works	Manila
Philippines. Office of the President	Manila

Singapore
Tien Wah Press, Ltd.	Singapore

Taiwan
China. National War College	Taipei
Fu Min Geographical Institute of Economic Development	Taipei

Sha, Hsüeh Chün   Taipei
T'ai-Wan Ta Hsüeh   Taipei
Taiwan.   National University   Taipei

Thailand
Thailand.   Department of Commercial
   Intelligence   Bangkok
Thailand.   Royal Thai Survey Department   Bangkok

Vietnam
Vietnam.   Dept. of Survey and Mapping   Hanoi
Vietnam.   Nha G'a'm-Dôc Khï-Tu'o'ng   Saigon

AUSTRALIA

Australia
Angus & Robertson   Sydney
Ampol Petroleum, Ltd.   Sydney
Australia.   Bureau of Mineral Resources,
   Geology and Geophysics   Adelaide
Australia.   Department of National
   Development   Canberra
Australia.   Division of Soils, Commonwealth
   Scientific and Industrial Research
   Organization   Canberra
Australian Educational Foundation, Pty, Ltd. Sydney
B. P. Australia, Ltd.   Melbourne
Colorgravure   Melbourne
Jacaranda   Brisbane
Martindale Press   Sydney
Motor Manual   Melbourne
Reader's Digest Association Pty, Ltd.   Sydney
Robinson, H. E. C. Pty, Ltd.   Sydney
The Age   Melbourne

New Zealand
New Zealand.   Atlas Committee   Wellington
New Zealand. National Airways Corporation   Wellington
New Zealand.   Town and Country Planning
   Branch   Wellington
Reed, A. W. & A. H.   Wellington
Shell Oil New Zealand, Ltd.   Wellington

EUROPE

Albania
Albania. Ministria e Aresimit dhe Kultures Tiranë
N. I. Sh. Mjete Mesimore e Sportive
  "Hamid Shijaku"   Tiranë

Austria
Austria. Akademie der Wissenschaften	Wien
Auto-Motor-und Radfahrerbund Österreichs	Wien
Buchgemeinschaft Donauland	Wien
Dom Verlag	Wien
Freytag-Berndt & Artaria	Wien
Geographishes Institut Wien	Wien
Hölder, Pichler Tempsky	Wien
Hölzel, Ed. Verlag	Wien
Internationaler Holzmarkt	Wien
Kaiser	Klagenfurt
Society of the Divine Word	Mödling
St. Gabriel Verlag	Mödling

Belgium
Asedi	Bruxelles
Belgium. Académie Royale des Sciences d'Outre-Mer	Bruxelles
Belgium. Centre d'Information et de Documentation du Congo Belge et du Ruanda-Urundi	Bruxelles
Belgium. Centre National de Recherches Scientifiques Souterraines	Liège
Belgium. Comité National de Géographie	Bruxelles
Belgium. Ministère des Travaux Publics et de la Reconstruction	Bruxelles
Contact	Anvers
De Sikkel	Anvers
Editions Meddens	Bruxelles
Editions R. de Rouck	Bruxelles
European Communities. Press and Information Service	Bruxelles
L'Institut National pour l'Etude Agronomique du Congo	Bruxelles
Mantniers, P.	Bruxelles
Plantyn	Anvers
Transportikronier	Anvers
Visscher	Bruxelles
Wesmael-Charlier	Namur

Bulgaria
   Bulgaria.　Akademya na Naukite　　　　　Sofia
   Bulgaria.　Glavno Upravlenie po Geodeziá
    i Kartografiá　　　　　　　　　　　　　　Sofia
   Bulgaria.　Muzei na Revolutsidnnoto
    Dvizhenie v Bŭlgariiá　　　　　　　　　Sofia

Czechoslovakia
   Czechoslovakia.　Akademie Véd　　　　　Praha
   Czechoslovakia.　Kartografické
    Nakladatelství　　　　　　　　　　　　Praha
   Czechoslovakia.　Komenium　　　　　　　Praha
   Czechoslovakia.　Ministerstvo Národnî
    Obrany　　　　　　　　　　　　　　　　Praha
   Czechoslovakia.　Státnî Nakl. Uĉebnic　　Praha
   Czechoslovakia.　Státnî Pedagogické Nakl.　Praha
   Czechoslovakia.　Státnî Zeměměřický a
    Kartografický Ústav　　　　　　　　　Praha
   Czechoslovakia.　Ústřednî Správa Geodesie
    a Kartografie　　　　　　　　　　　　Praha
   Czechoslovakia.　Ústřednî Ústav Geologický Praha
   Melantrich　　　　　　　　　　　　　　Praha
   Orbis　　　　　　　　　　　　　　　　　Praha

Denmark
   Denmark.　Geodaetisk Institut　　　　　København
   Gjellerups Forlag　　　　　　　　　　København
   Grafisk Forlag　　　　　　　　　　　　København
   Gyldendal　　　　　　　　　　　　　　København
   Hirschsprungs Forlag　　　　　　　　København
   Imperial Press　　　　　　　　　　　København
   Importbøger　　　　　　　　　　　　København
   Martins Forlag　　　　　　　　　　　København
   Munksgaard　　　　　　　　　　　　　København
   Normanns Forlag　　　　　　　　　　Odense
   Politikens Forlag　　　　　　　　　　København
   Reitzels, C. A. Forlag　　　　　　　　København
   Schultz　　　　　　　　　　　　　　　København
   Skandinavisk Bogforlag　　　　　　　København
   Skrifola　　　　　　　　　　　　　　København

Finland
   Maanmittaushallitus　　　　　　　　　Helsinki
   Otava　　　　　　　　　　　　　　　　Helsinki
   Söderström, Werner　　　　　　　　　Helsinki
   Suomen Maantieteellinen Seura　　　　Helsinki
   Tammi　　　　　　　　　　　　　　　Helsinki

Weilin & Co.	Helsinki
Yhtyneet Kuvalehdet	Helsinki

France
Blondel La Rougery	Paris
Bordos, H.	Paris
Colin	Paris
Delagrave	Paris
Didot-Bottin	Paris
Editions Alain	Paris
Editions Bordas	Paris
Editions du Centurion	Paris
Editions de l'École	Paris
Editions de Lyon	Lyon
Editions Sequoia	Paris
Foldex (France), Ltd.	Paris
France. Comité National de Géographie	Paris
France. Commissariat Général à la Productivité	Paris
France. Conseil National du Patronat Français	Paris
France. Institut Géographique National	Paris
France. La Documentation Française	Paris
France. Ministère de l'Équipement	Paris
France. Ministère des Postes et Télécommunications	Paris
France. Service de l'Économie Forestière	Paris
France. Sociètè Nationale des Chemins de Fer Français	Paris
Gallimard	Paris
Hachette	Paris
Hatier	Paris
IAC	Lyon
Imprimeries Oberthur	Rennes
Informations et Conjoncture	Paris
Journaux, André	Caen
Larousse	Paris
Le Carrousel Publicité	Tours
Librairie Mellottée	Paris
Livre de Poche	Paris
L'Oeuvre de la Propagation de la Foi	Paris
Michelin et Cie	Paris
Nathan, Fernand	Paris
Nouvelles de l'Enseignement	Paris
Peugeot	Paris
Quillet, A.	Paris
Sélection du Reader's Digest S. A. R. L.	Paris

Société des Pétroles Shell Berre	Paris
Société Européenne d'Études et d'Informa-	
tions	Paris
Société Française des Pétroles BP	Courbevoie,
	Seine
Stock	Paris
Tallandier	Paris

Germany
Accumulatoren-Fabrik, A. G.	Hannover
Akademie Verlag	Berlin
Allgemeiner Deutscher Automobil-Club	Kiel
Atlantik Verlag	Frankfurt
Autokarten und Reiseführer Verlag	Kiel
Bayerischer Schulbuch Verlag	München
Benziger & Co.	Einsiedeln
Bertelsmann, C.	Gütersloh
Beste, G. M. B. H.	Stuttgart
BLV Verlagsgesellschaft	München
BP Benzin & Petroleum Gesellschaft	Hamburg
Brockhaus, F. A.	Wiesbaden
Codex Verlag	Gundholzen
Columbus Verlag Oestergaard	Berlin
Continental Gummiwerke Kartographischer	
Verlag	Hannover
Deutsche Lufthansa	Köln
Deutsche Viscobil Öl Gesellschaft	Hamburg
Deutscher Bücherbund	Stuttgart
Deutscher Taschenbuch Verlag	München
Deutscher Zentralverlag VEB	Berlin
Droemer	München
Elwert Verlag	Marburg
Esso, A. G.	Hamburg
Europäischer Buchklub	Stuttgart
Fachbuchverlag, G. M. B. H.	Leipzig
Falk Verlag	Hamburg
Fischer, G.	Jena
Flemings Verlag	Hamburg
Frankfurt. Institut für Angewandte	
Geodäsie	Frankfurt
Frankfurt. Soziographisches Institut der	
Universität	Frankfurt
Freytag, G.	München
Germany. Akademie für Raumforschung	
und Landesplannung	Hannover
Germany. Deutscher Wetterdienst	Hamburg
Germany. Statistisches Bundesamt, Institut	

für Landeskunde und Institut für Raumforschung	Mainz
Goldmann Verlag	München
Haack, Hermann	Gotha
Haller Verlag	Berlin
Herder Verlag	Freiburg
Humboldt Verlag	Stuttgart
JRO Verlag	München
Keysersche Verlagsbuchhandlung, G.M.B.H.	Heidelberg
Klett Verlag	Stuttgart
Knaur, Th. Nachf.	München
Kohlhammer Verlag	Mainz
König, Hans, Verlag	Frankfurt
Landkartenverlag VEB	Berlin
Lehrmittel Verlag	Offenburg
Lingen	Köln
List, P.	München
Lux Verlag	München
Mairs Geographischer Verlag	Stuttgart
Meyer, Kartographisches Institut	Mannheim
Mohn	Gütersloh
Nomos Verlagsgesellschaft	Baden-Baden
Olbers Gesellschaft	Bremen
Oldenburger Verlagshaus	Oldenburg
Perthes, Justus	Gotha
Pfahl Verlag	Laupheim
Ravenstein Geographische Verlagsanstalt	Frankfurt
Reise und Verkehrsverlag	Stuttgart
Ruhr-Stickstoff, A. G.	Bochum
Siemens & Halske, A. G.	München
Springer Verlag	Berlin
Steiner Verlag	Wiesbaden
Südwest Verlag	München
Ullstein	Berlin
VEB Bibliographisches Institut	Leipzig
Velhagen & Klasing	Bielefeld
Verlag Die Gabe	Gütersloh
Verlag Enzyklopädie	Leipzig
Verlag Lebendiges Wissen	München
Verlag Sport & Technik	Berlin
Volk und Wissen Verlag	Berlin
Wenschow	München
Westermann, Georg	Braunschweig
Weststadt Verlag	München

Greece
   Greece. Ministry of National Economy   Athens
   Greece. National Statistical Service   Athens
   Greece. Statistikon Graphelon   Athens
   Hellēnike Leschē Autokinētou Kai
     Periēgēsēon   Athens

Gt. Britain
   Allan   London
   Arnold, E.   London
   Austin Motor Co. , Ltd.   Birmingham
   Automobile Association   London
   Bancroft & Co.   London
   Blackie & Son, Ltd.   London
   British Motor Corp. , Ltd.   London
   British Sulphur Corp. , Ltd.   London
   Burns & Oates, Ltd.   London
   Cassell   London
   Caxton Pub. Co.   London
   Clarendon Press   Oxford
   Collet   London
   Cranfield & Bonfiel Books   London
   Daily Express   London
   Dent, J. M.   London
   Ebury Press   London
   English University Press, Ltd.   London
   Evans Brothers   London
   Faber & Faber   London
   Gatrell, A. W. & Co. , Ltd.   London
   Geographers' Map Co.   Sevenoakes,
           Kent
   Geographia, Ltd.   London
   Geographical Projects, Ltd.   London
   Geo Publishing Co.   Oxford
   Gollancz, Victor   London
   Gt. Britain. Meteorological Office   London
   Gt. Britain. Ministry of Agriculture,
     Fisheries & Food   London
   Gt. Britain. Ministry of Housing and
     Local Government   London
   Heinemann   London
   Hulton Educational Publications, Ltd.   London
   Humphrey, H. A. Ltd.   London
   Kings College School   London
   Lloyd's Corp. of   London
   Longmans Green   London
   Lutterworth Press   London

MacDonald & Co., Ltd.	London
Macmillan & Co., Ltd.	London
Map Productions Ltd.	London
Meiklejohn	London
Methuen	London
Michelin Tyre Co.	Stoke-on-Trent
Murray, John	London
National Trust	London
Nelson-Doubleday	London
Nelson, Thomas & Sons, Ltd.	London
Newnes, George, Ltd.	London
Nuffield Organization	Oxford
Odhams Press Ltd.	London
Oxford University Press	London
Penguin Books	Harmondsworth
Pergamon Press, Ltd.	Oxford
Philip, George & Son, Ltd.	London
Railway Publications, Ltd.	London
Reader's Digest Association, Ltd.	London
Royal Automobile Club	London
Shell-Mex & BP Ltd.	London
Stanford, Edward	London
Technical Press, Ltd.	London
The Times Publishing Co.	London
Thomas, A.	Preston
Times of London	London
University of London Press	London
University Tutorial Press	London
Ward, Lock	London
Warne, F.	London
Weidenfeld & Nicolson	London
Wheaton & Co., Ltd.	Exeter

Hungary

Cartographia	Budapest
Geodéziai és Kartográfiai Intézet	Budapest
Kartográfiai Vállalat	Budapest
Országos Meteorológiai Intézet	Budapest
Ronai, Andras	Budapest
Tervgazdhsági Könyvkiadó	Budapest

Iceland

Rikisútgáfa Námsbóka	Reykjavik

Ireland

Dublin Institute for Advanced Studies	Dublin
Educational Company of Ireland, Ltd.	Dublin

Italy

AGIP	Milano
Automobile Club d'Italia	Roma
Consociazione Turistica Italiana	Milano
Curcio, A.	Roma
Edizioni Cremonese	Roma
Fabri	Milano
Fédération Internationale de l'Automobile	Roma
Istituto Geografico de Agostini	Novara
Istituto Geografico Editoriale Italiano	Roma
Istituto Italiano per L'Africa	Roma
Italatlas	Roma
Italgeo	Milano
Italy. Direzione Generale della Statistica	Roma
Italy. Istituto Geografico Militare	Firenze
Minerva Italica	Bergamo
Paravia, G. B.	Torino
Poligrafiche Bolis	Bergamo
Principato Giuseppe	Milano
Societa Cartografica G. De Agostini	Milano
Societa Editrice Internazionale	Torino
Studi Geo-Cartografici	Milano
Studio F. M. B.	Bologna
Touring Club Italiano	Milano
United Nations. Food and Agricultural Organization	Roma
Vallardi, A.	Milano
Zanchelli, Nicola	Bologna

Netherlands

Bootsma	's Gravenhage
Bosch & Keuning	Baarn
Brug Uitgeversbedrijf, N. V.	Amsterdam
Dijkstra	Zeist
Djambatan	Amsterdam
Duwaer, J. F. & Zonen	Amsterdam
Elsevier	Amsterdam
Katholier Sociaal-Kerkelijk Instituut	's Gravenhage
Meulenhoff, J. M.	Amsterdam
Netherlands. Bureau voor Wegen en Verkeersstatistiek	's Gravenhage
Netherlands. Department van Landbouw en Visscherij	Zwolle
Netherlands. Dienst Verkeersonderzoek	's Gravenhage
Netherlands. Ministerie van Marine	's Gravenhage
Netherlands. Staatsdrukkerij-en Uitgeverijbedrijf	's Gravenhage

Netherlands. Volkskundecommissie der Koninklijke Nederlandse Akademie van Wetenschappen	's Gravenhage
Nijgh & Van Ditmar	Rotterdam
Noordhoff, P.	Groningen
Smulders' Drukkerijen, N. V.	's Gravenhage
Stenvert	Apeldoorn
Ten Brink, H.	Meppel
Thieme, W. J.	Zutphen
Uitgeverij de Bezige Bij	Amsterdam
Versluys	Amsterdam
Wolters, J. B.	Groningen

Norway

Beste, A. S.	Oslo
Cappelens, J. W. Forlag, A. S.	Oslo
Damm, N. W. & Søn	Oslo
Dreyers Forlag	Oslo
Fabritius	Oslo
Fonna	Oslo
Kongelig Norsk Automobilklub	Oslo
Norway. Poststyret	Oslo
Norway. Statistik Sentralbyrå	Oslo
Norway. Vegdirektoratet	Oslo
Poståpnernes Landsforbund	Oslo

Poland

Ksiąznica-Atlas	Wrocław
Poland. Akademia Nauk	Warszawa
Poland. Centralny Urząd Geodezii i Kartografii	Warszawa
Poland. Instytut Geologiczny	Warszawa
Poland. Panstwowe Przeosiębiorstwo Wydawnictw Kartograficznych	Warszawa
Poland. Panstwowe Wydawnictw Naukowe	Warszawa
Poland. Słuzba Topograficzna Wojska Polskiego	Warszawa
Poland. Wydawn. Ministerstva Obrony Narodowej	Warszawa
Romer, Eugeniusz	Wrocław
Trzaska, Evert i Michalski, S. A.	Warszawa
Warszawa Universytet	Warszawa
Wjedza Powszechna	Krakow

Portugal

Instituto de Estudos Geograficos	Coimbra
Livraria Popular de F. Franco	Lisboa

Livraria Sá da Costa	Lisboa
Livraria Simões Lopes	Porto
Porto Editora	Porto
Portugal. Junta de Investigações do Ultramar	Lisboa
Silva, J. R.	Lisboa

Romania
Romania. Academia Republicii Socialiste	Bucuresti
Romania. Asociatia Automobiliştilor Din R. P. R.	Bucuresti
Romania. Editura Academiei Republici Populare Romine	Bucuresti
Romania. Editura de Stat Pentru Literatură Ştiinţifică	Bucuresti
Romania. Editura di Stat Didactică şi Pedagogică	Bucuresti
Romania. Editura Stiintifica	Bucuresti
Romania. Institutul Meteorologie	Bucuresti

Scotland
Bartholomew, John & Son, Ltd.	Edinburgh
Collins Clear-Type Press	Glasgow
Collins, William, Sons & Co., Ltd.	Glasgow
Edinburgh University Press	Edinburgh
Johnston, W. & A. K. & G. W. Bacon, Ltd.	Edinburgh
McDougall's Educational Co., Ltd.	Edinburgh
Oliver & Boyd	Edinburgh

Spain
Aguilar, S. A., de Ediciones	Madrid
Atheneum	Barcelona
Bosch	Barcelona
Compañia Mercantil Anónima Lïneas Aéreas Españolas	Madrid
E. D. A. F.	Madrid
Editorial Bello	Valencia
Editorial Francisco Seix, S. A.	Barcelona
Editorial Luis Vives, S. A.	Zaragoza
Editorial Miguel A. Salvatella	Barcelona
Editorial Seix Barral, S. A.	Barcelona
Editorial Teide	Barcelona
Editorial Vergara	Barcelona
Firestone-Hispania, S. A.	Bilbao
Hernando	Madrid
Litografïa de Fernández	Madrid

Martin, A.	Barcelona
Salinas Bellver, Salvador	Madrid
Spain. Cámeras Oficiales de Comercio, Industria y Navegación	Madrid
Spain. Comité Español de Riegos y Drenajes	Madrid
Spain. Consejo Superior de Investigaciones Científicas	Madrid
Spain. Direción General de Marruecos y Colonias e Instituto de Estudios Africanos	Madrid
Spain. Direción General de Montes, Caza y Pesca Fluvial	Madrid
Spain. Ejercito Servicio Geografico	Madrid
Spain. Instituto Geográfico y Catastral	Madrid
Spain. Ministerio de Obras Públicas	Madrid
Villarroya San Mateo, Antonio	Madrid

Sweden
Akademiförlaget	Göteborg
Aldus	Stockholm
Allhem	Malmö
Bergvalls Förlag	Stockholm
Bernces Förlag	Malmö
Bonnier	Stockholm
Carlson, A. V.	Stockholm
Esselte Map Service	Stockholm
Generalstabens Litografiska Anstalt	Stockholm
Gumperts Förlag	Göteborg
Kungliga Automobil Klubben	Stockholm
Lantbruksförbundets Tidskriftsaktiebolag	Stockholm
Motormännens Riksförbund	Stockholm
Natur Och Kultur Bokförlaget	Stockholm
Raben & Sjögren	Stockholm
Royal Automobile Club Sweden	Stockholm
Sohlmans Förlag, A. B.	Stockholm
Svenska Bokförlaget Norstedts	Stockholm
Sveriges Köpmannaförbund	Stockholm
Tidens Förlag	Stockholm

Switzerland
Buchclub Ex Libris	Zürich
Buchverlag Verlandsdruckerei	Bern
Editions Rencontre	Lausanne
Editions Stauffacher	Zürich
Europa Im Automobile A. G.	Zürich
Hallwag, A. G.	Bern

International Telecommunication Union   Geneva
Kantonaler Lehrmittel Verlag   Zürich
Kümmerly & Frey   Bern
Librairie Payot   Lausanne
Literarisches Institut   Basel
Nagel Publishers   Geneva
Orell Füssli, A. G.   Zürich
Sauerländer, H. R.   Aarau
Schweizer Reisekasse   Bern
Schweizer Volks-Buchgemeinde   Luzern
Schweizerische Gesellschaft für Volkskunde Basel
Switzerland. Konferenz der Kantonalen
   Erziehungsdirektoren   Zürich
Switzerland. Landestopographie   Wabern-Bern
United Nations Economic Commission
   for Europe   Geneva

Turkey
   Bir Yayinevi   Istanbul
   Kanaat Kitabevi   Istanbul
   Kanaat Yayinlari   Istanbul
   Milli Egitim Basimevi   Istanbul
   University of Istanbul   Istanbul

U. S. S. R.
   Novoe Vremya   Moskva
   U. S. S. R. Akademiia Nauk   Kiev
   U. S. S. R. Gidronet   Leningrad
   U. S. S. R. Glavnoe Upravlenie Geodezii I
      Kartografii   Moskva
   U. S. S. R. Voyenno-Morskoe Ministerstvo Moskva
   U. S. S. R. Voyenno-Topograficheskoe
      Upravlenie   Moskva

Wales
   Gwasg Prifysgol Cymru   Caerdydd
   Hughes & Son   Wrexham
   University of Wales Press   Cardiff

Yugoslavia
   Državana Založba Slovenije   Ljubljana
   Geokarta   Beograd
   Jugoslavenski Leksikografski Zavod   Zagreb
   Leksikografski Zavod Fnrj   Zagreb
   Savremena Shkola   Beograd
   Seljačka Sloga   Zagreb
   Turistička Štampa   Beograd

Učila	Zabreb
Vuk Karadžić	Beograd
Yugoslavia. Vojno-Istoriski Institut	Beograd
Znanje	Zagreb

NORTH AMERICA

Canada
   Canada. Department of Energy, Mines &
      Resources   Ottawa

Canada. Department of Energy, Mines & Resources	Ottawa
Canada. Department of Mines and Technical Surveys	Ottawa
Canada. Department of Transport	Ottawa
Canada. Surveys and Mapping Branch	Ottawa
Dent, J. M.	Toronto
Editions du Renouveau Pédagogique	Montreal
Encyclopedia Canadiana	Ottawa
Longmans, Green	Toronto
Ryerson Press	Toronto
Vilas Industries	Toronto

Costa Rica
Costa Rica. Ministerio de Economia y Hacienda	San José

El Salvador
Salvador. Direción General de Cartografîa	San Salvador
Salvador. Estadistica y Cencos	San Salvador
Salvador. Universidade Federal da Bahia, Centro de Estudos Afro-Orientais	San Salvador

Guatemala
Editorial Escolar "Piedra Santa"	Guatemala
Guatemala. Dirección General de Cartografia	Guatemala
Guatemala. Instituto Geográfico Nacional	Guatemala
Guatemala. Ministerio de Educación Pública	Guatemala
Guatemala. Observatorio Meteorológico y Estacion Sismográfia	Guatemala
Obiols, Alfredo	Guatemala

Mexico
Asociacion Nacional Automovilistica	Mexico, D. F.
Compañía Hulera Euzkadi, S. A.	Mexico, D. F.
Ediciones Ateneo	Mexico, D. F.

Edi-Mapas de Mexico	Mexico, D. F.
Editorial Grijalbo	Mexico, D. F.
Editorial Patria, S. A.	Mexico, D. F.
Editorial Porrúa, S. A.	Mexico, D. F.
Editorial Progreso	Mexico, D. F.
Fondo de Cultura Económica	Mexico, D. F.
Jackson, W. M. , Inc.	Mexico, D. F.
Mexico. Comisión Nacional de Caminos Vecinales	Mexico, D. F.
Mexico. Fondo de Cultura Economica	Mexico, D. F.
Mexico. Instituto Mexicano de Investigaciones Economicas	Mexico, D. F.
Mexico. Ministerio de Comunicaciones y Obras Públicas	Mexico, D. F.
Mexico. Secretariá de Comunicaciones y Transportes	Mexico, D. F.
Mexico. Universidad Nacional Autónoma	Mexico, D. F.
Reader's Digest Mexico, S. A.	Mexico, D. F.

Nicaragua
Castillo, Guillermo J.	Managua

Panama
Ediciones Oasis	Panama
Panama. Comisión del Atlas de Panamá	Panama

Puerto Rico
Puerto Rico. Dept. of Education	San Juan

U. S. A.
Abercrombie & Fitch	New York, N. Y.
Aldine Pub. Co.	Chicago, Ill.
Alpine Geographical Press	Champaign, Ill.
American Geographical Society	New York, N. Y.
American Heritage	New York, N. Y.
American Hotel Register Co.	Chicago, Ill.
American Map Co. , Inc.	New York, N. Y.
Association Press	New York, N. Y.
Augsburg Publishing House	Minneapolis, Minn.
Bantam Books	New York, N. Y.
Barnes & Noble, Inc.	New York, N. Y.
Better Camping Magazine	Milwaukee, Wisc
Bobley Pub. Corp.	Glen Cove, N. Y.
Bookcraft	Salt Lake City, Utah
Book Production Industries	Chicago, Ill.

Book Publishers Distributing Co.	Cincinnati, Ohio
Boy Scouts of America	New Brunswick, N. J.
Brown, W. C. Co.	Dubuque, Iowa
Camping Maps, U. S. A.	Montclair, N. J.
Catholic War Veterans	Washington, D. C.
Clapsy, E. M.	Dowagiac, Mich.
Collier, P. F. & Son, Corp.	New York, N. Y.
Consolidated Book Publishers	Chicago, Ill.
Container Corporation of America	Chicago, Ill.
Continental Oil Co.	Chicago, Ill.
Cooper Square Publishers	New York, N. Y.
Cram, George F. Co.	Indianapolis, Ind.
Crowell & Co.	New York, N. Y.
Dell Pub. Co.	New York, N. Y.
Denoyer-Geppert Co.	Chicago, Ill.
Deseret Book Co.	Salt Lake City, Utah
Diversified Map Corporation	St. Louis, Mo.
Dorsey Press	Homewood, Ill.
Doubleday	Garden City, N. Y.
Dover Publications	New York, N. Y.
Dutton, E. P. & Co.	New York, N. Y.
Editors Press Service	New York, N. Y.
Educational Book Club	Des Moines, Iowa
Encyclopaedia Britannica	Chicago, Ill.
European Road Guide, Inc.	Larchmont, N. Y.
Everton Publishers	Logan, Utah
Ezy Index	New York, N. Y.
Farmers Insurance Group	Los Angeles, Calif.
Fawcett Publications	Greenwich, Conn.
Field Enterprises Educational Corp.	Chicago, Ill.
Follett Educational Corp.	Chicago, Ill.
Garden City Books	Garden City, N. Y.
General Drafting Co.	Convent Station, N. J.
Geographia Map Co.	New York, N. Y.
Geographical Pub. Co.	Cleveland, Ohio
Ginn & Co.	Boston, Mass.
Golden Press	New York, N. Y.
Goushá, H. M. Co.	San José, Calif.
Greystone Press	New York, N. Y.

Grolier Society	New York, N. Y.
Grosset & Dunlap	New York, N. Y.
Halcyon House	Garden City, N. Y.
Hammond, Inc.	Maplewood, N. J.
Hanover House	Garden City, N. Y.
Harper & Row	New York, N. Y.
Harvard University Press	Cambridge, Mass.
Hawthorne Books	New York, N. Y.
Hearst Magazines, Inc.	New York, N. Y.
Hitt Label Co.	Los Angeles, Calif.
Holt	New York, N. Y.
Houghton Mifflin Co.	Boston, Mass.
Household Goods Carriers' Bureau	Washington, D. C.
Humble Travel Club	Houston, Tex.
Indiana University. Department of Geography	Bloomington, Ind.
Industrial Atlas Corporation	New York, N. Y.
International Bank for Reconstruction and Development	Washington, D. C.
International Publications Service	New York, N. Y.
Kalmbach Publishing Co.	Milwaukee, Wisc.
Kiplinger-Washington Editors, Inc.	Washington, D. C.
Macmillan Co.	New York, N. Y.
McGraw-Hill Book Co.	New York, N. Y.
Merrill, C. E. Co.	Columbus, Ohio
Moore, William L.	Mt. Vernon, Ill.
Munger Oil Information Service	Los Angeles, Calif.
National Bus Traffic Association	Chicago, Ill.
National Geographic Society	Washington, D. C.
National Safety Council	Chicago, Ill.
Nelson-Doubleday	New York, N. Y.
News Map of the Week, Inc.	Skokie, Ill.
New York Herald Tribune	New York, N. Y.
Oceana Publications	Dobbs Ferry, N. Y.
Odyssey Books	New York, N. Y.
Orbis Terrarum	New York, N. Y.
Ottenheimer Publishers, Inc.	Baltimore, Md.
Pan American Airways	New York, N. Y.
Pan American Union	Washington, D. C
Permabooks	New York, N. Y.
Petroleum Publishing Co.	Tulsa, Okla.

Philadelphia Inquirer	Philadelphia, Penna.
Pocket Books	New York, N. Y.
Praeger, Frederick A.	New York, N. Y.
Prentice-Hall	New York, N. Y.
Princeton University Press	Princeton, N. J.
Radio Amateur Callbook, Inc.	Chicago, Ill.
Rand McNally & Co.	Chicago, Ill.
Reader's Digest Association, Ltd.	Pleasantville, N. Y.
Replogle Globes, Inc.	Chicago, Ill.
Sadlier, W. H.	New York, N. Y.
Scholastic Book Service	New York, N. Y.
Scott, Foresman & Co.	Glenview, Ill.
Scribner, C.	New York, N. Y.
Sears Roebuck	Chicago, Ill.
Simmons-Boardman Books	New York, N. Y.
Simon & Schuster	New York, N. Y.
Spencer Press, Inc.	Chicago, Ill.
Standard International Library	New York, N. Y.
Standard Reference Works Pub. Co.	Brooklyn, N. Y.
Stein, Jack	Dayton, Ohio
St. Martin's Press	New York, N. Y.
Texana	Los Angeles, Calif.
Time-Life Books	New York, N. Y.
Time, Inc.	New York, N. Y.
Universal Guild	New York, N. Y.
University of Chicago Press	Chicago, Ill.
University of Michigan Press	Ann Arbor, Mich.
University of Texas	Austin, Texas
U. S. Aeronautical Chart and Information Center	St. Louis, Mo.
U. S. Aid Mission to Laos	Washington, D. C.
U. S. Army Natick Laboratories	Natick, Mass.
U. S. Central Intelligence Agency	Washington, D. C.
U. S. Department of Agriculture	Washington, D. C.
U. S. Department of Commerce	Washington, D. C.
U. S. Economic Development Administration	Washington, D. C.
U. S. Engineer Agency of Resources Inventories	Washington, D. C.
U. S. Engineer Resources Inventory Center	Washington, D. C.
U. S. Geological Survey	Washington, D. C.
U. S. Naval Oceanographic Office	Washington, D. C.
U. S. Topographic Command	Washington, D. C.
U. S. Weather Bureau	Washington, D. C.

Van Nostrad Co.	Princeton, N. J.
Walker, Gerald E.	Berkeley, Calif.
Water Information Center, Inc.	Port Washington, N. Y.
Watts	New York, N. Y.
Welch Scientific Co.	Chicago, Ill.
Westminster Press	Philadelphia, Penna.
Whittemore Associates	Needham Heights, Mass.
Wiley, John & Sons	New York, N. Y.
Wise, W. H.	New York, N. Y.
World Pub. Co.	Cleveland, Ohio
Yale University Press	New Haven, Conn.
Zondervan Pub. House	Grand Rapids, Mich.

SOUTH AMERICA

Argentina
Antonio, Roberto O.	Buenos Aires
Argentina. Instituto Geográfico Militar	Buenos Aires
Automóvil Club Argentino	Buenos Aires
Ediciones Libreria del Colegio	Buenos Aires
Editorial Campano	Buenos Aires
Editorial Mapa	Buenos Aires
Ford Motor Argentina	Buenos Aires
Granda, J. C.	Buenos Aires
Kapelusz y Cîa	Buenos Aires
Peuser, Ediciones Geográficas	Buenos Aires

Bolivia
Camacho Lara, René R.	La Paz
Ediciones Condarco	La Paz

Brazil
Alves, Francisco	Rio de Janeiro
Brazil. Companha Nacional de Material de Ensino	Rio de Janeiro
Brazil. Conselho Nacional de Geografia	Rio de Janeiro
Brazil. Instituto Brasileiro de Geografia e Estatistica	Rio de Janeiro
Brazil. Ministerio de Agricultura	Rio de Janeiro
Brazil. Ministerio da Educaçãoe Cultura	Rio de Janeiro
Brazil. Servicio de Meterologia	Rio de Janeiro

Brazil. Servicio Nacional de Recensamento	Rio de Janeiro
Edições Melhoramentos	São Paulo
Editôra Civilização Brasiliera, S. A.	Rio de Janeiro
Editôra do Brazil	São Paulo
Editôra FTD	São Paulo
Editôra Globo	Rio de Janeiro
Editôra Liceu	Rio de Janeiro
Editôra Minerva	Rio de Janeiro
Editôra Ypiranga	Rio de Janeiro
Livros Cadernos	Rio de Janeiro
Puma	Rio de Janeiro
Schaeffer, Juan E.	Rio de Janeiro

Chile

Chile. Instituto Geografico Militar	Santiago de Chile
Empresa Editora Zig Zag	Santiago de Chile
Kaplán Cojano, Oscar	Santiago de Chile
Liga Chileno-Alemana	Santiago de Chile

Colombia

Codazzi, Instituto Geográfico	Bogotá
Colombia. Banco de la Republica. Departmento de Investigaciones Economicas	Bogotá
Colombia. Ministerio de Obras Publicas	Bogotá
Compañia Suramericana de Seguros	Medellín

Ecuador

Ecuador. Ministerio de Relaciones Exteriores	Quito
Publicationes Educativas Ariel	Guayaquil
SAM	Quito

Paraguay

Machuca Martinez, Marcelino	Asunción

Peru

Editorial F. T. D.	Lima
Librería e Imprenta "Guía Lascano"	Lima
Peru. Dirección de Caminos	Lima

Surinam

Duif	Paramaribo

Uruguay
    Monteverde, A.   Montevideo

Venezuela
    Discolar   Caracas
    Ediciones Nueva Cadiz   Caracas
    Minerva Books   Caracas
    Pensamiento, Vivo   Caracas
    Venezuela. Consejo Nacional de Validad   Caracas
    Venezuela. Direccion de Plantificacion
      Agropecuaria   Caracas
    Venezuela. Ministerio de Agricultura   Caracas
    Venezuela. Ministerio de la Defensa   Caracas
    Venezuela. Ministerio de Obras Públicas   Caracas

Abercrombie & Fitch (New York, N. Y. , U. S. A.) 2134, 3445, 3594, 3711, 5001

Accumulatoren-Fabrik, A. G. (Hannover, Germany) 2781, 2782, 5002, 5003

Afrika Instituut (Pretoria, South Africa) 1787, 3989, 4189, 4455, 4469, 4977, 5503

Agip (Milano, Italy) 3062, 5004

Aguilar, S. A. , De Ediciones (Madrid, Spain) 309, 452, 598, 599, 600, 699, 700, 701, 836, 928, 929, 1014, 1015, 1138, 1139, 1140, 1270, 1271, 1369, 1396, 1397, 1398, 1399, 1498, 1499, 1500, 1571, 1601, 1602, 1603, 1604, 1605, 1707, 1708, 1709, 1710, 1711, 1773, 3209, 3210, 3211, 3212, 3213, 3214, 3215, 3216, 3217, 3218, 3219, 3220, 3221, 3222, 3223, 3224, 3225, 3226, 3227, 3228, 3229, 3230, 3231, 3232, 3233, 3234, 3904, 3952, 4190, 4191, 4192, 4193, 4194, 4195, 4196, 4197, 4198, 4199, 4200, 4201, 4202, 4203, 4204, 4205, 4206, 4207, 4208, 4209, 4210, 4211, 4212

Ahiever (Jerusalem, Israel) 2421, 4492

Akademie Verlag (Berlin, Germany) 2783, 4135

Akademiförlaget (Göteborg, Sweden) 837, 4213

Alain Editions - see Editions Alain

Albania, Ministria e Aresimit dhe Kultures (Tirane, Albania) 702, 838

Aldine Pub. Co. (Chicago, Ill. , U. S. A.) 1712, 2319, 4493

Aldus (Stockholm, Sweden) 930

Allan (London, England) 2943, 5504

Allgemeiner Deutscher Automobil-Club (Kiel, Germany) 2784, 5005

Allhem (Malmö, Sweden) 703

Alpine Geographical Press (Champaign, Ill. , U. S. A.) 3446, 3447, 3448, 3449, 3450, 3451, 3452, 3453, 3712, 3713, 3714, 3715, 3716, 3717, 3718, 3719, 4110, 4111, 4112, 4113, 4114, 4115, 4116, 4117, 5006, 5007, 5008, 5009, 5010, 5011, 5012, 5013

Alves, Francisco (Rio de Janeiro, Brazil) 310, 1606

American Geographical Society (New York, N. Y. , U. S. A.) 1893, 4945, 4959

American Heritage (New York, N. Y. , U. S. A.) 3720, 4494

American Hotel Register Co. (Chicago, Ill. , U. S. A.) 3454,
   3455, 3456, 3457, 3458, 3459, 3460, 3461, 3462, 3463,
   3464, 3465, 3466, 3467, 3468, 3469, 3470, 3471, 3472,
   3473, 3474, 3595, 3596, 3597, 3598, 3599, 3600, 3601,
   3602, 3603, 3604, 3605, 3606, 3607, 3608, 3609, 3610,
   3611, 3612, 3613, 3614, 3615, 3721, 3722, 3723, 3724,
   3725, 3726, 3727, 3728, 3729, 3730, 3731, 3732, 3733,
   3734, 3735, 3736, 3737, 3738, 3739, 3740, 3741, 5014,
   5015, 5016, 5017, 5018, 5019, 5020, 5021, 5022, 5023,
   5024, 5025, 5026, 5027, 5028, 5029, 5030, 5031, 5032,
   5033, 5034
American Map Co. , Inc. (New York, N. Y. , U. S. A.) 704,
   785, 1016, 1141, 1142, 1143, 1217, 1272, 1400, 1419,
   1501, 1607, 1713, 1948, 3475, 3476, 3477, 3742, 3743,
   3744, 3976, 3980, 4214, 4215, 4216
Ampol Petroleum, Ltd. (Sydney, Australia) 2527, 5035
Angus & Robertson (Sydney, Australia) 1949, 2528
Anokh, Hanok (Tel Aviv, Israel) 516
Antonio, Roberto O. (Buenos Aires, Argentina) 3905
Argentina. Instituto Geográfico Militar (Buenos Aires, Argen-
   tina) 2155, 3906, 3907, 3908, 3909, 3910, 3911, 4217,
   5036, 5505
Ariel, Publicationes Educativas - see Publicaciones Educa-
   tivas Ariel
Arnold, E. (London, England) 1788, 1897, 4495, 4496, 4497,
   4498, 4499
Aschehoug & Co. (Oslo, Norway) 1144, 1273, 1774, 4500
Asedi (Bruxelles, Belgium) 1608, 2659
Asociación Nacional Automovilística (México, D. F. , México)
   3616, 3617, 3618, 5037, 5038, 5039
Association Press (New York, N. Y. , U. S. A.) 4047
Ateneo Ediciones - see Ediciones Ateneo
Atheneum (Barcelona, Spain) 1502
Atlantik Refining Company of Africa (Cape Town, South
   Africa) 2234, 2257, 5040
Atlantik Verlag (Frankfurt, Germany) 1, 2, 84, 86, 160,
   228, 229, 230, 231, 270, 311, 380, 453, 454, 455, 456,
   705, 737, 2785, 2786, 2787, 2788, 2789, 4218, 4501,
   4502, 4503
Augsburg Publishing House (Minneapolis, Minn. , U. S. A.)
   4048, 4504
Austin Motor Co. , Ltd. (Birmingham, England) 2944, 2945,
   2946, 2947, 2948, 2949, 2950, 5041, 5042, 5043, 5044,
   5045, 5046, 5047
Australia. Bureau of Mineral Resources, Geology and Geophysics (Adelaide, Australia) 1936, 4470
Australia. Department of National Development (Canberra,

Australia) 2529, 2530, 4219, 4220

Australia. Division of Soils, Commonwealth Scientific and Industrial Research Organization (Canberra, Australia) 2531, 5499

Australian Educational Foundation, Pty., Ltd. (Sydney, Australia) 931, 2532

Austria. Akademie der Wissenschaften (Wien, Austria) 2604, 2605, 4451

Autokarten und Reiseführer Verlag (Kiel, Germany) 2790, 5048

Automobile Association (London, England) 3051, 5049

Automobile Association of Malaya (Penang, Malaysia) 2489, 5050

Automobile Association of South Africa (Johannesburg, South Africa) 1789, 1790, 2258, 5051, 5052

Automobile Club d'Italia (Roma, Italy) 1950, 1951, 3063, 3064, 5053, 5054, 5055, 5056

Auto-Motor-und Radfahrerbund Österreichs (Wien, Austria) 1952, 1953, 5057, 5058

Automóvil Club Argentino (Buenos Aires, Argentina) 3912, 5059

Bachtiar, A. (Djakarta, Indonesia) 232, 2392

Bacon, G. W. Ltd. - see Johnston, W. & A. K. (Edinburgh, Scotland)

Bancroft & Co. (London, England) 1274

Bantam Books (New York, N.Y., U.S.A.) 1145

Barnes & Noble, Inc. (New York, N.Y., U.S.A.) 772, 2135, 4221, 4505, 4506, 4507, 4508, 4509, 4510, 4511, 4512, 4513, 4514, 4515, 4516, 4517

Bartholomew, John & Son, Ltd. (Edinburgh, Scotland) 3, 52, 53, 54, 55, 75, 87, 93, 161, 233, 234, 278, 279, 280, 312, 348, 381, 403, 437, 457, 493, 494, 517, 518, 558, 601, 613, 706, 744, 773, 774, 808, 809, 822, 859, 914, 927, 932, 978, 1017, 1018, 1019, 1030, 1085, 1143, 1146, 1221, 1356, 1357, 1400, 1401, 1503, 1543, 1584, 1609, 1692, 1918, 1919, 1942, 1943, 1954, 1955, 2951, 2952, 2953, 2954, 2955, 2956, 2957, 2958, 2959, 2960, 2961, 2962, 2963, 2998, 3006, 3204, 3206, 3413, 3424, 3487, 3488, 4342, 4343, 4518, 4571, 4572, 4730, 4755, 4756, 5060, 5061, 5062, 5063, 5064, 5065, 5066, 5067, 5068, 5069, 5070, 5071, 5072, 5073, 5074, 5363, 5365, 5550

Bayerischer Schulbuch Verlag (München, Germany) 4519, 4520, 4521, 4522, 4523, 4524

Belgium. Académie Royale des Sciences d'Outre-Mer (Bruxelles, Belgium) 2181, 2192, 2193, 2239

Belgium. Centre d'Information et de Documentation du

Congo Belge et du Ruanda-Urundi (Bruxelles, Belgium)
   2182, 2183, 2194, 2195, 2240, 2241
Belgium. Centre National de Recherches Scientifiques Souter-
   raines (Liège, Belgium) 2660, 4134
Belgium. Comité National de Géographie (Bruxelles, Belgium)
   2661
Belgium. Ministère des Travaux Publics et de la Recon-
   struction (Bruxelles, Belgium) 2662, 4222
Bello, Editorial - see Editorial Bello
Ben-Eliyahu, Ephraim (Jerusalem, Israel) 2422, 4049
Benziger & Co. (Einsiedeln, Germany) 4050, 4525
Bergvalls Förlag (Stockholm, Sweden) 162, 458, 775, 933,
   1147
Bernces Förlag (Malmö, Sweden) 934
Bertelsmann, C. (Gütersloh, Germany) 313, 602, 776, 839,
   840, 868, 915, 946, 1020, 1021, 1022, 1084, 1148, 1275,
   1276, 1277, 1278, 1402, 1403, 1404, 1504, 1505, 1506,
   1507, 1774, 1956, 1957, 1958, 1959, 2072, 2791, 2792,
   2793, 5075, 5076, 5077
Beste, A. S. (Oslo, Norway) 1023, 1149, 1378
Beste, G. M. B. H. (Stuttgart, Germany) 1610
Better Camping Magazine (Milwaukee, Wisc. , U. S. A.) 3478,
   3745, 4118
Bir Yayinevi (Istanbul, Turkey) 841, 842, 1279, 1280, 1281
Blackie & Son, Ltd. (London, England) 1960, 1961, 2964,
   2965, 2966, 4970, 4971, 4972
Blondel La Rougery (Paris, France) 1962, 2730, 2731, 2732,
   5078, 5079, 5080, 5081
BLV Verlagsgesellschaft (München, Germany) 1963, 2794,
   3990, 4526
Bobley Pub. Corp. (Glen Cove, N. Y. , U. S. A.) 1643, 1714
Bolis, Ed. - see Poligrafiche Bolis
Bonnier (Stockholm, Sweden) 88
Bookcraft (Salt Lake City, Utah, U. S. A.) 3202, 4465
Book Production Industries (Chicago, Ill. , U. S. A.) 163, 603
Book Publishers Distributing Co. (Cincinnati, Ohio, U. S. A.)
   235
Bootsma ('s Gravenhage, Netherlands) 3090, 5082
Bordas - see Editions Bordas (Paris, France)
Bordos, H. (Paris, France) 236
Borneo Literature Bureau (Kuching, Borneo) 2490, 2491, 2492
Bosch (Barcelona, Spain) 519, 3235, 3236, 4223
Bosch & Keuning (Baarn, Netherlands) 4527
Bottin - see Didot-Bottin
Boy Scouts of America (New Brunswick, N. J. , U. S. A.) 3746,
   4119, 5083
B. P. Australia, Ltd. (Melbourne, Australia) 2533, 5084

BP Benzin & Petroleum Gesellschaft (Hamburg, Germany) 2795, 5085

B. P. Southern Africa Pty. , Ltd. (Cape Town, South Africa) 1791, 2259, 5086

Brazil. Companha Nacional de Material de Ensino (Rio de Janeiro, Brazil) 1282

Brazil. Conselho Nacional de Geografia (Rio de Janeiro, Brazil) 459, 935, 3923, 3924, 4224

Brazil. Instituto Brasileiro de Geografia e Estatistica (Rio de Janeiro, Brazil) 777, 3925, 3926, 3927, 3928, 4528

Brazil. Ministerio de Agricultura (Rio de Janeiro, Brazil) 3929, 4456

Brazil. Ministério da Educação e Cultura (Rio de Janeiro, Brazil) 3930, 3931, 3932, 4529, 4530, 4531, 4532

Brazil. Servicio de Meterologia (Rio de Janeiro, Brazil) 3933, 3934, 4136, 4137

Brazil. Serviço Nacional de Recensamento (Rio de Janeiro, Brazil) 3935, 4225

Brink, H. Ten - see Ten Brink, H.

British Motor Corp. , Ltd. (London, England) 2967, 2973, 5087, 5181

British Sulphur Corp. , Ltd. (London, England) 1283, 1715, 3991, 3992

Brockhaus, F. A. (Wiesbaden, Germany) 778, 1150

Brown, W. C. Co. (Dubuque, Iowa, U. S. A.) 779, 1611, 1792, 3747, 4024, 4025, 4138

Brug Uitgeversbedrijf, N. V. (Amsterdam, Netherlands) 707, 708, 936, 1508, 3091, 3092, 3093

Buchclub Ex Libris (Zürich, Switzerland) 1509

Buchgemeinschaft Donauland (Wien, Austria) 520, 1151, 1284, 1964, 2606, 2607, 5088

Buchverlag Verlandsdruckerei (Bern, Switzerland) 3282, 3993

Bulgaria. Akademiya na Naukite (Sofia, Bulgaria) 2679, 4533

Bulgaria. Glavno Upravlenie po Geodeziá i Kartografiá (Sofia, Bulgaria) 709, 1024, 1612, 2680, 2681, 2682, 5089

Bulgaria. Muzei na Revoliutsionnoto Dvizhenie Búlgariiá (Sofia, Bulgaria) 2683, 4534

Burns & Oates, Ltd. (London, England) 4051, 4052

Cadernos - see Livros Cadernos

Caltcx (Philippines) (Manila, Philippines) 2508, 5090

Camacho Lara, René R. (La Paz, Bolivia) 3922

Campano, Editorial - see Editorial Campano

Camping Maps, U. S. A. (Montclair, N. J. , U. S. A.) 3619, 3748, 3749, 4120, 4121

Canada. Department of Energy, Mines & Resources (Ottawa, Canada) 3479, 3480

Colombia. Ministerio de Obras Publicas (Bogotá, Colombia)
  3956, 5096
Colorgravure (Melbourne, Australia) 6, 2537, 2538
Columbus Verlag Oestergaard (Berlin, Germany) 7, 8, 168,
  269, 304, 461, 606, 689, 851, 1026, 1288, 1408, 2796,
  5097
Commission for Technical Cooperation in Africa South of the
  Sahara (Lagos, Nigeria) 1808, 4140
Compániá Hulera Euzkadi, S. A. (México, D. F., México)
  3620, 3621, 3622, 5098, 5099, 5100
Compañia Mercantil Anónima Líneas Aéreas Españolas
  (Madrid, Spain) 3237, 5506
Compañia Suramericana de Seguros (Medellín, Colombia) 3957
Condarco Ediciones - see Ediciones Condarco
Consociazione Turistica Italiana (Milano, Italy) 3065, 4231
Consolidated Book Publishers (Chicago, Ill., U. S. A.) 1155
Contact (Antwerpen, Belgium) 91
Container Corporation of America (Chicago, Ill., U. S. A.) 242
Continental Gummiwerke Kartographischer Verlag (Hannover,
  Germany) 1966, 1967, 1968, 1969, 1970, 1971, 2608,
  2663, 2664, 2797, 2798, 2799, 2800, 2801, 2802, 2803,
  2804, 2805, 2806, 2807, 2808, 3066, 3082, 3083, 3283,
  5101, 5102, 5103, 5104, 5105, 5106, 5107, 5108, 5109,
  5110, 5111, 5112, 5113, 5114, 5115, 5116
Continental Oil Co. (Chicago, Ill., U. S. A.) 3767, 3768,
  5189, 5190
Compano, Editorial - see Editorial Compano
Cooper Square Publishers (New York, N. Y., U. S. A.) 2156,
  4232, 4546
Costa Rica. Ministerio de Economia y Hacienda (San José,
  Costa Rica) 3579, 4233
Cram, George F. Co. (Indianapolis, Ind., U. S. A.) 9, 10,
  169, 314, 387, 462, 852, 853, 938, 1156, 4057
Cranfield & Bonfiel Books (London, England) 2968, 4927,
  5555
Cremonese, Edizioni - see Edizioni Cremonese
Crowell & Co. (New York, N. Y., U. S. A.) 11
Curcio, A. (Roma, Italy) 939
Czechoslovakia. Akademie Véd (Praha, Czechoslovakia) 4038,
  4039, 4040
Czechoslovakia. Kartografické Nakladatelství (Praha, Czech-
  oslovakia) 2684, 2685, 2686, 2687, 2688, 4547, 5117,
  5118, 5119
Czechoslovakia. Komenium (Praha, Czechoslovakia) 12
Czechoslovakia. Ministerstvo Národní Obrany (Praha,
  Czechoslovakia) 2689

Czechoslovakia. Státní Nakl. Ucebnic (Praha, Czechoslo-
    vakia) 170
Czechoslovakia. Státní Pedagogické Nakl.(Praha, Czecho-
    slovakia) 243
Czechoslovakia. Státní Zeměměřický a Kartografický Ústav
    (Praha, Czechoslovakia) 244
Czechoslovakia. Ústřední Správa Geodesie a Kartografie
    (Praha, Czechoslovakia) 92, 463, 464, 523, 524, 525, 526,
    607, 608, 609, 610, 710, 711, 712, 782, 783, 784, 854,
    855, 940, 1027, 1028, 1289, 1290, 1409, 1410, 1809,
    2690, 2691, 2692, 2693, 2694, 2695, 2696, 2697, 2698,
    2699, 2700, 2701, 2702, 2703, 2704, 2705, 2706, 2707,
    2708, 2709, 2710, 3323, 3324, 4141, 4234, 4457, 4471,
    4548, 4549, 4550, 4551, 4552, 4553, 4554, 4555, 4556,
    4978, 5120, 5121, 5122, 5123, 5124
Czechoslovakia. Ústřední Ústav Geologický (Praha, Czecho-
    slovakia) 2711, 4472

Daily Express (London, England) 2969, 5125
Damm, N. W. & Søn (Oslo, Norway) 1291
Dar Al-Ma'Ārif (Cairo, U. A. R. -Egypt) 171
Das Beste Verlag - see Verlag Das Beste
De Agostini, Istituto Geografico - see Istituto Geografico De
    Agostini
Delagrave (Paris, France) 245, 611, 1029, 1617
Dell Pub. Co. (New York, N. Y. , U. S. A.) 465, 856
Denmark. Geodaetisk Institut (København, Denmark) 2714,
    2715, 2716, 2717, 2718, 2719, 2720, 2721, 5126
Denoyer-Geppert Co. (Chicago, Ill. , U. S. A.) 172, 713, 714,
    857, 1292, 1411, 1810, 1811, 1899, 1900, 1972, 1973,
    1974, 1975, 2324, 3325, 3326, 3327, 3750, 3751, 4557,
    4558, 4559, 4560, 4561, 4562, 4563, 4564, 4565, 4566,
    4567
Dent, J. M. (London, England & Toronto, Canada) 93, 612,
    613, 614, 858, 859, 1030, 1293, 3484, 3485, 3486, 3487,
    3488, 4568, 4569, 4570, 4571, 4572
Deseret Book Co. (Salt Lake City, Utah, U. S. A.) 2970,
    3052, 3414, 4466, 4467
De Sikkel (Anvers, Belgium) 1412
Deutsche Lufthansa (Köln, Germany) 1618, 5507
Deutsche Viscobil Öl Gesellschaft (Hamburg, Germany) 2809,
    5127
Deutscher Bücherbund (Stuttgart, Germany) 1513, 1619, 4573
Deutscher Taschenbuch Verlag (München, Germany) 4574,
    4575, 4576, 4577
Deutscher Zentralverlag VEB. (Berlin, Germany) 2810, 5128
Didot-Bottin (Paris, France) 2736, 2737

Globo Editôra - see Editôra Globo
Golden Press (New York, N. Y. , U. S. A.) 1524
Goldmann Verlag (München, Germany) 393, 538, 867, 1042,
    1304, 1635
Gollancz, Victor (London, England) 1817
Goushá, H. M. Co. (San José, Calif. , U. S. A.) 2139, 2140,
    2141, 3493, 3494, 3495, 3496, 3497, 3498, 3499, 3500,
    3632, 3633, 3634, 3635, 3636, 3637, 3638, 3757, 3758,
    3759, 3766, 3767, 3768, 3769, 3770, 3771, 3772, 3773,
    3774, 3775, 3776, 3777, 3778, 5155, 5156, 5157, 5188,
    5189, 5190, 5191, 5192, 5193, 5194, 5195, 5196, 5197,
    5198, 5199, 5200
Grafisk Forlag (København, Denmark) 868
Granda, J. C. (Buenos Aires, Argentina) 1636
Greece. Ministry of National Economy (Athens, Greece) 2936
Greece. National Statistical Service (Athens, Greece) 2937,
    2938, 4260
Greece. Statistikon Graphelon (Athens, Greece) 2939, 4261
Greystone Press (New York, N. Y. , U. S. A.) 1424
Grijalbo, Editorial - see Editorial Grijalbo
Grolier Society (New York, N. Y. , U. S. A.) 183, 252, 1190,
    3501
Grosset & Dunlap (New York, N. Y. , U. S. A.) 869, 1525,
    3502, 3503, 3504, 3639, 3640, 3641, 3779, 3780, 3781,
    5201, 5202, 5203
Gt. Britain. Meteorological Office (London, England) 2980,
    4148
Gt. Britain. Ministry of Agriculture, Fisheries & Food
    (London, England) 2981, 3420, 4937
Gt. Britain. Ministry of Housing and Local Government
    (London, England) 2982, 3421
Guatemala. Dirección General de Cartografia (Guatemala,
    Guatemala) 3588
Guatemala. Instituto Geográfico Nacional (Guatemala,
    Guatemala) 3589
Guatemala. Ministerio de Educación Pública (Guatemala,
    Guatemala) 3590
Guatemala. Observatorio Meteorológico y Estacion
    Sismográfia (Guatemala, Guatemala) 3591, 4149
Guía Lascano - see Librería e Imprenta "Guía Lascano"
Gumperts Förlag (Göteborg, Sweden) 24, 25, 184, 870, 4262
Guruhi Jughrafiya (Teheran, Iran) 2419, 4150
Gwasg Prifysgol Cymru (Caerdydd, Wales) 3422, 4630
Gyldendal (København, Denmark) 26, 27, 101, 720, 871, 956,
    957, 1043, 1044, 1045, 1172, 1173, 1305, 1306, 1526,
    1637, 1638, 1728, 2722, 4263, 4264, 4265, 4266, 4267

Haack, Hermann (Gotha, Germany) 185, 253, 254, 394, 395,
    474, 539, 626, 627, 829, 872, 923, 958, 1046, 1047,
    1048, 1128, 1174, 1175, 1176, 1260, 1307, 1308, 1309,
    1389, 1425, 1426, 1527, 1528, 1639, 1640, 1702, 2825,
    2826, 2827, 2828, 2829, 2830, 2831, 2832, 2833, 2834,
    2835, 2836, 2837, 2838, 2839, 2840, 2841, 2842, 2843,
    2844, 2845, 2846, 2847, 2848, 2849, 2850, 3999, 4000,
    4268, 4269, 4270, 4271, 4272, 4273, 4631, 5204, 5205,
    5206, 5207, 5208, 5209, 5210, 5211, 5513, 5514, 5515,
    5516, 5517, 5518
Hachette (Paris, France) 28, 102, 255, 326, 475, 476, 540,
    541, 1310, 1427, 2760, 4632, 4633
Hai Kuang Ch'u Pan Shê (Hong Kong) 1904, 1905, 2499
Halcyon House (Garden City, N. Y. , U. S. A.) 29
Haller Verlag (Berlin, Germany) 103, 4459
Hallwag, A. G. (Bern, Switzerland) 1529, 2006, 2007, 2008,
    2009, 2010, 2011, 5212, 5213, 5214, 5215, 5216, 5217
Hammond, C. S. & Co. , Inc. - see Hammond, Inc.
Hammond, Inc. (Maplewood, N. J. , U. S. A.) 30, 31, 32, 33,
    34, 35, 36, 37, 98, 104, 105, 106, 107, 108, 109, 110,
    111, 112, 113, 182, 183, 186, 187, 188, 189, 190, 191,
    192, 193, 194, 235, 252, 256, 257, 258, 259, 260, 261,
    262, 263, 264, 265, 266, 294, 315, 327, 328, 329, 330,
    331, 332, 333, 334, 335, 336, 362, 363, 366, 378, 396,
    397, 398, 399, 400, 401, 431, 433, 465, 466, 467, 477,
    478, 479, 480, 481, 482, 483, 484, 485, 486, 505, 506,
    507, 509, 528, 542, 543, 544, 545, 546, 547, 548, 549,
    550, 582, 583, 615, 628, 629, 630, 631, 632, 633, 721,
    722, 723, 724, 725, 726, 727, 728, 760, 762, 789, 794,
    795, 796, 797, 798, 830, 856, 873, 874, 875, 876, 877,
    878, 879, 912, 941, 942, 947, 950, 959, 960, 961, 962,
    1031, 1049, 1050, 1051, 1052, 1053, 1054, 1055, 1056,
    1057, 1058, 1059, 1060, 1061, 1062, 1063, 1064, 1080,
    1092, 1145, 1177, 1178, 1179, 1180, 1181, 1182, 1183,
    1184, 1185, 1186, 1187, 1188, 1189, 1190, 1191, 1211,
    1219, 1220, 1249, 1311, 1312, 1313, 1314, 1315, 1316,
    1317, 1318, 1319, 1320, 1321, 1322, 1323, 1324, 1325,
    1382, 1424, 1428, 1429, 1430, 1431, 1432, 1433, 1434,
    1435, 1436, 1437, 1478, 1530, 1531, 1532, 1533, 1534,
    1535, 1536, 1537, 1538, 1539, 1540, 1558, 1641, 1642,
    1643, 1644, 1645, 1646, 1647, 1714, 1719, 1729, 1730,
    1731, 1732, 1733, 1734, 1735, 1736, 1737, 1738, 1739,
    1740, 1741, 2142, 2539, 2540, 2541, 2551, 2574, 3492,
    3501, 3505, 3506, 3507, 3508, 3509, 3510, 3511, 3512,
    3513, 3514, 3515, 3642, 3643, 3644, 3645, 3646, 3647,
    3709, 3710, 3746, 3782, 3783, 3784, 3785, 3786, 3787,
    3788, 3789, 3790, 3791, 3792, 3793, 3794, 3795, 3796,

Hulton Educational Publications, Ltd. (London, England) 1818, 1819, 4674
Humble Travel Club (Houston, Tex. , U. S. A.) 3760, 5172
Humboldt Verlag (Stuttgart, Germany) 269
Humphrey, H. A. , Ltd. (London, England) 2430, 4071, 4675

IAC (Lyon, France) 116, 800
Ichtiar (Djakarta, Indonesia) 2401
Imperial Press (København, Denmark) 2723, 2724, 5229, 5230
Importbøger (København, Denmark) 270
Imprimeries Oberthur (Rennes, France) 2761, 2762, 2763, 2764, 2765, 2766, 5520, 5521, 5522, 5523, 5524
India. Directorate General of Health Services (Delhi, India) 2373, 4961
India. Directorate of Economics and Statistics (Delhi, India) 2374, 2375, 4001, 4002
India. Information and Broadcasting Ministry (Calcutta, India) 2376, 4278
India. Ministry of Education and Scientific Research (Calcutta, India) 2377
India. National Atlas Organization (Calcutta, India) 2378
India. Survey of India (Dehra Dūn, India) 882, 965, 1067, 1199, 2379, 2380, 2381, 2382
Indian Book Depot & Map House (Delhi, India) 117, 2383, 2384, 4676
Indian Central Cotton Committee (Bombay, India) 2385
Indian Central Oilseeds Committee (Hyderabad, India) 2386
Indiana University. Department of Geography (Bloomington, Ind. , U. S. A.) 2014, 4279
Indonesia. Army Topographical Directorate (Djakarta, Indonesia) 2402, 4280
Indonesia. Badan Atlas Nacional (Djakarta, Indonesia) 2403, 4281
Industrial Atlas Corporation (New York, N. Y. , U. S. A.) 3803, 4473
Informations et Conjoncture (Paris, France) 966, 4474
Institut de Recherches Scientifiques du Cameroun (Yaoundé, Cameroun) 2189, 2190
Institut Fondamental d'Afrique Noire (Dakar, Senegal) 1820
Institut Français d'Afrique Noire (Dakar, Senegal) 1821, 4983
Institut Français d'Archéologie Orientale (Cairo, U. A. R. - Egypt) 2309, 4036, 4072
Instituto de Estudos Geograficos (Coimbra, Portugal) 3185, 3186, 3187, 4930
Instituto Gegráfico Codazzi - see Codazzi, Instituto Geográfico
International Bank for Reconstruction and Development (Washington, D. C. , U. S. A.) 1440, 1544, 1652, 1744,

4282, 4283, 4284, 4285, 4984, 4985, 4986, 4987
International Publications Service (New York, N. Y. , U. S. A.)
      1822, 4154
International Telecommunication Union (Geneva, Switzerland)
      2015, 4177, 4178
Internationaler Holzmarkt (Wien, Austria) 2655, 2656, 4460,
      4461
Israel. Department of Surveys (Jerusalem, Israel) 2427,
      2431, 2432, 4286, 4677, 4988
Israel. Mahleket Ha-Medidot (Jerusalem, Israel) 2433
Israel. Ministry of Labour (Jerusalem, Israel) 2434, 4678
Israel. Ministry of Survey (Tel Aviv, Israel) 2435
Israel. Tseva Haganah Le-Yisrael (Jerusalem, Israel) 2436,
      4679
Israel. University Press (Jerusalem, Israel) 2437, 4073, 4680
Istituto Geografico De Agostini (Novara, Italy) 17, 40, 118,
      176, 271, 338, 339, 340, 404, 488, 489, 731, 967, 968,
      969, 1068, 1069, 1070, 1071, 1072, 1073, 1074, 1075,
      1089, 1161, 1165, 1200, 1201, 1202, 1203, 1204, 1205,
      1218, 1279, 1280, 1281, 1327, 1328, 1329, 1330, 1331,
      1332, 1441, 1442, 1545, 1668, 1745, 1746, 1747, 1748,
      1780, 2016, 2017, 3067, 3068, 3069, 3070, 3188, 3922,
      3979, 4003, 4247, 4287, 4288, 4289, 4290, 4291, 4292,
      4681, 4682, 4683, 4684, 4685, 5231
Istituto Geografico Editoriale Italiano (Roma, Italy) 272, 341,
      4686
Istituto Italiano per l'Africa (Roma, Italy) 1823, 4687
Italatlas (Roma, Italy) 3071, 5232
Italgeo (Milano, Italy) 3072, 4688
Italy. Direzione Generale della Statistica (Roma, Itlay) 3073,
      4293
Italy. Istituto Geografico Militare (Firenze, Italy) 3074

Jacaranda (Brisbane, Australia) 1937, 1938, 2597, 2598
Jackson, W. M. , Inc. (México, D. F. , Mexico) 196
Japan. Un'Yashō Kankōkyoku (Tokyo, Japan) 2446
Jimbunsha (Tokyo, Japan) 2447, 2448, 2449, 2450
Johnston, W. & A. K. & G. W. Bacon, Ltd. (Edinburgh,
      Scotland) 119, 273, 405, 490, 637, 883, 1206, 1546, 2983,
      2984, 2985, 2986, 2987, 2988, 2989, 2990, 2991, 2992,
      3055, 3056, 3057, 3058, 3059, 4689, 5233, 5234, 5235,
      5236, 5237, 5238, 5239, 5240, 5241, 5242, 5243
Journaux, André (Caen, France) 1207
JRO Verlag (München, Germany) 41, 42, 120, 197, 274, 342,
      406, 491, 552, 732, 801, 884, 885, 1333, 1334, 1335,
      1336, 1337, 1338, 1339, 1340, 1443, 1444, 1547, 1548,
      1549, 2018, 2019, 2020, 2021, 2022, 2023, 2657, 2851,

2852, 2853, 2854, 2855, 2856, 2857, 2858, 2859, 3075, 3284, 4294, 4295, 4296, 5244, 5245, 5246, 5247, 5248, 5249, 5250, 5251, 5252, 5253, 5525
Jugoslavenski Leksikografski Zavod (Zagreb, Yugoslavia) 1076, 1445, 1446, 3429, 3430, 5254, 5255
Juta & Co., Ltd. (Cape Town, South Africa) 2264, 4690

Kaiser (Klagenfurt, Austria) 1341
Kalmbach Publishing Co. (Milwaukee, Wisc., U. S. A.) 3516, 3804, 4123, 5256
Kanaat Kitabevi (Istanbul, Turkey) 43
Kanaat Yayinlari (Istanbul, Turkey) 638, 886, 1342, 1343, 1344, 2024, 2025, 4691, 4692
Kantonaler Lehrmittel Verlag (Zürich, Switzerland) 343, 553, 639, 640, 970, 3285, 3286, 3287, 3288, 3289
Kapelusz y Cïa (Buenos Aires, Argentina) 1208, 4042, 4297
Kaplán Cojano, Oscar (Santiago de Chile, Chile) 802
Kartográfiai Vállalat (Budapest, Hungary) 407, 408, 554, 619, 641, 642, 643, 687, 733, 887, 971, 972, 973, 1077, 1078, 1345, 1346, 1347, 1447, 1448, 1449, 1550, 1653, 1654, 1655, 2026, 3037, 3038, 3039, 3040, 3041, 3042, 3043, 3044, 3045, 3046, 4298, 4299, 4300, 4301, 4693, 4694, 5257, 5258, 5259, 5260, 5261, 5262, 5263, 5264, 5265
Kartographisches Institut Meyer - see Meyer Kartographisches Institut
Katholiek Sociaal-Kerkelijk Instituut ('s Gravenhage, Netherlands) 2027, 4302, 4989
Keyser - see Keysersche Verlagsbuchhandlung, G. M. B. H.
Keysersche Verlagsbuchhandlung, G. M. B. H. (Heidelberg, Germany) 344, 409, 555, 556, 644, 974, 1079, 1209, 1210, 1551, 1656, 4695
Kim, Sang-Jin (Seoul, Korea) 2481
Kings College School (London, England) 3593, 4004
Kiplinger-Washington Editors, Inc. (Washington, D. C., U.S.A.) 1080, 1211,
Kishõ Kyõkai (Tokyo, Japan) 2451, 4155
Klett Verlag (Stuttgart, Germany) 275, 492
Knaur, Th. Nachf. (München, Germany) 410
Kohlhammer Verlag (Mainz, Germany) 2860
Kokusai Chicaku Kyõkai (Tokyo, Japan) 2452
Kongelig Norsk Automobilklub (Oslo, Norway) 3137, 3138, 5266, 5267
König, Hans, Verlag (Frankfurt, Germany) 2028, 2029, 2030, 2861, 2862, 2863, 2864, 5268, 5269, 5270, 5271, 5272
Ksiąznica-Atlas (Wrocław, Poland) 198, 3143, 3144, 3145, 4303, 4304, 4305, 4696, 4697
Kuang Hua Yü Ti Hsüeh Shê (Peking, China) 2330, 2331, 2332

Kümmerly & Frey (Bern, Switzerland) 121, 199, 276, 345,
    346, 645, 646, 734, 803, 804, 975, 976, 1212, 1450,
    1657, 1660, 1766, 2031, 2032, 2033, 2034, 2035, 2036,
    2037, 2038, 2039, 2040, 2041, 2103, 2110, 2865, 3290,
    3291, 3292, 3293, 3294, 3295, 3296, 3297, 3298, 3299,
    3300, 3301, 3302, 3303, 3304, 3305, 3306, 3307, 4105,
    4306, 4307, 4315, 4475, 5273, 5274, 5275, 5276, 5277,
    5278, 5279, 5280, 5281, 5282, 5283, 5284, 5285, 5286,
    5287, 5288, 5289, 5290, 5291, 5292, 5293, 5294, 5467
Kungliga Automobil Klubben (Stockholm, Sweden) 3273, 3274,
    5295, 5296

Landkartenverlag VEB. (Berlin, Germany) 2866, 2867, 2868,
    2869, 2870, 5297, 5298, 5299, 5300, 5301
Lantbruksforbundets Tidskriftsaktiebolag (Stockholm, Sweden)
    3275, 4005
Larousse (Paris, France) 44, 122, 557, 735, 1213, 1348,
    1451, 1452, 1453, 1749, 4308, 4309, 4310, 4311, 4312,
    4313
Lebanon. Direction des Affaires Géographiques (Beyrouth,
    Lebanon) 2486, 5302
Lebanon. Ministère du Plan (Beyrouth, Lebanon) 2487
Lebanon. Service Météorologique (Beyrouth, Lebanon) 2488,
    4156
Lebendiges Wissen - see Verlag Lebendiges Wissen
Le Carrousel Publicité (Tours, France) 2767, 5303
Lehrmittel Verlag (Offenburg, Germany) 4698
Leksikografski Zavod FNRJ (Zagreb, Yugoslavia) 888
Les Éditions de Lyon - see Editions de Lyon
Liang, Ch'i-Shan (Hong Kong) 2333
Librairie Mellottée (Paris, France) 2768, 5304
Librairie Payot (Lausanne, Switzerland) 411, 647, 736,
    3308, 3309, 3310
Libreria del Colegio Ediciones - see Ediciones Libreria del
    Colegio
Librería e Imprenta "Guía Lascano" (Lima, Peru) 3966,
    3967, 3968, 3969, 3970, 3971
Librería y Casa Editorial Hernando - see Hernando
Liceu Editora - see Editora Liceu
Liga Chileno-Alemana (Santiago de Chile, Chile) 3950, 3951,
    4699, 4700
Lingen (Köln, Germany) 1658
L'Institut National pour l'Étude Agronomique du Congo
    (Bruxelles, Belgium) 2187, 2199, 2245, 4006, 5500
List, P. - see also Atlantik Verlag (München, Germany)
    977, 1081, 1082, 1214, 1349, 1454, 1552, 1659, 1660,
    2871, 2872, 2873, 2874, 2875, 2876, 2877, 4314, 4315,
    4701, 4702, 4703, 4704, 4705

Mapa, Editorial - see Editorial Mapa
Map Productions, Ltd. (London, England) 2996, 5334
Map Studio Productions, Pty., Ltd. (Cape Town, South Africa)
    1836, 2221, 2226, 2237, 2266, 2310, 5335
Marco Surveys, Ltd. (Nairobi, Kenya) 1837, 4008
Mariam, Mesfin Wolde (Addis Ababa, Ethiopia) 2202, 4320
Martín, A. (Barcelona, Spain) 3249
Martindale Press (Sydney, Australia) 4718
Martins Forlag (København, Denmark) 890, 1083, 4321
McDougall's Educational Co. Ltd. (Edinburgh, Scotland) 51,
    126, 2267
McGraw-Hill Book Co. (New York, N.Y., U.S.A.) 52, 53,
    278, 348, 493, 978, 1084, 1085, 1662, 2439, 4077, 4719
Meddens Editions - see Editions Meddens
Meiklejohn (London, England) 54, 55, 279, 280, 494, 558
Melantrich (Praha, Czechoslovakia) 3331
Melhoramentos, Edições - see Edições Melhoramentos
Mellottée - see Libraire Mellottée
Merrill, C. E. Co. (Columbus, Ohio, U.S.A.) 56, 1216
Methuen (London, England) 1838, 2172, 3332, 4322, 4720,
    4721, 4722, 4723, 4724, 4725, 4726
Meulenhoff, J. M. (Amsterdam, Netherlands) 741, 1086,
    1555, 1663, 1664, 3098, 3099, 3100, 3101, 3102
México. Comisión Nacional de Caminos Vecinales (México,
    D. F., México) 3648, 3649, 5336, 5337
México. Fondo de Cultura Economica (México, D. F., México)
    3650, 4727
México. Instituto Mexicano de Investigaciones Economicas
    (México, D. F., México) 3651, 4104, 4323, 4990
México. Ministerio de Comunicaciones y Obras Públicas
    (México, D. F., México) 3652, 3653, 4179, 4180, 5526,
    5527
México. Secretaría de Comunicaciones y Transportes (México,
    D. F., México) 3654, 4181, 5528
México. Universidad Nacional Autónoma (México, D. F.,
    México) 3655, 3656, 4158
Meyer, Kartographisches Institut (Mannheim, Germany) 979,
    1087, 1351, 1456, 1556, 1665, 1750, 1751, 1781, 4043,
    4102, 4159, 4476, 4491, 4966, 4969, 5501
Michelin et Cie (Paris, France) 2769, 2770, 2771, 2772,
    2773, 2774, 4126, 5338, 5339, 5340, 5341, 5342, 5343
Michelin Tyre Co. (Stoke-on-Trent, England) 2997, 5344
Milli Egitim Basimevi (Istanbul, Turkey) 57, 3322
Minerva Books (Caracas, Venezuela) 1217, 3980
Minerva, Editôra - see Editôra Minerva
Minerva Italica (Bergamo, Italy) 4728
Moderna, Empresa - see Empresa Moderna

Mohn (Gütersloh, Germany) 4729
Monteverde, A. (Montevideo, Uruguay) 891, 1352
Moore, William L. (Mt. Vernon, Ill. , U. S. A.) 1353
Morocco. Comité National de Géographie (Rabat, Morocco) 2224
Motormännens Riksförbund (Stockholm, Sweden) 3276, 3277, 3278, 3279, 3280, 5345, 5346, 5347, 5348, 5349
Motor Manual (Melbourne, Australia) 2544, 2545, 2546, 2547, 2548, 2549, 2550, 5350, 5351, 5352, 5353, 5354, 5355, 5356
Munger Oil Information Service (Los Angeles, Calif. , U. S. A.) 1839, 1915, 4477
Munksgaard (København, Denmark) 1666
Murray, John (London, England) 1088, 2072

Nagel Publishers (Geneva, Switzerland) 1667
Nathan, Fernand (Paris, France) 58, 412, 559, 742, 743, 1089, 1218, 1668, 2191, 2201, 2298, 3250
National Bus Traffic Association (Chicago, Ill. , U. S. A.) 3518, 3657, 3809, 5357, 5529
National Geographic Society (Washington, D. C. , U. S. A.) 651, 1090, 1457, 3810, 3811
National Safety Council (Chicago, Ill. , U. S. A.) 3500, 3638, 3778, 5200
National Trust (London, England) 2998, 2999, 3424, 4730, 4731
Nationale Boekhandel (Kaapstad, South Africa) 2268, 4732
Natur Och Kultur Bokförlaget (Stockholm, Sweden) 495
Nelson-Doubleday (New York, N. Y. , U. S. A. and London, England) 1189, 1219, 2541, 2551
Nelson, Thomas & Sons, Ltd. (London, England) 652, 807, 892, 980, 1091, 1354, 1355, 1458, 1459, 1557, 1669, 1670, 1840, 1841, 1916, 2207, 2208, 2209, 2210, 2213, 2222, 2230, 2250, 2251, 2293, 2300, 2301, 2311, 2552, 3000, 3001, 3002, 3003, 3004, 3005, 3519, 3520, 3521, 3522, 3523, 3524, 3658, 3659, 3972, 4037, 4078, 4079, 4080, 4081, 4106, 4733, 4734, 4735, 4736, 4737, 4738, 4739, 4962, 4963, 4964, 4991, 5358
Nepal. Ministry of Information and Broadcasting (Kathmandu, Nepal) 2502
Netherlands. Bureau voor Wegen en Verkeersstatistiek ('s Gravenhage, Netherlands) 3103, 5359
Netherlands. Department van Landbouw en Visscherij (Zwolle, Netherlands) 3104, 4009
Netherlands. Dienst Verkeersonderzoek ('s Gravenhage, Netherlands) 3105, 5360
Netherlands. Ministerie van Marine ('s Gravenhage, Netherlands) 2599, 4160

Pensamiento Vivo (Caracas, Venezuela) 3981, 4348
Pergamon Press, Ltd. (Oxford, England) 1466, 1675
Permabooks (New York, N. Y. , U. S. A.) 61
Perthes, Justus (Gotha, Germany) 203, 204
Peru. Direccíon de Caminos (Lima, Peru) 3973, 5372
Petroleum Publishing Co. (Tulsa, Okla. , U. S. A.) 3531,
    3532, 3815, 3816, 4478, 4479
Peugeot (Paris, France) 2776, 5373
Peuser, Ediciones Geográficas (Buenos Aires, Argentina)
    131, 417, 1561, 1754, 3917, 3918, 3919, 3920, 3921
Pfahl Verlag (Laupheim, Germany) 132, 205, 352, 418, 419,
    566, 567, 658, 659, 660, 813, 1225, 4349, 4350, 4351,
    4758, 4759
Philadelphia Inquirer (Philadelphia, Penna. , U. S. A.) 133
Phil-Asian Publishers, Inc. (Manila, Philippines) 2509, 4760
Philip, George & Son, Ltd. (London, England) 24, 25, 62,
    63, 64, 65, 134, 135, 136, 184, 206, 207, 208, 209, 210,
    222, 283, 284, 285, 286, 287, 288, 353, 354, 355, 356,
    420, 421, 422, 423, 500, 501, 502, 568, 569, 570, 571,
    587, 661, 662, 663, 675, 714, 747, 748, 749, 750, 751,
    765, 772, 814, 815, 816, 817, 823, 895, 896, 897, 898,
    899, 983, 984, 1100, 1101, 1107, 1121, 1167, 1226,
    1227, 1228, 1294, 1361, 1362, 1363, 1364, 1368, 1467,
    1468, 1469, 1562, 1563, 1564, 1565, 1566, 1567, 1568,
    1676, 1677, 1712, 1755, 1756, 1757, 1758, 1810, 1849,
    1850, 1851, 1852, 1853, 1854, 1855, 1856, 1857, 1858,
    1859, 1860, 1861, 1862, 1863, 1864, 1865, 1866, 1867,
    1868, 1869, 2269, 2270, 2271, 2272, 2273, 2274, 2275,
    2276, 2277, 2278, 2279, 2280, 2281, 2282, 2283, 2284,
    2285, 2289, 2291, 2334, 2557, 2558, 2559, 2560, 2561,
    2562, 2563, 2564, 2565, 2566, 2567, 2568, 3014, 3015,
    3016, 3017, 3018, 3019, 3020, 3021, 3135, 3336, 3337,
    3533, 3534, 3574, 3817, 3818, 4083, 4084, 4085, 4086,
    4087, 4352, 4761, 4762, 4763, 4764, 4765, 4766, 4767,
    4768, 4769, 4770, 4771, 4772, 4773, 4774, 4775, 4776,
    4777, 4778, 4889, 4953, 4954, 4955, 5374, 5375, 5376,
    5377, 5378, 5379, 5380, 5381
Philippines. Agriculture and Natural Resources Dept.
    (Manila, Philippines) 2510, 4010
Philippines. Bureau of Public Works (Manila, Philippines)
    2511, 5382
Philippines. Office of the President. (Manila, Philippines)
    2512, 4353
Plantyn (Anvers, Belgium) 2083
Pocket Books (New York, N. Y. , U. S. A.) 140, 900
Poland. Akademia Nauk (Warszawa, Poland) 3146, 3147,
    3148, 3149, 3150, 3151, 4107, 4108, 4450, 4779, 4780,
    4941, 4993

Romer, Eugeniusz (Wroclaw, Poland) 144
Ronai, Andras (Budapest, Hungary) 3048, 4932
Royal Automobile Club (London, England) 2098, 2099, 2100,
    2101, 4129, 4130, 4131, 4132, 5447, 5448, 5449, 5450
Royal Automobile Club Sweden (Stockholm, Sweden) 2086,
    5389
Royal East African Automobile Assoc. (Nairobi, Kenya) 1874,
    5451
Ruhr-Stickstoff A. G. (Bochum, Germany) 2915, 4013
Ryerson Press (Toronto, Canada) 4811

Sá da Costa - see Livraria Sá da Costa
Sadiq Salih (Baghdad, Iraq) 71
Sadlier, W. H. (New York, N. Y. , U. S. A.) 433, 506, 1478
Salinas Bellver, Salvador (Madrid, Spain) 361, 672, 761
Salvador. Dirección General de Cartografía (San Salvador,
    El Salvador) 3583
Salvador. Estadistica y Cencos (San Salvador, El Salvador)
    3584, 4389
Salvador. Universidade Federal da Bahia, Centro de Estudos
    Afro-Orientais. (San Salvador, El Salvador) 3585, 4812
Salvatella, Editorial Miguel A - see Editorial Miguel A.
    Salvatella
SAM (Quito, Ecuador) 3961, 3962, 4813, 4814
Sauerländer, H. R. (Aarau, Switzerland) 3314, 3315, 3316,
    4815, 4816, 4817
Savremena Shkola (Beograd, Jugoslavia) 585
Schaeffer, Juan E. (Rio de Janeiro, Brazil) 1582
Scholastic Book Service (New York, N. Y. , U. S. A.) 762,
    1249
Schultz (København, Denmark) 72
Schweizer Reisekasse (Bern, Switzerland) 2102, 3317, 5452
Schweizer Volks-Buchgemeinde (Luzern, Switzerland) 145
Schweizerische Gesellschaft für Volkskunde (Basel, Switzer-
    land) 3318, 4454
Scott, Foresman & Co. (Glenview, Ill. , U. S. A.) 1765
Scribner, C. (New York, N. Y. , U. S. A.) 3885, 4818
Sears, Roebuck (Chicago, Ill. , U. S. A.) 362, 363, 507, 912
Seix Barral Editorial - see Editorial Seix Barral, S. A.
Seix Edtitorial - see Editorial Francisco Seix, S. A.
Sélection du Reader's Digest, S. A. R. L. (Paris, France)
    1479, 1766, 2777
Seljačka Sloga (Zagreb, Yugoslavia) 146, 147, 434
Senegal. Ministère du Plan et du Développement (Dakar,
    Senegal) 2247
Sequoia, Editions - see Editions Sequoia
Sha, Hsüeh-Chün (Taipei, Taiwan) 2335
Shell Company of South Africa, Ltd. (Cape Town, South
    Africa) 1875, 2286, 5453

Walker, Gerald E. (Berkeley, Calif., U. S. A.) 2130, 2131, 4438, 4439, 4891, 4892
Ward, Lock (London, England) 75
Warne, F. (London, England) 76
Warszawa Universytet (Warszawa, Poland) 1889
Water Information Center, Inc. (Port Washington, N. Y., U. S. A.) 3895, 3896, 4935, 4936
Watts (New York, N. Y., U. S. A.) 830
Weidenfeld & Nicolson (London, England) 2443, 3034, 3897, 4893, 4894, 4895, 4896
Weilin & Co. (Helsinki, Finland) 1391
Welch Scientific Co. (Chicago, Ill., U. S. A.) 1490
Wenschow (München, Germany) 77, 374, 447, 691, 1129, 2314
Wesmael-Charlier (Namur, Belgium) 306, 1491, 1492, 1493, 2132, 2200, 2673, 2674, 2675, 2676, 2677, 2678, 4897, 4898, 4899, 4900, 4901, 4902
Westermann, Georg (Braunschweig, Germany) 78, 79, 80, 81, 156, 157, 225, 226, 227, 307, 375, 376, 377, 448, 449, 596, 597, 692, 693, 694, 695, 696, 831, 832, 924, 1011, 1130, 1131, 1132, 1133, 1134, 1151, 1261, 1262, 1263, 1264, 1265, 1266, 1392, 1494, 1495, 1595, 1596, 1597, 1703, 1704, 1769, 1770, 1771, 1772, 1786, 2926, 2927, 2928, 2929, 2930, 2931, 2932, 2933, 2934, 4440, 4489, 4827, 4903, 4904, 4905, 4906, 4907, 4908, 4910, 4911, 4912, 4913, 4914
Westminster Press (Philadelphia, Penna., U. S. A.) 4097, 4098, 4915, 4916
Weststadt Verlag (München, Germany) 1135, 4441, 4958
Wheaton & Co., Ltd. (Exeter, England) 514, 1890, 1891, 1892, 3035, 4917
Whittemore Associates (Needham Heights, Mass., U. S. A.) 4099
Wiley, John & Sons (New York, N. Y., U. S. A.) 3575, 3898, 3899, 3900, 4490, 4918
Wise, W. H. (New York, N. Y., U. S. A.) 378
Wjedza Powszechna (Krakow, Poland) 1136, 2133
Wolters, J. B. (Groningen, Netherlands) 158, 308, 450, 515, 771, 925, 926, 1137, 1267, 1268, 1393, 1394, 1395, 1496, 1497, 1598, 1599, 1600, 1705, 2416, 2417, 2418, 3124, 3125, 3126, 3127, 3975, 4919
World Pub. Co. (Cleveland, Ohio, U. S. A.) 927, 2152, 2153, 2154, 3576, 3577, 3678, 3701, 3702, 3703, 3901, 3902, 3903, 4100, 5494, 5495, 5496

Ya Kuang Yü Ti Hsüeh Shê (Shanghai, China) 2360, 2361, 2362, 2363, 2364, 2365, 2366, 2367, 2368, 2369

Language Index

(German continued)

1779,	1781,	1786,	1816,
1898,	1952,	1953,	1957,
1958,	1959,	1963,	1964,
1966,	1967,	1968,	1969,
1970,	1971,	1988,	1989,
1990,	1991,	1997,	1998,
2000,	2006,	2018,	2019,
2020,	2021,	2022,	2023,
2028,	2029,	2030,	2031,
2032,	2033,	2034,	2035,
2036,	2037,	2038,	2039,
2049,	2050,	2051,	2052,
2053,	2054,	2055,	2056,
2057,	2058,	2059,	2060,
2061,	2062,	2063,	2064,
2065,	2066,	2067,	2068,
2069,	2070,	2074,	2088,
2089,	2090,	2091,	2092,
2093,	2094,	2095,	2096,
2097,	2102,	2109,	2125,
2126,	2128,	2129,	2218,
2306,	2307,	2391,	2426,
2442,	2604,	2605,	2606,
2607,	2608,	2609,	2610,
2611,	2612,	2613,	2614,
2615,	2616,	2617,	2618,
2619,	2620,	2621,	2622,
2623,	2624,	2625,	2626,
2627,	2628,	2629,	2630,
2631,	2632,	2633,	2634,
2635,	2636,	2637,	2638,
2639,	2640,	2641,	2642,
2643,	2644,	2645,	2646,
2647,	2648,	2649,	2650,
2651,	2652,	2653,	2654,
2655,	2656,	2657,	2658,
2663,	2664,	2670,	2671,
2674,	2675,	2676,	2677,
2678,	2781,	2782,	2783,
2784,	2785,	2786,	2787,
2788,	2789,	2790,	2791,
2792,	2793,	2794,	2795,
2796,	2797,	2798,	2799,
2800,	2801,	2802,	2803,
2804,	2805,	2806,	2807,
2808,	2809,	2810,	2811,
2812,	2813,	2814,	2815,
2816,	2817,	2818,	2819,
2820,	2821,	2822,	2823,
2824,	2825,	2826,	2827,
2828,	2829,	2830,	2831,
2832,	2833,	2834,	2835,
2836,	2837,	2838,	2839,
2840,	2841,	2842,	2843,
2844,	2845,	2846,	2847,
2848,	2849,	2850,	2851,
2852,	2853,	2854,	2855,
2856,	2857,	2858,	2859,
2860,	2861,	2862,	2863,
2864,	2865,	2866,	2867,
2868,	2869,	2870,	2871,
2872,	2873,	2874,	2875,
2876,	2877,	2878,	2879,
2880,	2881,	2882,	2883,
2884,	2885,	2886,	2887,
2888,	2889,	2890,	2891,
2892,	2893,	2894,	2895,
2896,	2897,	2898,	2899,
2900,	2901,	2904,	2905,
2906,	2907,	2908,	2909,
2910,	2911,	2912,	2913,
2914,	2915,	2916,	2917,
2918,	2919,	2920,	2921,
2922,	2923,	2924,	2925,
2926,	2927,	2928,	2929,
2930,	2931,	2932,	2933,
2934,	2935,	3066,	3075,
3077,	3082,	3083,	3085,
3088,	3089,	3113,	3114,
3282,	3283,	3284,	3286,
3287,	3288,	3289,	3291,
3292,	3293,	3294,	3295,
3296,	3297,	3298,	3299,
3300,	3301,	3302,	3303,
3304,	3305,	3306,	3307,
3312,	3313,	3314,	3315,
3316,	3317,	3318,	3319,
3320,	3321,	3990,	3993,
3999,	4000,	4013,	4014,
4023,	4027,	4028,	4029,
4030,	4031,	4032,	4043,
4050,	4059,	4096,	4102,
4105,	4128,	4135,	4143,

4300, 4301, 4693, 4694,
4932, 5257, 5258, 5259,
5260, 5261, 5262, 5263,
5264, 5265

ICELANDIC 998, 3050
INDONESIAN 94, 173, 232,
246, 247, 281, 350, 388,
413, 472, 527, 561, 622,
653, 679, 791, 2392, 2393,
2394, 2395, 2396, 2397,
2398, 2399, 2400, 2401,
2402, 2403, 2404, 2405,
2406, 2407, 2408, 2409,
2410, 2411, 2415, 2417,
4280, 4281, 4581
ITALIAN 40, 83, 118, 149,
159, 271, 272, 338, 339,
340, 341, 404, 488, 511,
586, 592, 639, 657, 676,
698, 717, 731, 746, 763,
812, 828, 921, 939, 967,
968, 969, 1068, 1069,
1070, 1074, 1200, 1201,
1204, 1224, 1234, 1269,
1327, 1328, 1330, 1331,
1441, 1545, 1578, 1627,
1693, 1694, 1701, 1745,
1746, 1747, 1780, 1823,
1894, 1950, 1951, 2016,
2017, 3062, 3063, 3064,
3065, 3067, 3068, 3069,
3070, 3071, 3073, 3074,
3076, 3078, 3079, 3080,
3081, 3285, 3311, 4122,
4231, 4287, 4288, 4289,
4290, 4291, 4292, 4293,
4392, 4402, 4432, 4681,
4682, 4683, 4684, 4685,
4686, 4687, 4688, 4728,
4875, 4876, 5004, 5053,
5054, 5055, 5056, 5231,
5232, 5458, 5459, 5473

JAPANESE 298, 365, 1379,
1480, 1706, 2446, 2447,
2448, 2449, 2450, 2451,

2452, 2453, 2454, 2455,
2456, 2457, 2458, 2459,
2460, 2461, 2462, 2463,
2465, 2466, 2467, 2468,
2469, 2470, 2471, 2472,
2473, 2474, 2475, 2476,
2478, 2479, 2480, 4155,
4447, 4830, 5472, 5498

KOREAN 2481, 2482, 2483

NORWEGIAN 89, 174, 237,
382, 952, 956, 1044, 1144,
1149, 1152, 1153, 1273,
1291, 1294, 1300, 1350,
1378, 1405, 1406, 1521,
1613, 1774, 1775, 3128,
3129, 3130, 3131, 3132,
3133, 3134, 3135, 3136,
3137, 3138, 3139, 3140,
3141, 3142, 4061, 4182,
4183, 4500, 4535, 4992,
5091, 5266, 5267, 5532

PERSIAN 2419, 4150
POLISH 144, 150, 198, 289,
357, 424, 425, 503, 504,
572, 573, 664, 665, 666,
752, 818, 901, 985, 986,
1102, 1103, 1104, 1105,
1106, 1136, 1229, 1230,
1231, 1232, 1365, 1366,
1367, 1367, 1470, 1471,
1569, 1570, 1678, 1759,
1889, 2133, 3143, 3144,
3145, 3146, 3147, 3148,
3149, 3150, 3151, 3152,
3153, 3154, 3158, 3159,
3160, 3161, 3162, 3163,
3164, 3165, 3166, 3167,
3168, 3169, 3170, 3171,
3172, 3173, 3174, 3175,
3176, 3177, 3178, 3179,
3180, 3181, 4107, 4108,
4109, 4303, 4304, 4305,
4450, 4480, 4481, 4696,
4697, 4779, 4780, 4781,

1390, 1445, 1446, 1483,
3428, 3429, 3430, 3431,
3432, 3433, 3434, 3435,
3436, 3437, 3438, 3440,
3441, 3442, 3443, 3444,
4239, 4259, 4448, 4449,
4831, 4923, 4924, 4925,
4926, 5254, 5255, 5474,
5475, 5476, 5477, 5478,
5479, 5480

SLOVAK   784, 1028, 2710

SPANISH   15, 16, 17, 114,
123, 131, 177, 196, 249,
309, 318, 319, 320, 361,
417, 452, 469, 489, 519,
530, 533, 535, 542, 587,
598, 599, 600, 620, 628,
672, 699, 700, 701, 715,
716, 761, 785, 788, 789,
797, 802, 836, 861, 891,
928, 929, 946, 1014,
1015, 1049, 1050, 1138,
1139, 1140, 1141, 1161,
1208, 1217, 1247, 1270,
1271, 1312, 1313, 1352,
1396, 1397, 1398, 1399,
1429, 1430, 1453, 1458,
1498, 1499, 1500, 1502,
1517, 1530, 1561, 1572,
1579, 1601, 1602, 1603,
1604, 1605, 1620, 1636,
1642, 1669, 1670, 1679,
1707, 1708, 1709, 1710,
1711, 1720, 1730, 1754,
1773, 1878, 2138, 2155,
2157, 2158, 2160, 2178,
2179, 3182, 3183, 3184,
3192, 3193, 3194, 3209,
3210, 3211, 3212, 3213,
3214, 3215, 3216, 3217,
3218, 3219, 3220, 3221,
3222, 3223, 3224, 3225,
3226, 3227, 3228, 3229,
3230, 3231, 3232, 3233,
3234, 3235, 3236, 3237,
3238, 3239, 3240, 3241,
3242, 3243, 3244, 3245,

3246, 3247, 3248, 3249,
3250, 3251, 3252, 3253,
3254, 3255, 3256, 3257,
3258, 3259, 3260, 3579,
3581, 3582, 3583, 3584,
3585, 3586, 3587, 3588,
3589, 3590, 3591, 3592,
3616, 3617, 3618, 3620,
3621, 3622, 3625, 3626,
3627, 3628, 3629, 3630,
3631, 3642, 3643, 3647,
3648, 3649, 3650, 3651,
3652, 3653, 3654, 3655,
3656, 3658, 3659, 3699,
3704, 3705, 3706, 3708,
3709, 3710, 3904, 3905,
3906, 3907, 3908, 3909,
3910, 3911, 3912, 3913,
3914, 3915, 3916, 3917,
3918, 3919, 3920, 3921,
3922, 3946, 3947, 3948,
3949, 3950, 3951, 3952,
3953, 3954, 3955, 3956,
3957, 3958, 3959, 3960,
3961, 3962, 3963, 3964,
3965, 3966, 3967, 3968,
3969, 3970, 3971, 3972,
3973, 3976, 3977, 3978,
3979, 3980, 3981, 3982,
3983, 3984, 3985, 3986,
3987, 3988, 3994, 4022,
4042, 4104, 4149, 4158,
4173, 4179, 4180, 4181,
4186, 4187, 4190, 4191,
4192, 4193, 4194, 4195,
4196, 4197, 4198, 4199,
4200, 4201, 4202, 4203,
4204, 4205, 4206, 4207,
4208, 4209, 4210, 4211,
4212, 4217, 4223, 4230,
4233, 4240, 4244, 4245,
4246, 4247, 4297, 4308,
4323, 4348, 4389, 4396,
4397, 4414, 4415, 4416,
4417, 4462, 4464, 4588,
4589, 4599, 4600, 4601,
4602, 4699, 4700, 4710,

Authors, Cartographers, Editors Index